国际组织文件翻译
实践教程

张晶晶 金丹 主编

清华大学出版社
北京

内 容 简 介

本书基于中国对外翻译有限公司（以下简称"中译公司"）自 1973 年以来，为联合国各机构及全球众多国际组织提供翻译服务的深厚积淀，由中译公司多位资深联合国译员执笔，带领读者步入联合国及国际组织文件翻译的大门。

中译公司作为中国翻译行业的"国家队"和联合国在华长期语言服务供应商，在编写本书时，主要从翻译实践角度出发，以多个层次呈现国际组织文件形式和涉及领域的多样性，内容涵盖人权、安全、维和、禁毒、经济、环境、文化、卫生、教育、科技等，基本囊括了联合国的主要工作领域，并侧重国际组织文件的翻译实操和技巧传授，辅以详尽的分析和指导，为读者剖析、展示翻译过程，达到帮助读者快速了解国际组织文件翻译，并有效提升翻译水平的目的。

本书封面贴有清华大学出版社防伪标签，无标签者不得销售。
版权所有，侵权必究。举报：010-62782989，beiqinquan@tup.tsinghua.edu.cn。

图书在版编目（CIP）数据

国际组织文件翻译实践教程 / 张晶晶，金丹主编 . — 北京：清华大学出版社，2022.9
ISBN 978-7-302-59995-1

Ⅰ.①国… Ⅱ.①张… ②金… Ⅲ.①国际组织—文件—翻译—教材 Ⅳ.① H315.9

中国版本图书馆 CIP 数据核字（2022）第 020257 号

责任编辑：刘士平
封面设计：常雪影
责任校对：袁　芳
责任印制：沈　露

出版发行：清华大学出版社
　　　　　网　　址：http://www.tup.com.cn, http://www.wqbook.com
　　　　　地　　址：北京清华大学学研大厦 A 座　　邮　　编：100084
　　　　　社 总 机：010-83470000　　邮　　购：010-62786544
　　　　　投稿与读者服务：010-62776969, c-service@tup.tsinghua.edu.cn
　　　　　质量反馈：010-62772015, zhiliang@tup.tsinghua.edu.cn
印 装 者：三河市龙大印装有限公司
经　　销：全国新华书店
开　　本：210mm×285mm　　印　张：33.25　　字　数：949 千字
版　　次：2022 年 11 月第 1 版　　印　次：2022 年 11 月第 1 次印刷
定　　价：128.00 元

产品编号：093632-01

编 委 会

主　编： 张晶晶　金　丹

副主编： 金文茜

编　委： 李长山　朱文君　张海英　李　菁　王雅琦
　　　　　黄世宪　于改革　盛　雪　陈轶欧　王　欣
　　　　　韩　洁　孙一冰　赵思雨　郗雨婷

PREFACE

在当前的国际形势下，编撰出版《国际组织文件翻译实践教程》十分及时，也非常实用。

一方面，国际形势出现了百年不遇的大变局，世界正处于大发展、大变革、大调整时期。全球国际力量对比发生变化，大国之间互动复杂，博弈加剧。全球热点问题频发，地区局势不稳，局部冲突不断，传统与非传统的安全议题联动蔓延。新冠疫情肆虐全球，严重影响经济和社会发展。随着国际形势的发展，联合国所肩负的历史使命和其在国际事务中的独特影响更加明显。中国作为世界第二大经济体，应该在国际社会发挥更大的作用，承担更多的国际义务。事实上，中国也在积极参与全球治理，贡献中国智慧、中国方案，中国在国际组织中更加活跃。

另一方面，翻译对国际组织的重要性，怎么强调都不为过。2018年8月，时任联合国大会和会议管理部助理秘书长Mr. Yohannes Mengesha在上海参加第18届世界翻译大会作主旨演讲时说，"The United Nations should be a centre for harmonizing the actions of nations in the pursuit of its principles and purposes. This basic mission of the Organization would clearly be impossible to achieve without translation and interpretation. The world's diverse cultural and linguistic communities and traditions could not agree on collective action to address international issues if they did not first understand each other clearly."联合国应成为协调各国行动以实现其原则和宗旨的中心。显然，没有口、笔译服务，该组织不可能实现这一基本的使命。来自不同语言、文化、传统背景的各国代表如果不能沟通，无法为解决国际问题需采取的集体行动达成一致，又怎么履行国际组织的崇高使命呢！

因此，培养更多优秀的翻译人才，让他们到国际组织或在国内承担国际组织文件翻译的任务，既能为国际组织培养优秀人才，也能为中国参与全球治理提供更好的语言服务。这是时代的召唤，也是我们义不容辞的职责。《国际组织文件翻译实践教程》的出版是培养优秀翻译人才的重要工具。

翻译是一种跨语言、跨文化的人际沟通、文化交流的活动和过程。联合国的各类文件，其书写和编撰有一定的规范。此外，联合国的很多文件是谈判妥协的结果，为了在不同意见之间架起桥梁，跨越政治和国家（political and national）分歧的鸿沟，各方不乏使用模棱两可的语言以便大家接受。翻译必须把握政治上的细微差别，准确把握精准的意思表达以及故意的模棱两可。国际组织的文件翻译，相比一般公文翻译，既有共性，也有特点。比如，国际组织的文件敏感度高、涵盖面广、信息量大、语言正式、术语多、用词严谨、选词精准，翻译国际组织的文件必须确保译文的规范性、准确性、完整性、可读性、严谨性。

作为本书的编写方，中国对外翻译有限公司长期为联合国系统提供语言服务，积累了丰富的经验，自1973年以来，培养了一大批熟悉联合国系统文件、符合政治性很强的国际组织对翻译要求的人才。此次，中国对外翻译有限公司倾心推出的这本《国际组织文件翻译实践教程》，对于有志从事国际组织文件翻译的青年有非常重要的参考价值和指导作用。我相信，这本教材的出版，一定会有利于培养出胜任国际组织文件翻译的优秀人才。

徐亚男

原中国驻特立尼达和多巴哥特命全权大使，

原联合国大会和会议管理部文件司中文处处长，原外交部翻译室主任

前言
FOREWORD

联合国文件翻译是正式公文类文件的翻译，一方面，它具有联合国文件的固有特色；另一方面，它也体现了国际组织公文类翻译的普遍规则。虽然联合国并未明文规定文件翻译的翻译原则和评判标准，但其总部及各办事处的中文翻译部门已经总结出一套行之有效的业务守则，即"完整、准确、通顺、术语、一致、风格"[①]。一般而言，联合国文件翻译工作均应秉持该守则行事。

然而知易行难。了解标准、熟知业务守则并不难，难的是付诸实践，并在实践中理解、融汇、体现各项评判标准和守则。联合国文件具有特殊性，在词汇、句法、术语、风格方面有诸多细致的要求，没有大量的实践，难以做到融汇于心，难以践行联合国翻译业务守则，而这也是培养联合国所需的文件翻译人才的痛点所在，因为这不仅需要大量的联合国文件作为实践素材，更重要的是，还需要熟知联合国翻译标准并有相关丰富经验的前辈予以细致指导，否则难免会让学习者有"入宝山而空回"，"不得其门而入"的感觉。

中国对外翻译有限公司（以下简称"中译公司"）作为中华人民共和国成立之后第一家国有翻译企业和联合国长期语言服务供应商，自中国重返联合国起，便持续不断地为以联合国为代表的国际组织提供翻译服务，积累了丰富的翻译经验，构建了庞大的国际组织语料库，培养了一大批熟稔联合国和国际组织翻译要求的专业翻译人才，从各方面来看，中译公司都可以承担起培养符合国际组织要求的高端翻译人才的重任。

本书在此背景下编写而成，旨在解决以下几个方面的难题。

（1）译者不甚了解以联合国为代表的国际组织的基本情况，不能根据不同国际机构的背景分析、理解原文。

（2）译者难以大量接触各种体裁的联合国文件，对联合国文件特有的词汇要求、语法特征、行文风格、文体特点缺乏感性的认识和实践，导致译文不符合联合国翻译标准。

（3）译者在翻译过程中缺乏切实的指导，难以深入掌握联合国文件的诸多标准化格式要求。

本书的特点如下。

选材广泛。本书所有学习材料均选自以联合国为代表的国际组织公开文件，从文件的形式上看，涵盖了会议文件、报告、呈文、出版物；从文件的内容上看，涉及人权、安全、维和、禁毒、经济、环境、

[①] 详见赵兴民著《联合国文件翻译案例讲评》。

文化、卫生、教育、科技等，基本涵盖联合国主要工作领域。

实践为主。本书从词汇、习惯表达、语法、行文风格、格式要求等多个方面展开了较为详尽的分析，不仅比较了联合国文件与非联合国文件之间的差别，还对比了联合国不同机构之间、联合国主要机构与专门机构之间、联合国与其他国际组织之间的文件翻译差异，为读者学习、掌握联合国系统以及诸多重要国际组织各类文件的特点提供了较为全面的指导。

本书独辟蹊径，不以翻译理论作为重点，而侧重于翻译实操，旨在按照一般的翻译流程，在译前准备（确定翻译策略）、翻译过程（运用翻译技巧处理文本）、译后审查（按照国际组织翻译标准核查译文）这三个步骤给予切实的指导。

本书的使用方法：基于联合国的工作范围，本书分为八个领域，每个领域为一章，分别为和平与安全、人权与人道、法律与法治、经济与金融、环境与发展、人文与社会、卫生与健康、科学与技术，共八章，每章包含若干篇章。

（1）在进入各章学习时，首先请仔细阅读"本章导言"部分。"本章导言"简要介绍了该章内所涉材料的类型、内容、翻译策略、重点翻译技巧、翻译评价标准等重要内容，旨在让读者对该章有一个较全面的了解，做好翻译准备。

（2）每个单元均包括"背景介绍""原文""分析点评"和"补充练习"（附答案）。"背景介绍"是对所选材料的简要说明。"原文"选自国际组织的各类典型文件。在"分析点评"部分（包括每段原文、翻译稿、审校稿和点评），首先，必要时以蓝色标记的方式指明原文中需要注意的翻译难点；然后，以批注形式对翻译稿中出现的问题予以简明扼要的提示；最后，在点评中详细解答翻译难点和出现的翻译问题。"补充练习"部分选取的材料与"原文"类似，以便读者开展同步练习。

（3）每章均附有"本章词汇"，其中既包括该章所选材料中涉及的重点词汇，也包括该章所涉领域的其他重要词汇。

随着中国加入国际组织的步伐加快，对能够熟练承担国际组织公文翻译任务的人才的需求也在不断地增加，中译公司顺应中国"走出去"的时代大潮流，选择在此时推出本书，正所谓"桐花万里丹山路，雏凤清于老凤声"，相信本书一定能帮助更多走向国际舞台的高端翻译人才打好基础，铺好道路。

张晶晶　金　丹

CONTENTS

第一章　和平与安全 1

第二章　人权与人道 65

第三章　法律与法治 133

第四章　经济与金融 207

第五章　环境与发展 289

第六章　人文与社会 349

第七章　卫生与健康 411

第八章　科学与技术 473

第一章 和平与安全

本章导言

和平与安全是人类永恒的追求，是世界人民的心之所向。1945年，在人类历经两次世界大战的蹂躏之后，"欲免后世再遭今代人类两度身历惨不堪言之战祸……"（《联合国宪章》序言），联合国宣布成立，并将"维持国际和平及安全"列为宗旨之一，承诺"为此目的：采取有效集体办法，以防止且消除对于和平之威胁，制止侵略行为或其他和平之破坏；并以和平方法且依正义及国际法之原则，调整或解决足以破坏和平之国际争端或情势"（《联合国宪章》第一章）。

根据《联合国宪章》，在联合国系统中，安全理事会对维护国际和平与安全负有主要责任，大会、秘书处及其他联合国办事处和机构互为补充，为促进和平与安全发挥重要作用。

安全理事会在接到关于威胁和平的投诉后，首先判断所称威胁或侵略行为是否存在，继而促请争端各方以和平手段解决争端，并建议调整方法或解决问题的条件。在调解无果的情况下，安理会可以采取经济制裁、国际军事行动等强制执行措施来维护或恢复国际和平与安全。几十年来，联合国通过安全理事会的行动，帮助结束或化解了无数次冲突。

大会是联合国主要的审议、决策和代表机构。根据《联合国宪章》，大会可以就维护国际和平与安全（包括裁军）提出建议。大会的六个主要委员会中有两个涉及和平与安全问题：第一委员会，负责裁军与国际安全有关方面的问题；第四委员会，负责审议非殖民化、外层空间国际合作、排雷行动等问题。

关于秘书处，根据《联合国宪章》第十五章，"秘书处置秘书长一人及本组织所需之办事人员若干人"，秘书长有权力"将其所认为可能威胁国际和平及安全之任何事件，提请安全理事会注意"。秘书长的最重要作用之一就是基于独立、公正和廉正，运用公开或私下的"斡旋"措施，防止国际争端出现、升级或扩散。

联合国维护国际和平与安全的努力主要涉及以下几个领域。

（1）预防性外交和调解——其主要表现为外交手段、斡旋及调解等，是减轻人类苦难，减少冲突及其后果带来的经济成本的最有效途径。

（2）维持和平——联合国维持和平行动是国际社会用以促进国际和平与安全的一个有效手段。

（3）建设和平——联合国建设和平活动旨在帮助国家走出冲突，减少再次陷入冲突的风险，并为建设可持续的和平与发展奠定基础。

（4）打击恐怖主义——近年来，倡导联合参与协调全球反恐斗争的呼声日高，在联合国系统框架内通过了多份反对恐怖主义的全球文书，特别是各会员国首次就反对恐怖主义达成的首个共同战略和业务框架《联合国全球反恐战略》。

（5）裁军——在裁军事务厅的支持下，大会及联合国其他机构致力推进裁军及核武器、化学武器、生物武器及其他大规模毁灭性武器和传统武器的不扩散。

鉴于维持国际和平与安全是联合国主要目的之一，具有重要地位，因此有关和平与安全的文件在联合国文件体系中数不胜数，且形式多样，主题繁杂。本章撷取十一份具有代表性的文件，择段为例，点评分析，以供读者学习。这十一份文件从对应机构上讲，涵盖联合国安全理事会、大会、秘书处以及不扩散核武器条约缔约国审议大会等其他联合国机构，除此之外，还有裁军谈判会议（非联合国直属机构，但与联合国联系极为密切）；在主题上分别涉及应对恐怖主义威胁、巴以冲突、维和行动、核裁军、核不扩散、禁核试核查活动、中东无核武器区，涵盖了前文中提到的预防性外交和调解、维持和平、建设和平、打击恐怖主义、裁军五个领域；从文件形式来说，既有秘书长/执行秘书的报告，也有会议逐字记录和简要记录，还有缔约国报告模板等。

和平与安全专题类文件具有联合国文件的一般性特点，语言平实、逻辑严密、遣词用语严谨，在涉及态度、立场、承诺等的情况下尤其如此。其特点主要体现在以下几个方面。

一、固定体例

在形式上有其特点，在翻译时有相应的固定体例规范可循。本章前三篇涉及逐字记录和简要记录，两者既有共同点，又有相异之处，特别是以第三人称进行记录的简要记录。例如，第二篇第1段中的"Mr. Kendrick (United States of America) said that his delegation continued…"，下划线部分需要处理为"美利坚合众国代表团"，而非"他的代表团"。这类固定体例规范详见正文。

二、专有词汇

和平与安全领域专有名词高频出现且一般有固定译法，例如，会议/机构名称、恐怖组织名称、核试验/核武器和核查方面的技术名词，特别是在裁军题材的文件中。例如，"weapons of mass destruction"（见本章第二篇和第八篇），常译为"大规模杀伤性武器"，在中国外交部的官方网站上，也经常会使用这一提法，但在联合国文件体系中，官方权威译文为"大规模毁灭性武器"。再例如，核不扩散专题类文件中经常出现"safeguards"一词（见第八篇），其标准译文为"保障监督"，而非"保障"或"保护"。面对这类专有名词和术语，译者在翻译时，需要查阅联合国词汇库和相关机构的网站。至于具体查阅方式，见本章详细介绍。

三、句法

本章涉及使用拆译法处理结构复杂的长句（见第一篇等）、灵活运用词性转化技巧（见第五篇等）以

及如何根据背景知识增译（见第二篇和第六篇等），力求在"授人以鱼"的同时"授人以渔"。

四、语篇

（一）背景知识对于准确翻译不可或缺，译者在翻译时，既要贴合原文，也要结合现实，灵活处理。例如：

1. 第六篇第1段"..., to date, not one weapon from within the five nuclear stockpiles recognized by the Treaty [on the Non-Proliferation of Nuclear Weapons] had been eliminated through multilateral negotiations envisaged under article VI."中，如将画线部分处理为"《条约》认可的五个核武库"，显然是按照字面直译的结果，并未译出原文的"所指"。如译者了解相关背景知识，知道《不扩散核武器条约》规定只有联合国五个常任理事国有权拥有核武器，就可以将译文具体丰满化，增译处理为"《条约》认可的五个核武器国家的核武器库存"。

2. 第九篇第2段"We firmly believe that the stagnation of the work of existing disarmament machinery under the aegis of the United Nations results not from imperfections in the machinery but from objective political realities and differences in States' priorities."中，如将下划线译为"联合国领导下的现有裁军机制"，则是对"under the aegis of"的意思理解不够到位，显然对相关背景知识欠缺了解：裁军谈判会议虽与联合国联系密切，但不是联合国的直属机构，不受联合国领导。因此译为"联合国支持下的"才是妥当的。

（二）文件的横向和纵向关联性强，是联合国文件的普遍特点，因此在翻译某份文件时，需耐心查阅参考其中提到的其他文件，例如在第八篇中，虽仅有六个段落，但多次援引大会第67/72号决议。详见本章第一篇、第六篇和第八篇。

联合国文件体系中的和平与安全专题类文件是对联合国在和平与安全领域相关工作、任务和挑战的直观反映。译者在翻译时，应针对上述特点，努力将自己置身文件编写者的高度，在进行相关文件查阅参考的基础上，联系具体背景，树立语篇意识，遵循既定体例规范，注意词汇处理细节，打磨翻译技巧。

背景介绍

以下材料选自安全理事会的会议逐字记录。该记录所涉内容为秘书长第六次报告（关于伊黎伊斯兰（达伊沙）对国际和平与安全构成的威胁以及联合国为支持会员国抵御这一威胁所做广泛努力）。所选段落摘自瑞典代表在会上的相关发言。

安全理事会是联合国六大机构之一，其职能和权力包括维护国际和平与安全、调查可能引起国际摩擦的任何争端或局势并就争端调解方法或解决条件提出建议，以及促请各会员国实施经济制裁和除使用武力以外的其他措施以防止或制止侵略等，详见《联合国宪章》第五章。

安全理事会的会议可以有逐字记录。逐字记录（第一人称完整会议记录）是对整场会议的同步记录，在结构上，将发言代表的发言内容逐字记录下来。各国/集团代表的发言用词严谨，特别是在表明本国立场态度或谈判达成决议/条约案文等情况下，译者应按第一人称翻译，需综合整篇发言的内容，细致揣摩发言者之意，不能擅自增减，更不能偏离原文。同时，这类文件中多会提到一份或多份信息文件并附有文件编号，应根据需要，通过文件编号在联合国正式文件系统（ODS）中进行查阅参考，以助做出准确翻译。请注意，如遇中国代表的发言，应查阅"中华人民共和国常驻联合国代表团"网站（内载中国代表在安全理事会和联合国大会会议上的发言稿），切勿自行翻译。

第一篇

原文

In doing so, it is of course important that the prosecution of suspected terrorists be carried out with full respect for human rights and the rule of law.

The transnational nature of many terrorist activities makes the prevention of terrorist acts by any one country alone more difficult.

We see a change in the tactics, forms and methods of actions by ISIL, who, under the new and changed conditions, are conducting terrorist attacks outside the conflict zones, with deliberate attempts to expand and strengthen the network of cells.

Those cells operate undetected, with a certain degree of autonomy, thereby making it difficult for Member States to identify them. It is therefore most critical to establish an effective mechanism for the exchange of information, at the international level, on foreign terrorist fighters, returnees and those who relocate.

The transfer of terrorist threats to other regions and the Security Council measures to counter them were therefore among the key topics on the agenda of the visits by the Chair of the Committee established pursuant to resolution 1267 (1999), concerning Al-Qaida and the Taliban and associated individuals and entities, to Malaysia and Singapore in August 2017 and to Afghanistan in October 2017.

请自行翻译后查看后文的分析点评

分析点评

第 1 段

In doing so, it is of course important that the prosecution of suspected terrorists be carried out with full respect for human rights and the rule of law.

翻译稿

在这样做的时候①，起诉恐怖主义嫌疑犯当然必须充分尊重人权和法治。

审校稿

当然，这样一来，在起诉恐怖分子嫌疑人时就必须充分尊重人权和法治。

点评

如果按照英文的顺序直译，中文是不通顺的。可以把副词 of course 单独拿出来，放在前面，这样更符合中文的表达习惯。另外，还可以将英文的主句部分"prosecution of suspected terrorists be carried out"作为时间状语，而把状语部分即"with full respect for human rights and the rule of law"的名词性结构变为动谓结构的主句部分，具体如审校稿所示。

第 2 段

The transnational nature of many terrorist activities makes the prevention of terrorist acts by any one country alone more difficult.

翻译稿

许多恐怖主义活动的跨国性质②使任何一个国家单独防止恐怖主义行为变得更加困难。

审校稿

很多恐怖主义活动具有跨国性质，这加大了各国单枪匹马独自防范恐怖主义的难度。

点评

本句的主语是名词性结构"The transnational nature of many terrorist activities"，

批注

① 直译并未体现与后句的逻辑联系。

② 受英文影响过重，中文表达不符合中文习惯。

如果按照英文顺序直译，意思好理解，但表述不地道，可以将主语部分拆开，单独译为一个主谓结构的句子，即"很多恐怖主义活动具有跨国性质"，并在后面用指定代词"这"进行指代承接，这样，译文通顺、流畅，符合中文表达习惯。

第3段

We see a change in the tactics, forms and methods of actions by ISIL, who, under the new and changed conditions, are conducting terrorist attacks outside the conflict zones, with deliberate attempts to expand and strengthen the network of cells.

【翻译稿】

我们看到伊斯兰国的战术、形式和行动方法发生了变化，他们在新的和已经变化的条件下在冲突地区以外进行恐怖袭击，蓄意企图扩大和加强组织网络。

【审校稿】

我们看到伊黎伊斯兰国恐怖分子在行动策略、形式和方法方面出现变化，他们根据已经发生变化的新情况，在冲突区域外发动恐怖袭击，蓄意试图扩大和加强基层组织网络。

【点评】

在联合国文件翻译中，表达的准确性至关重要，在本段中，"ISIL"的正确译法是"伊黎伊斯兰国"。另外，不同国家和不同组织对"伊斯兰国"的称呼不同，有的直接简称"伊斯兰国"，有的简称"达伊沙"，各自有不同的内涵，也代表了不同的政治含义，在翻译时一定要按原文的意思表达。单独来看，将"under the new and changed conditions"译为"在新的和已经变化的条件（情况）下"没有什么错误，但这不是此处要表达的意思，此处是说，恐怖分子根据新情况改变了行动方式。"network of cells"译为"基层组织网络"更准确。

第4段

Those cells operate undetected, with a certain degree of autonomy, thereby making it difficult for Member States to identify them. It is therefore most critical to establish an effective mechanism for the exchange of information, at the international level, on foreign terrorist fighters, returnees and those who relocate.

【翻译稿】

这些组织在未被发现的情况下运作，具有一定程度的自主性，因此，会员国很难识别它们。因此，最重要的是建立一个有效的机制，以便在国际一级交流关于外国恐怖分子战斗人员⑥、回返者和重新安置者的信息。

【审校稿】

这些基层组织秘密行动具有一定的自主权，这使会员国很难识别它们。因

批 注

① 专有名词翻译不准确。
② 译法生硬。
③ 意思不完整。

批 注

④ 直译不符合中文表达。
⑤ 也可以有另一种处理方式。
⑥ 词汇错误。

此，在国际层面建立一个有效机制，以交流外国恐怖主义作战人员、回返者和重新安置者方面的信息至关重要。

1. 将"operate undetected"译为"在未被发现的情况下运作"令人不明就里，实际上就是指"秘密行动"，"with a certain degree of autonomy"译为"具有一定的自主权"比"具有一定程度的自主性"更准确，而且更符合中文表达习惯。

2. 在联合国词库中，"foreign terrorist fighters"应译为"外国恐怖主义作战人员"，专业词汇一定要查，不能自己决定。另外，对"It is therefore most critical to..."也可以靠后处理，译为"……至关重要"。

第 5 段

The transfer of terrorist threats to other regions and the Security Council measures to counter them were therefore among the key topics on the agenda of the visits by the Chair of the Committee established pursuant to resolution 1267 (1999), concerning Al-Qaida and the Taliban and associated individuals and entities, to Malaysia and Singapore in August 2017 and to Afghanistan in October 2017.

因此，将恐怖主义威胁转移到其他区域①以及安全理事会为打击这些威胁采取的措施②是第1267（1999）号决议所设委员会主席在2017年8月访问马来西亚和新加坡以及2017年10月访问阿富汗议程上的关键议题之一，该决议是关于基地组织和塔利班以及相关个人和实体的③。

批 注

① 逻辑问题。
② 语言啰唆。
③ 处理方式错误。

因此，恐怖威胁转移到其他区域和安全理事会的反恐措施是关于基地组织和塔利班及关联个人和实体的安全理事会第1267（1999）号决议所设委员会主席2017年8月访问马来西亚和新加坡以及2017年10月访问阿富汗时议程上的关键议题之一。

本段话是一个主谓结构，主语部分是"The transfer of terrorist threats to other regions and the Security Council measures to counter them"，谓语部分是"were among the key topics on the agenda"，后面部分均为"agenda"的定语，其中，"concerning Al-Qaida and the Taliban and associated individuals and entities"所修饰的是"resolution 1267（1999）"，译者未能理清这一层关系，以致译文出错。另外，"Committee established pursuant to resolution 1267（1999）"应该译为"安全理事会第1267（1999）决议所设委员会"，这是联合国词汇中的固定译法，没有其他译法。译者在对该委员会名称不确定的情况下，应在安全理事会网站（"文件"板块下载按年份分列的决议）上查阅该项决议的具体内容，以助做出准确翻译。

补充练习

1. Notwithstanding the many measures taken by the international community to identify and block extremist Internet resources, the fighters and supporters of Da'esh continue to use the Internet and social networks, including the Dark Web encryption technology and communication tools, to disseminate, coordinate and conduct terrorist attacks and to promote their narratives. A stricter, well-coordinated regulation of the use of the Internet is therefore needed to identify and to prevent the spread of terrorist content. Complacency is harmful to our collective efforts to contain the spread of Da'esh propaganda via the Internet.

尽管国际社会为识别和阻断极端分子使用因特网资源采取了很多措施，但达伊沙的作战人员和支持者仍在继续利用因特网和社交媒体，包括利用暗网加密技术和各种通信工具，传播、协调和发动恐怖袭击，并宣传其言论。因此，需要更严格和协调一致地规范对因特网的使用，以识别和阻止恐怖主义内容的传播。骄傲自满对我们遏制达伊沙通过因特网传播恐怖主义的集体努力有害无益。

2. There have been terrorist attacks recently in Afghanistan, Iraq and Egypt, among other places, that have resulted in enormous casualties. As humankind's shared enemy, terrorism has ramifications that extend beyond national borders and that countries cannot deal with single-handedly. The international community should work to effectively implement the relevant Security Council resolutions, including resolutions 2253 (2015) and 2368 (2017) and join in combating the evolving threat of terrorism in line with its new trends and features.

近期，阿富汗、伊拉克、埃及等地发生恐怖袭击事件，造成重大伤亡。恐怖主义作为全人类公敌，影响超越国界，任何国家难以独自应对。国际社会应切实执行安理会第2253（2015）、2368（2017）号等各项有关决议，结合恐怖主义发展的新趋势和新特点，共同合作应对恐怖主义威胁。

背景介绍

以下两篇材料均为联合国大会特别政治和非殖民化委员会（第四委员会）会议简要记录。第二篇摘自美国代表团的发言，涉及"调查以色列侵害占领区巴勒斯坦人民和其他阿拉伯人人权的行为特别委员会的报告"。

第三篇摘自叙利亚代表团的发言,涉及"整个维持和平行动问题所有方面的全盘审查"。

联合国大会是联合国六大机构之一。《联合国宪章》对大会的职能和权利做了详细规定(见《联合国宪章》第四章)。

大会会议可以有逐字记录或简要记录。关于逐字记录,见上文第一篇的背景介绍。与之相对的简要记录是对会议的总结和概要记录,与逐字记录不同的是,简要记录是以第三人称对各位代表的发言进行记录,在翻译时,也要相应地转换,有相应的处理体例规范可循,下文点评分析部分将会具体提及。

第二篇

Mr. Kendrick (United States of America) said that his delegation continued to oppose the annual submission of unfair draft resolutions biased against Israel. Such a one-sided approach was unacceptable since it damaged the prospects for peace by undermining trust between the parties and creating an unhelpful international environment.

Member States continued to single out Israel with such draft resolutions, which condemned settlement activity but not violence. Israel was blamed for the situation in Gaza, while the only mention of Hamas took the form of praise for its political agreement with Fatah. The United States would, therefore, vote against such one-sided draft resolutions and encouraged other delegations to do so as well.

His delegation was especially concerned by draft resolutions proposing to renew the mandates of counterproductive, biased and unnecessary special committees, such as the Committee on the Exercise of the Inalienable Rights of the Palestinian People, supported by the Division for Palestinian Rights, and the Special Committee to Investigate Israeli Practices Affecting the Human Rights of the Palestinian People and Other Arabs of the Occupied Territories. Those bodies wasted limited United Nations resources, costing approximately $6.1 million in 2015, whilst they failed to contribute to peace in the region and instead perpetuated a United Nations bias against Israel.

请自行翻译后查看后文的分析点评

分析点评

第 1 段

Mr. Kendrick (United States of America) said that his delegation continued to oppose the annual submission of unfair draft resolutions biased against Israel. Such a one-sided approach was unacceptable since it damaged the prospects for peace by undermining trust between the parties and creating an unhelpful international environment.

翻译稿

肯德里克先生（美利坚合众国）说，他的代表团继续反对每年提交对以色列抱有偏见的不公正决议草案。这种一边倒的做法不可接受，因为它通过削弱各方之间的信任和形成对解决冲突毫无助益的国际环境，破坏了和平前景。

审校稿

Kendrick 先生（美利坚合众国）说，美国代表团依然反对每年提交对以色列抱有偏见的不公正决议草案的做法。这种一边倒的做法是不可接受的，因为它削弱了各方之间的信任，导致形成一种对解决冲突毫无助益的国际环境，从而破坏了和平前景。

点评

1. 简要记录的翻译在体例上有一些注意事项。就本例而言，除封面页外，人名一律不译，即使主席或报告员以本国代表身份发言时也不例外。另外，"her/his delegation"译为"××国代表团"（××国为发言者代表的国家）；同理，如果此处原文中出现"his/her country"，要处理为发言者所代表的国家的名称。

2. 英语句式向汉语句式的转换稍显生硬，见"since it damaged the prospects for peace by..."一句。"by"一词在表示方式时有多种处理方法，最常见的是"通过……（结果/目的）"，此外还有"……，从而（结果/目的）""（结果/目的），做法/方式是……"，该词是典型的英文逻辑连接词，而中文是"意会"语言，在表达时不译该词反而会更显流畅通顺。在此，译者将该词直接译为"通过"，显得生硬，审校稿将"by"后置翻译，采用"……，从而（结果/目的）"这种句式，效果就要好得多。

第 2 段

Member States continued to single out Israel with such draft resolutions, which condemned settlement activity but not violence. Israel was blamed for the situation in Gaza, while the only mention of Hamas took the form of praise for its political agreement with Fatah. The United States would, therefore, vote against such one-sided draft resolutions and encouraged other delegations to do so as well.

批 注

① 有体例规范可循。
② 有体例规范可循。
③ 有改进空间。

成员国①继续通过这种决议草案将矛头对准以色列，但②决议草案所谴责的对象却是定居点活动，而非暴力行为。以色列受到指责的原因在于加沙局势，而决议草案③中唯一提及哈马斯之处却是称赞其与法塔赫达成政治协议之举。因此，美国将对这种片面的决议草案投反对票，并鼓励其他代表团也这样做。

批 注

① 注意"会员国"和"成员国"的使用。
② 转折关系从何而来？
③ 突兀，缺乏逻辑性。

会员国继续用这种决议草案对以色列实行差别待遇，一味谴责定居点活动，却不谴责暴力行为。决议草案将加沙局势归咎于以色列，而唯一提及哈马斯之处却是称赞其与法塔赫达成政治协议之举。因此，美国将对这种片面的决议草案投反对票，并鼓励其他代表团也这样做。

1. 整体来说，此段虽短，但集中反映了背景介绍部分提到的简要记录特点，翻译时务必要把握发言背景，浏览简要记录里提到的委员会所讨论的报告或其他文件。这份简要记录反映的是有关代表团针对议程项目"调查以色列侵害占领区巴勒斯坦人民和其他阿拉伯人人权的行为特别委员会的报告"下提交的若干决议草案所做的发言。译者在落笔前可进一步浏览记录中提到的决议草案，了解更多详情。

2. "成员国"还是"会员国"？在联合国文件中，经常会遇到"member states"，具体如何处理，有规律可循，如果是相对于联合国而言，译为"会员国"，其他的（包括各委员会）一律为"成员国"，不过，教科文组织在称呼自己的成员时，也用"会员国"。

3. 关于"which"引导的主语从句，翻译稿存在没有依据而且错误的增译问题。"which"的先行词是"such draft resolutions"，结合前半句的"single out"（意为"treat or to speak about (someone or something in a group) in a way that is different from the way one treats or speaks about others"，即差别对待），以及第1点中提到的背景信息，即可明白美国代表所言之意，即决议草案只是谴责以色列一方的定居点活动，而不谴责另一方的暴力行为。

4. 关于"Israel was blamed for the situation in Gaza, while..."一句的处理，正如点评第1点所言，译者未弄清发言背景，以致出现了"只见树木不见森林"的译文。此句顺承前文，继续论述决议草案对以色列实行差别待遇，另外，结合后半句中的"the only mention of"，也可再次确定这一点。这样，大可把"决议草案"增译出来，处理为"决议草案将加沙局势归咎于⋯⋯，而⋯⋯却是称赞⋯⋯"，逻辑顺畅，而且"归咎"与"称赞"的对比再次突显出差别待遇。

第3段

His delegation was especially concerned by draft resolutions proposing to renew the mandates of counterproductive, biased and unnecessary special committees, such as the Committee on the Exercise of the Inalienable Rights of the Palestinian People, supported by the Division for Palestinian Rights, and the Special Committee to Investigate Israeli Practices Affecting the Human Rights of the Palestinian People and Other Arabs of the Occupied Territories. Those bodies wasted limited United Nations resources, costing approximately $6.1 million in 2015, whilst they failed to contribute to peace in the region and instead perpetuated a United Nations bias against Israel.

批注

① 见第 1 段。
② 定语太长，可读性差。

他的代表团①对提议延长巴勒斯坦人民权利司所支持的巴勒斯坦人民行使不可剥夺权利委员会以及调查以色列侵害占领区巴勒斯坦人民和其他阿拉伯人人权的行为特别委员会等心存偏见、起到反作用，而且没有必要的特别委员会的任务授权的决议草案尤为担忧②。这些机构浪费了有限的联合国资源，仅 2015 年就花费约 610 万美元，但它们并没有为该地区的和平做出贡献，相反却让联合国对以色列的偏见继续存在下来。

美国代表团对提议延长巴勒斯坦人民权利司所支持的巴勒斯坦人民行使不可剥夺权利委员会以及调查以色列侵害占领区巴勒斯坦人民和其他阿拉伯人人权的行为特别委员会等特别委员会的任务期限的决议草案尤感关切，这些特别委员会心存偏见，所起作用适得其反，实无存续之必要。这些机构浪费了有限的联合国资源，仅 2015 年就花费约 610 万美元，但它们非但没有为该地区的和平做出贡献，反倒让联合国对以色列的偏见继续延存。

化长句为短句的翻译技巧：见第一句的处理。该句虽长，但结构并不复杂，里面涉及两个较长的委员会名称，译者理解无误，但其余部分按照原文结构进行顺译，就显得头重脚轻，如果将"counterproductive, biased and unnecessary"拆分后置，重复译出"这些特别委员会"，另成一句，整个句子在结构上平衡，可读性也随之提高。其中，"unnecessary"一词结合前半句美国代表团对该决议草案的不满态度，将该词处理为"无存续之必要"。另外，"renew the mandates of"在联合国文件中也较为常见，一般译为"延长……任务期限"。

补充练习

1. The overwhelming support for the draft resolutions just adopted under agenda items 53 and 54 sent an unambiguous message to Israel to end its occupation of all the occupied Arab territories and to cease immediately all violations of human rights and international humanitarian law. The fact that only two delegations had voted against the draft resolution on the occupied Syrian Golan (A/C.4/72/L.25) reaffirmed that the attempt by Israel to annex the Syrian Golan was null and void and without international legal effect, in accordance with Security Council resolution 497 (1981).

议程项目 53 和 54 下刚刚通过的各项决议草案所获得的压倒性支持向以色列发出了明确的信息,即以色列应结束其对所有阿拉伯被占领土的占领,并立即停止一切侵犯人权和违反国际人道主义法的行为。只有两个代表团投票反对关于被占领的叙利亚戈兰的决议草案(A/C.4/72/L.25),这一事实再度表明,根据安全理事会第 497(1981)号决议,以色列企图吞并叙利亚戈兰的行为无效且不具国际法律效力。

2. The representative of Israel had made many errors which invalidated her statement. Firstly, the so-called Balfour Declaration, which Israel used to justify its crimes in Palestine, was not a valid document because it had been issued by a representative of the British occupying Power, who had not had any right to give away Palestinian territory. Secondly, the very concept of a Jewish State was inherently flawed; given that the United Nations functioned on the basis of national, not religious, borders, it made no more sense to establish a Jewish State than it would to establish individual States bringing together all the Muslim, Christian, Buddhist, Shinto, Confucian or pagan people in the world, respectively.

以色列代表的发言错误频出,属无效发言。首先,以色列用来开脱其所犯罪行的所谓《鲍尔弗宣言》并非有效文件,因为其发布人是占领国英国的一名代表,而该代表根本无权将巴勒斯坦领土拱手予以他人。其次,犹太国家这个概念本质上是存在缺陷的;鉴于联合国是以国家而非宗教为基础发挥职能,建立一个犹太国家与将全世界所有穆斯林、基督教、佛教、神道、儒教或异教徒分别招聚起来建立国家一样毫无意义。

第三篇

Although the concept of peacekeeping operations was not specifically mentioned in the Charter of the United Nations, they had become one of the Organization's primary tools to ease tensions, maintain peace and ensure an environment conducive to post-conflict peacebuilding. The principles set out in the Charter regarding the sovereignty, territorial integrity and political independence of States and non-intervention in the domestic affairs of States should be respected without discretionary decisions or politicization. It was also important to adhere to the basic principles of peacekeeping, namely, consent of the parties, impartiality and non-use of force except in self-defence and in defence of the mandate. Missions should cooperate with the host country in all matters pertaining to the forces deployed.

Although the Syrian Arab Republic supported the development of peacekeeping operations at all levels, the operations were no substitute for permanent solutions that addressed the root causes of conflict. All policy and strategy on peacekeeping operations must be developed and adopted through intergovernmental processes, and only the Special Committee on Peacekeeping Operations had the authority to deal with basic policy matters relating to peacekeeping operations, including ways of strengthening the Organization's capacity to undertake them.

Peacekeeping operations requiring the protection of civilians should do so without encroaching on the host country's primary responsibility in that regard. The protection of civilians should not be used as a pretext to interfere in a State's internal affairs; and it was vital to reach a common legal definition of civilian protection before establishing standards for the concept.

请自行翻译后查看后文的分析点评

分析点评

第 1 段

Although the concept of peacekeeping operations was not specifically mentioned in the Charter of the United Nations, they had become one of the Organization's primary tools to ease tensions, maintain peace and ensure an environment conducive to post-conflict peacebuilding. The principles set out in the Charter regarding the sovereignty, territorial integrity and political independence of States and non-intervention in the domestic affairs of States should be respected without discretionary decisions or politicization. It was also important to adhere to the basic principles of peacekeeping, namely, consent of the parties, impartiality and non-use of force except in self-defence and in defence of the mandate. Missions should cooperate with the host country in all matters pertaining to the forces deployed.

批 注

① 概念？还是行动？
② 哪个组织？
③ 欠精准。
④ 逻辑不通。
⑤ "基本原则"与"即"应紧挨。
⑥ 错译；形式欠妥。

尽管《联合国宪章》没有具体提到维持和平行动的概念，但它们①已成为本组织②缓解紧张局势、维持和平并确保有利于冲突后建设和平的环境的主要工具之一。应当尊重《宪章》中关于国家主权、领土完整和政治独立以及不干涉国家③内政的原则，而不必斟酌决定或政治化④。遵守维持和平的基本原则也很重要，即⑤当事方的同意、公正和不使用武力，除非是为了自卫和为任务规定辩护⑥。

特派团应在与部署部队有关的所有事项上与东道国合作。

虽然《联合国宪章》没有具体提及维持和平行动的概念，但是维持和平行动已经成为联合国缓和紧张局势、维护和平和确保为冲突后建设和平营造有利环境的主要工具之一。《宪章》中有关各国主权、领土完整和政治独立与不干涉各国内政的原则应当得到尊重，并且不得针对这些原则任意做出决定或将其政治化。此外，还必须恪守维持和平的各项基本原则，即各方同意、公正以及除非出于自卫和捍卫职责外不得使用武力。特派团应在与所部署部队有关的所有事项上与东道国合作。

1. 代词的处理：关于"they had become"，如直接译为"它们"，所指对象不够明确。英语中，代词使用较为频繁，而汉语中则较少使用"它/它们"来代指事物，因此，应将 it 或 they 所代指的具体内容翻译出来。

2. "the Organization"这类定冠词加中心词首字母大写的情况，通常须联系上下文将所指组织或机构明确地翻译出来，在联合国文本中出现 the Organization 且指代联合国时，一般不译为"本组织"或"该组织"，而应译为"联合国"；"states"和"parties"在大多数情况下译为"各国"和"各方"，以表明所描述的原则、准则、规范等广泛地适用于每个国家 / 当事方。

3. 关于"without discretionary decisions or politicization"，译者没有吃透原文，也没有理解该分句与前面主句之间的关系，对其进行了孤立的字面翻译，单看译文，读者难免一头雾水。审校稿中则明确地体现出原文的逻辑关系。

4. "It is important to..."这个句式在联合国文件中经常出现。如果……所代指的内容很短，一般可顺译为"……很重要"，如果……所代指的内容很长，再采用顺译法，就会出现头重脚轻的现象，因此，一般可以译为"应该/必须……，这一点至关重要"或"必须/务必要……"。在这里，采用后一种表述方式，还解决了翻译稿中"基本原则（也很重要）"和"即……"相隔的问题。

5. 关于"except（或 including）"的处理：如果后续内容较多或较长，可以将该短语单独列为小句，但如果像本段中这样，后续内容少而短，则通常应按"除 B 外的 A"这种形式翻译，以使全句更加紧凑，避免拖沓或语意模糊。再者，"consent of the parties""impartiality"和"non-use of force except in self-defence and in defence of the mandate"三者并列，词性统一，在译文中，也应尽量体现出这一风格。对比之下，翻译稿与审校稿高低立现。

第 2 段

Although the Syrian Arab Republic supported the development of peacekeeping operations at all levels, the operations were no substitute for permanent solutions that addressed the root causes of conflict. All policy and strategy on peacekeeping operations must be developed and adopted through intergovernmental processes, and only the Special Committee on Peacekeeping Operations had the authority to deal with basic policy matters relating to peacekeeping operations, including ways of strengthening the Organization's capacity to undertake them.

翻译稿

尽管阿拉伯叙利亚共和国支持各级维持和平行动的发展，但这些行动不能替代解决冲突根本原因的永久解决方案。必须通过政府间程序制定和采用有关维持和平行动的所有政策和战略，只有维持和平行动特别委员会才有权处理与维持和平行动有关的基本政策事项，包括加强本组织处理这些事项的能力。

批 注
① 调整语序。
② 指代不明，同第1段。

审校稿

尽管阿拉伯叙利亚共和国支持在各级发展维持和平行动，但维和行动不能代替解决冲突根源的永久解决方案。所有与维持和平行动有关的政策和战略，都必须通过政府间进程加以拟定和通过，而且只有维持和平行动特别委员会有权处理与维持和平行动有关的基本政策事项，包括如何加强联合国开展维持和平行动的能力。

点评

1. 名词/形容词作动词化处理：汉语中，动词非常活跃。在英汉翻译时，常常会用到名词/形容词作动词化处理这种技巧。这里的"were no substitute for"同样适用，可译为"不能替代"。

2. 英语被动句式的处理：在联合国文件中，英文被动句使用广泛，由于动作发出者不明，不易处理。在能够根据上下文确定动作发出者的情况下，一般可处理为"主谓宾"的主动句式；在无法确定或没有必要译明动作发出者的情况下，可借助"来""予以/加以"等词进行翻译，具体如审校稿所示。

第3段

Peacekeeping operations requiring the protection of civilians should do so without encroaching on the host country's primary responsibility in that regard. The protection of civilians should not be used as a pretext to interfere in a State's internal affairs; and it was vital to reach a common legal definition of civilian protection before establishing standards for the concept.

翻译稿

要求保护平民的维持和平行动应该这样做，而不会损害东道国在这方面的主要责任。保护平民不应作为干涉国家内政的借口；至关重要的是，在确立平民保护概念的标准之前，要达成一个共同的法律定义。

批 注
③ 错译；表述不明。
④ 理解错误。

审校稿

在执行维持和平行动过程中，如需保护平民，则在保护平民时，不得侵犯东道国在这方面的首要责任。保护平民不应被当作干涉一国内政的借口,而且必须要先就保护平民达成共同的法律定义,再针对这一概念确立标准,这一点至关重要。

1. 关于"Peacekeeping operations requiring the protection of civilians should do so without",翻译稿英文痕迹很重,显得畏首畏尾,让读者不明就里。"require"主要有"要求"和"需要"两个意思,根据上下文,此处应取"需要"之意;"so"和"in this regard"均是指"protection of civilians",即保护平民,"so"在前,应该明确翻译出来,"in this regard"按字面译为"在这方面"即可。此外,审校稿还在原文逻辑的基础上,引入了"如(果)",化长句为短句,让译文逻辑更清晰。

2. 在通过"before"连接两个行为或动作的句子中,不必将句式的翻译拘泥于"在……之前,……",也可以译为"先……,再……",使句子的连接更加通顺。此外,在处理这类句子时,一定要注意辨别时间、因果、逻辑顺序,确定之后再着手翻译,以免出现实质性错误。

3. 关于"it was vital to"的处理,参见第 1 段点评 4。

1. The government of Argentina had pledged to increase its contribution to peacekeeping operations at the recent United Nations Peacekeeping Defence Ministerial held in London. Over the years, operations had been deployed in increasingly perilous circumstances, with a greater requirement to protect civilians. The highly complex, multidimensional peacekeeping operations that had emerged as a result had provided a platform for sustainable development by promoting and protecting human rights, rebuilding institutions and consolidating democracy and the rule of law. Nevertheless, the changing reality of peacekeeping operations would require further reflection on how to strengthen their operational capacity.

参考译文

在最近于伦敦召开的联合国维持和平问题国防部长会议上,阿根廷政府承诺增派维持和平行动人员。多年来,维持和平行动的部署环境越来越危险,对平民保护提出了更高要求。维持和平行动也因此变得高度复杂且横跨多个层面,它促进和保护人权,重建各机构,巩固民主和法治,为可持续发展提供了平台。然而,面对维持和平行动不断变化的现实,必须进一步反思如何加强其行动能力。

2. The report of the High-level Independent Panel had rightly focused on conflict prevention and mediation, and on political solutions as drivers of the design

and deployment of peace operations, within the broader context of the new concept of sustainable peace set out in United Nations resolutions on the review of the peacebuilding architecture. While the basic principles of peacekeeping remained vital to mission success, they did not necessarily hinder the use of force in the protection of civilians as well as in self-defence or in defence of the peacekeeping mandate.

参考译文

联合国关于建设和平架构审查的各项决议提出了"可持续和平"这个新概念，顺应这一大背景，高级别独立小组适时将重点放在冲突预防和调解以及推动和平行动设计和部署的政治解决办法上。虽然维持和平基本原则仍然是特派团成功的关键，但这些原则不一定会妨碍为保护平民、自卫或捍卫维护和平的任务而使用武力。

背景介绍

以下两篇材料均选自联合国秘书长向联合国大会提交的报告。第四篇材料选自秘书长根据各国提交的材料，向大会提交的关于核裁军、以核武器进行威胁或使用核武器的合法性以及减少核危险的报告，其中介绍了各国为促进执行核裁军和不扩散协定而做出的努力，并整理汇编了会员国提交的意见。此篇所列段落具体摘自奥地利提交的材料。

第五篇材料节选自秘书长在大会第七十三届会议关于建立中东无核武器区的议程项目下提交的报告。为推进建立中东无核武器区，大会请秘书长根据现实局势，不断与中东各国和其他有关国家进行磋商并征求意见。该报告概述了秘书长从各国政府收到的答复。

根据《联合国宪章》规定，秘书长是联合国的"首席行政长官"，履行行政长官的职务，以及安理会、大会、经社理事会以及其他联合国机构"所托付之其他职务"，包括根据大会/安理会决议等，就特定问题向大会/安理会提交报告。

秘书长的报告（以及秘书长特别代表、其他机构执行秘书等的报告）一般围绕某一主题编写，主题在领域上跨度很大。在结构上，一般分为"背景介绍""正文（分段甚至分主题阐明问题）"和"结论（建议）"三个部分；在语言上，具有客观、平实、严谨的特点，大多没有非常复杂的结构，但逻辑紧密，不时涉及一些专有名词和术语。在翻译时须紧扣内容，细致入微，准确拿捏，在保证准确、规范的基础上形成与这一特殊主题相匹配的文风。

 第一章 和平与安全

 第四篇

 原文

Against the background of consistent Austrian support for nuclear disarmament efforts and its constitutional law (No. 149/1999) on a nuclear-free Austria, Austria strongly supports the conclusion and recommendations for follow-on actions agreed upon at the 2010 Review Conference of the Parties to the Treaty on the Non-Proliferation of Nuclear Weapons and is also particularly engaged in overcoming the current lack of effectiveness of the United Nations disarmament machinery, in particular that of the Conference on Disarmament, and the resulting absence of substantive multilateral disarmament negotiations.

Building notably on the 1996 advisory opinion of the International Court of Justice, Austria is convinced of the need to fundamentally change the discourse on nuclear weapons and to foster the understanding that any use of nuclear weapons would be morally repugnant and devastating in its effects on the whole world and all of humankind. Consequently, it is difficult to envisage how any use of nuclear weapons could be compatible with international law, in particular with the fundamental principles of international humanitarian law. Austria considers the mere existence of nuclear weapons to be unacceptable, given the risks of their use, either intentionally or by accident or mistake, and the resulting unacceptable humanitarian consequences.

请自行翻译后查看后文的分析点评

 分析点评

第 1 段

Against the background of consistent Austrian support for nuclear disarmament efforts and its constitutional law (No. 149/1999) on a nuclear-free Austria, Austria strongly supports the conclusion and recommendations for follow-on actions agreed upon at the 2010 Review Conference of the Parties to the Treaty on the Non-Proliferation of Nuclear Weapons and is also particularly engaged in overcoming the current lack of effectiveness of the United Nations disarmament machinery, in particular that of the Conference on Disarmament, and the resulting absence of substantive multilateral disarmament negotiations.

批 注
① 此处存在漏译。
② 不当增译。
③ 注意词汇变化转换。

奥地利素来支持核裁军努力，且通过了①关于无核奥地利的根本法（No. 149/1999），现在更是②大力支持关于《不扩散核武器条约》缔约国2010年审议大会达成的后续行动的结论和建议，并特别专注于克服联合国裁军机制，尤其是裁军谈判会议，目前缺乏效力的问题，以及由此导致的缺乏实质性多边裁军谈判③的问题。

奥地利一贯支持核裁军努力，根据这一背景及其关于无核奥地利的根本法（第149/1999号法），奥地利大力支持关于不扩散核武器条约缔约国2010年审议大会上商定的后续行动的结论和建议，并特别专注于克服联合国裁军机制，尤其是裁军谈判会议，目前缺乏效力的问题，以及由此导致的实质性多边裁军谈判迟迟无法举行的问题。

1. 增译/减译应有度。原文首先就提出了"Against the background of"，虽然"奥地利素来支持核裁军努力"确实是这一背景，但在翻译时不可如此缺省；另外，将"Austria strongly supports..."增译为"现在更是大力支持"，"更是"二字不仅画蛇添足，而且有失严谨。这也是联合国文件翻译的一大特点，容许适当灵活变通，但尽量不缺省漏译，也不随意增译。

2. 翻译技巧问题。关于"the resulting absence of substantive multilateral disarmament negotiations"，原译"导致的缺乏实质性多边裁决谈判的问题"并无错误，但由于汉语是形象语言，在表达的时候往往动词更具有动感和力度，故将"absence"改译为"未能举行"更能彰显力度。在英中翻译中词性变化转换（例如，名词和形容词动词化、动词名词化，甚至改用他词）这个技巧常常会用到，需要在实践中灵活运用。

第2段

Building notably on the 1996 advisory opinion of the International Court of Justice, Austria is convinced of the need to fundamentally change the discourse on nuclear weapons and to foster the understanding that any use of nuclear weapons would be morally repugnant and devastating in its effects on the whole world and all of humankind. Consequently, it is difficult to envisage how any use of nuclear weapons could be compatible with international law, in particular with the fundamental principles of international humanitarian law. Austria considers the mere existence of nuclear weapons to be unacceptable, given the risks of their use, either intentionally or by accident or mistake, and the resulting unacceptable humanitarian consequences.

批 注
④ 注意前后关系紧凑感。

特别是根据国际法院1996年的咨询意见，奥地利坚信④，必须从根本上改

变关于核武器的论述，促进了解[①]任何使用核武器都将为道德所不容，并将对整个世界和全人类造成破坏性影响。因此，奥地利认为很难设想使用核武器如何可以符合国际法，特别是国际人道主义法的基本原则[②]。奥地利认为，鉴于[③]使用核武器的危险，不管是有意还是无意抑或误用，以及由此导致的难以接受的人道主义后果，核武器存在本身就是不可接受的。

批 注

① 理解错误。
② 注意主语的适当省略。
③ 如若后置，效果会更好。

奥地利尤其依赖国际法院 1996 年的咨询意见，深信需要从根本上改变关于核武器的讨论，并促进达成如下谅解，即对核武器的任何使用都是令人憎恶的道德恶行，而且会对全世界和全人类造成毁灭性的影响。因此，很难想象核武器的使用如何能符合国际法，尤其是国际人道主义法的基本原则。奥地利认为，核武器的使用，不管是有意还是无意抑或误用，都有巨大风险，并造成难以承担的人道主义后果。有鉴于此，其存在本身就是不可接受的。

点 评

1. 第一句行文长达四行多，在翻译前务必要先理清句子结构和逻辑关系。首先，翻译稿依循原文结构，将"Building notably on"与后面的主语"Austria"分开，读来甚感突兀。将"奥地利"置于句首，主语明确，句子更显紧凑直观，可读性也随之增强。其次，"need"后面的"to fundamentally change"和"to foster the understanding that"二者为并列关系，用一个"并"字将二者连接起来，并用一个"即"字述明应该达成的谅解，结构严谨又意思明确。

2. 关于"it is difficult to envisage"，翻译稿为"奥地利认为很难设想"，其实这部分通篇都是关于奥地利，可适当省略主语，避免啰唆。

3. 最后一句也是长句，翻译稿同样是沿用了原文的句式结构。审校稿则另辟蹊径，先将"given"后面的两个短语转化为独立分句，紧接着再用"有鉴于此"体现因果关系，整个句子逻辑严密，表述清晰。

1. The Government of Iraq affirms that the only guarantee against the use or threat of use of nuclear weapons is the total elimination of nuclear weapons, in a gradual manner that will help to build confidence among States parties to the Treaty. It is necessary to reach agreement on the need for a binding international instrument under which nuclear-weapon States will provide assurances to non-nuclear-weapon States against the use or threat of use of nuclear weapons. Identifying the means by which significant progress towards this goal can be made would give States outside the Non-Proliferation Treaty incentives to accede to it.

伊拉克政府申明，不使用或威胁使用核武器的唯一保证是彻底消除核武器，

但消除工作须循序渐进，以助《条约》缔约国之间建立信任。有必要达成一项共识，即需要订立一份具有约束力的国际文书，由核武器国家据此向无核武器国家做出不使用或威胁使用核武器的保证。此外，还需查明哪些手段可帮助在实现这一目标方面取得重大进展，以此激励尚未加入的国家加入《不扩散核武器条约》。

2. In order to ensure transparency in transfers, and pursuant to its national legislation, Ukraine submits reports to IAEA on international transfers of specified equipment and non-nuclear material listed in Annex Ⅱ to the Protocol Additional to the Agreement between Ukraine and IAEA for the Application of Safeguards in Connection with the Treaty on the Non-Proliferation of Nuclear Weapons. Pursuant to paragraph 7.8 of the Understandings of the Zangger Committee, Ukraine submits reports to the Secretariat every year on the licences issued for the transfer, to non-nuclear-weapon States that are not parties to the Treaty, of goods specified in the trigger list and intended for peaceful purposes.

参考译文

为了确保转让透明，乌克兰根据本国法律法规，先后向原子能机构提交了多份报告，说明《乌克兰与国际原子能机构实施有关〈不扩散核武器条约〉保障监督的协定附加议定书》附件2所列指定设备及非核材料的国际转让情况。根据《桑戈委员会谅解》第7.8段，乌克兰每年向秘书处提交报告，汇报在向非《条约》缔约方的非核武器国家转让触发清单中明确规定且打算用于和平目的的商品方面的许可证签发情况。

第五篇

原文

At the meetings of the First Committee during the seventy-second session of the General Assembly, in October 2017, States continued to demonstrate support for the convening of a conference on the establishment of a Middle East zone free of nuclear weapons and all other weapons of mass destruction. While many States criticized the lack of progress toward a Middle East zone free of nuclear weapons and all other weapons of mass destruction, no new ideas were put forward and the two annual resolutions introduced by Egypt on the Middle East included only technical updates. The Russian Federation delivered a statement expressing concern for the lack of progress in convening the Conference on the nuclear-weapon-and other WMD-free zone in the Middle East and the negative impact this can have on the 2020 NPT Review Conference.

The two-State solution is the only realistic way to achieve an end to the conflict, an end to the occupation that began in 1967, resolution of all final status issues—including Jerusalem, borders, refugees and security—and the establishment of a sovereign, independent, contiguous and viable State of Palestine living side by side in peace with a secure State of Israel, in accordance with relevant resolutions of the Security Council, previous agreements, the Madrid Principles and the Quartet road map. I reaffirm my strong commitment to reaching a lasting and comprehensive peace in the Middle East.

The establishment of a MEWFZ would contribute to easing tensions and building confidence, promote peace process, strengthen global nuclear non-proliferation and disarmament norms and consolidate international efforts towards peace and security, taking into account the unique character of such a zone which goes beyond one category of weapons. Turkey firmly believes that the process for the establishment of MEWFZ should be accelerated, as delaying it indefinitely would undermine the credibility of the international non-proliferation regime. Turkey hopes that the challenge posed by this issue can be overcome in the forthcoming period. For this, all stakeholders concerned need to be emboldened to adopt constructive stances.

请自行翻译后查看后文的分析点评

分析点评

第1段

At the meetings of the First Committee during the seventy-second session of the General Assembly, in October 2017, States continued to demonstrate support for the convening of a conference on the establishment of a Middle East zone free of nuclear weapons and all other weapons mass destruction. While many States criticized the lack of progress toward a Middle East zone free of nuclear weapons and all other weapons of mass destruction, no new ideas were put forward and the two annual resolutions introduced by Egypt on the Middle East included only technical updates. The Russian Federation delivered a statement expressing concern for the lack of progress in convening the Conference on the nuclear-weapon-and other WMD-free zone in the Middle East and the negative impact this can have on the 2020 NPT Review Conference.

2017年10月，在大会第七十二届会议期间的第一委员会会议上①，各国继

批注

① 逻辑有误。

批注

① 句式待优化，术语错误。
② 表述不明。
③ 错译。
④ 欠严谨。
⑤ 错译。

续对召开一次关于建立中东无核武器及所有其他大规模杀伤性武器区的会议表示支持①。尽管许多国家批评在建立这一区域上②缺乏进展，但没有提出新的想法，并且埃及提出③的关于中东的两项年度决议④只涉及技术上的最新情况。俄罗斯联邦发表了一项声明⑤，其中就未能在召开会议建立此类区域取得进展及其对2020年审议大会可能产生的消极影响表达了关切。

审校稿

2017年10月，在大会第七十二届会议第一委员会会议上，各国继续表示支持召开一次关于建立中东无核武器及所有其他大规模毁灭性武器区的会议。许多国家批评建立中东无核武器及所有其他大规模毁灭性武器区的工作缺乏进展，但却无一提出新的想法，埃及就中东问题介绍的两项年度决议案也仅涉及技术上的更新。俄罗斯联邦在发言中对中东无核武器及所有其他大规模毁灭性武器区问题会议召开工作毫无进展及其可能对2020年审议大会产生的消极影响表示关切。

点评

1. 了解背景信息，对提高翻译准确性大有助益。对于"At the meetings of the First Committee during the seventy-second session of the General Assembly"，译者作了逐字翻译，但意思却大相径庭。联合国大会下设六个主要委员会，大会在每届会议开始时将议程项目分配给各主要委员会审议，其中第一委员会主要负责审议裁军与国际安全相关议题，该委员会并非是在大会第七十二届会议期间设立的。原翻译稿模糊了这一关系，容易造成歧义。

2. "to demonstrate support for"意为"对……表示支持"或者"表示支持……"，后者的表述优于前者，更为自然简便。

3. 术语处理欠缺严谨：①"WMD"为"大规模毁灭性武器"，这是联合国多语言术语库（UNTERM）中的官方译法。在翻译联合国文件时，如果遇到不确定的专有名词，不妨多查阅联合国多语言术语库（UNTERM）；原文前后三次提到"the Middle East zone free of nuclear weapons and all other weapons mass destruction"，分别针对"States""many states"和"The Russian Federation"而言，译者将后面两个分别省译为"这一区域"和"此类区域"，准确性欠佳，应该完整译出，不仅不显拖沓，反而更显清晰明确。②关于"the two annual resolutions introduced by Egypt"，译者处理为"埃及提出的……两项年度决议"，着实欠妥。首先，"resolution"在获得通过之前，只能成为"决议案"，通过之后，才可以称为"决议"。其次，"introduce"为"介绍"，"提出"的英文表述为"sponsor"，这两项决议案可能是由埃及和别的国家或由国家集团提出，由埃及在会上介绍。③在会上的"statement"，一般译为"发言"，而非声明。

第2段

The two-State solution is the only realistic way to achieve an end to the conflict, an end to the occupation that began in 1967, resolution of all final status issues—including Jerusalem, borders, refugees and security—and the establishment of a sovereign, independent, contiguous and viable State of Palestine living side by side in peace with a secure State of Israel, in accordance with relevant resolutions of the Security Council, previous agreements, the Madrid Principles and the Quartet road map. I reaffirm my strong commitment to reaching a lasting and comprehensive peace in the Middle East.

翻译稿

依照安全理事会的相关决议、以往协定、马德里原则和《四方路线图》，只有通过两国解决方案这一唯一现实途径，才能① 结束冲突、终止1967年以来的占领、解决全部最终地位问题（包括耶路撒冷、边界、难民和安全问题），并建立一个与安全的以色列国和平共处的享有主权、独立、毗连并自立② 的巴勒斯坦国。秘书长③ 重申其坚定地致力于实现中东全面持久和平。

批 注

① 强调程度与原文相比尚显不足。
② 词汇错译。
③ 注意第一人称和第三人称的区别。

审校稿

依照安全理事会相关决议、以往协定、马德里原则和《四方路线图》，要想结束冲突，终止1967年以来的占领，解决全部最终地位问题（包括耶路撒冷、边界、难民和安全问题），并建立一个与安全的以色列国毗邻而居、和平共处且享有主权、独立和有生存能力的巴勒斯坦国，两国解决方案是唯一切实可行的路径。我在此重申，本人将坚定地致力于实现中东持久全面和平。

点评

1. 第一句长达六行之多，而且涉及生僻词汇，有一定的难度。先看整个句子结构，说说翻译技巧。这句话的骨架为"The two-State solution is the only realistic way to achieve..., in accordance with..."，其中，"an end to the conflict" "an end to the occupation that..." 和 "the establishment of..." 为三个并列宾语。若按句子结构直译，即为"按照……，两国解决方案是实现……的唯一现实路径"，但三个并列宾语太长，显然不宜按照原文结构直译。译者对句子进行拆分，先将"The two-State solution is the only realistic way"译为一个独立分句，即"依照……，只有通过两国解决方案这一唯一现实途径，才能……"，这不失为一种好方法。但是，翻译稿对两国解决方案的强调和原文相比仍然较弱，采用"要想……两国解决方案是唯一切实可行的路径"这种方式将之后置，强调效果得到强化。

2. 再看第一句中的生僻词汇和分句处理。"viable"有两个意思：一是"feasible（切实可行的）"；二是"capable of developing and surviving independently（能独立发展/生存的）"，在这里，显然应取后者之意，译为"有生存能力的"，这是关于巴勒斯坦问题的政治话语中的惯用表述，强调的是国家的存活能力，而不是具有政治意味的"自立"。"contiguous"的意思是"touching or next to sth"（相邻/相近），在此，显然是指巴勒斯坦和以色列在地理上毗邻。在处理这个词时，需要注意一下中文和英文在行文规范上的差异。英文重"形合"，中文重"意合"，机械地按照英文"形合"的结构来处理，译为"享有主权、独立、毗连并自立",非常奇怪。译文中可"意合",将之前置,与修饰两国关系的"living side by side in peace with"合译为"毗邻而居、和平共处",其他三个单独修饰巴勒斯坦国家的词"sovereign""independent"和"viable"可以单独放在一起。

3. 关于"I reaffirm my strong commitment to",原文件并非简要记录,无须转化为第三人称,按第一人称翻译即可。另外,"commitment"意为"承诺",在这里,不妨将之动词化,处理成"致力于",更显妥帖。

第3段

The establishment of a MEWFZ would contribute to easing tensions and building confidence, promote peace process, strengthen global nuclear non-proliferation and disarmament norms and consolidate international efforts towards peace and security, taking into account the unique character of such a zone which goes beyond one category of weapons. Turkey firmly believes that the process for the establishment of MEWFZ should be accelerated, as delaying it indefinitely would undermine the credibility of the international non-proliferation regime. Turkey hopes that the challenge posed by this issue can be overcome in the forthcoming period. For this, all stakeholders concerned need to be emboldened to adopt constructive stances.

批注

① 术语错译,且与第1段中术语不一致。
② 理解与组句问题。
③ 偏离原文,不具体。
④ 推迟什么?

翻译稿

建立中东无核武器及所有其他大规模杀伤性武器及其运载系统区,将有助于缓和紧张局势和建立信任、推动和平进程、加强全球核不扩散和裁军规范和巩固为实现和平与安全所做的国际努力,同时考虑到这一区域的特殊性质,它超出了某一类武器的范围。土耳其坚信,建立此类区域③的进程应得以加快,因为推迟④势必将损害国际不扩散机制的公信力。土耳其希望能够在即将到来的时期内克服这一问题所带来的挑战。为实现这一目标,必须鼓励所有利益攸关方采取建设性的立场。

审校稿

考虑到无核武器区有其特殊性,所禁核武器不仅限于某一类,建立中东无核武器及所有其他大规模毁灭性武器区将有助于缓和紧张局势和建立信任,推动和平进程,加强全球核不扩散和裁军规范,巩固为实现和平与安全所做的国际努力。土耳其坚信,应加快中东无核区的建立进程,因为推迟该进程势必会损害国际不扩散制度的公信力。土耳其希望在下一阶段克服这个问题带来的挑战。为此,必须鼓励所有利益攸关方采取建设性立场。

点评

1. 关于"taking into account...beyond one category of weapons"一句,译者在该分句与主句间关系的处理上以及句意理解上均有问题。首先,"taking into account..."一句为条件状语,修饰"The establishment of a MEWFZ would

contribute to..., promote..., strengthen...and consolidate...,",二者之间为主次关系,表示在"考虑到……"的基础上/情况下,建立中东无核区所能带来的种种好处,按照汉语表达习惯,应该前置翻译。而翻译稿却沿用原文结构,将其放在主句之后,给人以二者并列的感觉。再来看句子本身,which 引导的定语从句所修饰的是"unique character of a zone",而译者没弄清楚这一点。显然,该分句不宜直译,宜进行拆译,即先译出无核区具有特殊性,再另起一句,补充说明特殊性在于这类区域内所禁止的武器"不仅限于某一类武器"。

2. 灵活运用省译与增译技巧。见"as delaying it..." 和"For this, all stakeholders..."这两句话的翻译处理。在前者中,"it"漏译,导致译文指代不明,应该承接上一句中的"中东无核区的建立进程",将"该进程"补译出来;而在后者中,译者却对"this"进行了扩充,有画蛇添足之嫌,因为上一句中已经明确交代了土耳其的希望,因此,"为此"二字足以承前启后。

补充练习

1. As mentioned in the Secretary-General's disarmament agenda entitled "Securing our Common Future" launched on 24 May 2018 in Geneva, the Secretary-General and the High Representative for Disarmament Affairs will work with Member States to strengthen and consolidate nuclear-weapon-free zones, including by facilitating enhanced cooperation and consultation between existing zones, encouraging nuclear-weapon States to adhere to the relevant protocols to the treaties establishing such zones, and supporting the further establishment of such zones, including in the Middle East.

参考译文

2018年5月24日,题为"确保我们共同的未来"的秘书长裁军议程在日内瓦启动。正如该议程所述,秘书长和裁军事务高级代表将与会员国一道,加强和巩固无核武器区,具体做法包括推动在现有无核武器区之间加强合作与协商,鼓励核武器国家加入关于建立无核武器区之条约的相关议定书,支持进一步建立无核武器区,包括中东无核武器区。

2. Ukraine is a member of the Treaty on Non-Proliferation of Nuclear Weapons since 1994 as a non-nuclear state. During 24 years of NPT membership, Ukraine has been fulfilling its obligations in accordance with the provisions of this international legal instrument. Furthermore, Ukraine keeps undertaking and efficiently implementing additional obligations in the framework of nuclear security summits. In particular, Ukraine refused to use highly enriched uranium and removed all of its stocks from its territory. In the course of the Washington

Nuclear Security Summit in March—April 2016, Ukraine on the highest political level reconfirmed its commitment to the principles of non-proliferation of nuclear weapons as a leading state in this process.

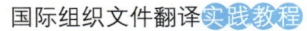

1994年，乌克兰作为无核国家加入《不扩散核武器条约》。在加入条约后的24年里，乌克兰一直按照该国际法律文书的规定履行义务。不仅如此，乌克兰还一直承担并有效履行核安保峰会框架下的其他义务。特别是，乌克兰拒绝使用高浓铀，并已将本国领土上的所有高浓铀库存清除完毕。在2016年3月和4月举行的华盛顿核安保峰会期间，乌克兰在最高政治层面重申，作为这一进程的主要参与国，乌克兰坚决恪守不扩散核武器原则。

背景介绍

以下两篇材料均选自不扩散核武器条约缔约国审议大会相关文件。第六篇选自不扩散核武器条约缔约国2015年审议大会的一份简要记录。所选段落摘自爱尔兰代表的发言。文件在形式上属于简要记录，关于风格特点和翻译注意事项，可参照联合国大会会议简要记录，详见本章第二篇背景介绍。

第七篇选自澳大利亚提交的关于2010年不扩散核武器条约缔约国审议大会商定行动计划执行情况的报告，主要内容为概述为执行《条约》各项条款所采取的步骤和措施。此类报告采用专用模板（均为图表）填写而成，因所选文字均选自表格所填内容，翻译风格上应简练、准确。

《不扩散核武器条约》（以下简称"《不扩散条约》"）旨在防止核武器及核武器技术的扩散，促进和平利用核能方面的合作，推进实现核裁军和全面彻底裁军的目标，是核武器国家在一项多边条约中对裁军目标做出的唯一具有约束力的承诺。《不扩散条约》（特别是第八条第3款）规定每五年对《条约》实施情况进行一次审议，即为审议大会。审议会议期间成立三个主要委员会，分别讨论不同议题，其中，第一委员会集中讨论条约中有关不扩散核武器、裁军和国际和平与安全（包括安全保障）条款的执行情况。审议大会及相关机构的文件多涉及专业术语，且术语多有固定译法，特别是在文件围绕某一主题详细展开时，更是如此，技术性很强。不仅如此，这类文件多会援引往届会议和联合国大会等机构的决议和决定以及其他成果/信息/工作文件，译者往往需要根据文件的文号或标题关键词在对应机构官方网站以及联合国正式文件系统（ODS）上进行查询。除语言和词汇本身外，掌握相关背景知识对于译者准确理解原文、妥善处理译文十分重要。这些特点在下文两篇材料中均有体现。

第六篇

While there had been considerable reductions in nuclear arsenals and the number of nuclear weapons was at its lowest level since the height of the cold war, to date, not one weapon from within the five nuclear stockpiles recognized by the Treaty had been eliminated through multilateral negotiations envisaged under article Ⅵ. The Treaty contained no arrangements for nuclear disarmament.

Given that nuclear weapons were widely judged to be bereft of moral justification and utilitarian value and had been shown to have appalling and indiscriminate destructive capacity, he questioned the reluctance to discuss legal pathways to eliminate them, as all States were obliged to do under the Treaty.

In view of current knowledge on the matter, the international community must determine whether it was prepared to continue to acquiesce to a situation where, sooner or later, a nuclear weapon may be either used or set off accidentally.

The compelling evidence about the devastating impact of nuclear weapons could not be ignored, nor could the ever-present risks of a nuclear weapon detonation and the inability of the international system to respond adequately thereto. Those factors underlined the clear and unambiguous Treaty obligation upon all States parties to enter into negotiations leading to effective measures for nuclear disarmament.

The working paper submitted by New Zealand on behalf of the New Agenda Coalition (NPT/CONF.2015/WP.9) was a constructive and cogent document which offered two possible pathways for pursuing effective measures for nuclear disarmament but did not seek to prescribe any particular legal instrument to be pursued through discussion between States.

However, it was no longer a question of whether those discussions should take place, nor was there any doubt as to the need for an agreed legal pathway to achieving nuclear disarmament.

请自行翻译后查看后文的分析点评

第1段

While there had been considerable reductions in nuclear arsenals and the number of nuclear weapons was at its lowest level since the height of the cold war, to date, not one weapon from within the five nuclear stockpiles recognized by the Treaty had been eliminated through multilateral negotiations envisaged under article Ⅵ. The Treaty contained no arrangements for nuclear disarmament.

虽然核武库已被大量削减，核武器数量仍处于冷战顶峰以来的最低水平，但是，迄今为止，没有通过第六条设想的多边谈判消除《条约》认可的五个核武库内的任何武器①。《条约》未载有针对核裁军的安排。

批 注

① 表述不清晰。

虽然核武库已被大幅削减，且核武器数量处于冷战高峰以来的最低水平，但到目前为止，在《条约》认可的五个核武器国家的核武器库存中，尚无一件核武器是通过第六条所设想的多边谈判消除的，因为《条约》中未规定任何核裁军安排。

点 评

总体上来讲，译者对本段话的字面理解基本到位，但译者对相关背景知识缺乏了解。《不扩散核武器条约》规定只有联合国五个常任理事国有权拥有核武器。但目前，五常之外好几个国家都拥有核武器。制约核扩散的国际法机制主要以《不扩散核武器条约》（NPT）和国际原子能机构（IAEA）为核心。但是，这个国际法机制并不完善，存在很多问题。

1. "five nuclear stockpiles" 是指五个核大国的核武器库存，"recognized by the Treaty" 作为定语修饰 "五个核大国的核武器库存"，结合上述背景知识，在此可以增译出 "五个核武器国家"，更加清晰准确。

2. 鉴于国际法机制并不完善这一背景知识，审校稿增译 "因为"，将最后一句与上一句连接起来，点明至今尚无一件核武器通过多边谈判消除的原因。

第 2 段

Given that nuclear weapons were widely judged to be bereft of moral justification and utilitarian value and had been shown to have appalling and indiscriminate destructive capacity, he questioned the reluctance to discuss legal pathways to eliminate them, as all States were obliged to do under the Treaty.

鉴于核武器被广泛评价为丧失道德合理性和功利价值②，并已被证明具有惊人和不加区分的破坏能力，他对不愿讨论消除核武器的法律途径提出质疑③，因为依据《条约》，所有国家都有义务这样做。

批 注

② 理解不到位，表述不当。
③ 不符合中文表述习惯。

核武器被普遍认为没有道义正当性和实用价值，并且已被证明具有骇人且不加区分的破坏能力，而有些国家却不愿意讨论消除核武器的法律途径，他对此表

示质疑，因为依据《条约》规定，所有国家都有义务这样做。

1. "moral justification"和"utilitarian value"两个名词的理解不透彻。"justification"为"正当理由"之意，"moral justification"是指"道义上的正当理由"或"道义上的正当性"，而在词典上，"utilitarian value"意为"功利价值""实用价值""实用性价值"，但结合本材料语境，即核武器破坏性太大，谁也不敢使用，在此应取"实用价值"或"实用性价值"之意。

2. 翻译技巧：打破句子结构，根据语意重组。翻译稿严格遵循了英文原文的句式结构，也因此受到束缚。审校稿在形式上略去了"Given"，将后面的两个分句翻译为独立的句子，并根据上下文增译出"有些国家却"。整个句子虽无"Given"，却更显条理清晰、逻辑严密。

第3段

In view of current knowledge on the matter, the international community must determine whether it was prepared to continue to acquiesce to a situation where, sooner or later, a nuclear weapon may be either used or set off accidentally.

鉴于目前对此事项①的认识，国际社会必须确定②是否准备继续默许这种情况，核武器早晚会被使用或意外爆炸③。

鉴于目前对这一问题的认识，国际社会必须决定是否准备继续默许核武器早晚会被使用或被意外引爆的情况。

批 注

① 表述不准确。
② 错译。
③ 处理方式不好。

1. "matter""determine"和"set off"的处理差强人意。"matter"可以译为"事项"，也可以译为"问题"，在本句中，译为"问题"更合适；"acquiesce"是"默许""默认"的意思；"set off"在此是指"引爆"核武器的意思，译者将其译为"爆炸"是不准确的。

2. "where"引导的定语部分并不长，拆开单译反而影响作者原意的表述，所以不拆为佳。

第4段

The compelling evidence about the devastating impact of nuclear weapons could not be ignored, nor could the ever-present risks of a nuclear weapon detonation and the inability of the international system to respond adequately thereto. Those factors underlined the clear and unambiguous Treaty obligation upon all States parties to enter into negotiations leading to effective measures for nuclear disarmament.

批注

① 处理方式不佳。
② 漏译了 risk。
③ 表达不准确。
④ 前面漏译 risk，导致这里的"对此"表述模糊，可能让人误解为"爆炸"而非"风险"。
⑤ 表述错误。
⑥ 表述欠佳。

翻译稿

不能忽视关于核武器的毁灭性影响的确信证据，也不能忽视核武器爆炸以及国际制度没有能力对此④做出适当响应⑤。这些因素强调了清晰和明确的《条约》义务，要求所有缔约国进行谈判⑥，产生切实的核裁军措施。

审校稿

核武器具有毁灭性的影响，而且相关证据确凿，这一点不容忽视；核武器爆炸的风险始终存在，而且国际社会无力充分应对这种风险，这一点也不容忽视。这些因素突出表明，所有缔约国都必须履行《条约》明确规定的义务，进行谈判并达成切实有效的核裁军措施。

点评

1. 翻译稿欠佳。第一句直译，读来令人费解。我们可以换种说法，比如"已有令人信服的证据证明核武器具有毁灭性的影响"，或再进一步改述为"核武器具有毁灭性的影响，而且相关证据确凿"，更显地道。"ever-present risks of..."可采用形容词"ever-present"动词化的处理方法，译为"核武器爆炸的风险始终存在"。

2. 在翻译过程中，必要时，不妨打破原有句子结构，根据语意重组。审校稿化短语为短句，呈排比句式，无论在形式上还是语言表达上，都力度十足。译者平时需要注意这种翻译技巧的积累，在实践中灵活运用。

3. 关于第二句，对"underline the...Treaty obligation"的处理较为生硬，应改述为"突出表明"。

第5段

The working paper submitted by New Zealand on behalf of the New Agenda Coalition (NPT/ CONF.2015/WP.9) was a constructive and cogent document which offered two possible pathways for pursuing effective measures for nuclear disarmament but did not seek to prescribe any particular legal instrument to be pursued through discussion between States.

批注

⑦ 表述不清。
⑧ 表述错误。

翻译稿

新西兰代表新议程联盟提交的工作文件（NPT/CONF.2015/WP.9）是一份建设性的和有说服力的文件，提供了制订切实的核裁军措施的两种可能途径，但未寻求通过各国之间的讨论制订任何具体的法律文书。

审校稿

新西兰代表新议程联盟提交的工作文件（NPT/CONF.2015/WP.9）颇具建设性和说服力，这份文件为寻找有效的核裁军措施提供了两种可能途径，而且没有对应通过国家间讨论制定何种具体的法律文书指手画脚。

1. "working paper" "document" 和 "which" 同指一份文件，翻译稿沿用原文句式，拖泥带水，弱化了可读性。将 "document" 略去不译，转而将 "which" 译为 "这份文件"（或 "该文件"），翻译稿的问题迎刃而解。

2. "prescribe" 在此意为 "state authoritatively or as a rule that (an action or procedure) should be carried out"，可引申为 "指手画脚"。

3. 此段中的核心在于工作文件 NPT/ CONF.2015/WP.9，为帮助理解本段以及下文内容，译者在时间允许的情况下，不妨根据文号 "NPT/ CONF.2015/WP.9" 在联合国正式文件系统（ODS）中或不扩散核武器条约缔约国 2015 年审议大会的网站上查阅，了解文件内容。

第 6 段

However, it was no longer a question of whether those discussions should take place, nor was there any doubt as to the need for an agreed legal pathway to achieving nuclear disarmament.

然而，是否应该进行讨论已不再是问题，同样没有疑问的是^①，必须有商定的法律途径来实现核裁军。

不过，是否应该进行这种讨论已不再是一个问题。同样，商定一种合法途径来实现核裁军的必要性也毋庸置疑。

批 注

① 有改进空间。

在英文中，"nor" 表示 "也不" 的意思，表明前面部分 "不……"，后面部分 "也不……"。结合本句来说，那就是 "是否应该进行这种讨论已不再是一个问题"，"需要商定一种合法途径来实现核裁军目标也不存在任何疑问"。审校稿在句子结构上作了调整，形式上更显工整，用词也更到位。

补充练习

1. Most of us were there in New York for last year's First Committee session, where this frustration led to action, supported by the majority of United Nations Member States, taking discussions and deliberations on issues on the Conference's agenda effectively outside of the Conference.

我们当中多数人参加了去年在纽约举行的第一委员会会议，会上，第一委员会不为这种挫败感所馁，奋然行动，在裁谈会之外就裁谈会议程上的各项议题展开了有益讨论和审议，这一行动得到了联合国大多数会员国的支持。

2. I firmly believe that outside developments bring a renewed sense of urgency to take on our obligation to continue to work towards a programme of work which covers every item on the Conference's agenda. The understanding of the Hungarian presidency is that under Rules 28 and 29 of the rules of procedure of the Conference it is our duty and obligation, as the first presidency of the annual session, to submit a draft programme of work for consideration and, if possible, adoption by the Conference.

我坚信，外部的事态发展给我们带来了新的紧迫感，促使我们担负起义务，继续努力制定一项涵盖裁谈会议程上所有项目的工作方案。作为主席国，匈牙利认为，根据裁谈会《议事规则》第 28 条和第 29 条，作为本届年会的第一任主席，我们有责任而且有义务提交一份工作方案草案，以供裁谈会审议，甚或通过。

3. I have already had, as incoming President, a number of opportunities to consult with regional groups as well as with individual member States about their views on how to best use the coming weeks to reach our common goal. My intention is to continue this intensive consultation process until a text emerges that has sufficiently broad support, and thus can be put formally before you.

作为继任主席，我多次有机会与各区域小组及具体成员国进行磋商，请它们就如何充分利用未来几周达成我们共同的目标发表看法。我打算继续这一密集磋商进程，直到达成一份得到充分广泛支持的案文并将其正式提交给你们。

4. During the weeks to come, in parallel with the general Conference proceedings, I will continue to reach out informally to member States as well as to regional groups in order to find the best formulation of the elements of a programme of work. I hope I can count on your cooperation and openness with regard to my plans.

在今后几周，我将在推进裁谈会一般会议程序的同时，继续同各成员国及各区域小组进行非正式接触，以期就工作方案各项内容达成最佳条文。关于我这些计划的实施，希望能够有幸仰仗各位的配合和开放姿态。

第七篇

Australia participated in several rounds of NPDI outreach to the P5 in Geneva (2014), New York (2014), London (2015), Washington (2016) and Geneva (2017). This afforded further opportunities to underline the importance of transparency. Australia also conducted joint representations with Japan in Moscow, as part of coordinated NPDI outreach to all the P5 capitals to discuss P5 national reports to the NPT.

We, as part of the NPDI, submitted a working paper on "Nuclear-weapon-free zones and negative security assurances" to the 2013 PrepCom, and a working paper on "Establishing a weapons-of-mass-destruction-free zone in the Middle East" to the 2014 PrepCom. These papers underlined that NWFZs are an important means for enhancing global and regional peace and security.

Australia maintains two diagnostic laboratories as part of the IAEA network of analytical laboratories.

At The Hague Nuclear Security Summit, Australia committed to realise or exceed the objectives of INFCIRC/225/Rev.5 as part of the joint statements on strengthening nuclear security implementation.

In addition to the TCF, Australia plays a key role in co-operation on the peaceful uses of nuclear energy in the Asia-Pacific region. Australia's nuclear-related agencies, the Australian Nuclear Science and Technology Organisation (ANSTO), the Australian Radiation Protection and Nuclear Safety Agency (ARPANSA) and the Australian Safeguards and Non-Proliferation Office (ASNO) continue to provide experts to the IAEA and to hold a range of meetings with regional counterparts, as part of bilateral cooperation agreements and IAEA projects.

请自行翻译后查看后文的分析点评

第 1 段

Australia participated in several rounds of NPDI outreach to the P5 in Geneva (2014), New York (2014), London (2015), Washington (2016) and Geneva (2017). This afforded further opportunities to underline the importance of transparency. Australia also conducted joint representations with Japan to Moscow, as part of coordinated NPDI outreach to all the P5 capitals to discuss P5 national reports to the NPT.

批注

① 谁与五常开展？澳大利亚还是不扩散与核裁军倡议组织？
② 若是与日本交涉，即为一对一，何来"联合"？
③ "capital city"有时也代指国家政府。
④ 译文西化腔。

翻译稿

澳大利亚参加了在日内瓦（2014年）、纽约（2014年）、伦敦（2015年）、华盛顿（2016年）、日内瓦（2017年）与五常开展的几轮不扩散与核裁军倡议组织外联活动，为强调透明度的重要性提供了进一步的机会。澳大利亚还在莫斯科与日本进行了联合交涉，作为与五常国家首都协调的不扩散核武器条约外联工作的一部分④，讨论五常向《不扩散条约》提交的国家报告。

审校稿

澳大利亚参加了不扩散与裁军倡议组织针对安理会五个常任理事国（五常）先后分别在日内瓦（2014年）、纽约（2014年）、伦敦（2015年）、华盛顿（2016年）和日内瓦（2017年）开展的几轮外联活动，这些外联活动为强调透明度的重要性提供了进一步的机会。在不扩散与裁军倡议组织针对五常国家政府协调开展外联以讨论五常提交不扩散条约机构的国家报告期间，澳大利亚还联合日本同莫斯科进行了交涉。

点评

1. 译文在形式上拘泥于原文。"NPDI outreach to the P5"，翻译稿"与五常开展的几轮不扩散与核裁军倡议组织外联活动"按照原文顺序，机械地将"不扩散与核裁军倡议组织（NPDI）"与"外联活动（outreach）"放在一起。其实，完全理解原文意思之后，大可像审校稿那般做适当调整，既能明确逻辑关系，又可增强译文可读性。

2. 对NPDI成员国相关背景信息了解不足。关于"conducted joint representations with Japan in Moscow"，先看"representation"，根据《韦氏词典》中"representation"第1d条释义 (1): a usually formal statement made against sth or to effect a change (2) a usually formal protest，所以处理为"交涉"是正确的。再结合上下文来看"joint representation"，前句提到NPDI针对安理会五常……开展了几轮外联活动，而根据背景信息，澳大利亚和日本均为NPDI成员国，所以说，应该是澳大利亚联合日本同莫斯科（代指俄罗斯，五常之一）进行了交涉。

3. "as part of"的处理洋味十足。在本段语境中，联合交涉是NDPI针对五常国家政府协调开展外联的一个工作步骤或一项活动，是在外联期间进行的，因此在理解透彻的基础上，大可转而采用其他更地道、更符合汉语习惯的表述。

第2段

We, as part of the NPDI, submitted a working paper on "Nuclear-weapon-free zones and negative security assurances" to the 2013 PrepCom, and a working paper on "Establishing a weapons-of-mass-destruction-free zone in the Middle East" to the 2014 PrepCom. These papers underlined that NWFZs are an important means for enhancing global and regional peace and security.

作为不扩散与裁军倡议组织的一分子,我们向 2013 年筹委会提交了一份关于"无核武器区与负面安全保证"的工作文件,并向 2014 年筹委会提交了一份关于"建立中东无大规模毁灭性武器区"的工作文件。这两份文件均强调指出,无核武器区是加强全球和区域和平与安全的一项重要手段。

作为不扩散与裁军倡议组织成员国,我国向 2013 年筹委会提交了一份关于"无核武器区与消极安全保证"的工作文件,后又向 2014 年筹委会提交了一份关于"建立中东无大规模毁灭性武器区"的工作文件。这两份工作文件均强调指出,无核武器区是加强全球和区域和平与安全的一项重要手段。

1. 关于"as part of the NPDI",根据背景知识可知,澳大利亚是 NPDI 的成员国之一,翻译稿中处理为"一分子",固然不能说错,但改为"成员国"后,要更加具体明确。

2. "negative security assurances"为"消极安全保证",而非"负面安全保证",与之对应的是"positive security assurances"(积极安全保证)。

第 3 段

Australia maintains two diagnostic laboratories as part of the IAEA network of analytical laboratories.

澳大利亚现维持着两间诊断实验室,这两间实验室是①原子能机构分析实验室网络的组成部分。

批 注

① 表述啰唆。

澳大利亚现维持着原子能机构分析实验室网络的两间诊断实验室。

翻译稿在形式上拘泥于英文原文,表述啰唆,形式拖沓。审校稿言简意赅,读来一目了然。

第 4 段

At The Hague Nuclear Security Summit, Australia committed to realise or exceed the objectives of INFCIRC/225/Rev.5 as part of the joint statements on strengthening nuclear security implementation.

在海牙核安全峰会上,澳大利亚在关于加强核保安执行情况的联合声明中

批 注

② 同一术语前后译法不一。

承诺达到或超过 INFCIRC/225/Rev.5 所载各项目标。

在海牙核安全峰会上，澳大利亚加入了关于加强核安全执行情况的联合声明，承诺完成甚至超额完成 INFCIRC/225/Rev.5 所载各项目标。

翻译稿对"as part of"的处理相对得当，但审校稿在准确把握原文意思的基础上，添加了"加入了"三个字，并用逗号拆分为两个分句，效果更上一层楼。

第 5 段

In addition to the TCF, Australia plays a key role in co-operation on the peaceful uses of nuclear energy in the Asia-Pacific region. Australia's nuclear-related agencies, the Australian Nuclear Science and Technology Organisation (ANSTO), the Australian Radiation Protection and Nuclear Safety Agency (ARPANSA) and the Australian Safeguards and Non-Proliferation Office (ASNO) continue to provide experts to the IAEA and to hold a range of meetings with regional counterparts, as part of bilateral cooperation agreements and IAEA projects.

除了技术合作基金外，澳大利亚在亚太地区和平利用核能的合作方面也发挥着关键作用。澳大利亚的核相关机构、澳大利亚核科学技术组织、澳大利亚辐射防护和核安全机构和澳大利亚保障监督和不扩散办公室继续向原子能机构提供专家，并与区域对口机构举行了一系列会议，<u>这些会议是双边合作协定和原子能机构项目的一部分</u>①。

批 注

① 译文拘泥于原文，理解错误且表述不通。

除技术合作基金外，澳大利亚在亚太地区和平利用核能的合作方面也发挥着关键作用。澳大利亚的核相关机构、澳大利亚核科学技术组织、澳大利亚辐射防护和核安全机构和澳大利亚保障监督和不扩散办公室还按照双边合作协定，在原子能机构项目中，一如既往地向原子能机构提供专家，并与区域对口机构举行了一系列会议。

点评

翻译稿太过拘泥于英文原文，不仅形式古板，而且后半句发生理解错误，以致表述不通。按照翻译稿的思维，后半句应作如下理解和处理：提供专家和举行会议均系按照双边合作协定的规定进行，是原子能机构项目的一部分。审校稿在完全理解这层意思的基础上，对句子作了调整优化，逻辑关系清晰，意思明确。

补充练习

1. Australia supports and promotes the role of women in disarmament, non-proliferation and arms control as part of its broader women, peace and security agenda which continues to be a key value and foreign policy priority for Australia. Gender is an issue of direct relevance to strengthening the NPT and has the potential to enhance the capability and effectiveness of NPT processes and their outcomes.

澳大利亚支持并促进妇女在裁军、不扩散、军控方面发挥作用，以落实其更广泛的妇女、和平与安全议程，这依然是澳大利亚的一项重要价值观，是澳大利亚的一个外交政策优先事项。性别平等问题直接关乎加强《不扩散条约》，甚或能够增强不扩散条约进程的能力和实效并扩大进程成果。

2. Australia is a longstanding contributor to the IAEA Technical Cooperation Fund (TCF). In 2015, Australia made a USD 20 000 in-kind contribution to the Sahel Project, hosting two fellows from the Sahel region. In 2015, Australia contributed EUR 600 000 to the Peaceful Uses Initiative to upgrade the nuclear applications laboratories at Seibersdorf as part of the IAEA's ReNuAL project.

澳大利亚是原子能机构技术合作基金的长期捐款国。2015年，澳大利亚以接待萨赫勒地区两名研究学员的形式为萨赫勒项目提供了价值20 000美元的实物捐助。2015年，澳大利亚向"和平利用核能倡议"捐款600 000欧元，用于塞伯斯多夫核应用实验室升级改造，这项工作是原子能机构"核应用实验室改造"项目的一部分。

背景介绍

以下三篇材料均来自2013年1月22日裁军谈判会议最后记录，其中第八篇和第九篇所选段落涉及爱尔兰代表在会上的发言，第十篇所选段落来自俄罗斯代表的发言。来源文件在形式上属于逐字记录，关于逐字记录类文件的特点和翻译注意事项，见本章第一篇的背景介绍部分。

裁军谈判会议（以下简称"裁谈会"）是目前国际社会唯一的多边裁军谈判机构，总部设在日内瓦。裁谈会的职权范围实际涵盖所有的多边军备控制和裁军问题。裁谈会每年举行三期会议，分别为期十周、七周和七周；裁谈会有自己的议事规则，以协商一致的方式通过决定，其会议形式有全体会议、非正式会议。

裁谈会不附属于联合国，但与联合国联系密切，每年向联合国大会提交其工作报告。裁谈会及其前身经过谈判先后达成了一系列重要的多边军备限制和裁军协定，如《不扩散核武器条约》《禁止发展、生产、储存和使用化学武器及销毁此种武器的公约》和《全面禁止核试验条约》。

裁谈会相关文件（包括报告和会议记录等）与上文提到的不扩散条约缔约国审议大会及相关机构的文件一样，遣词用语讲究，技术性也很强，往往涉及核试验、核武器和核武器核查等领域的背景知识和术语，而且在文件关联性方面，同样是旁征博引，在翻译时既要贴合原文字面意思，还需大量查阅参考资料。

第八篇

原文

Similarly, in its resolution 67/72 on the report of the Conference on Disarmament, the United Nations General Assembly noted with renewed concern that, despite the efforts of successive Presidents, the Conference on Disarmament has not yet succeeded in commencing its substantive work, including negotiations.

The General Assembly once again called upon this Conference to intensify further consultations and explore possibilities for overcoming its ongoing deadlock of well over a decade by adopting and implementing a balanced and comprehensive programme of work at the earliest possible date during its 2013 session, bearing in mind the decision on the programme of work adopted by the Conference on 29 May 2009 (CD/1864).

It also requested all States members to cooperate with the successive Presidents of the Conference in their efforts to guide the Conference to the early commencement of its substantive work, including negotiations, in its 2013 session.

Let me emphasize that for the European Union, the immediate commencement and early conclusion of negotiations in the Conference on Disarmament on fissile material cut-off treaty, on the basis of document CD/1299 and the mandate contained therein, and subsequently reiterated in CD/1864, remains a clear priority.

Launching and concluding these negotiations are urgent and important as an essential step to seek a safer world for all and to create the conditions for a world without nuclear weapons, in accordance with the goals of the Treaty on the Non-Proliferation of Nuclear Weapons. National security concerns, while legitimate, can and should be addressed as part of the negotiation process rather than as a prerequisite.

We also believe that confidence-building measures can be taken immediately, without the need to wait for the commencement of formal negotiations. This is the rationale behind our calling on all States possessing nuclear weapons to declare and uphold a moratorium on the production of fissile material for nuclear weapons or other nuclear explosive devices.

请自行翻译后查看后文的分析点评

第 1 段

Similarly, in its resolution 67/72 on the report of the Conference on Disarmament, the United Nations General Assembly noted with renewed concern that, despite the efforts of successive Presidents, the Conference on Disarmament has not yet succeeded in commencing its substantive work, including negotiations.

同样地，联合国大会在其关于裁军谈判会议报告的第 67/72 号决议中再次关切地指出①，虽然历任主席做了大量工作②，但裁军谈判会议尚未成功启动包括谈判在内的实质性工作。

批 注

① 理解错误。
② 过度翻译。

同样，联合国大会在其关于裁军谈判会议报告的第 67/72 号决议中再次关切地注意到，虽经历任主席努力，但裁军谈判会议至今仍未能开始其实质性工作，包括开展谈判。

点评

1. 翻译稿对本段的翻译基本准确，但对"efforts"的处理存在过度翻译现象，这里还是表示字面意思，即"努力"，原文未体现出"大量工作"的意思。在翻译联合国文件，特别是决议类文件时，语言要平实稳重，切勿过度翻译。

2. 所译文件中，如果提到其他参考文件（文件后面一般附有文号），特别是在以双引号形式直接引用具有约束性的大会、安理会等机构的决议时，务必要通过联合国正式文件系统（ODS）或相关机构官方网站等渠道进行查阅参考，根据决议内容作相应的翻译调整即可。以大会第 67/72 号决议为例，既可在联合国大会网站的"大会决议"栏目中查找，也可以通过文号"A/RES/67/72"（其中"A"代表 General Assembly；"RES"为"resolution"）在 ODS 系统进行查找。同理，若为安理会决议，则可在安理会网站上或通过文号"SC/RES/67/72"（其中"SC"代表"Security Council"）在 ODS 系统查找。本段中的"noted with renewed concern that..."在大会第 67/72 号决议（中文版）序言部分第 6 段的译文如下,"再次关切地注意到,尽管裁军谈判会议成员国和 2012 年会议历任主席做出努力……裁军谈判会议仍未能开始其实质性工作,包括按照大会 2011 年 12 月 2 日第 66/59 号决议的要求开展谈判,也未能商定工作方案"。

第 2 段

The General Assembly once again called upon this Conference to intensify further consultations and explore possibilities for overcoming its ongoing deadlock of well over a decade by adopting and implementing a balanced and comprehensive programme of work at the earliest possible date during its 2013 session, bearing in mind the decision on the programme of work adopted by the Conference on 29 May 2009 (CD/1864).

【翻译稿】

大会再次呼吁本届裁谈会加强进一步磋商,并根据裁谈会于 2009 年 5 月 29 日通过的关于工作方案的决定(CD/1864),探索通过在 2013 年会议期间,在最短时间内制定并实施一项均衡、综合的工作方案来打破持续 10 多年僵局的可能性。

批 注
① 逻辑错误。
② 处理方式不当。

【审校稿】

大会再次吁请裁军谈判会议铭记 2009 年 5 月 29 日裁谈会通过的关于工作方案的决定(CD/1864),进一步加强磋商,并探索各种可能性,以便在 2013 年会议期间打破十多年来的持续僵局,尽早通过和执行一份全面均衡的工作方案。

【点 评】

1. 专有名词译法固定:在联合国文件中,特别是在决议和决定中,"called upon"一般译为"吁请","programme of work"为"工作方案"。

2. "well over"是指"超过很多",与"a little over"是相对的,"well over 20 years old"是指二十多岁,应该指在 25 岁以上,而"a little over 20 years old"是指 20 岁出头,应该指二十一二岁,最多不超过 25 岁。"well over a decade"是指十多年。

3. 本段也是对大会第 67/72 号决议内容的转述,同上段点评 2,译前或翻译过程中如有查阅参考,定能有所启发。"bearing in mind"在联合国机构决议中一般翻译为"铭记",此处修饰的是裁谈会。

第 3 段

It also requested all States members to cooperate with the successive Presidents of the Conference in their efforts to guide the Conference to the early commencement of its substantive work, including negotiations, in its 2013 session.

批 注
③ 此处是指裁谈会成员国。

【翻译稿】

大会还请所有会员国配合裁谈会继任主席为指导裁谈会在 2013 年会议期

间早日启动包括谈判在内的实质性工作所做的工作^①。

审校稿

大会还请裁谈会所有成员国与裁谈会现任和继任主席合作，协助他们努力引导裁谈会在 2013 年会议期间及早开始包括谈判在内的实质性工作。

点评

1. "successive Presidents of the Conference" 字面意思是指裁谈会历任主席，包括前任、现任和继任主席，在此结合上下文，应为"现任和继任主席"。

2. "substantive work" 是指"实质性工作"，与"程序性工作"（procedural work）相对。

第 4 段

Let me emphasize that for the European Union, the immediate commencement and early conclusion of negotiations in the Conference on Disarmament on fissile material cut-off treaty, on the basis of document CD/1299 and the mandate contained therein, and subsequently reiterated in CD/1864, remains a clear priority.

翻译稿

让我强调一下，对欧洲联盟而言，根据 CD/1299 号文件以及载于该文件并随后在 CD/1864 号文件中得到重申的任务授权，在裁军谈判会议上立即启动并早日结束关于裂变材料禁产条约的谈判仍是一项明确的优先事项^②。

审校稿

在此请允许我强调指出，应根据 CD/1299 号文件以及该文件中载明且随后又在 CD/1864 号文件中予以重申的任务授权，在裁军谈判会议上立即启动并及早结束关于裂变材料禁产条约的谈判，这对欧洲联盟而言仍是一个明确的优先事项。

点评

翻译稿照搬原文结构，以长句"根据……任务授权，在裁军谈判会议上立即启动并早日结束……谈判"为主语，头重脚轻，易生歧义。

第 5 段

Launching and concluding these negotiations are urgent and important as an essential step to seek a safer world for all and to create the conditions for a world without nuclear weapons, in accordance with the goals of the Treaty on the Non-Proliferation of Nuclear Weapons. National security concerns, while legitimate, can and should be addressed as part of the negotiation process rather than as a prerequisite.

批注

① 拖沓。

② 译文头重脚轻。

批 注

① 处理方式不佳。
② 错译。

在依照《不扩散核武器条约》的目标寻求为所有人建立一个更加安全的世界以及为实现无核武器世界创造条件的道路上①，启动并结束这些谈判是必不可少的一步，极为紧迫和重要。在国家安全方面的关切是合理的，可以而且应该在谈判过程中进行解决，但不能将其作为首要问题予以解决②。

启动和结束这些谈判有其紧迫性和重要性，是根据《不扩散核武器条约》所定目标，为所有人建立一个更加安全的世界以及为建立一个无核武器世界创造条件所必不可少的一个步骤。国家安全关切固然合理正当，但只能而且应该在谈判进程中加以解决，而不应将之作为开启谈判的一项前提条件。

1. 关于第一句的处理，鉴于前段中提到谈判，在此应采取顺译法，承上启下，与上段紧凑地联系在一起，翻译稿打破英文句式结构，导致上下段中关于谈判的字眼相隔甚远，得不偿失。"as an essential step to seek a safer world for all and to create the conditions for a world without nuclear weapons" 是由介词加名词再加由动词不定式引导的目的状语组成的名词性结构，"as" 可以处理为 "是"。

2. "prerequisite" 应该理解为 "前提条件"，而不是 "首要问题"。

3. 注意不要漏译。翻译稿未体现出 "while legitimate" 这一让步状语。

第 6 段

We also believe that confidence-building measures can be taken immediately, without the need to wait for the commencement of formal negotiations. This is the rationale behind our calling on all States possessing nuclear weapons to declare and uphold a moratorium on the production of fissile material for nuclear weapons or other nuclear explosive devices.

批 注

③ 句子结构待改进。

我们还认为，可以立即采取建立信任措施，而无须等到正式谈判开始。这是我们呼吁所有拥有核武器的国家宣布并支持暂停生产核武器或其他核爆炸装置所用裂变材料的依据。③

我们还认为，可以立即采取建立信任措施，不需要等到正式谈判开始之后。也正是基于这一点，我们呼吁所有核武器国家宣布并维持暂停生产核武器或其他核爆炸装置所用裂变材料。

翻译技巧问题：第二句翻译稿沿用原文句式结构，拖沓且无节奏感，拆分后显得干脆利落。面对长句子，究竟是采取顺译法，还是打破原有句式结构进行重组，需要具体情况具体分析，要在实践中慢慢体会把握。"uphold"在此相当于"maintain"，意为"维持"。

补充练习

1. We cannot afford another year of fruitless consultations, procedural manoeuvres and the persistent abuse of the consensus rule. We have a clear call from the United Nations General Assembly to start substantial work, including negotiations in 2013. We will spare no efforts to work with you, Mr. President, to achieve this goal. We urge all member States of the Conference to engage constructively.

参考译文

如果协商无果、操纵程序和持续滥用协商一致原则的情况今年继续上演，后果我们无力承担。联合国大会明确要求我们在2013年就开始包括谈判在内的实质性工作。主席先生，我们会不遗余力地与您一道努力实现这一目标。我们也促请裁谈会所有成员国积极参与裁谈会的工作。

2. Taking into account the recent outcome of the First Committee, we should treat this session as the last one to start FMCT negotiations ourselves. Previous debates among experts on various formulas made it possible to exchange views and discuss different, often uneasy, practical and technical issues concerning fissile material. They added to the process of building confidence and mutual understanding. After such long preparations we should now launch the negotiations in accordance with our mandate.

参考译文

考虑到第一委员会最近取得的成果，我们应把本届会议当成是启动《禁产条约》谈判的最后一届会议。先前关于各类方案的专家辩论使各方得以就裂变材料问题交换意见并讨论其他一些实务和技术问题，这些问题大多令人深感不安。这些交流讨论为建立信任和互谅进程添砖加瓦。在做了这些长期准备之后，我们现在应该根据我们的任务授权启动谈判。

3. At the same time, we regret that, despite the decisions of the 2010 NPT Review Conference, the conference on the establishment of a Middle East zone free of nuclear weapons and all other weapons of mass destruction and their means of delivery did not take place. As one of the co-sponsors of the 1995 NPT Review Conference resolution on the Middle East, we have been working actively for the convening of that Conference. We intend to continue doing so, working closely with the other co-sponsors and the facilitator, Mr. Laajava.

与此同时，我们感到遗憾的是，尽管不扩散条约缔约国 2010 年审议大会做出了若干决定，但关于建立中东无核武器及所有其他大规模毁灭性武器及其运载系统区的国际会议并未举行。作为不扩散条约缔约国 1995 年审议大会关于中东地区决议的共同提案国之一，我们一直在为召开这一会议积极努力。我们打算密切协同其他共同提案国以及会议主持人拉亚瓦先生，一如既往地努力下去。

4. In addition, as underlined in the press statement of the Russian Ministry of Foreign Affairs, Russia, which is firmly committed to its obligations and mandate as co-convenor, considers that a decision to postpone the conference could be justified only if the countries of the Middle East granted clear consent and the future conference dates were fixed. We deeply regret that this has not occurred.

此外，正如俄罗斯外交部部长在新闻公报中所强调的，俄罗斯坚决致力于履行其作为共同召集人的义务和任务，认为要推迟召开会议，就必须先征得中东国家明确同意并重新确定会期，否则无正当理由作此决定。令我们深感遗憾的是，情况并非如此。

Since this Conference last met, there have been a number of developments which reveal growing impatience that we have failed to take forward our work since 1996.

However, in our view, the most serious challenge of 2013 could well be the continued deadlock in United Nations disarmament forums, first and foremost the Conference on Disarmament. We firmly believe that the stagnation of the work of existing disarmament machinery under the aegis of the United Nations results not from imperfections in the machinery but from objective political realities and differences in States' priorities.

In order to rectify the situation, we must work patiently and conscientiously to overcome conflicts, rather than breaking down the existing "triad" and creating alternative negotiating formats. Issues affecting the vital national security interests of States cannot be resolved through a simple vote. If we ignore this fact, we will be able to create only a semblance of moving forward, while in fact sowing even greater discord and worsening international conflict.

Unfortunately, the sixty-seventh session of the United Nations General Assembly adopted decisions that will effectively lead to the dispersion of the Conference agenda among other forums—notably the transfer of discussion of nuclear disarmament to the General Assembly.

That would carry the risk not only of maintaining the existing deadlock in the Conference, but also of fragmentation of multilateral disarmament and, ultimately, the collapse of the United Nations disarmament machinery as a whole.

To that end, as an interim measure, we have proposed that agreement should be reached on a programme of work involving in-depth discussion of the four core issues on the agenda—the prevention of an arms race in outer space, a fissile material cut-off treaty, negative security assurances and nuclear disarmament. That would allow us to gain time in order to continue seeking a compromise and start negotiations in the Conference.

请自行翻译后查看后文的分析点评

分析点评

第 1 段

Since this Conference last met, there have been a number of developments which reveal growing impatience that we have failed to take forward our work since 1996.

自上届裁谈会召开①以来，取得了一系列新进展②，这些进展表明我们逐渐失去耐心③，自 1996 年以来便一直未能推进工作。

自裁谈会上期会议以来，一系列事态接连发生，这些事态表明，眼见我们的工作自 1996 年以来便一直停滞不前，国际社会渐失耐心。

批 注

① 错译。
② 表达不准确。
③ 理解和表达错误。

1. 在本段中，"this Conference" 是 "the Conference on Disarmament"，即 "裁军谈判会议" 的简称，即 "裁谈会"，"last met" 是指上一期会议，而不是上届会议。关于这一点，如能了解相关背景信息，便可免去此错。裁谈会每年举行三期会议，第一期约 10 周，后两期各 7 周，各期会议又分别包括多次会议。

2. "a number of developments" 是指 "很多情况/事态发展"，是对客观事实的描述，不含 "进展" 之意。

3. 翻译技巧问题。此句虽不长，但包含多个信息单元，因此，宜采取拆译方法，处理为多个短句。

第 2 段

However, in our view, the most serious challenge of 2013 could well be the continued deadlock in United Nations disarmament forums, first and foremost the Conference on Disarmament. We firmly believe that the stagnation of the work of existing disarmament machinery under the aegis of the United Nations results not from imperfections in the machinery but from objective political realities and differences in States' priorities.

然而，我们认为，2013 年最严峻的挑战很可能是联合国裁军论坛持续面临的僵局，其中裁军谈判会议首当其冲①。我们坚信，联合国领导下②的现有裁军机制的工作出现停滞不前的原因不在于该机制自身的缺陷，而是因为客观的政治现实和各国优先事项的差异。

批 注
① 不严谨，不正确。
② 错译。

不过，我们认为，2013 年最严峻的挑战很可能在于以裁军谈判会议为首的各联合国裁军论坛继续处于僵局状态。我们深信，联合国支持下的现有裁军机制之所以出现工作停滞，原因不在于机制自身缺陷，而是在于客观政治现实和各国优先事项的差异。

在本段中，"continued deadlock"强调的是僵局仍然存在，可采用形容词动词化的技巧，处理为"继续处于僵局状态"；"first and foremost"是"首先""首要的是"或"最重要的是"，而"首当其冲"的对等英文表述通常是"bear the brunt of"，在这里，可灵活处理为"以……为首的"，与此同时，还要注意其所修饰的"forums"的复数细节；"under the aegis of"意为"with the protection or support of a particular organization or person（在……保护或支持下）"，无"领导之意"。再结合裁谈会不是联合国的直属机构这一背景知识，应翻译为"联合国支持下的"。

第 3 段

In order to rectify the situation, we must work patiently and conscientiously to overcome conflicts, rather than breaking down the existing "triad" and creating alternative negotiating formats. Issues affecting the vital national security interests of States cannot be resolved through a simple vote. If we ignore this fact, we will be able to create only a semblance of moving forward, while in fact sowing even greater discord and worsening international conflict.

为了改变这种状况,我们<u>务必耐心认真地开展工作来消除冲突</u>①,而不是打破现有的"<u>三合一</u>②"局面并<u>重新创建替代性</u>③的谈判论坛。仅仅依靠投票根本无法解决那些对至关重要的国家安全利益造成影响的问题。假若我们忽视了这个事实,我们只会制造出前进的假象,但实际却埋下了更加不和谐和国际冲突日益恶化的种子。

批 注

① 表述不够好。
② 错译。
③ 表述不好。

为了改变这种状况,我们必须认真和耐心地做工作,消除冲突,而不是打破现有的"三驾马车"局面和另寻替代谈判形式。关乎各国重要国家安全利益的问题单靠简单的投票无法解决。如果我们罔顾这个事实,我们只会貌似前进,但实际上却埋下更加不和谐的种子,导致国际冲突恶化。

在本段中,"triad"是"三驾马车"的意思,译者不求甚解,简单译为"三合一",着实不妥;"creating alternative negotiating formats"是创建替代性谈判形式,而不是"重新创建替代性的谈判论坛(forum)";"sowing"和"worsening"为并列关系。

第 4 段

Unfortunately, the sixty-seventh session of the United Nations General Assembly adopted decisions that will effectively lead to the dispersion of the Conference agenda among other forums—notably the transfer of discussion of nuclear disarmament to the General Assembly.

遗憾的是,<u>第六十七届联合国大会</u>④通过了<u>若干决定,这些决定</u>⑤将对裁谈会议程上的问题进行分解,其中一些由其他论坛代为处理⑥,尤其是关于核裁军的讨论将在<u>联合国大会</u>⑦上进行。

批 注

④ 错译。
⑤ 重复啰嗦。
⑥ 理解和表述错误。
⑦ 表述错误。

令人遗憾的是,联合国大会第六十七届会议通过的若干决定实际上会导致裁谈会议程被分散到其他论坛,特别是导致关于核裁军的讨论转到大会进行。

1. 在本段中,"that will effectively...among other forums"是一个定语从句,修饰的是"decisions",表示这些决定将会导致裁谈会的议程被分散到其他论坛,而译者将其译为"对裁谈会议程上的问题进行分解",完全理解错误;"×× session of the United Nations General Assembly"的正确译法是"联合国大会第 ×× 届会议",而非"第 ×× 届联合国大会",另外,单独提到"General

Assembly"时,简译为"大会"即可。

2. 从句式上讲,"大会通过了若干决定,这些决定将……",拖沓啰唆,审校稿改为"会议通过的若干决定实际上会……",简洁明了。

第5段

That would carry the risk not only of maintaining the existing deadlock in the Conference, but also of fragmentation of multilateral disarmament and, ultimately, the collapse of the United Nations disarmament machinery as a whole.

翻译稿

这种做法不仅会带来维持裁谈会现有僵局的风险,还会使多边裁军碎片化,并最终使整个联合国裁军机制崩溃。

审校稿

这种做法具有风险,不仅可能会导致裁谈会的现有僵局持续下去,而且可能会造成多边裁军领域四分五裂,并最终使整个联合国裁军机制崩溃。

点评

译者对原句中的"the risk not only of...but also of..."把握错误,"maintaining the existing deadlock"与"fragmentation of multilateral disarmament and, ultimately, the collapse of"为并列关系,而译者仅将"risk"与前半部分联系起来,导致错译。另外,"fragmentation"的意思是"(使)成碎片、(使)分裂、(使)分化",在这里,处理为"四分五裂"更便于读者理解。

第6段

To that end, as an interim measure, we have proposed that agreement should be reached on a programme of work involving in-depth discussion of the four core issues on the agenda—the prevention of an arms race in outer space, a fissile material cut-off treaty, negative security assurances and nuclear disarmament. That would allow us to gain time in order to continue seeking a compromise and start negotiations in the Conference.

翻译稿

为了实现这一目标并作为一项临时措施②,我们提议应就工作方案达成一致意见,对议程上的四大核心问题进行深入讨论——防止外层空间军备竞赛、裂变材料禁产条约、消极安全保证和核裁军③。这将为我们继续寻求妥协并在裁谈会上重启④谈判赢得时间。

审校稿

为此,作为一项临时措施,我们提议就议程上的四个核心问题展开深入讨论并在此基础上就工作方案达成一致,这四个核心问题分别是:防止外层空间军备

批 注

① 理解错误。

批 注

② 啰唆。
③ 逻辑关系混乱,且句子长。
④ 错译。

竞赛、裂变材料禁产条约、消极安全保证和核裁军。这将为我们继续寻求妥协和在裁谈会上开始谈判赢得时间。

1. 在英文中，"To that end"是一个极其常用的表述，表示"为此"的意思，没有必要译为"为了实现这一目标"。

2. 本句的主句为"we have proposed that agreement should be reached on a programme of work (involving...the agenda)"，也就是"我们提议就工作方案达成一致"，"involving in-depth discussion of..."意思是说"深入讨论"是"就工作方案达成一致"所必须经历的一个步骤或采取的一种方式。按照逻辑，先讨论，再达成一致意见，翻译稿逻辑颠倒。翻译稿中破折号"——"后面的内容与"四大核心问题"中间有字相隔，弱化了二者之间的同位关系，对此，审校稿先处理主句，再重复译出"这四个核心问题分别是："进行补充说明，从而使中文更加通顺，显得更有条理。

1. Finally, in April, the States party to the Convention on the Prohibition of the Development, Production, Stockpiling and Use of Chemical Weapons and on Their Destruction (CWC) will gather in The Hague for the third Review Conference. Since its entry into force in 1997, the CWC has made considerable progress towards eliminating, in a verifiable manner, an entire weapons category from global arsenals.

最后，《关于禁止发展、生产、储存和使用化学武器及销毁此种武器的公约》（《化学武器公约》）缔约国将在今年4月齐聚海牙，参加第三次审议会议。自1997年生效以来，《化学武器公约》已在通过可核查方式消除全球武库中所有化学武器类别方面取得相当大的进展。

2. It enjoys near-universal adherence. While there is never room for complacency with regard to weapons of mass destruction, this must be seen as a significant success story of the Conference on Disarmament. This Conference has shown itself capable of notable achievements. It is late in the day, but with political will and constructive engagement by all, it can and must do so again.

该公约几乎得到了普遍遵守。虽然在大规模毁灭性武器方面从来没有自满的余地，但这必须被视为裁军谈判会议的一项重大成就。裁谈会已经证明，它有能力取得显著成绩。虽然为时已晚，但有了各方的政治意愿和积极参与，裁谈会就能够而且必须再次取得显著成绩。

3. The development of transparency and confidence-building measures in outer space activities is an important component of the treaty on the prevention of the placement of weapons in outer space.

制定外层空间活动透明度和建立信任措施是关于防止在外层空间部署武器条约的一个重要组成部分。

In April 2013, Geneva will host a United Nations Institute for Disarmament Research conference on outer space security and the second session of the Group of Governmental Experts on Transparency and Confidence-building Measures in Outer Space Activities. We are counting on close cooperation between member States of the Conference on Disarmament and the Group.

The Russian delegation has repeatedly expressed its support for the start of negotiations on a fissile material cut-off treaty within the framework of a balanced programme of work and on the basis of the Shannon mandate. From our perspective, the drawing up of such a treaty could be a useful multilateral measure to strengthen the NPT regime and a step forward in nuclear disarmament.

That idea was at the core of the joint statement by concerned States in support of the Conference on Disarmament at the First Committee during the sixty-seventh session of the United Nations General Assembly. We are pleased that 17 countries, representing various groups and continents, associated themselves with it.

As Russian President Vladimir Putin underlined in his address to the Federal Assembly of the Russian Federation on 12 December 2012, "Russia stands for the principle of agreed and collective efforts in addressing current challenges" and is committed to building a nuclear-free world.

However, we should be mindful that in order to advance this process we must create the appropriate conditions, most importantly through maintaining global strategic stability; observing, in both word and deed, the principle of indivisible security; not placing the security of other States at risk through the pursuit of one's own security; and abandoning attempts to ensure dominance through military force.

请自行翻译后查看后文的分析点评

第1段

In April 2013, Geneva will host a United Nations Institute for Disarmament Research conference on outer space security and the second session of the Group of Governmental Experts on Transparency and Confidence-Building Measures in Outer Space Activities. We are counting on close cooperation between member States of the Conference on Disarmament and the Group.

2013年4月，联合国裁军研究所将在日内瓦就外层空间安全举行会议，联合国政府专家小组也将于日内瓦就外层空间活动的透明度和建立信任措施召开会议①。我们期待裁军谈判会议成员国和该专家组进行密切合作。

日内瓦将在2013年4月举办联合国裁军研究所外层空间安全问题会议和外层空间活动中的提高透明度和建立信任措施政府专家组第二届会议。我们期待裁军谈判会议成员国与该专家组开展密切合作。

在翻译稿中，有两个动作的行为者，即"联合国裁军研究所"和"联合国政府专家小组"，地点状语"日内瓦"出现了两次，虽然表达的内容是准确的，但行文风格不流畅，我们可以采用直译方式，直接将"Geneva"作为共同主语，这样译文就显得通顺多了。在中文中，这种表述其实很常见。比如，"北京将举办……会议"。

批 注

① 处理方式不当。

第2段

The Russian delegation has repeatedly expressed its support for the start of negotiations on a fissile material cut-off treaty within the framework of a balanced programme of work and on the basis of the Shannon mandate. From our perspective, the drawing up of such a treaty could be a useful multilateral measure to strengthen the NPT regime and a step forward in nuclear disarmament.

俄罗斯代表团一再表示，它②支持在均衡的工作方案框架下以及根据香农授权启动裂变材料禁产条约谈判。在我们看来，该条约的制定会成为加强《不扩散核武器条约》机制并推进核裁军进程的一项有效多边措施③。

俄罗斯代表团一再表示，支持在一个均衡的工作方案框架内并根据香农授权

批 注

② 可省译。
③ 错译；缩略语处理不当。

启动关于裂变材料禁产条约的谈判。在我们看来，起草该条约可成为加强《不扩散条约》体系的一项有效多边措施，并可进一步推进核裁军进程。

点评

1. 译者将"expressed its support for"逐字译为"一再表示，它支持"，"它"字多余，不符合汉语习惯。回想一下，外交部常用措辞"中方表示支持/欢迎……"。

2. 关于全称和缩略语的处理，在联合国文件翻译中，原文用缩略语的，中文译文也用缩略语，中文没有对应缩略语的，用全称。NPT的全称是《不扩散核武器条约》，简称为《不扩散条约》。因此，使用《不扩散条约》即可。

3. "could be"的宾语有两个，一个是"a useful multilateral measure to strengthen the NPT regime"，另一个是"a step forward..."，二者是并列的，翻译稿错误地将"to strengthen the NPT regime"和"a step forward..."理解为"a useful multilateral measure"的并列补语。

第 3 段

That idea was at the core of the joint statement by concerned States in support of the Conference on Disarmament at the First Committee during the sixty-seventh session of the United Nations General Assembly. We are pleased that 17 countries, representing various groups and continents, associated themselves with it.

翻译稿

这一设想①是支持裁军谈判会议的相关国家在联合国大会第六十七届会议期间，在第一委员会上发表的联合声明的核心事项②。我们感到欣慰的是，代表不同集团和大洲的17个国家发表了该声明③。

批 注

① 选词不好。
② 表达错误。
③ 错译。

审校稿

这一想法是有关国家在联合国大会第六十七届会议期间为支持裁军谈判会议而在第一委员会上所做联合发言的核心内容。让我们感到欣慰的是，有17个国家赞成该发言，它们代表了各集团和各大洲。

点评

1. 在本段中，"idea"译为"想法"比译为"设想"好。

2. 在这里，"joint statement"为联合发言，而不是联合声明。"at the core of the joint statement"应该是"联合发言的核心内容"而不是"核心事项"。

3. "associated themselves with"是表示"赞成……"或"赞同……"的意思，是指在一国代表发言之后其他国家表示赞同，而不是17个国家都作了这一发言；另外，在翻译稿，译者将定语"representing various groups and continents"前置翻译，修饰效果偏弱，后置译为"它们代表了各集团和各大洲"，则充分强调了这些国家代表性之广泛。

第 4 段

As Russian President Vladimir Putin underlined in his address to the Federal Assembly of the Russian Federation on 12 December 2012, "Russia stands for the principle of agreed and collective efforts in addressing current challenges" and is committed to building a nuclear-free world.

正如俄罗斯总统弗拉基米尔·普京在其于 2012 年 12 月 12 日向俄罗斯联邦联邦议会的致辞中所言①，"俄罗斯在解决当前挑战的过程中坚持协商一致②和集体努力原则"，俄罗斯③致力于建立无核世界。

批 注

① 与原文偏离。
② 错译。
③ 主语重复。

正如俄罗斯总统弗拉基米尔·普京在 2012 年 12 月 12 日向俄罗斯联邦联邦会议发表演讲时所强调的，"俄罗斯在应对当前挑战方面坚持商定并集体采取努力原则"，并致力于建立一个无核世界。

1. 在翻译稿中，译者将"underline"译为"所言"，所表达的含义显然弱于"强调"，与原文存在偏离；"agreed"是"商定"的意思，与"协商一致"还是有区别的。

2. 在翻译稿后半部分，主语"俄罗斯"出现了两次，保留一个即可。

第 5 段

However, we should be mindful that in order to advance this process we must create the appropriate conditions, most importantly through maintaining global strategic stability; observing, in both word and deed, the principle of indivisible security; not placing the security of other States at risk through the pursuit of one's own security; and abandoning attempts to ensure dominance through military force.

然而，我们应当注意的是，为了推动这个进程，我们必须创造合适的条件，最重要的是通过维护全球战略稳定来实现这一点；从言行上遵守不可分割安全原则；不为了追求自己国家的安全而使其他国家面临安全风险④；以及不试图⑤通过军事力量获取统治地位。

批 注

④ 表述不准确且啰唆。
⑤ 表述不准确。

然而，我们应当注意，为了推进这一进程，我们必须创造适当条件，其中最重要的是，要维护全球战略稳定；从言行上遵守安全不可分割原则；不为追求本国安全而危及其他国家的安全，以及放弃通过军事力量获取统治地位的企图。

1. 翻译稿基本再现了原文内容，但不够准确，而且表述方式也存在问题。"most importantly through"所接的内容包括"maintaining, observing, not placing 和 abandoning"，四者并列，而译者却仅仅将之与"maintaining"联系起来，将另外三项内容独立翻译。

2. "placing...at risk"字面意思是"让……面临风险"，在这里可以灵活一点，改为"危及"，简洁有力。

3. "abandoning attempts to"宜直译为"放弃……的企图"，较之翻译稿中的"不试图"，更为直接，从而更加铿锵有力，而且在句式上，也与前面三个分句保持了一致。

1. Now, while not enthusiastic about growing United Nations General Assembly involvement in the Conference's work, the United States assessed that the Canadian-sponsored FMCT resolution establishing a group of government experts, which is a standard practice based on consensus decision-making, did include sufficient safeguards that it would not undermine prospects for the Conference to engage on this vital objective.

参 考 译 文

美国虽然目前对联合国大会越来越多地参与裁谈会工作不甚感兴趣，但认为加拿大所提关于设立一个政府专家组的《禁产条约》决议案确实能够提供充分的保障监督，不会损害裁谈会实现这一重要目标的前景，是基于协商一致决策的标准做法。

2. Indeed, the Group of Governmental Experts could complement Conference efforts to make progress on FMCT in a manner that the Conference can—and we hope will—take up. We did not find this to be the case with the Open-Ended Working Group on nuclear disarmament, which is not consensus-based, circumvents the Conference and redirects its resources.

参 考 译 文

实际上，该政府专家组可对裁谈会的工作做出补充，以裁谈会能够接受且符合我们期望的方式在《禁产条约》问题上取得进展。我们认为核裁军问题不限成员名额工作组却是另一种情况，该小组不是以协商一致为基础，它绕开了裁谈会，而且改变了其资源流向。

3. Those principles are clearly jeopardized by unconstrained plans to create a

global ballistic missile defence; a reluctance to address the issue of prevention of the placement of weapons in outer space; a lack of progress in the ratification of the Comprehensive Nuclear-Test-Ban Treaty; and quantitative and qualitative imbalances in conventional weapons. Of course, all States that possess nuclear military potential should join the ongoing nuclear disarmament efforts step by step.

这些原则显然受到以下因素的损害：建立全球弹道导弹防御的计划不受约束；对于解决防止在外层空间部署武器问题态度勉强；在批准《全面禁止核试验条约》方面缺乏进展；以及常规武器在数量和质量方面均不平衡。当然，拥有核军事潜能的所有国家都应逐步加入现行核裁军努力。

4. Our position on this issue remains unchanged. However, we firmly believe that its discussion—and by this we refer to the proposal to end the production of fissile material—should take place exclusively within the framework of the Conference and involve all States that possess a nuclear military arsenal. Any other option would seriously diminish the effectiveness of work on the treaty and is unlikely to offer any added value.

我们在这一问题上的立场仍然没变。不过，我们坚信，相关讨论（我们指的是停止生产裂变材料的提案）只应在裁谈会框架内进行，而且所有拥有核军事武库的国家都应参与。任何其他备选方案都将严重削弱该条约相关工作的有效性，而且无法提供任何增加值。

背景介绍

本篇材料选自全面禁止核试验条约组织筹备委员会执行秘书关于2017年1月至6月期间核查相关活动的报告。

全面禁止核试验条约组织筹委会（以下简称"筹委会"）的职责是为《全面禁止核试验条约》生效做好各项准备工作。筹委会主要包括全会和临时技术秘书处。全会是筹委会的决策机构，每年召开两次全会，审议条约筹备相关事宜并做出决定。临时技术秘书处负责为国际监测系统提供技术和法律援助，并负责国际监测系统台站的监督、管理和维护，以及台站数据的接收、分析和处理。这类报告在结构上与秘书长的报告等文件（见本章第四篇的背景介绍）近似，但句子普遍偏长，而且技术性强，涉及很多核试验核查活动相关流程和技术的术语，有一定难度，翻译时须认真细致，多下一点功夫。

第十一篇

原文

The PTS continued to develop its capability for supportability analysis (formerly logistic support analysis) to improve planning for recapitalization and sustainment while ensuring overall station operational availability. This activity involved regular analyses of sparing, life cycle, mean time between failure, life time buy and efforts in recapitalization forecasting. The PTS continued to seek feedback from experienced users in order to increase the accuracy of its models, including projections of cost and downtime drivers in the IMS network. The PTS finalized the documentation associated with sparing optimization, focusing on processes and data structure, and continued to work on data extraction and transformation from DOTS and other PTS databases to enable support analysis.

Organization of the Infrasound Technology Workshop 2017, which will take place on 23—27 October 2017 in Tromsø, Norway, commenced in cooperation with NORSAR. This will follow on from the 2016 workshop held in November 2016 in Quito, Ecuador. The workshop will provide the opportunity to discuss the latest advances in infrasound technology and liaise with the atmospheric and space science community from northern Europe as synergies between infrasound and other observation technologies continue to expand.

The PTS organized a CTBT related session as part of the 2017 European Geosciences Union (EGU) General Assembly on 23—28 April in Vienna. The PTS installed a CTBTO booth and staff members were supported by interns and a CTBTO Youth Group member. Twelve PTS staff were submitting authors to the session on Research and Development in Nuclear Explosion Monitoring.

请自行翻译后查看后文的分析点评

分析点评

第 1 段

The PTS continued to develop its capability for supportability analysis (formerly logistic support analysis) to improve planning for recapitalization and sustainment while ensuring overall station operational availability. This activity involved regular analyses of sparing, life cycle, mean time between failure, life time buy and efforts in recapitalization forecasting. The PTS continued to seek feedback from experienced users in order to increase the accuracy of its models, including projections of cost and downtime drivers in the IMS network. The PTS finalized the documentation associated with sparing optimization, focusing on processes and data structure, and continued to work on data extraction and transformation from DOTS and other PTS databases to enable support analysis.

翻译稿

临时技术秘书处①继续发展其可支持性分析能力（原为后勤支助分析）②，以改善对资本结构调整和维持的规划，同时确保整体台站可用率。这项活动涉及定期分析闲置时间、使用周期、平均故障间隔时间、使用期限以及在资本结构调整预测方面的努力。临时技术秘书处继续请经验丰富的用户提供反馈意见③，以提高其模型的准确性，包括在预测国际监测系统网络成本和导致停机的因素方面的准确性。临时技术秘书处完成了与优化闲置时间有关的文件定稿，重点是各项进程和数据结构，并继续致力于从技术秘书处数据库和临时技术秘书处的其他数据库中提取和转换数据④，以助开展辅助分析。

批 注

① 应使用简称。
② 括号内容的位置错误。
③ 表述可进一步优化。
④ 不够准确。

审校稿

临时技秘处继续开发其保障性分析（原为后勤支助分析）能力，以改善资本结构调整和维持规划，同时确保整体台站可用率。这项活动涉及定期分析闲置时间、使用周期、平均故障间隔时间、使用期限，以及资本结构调整预测方面的努力。临时技秘处继续向经验丰富的用户征求反馈意见，以提高其模型的准确性，包括在预测国际监测系统网络成本和导致停机的因素方面的准确性。临时技秘处完成了有关优化闲置时间的文件，重点论述了流程和数据结构，同时还在一如既往地致力于利用技术秘书处数据库和临时技秘处其他数据库进行数据提取和转换工作，以助开展辅助分析。

点评

1. "PTS"是"Provisional Technical Secretariat"的简称，译文应与原文保持一致，在有简称可用的情况下，即应使用简称。另外，括号中的"logistic support analysis"实际与"supportability analysis"相对应，因此在译文中应该置于"能力"之前，这一点稍微细心即可避免。

2. 关于"to seek feedback from experienced users"，这句无论是在理解上还是翻译处理上，都无难点。翻译稿基本正确，但审校稿"向经验丰富的用户征求反馈意见"要更为地道。译者在翻译结束后，要尽量再从读者的角度去审视、修改译文。

3. 关于"data extraction and transformation from"，这种两个名词共用一个介词（"from"）的结构较为常见，在翻译时，需视具体情况分开处理或合并处理。在翻译稿中，译者将"data extraction from"译作"从……中提取数据"是没有问题的，但将"data transformation from"译作"从……中转换数据"则为不妥，译者被原文结构所束缚，没有考虑到实际情况，因为数据转换通常是一项独立工作,不需要"从……中转换"。其实,这句话是说从数据库中提取数据,再进行数据转换,只要弄清楚这一点,译文就基本不会出错。

第 2 段

Organization of the Infrasound Technology Workshop 2017, which will take place on 23—27 October 2017 in Tromsø, Norway, commenced in cooperation with NORSAR. This will follow on from the 2016 workshop held in November 2016 in Quito, Ecuador. The workshop will provide the opportunity to discuss the latest advances in infrasound technology and liaise with the atmospheric and space science community from northern Europe as synergies between infrasound and other observation technologies continue to expand.

开始与挪威地震台阵合作组织①将于 2017 年 10 月 23 日至 27 日在挪威特罗姆瑟举办的 2017 年次声技术讲习班。这将成为 2016 年 11 月在厄瓜多尔基多举行的 2016 年讲习班的延续②。由于次声和其他观测技术间的协同作用不断增强,在此次讲习班上,将有机会讨论次声技术最新进展并与北欧大气和空间科学界建立联系。

批 注

① 语义欠明。
② 理解错误,表述拗口。

现已着手与挪威地震台阵展开合作,共同组织将于 2017 年 10 月 23 日至 27 日在挪威特罗姆瑟举行的 2017 年次声技术讲习班。这期讲习班是 2016 年 11 月在厄瓜多尔基多举行的 2016 年讲习班的后续。随着次声观测技术和其他观测技术间的协同作用持续增强,届时将借讲习班之机,探讨次声技术最新进展并与北欧大气和空间科学界建立联系。

1. "Organization of the Infrasound Technology Workshop 2017, which…, commenced in cooperation with NORSAR" 一句看似较长,但若暂且忽略"which"引导的定语从句,则结构简单明了。翻译稿表述欠清晰。审校稿在句首添加了"现已"二字,并用一个逗号,将句子分为两个短句,无论是在表述习惯上,还是在语意清晰度上,较之翻译稿都有了很大改善。这种长句拆分为短句的方法在翻译中会经常用到。

2. 这一句的难点在于"follow on from",其英文释义为"to happen after something, and often as the next part or stage of it"(《麦克米伦词典》),与"follow-up"相近,因此处理为"……的后续"即可。

3. 关于"provide the opportunity(to do sth/for sth)",无论在理解上还是在翻译处理上,均无难点,在此要强调的是掌握多种表述方式,在具体情境中灵活运用。就这句而言,可以翻译为"这期讲习班将为探讨……并与……建立联系提供机会",也可以像审校稿这样,处理为"届时将借讲习班之机,探讨……并……"。

第3段

The PTS organized a CTBT related session as part of the 2017 European Geosciences Union (EGU) General Assembly on 23—28 April in Vienna. The PTS installed a CTBTO booth and staff members were supported by interns and a CTBTO Youth Group member. Twelve PTS staff were submitting authors to the session on Research and Development in Nuclear Explosion Monitoring.

翻译稿

临时技术秘书处于4月23日至28日在维也纳举办了一次与《禁核试条约》相关的会议，作为2017年欧洲地球科学联盟大会的一部分①。临时技术秘书处安装了一个禁核试组织专用的隔间②，实习生和禁核试组织青年团体成员充当后备工作人员③。临时技术秘书处的12名工作人员向核爆炸监测研发会议提交了④文件。

批 注

① 西化腔过浓。
② 错译。
③ 理解错误。
④ 意思不完整。

审校稿

在2017年4月23日至28日于维也纳举行的欧洲地球科学联盟大会期间，临时技术秘书处按照会议议程组织了一次与《禁核试条约》相关的会议。临时技术秘书处布置了一个禁核试组织的展台，几名实习生和禁核试组织青年小组的一名成员协助工作人员开展了会务工作。临时技术秘书处的12名工作人员给核爆炸监测研发会议撰写了稿件。

点 评

1. "booth"这个词确实有"隔间"的意思，但在这里，"booth"指的不是隔间，而是会议期间国际组织等相关方布置的展台。翻译的时候，基本词义可以作为参考，但译文还要结合具体语境，只有这样才能准确再现原文含义。

2. "as part of"意为"作为……的一部分"，但若在译文中作此直译，多数情况下有失妥当，要么显得洋味太浓，要么语意欠明。在本句语境中，"与《禁核试条约》相关的会议"既是大会的一项内容，必然是列入会议议程。因此，审校稿中处理为"在……大会期间，临时技术秘书处按照会议议程组织了一次与《禁核试条约》相关的会议"，意思清晰明了。关于"as part of"在具体语境下的翻译处理，参见第七篇。

3. 在翻译稿中，译者将"staff members were supported by"译作"充当后备人员"，错得有些离谱。另外还需要注意的是，"interns and a CTBTO Youth Group member"在翻译时要明确具体为"几名实习生和禁核试组织青年小组一名成员"，忠实再现原文单复数形式。

4. "submitting authors"的中心词是"author"，其职责不仅仅是提交文件，还包括前期撰稿。翻译稿只提到"提交"，未体现出"撰写"这层含义。

补充练习

1. The latest results of integrated testing of NET-VISA to estimate the effects

of running this new software in all stages of the IDC processing pipeline were made available on the IDC external database. The results include requested data from auxiliary seismic stations based on events produced by a version of NET-VISA that is capable of processing seismic, hydroacoustic and infrasound data. An interactive module has been developed and will be used from within the analyst review station to provide analysts with NET-VISA events, upon demand, in addition to the Standard Event List 3 automatic bulletin. This module is expected to be available to analysts during the third quarter of 2017.

为估计在国际数据中心流程的各个阶段运行"联网处理纵向综合地震分析软件"这一新软件的影响，对该软件进行了综合测试，最新测试结果现已在国际数据中心外部数据库中发布。测试取得的成果包括根据可处理地震、水声和次声数据的联网处理纵向综合地震分析软件生成的事件，向辅助地震台站请求获取数据。目前已开发出一个交互式模块，并将在分析员审查站内部使用，以便根据需求向分析员提供除标准事件清单 3 自动公报之外的由联网处理纵向综合地震分析软件生成的事件。这一模块预计将在 2017 年第三季度向分析员提供。

2. The IDC performs daily analysis of infrasound events hypothesized by the IDC automatic processing system. The IDC ensured the smooth integration of the new infrasound stations IS16 (China) and IS20 (Ecuador) into the IDC test bed in order to provide support to the IMS Division during installation and to prepare the transition of those stations to IDC operations. IDC supported the upgrade of infrasound station IS48 (Tunisia) to provide high quality data and processed results to IDC analysts and to guarantee high data availability.

国际数据中心对该中心自动处理系统假定的次声事件进行日常分析。在该中心的保障下，新次声台站 IS16（中国）和 IS20（厄瓜多尔）顺利并入国际数据中心测试平台，从而可在安装期间向国际监测系统司提供支助，并为这些台站在运行方面向国际数据中心看齐做准备。在国际数据中心的支助下，次声台站 IS48（突尼斯）实现升级，从而可向国际数据中心分析员提供高质量数据和处理结果，并确保较高的数据提供率。

本章词汇

acquiesce 默认；默许
agenda item 议程项目
arbitrary detention 任意拘留
assessed contribution 分摊会费
associated themselves with 赞成；赞同
bear in mind 牢记；铭记
bear the brunt of 首当其冲
bereave 丧失，失去
call on 呼吁；号召
call upon 呼吁；吁请
candidacy 候选国
capacity-building 能力建设
co-author of a resolution 决议的共同起草国 / 共同起草了……决议
compliance 履约（情况）、遵约（情况）、合规
comprehensive safeguards 全面保障监督
conclusion of negotiations 结束谈判
Conference on Disarmament 裁军谈判会议
confidence-building measure 建立信任措施
consensus decision 协商一致决定
constructive stances 建设性立场
contiguous 毗连
Committee established pursuant to resolution XX 第XX号决议所设委员会
deliberation 审议，审议意见
delegation 代表团
detonation 爆炸；起爆；引爆
developments 事态发展；情况；发展
disarmament 裁军；解除武装
disarmament process 裁军进程
dispersion 分散；散开
documentation 文献资料；证明文件；单证
draft resolution 决议草案
earmarking （资金或资源）专用 / 专款，指定用途款项
ecological safety 生态安全
eliminate 排除；清除；消除；（比赛中）淘汰；消灭
energy security 能源安全
engagement 接触，参与
envisage 想象；设想；展望
equipment checking 设备检查
extra-budgetary contribution 预算外捐款
fissile material 裂变材料
Fissile Material Cut-Off Treaty 《裂变材料禁产条约》
forced displacement 强迫 / 被迫流离失所，强迫迁离
fragmentation 碎裂；碎片化
genocide 灭绝种族
highly enriched uranium 高浓缩铀
holistic approach 整体方法
humanitarian matter 人道主义问题
illicit trafficking 非法贩运
inability 无能；无力；无法
indiscriminate 不加区分的；随意的；恣意的；不加选择的；不加分析的
in-kind support 实物支助
international instrument 国际文书
international non-proliferation regime 国际不扩散机制
Israeli/Jewish settlement 以色列 / 犹太定居点
joint representation 联合交涉
joint statement 联合声明；联合发言
justification 正当理由
low-enriched uranium 低浓缩铀
mandate 任务，任务授权，任务期限
Middle East zone free of nuclear weapons and all other weapons of mass destruction (MEWFZ) 中东无核武器及所有其他大规模毁灭性武器区
moratorium 暂停（试验）；中止
multilateral disarmament 多边裁军
negative/positive security assurance 消极 / 积极安全保证
network of cells 基层组织网络

note with renewed concern　再次关切地注意到
Non-proliferation Treaty (NPT) regime　《不扩散条约》机制
NPT Review Conference/Cycle　不扩散条约审议大会/周期
nuclear explosive devices　核爆炸装置
nuclear non-proliferation　核不扩散
nuclear safety　核安全
nuclear security　核安保，核保安
nuclear-weapon-free zone　无核武器区
nuclear weapon testing　核武器试验
on-site inspection　现场视察，现场核查
operation　业务活动，运行，运转
outreach　外联，推广
peaceful uses of nuclear energy　和平利用核能
prerequisite　前提条件；先决条件
prescribe　开药方；（硬性）规定；指手画脚
priority　优先事项；优先次序；重点
procedural manoeuvres　操纵程序
procedural work　程序性工作
programme budget implications　涉及方案预算问题
programme of work　工作方案
question　质疑；对……提出疑问；对……提出质疑
rationale　根本原因；基本原理；理论基础
recall　忆及，回顾
recipient nation　接受国
recognize　承认；认可

regular budget　正常预算
reluctance　不情愿；不愿意
reporting template　报告模板
resolution text　决议案文
results-oriented　注重成果的，以结果为导向的
right of reply　答辩权
security concerns　安全关切
self-determination　自决
set off　引发；触发；激起
sponsor　（决议的）提案国
staffing　人员配备
stockpile　库存；大量储备
substantive work　实质性工作
successive presidents　历任主席
table-top exercise　桌面演练，模拟演练
transit nation　过境国
Triad　三驾马车
under the aegis of　在……的支持/领导下；由……主办
under the auspices of the United Nations　在联合国主持下
underline　强调；突现；凸显
universalization　普遍性
utilitarian value　实用价值；实用性价值
verify/verification　核查
weapon of mass destruction　大规模毁灭性武器
well over　远远超过

第二章 人权与人道

本章导言

1948年12月10日，在巴黎召开的联合国大会以第217A(Ⅲ)号决议通过了《世界人权宣言》，这是人权史上具有里程碑意义的文件。作为所有国家和所有人民的共同成就，它第一次规定了基本人权应得到普遍保护，正是基于这项文书，联合国创立全面的人权法体系，其中包括经济权利、社会权利、文化权利以及政治权利和公民权利，界定的权利范围广泛，被国际社会普遍接受。为更好地增进和保护人权，协助各国政府履行自己的责任，联合国设立了多个人权机构和相关机制，涉及人权领域的方方面面。

联合国人权领域文件表述严谨，往往能够针对某个专题作深入分析，逻辑严密，表述精练，用词贴切。在翻译这类文件时，需要先把握住人权文件的特点，厘清原文的逻辑，谨慎选词，并用流畅连贯的中文进行表述。

联合国拥有众多人权机构和机制，日常文件类型复杂，语言风格也有所差异。本章共有十四篇材料，重点选取了几个具有代表性的人权机构的文件，介绍了这些机构文件的特点和相应的翻译技巧和方法。这些文件大致可以分为以下五类。

第一类，来文（本章第一篇和第二篇）。这类文件由核心人权条约机构（如禁止酷刑委员会）负责，有固定的格式，事实陈述往往占有很大比重，语言风格偏重叙述。在翻译时，可以灵活调整句子语序而不必字字句句对应原文，确保译文的可读性。

第二类，人权理事会普遍定期审议机制相关文件。这类文件类型众多，如利益攸关方就缔约国所提交材料的概述（本章第三篇和第四篇）、人权事务高级专员办事处办资料汇编（本章第五篇）、结论性意见（本章第六篇和第七篇）等。这类文件往往采用第三方视角对某个专题进行分析，语言平实客观。因此，在翻译这类文件时，要首先确保译文的准确性，不可因追求文字上的优美而偏离原文，导致译文有失客观。

第三类，人权状况特别报告员的报告（本章第十四篇）。这类文件重在客观论述事实，提醒缔约国注意本国存在的人权问题并提出改进建议。因此，文件通常文风平实，语言简练，同时，句式结构较长、句型复杂。在处理这类文件时，除了避免口语化用词之外，还要尽可能做到精练，酌情调整句子结构和语序，确保逻辑顺畅。

第四类，非政府组织向经济及社会理事会非政府组织委员会提交的材料（本章第八篇）。这类文件有固定格式，语言风格多样，在翻译时，如果遇到原文不是很规范的情况，要先把握句子的中心意思，理顺逻辑，避免完全按照原文的语序进行翻译。

第五类，简要记录（本章第十篇至第十三篇）。简要记录内容往往比较正式，从句式结构上看，经常会套有多个从句或非谓语成分。因此，在翻译时，要先明确发言的主题或重点，再确定核心句，最后把"旁枝末节"添加进去，形成逻辑鲜明、语义连贯、准确流畅的译文。

本章所选十四篇材料涵盖上述各机构文件，目的是尽可能全面地呈现人权领域最常见的文件类型，剖析文件特点，让大家熟悉这些领域和相应的翻译策略或技巧。

总的来说，翻译联合国人权与人道领域的相关文件时，应符合以下翻译标准。

（1）遣词造句力求准确，保持客观。

（2）理解无误，逻辑清晰。

（3）表达流畅，可读性强，符合中文表述习惯。

为达到上述标准，应重点掌握如下语言技巧。

一、词汇层面

（1）借助联合国官方词汇库（UNTERM）等工具，确保词义准确。联合国人权文件涉及专有词汇和术语，必须采用联合国的官方用法。例如第八篇第3段中的"human rights defenders"，这份文件属于人权文件，来自联合国日内瓦办事处，应选择UNTERM中的日内瓦用法，将"human rights defenders"译为"人权维护者"，而不用"人权捍卫者"。

（2）结合语境进行辨析，选择最佳词义。例如第七篇第2段中的"appreciate"一词，有"感谢"和"赞赏"的词义，在选词时同样需要结合语意进行辨别，不能一味地选择常见词义。

（3）适当引申。第一篇第2段中有"in the charge of"这个短语，如果按字面译为"负责"，无法挖掘出原文的隐藏含义。因此，不妨大胆引申，真正体现原文意图。

二、逻辑理解层面

（1）切分长句，提炼主干。例如，第二篇第1段的最后一句，原文颇为复杂，句子套句子，遇到这种情况，要先"抽丝剥茧"，确定核心句和从句（或非谓语成分），把切分后的小短句译出，再根据小短句之间的逻辑关系，按序排列，最后润色译文，确保句意无误，逻辑和表达顺畅。

（2）"瞻前顾后"，兼顾上下文逻辑。在处理联合国人权文件时，有时会被原文"牵着走"，只是"就词译词"，忽略段落、篇章的语境，导致译文前后不一致，逻辑不通。例如，第一篇第1段中的"officer"一词，翻译稿将第二次出现的"officers"译为"军官们"，显然没有呼应前文。再例如，第五篇第4段中"OHCHR noted that human rights violations documented from April to August 2018 included...which sometimes resulted in extrajudicial killings"一句，如果只是把"which"引导的定语从句按照字面意思译出，就无法体现出与前半句的逻辑关系，那么定语从句也就失去了它的意义。在遇到这种情况时，不妨根据上下文逻辑，选择适当的连接词将主从句进行衔接，而不要把两个句子孤零零地放在一起。

三、表达层面

（1）准确判断介词作用或修饰成分。例如第二篇第1段中的"When the facts occurred, X was a senior sergeant major...working at a military camp in Bujumbura..."一句。这里有一个介词"in"，作用是表明地点。由于在中文表达中，"在"一字就足以体现位置关系，没有必要紧跟原文，把"in"译为"位于"。再例如，第十一篇第1段中的"He said that many countries in Asia and the Pacific lacked..."一句，将"many countries in Asia and the Pacific"译为"亚洲及太平洋的许多国家"不太符合中文习惯，可以将这里的地点状语单独拿出来，译为"在亚洲及太平洋地区，很多国家……"。在处理介词时，经常会遇到类似的情况，要求译者先判断好介词的作用或者修饰成分，避免因为介词处理不当而导致译文不符合译入语的表达习惯。

（2）灵活调整句式结构或语序，确保译文的可读性。例如，第四篇第2段中的"Joint Submission 3 noted that there were high levels of discrimination and violence against lesbian, gay, bisexual, transgender and intersex persons in the country and that impunity for such acts was prevalent"一句，译为"联合来文3（JS3）指出，该国对女同性恋者、男同性恋者、双性恋者、跨性别者和双性人（LGBTI）人口的歧视和暴力程度很高，而且针对这种行为普遍存在有罪不罚的现象"，可读性较差，地道的中文并不会如此表述，改为"联署材料3指出，在该国，针对男女同性恋、双性恋、跨性别者和双性者群体的歧视和暴力现象严重，而且对于这类歧视和暴力行为，有罪不罚现象普遍"更流畅。

总的来说，联合国人权文件类型多样，各有特点。在翻译时，要根据文件类型和语言特点，确定语篇译文风格，选择相应的翻译策略或技巧。由于人权文件本身表述严谨，又往往涉及法律背景，所以对准确度的要求较高。无论是哪种类型的文件，都要求译者在选词、理解和表达上做到准确，在此基础上，可以适当调整句式和结构，使译文更符合读者的阅读习惯。因此，面对人权文件，译者要学会"带着镣铐跳舞"，重在把握好原文和译文之间的"度"。除了语言层面外，由于人权话题通常比较严肃，与我们的日常生活有着一定距离，译者平时也要留意语料和背景知识的积累，在翻译时方能得心应手。

背景介绍

以下两篇材料选自提交给禁止酷刑委员会的来文（communications）。禁止酷刑委员会1987年依据《禁止酷刑和其他残忍、不人道或有辱人格的待遇或处罚公约》第17条设立，负责监测缔约国履行该公约义务的情况。委员会的任务包括四项主要活动：审议缔约国定期送交的报告（《禁止酷刑公约》第19条）；在有确凿迹象显示在某一缔约国境内经常施行酷刑时进行秘密调查（《禁止酷刑公约》第20条）；审议声称因违反本公约条款而受害的个人所送交的来文（《禁止酷刑公约》第22条）；以及审议国家的申诉（《禁止酷刑公约》第21条）。声称因违反本公约条款而受害的个人，在用尽国内救济手段之后，可选择向该委员会提交呈文，申述冤情，请求该委员会对所涉缔约国做出指示。此类文件有严格的格式要求，分为五个部分，分别为"The facts as submitted by the complainant（申诉人陈述的事实）""The complaint（申诉）""State party's observations on admissibility and merits（缔约国关于可否受理和案情的意见）""Complainant's comments on admissibility and merits（申诉人关于可否受理和案情的评论）"和"Issues and proceedings before the Committee（委员会需处理的问题和议事情况）"。第一篇材料的主要内容涉及前两个部分，由申诉人提供，重在阐述事实，其风格随意，用词简单朴实，在翻译时应侧重于其易读性，以通顺达意作为主要评价标准，但也要注意尺度，不能大范围调整甚至删减，也不能因为其用词通俗而过度口语化。第二篇材料具体涉及来文的第五部分"委员会需处理的问题和议事情况"（Issues and proceedings before the Committee）。在该部分，委员会将按照《禁止酷刑公约》第22条第5款（a）项，审议能否受理该来文。如确认该来文可以受理，委员会将着手对涉及的案情（merits）开展审查。审查发现所涉缔约国确实违反《禁止酷刑公约》的，委员会将确认所涉违法事实，并促请缔约国采取措施纠正错误，赔偿受害人并采取的措施通报给委员会知晓。因此，文件的这一部分会多次直接或间接援引《禁止酷刑公约》的规定，文中会出现大量法律词汇，行文风格正式严肃，多使用结构复杂的长句。在翻译法律术语时，要注意采用其法律含义，而不是其常见词义；在拆解长句时，要注意保持其正式文件的严谨文风，避免因拆解为短句而过于跳脱和口语化。

The facts as submitted by the complainant

When the facts occurred, X was a senior sergeant major in the national army of Burundi and was working at a military camp in Bujumbura (run by the military police).

On 29 January 2010, at about 4:45 p.m., he went to the central market in Bujumbura. When he arrived at the market, he met three of his friends—B.N., E.E. and O.M., all of whom were non-commissioned officers. The three men proposed a foot race to one of the beaches on the shores of Lake Tanganyika, next to the port of Bujumbura. At about 5:45 p.m., when the four friends were on the beach, they suddenly heard shots fired in their direction. They tried to flee but then saw some 30 police officers running towards them, some in plain clothes—who they later found out were agents of the National Intelligence Service (SNR)—and others in military uniforms. The officers ordered all military personnel to remain at the scene. The complainant and the 12 other soldiers who were also there on the beach obeyed the order.

The complainant and the other soldiers were then rounded up in the middle of the beach before being quickly separated and each placed in the charge of two or three State officials. X was roughly seized by three officials, of whom one was a military officer and the other two SNR agents in plain clothes. Each SNR agent pointed a gun at each of the complainant's temples, while the military officer stood behind him, insulting him and accusing him of being a traitor and planning a coup d'état. The complainant was pushed to the ground and fell to his knees. Once he had been completely overpowered, he was brutally beaten; he received kicks to the chest, ribs and back to the accompaniment of violent insults, and also received blows to the head.

请自行翻译后查看后文的分析点评

第 1 段

The facts as submitted by the complainant

When the facts occurred, X was a senior sergeant major in the national army of Burundi and was working at a military camp in Bujumbura (run by the military police). On 29 January 2010, at about 4:45 p.m., he went to the central market in Bujumbura. When he arrived at the market, he met three of his friends—B.N., E.E. and O.M., all of whom were non-commissioned officers. The three men proposed a foot race to one of the beaches on the shores of Lake Tanganyika, next to the port of Bujumbura. At about 5:45 p.m., when the four friends were on the beach, they suddenly heard shots fired in their direction. They tried to flee but then saw some 30 police officers running towards them, some in plain clothes—who they later found out were agents of the National Intelligence Service (SNR)—and others in military uniforms. The officers ordered all military personnel to remain at the scene. The complainant and the 12 other soldiers who were also there on the beach obeyed the order.

批注

① 此类文件中,"complainant"一词专指"申诉人"。
② 中文表达受英文影响。
③ 非关键词,不必逐词译出。
④ 重复信息,可以省略。
⑤ 修饰成分,可与其修饰的成分合并,使译文更简洁。
⑥ 过于口语化。文件翻译大忌。
⑦ 用词不准确。
⑧ 用词不妥。"查明"一词暗示有职权这样做,并且正式开始了调查。与这些人的身份不符。
⑨ 错译。结合上文中的"police officers"来看,此处应是宪兵警官。

申诉人① 陈述的事实

<u>在事实发生时</u>②,X 是布隆迪国民军的一名高级军士长,<u>并在位于</u>③ Bujumbura 的一座军营(由宪兵队管理)里工作。2010 年 1 月 29 日下午 4 点 45 分前后,他来到 Bujumbura 中心市场。<u>当他到市场时</u>④,他遇到三位朋友(B.N.、E.E. 和 O.M.),<u>这三个人都是士官</u>⑤。这三人提议在紧邻 Bujumbura 港的 Tanganyika 湖岸一块沙滩上<u>搞一次</u>⑥竞走比赛。下午 5 时 45 分左右,这四位朋友在沙滩上突然听到有人朝他们这个方向开枪。他们试图<u>逃跑</u>⑦,但随后看到有大约 30 名警官在追他们,有些人穿便装(他们后来<u>查明</u>⑧这些人是国家情报局的特工),有些人穿军装。<u>军官们</u>⑨命令所有军人留在现场。申诉人与另外 12 名当时也在沙滩上的士兵服从了这一命令。

申诉人陈述的事实

事发时 X 是布隆迪国民军的一名高级军士长,在 Bujumbura 一处宪兵队管理的军营工作。2010 年 1 月 29 日下午 4 时 45 分前后,他前往 Bujumbura 中心市场,遇到三位士官朋友(B.N.、E.E. 和 O.M.)。这三人提议在紧邻 Bujumbura 港的 Tanganyika 湖岸沙滩上来一次竞走比赛。下午 5 时 45 分左右,这四人在沙滩上突然听到有人朝他们这个方向开枪。他们试图离开,但随后看到有大约 30 名宪警朝他们跑来,有些人穿便装(后来他们发现这些人是国家情报局的特工),有些人穿军装。宪警命令所有军人留在现场。申诉人与另外 12 名当时也在沙滩上的士兵服从了这一命令。

1. 介词处理不当。表示地点的介词"at"和"in",除非特指,否则通常无须译出。这不是译文正确与否的问题,而是译文是否符合译入语习惯的问题,细微之处拿捏不妥,往往导致读者看译文时虽然说不出具体原因,但总觉得不流畅。

2. 用词不妥。"national army of Burundi"是布隆迪的国民军,"military police"是该国的宪兵。提交给禁止酷刑委员会的呈文(submissions)来自不同国家,各国国情不同,同一类组织可能在不同国家有不同名称。譬如国家控制的军队,在甲国可能被称为"国民军",在乙国就被称为"自卫队",但英文表达都有可能是 national army。在翻译时要留心查阅各国国情,不能仅凭字面贸然翻译。

3. 本段译文中,出现多处常见词不准确、不妥当甚至错译的地方。例如"flea"在翻译稿中译为"逃跑",只是并未做坏事,为何要逃跑?译为"离开"即可。再例如 officer 一词,初次出现在倒数第二句,为"Police officers...",第二次出现在倒数第一句,为"officers...",明显均指"宪警",但翻译稿将第二次出现的 officers 译为"军官们",导致译文前后明显不一致。译员应时刻注意"锤炼言词",结合前后句、上下文来确定准确的词义。水浅石头多,在原文文本相对简单，理解难度低的时候，反而更容易忽视对字词准确含义的把握，这个问题值得引起重视。

第 2 段

The complainant and the other soldiers were then rounded up in the middle of the beach before being quickly separated and each placed in the charge of two or three State officials. X was roughly seized by three officials, of whom one was a military officer and the other two SNR agents in plain clothes. Each SNR agent pointed a gun at each of the complainant's temples, while the military officer stood behind him, insulting him and accusing him of being a traitor and planning a coup d'état. The complainant was pushed to the ground and fell to his knees. Once he had been completely overpowered, he was brutally beaten; he received kicks to the chest, ribs and back to the accompaniment of violent insults, and also received blows to the head.

批 注

① 主语相同，不必重复。
② "负责"一词意义不明。应当将原文中隐藏的含义译出。
③ "roughly"一词，是修饰句中的哪个成分的？
④ 此处是指上文中提及的"police officers"。
⑤ 参照第1段出现的"military police"，此处应当为宪兵。
⑥ 尽量使用主动态。

翻 译 稿

申诉人与其他士兵随后被围到沙滩中间，然后，他们①很快被分开，两三个国家官员负责一人②。X 大概③被三位官员④抓住，其中一人是军官⑤，另外两人是身穿便装的国家情报局特工。国家情报局特工每人手中一支枪，对着申诉人的两鬓，军官站在他后面，辱骂他，并指责他是叛徒和企图政变。申诉人被⑥推倒在地，并跪在地上。在他被完全压倒在地之后，他受到了残忍地殴打；有人踢他的胸部、肋骨和后背，并伴有暴力侮辱，还有人击打他的头部。

审 校 稿

申诉人与其他士兵随后被围到沙滩中间，然后很快被分开，每个人都由两三个国家官员控制。三人粗暴按住 X，其中一人是宪兵，另外两人是国家情报局便衣特工。申诉人两边太阳穴都被特工用枪指着，而那名宪兵站在他背后，辱骂他，斥责他是叛徒，策划政变。有人推搡着申诉人跪倒，把他压倒在地上残忍殴打；有人踢他的胸部、肋骨和后背，暴力侮辱他，还有人打他的头。

点 评

1. 本段的句子简单，却不容易处理，其中混杂出现主动句和被动句，描述的动作环环相扣，在处理时必须不断地"瞻前顾后"。"瞻前"是指要记得前面翻译的类似内容，不能译过就忘。例如，本段中出现的"military officer"一词，翻译稿译为"军官"，就是忘记第 1 段中曾出现"military police"一词，两者相互对应，都指宪兵。"顾后"是指要不断通过后续的翻译内容，对之前翻译的内容进行修正和监测。例如本段第一句出现的"in the charge of"一词，译为"负责"是一种权宜之计，其确切的含义并不是很清楚。通过后面的翻译，发现有三个人压制住申诉人对其施暴，这样一来，将该词组译为"控制"才能体现原文的意图。

2. 词义错误。第二句中的"roughly"作为副词，既有"大概，大约"的意思，也有"粗暴，粗鲁"的意思，无论从语法还是句意上分析，此处都应当是第二种意思。

3. 主动、被动语态把握不准。本段原文中多处出现被动态，在翻译时可尽量处理为主动态，以保证语言的流畅。

补充练习

Two SNR agents ripped off his T-shirt, which they then tore apart so they could use it to tie his hands behind his back. They ripped the laces from his shoes to reinforce the bonds around his wrists. Once his hands were bound behind his back and he was completely at the mercy of the State officials, they started beating him again, kicking him all over his body. They took his mobile phone, a sum of 33,000 Burundi francs (about US$20) and his identity card. When he protested, the officials began hitting him on the head again, sometimes with the butts of their rifles. As a result of this violent attack, the complainant lost consciousness for several minutes. When he came round, he felt sharp pain all over his body and noticed swelling in some places.

Colonel E.N. then ordered the State officials to separate the detained soldiers once again and to shoot anyone who moved. About 20 minutes later, the State officials bundled the complainant and the other detained soldiers into the back of a van. A few minutes before they were forced into the van, a journalist from Radio Publique Africaine arrived at the scene. She was nearly shot by a police officer. She has been able to testify that she saw people lying in the mud on the lake shore while their assailants stamped on their backs and, speaking in the national language, called them "thugs who want to shed blood yet again when so much blood has already been shed".

两个特工扯下他的T恤衫撕成布条，用这些布条将申诉人的两手绑在背后。又扯掉他的鞋带，用鞋带把他的手腕又绑了一道。他双手被绑在背后，只能任由国家官员摆布，这些人开始从头到脚地殴打他。他们从他身上拿走手机、33 000布隆迪法郎（约合20美元）和身份证。当他抗议时，这些人再次打他的头，有时还用步枪枪托打他。申诉人因这次暴力殴打失去意识好几分钟。恢复意识后，他浑身剧痛，还发现一些部位肿了起来。

E.N. 上校随后命令这些国家官员再次将被扣留的士兵们分开，士兵们敢动就开枪。大约20分钟之后，这些国家官员将申诉人及其他被扣留的士兵一起塞进一辆厢式货车。在他们被押上车之前几分钟，一位来自非洲公共广播电台的女记者赶到现场，却差一点被一名宪兵开枪击中。她能证明当时看到有人躺在湖边淤泥里，而说着布隆迪本国语言的施暴者猛踩这些人的背，她称这些施暴者是"在已经有这么多流血事件之后还想着杀戮的暴徒"。

第二章 人权与人道

第二篇

With regard to article 14 of the Convention, the Committee has taken note of the complainant's claim that he has not been the subject of any form of rehabilitation designed to ensure that he recovers as fully as possible in physical, psychological, social and financial terms. The Committee recalls that article 14 not only recognizes the right to fair and adequate compensation but also requires States parties to ensure that the victim of an act of torture obtains redress. The Committee refers to its general comment No. 3 (2012), in which it establishes that States parties should ensure that victims of torture or ill-treatment obtain full and effective redress and reparation, including compensation and the means for as full rehabilitation as possible. In view of the lack of a prompt and impartial investigation despite the complainant's numerous claims that he was tortured, which were corroborated by a range of evidence that the State party has not convincingly refuted, the Committee concludes that the State party breached its obligations under article 14 of the Convention.

With regard to the alleged violation of article 15 of the Convention, the Committee has noted the complainant's arguments that he was compelled to sign a statement attesting to his involvement in planning an alleged coup d'état, that he was convicted of military conspiracy on the basis of those confessions and that the State party has not carried out any investigations, despite his numerous complaints of torture. The Committee recalls that the broad scope of the prohibition in article 15 against invoking any statement that is established to have been made as a result of torture as evidence in any proceedings is a function of the absolute nature of the prohibition of torture and implies, consequently, an obligation for each State party to ascertain whether or not statements admitted as evidence in any proceedings for which it has jurisdiction have been made as a result of torture. In the present case, the State party has failed to conduct any such verification, and the Committee accordingly finds that it has violated the right of X under Article 15 of the Convention.

请自行翻译后查看后文的分析点评

第 1 段

With regard to article 14 of the Convention, the Committee has taken note of the complainant's claim that he has not been the subject of any form of rehabilitation designed to ensure that he recovers as fully as possible in physical, psychological, social and financial terms. The Committee recalls that article 14 not only recognizes the right to fair and adequate compensation but also requires States parties to ensure that the victim of an act of torture obtains redress. The Committee refers to its general comment No. 3 (2012), in which it establishes that States parties should ensure that victims of torture or ill-treatment obtain full and effective redress and reparation, including compensation and the means for as full rehabilitation as possible. In view of the lack of a prompt and impartial investigation despite the complainant's numerous claims that he was tortured, which were corroborated by a range of evidence that the State party has not convincingly refuted, the Committee concludes that the State party breached its obligations under article 14 of the Convention.

批注

① 同位语从句的常见处理方法。
② 此处没有"福祉"意义，不要添加原文没有的意思。
③ 全句多处与《公约》权威译本不符。
④ 译词不当。
⑤ which 引导的从句用来修饰句子中的哪个成分？

【翻译稿】

关于《公约》第14条，委员会注意到申诉人的主张，即①他未得到任何能够使他在身体、心理、社会和经济福祉②方面尽可能完全康复的援助。委员会回顾指出，第14条不仅承认公平和充分赔偿的权利，而且要求缔约国确保酷刑行为的受害人获得救济。③委员会提到其第3（2012）号一般性意见，在该意见中，委员会证实④缔约国应该确保酷刑或虐待行为的受害人获得包括尽可能完全康复所需的赔偿和手段在内的充分和有效救济和赔偿。尽管申诉人多次声称他受到酷刑，但缔约国仍然没有及时进行公正调查，这一点得到大量证据的证实，⑤而缔约国并没有对这些证据进行有说服力的反驳，有鉴于此，委员会得出结论，认为缔约国违反了《公约》第14条规定的义务。

【审校稿】

关于《公约》第14条，委员会注意到申诉人的主张，即他并未得到任何旨在确保其在身体、心理、社会和经济层面尽量完全恢复的复原措施。委员会回顾指出，第14条不仅承认获得公平和充分赔偿的权利，而且要求缔约国确保酷刑行为的受害人获得补偿。委员会提到其第3（2012）号一般性意见，在该意见中，委员会确定缔约国应该确保酷刑或虐待行为的受害人获得完全和有效的补偿和补救，包括赔偿和尽量完全复原的措施。尽管申诉人多次声称受到酷刑，缔约国仍然没有及时开展公正的调查，而且虽有大量证据证明申诉人遭受酷刑，但缔约国没有令人信服地反驳这些证据。有鉴于此，委员会得出结论，认为缔约国违反了《公约》第14条规定的义务。

【点评】

1. 本段提及《禁止酷刑公约》第14条，那么该条的原文是怎样的，其权威中文译本又是如何翻译的？负责任的译者应首先想到去查询，而不是预设目前看到的文件是百分百正确，另外，译者也不能自行翻译。经查，本段直接援引的"right to fair and adequate compensation"与《公约》原文相符，但联合国采纳的权威译本将其译为"获得公平和充分赔偿的权利"，应予以沿用，而不是自行译为"公平和充分赔偿的权利"。同样，rehabilitation 一词，在联合国语境下，虽然有"康复""恢复""善后"等多个意义，但前述权威译本将其译为"复原"，则必须予以沿用;"redress"一词为法律用语,虽有"司法救济""补偿补救"和"赔偿"等意,此处应从权威译本,为"补偿"。

2. 此处的"general comment"译作"一般性意见"。后面带编号时,译为第××号一般性意见。"establish"一词,在此类提交禁止酷刑委员会的呈文中,译为"确定",类似的还有establish precedent(确定先例),establish one's case(确定案件)。

3. 法律文本或不太正式的涉法文本中,时常出现近义词并列的现象。这样做通常是为了保证无遗漏,避免被钻空子,但汉语与英语并非完全对等,多个英文近义词往往共享同一个中文词,此时需要译者仔细辨别词义,必要时可适当增补词义,以体现近义词之间的区别。以本段出现的"obtain full and effective redress and reparation, including compensation..."一句为例,其中compensation,redress和reparation三词,均有补偿、赔偿之意,但从严格的法律意义而言,compensation是指对他人的损失给予价值相当的货币,或其他等价物,以使受损一方当事人恢复其原有状况,中文对应"赔偿";redress系指补偿、补救;reparation源自repair,强调对受损之处予以修理修补,虽然中文通常译为"赔偿",但更强调"补救"之意。因此,这句可译为"获得完全和有效的补偿和补救,包括赔偿……"

4. 本段最后一句是一个套叠长句,"In view of..."引导的原因状语从句中套叠了一个"despite"引导的让步状语从句,后者中又夹带一个定语从句"which were corroborated by..."。在处理这种复杂句时,可以将长句拆成多个短句,把较长的定语拿出来单独翻译为一个句子,通过重复提及定语的先行词,体现各个短句之间的关系。例如本句译文中重复提及"遭受酷刑"。

第2段

With regard to the alleged violation of Article 15 of the Convention, the Committee has noted the complainant's arguments that he was compelled to sign a statement attesting to his involvement in planning an alleged coup d'état, that he was convicted of military conspiracy on the basis of those confessions and that the State party has not carried out any investigations, despite his numerous complaints of torture. The Committee recalls that the broad scope of the prohibition in Article 15 against invoking any statement that is established to have been made as a result of torture as evidence in any proceedings is a function of the absolute nature of the prohibition of torture and implies, consequently, an obligation for each State party to ascertain whether or not statements admitted as evidence in any proceedings for which it has jurisdiction have been made as a result of torture. In the present case, the State party has failed to conduct any such verification, and the Committee accordingly finds that it has violated the right of X under Article 15 of the Convention.

关于被指控违反《公约》第15条,委员会注意到申诉人的论点,即他被

批 注

① 注意连续3个同位语从句。

批 注

① 漏译。
② 错译。

迫在证明他曾经参与谋划所谓政变的口供上签字,正是依据这些供词对他提起诉讼并判处他犯有军事阴谋罪,而尽管他多次申诉称遭受酷刑,但缔约国未进行任何调查。委员会回顾指出,第15条禁止援引任何业经确定系以酷刑手段取得的口供①,其中涉及的证据的范围②十分广泛,目的是绝对禁止酷刑,并因此也意味着每个缔约国有义务查明在其管辖下的任何诉讼程序中承认为证据的口供是否系以酷刑手段取得。在本案中,缔约国没有进行核实,因此,委员会裁定缔约国侵害了 X 依据《公约》第15条享有的权利。

◆ 审 校 稿

关于被指控违反《公约》第15条,委员会注意到申诉人的论据,即他被迫在证明他参与策划所谓政变的陈述上签字,这些供述成为判处他犯有军事共谋罪的依据,而尽管他多次控告称遭受酷刑,但缔约国未进行任何调查。委员会回顾指出,第15条广泛禁止在任何诉讼程序中援引任何业经确定系以酷刑手段取得的陈述,体现了禁止酷刑的绝对性,也意味着每个缔约国有义务查明其有权管辖的任何诉讼程序中作为证据接受的陈述是否系以酷刑手段取得。在本案中,缔约国没有进行核实,因此,委员会裁定缔约国侵害了 X 依据《公约》第15条所享有的权利。

◆ 点 评

1. 词义不准确。本段出现多个法律术语,包括 argument(理由、论据)、statement(陈述)、confession(供述)、convict(宣判……有罪)、conspiracy(共谋)、complaint(起诉、申诉)、proceeding(诉讼程序/听审)、jurisdiction(司法管辖权/法院的裁判权)和 find(裁断)。值得注意的是,这些术语也有非法律性质的词义,在翻译过程中,要根据文件的性质辨词选词。出现在涉法文件中时,采纳其法律术语词义,不能译为常见词义。

2. 错译、漏译。本段第二句的简要结构为:The Committee recalls the prohibition in article 15...is a function of the absolute nature of the prohibition of torture, and the prohibition implies an obligation for each State party。此句中的"absolute nature"意指禁止酷刑是一种不受任何限制的绝对权利,在任何情况下均不得施行酷刑。

◆ 补充练习

The Committee observes that the State party has merely denied and minimized the complainant's allegations of torture, without producing any convincing evidence to refute the acts described. Furthermore, the Committee notes the State party's argument that the injuries sustained by the complainant were caused by his resistance to law enforcement officials. However, corroborated and credible evidence reveals that the injuries occurred while the claimant was under the control of the State party's authorities. The Committee thereby deduces that acts of torture were inflicted on the complainant at the time of his arrest, as well as during subsequent interrogations, and concludes that all of these acts constituted a violation of article 1 of the Convention.

The Committee also notes the complainant's argument that article 11 was violated because the State party failed to conduct proper monitoring of the treatment he received while in detention. The Committee again recalls its latest concluding observations on Burundi, in which it expressed concern at: the excessive length of time during which people can be held in police custody; numerous instances in which the allowable duration of police custody has been exceeded; failures to keep registers on persons in custody or failures to ensure that such records are complete; failures to comply with fundamental legal safeguards for persons deprived of their liberty; the absence of provisions that guarantee access to a doctor and access to legal assistance for persons of limited means; and the excessive use of pretrial detention in the absence of regular reviews of its legality and of any limit on its total duration (see CAT/C/BDI/CO/2, para. 10). In the present case, the complainant appears to have remained outside judicial oversight until he was brought before a judge on 14 February 2010, 16 days after his arrest. In the absence of conclusive evidence from the State party that the complainant's detention was, in fact, placed under its supervision, the Committee finds that the State party has violated article 11 of the Convention.

委员会注意到，缔约国仅否认和淡化申诉人的酷刑指控，并没有提供任何令人信服的证据反驳申诉人描述的行为。另外，委员会还注意到缔约国的论据，即申诉人受伤是由于他抗拒执法人员所致。不过，已确认的可信证据表明，申诉人被缔约国主管当局控制之后才受伤。委员会由此推断，缔约国当局在抓捕申诉人以及随后的审讯期间对他实施了酷刑行为，并得出结论认为，所有这些行为都违反了《公约》第1条。

委员会还注意到申诉人的论点，即缔约国因未能适当监督他在被拘留期间受到的待遇而违反了第11条。委员会再次忆及其最近关于布隆迪的结论性意见，在该意见中，委员会对以下方面表示关切：警方超期羁押；存在多起法定羁押超期的情况；未登记在押人员，或未确保羁押记录完整；未能向被剥夺自由者提供基本法律保障；没有规定保障经济能力有限的人获得就医机会和法律援助；过度使用审前拘留措施，并且没有定期审查该措施的合法性，也没有定期审查对该措施总时长的任何限制（见CAT/C/BDI/CO/2，第10段）。本案中，在申诉人被捕16日之后也即直到2010年2月14日他被带见法官之前，他似乎一直都没有得到司法监督。缔约国没有提供确凿的证据说明事实上对拘留申诉人进行了司法监督，委员会因此裁定缔约国违反了《公约》第11条。

背景介绍

普遍定期审议是人权理事会的独特程序,涉及对所有193个联合国会员国的人权记录进行定期审议,其最终目标是改善每个国家的人权状况,并对全世界人民产生显著影响。

审议由理事会47个成员组成的普遍定期审议工作组主持进行。不过,任何联合国会员国都可以参与到与接受审议国家的讨论/对话中。由3个国家为一组的"三国小组"担任报告员,协助开展每个国家的审议工作。

审议所依据的文件包括:①受审议国家所提供的资料,其形式可以是"国家报告";②独立人权专家和小组的报告中;③来自非政府组织和国家人权机构等其他利益攸关方的材料。

在工作组完成国家审议后,三国小组撰写审议情况报告。

以下两篇材料来自人权事务高级专员办事处向该工作组提交的材料,分别涉及刚果共和国和多民族玻利维亚国的人权状况。本材料属于审议所依据的第③类文件,其内容包括各国向受审议国家提出的问题、评论和建议以及受审议国的回应,文件多处涉及政府机构、非政府组织以及法律法规的名称。在翻译此类文件时,应特别注意一些特有的问题:行文上,对客观事实材料的汇编与摘录,多为段落式呈现,每段内容相对较为独立;多使用有多重含义的平实词汇,但由于段落前后语境较少,需要根据所选文段的句式句型特征加以谨慎推敲;对于引用的非联合国框架内的材料,需要查明资料寻找准确出处。

第三篇

原文

Cultural Survival (CS) stated that most Pygmies have neither national identity cards nor birth registration. The result was lack of access to formal education and literacy training, and less employment opportunity leading to economic instability, discrimination and less political participation. CS recommended that Congo facilitate the acquisition of birth certificates and identity cards for forest-dwelling communities. CS noted that indigenous and rural children were vulnerable to trafficking in the form of forced labour and sexual exploitation. Both forced labour and sexual trafficking are often linked to crime networks.

JS1 stated that the application of children's rights was declining in Congo, specifically in the areas of health, education and recreation. As a result, many children, at social, family and school level, did not have access to health, justice, education, housing and access to basic needs. The most vulnerable children, street children, girls and boys, excluded from any health care system, were unable to access care as guaranteed in Congolese law.

AI reported that between 2014 and 2015, Congo engaged in unlawful mass expulsions of non-nationals, including refugees and asylum seekers, during the operation "Mbata ya Mokolo" (*Slap of the Elders* in Lingala) carried out by police in cities nationwide. AI recommended that Congo promptly adopt comprehensive asylum legislation, recognising in particular the right not to be subjected to *refoulement*, in line with international law; and ensure that a definition of discrimination, in line with international law, is included in the Criminal Code and that discrimination is prohibited in all its forms. JS1 reported that, although reliable data were not yet available, children in foster care, children accused of witchcraft, early marriages of girls, among other phenomena, continued to be a scourge with no sanction applied against the perpetrators of these violations.

请自行翻译后查看后文的分析点评

分析点评

第1段

Cultural Survival (CS) stated that most Pygmies have neither national identity cards nor birth registration. The result was lack of access to formal education and literacy training, and less employment opportunity leading to economic instability, discrimination and less political participation. CS recommended that Congo facilitate the acquisition of birth certificates and identity cards for forest-dwelling communities. CS noted that indigenous and rural children were vulnerable to trafficking in the form of forced labour and sexual exploitation. Both forced labour and sexual trafficking are often linked to crime networks.

文化生存组织指出，大部分俾格米人既没有国民身份，也没有出生登记。这种情况导致他们缺少正规教育和扫盲培训①，并且由于就业机会较少导致经济状况不稳定、遭受歧视和缺少政治参与。文化生存组织建议刚果促进丛居社区②获得出生证和身份证。文化生存组织指出，土著和农村儿童容易受到强迫劳动和性剥削形式的贩运。强迫劳动和性贩运往往依存于犯罪网络。

批注

① 理解不准确。
② 用词不准确。

文化生存组织指出，大部分俾格米人没有国民身份证，也没有出生登记。这种情况导致他们无法获得正规教育和扫盲培训，就业机会较少导致经济状况不稳定、遭受歧视和缺少政治参与。文化生存组织建议刚果为居住在山林的民众获得出生证和身份证提供便利。文化生存组织指出，土著儿童和农村儿童容易遭受以强迫劳动和性剥削为目的的贩运。强迫劳动和以性剥削为目的的贩运往往都与犯罪网络联系在一起。

点评

1. 词汇理解问题。见"The result was lack of access to..."一句。"lack access to"有多种处理方法,包括"缺少……途径、渠道""无法获得……"等。翻译稿中将该术语处理成"缺少",语义不完整。结合前半句的表述,我们可知"lack access to"是因"没有国民身份证、没有出生登记"导致的,即教育资源是客观存在的,但是由于一些人为原因导致他们没有办法接受教育,因此这句话的论述重点在于"无法获得教育",而不是"缺少教育资源"。

2. 用词不准确问题。见"forest-dwelling communities"。"communities"在联合国术语中多译为"社区、社群",但这不意味着所有定语加上"communities"都可以译作"……社区"。"communities"首先可以指代一种抽象概念,即在一定文化、地理区域基础上形成的"社区",也可以指在某一地理区域或某一领域具有共同特性的一群人,而此处"forest-dwelling communities"显然指的是具体的"人"的概念,而不是抽象的"社区"概念,因此译为"丛居社区"不当。在此处扩展一点,"communities"在译作"社区"时,有时也可以理解成特指某个群体,如"收容社区""农业社区""技术社区"等。

3. 对比理解。对于"in the form of"一词,"International Convention on the Elimination of All Forms of Racial Discrimination"(《消除一切形式种族歧视国际公约》)的标题采用的就是直译法,译为了"一切形式歧视",那么在此处为什么要译为"以……为目的"而不是"以……为形式"呢?原因在于,在处理同一个词语时,应当寻求的是功能对等,而不是词汇表面意思的对等。处理成"强迫劳动和性剥削形式的贩运",只是做到了形式上的对等,但没有真正理解"贩运"与"强迫劳动和性剥削"之间的实质关系。对于《消除一切形式种族歧视国际公约》,"种族歧视"是"歧视"的一种形式,与"性别歧视"等概念是对应的,而"贩运"和"性剥削"并不是"贩运"的一种形式,而是"贩运"的目的之一,要把握住这一点,寻求真正的功能对等,采用"以强迫劳动和性剥削为目的的贩运"这一译法。

第 2 段

JS1 stated that the application of children's rights was declining in Congo, specifically in the areas of health, education and recreation. As a result, many children, at social, family and school level, did not have access to health, justice, education, housing and access to basic needs. The most vulnerable children, street children, girls and boys, excluded from any health care system, were unable to access care as guaranteed in Congolese law.

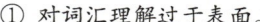

① 对词汇理解过于表面。

联署材料1指出,在刚果,儿童权利的适用情况① 正在退化,特别是在医疗

卫生保健、教育和娱乐领域。其结果是，社会、家庭和学校的儿童无法获得医疗卫生保健、司法、教育、住房机会，也无法满足基本需求。最脆弱的儿童、街头儿童、男童和女童被排除在任何医疗卫生保健系统之外，无法获得刚果法律所保障的医疗保健机会。

批 注

① 定语成分问题。

审校稿

联署材料1指出，在刚果，儿童享有的权利在不断减少，特别是在卫生、教育和娱乐领域。由此带来的结果是，许多儿童无法从社会、家庭和学校层面获得医疗保健、司法、教育和住房资源，也无法满足基本需求。被所有医疗保健系统排斥的最脆弱的儿童、街头儿童、男童和女童无法获取刚果法律保障的医疗保健机会。

点 评

1. 理解问题。见"application of children's rights"一句。翻译稿采用的依然是直译法，即译为"儿童权利的适用情况"。在此处，需要对"application"进行灵活处理。首先，"application"与"权利"搭配，不能完全取其本义"适用"的含义，可以理解为"权利"的执行，如果从这一点出发，也就不难理解审校稿采用"儿童享有的权利"这一译法。

2. 定语位置问题。见"As a result, many children, at social..."一句。在这句话中，"at social, family and school level"紧跟着"many children"出现，会使人误以为是"children"的定语，也就译为了"社会、家庭和学校的儿童"，但实际上，这个定语是用两个逗号隔开的，是一个插入成分，作为整句话的插入语。因此，"at social, family and school level"修饰的是整个句子，再结合语境理解，"儿童无法从社会、家庭和学校层面获得……资源"。再看"excluded from any health care system"一句。与上句话一样，也涉及定语位置问题。翻译稿处理为"最脆弱的儿童、街头儿童、男童和女童被排除在任何医疗卫生保健系统之外，无法获得……"将这个定语处理成了谓语成分，与后面句子主干"were unable to access care"形成并列。这种将定语转换成谓语的方法作为一种通行的翻译技巧没有问题，但要注意，"excluded from any health care system"修饰的主语是儿童，并且与定语"most vulnerable"并列，更为严谨的做法还是处理成定语，即按照审校稿"被所有医疗保健系统排斥的最脆弱的儿童、街头儿童、男童和女童无法获取……"处理。

第3段

AI reported that between 2014 and 2015, Congo engaged in unlawful mass expulsions of non-nationals, including refugees and asylum seekers, during the operation "Mbata ya Mokolo" (*Slap of the Elders* in Lingala) carried out by police in cities nationwide. AI recommended that Congo promptly adopt comprehensive asylum legislation, recognising in particular the right not to be subjected to *refoulement*, in line with international law; and ensure that a definition of discrimination, in line with international law, is included in the Criminal Code and that discrimination is prohibited in all its forms. JS1 reported that, although reliable data were not yet available, children in foster care, children accused of witchcraft, early marriages of girls, among other phenomena, continued to be a scourge with no sanction applied against the perpetrators of these violations.

批注
① 不求甚解的错译。
② 注意词汇的文化色彩。

大赦国际报告称，在2014—2015年，刚果警方在全国各城市开展了"Mbataya Mokolo"（林加拉语为殴打老人）运动①，并在其中策划了大规模非法驱逐非本国国民的活动，包括驱逐难民和寻求庇护者。大赦国际建议刚果依照国际法迅速通过全面的庇护法，特别承认不受驱回的权利；并确保按照国际法的规定将歧视的定义纳入《刑法典》，并禁止一切形式的歧视。联署材料1报告称，尽管没有提供可靠的数据，但寄养儿童、将儿童指为巫魔②、强迫女童早婚以及其他现象仍在作为一种悲剧上演，犯下侵权行为的肇事者也得不到制裁。

大赦国际报告称，刚果警方在2014—2015年在全国各地城市中开展"Mbataya Mokolo"（林加拉语为"长者的惩罚"）行动，期间大规模非法驱逐包括难民和寻求庇护者在内的非本国国民。大赦国际建议刚果根据国际法，迅速通过全面的庇护法，特别是承认不受驱回的权利；确保按照国际法的规定将歧视的定义纳入《刑法典》，并禁止一切形式的歧视。联署材料1报告称，尽管还没有可靠的数据，但儿童寄养、指责儿童是灾星、女童早婚以及其他现象仍是一种灾难，施害者没有受到处罚。

1. 敏感度问题。见"operation"一词。"operation"一词在联合国术语体系中有多种版本，既可以是"行动、活动"，也可以是"运动"，还可以是"业务活动"等。在文中，"operation"搭配的主语是"警方"，警方是不可能开展具有社会群体活动性质的"运动"的，只能是开展与之相对的"镇压行动"，因此在此处将"operation"理解成"campaign"（运动）不恰当。

2. 词汇的文化语境。见"children accused of witchcraft"一语。"witchcraft"直译为"巫魔"也不为错，没有充分体现对儿童歧视背后的文化内涵。根据上一段的"林加拉语"得知，这些侵犯人权的行动是在刚果偏远地区发生的，与"强迫女童早婚"一样，"witchcraft"也指代一种具有迷信、偏见色彩的活动。因此，可以联想到我们汉语文化语境，有"丧门星"这种带有歧视、迷信色彩的称呼，那么在翻译这个词时转化成"灾星"更符合汉语文化语境。

补充练习

JS1 stated that the Child Protection Act No. 4-2010 prohibited the deprivation of care of a child because of financial considerations in subsidized hospitals (art.26 al.4) and provided for criminal sanctions, disciplinary and administrative matters (art.104). However, no health facility provided free childcare. The failure of the public health service was increasingly leading the population to turn to the private sector whose rates increase from year to year, or to the informal sector.

JS4 stated that the prison organization of the Republic of Congo was composed in most cases of dilapidated buildings dating from the colonial period. These poor conditions had already been the subject of recommendations in the previous UPR cycle. Since 2010, the Government had expressed its desire to modernize the prison system by initiating a reform on prison management. Unfortunately, the prisons that were to be built had never been or had remained unfinished.

联署材料 1 指出,《儿童保护法》(第 4-2010 号法)禁止享受补贴的医院以财务问题为由拒绝为儿童提供医疗服务(第 26 条第 4 款),并对刑事处罚、纪律和行政事项做出了规定(第 104 条)。但是,没有卫生机构提供免费医疗服务。公共卫生服务的缺失导致越来越多的民众转向私营部门或非正规部门,而私营部门的收费逐年上涨。

联署材料 4 指出,刚果共和国的监狱大多由殖民时期的破旧建筑物改建而成。在上一个普遍定期审议周期已经就改善这种恶劣条件提出了建议。自 2010 年以来,政府一直表示渴望改革监狱管理,对监狱系统升级改造。遗憾的是,准备修建的监狱从未开工或至今仍未完成。

原文

Two submissions noted that the National Committee against Racism and All Forms of Discrimination was implementing the Multisectoral Plan to Eliminate Racism and All Forms of Discrimination (2016—2020). Joint Submission 15 recommended that the State allocate sufficient resources for the implementation of the Plan, strengthen departmental committees and take affirmative action in favour of vulnerable groups. Joint Submission 18 noted that discrimination against indigenous and campesino populations persisted.

Joint Submission 3 noted that there were high levels of discrimination and violence against lesbian, gay, bisexual, transgender and intersex persons in the country and that impunity for such acts was prevalent. Two submissions noted that the rights of women and lesbian, gay, bisexual, transgender and intersex persons were constantly being undermined by fundamentalist and conservative groups.

In 2016, the Inter-American Commission on Human Rights noted that the Plurinational Legislative Assembly had adopted the Gender Identity Act. Two submissions reported that, in 2017, the Plurinational Constitutional Court had declared this Act to be partially unconstitutional, stating that the right to gender identity did not involve access to all fundamental rights, including the right to marriage, adoption and parity in electoral processes.

请自行翻译后查看后文的分析点评

分析点评

第 1 段

Two submissions noted that the National Committee against Racism and All Forms of Discrimination was implementing the Multisectoral Plan to Eliminate Racism and All Forms of Discrimination (2016—2020). Joint Submission 15 recommended that the State allocate sufficient resources for the implementation of the Plan, strengthen departmental committees and take affirmative action in favour of vulnerable groups. Joint Submission 18 noted that discrimination against indigenous and campesino populations persisted.

批注
①② 联合国文件，"communication"和"submission"在特定情境下有固定译法。
③ 涉及玻利维亚行政区划，应查背景资料。

两份来文①注意到，反种族主义和一切形式歧视全国委员会正在执行"打击种族主义和一切形式歧视的多部门计划"（2016—2020 年）。联合来文②15（JS15）建议国家为执行该计划分配足够的资源，加强部门③委员会并采取有利于弱势群体的平权行动。联合来文 18（JS18）指出，针对土著人民和农民的歧视仍然存在。

两份材料指出，反种族主义和一切形式歧视全国委员会正在执行《打击种族主义和一切形式歧视多部门计划》（2016—2020 年）。联署材料 15 建议玻利维亚为该计划的执行工作划拨充足的资源，加强各省委员会并开展有利于弱势群体的平权行动。联署材料 18 指出，针对土著人民和农民的歧视仍然存在。

点评

1. 专有名词处理不当。此处"submission"为利益攸关方就多民族玻利维亚国提交的材料，统一译为"材料"，并非本章第一篇中提及的"来文"（communications）。"Joint Submission"译为"联署材料"。

2. 本段涉及玻利维亚行政区划信息，译者未加详查，以致错译。中国外交部网站"玻利维亚国家概况"页面显示玻利维亚"全国共分为九省，分别是……"（https://www.fmprc.gov.cn/），而以英文查询玻利维亚行政区划，可查到"Bolivia is a unitary state consisting of nine departments (Spanish: departamentos). Departments are the primary subdivisions of Bolivia."（https://en.wikipedia.org/wiki/Departments_of_Bolivia），由此可见，"department"是指省，而非部门。

第 2 段

Joint Submission 3 noted that there were high levels of discrimination and violence against lesbian, gay, bisexual, transgender and intersex persons in the country and that impunity for such acts was prevalent. Two submissions noted that the rights of women and lesbian, gay, bisexual, transgender and intersex persons were constantly being undermined by fundamentalist and conservative groups.

联合来文 3（JS3）指出，该国对女同性恋者、男同性恋者、双性恋者、跨性别者和双性人（LGBTI）[①]人口的歧视和暴力程度很高，而且针对这种行为普遍存在有罪不罚的现象。两份来文指出，妇女和女同性恋者、男同性恋者、双性恋者、跨性别者和双性人（LGBTI）的权利长期受到原教旨主义和保守派团体的攻击。

① 有固定译法，可查询词汇库。

联署材料 3 指出，在该国，针对男女同性恋、双性恋、跨性别者和双性者群体的歧视和暴力现象严重，而且对于这类歧视和暴力行为，有罪不罚现象普遍。两份材料指出，妇女和男女同性恋、双性恋、跨性别者和双性者的权利屡屡受到原教旨主义和保守派团体的攻击。

1. 专有名词处理不当。关于"Submission"和"Joint Submission"，见上段点评 1。关于"lesbian, gay, bisexual, transgender and intersex persons"，在 UN 文件翻译中有固定译法，如不确定，可查询联合国多语言术语库 UNTERM（https://conferences.unite.un.org/unterm/search?urlQuery=list%20of%20issues%20and%20questions）。

2. 表述西化，见翻译稿"人口的歧视和暴力程度很高，而且针对这种行为普遍存在有罪不罚的现象"，意思无误，但可读性明显欠缺。

第 3 段

In 2016, the Inter-American Commission on Human Rights noted that the Plurinational Legislative Assembly had adopted the Gender Identity Act. Two submissions reported that, in 2017, the Plurinational Constitutional Court had declared this Act to be partially unconstitutional, stating that the right to gender identity did not involve access to all fundamental rights, including the right to marriage, adoption and parity in electoral processes.

批注

① 原文无缩写，译文不必画蛇添足。
② 政府机构名称，需查背景资料，不可随便翻译。
③ 处理草率。

翻译稿

2016年，美洲人权委员会（IACHR）① 指出，多民族立法议会② 通过了《性别认同法》。两份来文报告，2017年，多民族宪法法院宣布该法部分违宪，表明③ 性别认同权并不包含获得所有基本权利，包括婚姻权、收养权和选举进程平等权。

审校稿

2016年，美洲人权委员会注意到，多民族立法大会通过了《性别认同法》。两份材料报告称，2017年，多民族宪法法院宣布该法部分规定违宪，指出性别认同权并不意味着获享包括婚姻权、收养权和选举平等权在内的所有基本权利。

点评

1. 政府机构名称翻译错误。"the Plurinational Legislative Assembly"实为"多民族立法大会"，而非"多民族立法议会"，仅一字之差，正确性和严谨性大打折扣。对于此类机构名称，译者应详查背景资料，不可随便翻译。就本材料而言，建议查询中国外交部网站"玻利维亚国家概况"页面或中国驻玻利维亚使馆、领事馆网站。

2. 部分词语处理不细致。关于"stating that"，这是现在分词引导的状语从句，是对前半句"多民族宪法法院宣布该法部分规定违宪"作补充说明。

补充练习

Centre Europe–Tiers Monde (CETIM) highlighted the key role played by the Plurinational State of Bolivia in the elaboration of the UN Declaration on the rights of peasants and other people working in rural areas.

The International Campaign to Abolish Nuclear Weapons (ICAN) welcomed that in 2018 the State had signed the UN Treaty on the Prohibition of Nuclear Weapons and urged to ratify it.

In 2017, the Inter-American Commission on Human Rights welcomed the State's ratification of the Inter-American Convention on Protecting the Human Rights of Older Persons.

Joint Submission 15 recommended that the State strengthen its relations with the Office of the United Nations High Commissioner for Human Rights.

参考译文

欧洲—第三世界中心强调了多民族玻利维亚国在制定《联合国农民和农村地区其他劳动者权利宣言》方面发挥的关键作用。

国际废除核武器运动欣见该国在2018年签署了《联合国禁止核武器条约》，并敦促该国批准该条约。

2017年，美洲人权委员会欣见该国批准《美洲保护老年人人权公约》。

联署材料15建议该国加强与联合国人权事务高级专员办事处（人权高专办）的关系。

背景介绍

本篇材料节选自联合国人权事务高级专员办事处向人权理事会普遍定期审议工作组会议提交的"尼加拉瓜资料汇编"，即属于审议所依据的第②类文件，此类报告系根据人权理事会第5/1号和第16/21号决议编写。在内容上，报告通常会涵盖国际义务的范围以及与国际人权机制和机构的合作、国家人权框架、参照适用的国际人道主义法履行国际人权义务的情况（贯穿各领域的问题、公民权利和政治权利、经济、社会及文化权利、特定个人或群体的权利、特定地区或领土）等部分。语言特点是文字简练，有时过于浓缩，而且多涉及政府机构、非政府组织以及法律法规的名称。在翻译时，需大量查阅背景资料，掌握词性转化，酌情增译，确保译文语言平实、客观。

第五篇

原文

In July 2018, OHCHR raised concern about the adoption of a law on money laundering and terrorism, with a very broad definition of terrorism, which could be use against people taking part in protests. It noted that, on 16 August 2018, the National Assembly adopted legislation to include new crimes relating to terrorism. OHCHR also noted that the trials of people charged in relation to the protests had serious flaws and did not observe due process, including the impartiality of the courts.

In November 2018, seven special procedures of the Human Rights Council condemned the alleged arbitrary detention of dozens of people, and the fact that some of them appeared to be facing trumped-up charges of terrorism.

In April 2018, the Secretary-General expressed his concern about the casualties in protests in Nicaragua. He called for restraint on all sides, and called upon the Government of Nicaragua to ensure the protection of human rights of all citizens, particularly the right to peaceful assembly and freedom of expression. The same month, four special procedures of the Human Rights Council stated that they were appalled at the violent response of Nicaraguan security forces to protests opposing social security reforms, and called upon the authorities to ensure that the fundamental freedoms of expression and peaceful assembly were respected.

OHCHR noted that human rights violations documented from April to August 2018 included the disproportionate use of force by the police, which sometimes resulted in extrajudicial killings; enforced disappearances; widespread arbitrary or illegal detentions; and ill-treatment and instances of torture and sexual violence in detention centres.

请自行翻译后查看后文的分析点评

分析点评

第 1 段

In July 2018, OHCHR raised concern about the adoption of a law on money laundering and terrorism, with a very broad definition of terrorism, which could be used against people taking part in protests. It noted that, on 16 August 2018, the National Assembly adopted legislation to include new crimes relating to terrorism. OHCHR also noted that the trials of people charged in relation to the protests had serious flaws and did not observe due process, including the impartiality of the courts.

2018 年 7 月，人权高专办对一项反洗钱和反恐法的通过表示担忧①，该法对恐怖主义的定义非常宽泛，可用于针对参加抗议活动的人民②。它③注意到，2018 年 8 月 16 日国民议会通过的新立法纳入了与恐怖主义相关的新罪行④。人权高专办还注意到，对被控与抗议活动相关者的审判存在严重缺陷，且未遵循正当法律程序，包括法院的公正性。

批 注

① "concern" 一词在联合国文件中有固定译法。
② 用词太宽泛。
③ 是谁？应具体化。
④ 可做微调。

2018 年 7 月，人权高专办对一部反洗钱和反恐怖主义法获得通过提出关切，因为该法对恐怖主义的定义极为宽泛，有可能用于打压抗议示威人士。人权高专办注意到，2018 年 8 月 16 日国民议会通过了有关立法，纳入了与恐怖主义有关的新罪名。人权高专办还注意到，对被控抗议活动相关罪名者的审判存在严重缺陷，没有遵循正当法律程序，包括法庭没有保持中立。

整体来说，翻译稿小瑕疵较多，影响了译文的整体质量。

1. 留心某些名词的译法，见 "raised concern"。在联合国文件体系中，"concern" 通常译为"关切"。

2. 酌情增译，见 "with a very broad definition of terrorism"，增译"因为"二字，明确提出关切的原因，增强逻辑清晰性。

3. 避免用"它",见"It noted that",从上下文来看,此处"It"显然是指"人权高专办",应具体化。

4. 掌握词性转化和句子拆分技巧,见"the National Assembly adopted legislation to include new crimes relating to terrorism",翻译稿沿用原文结构,将"to include"处理为目的状语从句,而审校稿则将之谓语化,处理为与"adopted"并列的动词,两相比较之下,后者的节奏感和语感更好。这种技巧只要用心,就可以熟能生巧。另外,从法律相关文本的角度来看,"to include new crimes relating to terrorism"处理为"纳入了与恐怖主义有关的新罪名"更为恰当。

第 2 段

In November 2018, seven special procedures of the Human Rights Council condemned the alleged arbitrary detention of dozens of people, and the fact that some of them appeared to be facing trumped-up charges of terrorism.

2018 年 11 月,七名人权理事会特别程序谴责了据称对数十人的任意拘留行为,其中一些人似乎面临着捏造的恐怖主义指控。

2018 年 11 月,人权理事会七项特别程序谴责据称任意拘留数十人的行为,其中有些人似乎还被扣上了莫须有的恐怖主义罪名。

1. 了解背景信息,见"seven special procedures of the Human Rights Council",此处错误使用量词,体现出译者对人权理事会特别程序缺乏了解。人权理事会特别程序是旨在从专题角度或具体国别角度对人权问题提供建议和报告的独立人权专家机制。特别程序系统是联合国人权机制的重要组成部分,涵盖公民、文化、经济、政治和社会等多方面的人权问题。特别程序由个人(被称为"特别报告员"或"独立专家")或由五名成员组成的工作组担任,在人权事务高级专员办事处(人权高专办)的支持下开展工作(欲了解更多信息,可查阅 https://www.ohchr.org/CH/HRBodies/SP/Pages/Introduction.aspx)。

2. 句子重心偏移,见"condemned the alleged arbitrary detention...and the fact that...",从原句结构来看,谓语动词是"condemned",宾语有两个"the alleged arbitrary detention"和"the fact that",为并列关系。翻译稿未将重心放在"condemned"上,虽无大错,却体现不出这种谓宾关系。除却结构问题,在遣词用字方面亦有进步空间。

第 3 段

In April 2018, the Secretary-General expressed his concern about the casualties in protests in Nicaragua. He called for restraint on all sides, and called upon the Government of Nicaragua to ensure the protection of human rights of all citizens,

批 注

① 注意不要被量词误导。

particularly the right to peaceful assembly and freedom of expression. The same month, four special procedures of the Human Rights Council stated that they were appalled at the violent response of Nicaraguan security forces to protests opposing social security reforms, and called upon the authorities to ensure that the fundamental freedoms of expression and peaceful assembly were respected.

批 注

① 同上文第 1 段。
② 同上文第 2 段。

翻译稿

2018 年 4 月，秘书长对尼加拉瓜抗议活动造成的人员伤亡表示忧心。他呼吁所有各方保持克制，并促请尼加拉瓜政府确保保护所有公民的人权，尤其是和平集会和表达自由的权利。同月，四名人权理事会特别程序表示，他们对尼加拉瓜安全部队对反对社会保障改革的抗议所做出的暴力反应感到震惊，并促请当局确保基本的表达自由及和平集会权利得到尊重。

审校稿

2018 年 4 月，秘书长对尼加拉瓜抗议活动期间发生的人员伤亡事件表示关切。他呼吁所有各方保持克制，并促请尼加拉瓜政府努力确保所有公民的人权，尤其是和平集会权和表达自由权得到保护。同月，人权理事会四项特别程序表示，尼加拉瓜安全部队针对反社会保障改革抗议采取的暴力应对方式令之惊骇，并促请当局努力确保基本的表达自由及和平集会自由得到尊重。

点评

1. 关于"expressed his concern"，见第 1 段批注①。
2. 关于"four special procedures of the Human Rights Council"，见第 2 段批注①。

第 4 段

OHCHR noted that human rights violations documented from April to August 2018 included the disproportionate use of force by the police, which sometimes resulted in extrajudicial killings; enforced disappearances; widespread arbitrary or illegal detentions; and ill-treatment and instances of torture and sexual violence in detention centres.

翻译稿

人权高专办注意到，2018 年 4 月至 8 月有记录的侵犯人权行为包括：警方过度使用武力，时而发生的法外处决；强迫失踪；任意拘留或非法拘留屡见不鲜；拘留中心发生的虐待以及酷刑和性暴力事件。

批 注

③ 与前一句逻辑关系不明。

审校稿

人权高专办注意到，2018 年 4 月至 8 月期间有案可查的侵犯人权行为包括：警方过度使用武力，甚或有法外处决之举；强迫失踪；任意或非法拘留现象屡见不鲜；拘留中心内虐待以及酷刑和性暴力事件时有发生。

整体来看，本段原文呈总分结构，以分号相隔的四个并列分句均为名词短语形式，在翻译时，4个并列分句也应尽量做到句式一致，同时兼顾细节。

1. 关于第1个分句"the disproportionate use of force by the police, which sometimes resulted in extrajudicial killings"，译者将名词"use"动词化，处理为陈述句，意为"警方武力的使用不符合比例原则"，译为"警方过度使用武力"正确妥当，但在"which sometimes resulted in extrajudicial killings"的处理上存在问题，"时而发生的法外处决"不仅没有体现出与前半句的逻辑关系，甚至还给人以不知所云的感觉。

2. 关于第2个分句，只有两个单词，无更多信息，无技巧可谈，按原文直译便可。

3. 关于第3个分句"widespread arbitrary or illegal detentions"，译者巧妙地将形容词动词化，处理为"任意拘留或非法拘留屡见不鲜"，十分妥帖。

4. 关于第4个分句"ill-treatment and instances of torture and sexual violence in detention centres"，译者按照原文句式处理为名词性短语，译文正确，但与前几句在句式上欠缺一致性。从复数名词"instances"可见虐待以及酷刑和性暴力事件并非个案，可酌情增译"时有发生"，从而在句式上与前面保持一致。

1. OHCHR noted that, given their scope and persistence, the protests, which had been ongoing since April 2018, appeared to be the result of deep-rooted grievances. Since the presidential elections of 2006, the institutional framework had weakened, with a gradual concentration of the different State powers in the hands of the ruling party. This had contributed to reduced civic space, lack of independence of the judiciary and the national human rights institution, recurrent allegations of corruption and electoral fraud and media censorship, and high levels of impunity, among other issues.

参考译文

人权高专办指出，抗议活动自2018年4月以来持续至今，从其范围和持续性来看，这些抗议活动似乎是由根深蒂固的不满情绪所致。自2006年总统选举以来，该国体制框架不断遭到削弱，各项国家大权被逐渐攥入执政党手中。这导致公民空间收窄，司法机关和国家人权机构丧失独立性，关于腐败和选举舞弊以及媒体审查的指控层出不穷，以及严重的有罪不罚现象等情形。

2. In July 2018, the United Nations High Commissioner for Human Rights stated that the violence and repression seen in Nicaragua since demonstrations began in April were products of the systematic erosion of human rights over the years, and highlighted the overall fragility of institutions and the rule of law.

参考译文

2018年7月，联合国人权事务高级专员指出，自4月示威活动开始以来，尼加拉瓜境内发生的暴力和镇压事件是经年累月有系统地侵犯人权的恶果，并强调指出，该国的制度和法治整体脆弱不堪。

背景介绍

以下两篇材料节选自联合国消除对妇女歧视委员会（CEDAW）。联合国消除对妇女歧视委员会于1982年建立，是由全球23位妇女问题专家组成的专家机构。所选材料是委员会针对消除对妇女一切形式歧视公约缔约国提交的公约履行情况报告以及在会上与受审议国家进行的互动讨论口头得出的结论性意见，其结构通常为：委员会审议国别报告——指出赞赏之处和积极方面——列明关注的主要领域及建议——后续落实及下次报告的编写，其特点是涉及不同国家的司法行政制度、部委名称和法律法规。在翻译此类文件时，应把握的要点是：注意语气，委员会作为监测机构，在客观论述事实和提出建议部分的表达、措辞、语气轻重是不同的，因此要谨慎处理细微的逻辑关系，尽可能站在委员会立场去推敲每个词的用意；表达简洁、通顺，特别在提出建议段落，让句子读起来简洁有力，起到建议所应起到的效果。

第六篇

原文

The Committee welcomes the establishment of the Gender Affairs Department within the new Ministry of Nationality, Immigration and Gender Affairs and the establishment of the national gender machinery satellite offices. It notes that the State party has increased funding and staff for the national machinery for the advancement of women notwithstanding general budgetary constraints and that the National Gender Commission has a clear mandate to monitor and evaluate the implementation of gender policies. The Committee remains concerned, however, about the lack of adequate gender-responsive budgeting and technical capacity in the national machinery for the advancement of women and the absence of similar mechanisms at the local level.

The Committee acknowledges the efforts made by the State party to combat discriminatory gender stereotypes and harmful practices, including the adoption of the national policy on gender and development. It also notes that the number of women traditional leaders has increased, which is a positive change in social and cultural norms in the State party. The Committee is concerned, however, about the persistence of harmful practices, including child marriage, and deep-rooted stereotypes regarding the roles and responsibilities of men and women in the family and the community. It is further concerned about the lack of mechanisms to monitor and evaluate the implementation of the national policy on gender and development, with a view to changing such stereotypes and harmful practices.

The Committee recommends that the State party continue its efforts to facilitate escorts for children on their way to and from school, as well as the establishment of a hotline for children to report abuses, and provide information on the number of prosecutions of and sentences imposed on perpetrators, including teachers, of sexual abuse against girls in educational settings in its next periodic report.

请自行翻译后查看后文的分析点评

分析点评

第 1 段

The Committee welcomes the establishment of the Gender Affairs Department within the new Ministry of Nationality, Immigration and Gender Affairs and the establishment of the national gender machinery satellite offices. It notes that the State party has increased funding and staff for the national machinery for the advancement of women notwithstanding general budgetary constraints and that the National Gender Commission has a clear mandate to monitor and evaluate the implementation of gender policies. The Committee remains concerned, however, about the lack of adequate gender-responsive budgeting and technical capacity in the national machinery for the advancement of women and the absence of similar mechanisms at the local level.

委员会欢迎在新成立的国籍、移民和性别事务部内设立了性别平等事务司,并成立了国家性别平等机制卫星办公室①。委员会注意到,缔约国没有考虑一般预算限制,增加了国家提高妇女地位机制的资金和工作人员,而且全国性别平等委员会负有监测和评价性别平等政策执行情况的明确任务②。然而,委员会仍然感到关切的是,国家提高妇女地位机制缺乏性别反应预算编制和技术能力,而且在地方一级缺乏类似的机制。

批 注

① 将词汇放在语境中理解。
② 句子逻辑关系理解有误。

委员会欢迎在新成立的国籍、移民和性别事务部设立性别平等事务司,并成

立国家性别平等机制分支办事处。委员会注意到,尽管存在一般预算限制,缔约国仍为提高妇女地位国家机构增加了资金和工作人员,而且国家性别平等委员会负有监测和评价性别平等政策执行情况的明确任务。然而,委员会仍然感到关切的是,提高妇女地位国家机构缺乏促进性别平等预算编制和技术能力,而且地方一级缺乏类似的机制。

1. 词汇查询和常规用法问题。见"National Gender Commission"和"national machinery for the advancement of women"。"national"和"commission"连用时,在联合国术语系统中有两种译法,可以是"国家",如"National Commission against Addictions",译为"国家反吸毒委员会",也可以是"全国",如"National Commission for Human Rights",译为"全国人权委员会",当然还有"national"搭配"assembly"的情况,可根据不同国家规定,译为"国民议会""全国代表大会""国民大会""国会"等。总之,"national"一词在处理时要谨慎细心,要从联合国术语库(UNTERM portal)中找到相关依据,其次可以参考各国向人权报告委员会、妇女委员会等条约人权机构提交的国别人权报告寻找准确译法。同理,"national machinery for the advancement of women"一词也应当在联合国术语库中找到权威译法,即"提高妇女地位国家机构",而不是"国家提高妇女地位机制"。"machinery"一词,在联合国文件中也有两种译法。一般来说,"machinery"多指一种抽象"机制",如"gender machinery",译为"性别平等机制",在这种情况下其含义就相当于"mechanism",但在与具体的词汇,如"national"搭配时,可以理解为"国家机构"。

2. 词汇不准确问题。见"national gender machinery satellite offices"一词。"satellite offices"一词,如果不细读原文,可以直译为"卫星办公室",在联合国文件中,也有这种译法,如"BeiDou Navigation Satellite Office"就译为"北斗导航卫星办公室",但是,还是要根据不同文本的具体含义来定夺。在本文中,"satellite offices"是复数形式,且不是专有名词,可以理解为国家性别平等机构的多个"branches",即"分支机构",是一种在各地区都有分布的组织形式,因此译为"分支办事处"比"卫星办公室"更符合语境,也更清楚了然。

3. 转折句理解问题。见"It notes that the State party has increased funding and staff for the national machinery..."一句。该句为转折关系,翻译稿译为并列关系,体现不出原文中的赞扬意味。在处理转折句时,要拿捏分句与分句之间细微的逻辑关系,不要有意弱化或加强原文应有的逻辑语气。

第 2 段

The Committee acknowledges the efforts made by the State party to combat discriminatory gender stereotypes and harmful practices, including the adoption of the national policy on gender and development. It also notes that the number of women traditional leaders has increased, which is a positive change in social and cultural norms in the State party. The Committee is concerned, however, about the persistence of harmful practices, including child marriage, and deep-rooted stereotypes regarding the roles and responsibilities of men and women in the family and the community. It is further concerned about the lack of mechanisms to monitor and evaluate the implementation of the national policy on gender and development, with a view to changing such stereotypes and harmful practices.

委员会承认缔约国为消除歧视性的性别陈规定型观念和有害做法所做的努力，包括通过了《国家性别与发展政策》。委员会还注意到，女性传统领导人的数量有所增加，这是缔约国社会和文化规范的一个积极变化。然而，委员会感到关切的是，包括童婚和对男女在家庭和社区中角色和责任的根深蒂固观念在内的有害传统习俗持续存在①。委员会还感到关切的是，缺乏用于改变此类陈规定型观念和有害做法的监测和评价《国家性别与发展政策》执行情况的机制。

批 注

① 句子过长，可读性差。

委员会承认缔约国为消除歧视性的性别陈规定型观念和有害做法所做的努力，包括通过了《性别平等与发展问题国家政策》。委员会还注意到，女性部落首领的人数有所增加，这是缔约国社会和文化规范方面的一个积极变化。然而，委员会感到关切的是，有害习俗，包括童婚以及有关男女在家庭和社区中角色和责任的根深蒂固的陈规定型观念持续存在。委员会还感到关切的是，缺少为了改变此类陈规定型观念和有害做法而对《性别平等与发展问题国家政策》的执行情况开展监测和评价的机制。

1. 用词问题。见"women traditional leaders"一句。"traditional leaders"在联合国文件中既可以译为"传统领导人"，也可以译为"部落首领"，具体还应根据文件描述的情况决定。所以，"women traditional leaders"，既可以译为"妇女传统领导人"，也可译为"女性部落首领"，多指传统社会体制下参与管理的妇女，与之相对的是，"women leaders"一般是现代意义上的"女性领导人"或"妇女领袖"。

2. "including"处理问题。见"The Committee is concerned, however, about the persistence of harmful practices, including child marriage..."一句。在处理"including"一词时，尽量不要机械地统一处理成"包括……在内"。"including"放在不同语境、不同结构句子中处理方法也不一样，应当考虑的两点是：一是"including"后面的内容是否重要，是否需要强调；二是句子是否较长。针对第一种情况，如原文中"including child marriage"，很明显"童婚"是一个重点强调的有害习俗，处理成"包括童婚……在内的有害习俗"不是很得当，可以在此处断句，重点将"童婚"提出来；针对第二种情况，如果句子很长，后接词汇过多，不妨译为"童婚等有害习俗"，这样让句子更紧凑，读起来也更通顺。

第 3 段

The Committee recommends that the State party continue its efforts to facilitate escorts for children on their way to and from school, as well as the establishment of a hotline for children to report abuses, and provide information on the number of prosecutions of and sentences imposed on perpetrators, including teachers, of sexual abuse against girls in educational settings in its next periodic report.

批 注

① 表达不当。
② 理解错误。

【翻译稿】

继续努力促进①护送儿童上学和放学，以及为儿童设立举报虐待行为的热线，并在下一次定期报告中提供资料，说明起诉和判决在教育环境中对女童实施性虐待的包括教师在内的施害者人数。②

【审校稿】

继续努力为护送儿童上下学提供便利，促进设立供儿童举报虐待行为的热线，并在下一次定期报告中提供资料，说明在教育环境中对女童实施性虐待的教师等施害者受到起诉和判刑的数量。

【点评】

1. "facilitate"一词在联合国文件中为"促进、帮助、提供便利"等意义，可视具体语境，采用"一词多译"的办法，达到通畅易懂的目的。

2. 理解错误。译文出现的错误是将"number"理解成了修饰"perpetrators"，而"number"的修饰对象是"prosecutions of and sentences"，因此处理成"说明起诉和判决……施害者人数"实属错误，应当译为"说明施害者……受到起诉和判刑的数量"。

补充练习

The Committee notes that the State party has a dual legal system in which customary and statutory law are both applicable and that the Customary Law Act provides that customary law is valid only to the extent to which it "is not incompatible with the provisions of any written law or contrary to morality, humanity or natural justice". It is concerned, however, that some elements of customary law are not in compliance with the Convention. The Committee is also concerned that inadequate capacity and resources have delayed the process of incorporating the Convention into national legislation and that there is no timetable for the completion of the process. It is further concerned that the State party has not ratified the Protocol to the African Charter on Human and People's Rights on the Rights of Women in Africa.

The Committee reiterates its previous recommendation (CEDAW/C/BOT/CO/3, para. 10) and draws the attention of the State party to target 5.1 of the Sustainable

Development Goals, to end all forms of discrimination against all women and girls everywhere. It recommends that the State party adopt in the Constitution and other national laws, without delay, a comprehensive definition of discrimination against women, covering all prohibited grounds of discrimination, encompassing direct and indirect discrimination in the public and private spheres, in line with article 1 of the Convention.

委员会注意到，缔约国有一个同时适用习惯法和成文法的双轨法律制度，并且《习惯法法案》规定，习惯法只在其"不与任何成文法的规定相抵触，或与道德、人道或自然正义相冲突"的情况下才有效。然而，委员会感到关切的是，习惯法中的某些要件与《公约》不一致。委员会还感到关切的是，能力和资源不足延缓了缔约国将《公约》纳入其国家立法的进程，而且缔约国没有设定完成这项进程的时间表。委员会还感到关切的是，缔约国尚未批准《非洲人权和民族权宪章关于非洲妇女权利的议定书》。

委员会重申其之前的建议（CEDAW/C/BOT/CO/3，第10段），提请缔约国注意关于在世界各地消除对妇女和女童一切形式的歧视的可持续发展目标之具体目标 5.1。委员会建议缔约国依照《公约》第一条，毫不拖延地在《宪法》和其他国家法律中采用对歧视妇女的全面定义，涵盖所有受到禁止的歧视理由，包括公私领域的直接和间接歧视在内。

第七篇

The Committee considered the ninth periodic report of Colombia (CEDAW/C/COL/9) at its 1661st and 1662nd meetings (see CEDAW/C/SR.1661 and CEDAW/C/SR.1662), held on 19 February 2019. The Committee's list of issues and questions is contained in CEDAW/C/COL/Q/9, and the responses of the State party are contained in CEDAW/C/COL/Q/9/Add.1.

The Committee appreciates the submission by the State party of its ninth periodic report. It also appreciates the State party's follow-up report to the previous concluding observations of the Committee (CEDAW/C/COL/CO/7-8/Add.1) and its written replies to the list of issues and questions raised by the pre-sessional working group, as well as the oral presentation by the delegation and the further clarifications provided in response to the questions posed orally by the Committee during the dialogue.

The Committee commends the State party on its delegation, which was headed by the Deputy Minister for Multilateral Affairs, Adriana Mejia Hernandez, and included representatives of the Ministry of the Interior, the Attorney General's Office, the Constitutional Court, the Congress, the National Gender Commission of the Judiciary, the Office of the Presidential Council for Women's Equity, the Ministry of Foreign Affairs and the Permanent Mission of Colombia to the United Nations Office and other international organizations in Geneva.

The Committee welcomes the progress achieved since the consideration in 2013 of the State party's combined seventh and eight periodic reports (CEDAW/C/COL/7-8) in undertaking legislative reforms, in particular the adoption of the following (followed by a list of resolutions/acts/decrees adopted).

请自行翻译后查看后文的分析点评

分析点评

第 1 段

The Committee considered the ninth periodic report of Colombia (CEDAW/C/COL/9) at its 1661st and 1662nd meetings (see CEDAW/C/SR.1661 and CEDAW/C/SR.1662), held on 19 February 2019. The Committee's list of issues and questions is contained in CEDAW/C/COL/Q/9, and the responses of the State party are contained in CEDAW/C/COL/Q/9/Add.1.

批注

① 在联合国文件翻译中，某些词与常规译法有别。
② 一个专有名词，处理时粗心。
③ 增译。

翻译稿

委员会在2019年2月19日举行的第1661次和第1662次会议（见CEDAW/C/SR.1661和CEDAW/C/SR.1662）上考虑①了哥伦比亚的第九次定期报告（CEDAW/C/COL/9）。委员会的议题清单和问题②包含于CEDAW/C/COL/Q/9号文件，哥伦比亚方面③的答复包含于CEDAW/C/COL/Q/9/Add.1号文件。

审校稿

委员会在2019年2月19日举行的第1661次和第1662次会议（见CEDAW/C/SR.1661和CEDAW/C/SR.1662）上审议了哥伦比亚的第九次定期报告（CEDAW/C/COL/9）。委员会的议题和问题清单载于CEDAW/C/COL/Q/9号文件，哥伦比亚的答复载于CEDAW/C/COL/Q/9/Add.1号文件。

点评

1. 专有名词有专门译法。"consider"一词在联合国文件翻译中，特别是用于指代对报告的审评时，一般处理为"审议"，而非"考虑"。

2. 未查参考。"list of issues and questions"构成专有名词，是否为专有名

词，可通过两种方式进行判断和处理，一是从语法上，后面为"is"，可见主语是"issues"和"questions"共同组成的"list"而非"list of issues"+"questions"；二是根据文号（document symbol）在联合国正式文件系统（United Nations Official Document System, ODS）进行查阅。这既是在翻译联合国文件时需要掌握的一项技巧，也是经常需要做的一项工作。以此段为例，不过数行，却列出了四份文件的文号。这些文件，有时联合国语文部门会随待翻译文件一并提供，有时需要译者根据文件编号或文件标题在 ODS 系统上查询。

第 2 段

The Committee appreciates the submission by the State party of its ninth periodic report. It also appreciates the State party's follow-up report to the previous concluding observations of the Committee (CEDAW/C/COL/CO/7–8/Add.1) and its written replies to the list of issues and questions raised by the pre-sessional working group, as well as the oral presentation by the delegation and the further clarifications provided in response to the questions posed orally by the Committee during the dialogue.

委员会感谢①缔约国提交第九次定期报告。委员会还感谢缔约国对②委员会之前提出的结论性意见提交后续报告（CEDAW/C/COL/CO/7–8/Add.1），以及对会前工作组提出的问题和议题清单做出书面回复，并感谢代表团做出口头介绍，以及在对话期间对委员会口头提问做出进一步说明③。

批 注

① 注意还有别的译法。
② "to"一词理解有误。
③ 对审议流程了解不够，以至于逻辑有误，应查询背景资料。

委员会赞赏缔约国提交第九次定期报告。委员会还赞赏缔约国根据委员会先前所提结论性意见提交后续报告（CEDAW/C/COL/CO/7–8/Add.1），并针对会前工作组提出的议题和问题清单做出书面回复，同时还赞赏代表团在对话期间做出口头介绍，并针对委员会口头提问做出进一步说明。

1. 词汇不准确。"appreciate"一词在联合国文件中可译为"感谢""赞扬""赞赏"。

2. 译者对审议流程不明。委员会对国别报告的审议进程其实就是委员会对受审议国家提交的定期报告、后续报告和对会前工作组所提问题清单做出的书面回复进行审议并在会上与受审议国家进行互动讨论（即受审议国家在会上对话期间做出口头介绍并对委员会口头提问做出进一步说明）的过程。了解这一点，处理起来逻辑自明。

第 3 段

The Committee commends the State party on its delegation, which was headed by the Deputy Minister for Multilateral Affairs, Adriana Mejia Hernandez, and included representatives of the Ministry of the Interior, the Attorney General's Office, the

Constitutional Court, the Congress, the National Gender Commission of the Judiciary, the Office of the Presidential Council for Women's Equity, the Ministry of Foreign Affairs and the Permanent Mission of Colombia to the United Nations Office and other international organizations in Geneva.

批注

① 称赞的对象是缔约国还是代表团？
② 国家机构名称处理不当。
③ 理解错误。
④ 这些国际组织和后面的日内瓦是何关系？

委员会赞扬以多边事务副部长 Adriana Mejia Hernandez 女士为首的缔约国代表团①。代表团成员还包括内政部、总检察长办公室、宪法法院、国会、国家司法机关性别委员会②、妇女平等总统委员会③、外交部及哥伦比亚常驻联合国日内瓦办事处和其他国际组织④代表团的代表。

委员会称赞缔约国派出由多边事务副部长 Adriana Mejia Hernandez 女士率领的代表团。代表团成员分别来自内政部、总检察长办公室、宪法法院、国会、司法部国家性别平等委员会、总统理事会妇女平权办公室、外交部和哥伦比亚常驻联合国日内瓦办事处和日内瓦其他国际组织代表团。

1. 国家机构名称处理不当。关于"commends the State party on its delegation"，称赞的直接宾语是"the State party"，介词"on"点明称赞的事由，译者将二者颠倒。

2. 理解错误。关于缔约国政府机构的名称，译者对背景资料查询不到位。一般情况下，各国部委名称等均可在中国外交部官方网站"国家和组织"部分相应的国家页面查询到，对于一些较为生僻的机构名称，可通过关键词检索查询相关信息，再作处理。本段中的"National Gender Commission of the Judiciary"，通过关键词检索可查询到 https://www.ohchr.org/en/NewsEvents/Pages/DisplayNews.aspx?NewsID=24182&LangID=E，并看到下述信息"National Gender Commission of the Ministry of Justice"以及"the National Gender Commission had been set up in the judiciary to promote gender mainstreaming and the institutionalization of gender equality in the work of imparting justice"，交叉判断之下，可确定是"司法部国家性别平等委员会"。

3. 表述不明确。关于"the United Nations Office and other international organizations in Geneva"，须重复译出"日内瓦"，以明确参加会议的除了哥伦比亚常驻联合国日内瓦办事处的代表，还有日内瓦其他国际组织代表团（而非常驻其他地方国际组织代表团）的代表。

第 4 段

The Committee welcomes the progress achieved since the consideration in 2013 of the State party's combined seventh and eight periodic reports (CEDAW/C/COL/7-8) in undertaking legislative reforms, in particular the adoption of the following (followed by a list of resolutions/acts/decrees adopted).

翻译稿

委员会欢迎①缔约国自 2013 年审议其第七次和第八次合并定期报告②（CEDAW/C/COL/7-8）以来进行立法改革的进展，特别是通过了：以下决议、法案和法令（清单如下）。

审校稿

委员会欣见，自 2013 年审议缔约国第七至第八次合并定期报告（CEDAW/C/COL/7-8）以来，该国立法改革进展不断，特别是通过了以下决议、法案和法令（清单如下）。

点评

句子处理欠妥。本段原文只有一句话，除却 "combined seventh and eight periodic reports" 有固定译法之外，长句可拆分为小分句，译文可读性随之提高。

批注

① 其他译法。
② 有固定译法。另外，此句译文逻辑不明。

补充练习

The Committee welcomes the international support for the Sustainable Development Goals and calls for the realization of de jure (legal) and de facto (substantive) gender equality, in accordance with the provisions of the Convention, throughout the process of implementing the 2030 Agenda for Sustainable Development. The Committee recalls the importance of Goal 5 and of the mainstreaming of the principles of equality and non-discrimination throughout all 17 Goals. It urges the State party to recognize women as the driving force of the sustainable development of the State party and to adopt relevant policies and strategies to that effect.

The Committee stresses the crucial role of the legislative power in ensuring the full implementation of the Convention (see A/65/38, part two, annex Ⅵ). It invites the Congress, in line with its mandate, to take the necessary steps regarding the implementation of the present concluding observations between now and the submission of the next periodic report under the Convention.

参考译文

委员会欢迎国际社会支持可持续发展目标，并吁请在执行《2030 年可持续发展议程》的整个进程中，根据《公约》规定实现法律上和实质性的性别平等。委员会忆及目标 5 以及将平等和不歧视原则纳入所有 17 项目标的主流的重要性。委员会敦促缔约国承认妇女是推动实现该国可持续发展的一支力量，并为此通过相关政策和战略。

委员会强调立法权在确保充分执行《公约》方面的关键作用（见 A/65/38，第二部分，附件六）。委员会请国会依照其授权，为从现在起到《公约》规定的下个报告期之前执行本结论性意见采取必要步骤。

背景介绍

本篇材料选自经济及社会理事会非政府组织委员会,涉及非政府组织为获得经社理事会咨商地位所提交的申请。

非政府组织委员会审查该申请材料后,将做出是否接受该申请的决定(实际上是一种建议),该非政府组织将有机会获得经社理事会的咨商地位。在委员会下一次会议上(通常于同年七月召开),经社理事会将审查该建议,并做出最终推荐决定,这时非政府组织才会被授予咨商地位。

提交材料的非政府组织有相当一部分来自非英语国家,因此原文的英文行文并不流畅,甚至会出现错误。在翻译这类文件时,不要被原文束缚住,要"不畏浮云遮望眼",在厘清句子结构、理解句子意义的基础上,大胆调整句子语序,用连贯流畅的中文表达出来。

第八篇

原文

The Federation is a human rights NGO which brings together 19 associations of families of the desaparecidos, or disappeared people, in Latin America and the Caribbean from 13 countries. Its central concern is with the phenomenon of forced disappearance in Latin America and around the world.

The Federation is working to achieve global ratification of the International Convention for the Protection of All Persons from Enforced Disappearance by working through the embassies and foreign ministries of countries that have not yet ratified the Convention.

Canadian Human Rights Watch is a committee of lawyers dedicated to promoting the rule of law and human rights internationally by protecting human rights defenders and advocacy rights and by engaging in research and education relating to the rule of law and advocacy rights.

The organization contributed to the work of the United Nations by promoting universal implementation and enforcement of international human rights laws and standards and the rule of law.

The organization participated in the work of the Human Rights Council by attending its sessions, providing written statements and oral interventions, organizing and attending side events, meeting with United Nations officials and State representatives, participating in the universal periodic review process and attending meetings.

请自行翻译后查看后文的分析点评

分析点评

第 1 段

The Federation is a human rights NGO which brings together 19 associations of families of the *desaparecidos*, or disappeared people, in Latin America and the Caribbean from 13 countries. Its central concern is with the phenomenon of forced disappearance in Latin America and around the world.

翻译稿

该联合会是一个人权非政府组织，来自拉丁美洲和加勒比地区 13 个国家的 19 个失踪人口协会。它的 是拉丁美洲和世界各地的强迫失踪现象。

批 注

① 受英文影响，不符合中文表述习惯。
② 错译。
③ 不准确且表达不符合中文表述习惯。

审校稿

该联合会是一个人权非政府组织，由来自拉丁美洲和加勒比 13 个国家的 19 个失踪者亲属协会组成。它的核心关切是拉丁美洲及世界各地存在的强迫失踪现象。

点评

1. 表述不符合中文表达习惯。"brings together" 意思是"集合，聚集"，在这里，将其直译为"汇集"或"聚集"受英文影响，不符合中文表述习惯，可将其译为"由……组成"或"会员包括"。

2. 错译。在本句中，"families" 是 "family" 的复数形式，不是指家庭，而是指亲属，理解有误，属于错译。

3. 不准确且表达不符合中文表述习惯。"central concern" 译为"核心关切"比"核心关注点"更好。

第 2 段

The Federation is working to achieve global ratification of the International Convention for the Protection of All Persons from Enforced Disappearance by working through the embassies and foreign ministries of countries that have not yet ratified the Convention.

翻译稿

该联合会正在努力实现全球批准《保护所有人免遭强迫失踪国际公约》，

批 注

① 处理方式欠妥。

取的方式是通过那些尚未批准该公约的国家的驻外大使馆和外交部开展工作。

审校稿

对于那些尚未批准《保护所有人免遭强迫失踪国际公约》的国家，该联合会正在透过这些国家的驻外大使馆和外交部对其做工作，以期实现全球批准该《公约》。

点评

1. 过于贴合原文句式结构。译者完全按照英文顺序，亦步亦趋，不敢放开手脚，造成对"by working"引导的从句的处理不理想。

2. 理解有误。通过驻外大使馆和外交部开展工作，其工作的对象当然是大使馆和外交部，也就是说，通过游说大使馆和外交部，使之能够对本国政府做工作，以便批准《公约》。联合会要做工作的对象当然是那些未批准《公约》的国家，对于已经批准的国家，做工作显然对批准《公约》没有意义。

3. 介词处理不到位。将"by working"等由 by 加动词结构译为"采取的方式"属于没有办法的办法，当属匠心独具。问题是，此处这种处理导致出现歧义。如果调整一下句子的先后顺序，可能就不会存在这个问题。另外，将"through"译为"透过"似乎比"通过"更好，意指联合会对这些国家的驻外使馆或外交部做工作，以期通过它们来说服其本国政府批准《公约》。

第 3 段

Canadian Human Rights Watch is a committee of lawyers dedicated to promoting the rule of law and human rights internationally by protecting human rights defenders and advocacy rights and by engaging in research and education relating to the rule of law and advocacy rights.

批 注

② 专有名称，错译。
③ 专有名称，错译。
④ 令人费解。

翻译稿

加拿大人权观察是一个由律师组成的委员会，致力于通过保护人权捍卫者和倡导权以及从事与法治和倡导权有关的研究和教育，促进国际法治和人权。

审校稿

加拿大律师人权观察是一个律师委员会，通过保护人权维护者和倡导权利，以及通过参与有关法治和倡导权利方面的研究和教育工作，致力于在国际一级促进法治和人权。

点评

1. 词义错误。译稿将"Canadian Human Rights Watch"译为加拿大人权观察，属于按字面翻译，但在当时的联合国词库中，这个组织的译名为"加拿大律师人权观察"，故在翻译时应尽量查联合国词库，实在没有的，才可按字面意思翻译。否则，就可能出问题。

2. 理解有误。译稿按英文顺序翻译，应该说所有要素都基本上得到准确表达，将"dedicated to"引导的定语从句处理成一个主句是一种很好的处理方式，但对"by"引导的状语部分的位置安排不够好，可以稍作调整。

3. 表述不到位。至于"internationally"，是指"at the international level"，表示是在国际层面或国际一级促进法治和人权，其中包括在国际一级促进国内法治和人权，而不是单纯的国际法治和人权。

4. 词义错误。因为本文件属于人权文件，来自联合国日内瓦办事处，应选择 UNTERM 中的日内瓦用法，所以"human rights defenders"应译"人权维护者"，而不用"人权捍卫者"，"advocacy rights"译为"倡导权利"比译为"倡导权"好。

第 4 段

The organization contributed to the work of the United Nations by promoting universal implementation and enforcement of international human rights laws and standards and the rule of law.

该组织为联合国的工作做出了贡献，采取的方式是促进普遍实施和执行国际人权法律和标准以及法治。

该组织通过促进普遍实施和执行各项国际人权法律及标准和法治，为联合国的工作做出贡献。

介词处理欠妥。在联合国文件翻译中，不建议将 by 引导的状语译为"采取的方式是……""采取的具体方式……"，只要改变一下译文顺序，这个问题就可以迎刃而解。

第 5 段

The organization participated in the work of the Human Rights Council by attending its sessions, providing written statements and oral interventions, organizing and attending side events, meeting with United Nations officials and State representatives, participating in the universal periodic review process and attending meetings.

该组织参加人权理事会的工作，出席其届会，提供书面发言和口头干预，组织和出席会外活动，会见联合国官员和国家代表，参加普遍定期审议过程和出席会议。

该组织参与人权理事会工作的方式包括：参加其各届会议、提供书面陈述和

批　注

① 错译。

口头发言、组织和参加各种会外活动、与联合国官员及各国代表会面、参加普遍定期审议进程和出席各种会议。

1. 理解不准确。本句是一个简单句，主句是"The organization participated in the work of the Human Rights Council"，后面都是介词"by"+动名词结构，表示该组织参与人权理事会工作的具体内容。译稿将所有动词并列起来，没有体现它们之间的关系。

2. 词义错误。在这里，"intervention"不是"干涉、干预"的意思，是指"发言"，系译者未结合上下文语境造成的理解错误。

补充练习

The Federation's main contribution to the work of the United Nations has been through the Human Rights Council. It is well known and respected for its work on forced disappearances, representing the perspective of the families of the *desaparecidos*.

The Federation believes that it is impossible to separate the issue of enforced disappearance from that of human rights and the achievement of the Millennium Development Goals, since development is based on democratic governance, the rule of law, respect for human rights, peace and security, which is the focus of the Federation's work.

The organization's mission has been and remains: (a) to campaign for human rights defenders whose rights, safety and/or independence are threatened because of their human rights advocacy; (b) to produce legal analyses of national and international laws and standards relevant to advocacy rights and the rule of law; (c) to work in cooperation with other NGOs; and (d) to engage in human rights education and training and in law reform in areas related to the rule of law and advocacy rights.

To promote respect and understanding for human rights and the rule of law, the organization conducted advocacy, education and research and worked in cooperation with other human rights organizations. Its work included in-country investigations; trial monitoring; letters, reports and amicus briefs; legal research; and free classroom and online education. It provided written and oral statements to the Human Rights Council and organized and attended side events in Geneva; submitted reports to treaty bodies, the Office of the United Nations High Commissioner for Human Rights (OHCHR) and special procedures of the Council and attended their meetings.

The organization made 20 oral interventions, often jointly with other NGOs, on prevention and punishment of attacks on human rights defenders, education, accountability, independence of lawyers and judges, advocacy rights and other issues of concern.

该联合会对联合国工作的主要贡献一直是透过人权理事会做出的。它在强迫失踪方面所做的工作众所周知，并且受到普遍尊重，代表了失踪者家属的观点。

该联合会认为，不能将强迫失踪问题与人权以及实现千年发展目标问题分开，因为发展是以民主治理、法治、尊重人权、和平与安全为基础，是该联合会的工作重心。

该组织的使命一直且仍然是：(a) 为保护那些因为倡导人权而使其权利、安全和（或）独立受到威胁的人权维护者而开展运动；(b) 对有关倡导权利和法治的国内及国际法律和标准进行法律分析；(c) 与其他非政府组织开展合作；(d) 参与人权教育和培训活动，并参与法治和倡导权利相关领域的法律改革。

为了促进尊重和理解人权和法治，该组织开展宣传、教育和研究，并且与其他人权组织开展合作。它的工作包括开展国内调查；进行审判监督；写信、写报告以及出庭陈述；开展法律研究；以及开设免费课程和在线教育。它向人权理事会提供书面和口头陈述，并组织和参加在日内瓦举行的会外活动；向各种条约机构、联合国人权事务高级专员办事处（人权高专办）以及经社理事会的特别程序提交报告，并且参加它们的会议。

该组织就如何预防和处罚袭击人权维护者的行为、教育、问责、律师和法官的独立性、倡导权利及其他重要问题做了20次口头发言，通常是与其他非政府组织共同发言。

背景介绍

本篇材料选自联合国人权事务高级专员办事处（人权高专办）关于科摩罗的人权报告，概述了科摩罗现存的人权问题并提出了相应的建议。人权高专办是联合国在人权方面的主导实体，主要任务是防止侵犯人权行为、保证所有人权得到尊重、促进国际合作以保护人权、协调联合国内所有相关活动以及加强和简化联合国系统人权领域的工作。人权报告的行文特点是语言简练，句式不复杂，但涉及较多法律词汇和联合国专有词汇，因此，译文须做到语言平实、用词准确、表达简洁。

第九篇

原文

The ILO Committee of Experts noted that the capacity of schools was very limited and that some primary and secondary schools were obliged to refuse to enrol certain children of school age. Consequently, a large number of children, particularly from poor families and disadvantaged backgrounds, were deprived of an education. It requested that the Comoros intensify its efforts to increase the school attendance rate and reduce the drop-out rate, especially among girls, in order to prevent children under 15 years of age from working.

While to its knowledge, there were currently no asylum seekers, refugees or stateless persons in the country, UNHCR was concerned that the Comoros did not have a national legislative framework on asylum or any laws or procedures that clearly established the rights and safeguards to which asylum seekers and refugees were entitled. UNHCR recommended that the Comoros enact national asylum legislation and establish a functioning national asylum framework for ensuring international protection, which included procedures for refugee status determination in line with international standards.

UNHCR regretted the lack of laws establishing procedures for statelessness status determination or providing a framework for the protection for stateless persons in the country. Additionally, the Comorian nationality law provided no legal safeguard that children born in the country who would otherwise be stateless acquired nationality by operation of the law. UNHCR recommended that the Comoros amend law No. 79-12 of 1979 on nationality to enable children born in the Comoros who would otherwise be stateless to acquire Comorian nationality by operation of the law.

请自行翻译后查看后文的分析点评

分析点评

第 1 段

The ILO Committee of Experts noted that the capacity of schools was very limited and that some primary and secondary schools were obliged to refuse to enrol certain children of school age. Consequently, a large number of children, particularly from poor families and disadvantaged backgrounds, were deprived of an education. It requested that the Comoros intensify its efforts to increase the school attendance rate and reduce the drop-out rate, especially among girls, in order to prevent children under 15 years of age from working.

劳工组织专家委员会注意到，学校的能力非常有限，一些小学和中学都不得不拒绝某些学龄儿童入学。因此，大量儿童，特别是贫困家庭和处境不利的儿童被剥夺了受教育权。它①请科摩罗加大力度提高儿童入学率并降低辍学率，尤其是女孩的辍学率②，以防止未满15岁的儿童工作。

批 注

① "它"是指谁？
② "girl"的译法？这里是否仅指辍学率？

劳工组织专家委员会注意到，学校的能力非常有限，一些小学和中学不得不拒绝某些学龄儿童入学。因此，大量儿童，特别是贫困家庭和处境不利的儿童被剥夺了受教育权。委员会请科摩罗加大力度提高儿童尤其是女童的入学率并降低其辍学率，以防止未满15岁的儿童参加工作。

1. 指代不明。原文中的"It"显然指的是第一句中的劳工组织专家委员会，所以这里处理成"委员会"而不是"它"，这种处理方式指代更明确、更正式，能避免歧义。

2. 用词不准确。在联合国文件中，尤其是人权文件，"girl"一词频频出现，但与我们日常的处理方法不同，这里不译作"女孩"，而是"女童"，一方面是因为这种表述更正式，符合联合国文件的表述习惯，另一方面是因为"女童"专指未成年人，指向性强。与此类似还有"boy"，即"男童"而不是"男孩"。

3. 理解问题。"especially among girls"以插入语形式出现，起到补充说明的作用。这句的难点在于前面有两个并列成分，一个是提高入学率，另一个是降低辍学率，而按照就近原则，容易把插入语成分与最靠近它的成分联系起来，但这有时会造成错译，所以除了从语法结构上分析之外，还应结合上下文准确理解原文意思。这句是讲要提高所有儿童入学率并降低辍学率，女童属于儿童的范畴，而且是要重点关注的，所以"especially among girls"紧跟在前面两个并列成分之后，而不是仅指"辍学率"。

第 2 段

While to its knowledge, there were currently no asylum seekers, refugees or stateless persons in the country, UNHCR was concerned that the Comoros did not have a national legislative framework on asylum or any laws or procedures that clearly established the rights and safeguards to which asylum seekers and refugees were entitled.

尽管难民署了解到该国目前尚无寻求庇护者、难民或无国籍人，但它感到关切的是，科摩罗没有明确规定寻求庇护者和难民应得权利和保障的有关庇护的[①]国家立法框架或任何法律和程序。

批 注

① 语句太长，可读性差。

尽管难民署了解到科摩罗目前尚无寻求庇护者、难民或无国籍人，但它仍然关切的是，科摩罗没有关于庇护的国家立法框架或任何法律和程序，没有明确规定寻求庇护者和难民应享有的权利和保障。

介词处理。对于介词"on",一种常见的方式是将其译为"关于",但如果"on"后面的内容过长,就容易造成定语过长,影响译文可读性,所以可结合上下文灵活处理,例如译为"说明""规定",但切忌脱离原文。

第 3 段

UNHCR regretted the lack of laws establishing procedures for statelessness status determination or providing a framework for the protection for stateless persons in the country. Additionally, the Comorian nationality law provided no legal safeguard that children born in the country who would otherwise be stateless acquired nationality by operation of the law. UNHCR recommended that the Comoros amend law No. 79-12 of 1979 on nationality to enable children born in the Comoros who would otherwise be stateless to acquire Comorian nationality by operation of the law.

难民署感到遗憾的是,该国① 内缺乏设立无国籍身份确定程序或者提供无国籍人保护框架的法律。此外,科摩罗的国籍法没有为在该国出生的、如不给予国籍便会成为无国籍人的儿童依法② 提供法律保障。难民署建议科摩罗修订③《关于国籍的1979年第79-12号法》,使在科摩罗出生的、如不给予国籍便会成为无国籍人的儿童依法获得科摩罗国籍。

批 注

① 哪国?
② 跟在谁的后面?
③ 用词有误。

难民署感到遗憾的是,科摩罗缺少设立无国籍身份确定程序或者提供无国籍人保护框架的法律。另外,科摩罗《国籍法》没有为在该国出生的、如不给予国籍便会成为无国籍人的儿童提供可依法获得国籍的法律保障。难民署建议科摩罗修正《1979年关于国籍的第79-12号法》,使在科摩罗出生的、如不给予国籍便会成为无国籍人的儿童依法获得科摩罗国籍。

1. 指代不明确。"该国"到底是指哪国?结合上下文可知这个国家指的是科摩罗,所以应在译文中体现出来,避免指代不明。

2. 状语理解问题。原文中的"by operation of the law"作为状语出现在句末,如果将其理解为修饰整句的动作,显然不合逻辑,因为国籍法已经是法律了,不存在依法或不依法的问题,所以,"by operation of the law"修饰的是"acquired",即"依法获得"。

3. 用词不准确。"amend"一词应为"修正"而不是"修订"。在涉及法律文书时,通常使用"修正",与其对应的还有"amendment",即修正案,而"修订"一般用"revise"。另外,从语义上讲,"修正"比"修订"更加正式。

补充练习

The ILO Committee of Experts noted that section 7 of the Labour Code provided that persons who had left their jobs or occupation could continue to be members of a trade union for a maximum of two years, provided that they had been in that occupation for at least one year. The ILO Committee requested that the Comoros take the necessary measures to amend section 7 of the Labour Code so that the question of continued membership of a trade union was determined by the constitutions and rules of the trade union in question.

The ILO Committee of Experts was concerned that child labour was a visible phenomenon in the country, particularly as a result of poverty and of the low school enrolment rate in some cases. It strongly encouraged the Comoros to take the necessary steps to make education compulsory until the minimum age for admission to employment, namely 15 years.

劳工组织专家委员会注意到,《劳动法》第 7 条规定,离职者仍可继续成为工会会员,但最多不超过两年,条件是他们至少任职一年。劳工组织委员会请科摩罗采取必要措施修正《劳动法》第 7 条,以便将工会会籍问题交由相关工会的章程和规则决定。

劳工组织专家委员会感到关切的是,科摩罗的童工现象非常普遍,这尤其是因为贫困和某些情况下的低入学率造成的。委员会大力鼓励科摩罗采取必要措施,为尚未达到最低就业年龄的儿童,即 15 岁以下的儿童提供义务教育。

背景介绍

以下四篇材料均选自简要记录。前三篇来自《残疾人权利公约》缔约国会议简要记录,第四篇来自联合国大会社会、人道主义和文化委员会(第三委员会)简要记录。

《残疾人权利公约》缔约国每年就《公约》的执行情况进行审议,以确保全球残疾人享有其所应有的权利和基本自由。第三委员会的重要工作是审查人权问题。简要记录是对会议的总结和概要,通常涉及会上的发言,内容往往比较正式,句式结构有时会很复杂,套有多个从句或非谓语成分。因此,在翻译时,要"抽丝剥茧",先明确发言的主题或重点,再确定核心句,最后把"旁枝末节"添加进去,形成逻辑鲜明、语义连贯、准确流畅的译文。

第十篇

In many ways, the Committee on the Rights of Persons with Disabilities had broken new ground.

However, every effort must be made to achieve a better regional and gender balance among its members.

The participation of persons with disabilities and their representative organizations in the implementation of the Convention was a fundamental principle of the human rights-based approach to disability.

He wished to commend the President and Vice-Presidents for their efforts to increase the involvement of persons with disabilities in the preparations for the Conference and as panelists, and he encouraged them to adopt rules on such participation.

OHCHR appealed to Member States to commit to actively including persons with disabilities in the negotiations of the global compact for migration, and in the comprehensive refugee response framework.

请自行翻译后查看后文的分析点评

第1段

In many ways, the Committee on the Rights of Persons with Disabilities had broken new ground.

批 注

① 中文所表达的含义与英文所要表达的含义不同。

残疾人权利委员会在许多方面开辟了新天地①。

残疾人权利委员会在许多方面取得了新的突破。

译文表达不准确。虽然"broken new ground"也有开辟新天地的译法，但与本文上下文不符。"break new ground"的意思是"开辟新领域；开创新方法"，也可译为"取得新的进展（突破）"。在本句中，译为"取得新的进展（突破）"

比"开辟新天地"好。

第2段

However, every effort must be made to achieve a better regional and gender balance among its members.

然而，每一分努力的目的① 都必须是为了在其成员之间实现更好的区域和性别均衡。

批 注

① 不符合中文表达习惯。

然而，一切努力都必须是为了在其成员之间实现更好的区域和性别均衡。

译文晦涩，表述欠佳。译文理解和表达基本正确，但不是地道的中文。

第3段

The participation of persons with disabilities and their representative organizations in the implementation of the Convention was a fundamental principle of the human rights-based approach to disability.

残疾人及其代表组织参与《公约》的执行是残疾问题基于人权的办法② 的基本原则。

批 注

② 译法生硬，未能表达原文意涵。

残疾人及其代表组织参与执行《公约》是采取立足人权的办法处理残疾问题的一项基本原则。

不符合中文表达习惯。对于"human rights-based"一词，纽约总部的译法一般是"立足人权/注重人权的"，在本段中，"human rights-based approach to disability"是指在涉及残疾人的问题上采取立足人权（注重人权）的办法。

第4段

He wished to commend the President and Vice-Presidents for their efforts to increase the involvement of persons with disabilities in the preparations for the Conference and as panelists, and he encouraged them to adopt rules on such participation.

他谨此赞扬主席和各位副主席所做的努力，他们增加了③ 残疾人对会

批 注

③ 该句的主语辨识有误。

议筹备工作和作为专题讨论嘉宾的参与，他还鼓励他们通过关于这类参与的规则。

他要赞扬主席和副主席为促进残疾人参与会议筹备工作以及作为专题讨论嘉宾参与会议所做出的努力，并鼓励他们通过关于此类参与的规则。

认错句子主语。"for their efforts to increase the involvement..."是指"为了增加（促进）……参与而做出的努力"，"Panelists"是指残疾人。翻译稿对原文的处理方式不恰当，使译文出现了两个主语，致使译文结构散乱，不符合中文表达习惯。

第 5 段

OHCHR appealed to Member States to commit to actively including persons with disabilities in the negotiations of the global compact for migration, and in the comprehensive refugee response framework.

人权高专办呼吁各会员国做出承诺，积极地将残疾人纳入[①]关于全球移民契约的谈判和难民问题全面响应框架。

人权高专办呼吁各会员国做出承诺，积极让残疾人参与"移民问题全球契约"谈判和难民问题全面响应框架。

表达欠妥。翻译稿的理解和表达基本正确，但对"including"一词的处理不理想，这里实际是让残疾人参与"移民问题全球契约"和难民问题全面响应框架。

批　注

① 表达欠妥。

补充练习

However, owing to a funding shortfall, persons with disabilities, among others, continued to be left behind in programming.

UNHCR was grateful for the support of donors, but at the point of delivery it was acutely aware of the impact of funding and staffing shortfalls.

UNHCR had played an active role at the World Humanitarian Summit in championing the Charter on Inclusion of Persons with Disabilities in Humanitarian Action, and was committed to its promotion.

参考译文

不过，由于缺少资金，在方案编制方面依然对残疾人考虑不足。

难民署感谢捐助者的支助，但在落实资助项目时，难民署强烈意识到缺少资金和人员带来的影响。

在世界人道主义峰会通过《残疾人参与人道主义行动章程》的过程中，难民署发挥了积极作用，并致力于宣传该章程。

第十一篇

原文

The work of UNHCR was grounded in the Convention, and the organization strove to listen to people's specific needs and adjust its programming accordingly.

UNHCR also participated in the task team created by the Inter-Agency Standing Committee to coordinate global guidelines for the full and respectful inclusion of persons with disabilities in humanitarian action.

The New York Declaration for Refugees and Migrants, the comprehensive refugee response framework and the work towards the adoption of a compact on refugees and a compact on migrants was a platform that could be used to lobby for greater inclusion of persons with disabilities in specific aspects of the response to displacement.

UNHCR considered itself a leader in knowledge of displacement. However, when it came to responding to the specificities of the needs of persons with disabilities in a displacement context, the organization acknowledged that it had much to learn and that it could only make progress by working directly with persons with disabilities and their representative organizations. However, it was firmly committed to so doing.

Mr. Decorte (Acting Director and Officer-in-Charge of New York Office, United Nations Human Settlements Programme (UN-Habitat)) said that his organization had made a new commitment in the form of the New Urban Agenda.

请自行翻译后查看后文的分析点评

分析点评

第1段

The work of UNHCR was grounded in the Convention, and the organization strove to listen to people's specific needs and adjust its programming accordingly.

《公约》是难民署工作的基础，且该组织①努力听取人们的具体需要，并据此调整其方案拟定。

批 注

① 注意句子的真正主语。

审 校 稿

难民署以《公约》为基础开展工作，努力倾听人们的具体需要，并据此调整其方案编制工作。

点 评

句子结构把握不准。原文出现了两个主语，但实际的动作是由难民署发出的。因此，审校稿略作调整，将难民署作为整个句子的主语。另外，"programming"一词可译为"方案拟订"，也可译为"方案编制"。后者是联合国纽约总部采纳的译法。鉴于本材料选自纽约总部的文件，此处应译为"方案编制"。

第 2 段

UNHCR also participated in the task team created by the Inter-Agency Standing Committee to coordinate global guidelines for the full and respectful inclusion of persons with disabilities in humanitarian action.

难民署还参与了由机构间常设委员会创立②的工作组③，为将残疾人充分且尊重地纳入④人道主义行动的全球准则开展协调工作。

批 注

② 用词不准确。
③ 用词错误。
④ 中文看不懂。

审 校 稿

难民署还参加了机构间常设委员会设立的任务小组，协调残疾人充分和体面地参与人道主义行动全球准则的制定工作。

点 评

1. 用词不准确。"create"通常译为"设立"。
2. 用词错误。"task team"可译为"任务小组"，不是"工作组"，工作组是"working group"。
3. 中文表述不地道。"为将残疾人充分且尊重地纳入人道主义行动的全球准则开展协调工作"让人不明所以，其实，可将"respectful"理解为"受人尊重的、体面的"。因此，我们可以将这句话改为"协调残疾人充分和体面地参与人道主义行动全球准则的制定工作"。

第 3 段

The New York Declaration for Refugees and Migrants, the comprehensive refugee response framework and the work towards the adoption of a compact on refugees and a

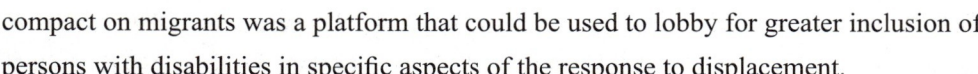

compact on migrants was a platform that could be used to lobby for greater inclusion of persons with disabilities in specific aspects of the response to displacement.

《关于难民和移民的纽约宣言》、难民问题全面响应框架以及为通过一项难民契约和一项移民契约①所做的工作，这些构成了一个平台，可以用于开展游说工作，使残疾人更多地被纳入流离失所应对措施的具体方面②。

批 注

① 啰唆。
② 不符合中文表达习惯。

《关于难民和移民的纽约宣言》、难民问题全面响应框架以及为通过难民契约和移民契约所做的工作都是可以利用的平台，可以用于开展游说工作，让残疾人更多地参与应对流离失所的具体问题。

表述啰唆，译文未加锤炼。将"inclusion"译为"纳入"，句子就成了被动句，译为"参与"，句子就成了主动句，相比之下，后者更为顺畅。

第 4 段

UNHCR considered itself a leader in knowledge of displacement. However, when it came to responding to the specificities of the needs of persons with disabilities in a displacement context, the organization acknowledged that it had much to learn and that it could only make progress by working directly with persons with disabilities and their representative organizations. However, it was firmly committed to so doing.

难民署自认为在流离失所问题方面具有最完备的知识③。然而，在流离失所背景下应对残疾人的具体需要时，该组织承认自己还有很多东西需要学习，并且只有直接面对残疾人及其代表组织开展工作，该组织才能取得进展。然而，难民署致力于这方面的工作。

批 注

③ 表达不准确。

难民署自认为在了解流离失所问题方面最有发言权。然而，在涉及流离失所背景下应对残疾人需求的特殊性时，难民署承认自己要学的东西还很多，只有直接与残疾人及其代表组织合作，才能取得进展。尽管如此，难民署仍坚定致力于这样做。

表达不准确。将"a leader in knowledge of displacement"译为"在流离失所问题方面具有最完备的知识"让人费解，其实，可以将"knowledge"理解为"了解"，这样读者更容易理解原文。因此，将其译为"在了解流离失所问题方面最有发言权"更符合中文的表达习惯。"specificities of the needs of persons with disabilities"是指"残疾人需求的特殊性"而不是"残疾人的具体需要",不可以将二者混淆。"committed to so doing"可以译为"致力于这样做"。

第5段

Mr. Decorte (Acting Director and Officer-in-Charge of New York Office, United Nations Human Settlements Programme (UN-Habitat)) said that his organization had made a new commitment in the form of the New Urban Agenda.

Decorte 先生(联合国人类住区规划署(人居署)代理主任兼纽约办事处主任①)说,人居署已经以《新城市议程》的形式②做出了一项新的承诺。

批 注
① 逻辑关系错误。
② 译文生硬。

Decorte 先生(联合国人类住区规划署(人居署)纽约办事处代理主任和临时负责人)说,人居署通过《新城市议程》做出新的承诺。

逻辑关系错误。"Acting Director and Officer-in-Charge of New York Office, United Nations Human Settlements Programme"的意思是"联合国人类住区规划署纽约办事处代理主任和临时负责人"。其中,"Officer-in-Charge"是临时负责人的意思,其含义是,负责人不在,由其担任"临时负责人",不可能由人居署的代理主任来兼任纽约办事处的临时负责人,只能是从办事处内部找人临时负责一下。

补充练习

It had produced guidelines and handbooks on subjects such as physical access to housing and general accessibility to cities.

In addition, it had launched a number of pilot projects; in Nairobi, UN-Habitat was working with small private bus operators to improve access to transport for persons with disabilities and show how that would deliver benefits for all.

人居署围绕实际获得住房和城市一般无障碍设施等主题编写了准则和手册。

此外,人居署还推出了若干试点项目;在内罗毕,人居署与小型私人巴士经营者合作,改进交通无障碍设施以方便残疾人使用,向人们证明这一做法将使所有人获益。

第二章 人权与人道

第十二篇

原文

He said that many countries in Asia and the Pacific lacked appropriate services for early-childhood disability detection and intervention and disability-inclusive education management.

She said that the Short Set of Questions on Disability prepared by the Washington Group on Disability Statistics, which was an appropriate and broadly tested methodology, should be used as a tool to disaggregate data by disability, particularly in household surveys and national censuses.

She also asked whether accessibility and the inclusion of persons with disabilities could be included as parameters for rating cities and municipalities.

At its sixteenth and seventeenth sessions, the Committee had considered 15 initial State party reports, had adopted concluding observations, including recommendations regarding the implementation of the Sustainable Development Goals, and had initiated the second reporting cycle under the simplified reporting procedures for four States parties.

The Committee had adopted two general comments, on women and girls with disabilities and on the right to inclusive education, and it was currently working on two additional draft general comments, on the right to live independently in the community and on non-discrimination and equality, for which written submissions could be made until 30 June 2017.

请自行翻译后查看后文的分析点评

分析点评

第1段

He said that many countries in Asia and the Pacific lacked appropriate services for early-childhood disability detection and intervention and disability-inclusive education management.

翻译稿

他说，亚洲及太平洋的①许多国家在早期儿童②残疾检测和干预以及兼顾残疾问题的教育管理方面缺乏适当的服务。

审校稿

他说，在亚洲及太平洋地区，很多国家在婴幼儿残疾检测和干预以及兼顾残

批 注

① 表达欠佳。
② 错译。

疾问题的教育管理方面缺乏适当的服务。

1. 表达欠妥。如何切分句子？本段是一个很好的例子。可以将地点状语单独拿出来，译为"在亚洲及太平洋地区，很多国家……"，可避免主语过长，也可避免可能的歧义。

2. 错译。译者将"early-childhood disability detection"译为"早期儿童残疾检测"，是望文生义，"early-childhood"应该译为"婴幼儿"。

第 2 段

She said that the Short Set of Questions on Disability prepared by the Washington Group on Disability Statistics, which was an appropriate and broadly tested methodology, should be used as a tool to disaggregate data by disability, particularly in household surveys and national censuses.

她说，由残疾统计华盛顿小组编制的残疾状况简易问题集是适当的且经过广泛测试的方法①，该问题集应当作为工作用来按残疾状况进行分类②，特别是用于家庭调查和全国人口普查。

批 注

① 西化腔。
② 表达不恰当且有打字错误。

她说，残疾统计华盛顿小组编写的《简易残疾问题集》是经过广泛检验的适当方法，应作为收集残疾分类数据的工具，特别是用于住户调查和国家人口普查。

1. 过于直译。将"which was an appropriate and broadly tested methodology"译为"是适当的且经过广泛测试的方法"，是中文表述按英文走的典型表现。

2. 表达不恰当。将"as a tool to disaggregate data by disability"译为"作为工作用来按残疾状况进行分类"欠妥，这里存在译者打字错误的情况，即译者想说的是"作为工具用来按残疾状况进行分类"。即使如此，也不够好，可以将其修改为"作为收集残疾分类数据的工具"。

第 3 段

She also asked whether accessibility and the inclusion of persons with disabilities could be included as parameters for rating cities and municipalities.

批 注

③ 译文处理得不够好。
④ 译法不到位。

她还问道，是否可以纳入有关残疾人的无障碍问题和包容性问题作为③城市和都市评级的参数④。

她还询问是否可以将无障碍设施和允许残疾人加入的情况列为城市和都市评级标准。

1. 理解不到位。翻译稿将"whether accessibility and the inclusion of persons with disabilities could be included as parameters"译为"是否可以纳入有关残疾人的无障碍问题和包容性问题作为"不够准确,"inclusion of persons with disabilities"应该是"允许残疾人加入"的意思,"be included as"可以被理解为"被允许列为、被列为"的意思,这句话可改为"将无障碍设施和允许残疾人加入的情况列为"。

2. 词义不准确。将"parameters"译为"参数",但中文一般不会这么说,可以将其译为"标准"。

第 4 段

At its sixteenth and seventeenth sessions, the Committee had considered 15 initial State party reports, had adopted concluding observations, including recommendations regarding the implementation of the Sustainable Development Goals, and had initiated the second reporting cycle under the simplified reporting procedures for four States parties.

委员会在其第十六和十七届会议上审议了15个初始缔约国的报告①,通过了结论意见②,其中包括关于落实可持续发展目标的建议,并且根据简化报告程序,针对四个缔约国启动了第二个报告周期。

批 注

① 翻译错误。
② 不准确。

残疾人权利委员会第十六届和第十七届会议审议了15份缔约国初次报告,通过了结论性意见,其中包括关于落实可持续发展目标的建议,并根据简化报告程序,启动了对4个缔约国的第二个报告周期。

1. 理解错误。在本段中,"15 initial State party reports"的意思是"15份缔约国的初次报告",不能译为"15个初始缔约国的报告",数量词修饰的是报告,是指有15份报告,而不是15个缔约国。另外,"initial reports"是指初次报告。

2. 词义不准确。在联合国文件中,"concluding observations"译为"结论性意见",不译"结论意见"。

第 5 段

The Committee had adopted two general comments, on women and girls with disabilities and on the right to inclusive education, and it was currently working on two additional draft general comments, on the right to live independently in the community and on non-discrimination and equality, for which written submissions could be made until 30 June 2017.

批 注

① 术语不准确。
② 表达欠妥。
③ 有歧义。

【翻译稿】

委员会通过了两项一般性评论①，分别关于残疾妇女和女童以及全纳教育权，目前，委员会正在拟定另外两项一般性评论草案，分别关于有权在社区独立生活②以及不歧视和平等，到 2017 年 6 月 30 日可做出书面提交③。

【审校稿】

残疾人权利委员会通过了两项一般性意见，一项涉及残疾妇女和女童问题，另一项涉及全纳教育权问题。目前，委员会正在拟定另外两项一般性意见草案，分别涉及在社区中独立生活的权利和不歧视与平等问题，可在 2017 年 6 月 30 日前提交书面材料。

【点评】

1. 术语不准确。在联合国词汇中，"general comments"有"一般性意见"和"一般性评论"两种译法，但本文讲的是残疾人权利委员会通过的内容，当然是"一般性意见"，而一般性评论是指与会人员在会上所做一般性讲话。例如"general comment No.1"可译为"第 1 号一般性意见"。

2. 可读性有待提高。翻译稿将"on women and girls with disabilities and on the right to inclusive education"译为"分别关于残疾妇女和女童以及全纳教育权"，从理解方面来讲，没有错误，但改为"一项涉及残疾妇女和女童问题，另一项涉及全纳教育权问题"更好。

3. 有歧义。"有权在社区独立生活"只是一项权利，"在社区独立生活的权利"可以是多项权利的集合，而且更适合与后面的名词性结构并列。将"for which written submissions could be made until 30 June 2017"译为"到 2017 年 6 月 30 日做出书面提交"不好，中文不会这样表述，可以将其改为"可在 2017 年 6 月 30 日前提交书面材料"。

【补充练习】

The Committee had also received over 300 communications and had registered 37 cases. It had taken final decisions in 15 cases, adopted eight views with violations, two views without violations, and had taken five decisions of inadmissibility.

The Statistical Commission must heed the call made by Member States in General Assembly Resolution 71/165 to incorporate the Washington Group's guidelines.

【参考译文】

委员会还收到了 300 多份来文，登记了 37 起案件，并就 15 起案件做出了最后决定。在通过的意见中，有8项意见认为存在违反《公约》的行为，有2项意见认为不存在违反《公约》的行为，委员会还就5个案件的可否受理问题做出了决定。

统计委员会必须响应会员国在大会第71/165号决议中发出的号召，采取华盛顿小组制定的准则。

原文

Sterilizations often supported the impunity of perpetrators of violence against women by eliminating the consequences of sexual abuse. For women with disabilities who had low self-esteem and little access to information on their rights, reporting violence or abuse was complicated. Quality inclusive education for girls with disabilities in mainstream schools with other girls was needed. It was also important to improve access to information and remove barriers in communication so that women with disabilities who had difficulty communicating could express their expectations and concerns. An opportunity was at hand to establish a joint international campaign to promote the elimination of forced sterilization, abortions and other practices against the physical integrity of women with disabilities.

Regarding the disaggregation of statistical data, it would not be possible to evaluate progress on and achieve the objectives of the 2030 Agenda without data disaggregated by gender and disability. She agreed that the Washington Group methods could be used for disaggregation by disability. The current report focused on the situation of young women and girls to address the serious violations they faced and raise awareness, but she would be working with the Independent Expert on the enjoyment of all human rights by older persons to address the tremendous needs of adult and older women with disabilities at an expert meeting on the intersection of disability and older persons.

请自行翻译后查看后文的分析点评

分析点评

第1段

Sterilizations often supported the impunity of perpetrators of violence against women by eliminating the consequences of sexual abuse. For women with disabilities who had low self-esteem and little access to information on their rights, reporting violence or abuse was complicated. Quality inclusive education for girls with disabilities in mainstream schools with other girls was needed. It was also important to improve access to information and remove barriers in communication so that women with disabilities who had difficulty communicating could express their expectations and concerns. An opportunity was at hand to establish a joint international campaign to promote the elimination of forced sterilization, abortions and other practices against the physical integrity of women with disabilities.

批 注

① 照搬原文。
② 容易引起歧义，"绝育"为什么能"支持"有罪不罚？
③ 用词不当。
④ 照搬原文，未灵活处理。

绝育常常通过①消除性虐待的后果，支持②对暴力侵害妇女行为的犯罪者实施有罪不罚。对于缺乏自尊且几乎无法获得关于其权利的信息的残疾妇女来说，报告③暴力行为或虐待十分复杂。需要在主流学校为残疾女童在其他女童中间开展高质量的包容教育。还必须改善获取信息的机会和移除交流障碍，从而使在交流方面存在困难的残疾妇女能够表达她们的期待和关切。我们现在有机会④开展一项联合国际运动，从而促进消除破坏残疾妇女人身安全的强迫绝育、堕胎和其他做法。

由于绝育能掩盖性虐待的后果，所以常常助长暴力侵害妇女行为实施者免受惩罚。对于缺乏自尊且几乎无法了解自身权利的残疾妇女来说，举报暴力或虐待行为是一个复杂的问题。需要在主流学校为残疾女童及其他女童一起开展优质的全纳教育。还必须改善获取信息的机会和消除交流障碍，以便在交流方面存在困难的残疾妇女能够表达她们的期待和关切。摆在我们面前的一个机会是开展一项联合国际运动，促进消除危害残疾妇女人身安全的强迫绝育、堕胎和其他做法。

1. 造成歧义。这句的主语是"Sterilizations"，不可能做出"支持"这个动作，所以在这里"support"不完全是支持的意思，而是助长，使不良情况恶化的意思。

2. 介词处理不当。在这句话中，乍一看"by"似乎表示的是一种手段或途径，所以原译文将其处理成"通过"，但这句话有隐含的逻辑关系，与前一句构成因果。在翻译过程中，尤其是遇到介词、非谓语结构或连词时，要认真考虑原文的逻辑关系，正确理解原文意思，灵活调整语序，确保不被原文"牵着走"。

3. 用词不当。"report"通常处理成"报告""报道"或"汇报"，但在这句话中，这3个词意似乎都略轻，原文实际是说对暴力或虐待行为举报，翻译时要认真考虑词义，保证用词的准确、到位。

4. 表达不到位。原译文已经将意思表达了出来，但语义略轻，没有体现出原文的一种迫切性，意思上来说与原文略有出入。

第2段

Regarding the disaggregation of statistical data, it would not be possible to evaluate progress on and achieve the objectives of the 2030 Agenda without data disaggregated by gender and disability. She agreed that the Washington Group methods could be used for disaggregation by disability. The current report focused on the situation of young women and girls to address the serious violations they faced and raise awareness, but she would be working with the Independent Expert on the enjoyment of all human rights by older persons to address the tremendous needs of adult and older women with disabilities at an expert meeting on the intersection of disability and older persons.

统计数据分列，如果没有根据性别和残疾分列的数据，评价《2030年议程》的进展和实现其目标则将不可能完成。她同意华盛顿小组的方法可用于残疾状况的分列。本报告侧重于青年妇女和女童的状况，以处理她们面对的严重侵犯人权的情况并提高认识，但她将在一场关于残疾和老年人的交叉问题专家会议上，与老年人享受所有人权问题独立专家合作[1] 解决[2] 残疾成年和老年妇女的巨大需求。

批 注

[1] 不准确。
[2] 过于绝对。

关于分列统计数据，如果没有根据性别和残疾状况分列的数据，就无法评价《2030年议程》的进展情况和实现其目标。她同意华盛顿小组的方法可用于分列残疾状况。本报告侧重于年轻妇女和女童的状况，以处理她们面对的严重侵犯人权行为并提高认识，但她将在残疾和老年人交叉问题专家会议上，与老年人享有所有人权问题独立专家共同探讨残疾成人和老年妇女的巨大需求。

词义错误。关于"work with"在本句中的用法，最后一句很关键，它提到了一场会议，也就是说报告员将在会议上与独立专家一起做某件事。如果用"合作"，过于正式，在会议上不是合作，而是共同、一起做一件事。同理，在会议上是无法解决需求的，因为会议只能提出一些举措或者建议，至于能否解决要看会议结束后的落实工作，所以在这里"address"不是最常见的"解决"，而是"探讨"，后面的词义在一些报告或正式文件中也常常出现。

补充练习

Ensuring access to sexual and reproductive health, a healthy life, and empowerment of women with disabilities would help girls with disabilities to feel self-confident and defend and value themselves. Women with disabilities grew up at a disadvantage in an unsupportive environment where they did not fit any of the social moulds for women or mothers and were not considered sexually attractive. Girls with disabilities must know that they could decide on their own fate, sexuality, fertility and physical integrity with full independence and the same professional and personal development options as others.

参考译文

确保残疾妇女获得性和生殖健康、健康的生活和增强其权能将有助于残疾女童建立自信,维护并重视自己。残疾妇女处于弱势地位,成长环境不利,在这样的环境下,她们不符合任何妇女或母亲的社会模型,并被视为不具有性吸引力。残疾女童必须明白,她们可以完全独立地决定自己的命运、性、生育和人身安全,并且可以与其他人一样选择职业和个人发展。

背景介绍

本篇材料选自人权状况特别报告员的报告。特别报告员身处人权保护工作的第一线,通过"特别程序"调查人权侵犯事件并介入个别侵权案件和紧急状况。这些人权专家以私人身份独立开展调查,最长任期为六年,工作没有酬劳,目前经特别程序授权的此类专家超过30名。人权状况特别报告员的报告重在客观论述事实,提醒缔约国注意本国存在的人权问题并提出改进建议。因此,这类报告通常文风平实,语言简练、准确,又因为涉及人权问题,句式结构较长、句型复杂。在处理这类文件时,除了避免口语化用词之外,还要尽可能做到精炼,酌情调整句子结构和语序,确保逻辑顺畅。

第十四篇

原文

The way in which elections have been conducted in the past has been criticized for a lack of compliance with international standards. The United Nations and other inter-governmental bodies have repeatedly called on the Government to address shortcomings and implement reforms. Most of those recommendations have yet to be implemented. The lack of substantial reform implies that the legal and institutional structure for the holding of elections remains conducive to practices that undermine the integrity of electoral processes. The Government's reluctance to implement recommendations indicates a lack of willingness to guarantee pluralistic and transparent conditions for elections.

The wider legal and institutional environment remains hostile to dissident opinions and unduly restricts civil and political rights. Disproportionate and discriminatory restrictions on freedom of opinion and expression, freedom of assembly and freedom of association were highlighted in the previous report of the Special Rapporteur (A/HRC/41/52). They have an adverse impact on civil society and are particularly worrisome, given that respect for fundamental freedoms is essential in electoral processes. Recent adverse developments in the media do not augur well for any improvement in the situation.

请自行翻译后查看后文的分析点评

分析点评

第 1 段

The way in which elections have been conducted in the past has been criticized for a lack of compliance with international standards. The United Nations and other inter-governmental bodies have repeatedly called on the Government to address shortcomings and implement reforms. Most of those recommendations have yet to be implemented. The lack of substantial reform implies that the legal and institutional structure for the holding of elections remains conducive to practices that undermine the integrity of electoral processes. The Government's reluctance to implement recommendations indicates a lack of willingness to guarantee pluralistic and transparent conditions for elections.

过去选举的方式因不符合国际标准而受到批评。联合国和其他政府间机构一再呼吁政府①解决不足，实施改革。这些建议大部分尚未付诸实施。缺乏实质性改革意味着，举行选举的法律和体制结构依然会导致损害选举进程整体性②的做法。政府不愿意执行建议，表明其缺乏意愿保证选举的多元化和透明性的条件。

过去的选举方式因不符合国际标准而受到批评。联合国和其他政府间机构一再呼吁白俄罗斯政府解决不足之处，实施改革。这些建议大部分尚未得到实施。缺乏实质性改革意味着，举行选举的法律和体制结构依然会带来破坏选举进程完整性的做法。白俄罗斯政府不愿落实相关建议，表明其缺乏保证选举条件多元透明的意愿。

批 注

① 哪个政府？
② 表述不确切。

1. 由于本文是白俄罗斯人权状况特别报告员的报告，所以通篇论述的是白俄罗斯这个国家的人权状况，在遇到"government"时，完全可以处理成"白俄罗斯政府"，否则指代不明。

2. 这一句涉及选词、用词的问题。"integrity"确实有整体性的意思，但在本句中，这个词义是说确保选举进程的完整性，也就是从选举人投票开始就应该遵循既定程序，所有环节缺一不可，重点强调的是"完整"而不是整体性。关于"undermine"，与"完整性"搭配的词义是"破坏"而不是"损害"。

第 2 段

The wider legal and institutional environment remains hostile to dissident opinions and unduly restricts civil and political rights. Disproportionate and discriminatory restrictions on freedom of opinion and expression, freedom of assembly and freedom of association were highlighted in the previous report of the Special Rapporteur (A/HRC/41/52). They have an adverse impact on civil society and are particularly worrisome, given that respect for fundamental freedoms is essential in electoral processes. Recent adverse developments in the media do not augur well for any improvement in the situation.

更广泛的法律和体制环境仍然对持不同政见者的观点充满敌意，且不恰当地限制了公民权利和政治权利。关于对意见自由和表达自由、集会自由以及结社自由的不相称的和歧视性的限制，在报告员之前的报告中（A/HRC/41/52）已被着重强调①。这些限制对民间社会有不利影响，而且考虑到尊重基本自由在选举中十分重要②，这些限制尤其令人担忧。最近媒体的不利发展未预示状况有任何改善。

批 注

① 不够准确。
② 词义略轻。

更广泛的法律和体制环境仍然对持不同政见者的观点充满敌意，而且不当地限制了公民权利和政治权利。特别报告员在上一份报告（A/HRC/41/52）中着重论述了对意见和表达自由、集会自由及结社自由过度且具有歧视性的限制。这些限制给民间社会造成负面影响，而且鉴于尊重基本自由在选举进程中必不可少，这些限制尤其令人担忧。最近媒体的不利发展并未预示情况有任何改善。

1. 这段谈及特别报告员在以往报告中重点探讨的内容，"highlight"的确有"强调"的意思，但在这里并不合适，因为强调的内容通常是需要做出的改善，而这里提到的"限制"显然是负面内容，所以不能用"强调"，而是着重论述。

2. 原译文的词义略轻，无法体现原文对尊重基本自由的重视，用"必不可少"一词更好。

补充练习

Ahead of the coming electoral cycle, the Special Rapporteur wishes to recall the universality and indivisibility of human rights in electoral processes. She believes that the current situation should be examined in order to understand whether conditions are being met to hold elections according to international human rights standards and allow citizens to fully enjoy their right to participate in public affairs.

参考译文

在即将到来的选举周期之前，特别报告员希望回顾选举进程中人权的普遍性和不可分割性。她认为，应当对目前的情况进行审查，以了解是否符合按照国际人权标准举行选举的条件，以及使公民充分享有参与公共事务的权利。

本章词汇

asylum seeker　寻求庇护者
access to information　信息获取
Committee on the Rights of Persons with Disabilities　残疾人权利委员会
democratic governance　民主治理
electoral process　选举进程
expulsion　驱逐
early marriage　早婚
child marriage　童婚
freedom of opinion and expression　意见和表达自由
freedom of assembly　集会自由
freedom of association　结社自由
forced disappearance　强迫失踪
enforced disappearance　强迫失踪
forced labour　强迫劳动
gender-responsive law　促进性别平等的法律
human rights defender　人权维护者
Human Rights Council　人权理事会
International Convention for the Protection of All Persons from Enforced Disappearance　《保护所有人免遭强迫失踪国际公约》
international human rights standards　国际人权标准
informal sector　非正规部门
impunity　有罪不罚
inclusive education　全纳教育
Office of the United Nations High Commissioner for Human Rights (OHCHR)　联合国人权事务高级专员办事处（人权高专办）
refugee status determination　难民身份确定
rule of law　法治
stateless person　无国籍者
side event　会外活动
sexual exploitation　性剥削
sexual trafficking　性贩运
universal periodic review　普遍定期审议
submission　呈文、材料
communication　来文
right to fair and adequate compensation　获得公平和充分赔偿的权利
admissibility　可否受理
complainant　申诉人
complaint　申诉
merits　案情实质
concluding observations　结论性意见
general comment　一般性意见；一般性评论
Issues and Proceedings before the Committee　委员会需处理的问题和议事情况
argument　理由、论据
statement　陈述
confession　供述
convict　宣判……有罪
conspiracy　共谋
jurisdiction　司法管辖权/法院的裁判权
accuse of　指控、控告
joint submission　联署材料
concern　关切、关注
Special Rapporteur　特别报告员
special procedure　特别程序
human rights violation　侵犯人权
disproportionate use　过度使用
extrajudicial killings　法外处决
arbitrary detention　任意拘留
ill-treatment　虐待
torture　酷刑
machinery　机制；机构
prosecution　起诉
sentence　判决
perpetrator　犯罪人、施害者
consider　考虑；审议
review　审查
oral presentation　口头介绍
periodic report　定期报告
universal implementation　普遍实施
drop-out rate　辍学率

gender balance   性别均衡
human rights-based   立足人权 / 注重人权的
task team   任务小组
working group   工作组
response framework   响应框架
early-childhood   儿童早期
initial report   初次报告
reporting cycle   报告周期
simplified reporting procedure   简化报告程序
written submissions   书面材料
forced sterilization   强迫绝育
sexual and reproductive health   性健康和生殖健康
empowerment of women   增强妇女权能
accessibility   无障碍
persons with disabilities   残疾人
impartial investigation   公正调查
establish precedent   确定先例
domestic remedies   国内补救办法
proper monitoring   适当监督

legal safeguard   法律保障
police custody   警方羁押
crime network   犯罪网络
indigenous children   土著儿童
International Convention on the Elimination of All Forms of Racial Discrimination   《消除一切形式种族歧视国际公约》
street children   街头儿童
Inter-American Commission on Human Rights   美洲人权委员会
fundamental rights   基本权利
vulnerable groups   弱势群体
lesbian, gay, bisexual, transgender and intersex persons   男女同性恋、双性恋、跨性别者和双性者
money laundering   洗钱
due process   正当程序
impartiality   公正
institutional framework   体制框架

第三章

法律与法治

本章导言

联合国是全球最大的国际组织,全世界有 197 个独立国家,联合国会员国就有 193 个。联合国系统是指联合国自身及多个附属机构,例如基金(儿童基金会、人口基金等)、方案(环境署、开发署、毒品和犯罪问题办公室等)、专门机构(世界卫生组织、教科文组织、世界知识产权组织等),其他联合国实体和机构(艾滋病规划署、难民署、妇女署等)及相关组织(国际原子能机构、禁止化学武器组织)等。

各机构都有内部章程条例,还有机构(裁军谈判会议、国际法委员会)专门谈判和制订国际条约,这些工作都与法律和法制有关。

联合国的法律类文件主要有《联合国法律年鉴》,国际法委员会的年度报告和简要记录,人权理事会的报告或来文,消除对妇女歧视委员会的报告,联合国毒品和犯罪问题办公室的文件(例如,本章所选涉及反腐败和打击有组织犯罪的文件),联合国贸易和发展会议的文件,世界知识产权组织的文件(保护产权、解决产权争议的法律文件)等。

法律类文件一般涉及重要利益和是非,摆事实,讲规则,鲜有主观色彩。国际协定、条约或公约更是如此。法律类文件用词比较正式,多专业术语,甚至外来语,但少用成语或比喻,也不用俚语。

法律类文件的难点首先体现在词汇方面。

一、专有名词

联合国文件中专有名词多不胜数,有机构、基金、方案、计划、项目、纲领等,一般都要先查联合国词汇,有定译的用定译,没有再自译。例如,"Article 2 (of Convention against Corruption)"不译为"《反腐败公约》第 2 条",而要按照已有的联合国权威中文本译为"《反腐败公约》第二条"。

二、拉丁文/法语

例1 In their appeal, the defence also underlined that the factual circumstances of the alleged crime, including the *mens rea* and *actus reus*, were not established or proven beyond reasonable doubt.

辩方在上诉中还强调,所控罪行的实际情况,包括犯罪意图和犯罪行为,没有得到确凿无疑地证实或证明。

其中的斜体字 *mens rea* 和 *actus reus*,都是拉丁文,意思分别是"犯罪意图"和"犯罪行为"。

例2 The conviction and sentence handed down against the author did not constitute a violation of the *non bis in idem* principle.

对提交人的定罪和判刑并不违反一事不再理原则。

其中的斜体字 *non bis in idem* 是拉丁文,意思是"一罪不二审"或"一事不再理"。"一事不再理"更接近拉丁文的字面意思。

例3 Restrictions on freedom of movement, as described in Article 4, either relate to *force majeure* cases, state of emergency, civil protection, public health threat or to coercive measures and must abide by the principles of equality, proportionality and non-discrimination.

第4条所述的行动自由限制,要么涉及不可抗力案件、紧急状态、公民保护、公共健康威胁,要么涉及强制措施,因此必须遵守平等、相称和非歧视原则。其中斜体字 *force majeure* 是法文,意思是"不可抗力"。这个法文词在英文合同中用得最普遍,在联合国文件用得也很多。与它意思相近的拉丁文"vis major",却几乎不见使用,意思相当的英文"irresistible force"(见 *Merriam Webster's Dictionary of Law*)也使用极少,目前只找到了一个例子:In that regard, Koskenniemi had written that the relationship between *jus cogens* and persistent objection was a point where an irresistible force and an immovable object of international legal theory collided.(在这方面,科斯肯涅米写道,强行法与一贯反对之间的关系就是不可抗力与国际法律理论不可动摇的目标发生碰撞的一个点。)

三、法律专业术语

例1 This inviolability is embodied in various international treaties and essentially covers persons who, in accordance with international law, enjoy some kind of personal immunity. This is particularly true of diplomatic agents, members of special missions, representatives to international organizations, or persons who represent the State in an international body or at a conference.

这种不可侵犯权体现在各种国际条约中,基本上涵盖了根据国际法享有某种形式的属人豁免的人,尤其是外交人员、特别使团成员、国际组织代表或国家派往国际机构或会议的代表。其中 inviolability 意为"不可侵犯权、不可侵犯性";personal immunity 意为"属人豁免""个人豁免权",而不是"个人免疫力"。

例2 Deprivation of life involves intentional or otherwise foreseeable and preventable life-terminating harm or injury, caused by an act or omission.

剥夺生命涉及由作为或不作为造成的故意或其他可预见和可预防的终止生命的损伤或伤害。

其中,act or omission 在法律文件中译为"作为或不作为"。

法律术语的翻译,有时会历经多代翻译工作者或有关专家的努力,如 act 一度译为"法案",但查询 P.H. Collins 主编的 *Law Dictionary* (2nd ed) 的注释，其意为"Before an Act becomes law, it is presented to Parliament in the form of a Bill"，换言之，就是 Act 在议会通过之前称 Bill，通过之后才是"Law（法）"。如 Marriage Act 译为《婚姻法》，Companies Act 译为《公司法》。

四、宰熟词

有些英文词是翻译人士早就学过的，都像多年的同桌一样熟悉，却不知道在法律中有特别的意义。
例如：
The Court found that a legal void made it impossible for the applicant to exercise her voting rights and her right to stand in local elections for a prolonged time.
原译：法院认定，法律上的无效使原告长期无法行使其投票权和参加地方选举的权利。
其中的 found 一词，单词原形是 find，在本句的语境中，其意既不是"发现"，也不是"认定"，而是"裁定"，因为 Law[with clause](of a judge or court)rule; decide—Noxd（《新牛津英语词典》）。

五、同一术语在不同条约或组织有不同的译法

Undue Advantage：在《联合国反腐败公约》中译为"不正当好处"，而在《联合国打击跨国有组织犯罪公约》中译为"不应有的好处"。
Dispute Resolution：一般联合国机构都译为"争端解决"，产权组织译为"争议解决"。
Programme：一般联合国机构都译为"方案"，产权组织则统统译为"计划"。

除词汇外，法律英文的句子较长，多是复杂句，有很多定语、状语、补语等成分，特别是介词引导的定状补。总的处理原则是弄清语法结构和逻辑关系，这要求译者熟悉相关内容。所涉情况复杂，详见本章译例分析。

背景介绍

本章第一篇至第五篇选自国际法委员会临时简要记录,主要内容是条约的暂时适用(Provisional application of treaties)。

国际法委员会由联合国大会于 1947 年成立。现有委员 34 人。委员由联合国会员国政府提名,联合国大会选举,代表世界各主要文明形式和主要法系,以个人身份服务,任期五年。委员会的宗旨是促进"国际法的逐渐发展与编纂",负责专题众多,已完成的专题有《海洋法公约》《维也纳条约法公约》等,现有专题包括"国家责任""关于国际法不加禁止的行为所产生的损害性后果的国际责任""对条约的保留"等。

国际法委员会简要记录的语言特点是措辞正式,句子长而复杂。

第一篇

原文

He endorsed the Special Rapporteur's intended focus on the legal effects that the provisional application of treaties had at international level. It was important to understand the practice of different States. The Commission had hoped to receive more responses to its enquiries in that regard, and more information would be required before the Special Rapporteur could reach conclusions on the subject.

When considering the possible legal effects of provisional application, the Commission had to reconcile the objective of enhancing the legitimacy and legal certainty of provisional application with that of responding appropriately to potential concerns of States that there might be a lesser incentive to ratify a treaty when it was recognized that provisional application produced legal effects.

请自行翻译后查看后文的分析点评

分析点评

第 1 段

He endorsed the Special Rapporteur's intended focus on the legal effects that the provisional application of treaties had at international level. It was important to understand the practice of different States. The Commission had hoped to receive more responses to its enquiries in that regard, and more information would be required before the Special Rapporteur could reach conclusions on the subject.

他赞成特别报告员打算重点①关注条约的暂时适用在国际层面的法律效力。了解不同国家的做法非常重要。在这方面，委员会希望收到更多对其问询②的答复，在特别报告员就此主题做出结论前将需要更多信息。

批 注

① 可商。
② 错译。

他赞成特别报告员的打算，即重点关注条约的暂时适用在国际层面的法律效力。了解不同国家的做法非常重要。在这方面，委员会希望收到更多对其调查的答复，在特别报告员就本专题做出结论前将需要更多信息。

1. "He endorsed the Special Rapporteur's intended focus on…"译为"他赞成特别报告员打算重点关注……"，并不错，但也可以有其他译法，如译为"他赞成特别报告员的打算，即重点……"或"他赞成特别报告员侧重条约暂时适用在国际层面的法律效力的打算"；这就是常说的所谓"词类转换"。

Rapporteur 来自法文，拼写和发音几乎保持原样。一般英汉词典都译为"特派调查员""会务报告人""调查员""报告员""报告人""汇报人""报告起草人"等，不一而足；联合国则译为"报告员"，如 chief rapporteur 译为"首席报告员"，case rapporteur 译为"个案报告员"。

联合国最多的是 special rapporteur 译为"特别报告员"。如 Special Rapporteur on the situation of human rights 译为"人权状况特别报告员"，Special Rapporteur on the right to education 译为"受教育权特别报告员"，Special Rapporteur on the right to development 译为"发展权特别报告员"，Special Rapporteur on minority issues 译为"少数群体特别报告员"，Special Rapporteur on the right to food 译为"食物权特别报告员"，Special Rapporteur on the right to privacy 译为"隐私权特别报告员"，special rapporteur on torture 译为"酷刑问题特别报告"，等等。

顺便提一下，special rapporteur on torture 是简称，全称是 Special Rapporteur on torture and other cruel, inhuman or degrading treatment or punishment，即"酷刑和其他残忍、不人道或有辱人格的待遇或处罚特别报告员"。有的英汉词典译为"关于酷刑的特别调查员"，与联合国官方译法不同。

2. provisional application of treaties 译为"条约的暂时适用"，其中的"application"与条约、公约、条例等搭配，一般都译为"适用"。

3. Enquiry 既有"问询"，也有"调查"，此处主语是 Commission，即国际法委员会，当译为"调查"。

第 2 段

When considering the possible legal effects of provisional application, the Commission had to reconcile the objective of enhancing the legitimacy and legal certainty of provisional application with that of responding appropriately to potential concerns of States that there might be a lesser incentive to ratify a treaty when it was recognized that provisional application produced legal effects.

在考虑①暂时适用可能的法律效力时，委员会必须将加强暂时适用正当性和法律上可靠性②的目标，与在承认暂时适用产生法律效力时适当回应可能缺乏③批准一份条约的动机的各国的潜在关切的目标相协调。

批 注

① 不当。
② 不准确。
③ 不准确。

在审议暂时适用可能的法律效力时，委员会必须得调和两个目标，既要加强暂时适用的合法性和法律确定性，又要适当回应各国可能产生的关切，也即如果承认条约的暂时适用会产生法律效力，或许会减少批准条约的动力。

点 评

1. Commission，即 International Law Commission（国际法委员会）的任务主要是逐渐发展和编纂国际法，所以 consider 在国际法委员会的语境中，一般都译"审议"，不译"考虑"。

2. legitimacy：在一般语境中译为"正当性"，似无不可；但在这里只能译为"合法性"。

3. legal certainty：译为"法律上可靠性"④，这种理解不正确；《英汉法律词典》中的解释是"法律的确定性，法律上的确定性"，联合国词汇直接译为"法律确定性"。

批 注

④ 不准确。

4. reconcile ~ sth (with sth): to find an acceptable way of dealing with two or more ideas, needs, etc. that seem to be opposed to each other，使和谐一致；调和；使配合。

这是英语常用句式，如果 reconcile 和 with 连接的成分较短，那还好处理。

例如：

That raised the question of how to reconcile variability and clarity.

这就提出了如何调和变化性和明确性的问题。

又如：

The death penalty could not be reconciled with full respect for the right to life, and abolition of the death penalty was both desirable and necessary for the enhancement of human dignity and the progressive development of human rights.

死刑与充分尊重生命权不可调和。为了强化人类尊严、促进人权逐步发展，废除死刑不仅合乎需要，而且十分必要。

但在本句中，reconcile 和 with 后面所接成分都很长，with 后面所接成分还特别复杂，翻译稿至少有三点不足。

（1）除了 legitimacy 和 legal certainty 翻译不当，把 lesser incentive 译为"缺乏……动机"也不正确，没有译出"lesser"的真正意思。

（2）对 when 从句所修饰的对象理解错误。

（3）"……批准一份条约的动机的各国的潜在关切的目标……"，连用四个"的"，正是台湾著名诗人、散文家和翻译家余光中所谓的"的的不休"，也是现代白话文常犯的毛病。四个"的"，让人一时很难看清彼此的修饰关系。

审校稿抛开原文的形式，采取先总后分的叙述方式，先说"调和两个目标"，再分说两个目标，"既……"讲第一个目标，"又……"讲第二个目标，层次分明，译意清楚。

当然，reconcile 若译为"兼顾"，也不错。

Subject to the availability of extrabudgetary resources, the Secretariat should conduct research with a view to preparing a discussion paper that would map an overview of practical considerations and challenges that authorities encounter, as well as lessons they have learned and good practices they have identified, in reconciling the need for observing and protecting the human rights of the person sought with the effectiveness of extradition proceedings, and in addressing efficiently the interplay between, on one hand, refugee and asylum proceedings and, on the other, extradition proceedings.

参考译文

秘书处应根据预算外资源的可得情况开展研究，以便编写一份讨论文件，概述实际考虑因素和主管部门在平衡遵守和保护被请求引渡人的人权与引渡程序的效力的必要性及有效处理难民和庇护程序与引渡程序之间相互关系方面面临的挑战，以及它们吸取的经验教训和查明的良好做法。

原文

The identification of four types of situations in which a treaty might be applied provisionally was undeniably useful in explaining how provisional application might come about, but less so in identifying its effects, which would not depend on the form in which States expressed their will to apply a treaty provisionally. She questioned some of the statements made in the report concerning the nature of that will: paragraphs 35 (d), 36, 38 and 54, in particular, reflected a tendency to regard provisional application as the result of a State's unilateral declaration. Although the report seemed to restrict such effects to situations in which a treaty contained no obligation concerning its provisional application, she did not share that conclusion. Rather, provisional application should be seen as a specific aspect of the law of treaties based on the consent or agreement of States or international organizations, which could be deduced from article 25 of the Vienna Convention. The two options provided in that article—a specific treaty provision or another form of agreement between negotiating States—both relied on consent between parties; neither could therefore be viewed as a unilateral act *stricto sensu*. Even an individual declaration by a State indicating that it would (or would not) apply a treaty not yet in force would be based on the relevant agreed provision of the treaty in question.

请自行翻译后查看后文的分析点评

分析点评

批 注

① 理解有误。
② 处理不佳。
③ 错译。
④ 可商。
⑤ 可改进。
⑥ 粗心之误。
⑦ 理解错误。
⑧ 不妥。

在解释如何施行暂时适用的过程中①，确认可暂时适用一份条约的四种情形毫无疑问是非常有用的，但在确认其效力（不会依赖于各国表达其暂时适用一份条约的意愿的形式②）的过程中，则不会那么有用。她对报告中就这种意愿的性质所做的一些声明提出了质疑：第35（d）、36、38和54段，特别是反映了一种将暂时适用作为一国单方宣告③的结果的倾向。尽管报告看起来将这种效力局限于一份条约不包含关于其临时适用的义务的情形，但她并未认同这个结论。而且④，暂时适用应被看作是基于各国或国际组织同意或达成一致的条约法的特定方面⑤，这可从《维也纳公约》第二十五条推论中⑥。该条中规定的两个选项——谈判国之间的特定条约条款或另外形式的协定⑦——都依赖于各方之间的同意；因此，严格地说也⑧不能被看作是一种单方面行为。即使一国单独宣布其会（或不会）适用一份尚未生效的条约，也将以所述条约相关商定条款为基础。

确认可暂时适用一份条约的四种情形毫无疑问在解释暂时适用可能会如何发生的情形方面是非常有用的，但在确认其效力方面，则不会那么有用，因为条约效力不会取决于各国表达其暂时适用一份条约的意愿的形式。她对报告中就这种意愿的性质所做的一些声明提出了质疑：第35（d）、36、38和54段，特别反映了一种将暂时适用作为一国单方面声明的结果的倾向。尽管报告看起来将这种效力局限于一份条约未载有其临时适用义务的情形，但她并未认同这个结论。相反，暂时适用应被看作是条约法基于各国或国际组织同意或达成一致的特定方面，这可从《维也纳公约》第25条中推出。该条中规定的两个选择——条约明确规定或谈判国之间另有协定——都依赖于各方之间的同意；因此，二者也均不能被看作是一种狭义的单方面行为。即使一国申明其会（或不会）适用一份尚未生效条约的具体声明，也将以所述条约相关商定条款为基础。

1. 在翻译第 1 句 "The identification of four types of situation...was undeniably useful in explaining how provisional application might come about, but less so in identifying its effects..." 时，应注意以下三点。

（1）"in explaining how provisional application might come about" 这一介词短语修饰 "useful"，与 "in identifying its effects" 所修饰的 "so" 含义相同，翻译稿把它放在全句句首，就修饰整个句子了，所以理解不当。

（2）"in explaining how provisional application might come about" 译为"在解释如何施行暂时适用的过程中"，不够严谨；come about 等于 happen，不是"实施"。

（3）"which would not depend on the form in which States expressed their will to apply a treaty provisionally"，这是一个非限定性定语从句，像翻译稿那样处理也凑合，按原文顺序放在最后译更好。

2. 第 2 句中 "unilateral declaration" 不译"单方宣告"，统译为"单方面声明"。

3. 在翻译第 4 句 "Rather, provisional application should be seen...from Article 25 of the Vienna Convention" 时，应注意以下三点。

（1）上一句 "Although the report seemed to...she did not share that conclusion" 是说这位发言的委员不同意报告中给出的结论，本句是说该委员提出了不同的观点。

此处 "Rather" 应选择《牛津高阶英汉双解词典》的第 4 个义项，"used to introduce an idea that is different or opposite to the idea that you have stated previously"，译为"相反"。

（2）"agreement" 可以译为"意思表示一致"（《英汉法律词典》)，但与 "consent" 有点重复，译为"协定"似乎更好，也更与《维也纳条约法公约》第 25 条的规定吻合。

（3）"从《维也纳公约》第二十五条推论中"，把 "deduced from" 译为"推论中"，当是疏忽之误，应译为"……中推论出来"。

4. 在翻译第 5 句 "The two options provided..." 时，应注意以下三点。

（1）把 "a specific treaty provision or another form of agreement between negotiating States" 译为"谈判国之间的特定条约条款或另外形式的协定"，纯从语法的角度看，似乎也可以这么理解，但与《维也纳条约法公约》第 25 条的规定不符：

"1. A treaty or a part of a treaty is applied provisionally pending its entry into force if:

（a）the treaty itself so provides; or

（b）the negotiating States have in some other manner so agreed."

中文译文：

"1. 条约或条约之一部分于条约生效前在下列情形下暂时适用：

（a）条约本身如此规定；或

（b）谈判国以其他方式协议如此办理。"

看到这款规定之后，就会明白当译为"条约明确规定或谈判国之间另有协定"，这里的"specific"，当然也可以译为"具体"。

这个问题是专业翻译常见的问题，既要求译者语言功夫扎实，又要求译者熟悉或查出相关内容。

（2）此处的"neither"未译；但该词有强调的作用，意思是"not one nor the other of two things or people"，所以最好译"两者都不"或"两者均不"。

（3）"*stricto sensu*"是拉丁文，《韦氏大学英语词典》给出的解释是"in a narrow or strict sense"，即"狭义的或严格意义的"。在此处，当理解为修饰"a unilateral act"。

Practice suggested that provisional application of a treaty need be neither uniform nor universal. The Special Rapporteur seemed to accept the possibility of a "multilayer" model; however, the matter should be considered in terms of both the distinction between bilateral and multilateral treaties and the different legal effects that might arise between States that accepted—implicitly or explicitly—or rejected the provisional application of a particular treaty.

参考译文

实践表明，一份条约的暂时适用既不需要统一，也不需要通行。特别报告员看起来接受了"多层次"模式的可能性；但是，这个问题应当从双边和多边条约之间的差别及特定条约在接受（暗示或明示）或拒绝其暂时适用的各国之间可能产生不同的法律效力这两个方面予以审议。

原文

The provisional application of a treaty resulted from an agreement between negotiating States if provided for in the treaty itself, by means of a separate agreement or if the negotiating States "in some other manner so agreed". That formulation presented negotiating States with a broad range of options, which could include an implicit agreement or a unilateral declaration by a State. It was necessary to consider carefully whether the mere fact of making a unilateral declaration could, of itself, result in a provisional application, since, on the one hand, article 25 of the Vienna Convention did not expressly refer to unilateral declarations, and on the other, such authorization risked compromising the legal certainty of the law of treaties.

Mr. Hassouna said that the Special Rapporteur should elaborate on the relationship between provisional application and entry into force, since some States saw those two procedures as separate and governed by distinct legal regimes, while others saw them as legally indistinguishable. In view of the fact that during the discussion in the Sixth Committee many States had indicated that recourse to provisional application should be subject to the relevant provisions of domestic law, the Special Rapporteur should clarify the situations in which domestic law was either relevant or irrelevant. Doing so did not require a comparative study of States' domestic legislation on the provisional application of treaties, nor was it the Commission's role to undertake such a study. Rather, its role was to identify the practice of States in the area of international law, and domestic law was relevant in that matter only to the extent that it involved the application of international law concepts, rights, obligations or procedures.

请自行翻译后查看后文的分析点评

分析点评

第 1 段

The provisional application of a treaty resulted from an agreement between negotiating States if provided for in the treaty itself, by means of a separate agreement or if the negotiating States "in some other manner so agreed". That formulation presented negotiating States with a broad range of options, which could include an implicit agreement or a unilateral declaration by a State. It was necessary to consider carefully whether the mere fact of making a unilateral declaration could, of itself, result in a provisional application, since, on the one hand, article 25 of the Vienna Convention did not expressly refer to unilateral declarations, and on the other, such authorization risked compromising the legal certainty of the law of treaties.

翻译稿

如果条约本身通过单独协定的方式做出规定，或是谈判国"以某种其他方式达成一致①"，那么一份条约的暂时适用就源于谈判国之间的协定。这种表述为谈判国提供了广泛的选择，这可包括一份含糊的协定②，或一国的单方宣告。有必要审慎考虑做出单方宣告本身是否会导致暂时适用，一方面，因为《维也纳公约》第二十五条并未明确提及单方宣告；另一方面，这类授权可能会危及条约法的法律可靠性。

批 注

① 注意引号中的文字。
② 不准确。

如果条约本身通过单独协定的方式做出规定，或是谈判国"以其他方式协议如此办理"，那么一份条约的暂时适用就源于谈判国之间的协定。这种表述为谈判国提供了广泛的选择，这可包括一份默示协定，或一国的单方面声明。有必要仔细审议仅仅做出单方面声明本身是否会导致暂时适用，一方面，因为《维也纳公约》第 25 条并未明确提及单方面声明；另一方面，这类授权可能会危及条约法的法律确定性。

1. "in some other manner so agreed"放在引号内，表明是引文，不可自译，须查出其出处。翻译稿没有做到这一点；它出自《维也纳条约法公约》第 25 条 "(b) the negotiating States have in some other manner so agreed"。

中文译文是"(b) 谈判国以其他方式协议如此办理"。

2. "formulation"在联合国文件中有多种意思，如 *formulation* of reservations 意思是"提具保留"；Project *Formulation* Framework 意思是"项目拟订框架"；compromise *formulation* 意思是"折中提法"。在本文中，也是"提法、表述或措辞"之意。

3. "implicit agreement"不译"含糊的协定"，而译"默示协定"。其他专门术语诸如"unilateral declaration"（单方面声明）、"legal certainty"（法律确定性）等，别处已说过，不再重提。

第 2 段

Mr. Hassouna said that the Special Rapporteur should elaborate on the relationship between provisional application and entry into force, since some States saw those two procedures as separate and governed by distinct legal regimes, while others saw them as legally indistinguishable. In view of the fact that during the discussion in the Sixth Committee many States had indicated that recourse to provisional application should be subject to the relevant provisions of domestic law, the Special Rapporteur should clarify the situations in which domestic law was either relevant or irrelevant. Doing so did not require a comparative study of States' domestic legislation on the provisional application of treaties, nor was it the Commission's role to undertake such a study. Rather, its role was to identify the practice of States in the area of international law, and domestic law was relevant in that matter only to the extent that it involved the application of international law concepts, rights, obligations or procedures.

哈苏纳先生说，特别报告员应详细阐述暂时适用和生效之间的关系，因为一些国家认为这两个程序是割裂①的，受截然不同的法律制度管辖，而其他人则认为它们在法律上是不能区分的。考虑到在第六委员会讨论期间，许多国家指出，暂时适用的追索权②应受国内法相关条款的管辖，特别报告员应澄清与国内法相关或不相关的情形。这样做③并不需要对各国关于条约暂时适用的国内立法进行

① 不准确。
② 不当。
③ 应当译出具体所指。

对比研究，而且委员会也没有这个职责去开展这样的研究。而且，其角色是确认在国际法领域各国的做法，以及<u>在这个问题上国内法与其相关的程度仅达到涉及国际法概念、权利、义务或程序的程度</u>①。

批 注

① 啰唆不清。

哈苏纳先生说，特别报告员应详细阐述暂时适用和生效之间的关系，因为一些国家认为这两个程序是分立的，受截然不同的法律制度管辖，而其他国家则认为它们在法律上无法区分。考虑到在第六委员会讨论期间，许多国家指出，诉诸暂时适用应受国内法相关条款的管辖，特别报告员应澄清国内法相关或不相关的情形。澄清并不需要对各国关于条约暂时适用的国内立法进行比较研究，而且委员会也没有这个职责去开展这样的研究。相反，其角色是确认在国际法领域里的国家实践，并且国内法只在涉及适用国际法概念、权利、义务或程序的程度上才与这一问题有关。

1. 第一句中的"saw those two procedures as separate"，"separate"的意思是"not joined to or touching something else"，即"独立的，分开的"，译为"割裂"有点不妥。

2.（1）把第二句中的"recourse to provisional application"译为"暂时适用的追索权"，显然错误。"Recourse"，《美国传统词典》的解释是："*Law* The right to demand payment from the endorser of a commercial paper when the first party liable fails to pay." 一看到这个英文定义，就知道"追索权"是指"commercial paper"（商业票据）的持有人在"first party liable"（第一责任方）不能付款时要求"endorser"（票据背书人）付款的权利，显然与"provisional application"无关。此处"recourse"的意思是"a source of help or strength: RESORT"，也即求助、借助，或诉诸，法律上常译为"诉诸"。

（2）"subject to"是联合国文件中常用短语，be subject to a rule/law/penalty etc. 就是 obey 的意思，译为"受……管辖"，也不算错。

3. Doing so 是指上句的"clarify"，英文为避免重复而这样措辞，译为"这样做"没错，若译为"澄清"，即重复一下，则意思更明白，行文也更流畅。

4. "and domestic law was relevant in that matter..."一句，译文有两个不足。

（1）"and"译为"以及"不妥，当译为"并且"，因为这是与前一个分句并列的句子。

（2）"在这个问题上国内法与其相关的程度仅达到涉及国际法概念、权利、义务或程序的程度"，虽然译者很用心，但效果不理想，"其"所指不是很清楚，行文又相当啰唆。

补充练习

It might be appropriate to take account of domestic legislation, insofar as that legislation determined recourse to provisional application. Practice varied greatly in that regard: in some States, provisional application was limited to treaties dealing with specific matters, such as trade; in others, provisional application was not permitted; and in yet others, recourse was had to provisional application even in the absence of specific legislation in that connection.

在国内立法决定诉诸暂时适用的情况下，宜考虑到国内立法。在这方面，各国的实践迥异：在一些国家中，暂时适用仅限于涉及贸易等特定问题的条约；在其他一些国家中，暂时适用不被允许；而在另外一些国家，甚至在缺乏这方面具体立法的情况下，也不得不诉诸暂时适用。

第四篇

原文

Ms. Jacobsson said that she supported the Special Rapporteur's proposal to exclude from the topic the legal effects of the provisional application of treaties at the domestic level and the conclusion that the provisional application of treaties created a legal relationship and therefore produced legal effects. She also shared his view that a comparative analysis of domestic law was not necessary. In view of his contention that the entry into force of a treaty fell under a different legal regime than its provisional application, it would be helpful if, in a future report, he could elaborate on the difference between the two, which was not always obvious. Similarly, the distinction between a unilateral act of a State and the provisional application of a treaty required further consideration, since a unilateral act of a State could not create any rights for that State beyond what was accepted by other States, but it might create obligations; while the provisional application of a treaty could entail the conferral of rights on the State that had decided to apply a treaty provisionally.

Lastly, she supported the Special Rapporteur's plan to address in future reports the provisional application of treaties by international organizations, since agreements between the European Union and third States could serve as interesting examples of legally acceptable solutions to the provisional application of treaties between two parties.

请自行翻译后查看后文的分析点评

第1段

Ms. Jacobsson said that she supported the Special Rapporteur's proposal to exclude from the topic the legal effects of the provisional application of treaties at the domestic level and the conclusion that the provisional application of treaties created a legal relationship and therefore produced legal effects. She also shared his view that a comparative analysis of domestic law was not necessary. In view of his contention that the entry into force of a treaty fell under a different legal regime than its provisional application, it would be helpful if, in a future report, he could elaborate on the difference between the two, which was not always obvious. Similarly, the distinction between a unilateral act of a State and the provisional application of a treaty required further consideration, since a unilateral act of a State could not create any rights for that State beyond what was accepted by other States, but it might create obligations; while the provisional application of a treaty could entail the conferral of rights on the State that had decided to apply a treaty provisionally.

雅各布松女士说，她支持特别报告员的建议，①不将条约暂时适用的法律效力问题包括在国内层面，以及条约的暂时适用建立了一种法律关系并因此产生了法律效力的结论。她还赞同特别报告员的看法，即对国内法的对比分析没有必要②。关于③他提出的一份条约生效被归入不同的法律制度而不是其暂时适用的论点，如果在将来的报告中，他能够详细阐述二者之间并不总是非常明显的区别，会非常有用。同样，一国的单方面行为和一份条约的暂时适用之间的差别也需要进一步审议，因为一国的单方面行为不能产生超出其他国家已经接受的范围之外的权利，但这会产生义务；然而条约的暂时适用可伴随④已经决定暂时适用一份条约的国家获得⑤权利。

批 注

① 不合惯例。
② 可改进。
③ 有误。
④ 不准确。
⑤ 有误。

雅各布松女士说，她支持特别报告员主张本专题不包含国家层面条约暂时适用的法律效力的提议，也支持条约的暂时适用产生了一种法律关系并因此产生了法律效力的结论。她还赞同特别报告员的看法，不必对国内法进行比较分析。鉴于他主张条约生效与条约暂时适用归入不同的法律制度，如果在将来的报告中，他能够详细阐述二者之间并不总是非常明显的区别，会非常有用。同样，一国的单方面行为和一份条约的暂时适用之间的区别也需要进一步审议，因为一国的单方面行为不可能为其创立超出其他国家接受范围之外的任何权利，却会产生义务；而条约的暂时适用可能要求赋予已经决定暂时适用一份条约的国家以权利。

点评

1. 第一句中，"support"带两个宾语，一是"Special Rapporteur's proposal"，二是"the conclusion"，但二者定语都比较长。如果译为"支持……提议和……结论"，中间不加标点，就显得句子太长，读起来费力。如果把"以及"改译为"也支持"，变成"支持……提议，也支持……"，则既明快，又符合中文表达习惯，因为中文多用动词。

2. 第二句"She also shared his view that a comparative analysis of domestic law was not necessary"，翻译稿的处理可以接受，但审校稿的处理更地道。

3. Share somebody's view，字面意思就是"共有某人的观点或看法"，照中文的说法，译为"认同某人看法""赞同某人的看法""与某人有同样的看法""像某人一样，也认为"等，也未尝不可。

4. 第三句，把"In view of"译为"关于"可能是笔误；翻译稿将"In view of his contention..."分句译为"……的论点"，是常规译法，另外也可以按照英文顺序翻译，只要把"contention"（论点、看法）改为"主张"就可以。

5. "while the provisional application of a treaty could entail the conferral of rights..."一句，"entail"和"conferral"都译错："entail"是"make (sth.) necessary; involve"（《牛津高阶英汉双解词典》），即"要求，或涉及"；"conferral"是"confer"的名词形式，"confer"的意思是"[transitive] FORMAL to give something such as authority, a legal right, or an honor to someone"（《麦克米伦高阶英汉双解词典》），即"授予、赋予"。

第 2 段

Lastly, she supported the Special Rapporteur's plan to address^① in future reports the provisional application of treaties by international organizations, since agreements between the European Union and third States could serve as interesting examples of legally acceptable solutions to the provisional application of treaties between two parties.^②

批注
① 联合国的正式措辞。
② 可以有不同译法。

翻译稿

最后，她支持特别报告员的计划，在未来的报告中解决国际组织的条约暂时适用问题，因为欧洲联盟和第三国之间的协定可作为两方之间条约暂时适用法律上可接受解决方案的有趣范例^③。

批注
③ 常规译法。

审校稿

最后，她支持特别报告员的计划，在未来的报告中解决国际组织的条约暂时适用问题，因为欧洲联盟和第三国之间的协定可作为有趣的范例，是法律上可接受的解决方案，可解决在两方之间暂时适用条约问题。

点评

1. "...address^④ in future reports the provisional application of treaties by

批注
④ 联合国的正式措辞。

international organizations"中的"address",是及物动词,《牛津高阶英汉双解词典》的解释是:"~ (yourself to) sth (*formal*): to think about a problem or a situation and decide how you are going to deal with it 设法解决;处理;对付"。《韦氏大学英语词典》的解释更细致一些:"2. a: to direct the efforts or attention of (oneself)"; b: to deal with, TREAT"。

例如:

address development goals(努力)实现发展目标

address the challenge of financing 应对筹资挑战或克服筹资困难

address child and women abductions 处理儿童妇女绑架问题

address key performance issues 解决主要业绩问题

address the special development needs and challenges of landlocked developing countries 应对内陆发展中国家的发展需要与挑战

address homelessness 解决无家可归问题

2. 这一句译文采取了常规译法,也就是基本按照英文的语法句式进行翻译,没有对英文句子成分做大的调整。虽然译文句子很长,成分也颇为复杂,但不影响理解,因此这种译法是可行的;当然通过合理拆分,采用增译的手法也可以译为短句。

Mr. Candioti said that he agreed with the Special Rapporteur's approach of focusing on the legal effects of the provisional application of treaties. He also agreed that a clear distinction should be made between the provisional entry into force of a treaty and the provisional application of that treaty.

参考译文

坎迪奥蒂先生说,他同意特别报告员将重点放在条约暂时适用的法律效力上的做法。他还同意应在一份条约临时生效和该条约暂时适用之间做出明确区分。

He further agreed that, at least at the present stage, the Commission should deal with the topic solely from an international law perspective and not consider questions relating to the domestic law of States. However, such questions could not be ignored.

He shared Mr. Park's views on the matter, in particular with regard to the relevance of articles 27 and 49 of the Vienna Convention. However, the Commission must seek primarily to clarify the scope, modalities and effects of provisional application within the framework of the international law of treaties in order, among other things, to contribute to a better understanding of the implications for States of any decision to apply a treaty provisionally.

As to the source of obligations, the Special Rapporteur's identification of at least four types of situations in which provisional application could result from an agreement was helpful. With regard to the last of the situations mentioned, namely that of a treaty that said absolutely nothing about provisional application, he said that it should be analysed in the light of the requirement set out in article 25, paragraph 1, of the 1969 Vienna Convention that the negotiating States must have agreed to apply a treaty provisionally. That analysis was called for in view of the Special Rapporteur's assertion that, in certain cases, the decision of a State to apply a treaty provisionally was an autonomous unilateral act, governed only by the intentions of the State in question.

请自行翻译后查看后文的分析点评

分析点评

第1段

He further agreed that, at least at the present stage, the Commission should deal with the topic solely from an international law perspective and not consider questions relating to the domestic law of States. However, such questions could not be ignored. He shared Mr. Park's views on the matter, in particular with regard to the relevance of articles 27 and 49 of the Vienna Convention. However, the Commission must seek primarily to clarify the scope, modalities and effects of provisional application within the framework of the international law of treaties in order, among other things, to contribute to a better understanding of the implications for States of any decision to apply a treaty provisionally.

他还同意，至少在目前阶段，委员会应仅从国际法角度处理这个主题①，而不考虑与各国国内法有关的问题。但是，这类问题不能被忽视。在这个问题上，他认同 Park 先生②的观点，特别是关于《维也纳公约》第二十七条和第四十九条之间的相关性。但是，委员会必须首先阐明暂时适用在条约国际法框架内的范围、方式和效力，以便除其他以外更好地理解各国决定暂时适用一份条约③的影响。

他还同意，至少在目前阶段，委员会应仅从国际法角度处理本专题，而不审

批 注

① 不合惯例。
② 不合要求。
③ 理解有误。

议与各国国内法有关的问题。但是，这类问题不容忽视。在这个问题上，特别是关于《维也纳公约》第 27 条和第 49 条的相关性，他认同朴先生的观点。但是，委员会必须首先在条约国际法框架内阐明暂时适用的范围、方式和效力，以便除其他以外，协助更好地理解任何暂时适用一份条约的决定对各国的影响。

1. "topic" 一般译为"专题"，特别是在国际法委员会的文件中。

2. 第三句 "He shared Mr. Park's views...49 of the Vienna Convention" 翻译稿有两个问题。

（1）Park 先生的姓未译。国际法委员会的文件要求把所有委员的名字都译出，而且不能随意自译，有统一译名的要用统一译名。Park 先生是委员会委员，所以应当译出，但是不能照一般的英文人名进行音译，因为他是韩国人，Park 是他的姓，要译为"朴"。

（2）在英文中，"the matter" 和 "in particular with regard to the relevance of..." 是紧密相连的，翻译稿的处理有隔断之嫌，况且"特别是关于……相关性"的说法也有不完整之感。解决办法有两个：一是审校稿的处理；二是增译为"特别是对……相关性的看法"。

3. 第四句，翻译稿把 "the implications for States of any decision to apply a treaty provisionally" 理解成了 "the implications for States' decision to apply a treaty provisionally"，显然不当；英文的意思是说 "the implications of any decision to apply a treaty provisionally" "for States"，但这样写不合英语惯例。

另外，还需要特别注意，"implication" 在联合国文件中常用，所用义项就是 "a possible future effect or result of an action, event, decision etc.（行动、事件、决定等的）可能的影响"，详见《朗文当代高级英语辞典》。

联合国文件有一些特定的译法，最好照用，如 "humanitarian implications"（所涉人道主义问题）、"financial implications"（所涉经费问题）、"administrative implications"（所涉行政问题）、"programme budget implication"（所涉方案预算问题）等。

第 2 段

As to the source of obligations, the Special Rapporteur's identification of at least four types of situations in which provisional application could result from an agreement was helpful. With regard to the last of the situations mentioned, namely that of a treaty that said absolutely nothing about provisional application, he said that it should be analysed in the light of the requirement set out in article 25, paragraph 1, of the 1969 Vienna Convention that the negotiating States must have agreed to apply a treaty provisionally. That analysis was called for in view of the Special Rapporteur's assertion that, in certain cases, the decision of a State to apply a treaty provisionally was an autonomous unilateral act, governed only by the intentions of the State in question.

批 注

① 看错字。
② 稍显口语化。
③ 误看成另一个词。
④ 不搭配。

关于立法的①来源，特别报告员确定暂时适用可源于协定的至少四种情形，这非常有益。关于提到的最后一种情形，即一份条约绝口②不提暂时适用的情形，他说，应当根据 1969 年《维也纳公约》第二十五条第 1 款中确定的要求，即谈判国必须同意了暂时适用一份条约来进行分析。要求采取这种分析是考虑到特别报告员认为，在某些情况下，一个国家暂时适用一份条约的决定是一项一致③的单边行为，只受所述国家的意图管辖④。

关于义务的来源，特别报告员确定暂时适用可源于协定的至少四种情形，这非常有益。关于所述最后一种情形，即一份条约只字不提暂时适用的情形，他说，应当根据 1969 年《维也纳公约》第 25 条第 1 款中确定的要求，即谈判国必须已同意了暂时适用一份条约来进行分析。之所以要求做这种分析，是因为特别报告员认为，在某些情况下，一个国家暂时适用一份条约的决定是一项自主的单方面行为，只受有关国家的意图支配。

1. 把"obligations"（义务）误看成了"legislation"（立法）。

2. 把"said absolutely nothing about..."译为"绝口不提"很好，不过稍显口语化，译为"绝对只字不提"，更书面化。从中文表达出发，"绝对"也可以省略，"只字不提"就是"绝口不提"。

3. 最后一句有两个不足，一是把"autonomous"（自动的、自主的）误看作"unanimous"（一致）；二是把"govern"译为"管辖"，与中文"意图"不搭配。

补充练习

Since it was a well-accepted proposition that the provisional application of treaties produced binding legal effects, the Special Rapporteur should focus his efforts in future reports on situations of uncertainty surrounding those legal effects. The two conditions set out in Article 25 of the Vienna Convention could be interpreted as meaning that when a State made a unilateral decision to provisionally apply a treaty, and when such application was not provided for in the treaty itself, the other States parties had to agree to its unilateral undertaking. Yet the excerpt concerning unilateral declarations from the judgment of the International Court of Justice in the *Nuclear Tests (Australia v. France)* case, which was reproduced in paragraph 37 of the report, indicated that no subsequent acceptance of the unilateral declaration by other States was required. If that interpretation applied to a unilateral declaration of the provisional application of a treaty, then the Special Rapporteur should clarify how it could be reconciled with the two possibilities envisaged in Article 25 of the Vienna Convention. Similarly, the relationship or distinction between a unilateral undertaking and a provisional application of a treaty should also be clarified.

既然条约的暂时适用产生具有约束力的法律效力是广为接受的主张，特别报告员就应在今后的报告里集中精力探讨围绕着这些法律效力的不确定性情形。《维也纳公约》第25条中确立的两种情形可解释为，当一国单方决定暂时适用一项条约，而且当这类适用在条约本身并未做出规定时，其他缔约方必须同意其单方面承诺。报告第37段转载的有关单方面声明的摘录，出自国际法院在核试验（澳大利亚诉法国）案中的判决；摘录指出，不需要其他国家随后接受单方面声明。如果这种解释适用于一份条约暂时适用的单方面声明，那么特别报告员应说明它如何与《维也纳公约》第25条中设想的两种可能协调起来。同样，一份条约的单方承诺和暂时适用之间的关系或区别，也应当予以说明。

背景介绍

世界知识产权组织（以下简称产权组织）是联合国的一个专门机构，1967年根据《世界知识产权组织公约》设立，总部设在瑞士日内瓦。产权组织是一个知识产权服务、政策、信息与合作的全球论坛，旨在领导发展一个平衡有效的国际知识产权体系，促进创新创造，造福万众。以下第六篇至第十篇材料选自知识产权组织专门文件《当国际私法遇到知识产权法——法官指南》。国际私法涉及跨越国界的私人当事方之间的关系，而知识产权在主权领土范围内保护技术、外观设计、品牌、文学艺术作品等知识财产。全球化促使知识财产超出国界，走向全球，单靠知识产权已经无法解决相关法律问题，这就需要借助国际私法。

《指南》由法官撰写，供法官使用，语言简明，实例丰富，重点介绍了这一复杂领域的主要问题，旨在协助许多不同国家的法官和律师做出知情决定。

第六篇

Private international law, which concerns relations between private parties across national borders, becomes more relevant when facing the challenges unearthed by the heightened mobility of intellectual property and the globalized nature of commercial dealings. This intersection between intellectual property and private international law has naturally drawn considerable academic and judicial attention, as it raises important questions as to which court has jurisdiction to adjudicate cross-border disputes on intellectual property, which law is to be applied, and whether foreign intellectual property-related judgments can be recognized and enforced.

As international organizations concerned, respectively, with private international law and intellectual property, the Hague Conference on Private International Law and the World Intellectual Property Organization jointly recognized the need to address the intersection of private international law and intellectual property. The product of our partnership is this Guide, intended as a practical means of supporting the work of judges and lawyers around the world.

This Guide benefited greatly from external reviews of the draft text by Professor Pedro de Miguel Asensio, Complutense University of Madrid; Professor Marcelo De Nardi, Unisinos University; Professor Toshiyuki Kono, Kyushu University; Professor Axel Metzger, Humboldt University; and Professor Marketa Trimble, University of Nevada.

请自行翻译后查看后文的分析点评

分析点评

第 1 段

Private international law, which concerns relations between private parties across national borders, becomes more relevant when facing the challenges unearthed by the heightened mobility of intellectual property and the globalized nature of commercial dealings. This intersection between intellectual property and private international law has naturally drawn considerable academic and judicial attention, as it raises important questions as to which court has jurisdiction to adjudicate cross-border disputes on intellectual property, which law is to be applied, and whether foreign intellectual property-related judgments can be recognized and enforced.

国际私法涉及跨国私人当事方①之间的关系，面对知识产权流动性增强和商业交易全球化带来的挑战，国际私法②变得更加重要。知识产权和国际私法之间的这种交叉自然引起了学术界和司法界的极大关注，因为它提出了一些重要问题，如③哪个法院有权裁决关于知识产权的跨国界争端，将适用哪部法律，以及外国知识产权相关判决是否能够得到承认和执行。

批 注

① 处理得当。
② 重复主语也可以。
③ 短语理解不准确。

国际私法涉及跨越国界的私人当事方之间的关系，在面对知识产权流动性增强和商业交易全球化带来的挑战时，变得更加重要。知识产权和国际私法之间的这种交集自然引起了学术界和司法界相当大的关注，因为它提出了一些重要问题，涉及哪个法院有权裁决知识产权跨境争议，哪种法律适用，外国知识产权相关判决是否能够得到承认和执行。

1. 本段所用专门术语：

（1）private international law：《元照英美法词典》称它等同于"international private law"，一般译为"国际私法"；也有个别法律词典将其译为"私国际法"。本文采用通行的译法。

（2）private party：私人当事方。

（3）intellectual property：知识产权。

（4）dispute：有"争议、争端、纠纷"等多种译法，本段根据产权组织 alternative dispute resolution（ADR）（替代性争议解决）机制，译为"争议"。

2.（1）在第 1 句中，"which"引导一个非限制性定语从句，译文省去关系代词"which"，直接把定语译为谓语。这样处理，文从字顺，简明扼要。

（2）译文省去"when"而重复一次主语，这种处理方法没有问题，但句子标点可相应地改为"国际私法……关系；面对知识产权流动性增强和商业交易全球化带来的挑战，国际法变得更加重要"。

（3）"unearth"在此使用引申义"2: to make known or public: bring to light"（《韦氏大学英语词典》），中文译为"带来"。

（4）"heightened mobility of intellectual property"本是名词词组，直译就是"知识产权被增强的流动（性）"，中文译为"知识产权流动性增强"更自然。

（5）"globalized nature of commercial dealings"也是名词词组，直译就是"商业交易的全球化性质"，中文译为"商业交易全球化"，省去了"nature"更自然，使"全球化"与"增强"并列。

3.（1）第 2 句中的"drawn considerable academic and judicial attention"没有字对字地直译，而译为"引起了学术界和司法界的极大关注"，这样更自然。只是"considerable"译为"极大"不恰当。

（2）"it raises important questions as to..."，介词"as to"引导三个宾语，常规译法是"因为它就哪个法院有权裁决知识产权跨境争议，哪种法律适用，外国知识产权相关判决是否能够得到承认和执行提出了重要问题"。

译文另辟蹊径，处理得很精彩，把"as to"译为"如"，虽不准确，却基本保证了全句的意思，行文更自然。审校稿将"as to"译为"涉及"，很准确，行文也一样顺畅。

第 2 段

As international organizations concerned, respectively, with private international law and intellectual property, the Hague Conference on Private International Law and the World Intellectual Property Organization jointly recognized the need to address the intersection of private international law and intellectual property. The product of our partnership is this Guide, intended as a practical means of supporting the work of judges and lawyers around the world.

作为分别与国际私法和知识产权有关的国际组织①，海牙国际私法会议和世界知识产权组织共同认识到需要解决国际私法和知识产权的交叉问题。我们合作的成果是本指南②，旨在作为支持世界各地法官和律师工作的实用手段。

批 注

① 过于拘泥原文语法结构。
② 如调整语序，效果会更好。

海牙国际私法会议和世界知识产权组织作为国际组织，分别涉及国际私法和知识产权，它们共同认识到有必要解决国际私法和知识产权的交集问题。本指南就是我们彼此合作的成果，旨在以此方式实际支持世界各地法官和律师的工作。

1. 第1句的译文是常规译法，并没有错误。以介词"as"引导长长的名词词组放在句首，然后再给出主语，这种结构在英语里很自然，译为中文则以将主语放在句首为佳。

2. 第2句，原译并不错，但"intended..."为定语，是修饰"guide"的，在译文按语法来讲，就成了修饰"product"的。中文也有这样的句式，只是理解起来要费点脑筋。改译后，就消除了这个问题，再把定语转译为谓语，非常自然。

第3段

This Guide benefited greatly from external reviews of the draft text by Professor Pedro de Miguel Asensio, Complutense University of Madrid; Professor Marcelo De Nardi, Unisinos University; Professor Toshiyuki Kono, Kyushu University; Professor Axel Metzger, Humboldt University; and Professor Marketa Trimble, University of Nevada.

本指南极大地受益于③ 马德里康普顿斯大学的 Pedro de Miguel Asseno 教授、（巴西）乌尼西索斯大学的 Marcelo de Nardi 教授、九州大学的 Toshiyuki Kono 教授、洪堡大学的 Axel Metzger 教授和内华达大学的 Marketa Trimble 教授对指南草案的外部审查。

批 注

③ 过分拘泥于英文表达，可译得更地道一点。

本《指南》承蒙马德里康普顿斯大学的 Pedro de Miguel Asseno 教授、（巴西）乌尼西索斯大学的 Marcelo de Nardi 教授、九州大学的 Toshiyuki Kono 教授、洪堡大学的 Axel Metzger 教授和内华达大学的 Marketa Trimble 教授对本《指南》

草案的外部审查，受益匪浅。

此段就一句话，结构极简单，原译也属常规译法，勉强可以接受。"benefited greatly from something"译为"极大受益于……"没问题，但按照中文地道的说法，至少也应当译为"承蒙……，受益匪浅"。

There are also non-binding instruments dealing with IP and PIL, for example, the 2015 HCCH Principles on Choice of Law in International Commercial Contracts (HCCH Principles). The Principles provide a comprehensive blueprint to guide users in creating, reforming or interpreting choice of law regimes at the national, regional or international level. They endorse party autonomy by giving practical effect to the choice made by parties to a commercial transaction as to the law governing their contractual relationships. They are relevant to international contracts concerning IP rights, such as IP licensing contracts and IP transfer contracts, which often contain the parties' choice of applicable law.

参考译文

还有一些不具约束力的文书涉及知识产权和国际私法，例如，《2015年海牙国际私法会议国际商业合同法律选择原则》(《海牙国际私法会议原则》，以下简称《原则》)。《原则》提供了一个全面的蓝图，以指导用户在国家、区域或国际各级创建、改革或解释法律选择制度。它们认可当事人意思自治，赋予商业交易当事人就管辖其合同关系的法律所做的选择以实际效力。它们涉及与知识产权权利有关的国际合同，如知识产权许可合同和知识产权转让合同，这些合同通常包含当事方对适用法律的选择。

This Guide is a pragmatic tool, written by judges, for judges. Experts who specialize in one of the two fields of law will gain a reliable overview of how these fields intertwine. The Guide does not claim to offer an exhaustive treatment of the law in all areas, but rather elucidate the operation of private international law in intellectual property matters with illustrative references to selected international and regional instruments and national laws. It is our hope that readers will be better placed to apply the laws of their own jurisdiction, supported by an awareness of key issues concerning jurisdiction of the courts, applicable law, the recognition and enforcement of judgments, and judicial cooperation in cross-border intellectual property disputes.

The Guide should be considered as a stepping-stone that will help judges and lawyers when they are resolving cross-border IP law issues. It does not advocate any particular approach to substantive issues of law or provide any solutions in individual cases; rather, by highlighting the main issues in this complex area, it aims to assist judges and lawyers in many different States to make informed decisions.

Parties may resort to different dispute resolution mechanisms, including court adjudication, IP administrative procedures and alternative dispute resolution (ADR) procedures such as arbitration, mediation and conciliation. If a dispute is brought before a court, and parties, IP rights or activities based in foreign States are involved, this may raise PIL issues, such as contested views as to the competence of the court, the law applicable to the dispute, and the recognition and enforcement of foreign judgments. The manner in which these issues are addressed by courts in cross-border IP disputes can contribute to enhanced IP enforcement, improve the predictability and finality of court proceedings, avoid concerns about redundant or inadequate liability, preserve the public resources of the courts as well as the private resources of the parties, and ultimately facilitate the sound administration of justice.

请自行翻译后查看后文的分析点评

第1段

This Guide is a pragmatic tool, written by judges, for judges. Experts who specialize in one of the two fields of law will gain a reliable overview of how these fields intertwine. The Guide does not claim to offer an exhaustive treatment of the law in all areas, but rather elucidate the operation of private international law in intellectual property matters with illustrative references to selected international and regional instruments and national laws. It is our hope that readers will be better placed to apply the laws of their own jurisdiction, supported by an awareness of key issues concerning jurisdiction of the courts, applicable law, the recognition and enforcement of judgments, and judicial cooperation in cross-border intellectual property disputes.

① 可略去不译。

翻译稿

本指南是法官为法官编写的实用工具。专攻① 这两个法律领域之一的专家将获得关于这些领域如何相互交织的可靠概述。《指南》并未声称对所有领域的法律都进行了详尽的论述，而是阐明了国际私法在知识产权事务中的运作，并举例说明了某些国际和区域文书及国家法律①。我们希望读者能够更好地适用自己管辖范围内的法律，同时了解有关法院管辖权、适用法律、判决的承认和执行以及跨境知识产权纠纷司法合作等关键问题。

批　注

① 此句有两处可以商榷。

本指南是一种实用工具，由法官撰写，供法官使用。这两个法律领域之一的专家将获得关于这些领域如何相互交织的可靠概述。指南并未自诩详尽论述了所有领域的法律，却阐明了国际私法在知识产权事务中的运作情况，还引用某些国际和区域文书及国家法律加以具体说明。我们希望读者能够更好地适用其本法域的法律，同时了解有关法院管辖权、适用法律、判决的承认和执行及解决跨境知识产权争议司法合作等关键问题。

1. 原文第 2 句，"Experts who specialize in one of the two fields of law"的核心意义是"Experts in one of the two fields of law"。某领域专家，当然是专门从事某个领域研究的人，即专攻某一领域的人，翻译时再强调"专攻"（specialize in）一词，就没有必要了。要注意的是，英文使用"specialize in"是出于语法上的要求，并非语义上的必然。

2. 第 3 句，译文有两点值得注意。

（1）"exhaustive treatment"，与其译为"对……进行详尽论述"，不如简单译为"详尽论述……"。

（2）"with illustrative references to selected international and regional instruments"是介词短语作状语，修饰"elucidate"。译文改为句子更符合中文习惯。"illustrative references"直译就是"说明性的引用"，译为"引用……具体加以说明"更流畅。"selected"的字面意思是"被选择的"，也就是说不是全部的，所以译为"某些"意思不错；当然，译为"部分"也可以。

3. 第 4 句

（1）"be better placed to"是成语，意思是"能更好地做某事"，后接不定式。在《牛津英汉高级双解词典》中，be well, ideally, uniquely, better, etc. placed for sth/to do sth 被解释为"to be in a good, very good, etc. position or have a good, etc. opportunity to do sth 有良好的（或理想的、独特的等）机遇；处于有利等的位置"。

（2）"supported by..."是过去分词短语作补语，很长，如果译为"得到……支持""在……支持下"或"以……为支持"，都难免行文冗长，改译为"同时还要"，既译出了"support"的意思，又很地道。

（3）专门术语①"jurisdiction"，本句两次使用，第一个是指"管辖区域、管辖范围"，最新的译法为"法域"；第二个是指"管辖权，审判权"。

② "applicable law"，《英汉法律词典》的解释是"可适用的法律；（国际私

法）准据法，法律适用法"，本《指南》涉及知识产权与国际私法交集问题，所以采用"准据法"。

第 2 段

The Guide should be considered as a stepping-stone that will help judges and lawyers when they are resolving cross-border IP law issues. It does not advocate any particular approach to substantive issues of law or provide any solutions in individual cases; rather, by highlighting the main issues in this complex area, it aims to assist judges and lawyers in many different States to make informed decisions.

批 注

① 常规译法。
② 参见表示方式的介词"by"就译为"通过……"，未免英文腔调过重。

翻 译 稿

该指南应被视为在法官和律师解决跨国知识产权法问题时有所帮助的垫脚石。它不主张对法律的实质性问题采取任何特定的办法，也不在个别案件中提供任何解决办法；相反，通过强调这一复杂领域的主要问题，它旨在协助许多不同国家的法官和律师做出知情的决定。

审 校 稿

《指南》应当用作一种得力工具，帮助法官和律师解决跨境知识产权法问题。它既未针对法律的实质性问题倡导任何特定的办法，也未就个体案件提供任何解决办法；相反，它突出了这一复杂领域的主要问题，旨在协助许多不同国家的法官和律师做出知情决定。

点 评

1. 第 1 句，原译并不错，不过也可以有其他处理方法。①"stepping stone"在此处用的是引申意义，"a means of progress or advancement"（《韦氏大学英语词典》）或者"something that allows you to make progress or begin to achieve sth"（《牛津高阶英汉双解词典》），中文不妨译为"顺手工具、得力工具"。②"help judges and lawyers when they are resolving cross-border IP law issues"，"在法官和律师解决跨国知识产权法问题时帮助他们"，是死扣字面的常规译法，实际意思就是帮助他们解决问题。

2. 第 2 句："...by highlighting the main issues in this complex area, it aims to assist judges..."，可以把主语提前，从而略去介词"by"，会译得更加自然。

第 3 段

Parties may resort to different dispute resolution mechanisms, including court adjudication, IP administrative procedures and alternative dispute resolution (ADR) procedures such as arbitration, mediation and conciliation. If a dispute is brought before a court, and parties, IP rights or activities based in foreign States are involved, this may raise PIL issues, such as contested views as to the competence of the court, the law applicable to the dispute, and the recognition and enforcement of foreign judgments. The manner in which these issues are addressed by courts in cross-border IP disputes can contribute to enhanced IP enforcement, improve the predictability and finality of court proceedings, avoid concerns about redundant or inadequate liability, preserve the public resources of the courts as well as the private resources of the parties, and ultimately facilitate the sound administration of justice.

各方可以诉诸不同的争端解决机制，包括法院裁决、知识产权行政程序和替代争端解决程序①，如仲裁、调解和和解。如果争端提交法院，涉及当事方、知识产权或在外国②的活动，这可能会引起 PIL 问题，例如对法院权限、适用于争端的法律以及承认和执行外国判决的争议性意见。法院在跨国知识产权纠纷③ 中处理这些问题的方式有助于加强知识产权执法，提高法院诉讼程序的可预测性和终结性，避免对冗余或不充分赔偿责任的担忧，保护法院的公共资源和当事人的私人资源，并最终促进良好的司法管理④。

批 注

① 术语翻译不专业。
② 有不当省略。
③ 术语翻译不专业。
④ 译法可商。

各方可以诉诸不同的争议解决机制，包括法院裁判、知识产权行政程序和替代性争议解决（ADR），如仲裁、调解和和解。如果争议提交法院，涉及当事方、知识产权或以外国为基地开展的活动，这可能会引起国际私法问题，例如对法院权限、争议的适用法律及承认和执行外国判决产生有争议性的意见。法院在跨境知识产权争议中处理这些问题的方式有助于加强知识产权执法，提高法院诉讼程序的可预测性和终结性，免得担心赔偿责任过大或不足，保护法院的公共资源和当事人的私人资源，并最终促进司法的健全。

1. 这段文字，法律术语特别多，dispute resolution mechanisms（一般译为"争端解决机制"，这里为照应产权组织的惯例，译为"争议解决机制"）、court adjudication（法院裁判）、arbitration（仲裁）、mediation（调解）、conciliation（和解）、competence (of the court)（权限，指法院处理特殊事务的权力，有时可与 jurisdiction（管辖权）同义，见《英汉法律用语词典》)译得都很准确，很专业。但 alternative dispute resolution (ADR)，按照产权组织的固定译法应当是"替代性争议解决（ADR）"，不译为"替代争端解决"。PIL 是简称，全称为 private international law，因中文没相应的简称，只好使用全称"国际私法"。

2. activities based in foreign States：以不省略"based"，译为"以外国为基地开展的活动"为好。

3. cross-border IP disputes："跨境知识产权争议"。"dispute"有"纠纷"的译法，本文统一译为"争议"。

4. administration of justice，《英汉双解法律词典》的解释是"providing justice"，即"司法、执法"，而不是"司法管理"。动词是"administer justice"，也就是 to provide justice，司法，执法。

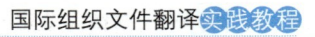

OAPI rights, while deriving from a uniform administrative system, are enforced in national civil and criminal courts which apply the legislation of each of the Member States in which they have effect. For patents, the Bangui Agreement specifies jurisdiction, stating that the owner of the patent has the right to institute legal proceedings before the court of the place of the infringement.

OAPI① 权利虽然源于统一的行政管理制度，但在国家民事和刑事法院强制执行，这些法院适用 OAPI 权利生效的各成员国的立法。对于专利，《班吉协定》明确规定了管辖权，指出专利所有人有权向侵权地法院提起法律诉讼。

第八篇

Party A owns the copyright in a film script in States X and Y. In State Z, the term of copyright protection has expired and the work is in the public domain. Party B, resident in State Z, distributes the film through the Internet via a server in State Z, making it accessible worldwide, including in States X and Y. Party A initiates proceedings in State X, where it is resident and where it owns a valid copyright, and claims damages for infringement in States X, Y and Z.

For example, while European patents under the EPC are enforced at the national level, a Unitary Patent Protection (UPP) system, building on the EPC through EU Regulations 1257/2012 and 1260/2012, will make it possible to acquire unitary effect for a European patent in up to 25 EU Member States (i.e. those which have so far signed the Agreement on a Unified Patent Court (UPC)). This Agreement establishes a court system consisting of a Court of First Instance, a Court of Appeal and a Registry which are separate from national court systems. The UPC will, as a general rule, have exclusive competence in civil litigation on matters related to European patents with unitary effect, classical European patents, supplementary protection certificates issued for a product covered by such a patent, and European patent applications.

请自行翻译后查看后文的分析点评

---

① OAPI = African Intellectual Property Organization，非洲知识产权组织。

分析点评

第 1 段

Party A owns the copyright in a film script in States X and Y. In State Z, the term of copyright protection has expired and the work is in the public domain. Party B, resident in State Z, distributes the film through the Internet via a server in State Z, making it accessible worldwide, including in States X and Y. Party A initiates proceedings in State X, where it is resident and where it owns a valid copyright, and claims damages for infringement in States X, Y and Z.

甲方在 X 和 Y 国拥有电影剧本的版权。在 Z 国，版权保护期已经届满，作品属于公有领域。B 方①，居住在 Z 国，通过 Z 国的服务器通过② 互联网发行影片，使其在世界各地都可以访问，包括在 X 和 Y 国。甲方在 X 国提起诉讼，在 X 国，在那里它拥有有效的版权，并在 X、Y 和 Z 国要求侵权损害赔偿。

甲方在 X 和 Y 国拥有电影剧本的版权。在 Z 国，版权保护期限已过，作品属于公共领域。居住在 Z 国的乙方通过 Z 国的服务器在互联网上分发该电影，使世界各地，包括 X 和 Y 国，都可以观看该影片。甲方在 X 国提起诉讼，它是 X 国居民，在 X 国拥有有效版权，并在 X、Y 和 Z 国要求侵权损害赔偿。

批 注

① 译法不一致。
② 同一句中两次使用"通过"，太单调乏味。

点评

1. Party B：翻译，尤其是专业材料翻译，要保持用语统一。前面把"Party A"译为"甲方"，"Party B"就应当相应地译为"乙方"。如想保留"B 方"，最好把"Party A"译为"A 方"。

2. 第 3 句"Party B, resident in State Z...including in States X and Y"，① 英文使用了"through"和"via"，二者均表示手段或方式，原译紧跟英文译出两个"通过"，意思不错，但行文不美，需要适当变通；② 把 it 还原为所代名词很自然。英文多用代词，中文用得少，所以有时把代词还原成所代的名词会更地道。

3. 第 4 句"Party A initiates proceedings in State X,...infringement in States X, Y and Z"，把 where 还原为所代名词"State X"，会更清楚，更自然。

第 2 段

For example, while European patents under the EPC are enforced at the national level, a Unitary Patent Protection (UPP) system, building on the EPC through EU Regulations 1257/2012 and 1260/2012, will make it possible to acquire unitary effect for a European patent in up to 25 EU Member States (i.e. those which have so far signed the Agreement on a Unified Patent Court (UPC)). This Agreement establishes a court system consisting of a Court of First Instance, a Court of Appeal and a Registry which are separate from national court systems. The UPC will, as a general rule, have exclusive competence in civil litigation on matters related to European patents with unitary effect, classical European patents, supplementary protection certificates issued for a product covered by such a patent, and European patent applications.

例如，虽然《欧洲专利公约》下的欧洲专利是在国家一级实施的，但通过欧盟第 1257/2012 号和第 1260/2012 号条例建立在《欧洲专利公约》基础上的单一专利保护（UPP）制度，将使欧洲专利在多达 25 个欧盟成员国（即迄今已签署《统一专利法院协定》）获得单一效力成为可能。该协议建立了一个法院系统，由独立于国家法院系统的一审法院、上诉法院和书记官处组成。一般而言，统一产品委员会①将在与具有统一效力的欧洲专利、经典欧洲专利、为该专利所涵盖的产品颁发的补充保护证书②以及欧洲专利申请有关的事项上拥有民事诉讼的专属权限。

批 注

① 当属打字错误，正确译法是"统一专利法院"。
② 太拘泥于英文。

例如，虽然《欧洲专利公约》下的欧洲专利是在国家一级实施的，但基于《欧洲专利公约》的统一专利保护（UPP）制度，通过欧盟第 1257/2012 号和第 1260/2012 号条例，将使一项欧洲专利在多达 25 个欧盟成员国（即迄今已签署《统一专利法院（UPC）协定》的欧盟成员国）获得统一效力成为可能。该协定建立了一个法院系统，由独立于国家法院系统的一审法院、上诉法院和书记官处组成。一般而言，统一专利法院将拥有民事诉讼的专属管辖权，审理涉及具有统一效力的欧洲专利、经典欧洲专利、为此类专利所涵盖产品颁发的补充保护证书以及欧洲专利申请的问题。

点 评

1. 第 1 句 "...while European patents under the EPC are enforced at the national level, a Unitary Patent Protection (UPP) system,...will make it possible...", 有两点需要注意。

（1）EPC = European Patent Convention，《欧洲专利公约》。

（2）"enforce" 用于专利时的专业译法就是"实施"；在其他语境则可以灵活运用，如：~ a law（实施法律）/ ~ discipline（执行纪律）。

2. 第 2 句 "This Agreement establishes a court system consisting of a Court of First Instance...", 有四点需要注意。

（1）"agreement" 虽然在国内的合同中多译为"协议"，但在联合国文件中通常译为"协定"。译者前面把 "the Agreement on a Unified Patent Court" 译为《统一专利法院（UPC）协定》，原文中出现的 "This Agreement" 即指该《协定》，却译为"协议"，既不统一，也有失严谨。

（2）"Court of First Instance" 译为"一审法院"。注意，此处的 "instance" 不是在 "for instance" 中所用的义项，而是"审级"的意思（《元照英美法词典》），例如，"instance (or level) of court"（法院审级），"first instance"（初审、一审），"second instance"（二审）。

（3）"Registry"：书记官处（国际法院），见《英汉法律词典》。

（4）"consist of" 通常译为"由……组成"，此处也可译为"设有"。

3. 最后一句 "The UPC will, as a general rule, have exclusive competence in civil litigation on matters related to...European patent applications"，句子较长，比较复杂，要译好必须恰当处理介词。

（1）先从 "civil litigation" 断句，将句子的前一部分译为"统一专利法院将拥有民事诉讼的专属管辖权"，把握住主要意思。

（2）联系法院的职能及其 "exclusive competence"（"专属权限"，此处实指"专属管辖权"）来理解 "on matters related to" 中的介词 "on"："在……方面"的专属管辖权或专属裁判权，实际上就是有专门的权力审判什么事，所以可译为动词"审理"。这样，既能打破英文句法的束缚，又符合中文多用动词的习惯。

Parties A and B, resident in States X and Y respectively, enter into a license agreement regarding the distribution of the goods produced using a technology patented by Party A in States X and Y. The license is governed by the law of State X. A dispute over an alleged breach of the license arises and Party A initiates a court proceeding in State X, where it is habitually resident. Instead of, or as well as, bringing claims under the licensing agreement, Party A claims patent infringement by Party B in States X and Y. Party B counterclaims that Party A's patents in both States are invalid.

甲、乙双方分别居住在 X 国和 Y 国，就分销使用甲方在 X 国和 Y 国获得专利的技术生产的货物达成许可协议。许可受 X 国法律管辖。因指控违反许可而产生争议，甲方将在其惯常居住地 X 国提起法院诉讼。甲方不根据许可协议提出索赔，或根据许可协议提出索赔，均声称乙方在 X 国和 Y 国侵犯专利。乙方反诉，称甲方在这两个国家的专利无效。

In most cases, IP rights are obtained through national processes in each country for which protection is sought, and as seen above, these national rights are mutually independent. Some IP rights, however, come into existence through international or regional IP instruments that facilitate protection across borders or that grant IP rights transcending borders. These instruments either result in the obtainment of a bundle of national and regional territorial rights through a single international or regional application, or grant unitary, "supranational" rights through one registration.

A common approach is that the court of the State in which the defendant is domiciled will have jurisdiction over that defendant, including with respect to facts occurring outside that State. PIL questions frequently require determination of a party's "domicile", "residence" or "habitual residence", which essentially focuses on a person's "principal home". The question of where a person is "at home" is generally determined according to the law of the State in which the action is brought (*lex fori*). For example, Brussels I*a* Regulation Article 4 confers "general jurisdiction" to the courts of the Member State where the defendant is domiciled, which will have jurisdiction to grant remedies in all relevant territories including for the harm outside the forum. In Australia, this is a connecting factor; see part Ⅲ.C.2 below.

请自行翻译后查看后文的分析点评

分析点评

第 1 段

In most cases, IP rights are obtained through national processes in each country for which protection is sought, and as seen above, these national rights are mutually independent. Some IP rights, however, come into existence through international or regional IP instruments that facilitate protection across borders or that grant IP rights transcending borders. These instruments either result in the obtainment of a bundle of national and regional territorial rights through a single international or regional application, or grant unitary, "supranational" rights through one registration.

 翻译稿

在大多数情况下，知识产权①是通过每个寻求保护的国家的国家程序②获得的，如上所述，这些国家的权利是相互独立的。然而，一些知识产权是通过国际或区域知识产权文书产生的，这些文书促进了跨国界的保护，或者授予了超越国界的知识产权。这些文书要么通过单一的国际或区域申请获得一系列国家和区域领土③权利，要么通过一次登记授予单一的"超国家"权利。

批 注
① 术语翻译不准确。
② 译文拘泥于原文，有点晦涩。
③ 专门术语理解错误。

 审校稿

在大多数情况下，知识产权权利是寻求每个国家的保护，通过其国家程序获

得的;如上所述,这些国家赋予的权利都是相互独立的。然而,有些知识产权权利是通过国际或区域知识产权文书产生的,这些文书促进跨境保护,或者授予超越国境的知识产权权利。这些文书要么通过单一的国际或区域申请获得一系列国家和区域的地域性权利,要么通过一次注册授予单一的"超国家"权利。

1. 第 1 句 "In most cases, IP rights are obtained through national processes in each country for which protection is sought...",如照英文结构译出,如翻译稿那样,难免晦涩;可以先把"in each country for which protection is sought"译为谓语,"寻求每个国家的保护",再把英文的真正谓语译为"通过其国家程序获得的",就明白易懂了,也完整传达原文的意思。

另外,专门术语"IP rights"中的 IP 是"intellectual property"的缩写,通常译为"知识产权","IP rights"译为"知识产权权利"。

2. 第 2 句 "Some IP rights...come into existence through international or regional IP instruments that facilitate protection across borders or that grant IP rights transcending borders",大致有两种翻译方式。

(1)照英文语法结构,译为一句。

"然而,有些知识产权是通过促进了跨境保护或授予超越国界的知识产权的国际或区域知识产权文书产生的。"

(2)如翻译稿或审校稿那样,在"instruments"后断开,因关系代词 That = international or regional IP instruments,可以把它还原为"these instruments",把整个定语从句单译为一句。

3. 第 3 句 "These instruments either result in the obtainment of a bundle of national and regional territorial rights...",有两点需要注意。

(1)因为上一句把"that"译为了"these instruments",所以为了行文简洁,此句可与上句并为一句,省去主语"these instruments"不译,直接译谓语部分;当然,本句也可以像原文一样,单独成句。

(2) territorial rights:地域性权利。版权是自动获得的权利,无须申请;知识产权权利则需要申请、授予,而且在非授权国家或地域不受保护,所以是"territorial",是"地域性的",也就是说是有地理范围的。

第 2 段

A common approach is that the court of the State in which the defendant is domiciled will have jurisdiction over that defendant, including with respect to facts occurring outside that State. PIL questions frequently require determination of a party's "domicile" "residence" or "habitual residence", which essentially focuses on a person's "principal home". The question of where a person is "at home" is generally determined according to the law of the State in which the action is brought (*lex fori*). For example, Brussels I*a* Regulation Article 4 confers "general jurisdiction" to the courts of the Member State where the defendant is domiciled, which will have jurisdiction to grant remedies in all relevant territories including for the harm outside the forum. In Australia, this is a connecting factor; see part Ⅲ.C.2 below.

批 注

① 术语错译。
② 未译。
③ 译名错误。

 翻译稿

一种常见的做法是，被告所在国的法院将对该被告拥有管辖权，包括对发生在该国以外的事实的管辖权。PIL 问题经常需要确定当事人的"住所""住所"或"惯常住所"①，主要集中在一个人的"主要住所"。一个人哪里"是家"的问题一般是根据提起诉讼的国家的法律确定的（Fori 法②）。例如，布鲁塞尔 Ia 条例③第 4 条授予被告居住地成员国的法院"一般管辖权"，该法院将有管辖权在所有相关领土内给予补救，包括对法院以外的损害给予补救。

在澳大利亚，这是一个连接因素；见下文第Ⅲ.C.2 部分。

 审校稿

通常做法是，被告居住国的法院将对被告拥有管辖权，包括对发生在该国以外的事实拥有管辖权。国际私法问题经常需要确定当事人的"住所""居所"或"惯常居所"，本质上都侧重一个人的"主要寓所"。一个人哪里"是家"的问题一般是根据起诉地国家的法律（法院地法）确定。例如，《布鲁塞尔条例 Ia》第 4 条授予被告常住地成员国的法院"一般管辖权"，该法院将有管辖权在所有相关领土内给予补救，包括对诉讼地以外的损害给予补救。在澳大利亚，这是一个连接因素；见下文第三部分 C.2。

 点评

此段术语很多，不熟悉相关知识的人难免出错。

（1）domicile：住所，不要与"residence"混淆。

（2）residence：居所。

（3）habitual residence：常居地，惯常居所。

（4）*lex fori*：是拉丁语，即 law of the forum; lex ordinandi, 意思是"法院地法；诉讼地法；审判地法"。详见《元照英美法词典》和《英汉法律词典》。此处的"*lex fori*"就是指"the law of the State in which the action is brought"。译者不懂，也没有广泛查阅专业词典，所以错译为"Fori 法"。

（5）"the action is brought" 中的"action" 使用的是法律专门意义，即"诉讼"。

（6）Brussels I*a* Regulation：《布鲁塞尔条例 I*a*》。

（7）general jurisdiction：普通管辖权，一般管辖权。

（8）remedies：补救（措施），国际法中也常译为"救济"。但"principal home"不是法律术语。

补充练习

In a dispute as to whether a work is copyright protectable, the parties have reached an agreement on the applicable law. After identifying the legal question (i.e., is the work protectable?) and characterizing the legal question (as one pertaining to copyright law), the court will apply the choice of law rules in order to decide the validity of the choice of law agreement. Here, this could be the law of the creator's "principal home" (which could be the creator's "domicile" "residence" or "habitual residence"). If this law prohibits parties from agreeing a different applicable law, the court should hold the choice of law agreement invalid. (Note that the court may already have decided this issue when considering the overriding mandatory rules.) If the law of the creator's "principal home" does not prescribe that its law must apply, parties may agree on a different set of rules and their choice of law agreement will be valid.

在关于某一作品是否可受版权保护的争议当中，当事方就准据法达成协议。在确定了法律问题（即，该作品是否可受保护？）并将法律问题定性（如与版权法有关的问题）之后，法院将适用法律选择规则来决定法律选择协定的有效性。在此情况下，可以适用创作人"主要寓所"（可以是创作人的"住所""居所"或"惯常居所"）的法律。如果该法禁止当事方商定不同的准据法，则法院应当裁定法律选择协定无效。（注意，法院在考虑适用高于一切的强制性规则时可能已经就此问题做出裁决。）如果创作人"主要寓所"所在地的法律没有规定必须适用其法律，则当事方可以另外商定一套规则，其法律选择协定也将是有效的。

Title or validity of immovable property may be an exception, on the basis that it is a right created by a foreign State. Similarly, the court may not have jurisdiction to decide claims of title or rights to foreign IP. However, a question may arise as to whether this exception only applies to registered rights (such as patents or trademarks) or whether it applies to rights that exist automatically (such as copyright). In addition, a court may be willing to decide a question of title or validity when that question arises incidentally in an action over which the court has jurisdiction, such as a contractual dispute (preliminary question); see part Ⅲ.C.4.

A non-exclusive choice of court clause may establish a connecting factor or may influence the court's discretion. Generally, an exclusive choice of court clause should be enforced unless there are good reasons for not doing so. Grounds for not enforcing such a clause may include public policy grounds.

The **HCCH Choice of Court Convention** deals with the effectiveness of exclusive choice of court agreements. It is based on three key obligations: 1) the chosen court must hear the dispute, unless the agreement is null and void as to its substantive validity under the law of the State of the chosen court; 2) any non-chosen court must suspend or dismiss proceedings to which an exclusive choice of court agreement applies; and 3) a judgment given by the chosen court must be recognized and enforced in other Contracting Parties.

请自行翻译后查看后文的分析点评

分析点评

第 1 段

Title or validity of immovable property may be an exception, on the basis that it is a right created by a foreign State. Similarly, the court may not have jurisdiction to decide claims of title or rights to foreign IP. However, a question may arise as to whether this exception only applies to registered rights (such as patents or trademarks) or whether it applies to rights that exist automatically (such as copyright). In addition, a court may be willing to decide a question of title or validity when that question arises incidentally in an action over which the court has jurisdiction, such as a contractual dispute (preliminary question); see Part Ⅲ.C.4.

翻译稿

不动产的所有权或有效性可能是一个例外，①它是一项由外国设定的权利。同样，法院可能没有管辖权决定外国知识产权的所有权或权利主张。然而，可能会出现这样一个问题，即这一例外是否仅适用于已注册的权利（如专利或商标）或是否适用于自动存在的权利（如版权）。此外，当所有权或有效性问题在法院有管辖权的诉讼中偶然出现时，法院可能愿意决定该②，如合同争议（初步问题）；见第三部分 C.4。

批 注

① 译得精彩。
② 可译得更简短。

审校稿

不动产的所有权或有效性可能是一个例外，因为它是一项外国设定的权利。同样，法院可能没有管辖权决定外国知识产权的所有权或权利主张。然而，问题可能是，这一例外是否仅适用于已注册的权利（如专利或商标）或是否适用于自动存在的权利（如版权）。此外，在法院有管辖权的诉讼中，如果偶尔出现所有权或有效性问题，法院可能愿意裁决该问题，如合同争议（初步问题）；见第三部分 C.4。

点评

1. "on the basis" 通常都译为 "基于、根据、依据或在……基础上"，在这里，basis 的意思是 "3.[C] [usually sing.U] the important facts, ideas or events that support sth and that it can develop from 基础；要素；基点"（《牛津高阶英汉双解词典》）但这个义项用在本句则不妥，因为 basis 在本句中的意思是 "1.[sing.] the reason why people take a particular action 原因；缘由"（《牛津高阶英汉双解词典》），该词典举出的例句如下：She was chosen for the job on the basis of her qualifications. 她因资历适合而获选担任这项工作。Some videos have been banned on the basis that they are too violent. 有些录像因带暴力镜头过多而被查禁。所以，翻译稿译 "因为"，非常正确。

2. 第 3 句 "a question may arise as to..."，其中 "as to" 的意思是 "as for, about"（《韦氏大学英语词典》），整句直译就是 "关于……可能出现问题"，或 "一个关于……的问题可能出现"，换言之，就是 "问题可能是"。译为 "可能会出现这样一个问题，即"，既有失简洁，又不太自然。

3. 第 4 句，原译并不错，但若采取 "化境" 标准，可译得更简短明了，如审校稿那样。

第 2 段

A non-exclusive choice of court clause may establish a connecting factor or may influence the court's discretion. Generally, an exclusive choice of court clause should be enforced unless there are good reasons for not doing so. Grounds for not enforcing such a clause may include public policy grounds.

翻译稿

非排他性的法院选择条款可能确立一个联系①因素，或者可能影响法院的自由裁量权。一般而言，除非有充分理由不这样做②，否则应强制执行排他性的法院选择条款。不执行此类条款的理由可能包括公共政策方面的理由。

批 注

① 不准确。
② 翻译不当。

审校稿

非排他性的法院选择条款可能确立一个连接因素，或者可能影响法院的自由裁量权。一般而言，除非有充分理由，否则应强制执行排他性的法院选择条款。不执行此类条款可能包括公共政策方面的原因。

点评

1. connecting factor，照例译为 "连接因素"。

2. 在第 2 句中，"doing so" 指的是 "enforce an exclusive choice of court clause"。根据汉语行文习惯，代词不能先于所指之词而出现，所以应译为："一般而言，除非有充分的理由不强制执行排他性法院选择条款，否则就应当这样做。" 这样译，有可能引起误会，因为不清楚 "这样做" 究竟是怎么做，是应当 "强制执行"，还是 "不强制执行"？因此，最好改为："一般而言，除非有充分的理由不强制执行排他性法院选择条款,否则就应当强制执行。"但为了行文简洁,当如审校稿那样处理,把"doing so"略去不译。当然,也可以顺译为:"一般而言,应当强制执行排他性法院选择条款,不执行理由充足者除外。"

第 3 段

The **HCCH Choice of Court Convention** deals with the effectiveness of exclusive choice of court agreements. It is based on three key obligations: 1) the chosen court must hear the dispute, unless the agreement is null and void as to its substantive validity under the law of the State of the chosen court; 2) any non-chosen court must suspend or dismiss proceedings to which an exclusive choice of court agreement applies; and 3) a judgment given by the chosen court must be recognized and enforced in other Contracting Parties.

《HCCH 法院选择公约》涉及排他性法院选择协议的效力。它基于三项关键义务:1)选定的法院必须审理争议,除非根据选定法院所在国的法律,该协议的实质有效性①无效;2)任何未选定的法院必须中止或驳回排他性法院选择协议适用的程序;3)由选定法院做出的判决必须在其他缔约方得到承认和执行。

批 注

① 译得不够准确。

《海牙国际私法会议法院选择公约》涉及排他性法院选择协定的效力。它基于三项关键义务:1)选定的法院必须审理争议,除非根据选定法院所在国的法律,该协定的实质性效力无效;2)任何未选定的法院必须中止或驳回排他性法院选择协定适用的程序;3)由选定法院做出的判决必须在其他缔约方得到承认和执行。

1. null and void:系法律惯用语,意思是"having no force, binding power, or validity"(《韦氏大学英语词典》)或"having no legal force"(《剑桥高级学习词典》),《元照英美法词典》将其译为"无效的;无法律约束力的"。

2. substantive validity:法律专门术语,译为"实质性效力;实体法上的效力"(《英汉法律词典》)。

补充练习

In some jurisdictions, in particular common law countries, even if a court is competent to hear a dispute, it may nevertheless decline to hear it on the basis that it is clearly an inappropriate forum.

参考译文

在某些法域,特别是英美法系国家,法院即使有权审理争议,也可以拒绝审理,理由是该法院显然不适宜审理此案。

背景介绍

位于荷兰海牙的国际法院是负责解决主权国家政府间争端的联合国专门机构,负有特殊的职能。了解国际法院的背景、运作方式及其与其他联合国机构之间的关系,有助于就联合国法律类文件中的一些特殊表达、固有概念形成更为清晰的认识,为翻译其他同类文件提供背景知识。以下第十一篇和第十二篇选自国际法院出版物,涉及国际法院的人员设置、办案流程、职能分管等方面内容,翻译时需注意:

(1)理解并准确判断"宰熟词",注意这些词汇在司法领域的特殊意义。
(2)处理好无主语句和逻辑关系不明朗的复杂句。

第十一篇

原文

If the Court does not have a judge of the nationality of the States parties to a particular case, those States can each choose what is known as a judge ad hoc. These judges can be of any nationality, and have exactly the same rights and duties as elected judges. Every three years, the Court elects its President and Vice-President. The President chairs all sittings of the Court: he or she directs its work and supervises its administration. The Court is administratively independent. It is the only principal organ of the United Nations that is not assisted by the UN Secretariat.

States are sovereign: they are free to choose how to resolve their disputes. The Court can therefore only hear a case if the States involved have freely consented to having the case referred to it. In most instances, States appear before the Court on the basis of an international treaty. Once the Court has been seized, the proceedings take place in two phases. First, the States submit their arguments, evidence and submissions in writing, then their representatives and lawyers deliver oral arguments before the Court during hearings. At the end of each State party's oral argument, the

Agent presents the final submissions, stating what his or her Government "respectfully requests the Court to adjudge and declare".

Judgments are read out at public sitting. They conclude with an operative part, in which the Court gives its decision in respect of each of the points at issue. The President reads the operative part of a judgment: "For these reasons, the Court, by...votes to..., finds that..." All the Court's judgments are final and without appeal. It should be noted that, in accepting the Court's jurisdiction, the States concerned undertake ipso facto to comply with its decisions, which are all binding on the Parties.

请自行翻译后查看后文的分析点评

分析点评

第 1 段

If the Court does not have a judge of the nationality of the States parties to a particular case, those States can each choose what is known as a judge ad hoc. These judges can be of any nationality, and have exactly the same rights and duties as elected judges. Every three years, the Court elects its President and Vice-President. The President chairs all sittings of the Court: he or she directs its work and supervises its administration. The Court is administratively independent. It is the only principal organ of the United Nations that is not assisted by the UN Secretariat.

批 注
① 用词错误。
② 重复。
③ 用词不准确。

如果国际法院没有一名法官属某案所涉缔约之国籍，每个缔约国① 就可以选择一名法官，也就是专案法官。这些法官可来自任何国家，并可与国际法院法官享有完全相同的权利和义务。国际法院每三年举行一次院长和副院长的选举。院长主持国际法院的所有开庭：他或她② 指导国际法院的工作并监督法院的管理。国际法院在行政上保持独立。在联合国的主要机构中，它是唯一不受联合国秘书处协助的机构③。

如果国际法院任何法官均不具有特定案件当事国的国籍，那么每个当事国可以选派一名专案法官。这些法官可具有任何国家的国籍，与选举出的法官享有完全相同的权利并承担完全相同的义务。国际法院每三年举行一次院长和副院长的选举。院长主持国际法院的所有庭审：指导国际法院的工作并监督国际法院的管理。国际法院在行政上保持独立。它是联合国唯一不依靠联合国秘书处协助的主要机关。

点评

1. 用词问题。可以看出，译者对词汇的驾驭并不是很灵活，在译文中，分别出现了用词错误、用词不准和重复这三个问题。其中，第一个是用词错误，体现在对于诸如"States parties"这样的宰熟词，未经深入思考就译为了"缔约国"。虽然"States parties"在大多数情况下可译为"缔约国"，但是在本文语境中，因涉及国际争端问题，因此，相对于国际法院应当译为"当事国"；第二个是用词不准问题，如"principal organ"一词。"Principal organ"，在《联合国宪章》中文版中译为"主要机关"，国际法院是联合国的六个主要机关之一。"Organ"通常译为"机关"，"agency"或"body"多译为"机构"；第三个是用词重复问题，见"he or she directs its work"，在此处"he or she"指的就是"The President"，而前面已经出现或这一术语，再出现指示代词时，就不必重复。

2. 增译加强表达。见"These judges can be of any nationality, and have exactly the same rights and duties as elected judges."一句。通过对比译文与审校稿，我们可以看出，审校稿相对高明之处在于补充了一些字面表达所局限的内容，因此更便于我们理解。通过将"any nationality"增译为"具有任何国家的国籍"，传达出"对法官国籍不作任何要求"这一深层含义，而将译文中的"享有完全相同的权利和义务"增译为"享有完全相同的权利并承担完全相同的义务"，则将隐藏含义"在享有权利上对等，并且在履行义务上对等"的这层含义也传达了出来，因此与上下文连通起来一气呵成，更有助于理解与表达。

第2段

States are sovereign: they are free to choose how to resolve their disputes. The Court can therefore only hear a case if the States involved have freely consented to having the case referred to it. In most instances, States appear before the Court on the basis of an international treaty. Once the Court has been seized, the proceedings take place in two phases. First, the States submit their arguments, evidence and submissions in writing, then their representatives and lawyers deliver oral arguments before the Court during hearings. At the end of each State party's oral argument, the Agent presents the final submissions, stating what his or her Government "respectfully requests the Court to adjudge and declare".

翻译稿

主权国家：它们可以自由选择如何解决各自的纠纷。① 因此，只有在所涉国家自愿允许国际提起案件的情况下，国际法院才可予以审理②。在大多数情况下，各国依据某项国际条约在国际法院出庭。一旦国际法院接受审理，诉讼程序便分两个阶段进行。首先，各国以书面形式提交各自的论点、证据和辩护意见，随后，各国代表和律师在国际法院的听证会上进行口头辩论。在每个缔约国做完口头辩论后，代理人提出最后辩护意见，表示或她的政府"谨请求国际法院裁定并宣告"。

批注

① 理解不准确。
② 表达不通顺；逻辑有问题。

国家享有主权：它们可以自由选择解决纠纷的方式。因此，只有在当事国自由同意将案件提交国际法院的情况下，国际法院才可以审理。在大多数情况下，国家会依据某项国际条约在国际法院出庭。一旦国际法院受理，诉讼程序将分为两个阶段进行。首先，各国以书面形式提交各自的论点、证据和意见；其次，各国代表和律师在国际法院审理期间进行口头辩论。每个当事国结束口头辩论后，代理人将提出最后意见，表示本国政府"恭请国际法院判决并宣布"的事宜。

1. 理解问题。见"States are sovereign: they are free to choose how to resolve their disputes."一句。译者将"States are sovereign"译为了"主权国家"，并将"they are free to choose how to resolve their disputes"译为了"可以自由选择如何解决各自的纠纷"，实际上偏离了原文的重心。前半句用一个系表结构代出，是为了强调国家具有的条件，而不是国家本身。因此，将这句话理解成"主权国家"偏离了重心，也偷换了概念，因为"国家享有主权"和"主权国家"显然不是一个概念，前者还涉及准主权国以及观察员国等其他情况。在后半句话中，"如何解决各自的纠纷"与"解决纠纷的方式"虽然是不同表达方式问题，但也存在重心的偏差，将"方式"放在句末作为句子的落脚点，会加强这种强调作用。

2. 表达不通顺问题。见"The Court can therefore only hear a case if the States involved have freely consented to having the case referred to it."一句。译文读起来很不通顺，也无从得知案件到底是由谁提起、由谁受理，可能是译者对"consented to having the case referred to it"这个结构理解有问题。在法律类文件中，句子的主被动切换以及主语"隐形"的情况经常出现，这就需要我们判断出真正的主语。显然，这句话的原型是"have...done"结构，这个结构有两个常见的含义，一个是"派/请别人来完成"，另一个是"自己完成"。而"referred to"（提交案件）显然不是由国际法院或其他机构完成的，国际法院是负责审理的，那么只能说当事国自行转交，因此取第二种含义。要注意的是，虽然"refer to"在很多情况下译为"转交""转介"，相当于"transfer to"，但在整段语境中，并未提到第三方中介机构。因此，可以理解为各当事国自行提交国际法院，因此译为"提交"更合适。

第 3 段

Judgments are read out at public sitting. They conclude with an operative part, in which the Court gives its decision① in respect of each of the points at issue. The President reads the operative part of a judgment: "For these reasons, the Court, by...votes to..., finds that..." All the Court's judgments are final and without appeal. It should be noted that, in accepting the Court's jurisdiction, the States concerned undertake ipso facto to comply with its decisions, which are all binding on the Parties.

批注

① 理解有问题。

在公开开庭时宣读判决。他们最后进入执行部分，国际法院就每一个争议之点给出决定意见。① 院长宣读判决的执行部分："基于上述原因，国际法院，通过……票决……，认定……" 国际法院的全部判决系属确定，不得上诉。应当指出的是，所涉国承认国际法院的管辖权② 也就要在事实上服从其决定，因为这些决定对当事方有约束力。

> 批 注
> ① 表达有问题。
> ② 理解有问题。

判决在公开审讯中宣读。判决最后是执行部分，国际法院在该部分就每一个争议点做出裁决。院长宣读判决的执行部分："基于上述原因，国际法院以……票对……票裁定……"，国际法院的全部判决均为最终判决，不得上诉。应当指出的是，当事国接受国际法院管辖，当然也就承诺了服从其裁决，这些裁决对各当事方都具有约束力。

理解问题。译文中有两处比较明显的理解问题，分别可见"in which the Court gives its decision③ in respect of each of the points at issue"及"It should be noted that, in accepting the Court's jurisdiction"。译文对这两句话的理解错误有共通之处，主要在于对法律用语的固定表达不熟悉，照搬字面意思，忽视其深层含义。如在"give its decisions"中，"decisions"并非大会等机构所做的决定意见，此处专指司法机构所做的、具有法律效力的"裁决"。因此，译为"裁决"比较合适；而在"in accepting the Court's jurisdiction"中，也是过于照搬原文字面意思，"accepting"虽有承认的意思，但在法律用语中更侧重于"subject to"的含义，因此"接受管辖"才是准确译法。另外，在联合国术语库中，"jurisdiction"既可以译为"管辖权"，也可以译为"管辖范围"或"管辖"，在文中并没有明显的"范围"或"权利"的含义，因此按照译文作过度处理是不恰当的。

> 批 注
> ③ 理解有问题。

1. If a State refuses to abide by a decision of the Court, the opposing State may have recourse to the Security Council, which may, under Article 94 of the Charter of the United Nations, make recommendations or decide upon measures to be taken to give effect to the judgment. Given the great legal, moral and diplomatic authority with which decisions of the Court are invested, it is however extremely rare for this to happen.

参考译文

如果一国拒绝服从国际法院的裁决，对方国家可诉诸安全理事会，安全理事会可根据《联合国宪章》第九十四条提出建议或决定要采取的措施以执行判决。然而,鉴于国际法院的裁决在法律、道义和外交上具有极大的权威性,这种情况极为罕见。

2. On very many occasions, and on all continents, the Court has helped to defuse crises, to normalize relations between States and to restart deadlocked negotiations, either through the settlement of disputes by judicial means or by stating the law in respect of a particular question.

许多情况下,国际法院要么以司法手段解决争端,要么阐明有关某一具体问题的法律,在各大洲帮助化解危机,帮助实现国家间关系的正常化,以及帮助重启陷入僵局的谈判。

第十二篇

原文

Regarding the court's failure to call and question independent experts, the State party submits that not only did the police conduct an expert analysis, they also questioned and took the testimonies of two additional experts.

The verdict of the trial court and the decision of the appellate instances are thus supported by the evidence adduced during those proceedings.

The findings of expert analyses by other experts could not have been admitted as evidence, because those analyses had been conducted in violation of the requirements of the Criminal Procedure Code.

请自行翻译后查看后文的分析点评

分析点评

第 1 段

Regarding the court's failure to call and question independent experts, the State party submits that not only did the police conduct an expert analysis, they also questioned and took the testimonies of two additional experts.

关于法院未能传唤和审问① 独立专家，缔约国称②，不仅警方进行了专家分析，他们还审问并提取③ 了另外两名专家的证词。

关于法院未能传唤和讯问独立专家问题，当事国主张，不仅警方进行了专家分析，他们还讯问了另外两名专家并进行了取证。

在本句中，"question"作为动词使用，表示"向……提出问题；询问；盘问"之意。由于法院与独立专家之间的关系，法院不可能对独立专家进行审问，因此，译者存在用词不当的问题。另外，在"the State party submits that"中，"submit"应译为"主张"。句中"questioned and took the testimonies"应为"讯问……并对……进行取证"之意。

> 批 注
>
> ① 错译。
> ② 不准确。
> ③ 错译。

第 2 段

The verdict of the trial court and the decision of the appellate instances are thus supported by the evidence adduced during those proceedings.

因此，这些程序中举出的证据证明了法院审判的判决和上诉诉讼的决定④。

因此，初审法院的判决和上诉法院的裁决得到了诉讼期间所举证证据的支持。

"trial court"应为"初审法院"，而不是"法院审判"。句中"decision"应译为"裁决"，而不是"决定"。这句话的主要意思是"初审法院的判决和上诉法院的裁决得到了所提证据的支持"。

> 批 注
>
> ④ 存在错译和表达不准确的问题。

第 3 段

The findings of expert analyses by other experts could not have been admitted as evidence, because those analyses had been conducted in violation of the requirements of the Criminal Procedure Code.

其他专家的专家分析结果不能⑤ 作为证据，因为这些分析的进行⑥ 违反了《刑事诉讼法》的要求。

> 批 注
>
> ⑤ 错译。
> ⑥ 表达不准确。

其他专家的专家分析结果本不能作为证据予以采信，因为这些分析的开展方式违反了《刑事诉讼法》的要求。

在本句的前半部分，"could not have been admitted"使用的是虚拟语态，应该表示"本不能怎么样"，而译者没有译出这一点。而"those analyses had been conducted in violation of the requirements of the Criminal Procedure Code"强调的不是"analyses"违反了《刑事诉讼法》的要求，而是进行这些分析的方式违反了相关要求。

补充练习

While an island is defined as being "naturally formed", there is no definition under the United Nations Convention on the Law of the Sea or the 1958 Conventions or other codified sources of international law as to generally accepted criteria for what is an "artificial" island.

虽然岛屿被界定为"自然形成的"，但对于何为"人工"岛屿，《联合国海洋法公约》、1958年《公约》或其他已编纂的国际法渊源均未界定普遍公认的标准。

背景介绍

以下第十三篇和第十四篇材料均涉及《联合国打击跨国有组织犯罪公约》（以下简称为《公约》）。第十三篇为公约秘书处编写的背景文件，其中概述了《公约》所载的报告要求，以及公约缔约方会议最近赋予的这方面任务授权，描述了收集和传播信息的现有工具，并探讨了如何利用这些信息提供技术援助。最后，该文件就如何改进信息的收集、传播和分析及进一步利用这些信息提供技术援助提出了建议。

第十四篇为秘书处为协助偷运移民问题工作组开展讨论而编写的背景文件，其中概述工作组以往就相关议程项目开展的工作，列出可供讨论的问题，概要介绍主要问题和对各国应对工作的指导意见，并介绍了旨在协助各国实施《偷运移民议定书》的主要工具和推荐资源。

第十三篇

For the tertiary level of education, the Office will develop concise, multidisciplinary and interactive syllabuses on organized crime training and a model course in stand-alone modular format. The material is to include a list of bibliographic resources that can also be made available in SHERLOC, as well as a website dedicated to Education for Justice. The primary target groups will be undergraduate students and students at higher vocational training institutes for practitioners in disciplines that include, but are not necessarily limited to, law, criminology, political science, psychology, sociology, anthropology, international relations and economics.

The information on competent national authorities is continuously updated. Access is reserved for designated competent national authorities and is password-protected. The 2017 issue of the directory will be published at the end of the year.

The respondents indicated that they used SHERLOC mostly to consult legal provisions, obtain information on competent national authorities, support the domestic policymaking process, analyse case law and obtain information on countries' compliance with the Organized Crime Convention and the Protocols thereto.

The information in SHERLOC is obtained in a number of ways. First and foremost, the SHERLOC team receives legislation and case law directly from the Permanent Missions of Member States. Information is also received from various government ministries and criminal justice practitioners within Governments. Secondly, volunteers including law students and legal practitioners conduct research and send legislation and case law to the SHERLOC team within UNODC. Finally, the Office conducts research in the context of technical assistance activities. Information received from volunteers or gathered through the Office's own research is subsequently verified with the relevant permanent missions before it is uploaded to SHERLOC.

请自行翻译后查看后文的分析点评

第 1 段

For the tertiary level of education, the Office will develop concise, multidisciplinary and interactive syllabuses on organized crime training and a model course in stand-alone modular format. The material is to include a list of bibliographic resources that can also be made available in SHERLOC, as well as a website dedicated to Education for Justice. The primary target groups will be undergraduate students and students at higher vocational training institutes for practitioners in disciplines that include, but are not necessarily limited to, law, criminology, political science, psychology, sociology, anthropology, international relations and economics.

批注

① 表述不准确，造成误解。
② 漏译。
③ 理解错误。
④ 理解错误。

在高等教育方面，毒品和犯罪问题办公室将编写简明、多学科和互动式的有组织犯罪培训教学大纲①，还将单独设置一个单元②的示范课程。该材料将列出文献资源（这些资源也可在夏洛克门户网站上查阅），以及教育促进正义举措的专门网站③。主要目标群体是本科生和高等职业培训机构的学生，旨在将他们培养成以下学科（包括但不限于）的从业人员④：法律、犯罪学、政治学、心理学、社会学、人类学、国际关系和经济学。

在高等教育方面，毒品和犯罪问题办公室将编写简明、多学科、互动式的有组织犯罪问题培训教学大纲，还将单独制作一个独立模块形式的示范课程。材料将列出文献资源，这些资源也可在夏洛克门户网站和教育促进正义举措的专门网站发布。主要目标群体是本科生和培养（包括但不限于）以下学科从业人员的高等职业培训机构的学生：法律、犯罪学、政治学、心理学、社会学、人类学、国际关系和经济学。

1. 原文中的"syllabuses on organized crime training"，从字面上看是"关于有组织犯罪培训的教学大纲"，但这种表述不够确切，容易让人产生误解："有组织犯罪培训"是指什么？培训有组织犯罪？这显然不合常理。其实，这里是说就有组织犯罪相关问题进行培训。原译文没有体现这层含义，不够准确，容易让人误解。

2. 漏译。原文中的"stand-alone modular format"是指以独立模块为形式。翻译稿漏译了"format"，只提到了"单元"，显然是错误的。

3. 理解有误。第2句话的主句是"The material is to include a list of bibliographic resources"，后面的"that"引导了一个定语从句，修饰先行词"resources"，而这个定语从句中的"SHERLOC"和"a website"是并列成分，意思是这种资源可以通过这两种途径发布。原译文理解有误，没有厘清句子的层次结构，尤其是没辨明"as well as"引导的部分究竟与谁并列，误以为"bibliographic resources"与"a website"并列，如果真如此，就是说该材料将列出文献资源和一个网站，为何要列一个网站呢？从语义和逻辑上都说不通。

4. 第3句话的难点在于"students at higher vocational training institutes for practitioners in disciplines"。原译文中的前半段问题不大，确实是"高等职业培训机构的学生"，问题在于后半段，也就是"for practitioners in disciplines"。

原译文将"for"理解成表示目的,这没有问题,但关键是"for practitioners in disciplines"修饰的是前面整个句子还是仅修饰"vocational training institutes"。根据就近原则,我们暂且先把它理解成修饰"vocational training institutes",那么这部分的意思就是"培养(以下)学科从业人员的高等职业培训机构",既然是职业培训机构,培养专门的从业人员完全说得通。但如果把这个部分理解成修饰前面的整个句子,也就是原译文的理解,则非常牵强,逻辑上走不通。

第 2 段

The information on competent national authorities is continuously updated. Access is reserved for designated competent national authorities and is password-protected. The 2017 issue of the directory will be published at the end of the year.

国家主管部门的信息不断更新。指定的国家主管部门的访问权得到保留①并受密码保护。2017 年的目录发行本将在年底出版。

国家主管部门的信息不断更新,仅供指定的国家主管部门访问并受密码保护。2017 年版名录将在年底发布。

这一段的难点在于第二句话中的"Access is reserved for designated competent national authorities"。从字面上看,意思是"指定的国家主管部门的访问权得到保留",但这种译法很晦涩,只把字面意思翻了出来,让人不明白原文究竟想说什么。归根结底,还是没有理解原文真正的含义。"Access is reserved for"的意思是"为……保留访问权",而"为……保留"其实是说"只有……才能",所以原译文被修改为"仅供指定的国家主管部门访问"。这样一来,译文意思就清楚明了。

第 3 段

The respondents indicated that they used SHERLOC mostly to consult legal provisions, obtain information on competent national authorities, support the domestic policymaking process, analyse case law and obtain information on countries' compliance with the Organized Crime Convention and the Protocols thereto.

调查对象指出,他们使用夏洛克门户网站主要是为了查看法律条款、获取国家主管部门的信息,为国内决策进程提供支持,分析判例法以及获取各国遵守《有组织犯罪公约》及其各项议定书情况的信息②。

批 注

① 译文晦涩,没有表达出句子的真正含义。

批 注

② 表述不到位。

调查答复者指出,他们使用夏洛克门户网站主要是为了查看法律条款、获取国家主管部门的信息,为国内决策进程提供支持,分析判例法以及了解各国遵守《有组织犯罪公约》及其各项议定书的情况。

【点评】

这句话最后一部分的问题在于表述不到位。关于"information on...",通常的译法是"关于……的信息""关于……的资料"。原译文将"information on countries' compliance with the Organized Crime Convention and the Protocols thereto"译为"各国遵守《有组织犯罪公约》及其各项议定书情况的信息",这似乎也说得通,但可读性较差。"关于某种情况的信息"并不是很容易理解。其实,这句话的意思是说获取信息、了解这方面的情况。修改后的译文对介词"on"做了一个调整,将其译为一个贴近原意的动词"了解",这样既能避免"on"后面的成分在译文中过长,又能准确再现原文的意思。

第 4 段

The information in SHERLOC is obtained in a number of ways. First and foremost, the SHERLOC team receives legislation and case law directly from the Permanent Missions of Member States. Information is also received from various government ministries and criminal justice practitioners within Governments. Secondly, volunteers including law students and legal practitioners conduct research and send legislation and case law to the SHERLOC team within UNODC. Finally, the Office conducts research in the context of technical assistance activities. Information received from volunteers or gathered through the Office's own research is subsequently verified with the relevant permanent missions before it is uploaded to SHERLOC.

批 注

① 时态错误。
② 表述不完整。
③ 理解错误。
④ 表述不完整。

夏洛克门户网站上的信息可通过多种方式获得①。首先,夏洛克门户网站小组直接从各会员国常驻代表团获取立法和判例法②。还从政府各部委和各国政府内部的刑事司法从业人员处获取资料。其次,志愿者(法律专业学生)和法律从业人员③ 开展研究并向毒品和犯罪问题办公室内部的夏洛克门户网站小组传送立法和判例法④。最后,毒品和犯罪问题办公室在技术援助活动中开展研究。从志愿者处获得的资料或毒品和犯罪问题办公室通过自己的研究收集到的资料随后会向相关常驻代表团核实,之后再上传夏洛克门户网站。

夏洛克门户网站上的信息是通过多种方式获得的。首先,夏洛克门户网站小组直接从各会员国常驻代表团获取立法和判例法资料。还从政府各部委和各国政府内部的刑事司法从业人员处获取资料。其次,包括法律专业学生和法律从业人员在内的志愿者开展研究并向毒品和犯罪问题办公室内部的夏洛克门户网站小组传送立法和判例法资料。最后，毒品和犯罪问题办公室在技术援助活动中开展研究。从志愿者处获得的资料或毒品和犯罪问题办公室通过自己的研究收集到的资料随后会向相关常驻代表团核实，之后再上传到夏洛克门户网站。

1. "legislation and case law"确实是"立法和判例法"，但原译文中"获取立法和判例法"让人摸不着头脑。什么叫获取立法和判例法？其实，这里指的不是具体的立法和判例法，而是立法和判例法相关资料。原译文表述不完整，引发误解。

2. 原译文中关于这一部分的理解错误："volunteers including law students and legal practitioners"中的"including"有两个宾语：一个是"law students"，另一个是"legal practitioners"，两者都属于"volunteer"，而原译文将"volunteer"看作只包含"law students"，理解有误。

UNODC will commence the development of a simplified web-based tool for gathering comprehensive information on the implementation of the Organized Crime Convention and the Protocols thereto. The tool will be added to SHERLOC as another component. Focal points can be given accounts with password protection or, if required, a paper-based questionnaire in case of difficulties with Internet connectivity. In that way, States parties can easily and quickly input, update or verify national information on legislation and jurisprudence, appoint focal points for ease of communication with the Secretariat and provide analysis on key legal issues in their legislation and case law.

Should States find it useful, a function to request technical assistance could be added to the portal. The information available in SHERLOC could be used as a first step to carry out desk reviews or to assess legislative assistance needs in States requesting such assistance.

参考译文

毒品和犯罪问题办公室将开始开发一套简化版的网络工具，以全面收集《有组织犯罪公约》及其各项议定书实施情况的资料。该工具将添加到夏洛克门户网站上，作为另一个组成部分。可以给联络点设置一个有密码保护的账号，或者如果需要，在互联网连接困难的情况下向其发放纸质调查表。如此一来，缔约国可方便迅速地输入、更新或核实本国有关立法和判例的信息，指定联络点以方便与秘书处联络，并就本国立法和判例法中关键法律问题提供分析。

如果各国认为请求技术援助功能有帮助，可在门户网站上添加这项功能。夏洛克门户网站上的现有资料可作为开展案头审议或评估立法援助请求国的立法援助需求的第一步。

第十四篇

At its second meeting, held in 2013, the Working Group recommended to the Conference that the following topics, inter alia, be considered at future meetings of the Working Group: organized crime aspects of the smuggling of migrants, including financial investigations and responses targeting the proceeds of crime; and criminal justice responses, including investigation and prosecution of the perpetrators. The Working Group also recommended that, pursuant to Article 20 of the Convention, and in accordance with national legislation, States parties should make use of a range of special investigative techniques in smuggling of migrants cases, commensurate with the needs of any specific investigation, as an effective means of gathering intelligence and evidence.

At its third meeting, held in 2015, the Working Group recommended to the Conference that States enhance the use of the Organized Crime Convention and the Smuggling of Migrants Protocol as the basis for international cooperation aimed at facilitating extradition and the widest possible measure of mutual legal assistance in smuggling of migrants cases, in accordance with Articles 16 and 18 of the Convention.

Matters related to international cooperation in criminal matters are dealt with in the Organized Crime Convention, as are the crimes that often accompany the smuggling of migrants: participation in an organized criminal group, corruption, obstruction of justice and money-laundering. It is therefore essential that the Smuggling of Migrants Protocol be read and applied in conjunction with the Convention and that national legislation to address the smuggling of migrants be developed to implement not only the Protocol, but also the Convention itself.

请自行翻译后查看后文的分析点评

第1段

At its second meeting, held in 2013, the Working Group recommended to the Conference that the following topics, inter alia, be considered at future meetings of the Working Group: organized crime aspects of the smuggling of migrants, including financial investigations and responses targeting the proceeds of crime; and criminal justice responses, including investigation and prosecution of the perpetrators. The

Working Group also recommended that, pursuant to Article 20 of the Convention, and in accordance with national legislation, States parties should make use of a range of special investigative techniques in smuggling of migrants cases, commensurate with the needs of any specific investigation, as an effective means of gathering intelligence and evidence.

工作组在其于 2013 年举行的第二次会议上建议缔约方会议在今后的工作组会议上特别审议下列议题：偷运移民的有组织犯罪方面，包括金融调查和针对犯罪收益的对策①；及刑事司法对策，包括调查和起诉实施者。根据《公约》第二十条和国家立法，工作组还建议②缔约国在偷运移民案件中使用符合具体调查需求的一系列特别调查手段，作为收集情报和证据的有效途径。

批 注

① 理解有误，target 具体指的是什么？
② 语法结构错误。

工作组在 2013 年举行的第二次会议上向缔约方会议建议，在将来的工作组会议上特别审议下列议题：偷运移民的有组织犯罪方面，包括针对犯罪所得的金融调查和对策；刑事司法对策，包括调查和起诉犯罪人。工作组还建议缔约国根据《公约》第二十条和国家立法，在偷运移民案件中使用符合具体调查需求的一系列特别调查手段，作为收集情报和证据的有效途径。

1. 原文中的"response"一词有多个词义，例如"应对""响应""反应""对策"等，具体选择哪个词义，需要结合上下文确定。在这句话中，重点是"proceeds of crime"，即"犯罪所得"，无论是"financial investigations"（金融调查）还是"responses"（对策），针对的都是"proceeds of crime"（犯罪所得）。原译文此处理解有误，误将"targeting the proceeds of crime"这个分词结构看成是只修饰"responses"，实际上该结构修饰的是"financial investigations"和"responses"两个部分。

2. 语法结构问题。"pursuant to Article 20 of the Convention, and in accordance with national legislation"这部分在"recommended that"之后，也就是说"根据《公约》第二十条和国家立法"应该包含在工作组的建议之内，也即工作组建议缔约国"根据《公约》第二十条和国家立法"采取一些措施，而原译文把"pursuant to Article 20 of the Convention, and in accordance with national legislation"这个宾语从句中的成分挪到了主句，语法结构出现错误，不仅没有体现原文的意思，甚至颠倒了主次。

第 2 段

At its third meeting, held in 2015, the Working Group recommended to the Conference that States enhance the use of the Organized Crime Convention and the Smuggling of Migrants Protocol as the basis for international cooperation aimed at facilitating extradition and the widest possible measure of mutual legal assistance in smuggling of migrants cases, in accordance with articles 16 and 18 of the Convention.

批 注

① 首次出现，应用全称。
② 理解有误。

 翻译稿

工作组在其于2015年举行的第三次会议上向缔约方会议建议，各国应当按照《公约》①第16条和第18条，更多地将《有组织犯罪公约》和《偷运移民议定书》用作开展国际合作以便利引渡和在偷运移民案件中尽可能广泛地提供司法协助的依据②。

 审校稿

工作组在2015年举行的第三次会议上向缔约方会议建议，各国应当按照《有组织犯罪公约》第16条和第18条，更多地以《公约》和《偷运移民议定书》为依据开展国际合作，以便利引渡和在偷运移民案件中尽可能广泛地提供司法协助。

 点评

1. 这一段出现了一项公约（《有组织犯罪公约》），并且出现了两次。无论是英文还是中文，如果某公约的名称先后出现两次，那么至少在第一次出现的时候应用全称。通过对比原文和译文可以发现，由于译文的句子结构作了调整，没有完全对应原文，所以原文中的简称被调到了译文中应使用全称的位置，那么在将原文译为中文时，应做出相应的调整，而不是一味地遵循原文格式。

2. "as the basis for"这句话是个难点，陷阱比较多。这句话看似可以有多种断句方式，第一种是将"as the basis for"和"the widest possible measure"看成并列成分，这种断句方式也是原译文采用的方式；第二种是将"facilitating extradition"和"the widest possible measure"看成并列成分，也就是它们都跟在"aimed at"之后。仅从字面上来看，略有难度，但我们可以充分利用原文信息。原文最后一句很关键，给出了两项公约条款。查阅一下《有组织犯罪公约》第16条和第18条，会发现这两条主要述及"引渡"和"司法协助"。如果按照第一种方式，重心变成了"国际合作"和"司法协助"，显然与公约条款的内容不符。因此，应该使用第二种方式。这样一来，原文强调加强国际合作以便利引渡和提供司法协助就完全说得通了。

第3段

Matters related to international cooperation in criminal matters are dealt with in the Organized Crime Convention, as are the crimes that often accompany the smuggling of migrants: participation in an organized criminal group, corruption, obstruction of justice and money-laundering. It is therefore essential that the Smuggling of Migrants Protocol be read and applied in conjunction with the Convention and that national legislation to address the smuggling of migrants be developed to implement not only the Protocol, but also the Convention itself.

翻译稿

与刑事事项国际合作有关的事项被列入了①《有组织犯罪公约》，同样被列入的还有通常伴随偷运移民行为的犯罪：加入有组织犯罪集团、腐败、妨害司法和洗钱。因此，必须结合《公约》来解读和适用《偷运移民议定书》，制定②用于处理偷运移民行为的国家法律不仅是为了③执行《议定书》，也是为了执行《公约》本身。

批 注

① 措辞不当。
② 语法结构错误。
③ 理解有误。

审校稿

《有组织犯罪公约》除了述及与刑事事项国际合作有关的事项之外，还述及了通常伴随偷运移民行为的犯罪：加入有组织犯罪集团、腐败、妨害司法和洗钱。因此，必须结合《公约》来解读和适用《偷运移民议定书》，还必须制定用于处理偷运移民行为的国家法律，以实施《议定书》和《公约》本身。

点评

1. "deal with"这个短语最常见的意思是"处理、应对"，但在涉及文件、文书时，通常是"述及、论及"的意思。原译文将这个短语处理成"列入"，乍一看似乎也有些道理，但《有组织犯罪公约》早已成为一项十分成熟的国际文书，"列入"不仅无法体现这种含义，还会造成一种错觉，让读者以为《公约》和日常文件或决议一样，可以随时列入新的事项，这显然不符合常理。因此，修改后的译文将"deal with"译为"述及"。此外原译文使用了被动句，但如果能够找到主语，应尽量减少被动句的使用，加强可读性。

2. "It is therefore essential"后面跟了两个宾语从句，一个是"that the Smuggling of Migrants Protocol be read..."，另一个是"that national legislation to address the smuggling of migrants..."，原译文将"essential"译为"必须"，没有问题，但第二个宾语从句没有体现出这个意思，语义上不连贯，可增译"还必须"。另外，第二个宾语从句的重心是制定法律，而不是制定法律的目的，原译文的语句结构显然将重心放在目的上，与原文有出入。

补充练习

Mutual legal assistance is another important tool that can support investigations into and the prosecution of smugglers of migrants. Article 3 of the Smuggling of Migrants Protocol defines the smuggling of migrants as an act committed to obtain a financial or other material benefit. Therefore, those who procure their own illegal entry or who procure the illegal entry of others for reasons other than financial or other material benefit, such as individuals smuggling family members or charitable organizations assisting in the movement of refugees or asylum seekers, are outside the definition. As the element of financial or other material benefit is vital in smuggling of migrants cases, it is crucial that authorities acquire relevant information in a timely manner, in particular financial information.

As it is a form of crime that transcends borders, the smuggling of migrants can be countered only by a cross-border law enforcement response. The mandatory provisions of article 27 of the Convention, on law enforcement cooperation, offer guidance and a basis for informal operational cooperation.

司法协助是支持调查和起诉偷运移民者的另一项重要手段。《偷运移民议定书》第3条对偷运移民的定义是，为获取金钱或其他物质利益而实施的一种行为。因此，那些自身设法非法入境或并非以金钱或其他物质利益为目的安排他人非法入境的人员，例如，偷运其家人的个人或协助难民或寻求庇护者迁移的慈善组织不在该定义之列。鉴于金钱或其他物质利益这个要件在偷运移民案件中至关重要，所以当局务必及时获取相关信息，特别是财务信息。

由于偷运移民是一种跨越国界的犯罪形式，所以只能通过跨境执法对策予以打击。《公约》有关执法合作的第27条的强制性规定为非正式行动合作提供了指导和依据。

背景介绍

以下第十五篇和第十六篇均涉及《联合国反腐败公约》，来自公约缔约国会议实施情况审议组。该审议组根据联合国反腐败公约缔约国会议第3/1号决议设立，其职能是通盘审议各国实施公约的情况，以找出这方面的挑战和良好做法，并审议技术援助需求，以便确保公约的有效实施。

此类文件的结构通常为：按《公约》条款，分列实施情况评述、成功经验和良好做法、实施方面的挑战。其特点主要有两个：一是文件紧贴《公约》，按照《公约》章和条款的顺序编写。在翻译时，须紧密结合《公约》条款进行理解和翻译；二是普遍涉及具体国家的司法行政制度、部委机关名称和法律法规。翻译时应主动查询各国的相关制度，不能套用中国国内的制度处理。

第十五篇

Money-laundering, concealment (arts. 23 and 24)

Money-laundering is criminalized (sect. 243, Crimes Act (CA)). All offences punishable under domestic law and acts committed abroad that would be offences in

New Zealand had they been committed there are predicate offences.

If a perpetrator of the predicate offence "deals" with the property proceeds of crime (sect. 243(1), CA), he or she also commits money-laundering and can be prosecuted for both offences.

Concealment is criminalized (sect. 243 (3), CA).

Embezzlement, abuse of functions and illicit enrichment (arts. 17, 19, 20 and 22)

In the absence of a specific embezzlement offence, theft by a person in a special relationship (sect. 220, CA) and criminal breach of trust (sect. 229, CA) are criminalized. Apart from the corrupt use of information (sect. 105(A), CA), abuse of functions is not criminalized as separate offence, but can be covered by section 105, CA. Illicit enrichment is not criminalized.

请自行翻译后查看后文的分析点评

分析点评

第 1 段

Money-laundering, concealment (arts. 23 and 24)

Money-laundering is criminalized (sect. 243, Crimes Act (CA)). All offences punishable under domestic law and acts committed abroad that would be offences in New Zealand had they been committed there are predicate offences.

If a perpetrator of the predicate offence "deals" with the property proceeds of crime (sect. 243(1), CA), he or she also commits money-laundering and can be prosecuted for both offences.

Concealment is criminalized (sect. 243 (3), CA).

洗钱、隐瞒①（第 23 条和第 24 条）

规定洗钱为犯罪②（《犯罪法》第 243 条）。根据国内法应予惩处的一切犯罪行为及在国外实施的行为在新西兰应列为犯罪时③属于上游犯罪。

实施上游犯罪的人"处理"④犯罪所得收益（《犯罪法》第 243 条第 1 款），则他/她⑤同时犯有洗钱罪，可以就这两种罪行予以起诉⑥。

规定窝赃为犯罪（《犯罪法》第 243 条第 3 款）。

批 注

① 《公约》条款请勿自行翻译。
② 被动句的处理问题。
③ 表述不清晰。句子重心偏移的问题。
④ 用词欠精确的问题。
⑤ 是否一定要译出？
⑥ 另增主语的问题。

洗钱、窝赃（第二十三条、第二十四条）

洗钱被定为犯罪（《犯罪法》第 243 节）。依据新西兰国内法应受惩处的一切犯罪行为及虽在国外实施但在新西兰属于犯罪的行为，均为上游犯罪。

实施上游犯罪的人若"处置"犯罪所得财产，也就犯了洗钱罪，可因这两种罪行被起诉。

窝赃被定为犯罪（《犯罪法》第 243（3）节）。

1. 凡涉及规约（statute）、条约（treaty）、公约（convention）等正式法律文书及其内容时，均需遵照权威官方译本，无此类译本的，可斟酌自行翻译。Money-laundering, concealment (arts. 23 and 24)，来自《联合国反腐败公约》的摘抄内容，应遵照其官方译本，其中"concealment"为"窝赃"，"arts. 23"为"第二十三条"，不能自行译为"隐瞒"和"第 23 条"。

2. 见"All offences...and acts committed abroad...are predicate offences."一句。此句中的 offences 和 acts 为双主语，二者并重，均指"行为"。"acts committed abroad that would be offences in New Zealand had they been committed there"是一个短语，中心词是"acts"，带有两个定语：一是过去分词"committed abroad"，意为"在国外实施的"；二是从句"that would be offences in New Zealand had they been committed there"，意思是"若在新西兰实施也属犯罪的"。译者译为"国外实施的行为在新西兰应列为犯罪时"，问题之一是重心没有放在"行为"一词上，问题之二是结构上未能表现出与 offences 的双主语并列关系。该译文没有重大错误，但谈不上是好的译文。在审校稿中，此句改为"……一切犯罪行为和……属于犯罪的行为"，较好地解决了上述两个问题。

3. 见"If a perpetrator..., he or she also commits...and can be prosecuted for both offences."一句。此句主语为 perpetrator，he or she 也是指 perpetrator，既然如此，不必译为"他或她"，否则有失简练。此句译文最大的不妥之处在于"妄加主语"——将"can be prosecuted for both offences"处理为"可以就这两种罪行予以起诉"，隐晦地增加了一个"起诉人"作为第二个主语，犹如另起新句，并将 perpetrator 降格为新句中的宾语，转折突兀，文气不通，逻辑不畅，是译文中最明显的败笔。

第 2 段

Embezzlement, abuse of functions and illicit enrichment (arts. 17, 19, 20 and 22)

In the absence of a specific embezzlement offence, theft by a person in a special relationship (sect. 220, CA) and criminal breach of trust (sect. 229, CA) are criminalized.

Apart from the corrupt use of information (sect. 105(A), CA), abuse of functions is not criminalized as separate offence, but can be covered by section 105, CA.

Illicit enrichment is not criminalized.

贪污、滥用职能和非法获益（第 17 条、第 19 条、第 20 条和第 22 条①）
在缺乏具体贪污罪行②的情况下，盗窃特殊关系人（第 220 节，《犯罪法》）和背信犯罪（第 229 节，《犯罪法》）均属犯罪行为。

批 注

① 见上一段点评 1。
② 理解各分句之间关系的问题。

除滥用信息外（，《犯罪法》），滥用职能并不独立成罪，但《犯罪法》第 105 条予以涵盖。

非法获益不属于犯罪行为。

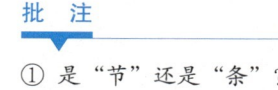

① 是"节"还是"条"？

贪污、滥用职权和资产非法增加（第十七条、第十九条、第二十条和第二十二条）

法律未规定具体的贪污罪，但把特殊关系人士的盗窃行为（《犯罪法》第 220 节）以及背信罪（《犯罪法》第 229 节）定为犯罪。

除滥用信息外（《犯罪法》第 105(A) 节），法律未将滥用职权规定为单独犯罪，但《犯罪法》第 105 节有相关规定。

法律未规定资产非法增加为犯罪。

1. 见 "In the absence of a specific embezzlement offence..." 一句，正确的理解应为 "While not establishing a specific embezzlement offence, but..."，而不是 "In case of not establishing a specific embezzlement offence, then..."。这里是转折关系，而不是条件关系。

2. 见 "..., but can be covered..." 一句。"cover" 一词，需译出其隐含意义，有依据地增译。

3. 见 "section" 一词，法律法规根据内容需要可以分为编（part）、章（chapter）、节（section）、条（article）、款（paragraph）、项（subparagraph）、目（item）。其中，section 一般译为"节"。

Bribery and trading in influence (arts. 15, 16, 18 and 21)

Active and passive bribery of national public officials is criminalized (sects. 100–105, CA). While the promise of an undue advantage is not explicitly included, the provisions are formulated broadly and the judiciary has interpreted them to also cover promises (*Field v. R [2011] NZSC 129*). Jurisprudence has established a *de minimis* defence in relation to "gifts of token value which are just part of the usual courtesies of life" (*Field v. R [2011] NZSC 129*).

参考译文

贿赂和影响力交易（第十五条、第十六条、第十八条和第二十一条）

法律规定国家公职人员行贿受贿为犯罪（《犯罪法》第 100～105 条）。有关条款未明确涵盖许诺给予不正当好处，但措辞宽泛，已被司法机关解释为也涵盖了这种许诺（Field 诉 R [2011] NZSC 129）。判例已确立了对于"出于礼节而赠予的具有象征价值的礼品"的答辩，法律不问琐事（Field 诉 R [2011] NZSC 129）。

第十六篇

原文

More States confirmed the possibility of relying on the Convention as a legal basis for mutual legal assistance than is the case for extradition. Article 46 itself has been invoked and has served as the legal basis for providing assistance on numerous occasions. Many States parties reported having made and/or received at least one request using the Convention as a legal basis; that was often commended as a good practice by the reviewers. For example, one State party reported that its legislation on mutual legal assistance was complemented by special regulations facilitating the submission and receipt of mutual legal assistance requests to and from States parties to the Convention for Convention offences. The central authority of another party may be contacted by requesting countries and may suggest, if need be, the most appropriate legal basis to ensure the most efficient execution of the request.

Another State's central authority frequently carries out informal consultations before formal mutual legal assistance requests are received, and it is a common practice to accept and review draft requests before the submission of a formal request. One State party reported that the staff of its central authority engaged in constant, near-daily communication with counterparts in countries that had submitted a large number of requests for mutual legal assistance. The central authority also seeks to have regular annual consultations with its main partners in the areas of extradition and mutual legal assistance.

请自行翻译后查看后文的分析点评

分析点评

第 1 段

More States confirmed the possibility of relying on the Convention as a legal basis for mutual legal assistance than is the case for extradition. Article 46 itself has been invoked and has served as the legal basis for providing assistance on numerous occasions. Many States parties reported having made and/or received at least one request using the Convention as a legal basis; that was often commended as a good practice by the reviewers. For example, one State party reported that its legislation on mutual legal assistance was complemented by special regulations facilitating the submission and receipt of mutual legal assistance requests to and from States parties to the Convention for Convention offences.

与引渡相比①，更多国家确认有可能将《公约》作为司法协助的法律依据。第四十六条本身已被多次援引和作为提供援助的法律依据。许多缔约国报告说，他们将《公约》作为法律依据，已经提出和（或者）收到了一条请求②；这经常被③审议人员称赞为一种良好做法。例如，一个缔约国报告说，其关于司法协助的立法得到了关于《公约》罪行的特别条例的补充④，便于向《公约》缔约国提交和从《公约》缔约国接收司法协助请求。

批 注

① 主语混乱。
② 漏译。
③ 可以换个说法。
④ 语意不明，逻辑错误，可读性差。

确认有可能以《公约》作为司法协助的法律依据的国家多于以《公约》作为引渡的法律依据的国家。第四十六条本身已被多次援引并作为提供援助的法律依据。许多缔约国报告称，它们利用《公约》作为法律依据已经提出和（或）收到了至少一项请求；审议人员经常称赞这是一种良好做法。例如，一个缔约国报告称，其关于司法协助的立法已做了补充，即便利《公约》缔约国之间就《公约》规定罪行提交和接收司法协助请求的专项条例。

1. 第 1 句话的主语是国家，因此进行比较的应该是国家，而不是"引渡"与"国家"。

2. 第 3 句原文有"at least"，译文漏译。

3. 最后一句"For example...its legislation on mutual legal assistance was complemented by special regulations facilitating the submission and receipt...requests to and from States parties to the Convention for Convention offences"，"facilitating"是一个非谓语结构，现在分词表主动，作定语，修饰的是"special regulations"，翻译稿将该词理解成了单独的结构，完全没有体现这种逻辑关系。

第 2 段

Another State's central authority frequently carries out informal consultations before formal mutual legal assistance requests are received, and it is a common practice to accept and review draft requests before the submission of a formal request. One State party reported that the staff of its central authority engaged in constant, near-daily communication with counterparts in countries that had submitted a large number of requests for mutual legal assistance.

另一个国家的中央机关经常在收到正式司法协助请求之前进行非正式磋商，在正式请求提交之前接受和审查请求草案是一种惯常做法。一个缔约国报告说，其中央机关的工作人员与提交了大量司法协助请求的国家的对应方进行了经常的、几乎每日的交流⑤。

批 注

⑤ 逻辑不通；可读性差。

另一个国家的中央机关经常在收到正式司法协助请求之前进行非正式磋商，在提交正式请求之前接受和审查请求书草案是一种常见的做法。有一个缔约国报告称，其中央机关的工作人员几乎每天都在不断地与提交了大量司法协助请求的国家的对应方进行通信。

翻译稿将若干时间状语简单地罗列，导致语句不通顺，可读性差，在翻译时要避免这种情况。在理解原文的基础上，可以灵活调整词的位置，确保可读性。

With regard to extradition, the vast majority of States parties did not require implementing legislation for consultations to be held, either because they regarded the duty of consultation as part of international comity or practice, or they considered article 44, paragraph 17, of the Convention to be directly applicable and self-executing in their legal systems. In some cases, a lack of both legislation and practice has resulted in the non-implementation of the requirement, and recommendations were issued for the States parties involved to consult with the requesting party before refusing extradition.

参考译文

关于引渡，绝大多数缔约国并没有要求为举行磋商而执行立法，原因或是它们认为磋商的义务是国际礼让或惯例的一部分，或者它们认为在其本国法律制度中，《公约》第四十四条第十七款可以直接适用和自动执行。在某些情况下，由于缺乏立法和实践，导致该规定未能得到执行，建议有关缔约国在拒绝引渡前与请求国进行磋商。

背景介绍

本篇选自秘书长报告。该报告系根据大会第68/192号、第70/176号、第71/209号和第71/287号决议编写而成，概述了联合国毒品和犯罪问题办公室为支持会员国努力打击跨国有组织犯罪、腐败和恐怖主义及预防犯罪和强化刑事司法系统以加强法治而开展的活动情况。报告还提及与该办公室的治理和财务状况有关的动态，并载有关于各国批准或加入《联合国打击跨国有组织犯罪公约》及其各项议定书和《联合国反腐败公约》的情况的信息，以及有关新出现的政策问题及其对策和旨在加强联合国预防犯罪和刑事司法方案的建议的信息。

第十七篇

The present report provides a brief overview of efforts undertaken by UNODC, as requested by the General Assembly in its resolution 71/209. The report also provides a brief overview of the progress made in the implementation by the United Nations system of the United Nations Global Plan of Action to Combat Trafficking in Persons, adopted by the Assembly in its resolution 64/293.

UNODC also continued to provide robust training on respecting human rights while countering terrorism. In that context, UNODC assisted countries of the Sahel and the Middle East and North Africa region on, inter alia, dealing with situations in which children are recruited and exploited by terrorist and violent extremist groups, and partnered with OHCHR to initiate assistance on gender dimensions in criminal justice responses to terrorism.

The Office is strengthening its cooperation with national and local government structures to address issues related to urban governance and the impact of crime and gang-related violence, including in the context of the New Urban Agenda. In that connection, the Office organized a side event at the United Nations Conference on Housing and Sustainable Urban Development (Habitat Ⅲ), held in Quito from 17 to 20 October 2016, on the impact of organized crime on city safety, in partnership with UN-Habitat and UN-Women.

请自行翻译后查看后文的分析点评

第 1 段

The present report provides a brief overview of efforts undertaken by UNODC, as requested by the General Assembly in its resolution 71/209. The report also provides a brief overview of the progress made in the implementation by the United Nations system of the United Nations Global Plan of Action to Combat Trafficking in Persons, adopted by the Assembly in its resolution 64/293.

本报告根据大会第 71/209 号决议提出的请求①，概述了毒品和犯罪问题办公室所做的努力。报告还简要概述了联合国系统在执行大会第 64/293 号决议通过

批 注

① 理解有误。

的《联合国打击贩运人口的全球行动计划》方面取得的进展。

本报告概述了毒品和犯罪问题办公室根据大会第71/209号决议提出的请求所做的努力。报告还简要概述了联合国系统在执行大会第64/293号决议通过的《联合国打击贩运人口的全球行动计划》方面取得的进展。

译文出现错误的地方在于"as requested by the General Assembly in its resolution 71/209"。其中"as"引导非限制性定语从句,但从结构上分析,as既可以指逗号前面整个句子的内容,也可以按照就近原则指代离它位置较近的内容,所以这句话的难点在于"as requested by the General Assembly in its Resolution 71/209"修饰的是"The present report"(即,报告根据大会决议提出的请求概述了毒品和犯罪问题办公室的努力),还是"efforts undertaken by UNODC"(即,毒品和犯罪问题办公室根据大会请求做出了努力)。仅从本句的行文来看,并不好判断,需要查询句子中提及的大会第71/209号决议予以佐证。经查,该决议涉及毒品和犯罪问题办公室今后应采取的措施,因此前述第二种理解是正确的。

第 2 段

UNODC also continued to provide robust training on respecting human rights while countering terrorism. In that context, UNODC assisted countries of the Sahel and the Middle East and North Africa region on, inter alia, dealing with situations in which children are recruited and exploited by terrorist and violent extremist groups, and partnered with OHCHR to initiate assistance on gender dimensions in criminal justice responses to terrorism.

毒品和犯罪问题办公室还继续提供关于在打击恐怖主义的同时尊重人权的有力培训。在这方面,毒品和犯罪问题办公室协助萨赫勒及中东和北非区域的国家处理尤其是恐怖主义和暴力极端主义集团招募或剥削儿童的情况,并在应对恐怖主义的刑事司法对策中与人权高专办合作启动性别层面的援助①。

毒品和犯罪问题办公室还继续提供关于在打击恐怖主义的同时尊重人权的有力培训。在这方面,毒品和犯罪问题办公室协助萨赫勒及中东和北非区域的国家处理尤其是恐怖主义和暴力极端主义集团招募或剥削儿童的情况,并与人权高专办合作发起在应对恐怖主义的刑事司法对策中提供性别层面的援助。

翻译稿最后一个句子理解有误。要理解这句话的含义,首先需要理清句子

> 批 注
> ① 理解错误。

层次。这句话的主要结构是毒品和犯罪问题办公室与人权高专办合作，合作的内容是发起性别层面的援助，而这种援助是在应对恐怖主义的刑事司法对策中提供的。翻译稿错在认为介词结构"in criminal justice responses to terrorism"修饰整句话，而通过上文的分析可知，这部分修饰的是"assistance on gender dimensions"。此外，翻译稿可读性差，症结在于对介词结构的把握不够，没有正确分析句子成分，造成被原文"牵着走"的后果。

第3段

The Office is strengthening its cooperation with national and local government structures to address issues related to urban governance and the impact of crime and gang-related violence, including in the context of the New Urban Agenda. In that connection, the Office organized a side event at the United Nations Conference on Housing and Sustainable Urban Development (Habitat III), held in Quito from 17 to 20 October 2016, on the impact of organized crime on city safety, in partnership with UN-Habitat and UN-Women.

毒品和犯罪问题办公室正在加强与国家和地方政府机构的合作，以解决城市治理相关问题和犯罪与帮派相关暴力行为的影响，包括在《新城市议程》范围内①。在这方面，毒品和犯罪问题办公室与人居署和妇女署合作组织了一次于2016年10月17日至20日举行的②联合国住房和城市可持续发展大会（人居三大会）的会外活动③，内容关于有组织犯罪对城市安全的影响。

批 注

① 表述不完整。
② 产生歧义。
③ 理解错误。

毒品和犯罪问题办公室正在加强与国家和地方政府机构的合作，以解决城市治理相关问题和犯罪与帮派相关暴力行为的影响，包括在《新城市议程》范围内加强这种合作。在这方面，毒品和犯罪问题办公室乘联合国住房和城市可持续发展大会（人居三）2016年10月17日至20日在基多举行之机，与人居署和妇女署合作组织了一次会外活动，探讨有组织犯罪对城市安全的影响。

1. 表述不完整。第一句中的"including in the context of the New Urban Agenda"指的是前半句提到的毒品和犯罪问题办公室与国家和地方政府机构加强合作，起到补充说明的作用，明确了加强合作的范围。但翻译稿没有体现出这种含义，未指明是在《新城市议程》范围内加强合作还是在《新城市议程》范围内解决问题和影响，容易造成误解，而审校稿又重复了一遍"加强这种合作"，马上使语义更明确。遇到类似的句子或插入语，可以采用这种增译技巧，适当重复一下前文内容，目的是明确语义，避免造成歧义和误解。

2. 在第2句中，"held in Quito from 17 to 20 October 2016"修饰的是人居三

大会。那么如何判断这个日期指的不是"side event"（会外活动）而是人居三大会呢？只要通过网络查询，就会发现人居三大会确实在2016年10月17日至20日举行。另外，按照常理，会外活动的举办时间通常较短，不会持续很多天。在明确这一点后，会发现原译文没有明确指出该日期是会外活动的举办日期还是人居三大会的日期，容易产生歧义，而审校稿对此作了明确区分。

3. 理解有误。原文提到"a side event at the United Nations Conference on Housing and Sustainable Urban Development"，不是说会外活动是在人居三大会上举办的，而是在此期间（包括休会期间）举办的。翻译稿将"at"理解成在会上，不够准确。

补充练习

The UNODC counter-terrorism legal training curriculum was complemented with a new module on the international legal framework against chemical, biological, radiological and nuclear terrorism. The module on the universal legal framework against terrorism is now under revision, and an additional new publication on countering terrorism in the international legal context is under development. Furthermore, the Office produced a version of the training module entitled Human Rights and Criminal Justice Responses to Terrorism adapted to the counter-terrorism law of Kenya. The Office also finalized training materials for criminal justice training institutions from South-Eastern Europe on prosecution and investigation in foreign terrorist fighter-related cases.

The Office further strengthened partnerships with entities of the Counter-Terrorism Implementation Task Force, including through co-chairing three Task Force working groups. Taking into account its mandate on terrorism prevention, UNODC plays an important role in overall United Nations efforts to support Member States in their implementation of the United Nations Global Counter-Terrorism Strategy. More specifically, 50 per cent of the projects under pillar III of the Strategy, on capacity-building, are implemented by UNODC.

毒品和犯罪问题办公室的反恐法律培训课程补充了有关打击化学、生物、辐射和核恐怖主义国际法律框架的新模块。目前正在修订关于全球反恐法律框架的模块，另外，正在编写一部在国际法范畴内反恐的新出版物。此外，毒品和犯罪问题办公室根据肯尼亚的反恐法律编写了一版题为"人权和应对恐怖主义的刑事司法对策"的培训模块。毒品和犯罪问题办公室还完成了为东南欧的刑事司法培训机构编写的关于起诉和调查外国恐怖主义作战人员相关案件的培训材料的定稿。

通过共同主持反恐执行工作队三个工作组的工作等，毒品和犯罪问题办公室进一步加强了与该工作队各实体的伙伴关系。考虑到其关于预防恐怖主义的任务授权，毒品和犯罪问题办公室在联合国为支持会员国执行《联合国全球反恐战略》做出整体努力方面发挥重要作用。更具体而言，关于能力建设的《战略》支柱三下50%的项目由毒品和犯罪问题办公室实施。

背景介绍

本篇选自联合国儿童基金会与承包商订立的服务合同。儿基会是联合国大会根据1946年12月11日第57(1)号决议设立的国际政府间组织，系联合国附属机构，致力于与世界各国的政府、民间社会组织和其他合作伙伴合作，在《儿童权利公约》的指导下，促进儿童的生存权、受保护权、发展权和参与权。此类材料属于合同法律文件的范畴，无论是中文还是英文，在用语上都自成一格，有鲜明的用词特点。其翻译要求严谨，译者须做到用词准确，使译文具有法律文件的严谨性、准确性、权威性。

第十八篇

原文

This Contract is entered into by the Parties under the Long Term Agreement-Service (LTA-S) and is subject to the LTA-S.

This contract (the or this "Contract") comprises: (a) this document (including any Special Terms and Conditions set out at Section 4 below); (b) the LTA-S; (c) the UNICEF General Terms and Conditions of Contract (Services) attached as Annex A; and (d) the other annexes (if any) attached to this document. Subject to any changes agreed pursuant to Article 3.6 of the LTA-S, in the case of any inconsistencies between the terms of this Contract and the terms of the LTA-S, the terms of the LTA-S will prevail over the terms of this Contract, except with regard to the specifications or technical requirements specified in this Contract which will prevail over the LTA-S. Capitalized terms used but not defined in this Contract have the meaning given to them in the UNICEF General Terms and Conditions of Contract (Services).

请自行翻译后查看后文的分析点评

分析点评

第 1 段

This Contract is entered into by the Parties under the Long Term Agreement-Service (LTA-S) and is subject to the LTA-S.

本合同由双方根据《长期服务安排》签订,并受《长期服务安排》约束。

本合同系由双方根据《服务长期安排》订立,受《服务长期安排》约束。

本段难度不大,翻译稿也较为到位,审校稿增加了一个"系"字,并将"签订"改为"订立",更好地体现了法律文件的严谨性和规范性。本段中有两个合同法律文件中经常使用的表述。

1. "This Contract is entered into by"译为"本合同系由……订立",典型的被动句转主动句。

2. "be subject to"这一短语经常出现在条件性、约束性或限制性语境下,在英文法律文件中频繁可见。在法律翻译英译汉中,有多种译法,包括"除非……,否则……""须……""在不抵触……情形下""以……为条件""根据……规定""除……另有规定外"和"受……约束"等。虽然各种译法都不尽相同,但核心意思大同小异,都是指"受制于"有关条款或须"依照"有关条款办事,具体该作何译,须视上下文而定。

第 2 段

This contract (the or this "Contract") comprises: (a) this document (including any Special Terms and Conditions set out at Section 4 below); (b) the LTA-S; (c) the UNICEF General Terms and Conditions of Contract (Services) attached as Annex A; and (d) the other annexes (if any) attached to this document. Subject to any changes agreed pursuant to Article 3.6 of the LTA-S, in the case of any inconsistencies between the terms of this Contract and the terms of the LTA-S, the terms of the LTA-S will prevail over the terms of this Contract, except with regard to the specifications or technical requirements specified in this Contract which will prevail over the LTA-S. Capitalized terms used but not defined in this Contract have the meaning given to them in the UNICEF General Terms and Conditions of Contract (Services).

① 可进一步明确化。

本合同("合同"或"本合同")包括①:(a)本文件(包括下文第 4 节所述

第三章 法律与法治

批 注

① 不够简洁明确。
② 累赘，形式上拘泥于原文。
③ 中文中有大小写之分吗？

任何特殊条款和条件）；（b）《长期服务安排》；（c）儿童基金会作为附件 A 随附的①《合同（服务）一般条款和条件》；（d）本文件所附的其他附件（如果有的话）②。除须遵守根据《长期服务安排》第 3.6 条商定的任何变更以外，如果本合同的条款与《长期服务安排》的条款有任何不一致之处，《长期服务安排》的条款优先于本合同条款，但本合同明确规定的规格或技术要求将优先于《长期服务安排》。本合同中使用但未定义的大写术语③具有在儿基会《合同（服务）一般条款和条件》中赋予它们的含义。

本合同（"合同"或"本合同"）由以下文件构成：（a）本文件（包括下文第 4 条所述任何特殊条款和条件）；（b）《服务长期安排》；（c）附件 A 儿基会《合同通用条款和条件（服务类）》；以及（d）本文件的任何其他附件。除根据《服务长期安排》第 3.6 条商定任何变更外，如果本合同所载条款与《服务长期安排》所载条款存在任何不一致之处，《服务长期安排》所载条款优先于本合同所载条款，但在本合同明确规定的服务规格或技术要求方面，本合同优先于《服务长期安排》。本合同中使用大号字体显示但未给出定义的术语一律以儿基会《合同通用条款和条件（服务类）》中规定的相应含义为准。

点 评

原文难度不高，但翻译稿细节处理不到位，有失严谨。

1. 在第 1 句中，"comprise"可译为"包括"或"由……构成"，意思一样，但后者更能明确体现合同与后述文件之间的关系，而且相较于前者，在中文法律文件中也更常见。

2. 关于"the UNICEF General Terms and Conditions of Contract (Services) attached as Annex A"，译稿为典型的直译，不能算错，但读着别扭。原文的意思其实是：采用附件 A 的形式附上该《一般条款和条件》。因此审校稿将之改为"附件 A 儿基会《合同通用条款和条件（服务类）》"，达到了两重效果：一、这句译文本身更加简洁明确；二、整段结构更加紧凑清晰，"本合同由以下文件构成：（a）本文件；（b）《安排》；（c）附件 A（比较原译"儿童基金会作为附件 A 随附的"）；以及（d）……"。

3. "(if any)"：此短语常以括号形式出现在句末，起到"兜底"的作用，意思是：若有，即为合同构成部分，若无，则无。很多译者都会处理为"（若有 / 如有 / 如果有的话）"，但在中文法律文件中根本看不到这样的表述，而是以"任何"代之。因此，审校稿将之改为"本文件的任何其他附件"。两相比较，后者更简洁、更达意且更符合中文表达习惯。

4. 常识性错误，见"Capitalized terms"引领的一句的处理。首先，英文中存在字母大小写之分，有时会整个单词或短语用大写字母显示，以示强调；而在中文中则无大小写之分，但对于意欲着重强调部分，会采用有别于文本字体的大号字体或其他字体或者下划线的形式，在此处理为"使用大号字体显示"，在形式和意思上与原文最为贴近。其次，"具有《一般条款和条件》中赋予它们的含义"，又是翻译腔十足的直译，经审校稿修改后，就地道多了。

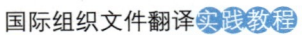

This Contract will be a binding contract between UNICEF and the Contractor when UNICEF receives a copy of this Contract counter-signed by the Contractor. The effective date of this Contract will be the date UNICEF receives the counter-signed copy.

The term of this Contract will be for the period stated on the first page of this Contract.

UNICEF can cancel this Contract upon written notice (including by email) to the Contractor without any liability for cancellation charges or any other liability of any kind, provided that notice of such cancellation is given prior to the scheduled start date for performance of the Services.

儿基会一经收到承包商会签的本合同副本，本合同即构成儿基会与承包商之间具有约束力的合同。儿基会收到会签副本之日为本合同的生效日期。

本合同的有效期限为本合同第一页上载明的时间段。

儿基会可在向承包商发出书面通知（包括通过电子邮件）之后取消本合同，而无须承担任何偿付取消费用的责任或任何其他责任，但前提是儿基会必须在预定的开始提供服务日期之前发出此等取消通知。

本章词汇

mens rea 〈拉〉犯意，犯罪意图
actus reus 〈拉〉犯罪行为
force majeure 〈法〉不可抗力
find 判定，裁定
dispute resolution 争端解决（联合国总部）
rapporteur 〈法〉报告员
special rapporteur 特别报告员
provisional application of treaties 条约的暂时适用
legal certainty 法律确定性
unilateral declaration 单方面声明
implicit agreement 默示协定
topic 专题
private international law 国际私法
administration of justice 司法、执法
arbitration 仲裁（指争议双方当事人将其争议提交给中立的第三方（即仲裁员）来审理并做出裁决的争议解决方法）
agreement on arbitration 仲裁协定 = arbitration agreement
commercial arbitration 商业仲裁
place of arbitration 仲裁地点
arbitration proceedings /process 仲裁程序
arbitration clause 仲裁条款
grievance arbitration 申诉仲裁
rights arbitration 权利仲裁
award 裁决
arbitration award 仲裁裁决
arbitrator 仲裁员，仲裁人
umpire 首席仲裁员
adjudication n. ①审判；裁判，指解决争议或裁决案件的法律程序或过程。②判决
judgment n. 判决 法庭对案件各方当事人的权利和义务或是否承担责任问题做出的最后决定。在诉讼实践中，与"decision"作为同义词互换使用；在刑事诉讼中，"sentence"与"judgment"同义
mediation 调解
conciliation 和解

Court of First Instance 一审法院
territorial rights 地域性权限
domicile 住所，不得与"residence"混淆
residence 居所
lex fori 〈拉〉法院地法；诉讼地法；审判地法
null and void 无效
substantive validity 实质性效力
opinio juris 法律确信
part 部分
chapter 章
section 节
article 条
paragraph 款
subparagraph 项
item 目
criminal justice 刑事司法
concealment 窝赃
embezzlement 贪污
national legislation 国家立法
source 渊源（法律上）
　　如：sources of international law 国际法的渊源
source of law 法律渊源 = fons juris〈拉〉
act 法（不译"法案"）
act or omission 作为或不作为
cause of action 诉因，诉讼理由
right of action 起诉权
personal action 对人诉讼
action in personam 对人诉讼
action in rem 对物诉讼
aggravating circumstances 加重处罚情节
criminal cases 刑事案件
criminal act 犯罪行为
criminal action = criminal suit 刑事诉讼（不要译"犯罪行动"）
criminal attempt 犯罪未遂
criminal code 刑法
Criminal Code《刑法典》
criminal law 刑法

criminal offence　刑事罪
jurisprudence　①法理学，②判例（联合国文件中常用此义）
trading in influence　影响力交易
abuse of functions　滥用职权
proceeds of crime　犯罪所得
undue advantage　不正当好处
expert evaluation　鉴定结论
predicate offence　上游犯罪
illicit enrichment　资产非法增加
bona fide third parties　善意第三人
special investigative techniques　特殊侦查手段
reversal of the burden of proof　举证责任倒置
bail while awaiting trial　取保候审
plea bargaining　控辩交易
mitigating factor　减轻处罚因素
extenuating circumstances　罪行减轻情节
presumption of innocence　无罪推定
beneficial owner　实际受益人
financial disclosure system　财产申报制度
criminal association　犯罪团伙
infiltrator agent　卧底特工
corroborating evidence　补强证据/佐证
double jeopardy　双重危险/双重追诉
non bis in idem　〈拉〉一罪不二审/一事不再理
cases of grand corruption　严重腐败案件，腐败大案

inchoate offences/inchoate crime　初始罪
jus cogens　〈拉〉强行法
jus soli　〈拉〉出生地法、出生地主义
jus sanguinis　〈拉〉血统制、血统主义
applicable law　准据法（联合国之外，也有译"可适用的法律"的）
remedy　救济、补救办法、补救
domestic law　本国法律
national law　本国法
perpetrator　实施者
the accused　被告
accused person　被控告人
accused offenders　被告犯罪的人
the alleged offender　被指控人；被指控犯罪的人
offender　犯罪的人
intentional ignorance　故作不知
wilful blindness　故意无视
territorial principle　属地原则
passive personality principle　被动属人原则
active personality jurisdiction　主动属人管辖权
personal immunity　属人豁免
ratione personae jurisdiction　属人管辖（权）
joint criminal enterprise　共同犯罪事业
production of document(s)　出示文件，出示证件
production of evidence　提供证据，出示证据
dual criminality　双重犯罪
enabling statute　授权法

第四章

经济与金融

本章导言

经济与金融类的文件专业性强、涵盖面广、种类多样、性质各异、内容丰富，是一个值得深入学习和探索的领域。

联合国经济与金融类文件可谓这一领域的"集大成者"，从纵观全局的全球经济展望、贸易规则、金融合作，到着眼于细处的特定行业、特定部门、特定业务及特定操作，几乎无不涉及。联合国在该领域的文件主要分为以下几种类型：①会议文件；②出版物；③财政预算和统计报告；④其他国际组织提交的信息报告和资料。本章材料分别选自国际货币基金组织的主要出版物和文件、联合国国际贸易法委员会的文件以及经合组织的文件。

联合国经济与金融类文件具有鲜明的特征。

（1）广泛涉及多个方面，包括但不限于金融、政治（国际组织行动、各国政策和外交工作等）、经济、法律（公约、条约、协议等）以及环境（各地区的地理和气候特征）。

（2）类型和体裁多种多样。仅就具有高度代表性的国际货币基金组织文件来说，主要包括：①出版物，例如《世界经济展望》；②项目文件，例如各国与国际货币基金组织联合开展的培训项目；③各类发言稿，例如货币基金组织总裁讲话稿；④网络媒体发布内容，例如各类博客。

（3）具有高度的专业性，最明显的表现是专业术语来源广泛、数量巨大。在翻译时必须采用来自各机构术语表的经济与金融术语，超出范围的其他术语，则应查证联合国词汇库、相关领域权威机构的作准文件和行业惯用语等。

（4）从此类文件自身的行文风格来看，经济学和金融学专业逻辑性强，多涉及数据资料，这就决定了语言的表达必然严谨。具体而言，句子的结构相对复杂，不但长且插入成分多，同时句子内部条分缕析，句段之间逻辑关系严整。

根据联合国经济类文件的上述特点，译文一方面要体现文件的专业性，另一方面应通过使用各种翻译技巧，尽可能提升文件的可读性。这要求译员做到以下几点。

首先，从背景知识来说，必须注重积累专业知识，尤其是经济与金融领域的专业知识。不但必须

"知其然",还要"知其所以然",翻译起来才能达意、通畅,并具有专业性。

其次,从工作态度来说,译者必须以严谨的态度对待遇到的专业术语,遵守相关的术语表、词汇库以及权威机构的作准文件和行业惯用语的规定。对于词义单一的行业术语,坚持直译;对于在经济领域具有特殊含义的非专业术语,应根据语境把握词义;摒弃"不懂装懂"的习惯,始终以理解为前提进行翻译。例如,"fundamentals"一般情况下意思是"基本原理",而在经济与金融领域则多半是"(经济)基本面";"commodity"通常意思是"商品",而在经济与金融领域往往需要翻成"大宗商品";"deficit"在"fiscal deficit"中是"赤字",而在"trade deficit"中为"逆差"。

最后,从方法技能来说,在理解和翻译复杂的长句段时,注意细致拆解句段结构,结合主旨和上下文认真分析判断句意和功能,尤其要注意各种副词、连词以及标点符号的使用和位置。特别是,要考虑译文的类型、体裁和读者群,并从这些角度出发考虑译文的可读性、措辞和风格。

联合国经济与金融类文件是联合国的一类专业性文件,与普通经济与金融类文件存在共性,同时具有其特殊性。致力于投身联合国经济与金融类文件翻译工作的人员需要夯实自身英语基础知识,提升英语综合能力,同时扩大和深化经济与金融领域的专业知识,在明确并遵守联合国文件翻译要求的前提下,努力追求"信达雅"。

背景介绍

以下十篇材料均选自国际货币基金组织《世界经济展望》,分别涉及如下主题:增长减缓,复苏不稳;企业市场支配力的增长及其宏观经济效应;资本货物价格以及全球前景和政策。

国际货币基金组织的主要宗旨是确保稳定国际货币体系,也即稳定各国(及其公民)相互交易所依赖的汇率体系及国际支付体系。该组织的文件和出版物高度集中地体现了联合国经济与金融类文件的特征。

《世界经济展望》是国际货币基金组织的主要出版物之一,旨在定期提供该组织对全球前景的评估,内容包括工作人员对全球层面、主要国家组(按地区和经济发展阶段等划分)和许多单个国家的经济发展的分析和预测,重点是经济政策问题以及对经济发展和前景的分析。该出版物通常每年出版两期,既是国际货币与金融委员会的会议文件,又是国际货币基金组织进行全球监督活动的主要工具。

从翻译角度看,该出版物的内容特点有:时事性较强,每期均体现根据近期全球经济发展趋势做出的各项预测和相关调整,并分析研究最近的重大事件或突出问题的影响;广泛涉及多个方面,包括但不限于金融、政治(国际组织行动、各国政策和外交工作等)、经济、法律(公约、条约、协议等)以及环境(各地区的地理和气候特征);具有高度的专业性;专业术语来源广泛,数量巨大;句段之间和内部逻辑关系严密,结构相对复杂,且多涉及数据资料。

在翻译过程中,经济与金融类的术语应以国际货币基金组织术语表为准,其他术语可以查阅联合国词汇库、相关领域权威机构(主要是中国人民银行、中国外交部、中国国家税务总局等)、作准文件(公约、条约、协议文本)和行业惯用语;在理解和翻译复杂的长句段时,应当在细致分析语法结构的基础上拆解句段,结合主旨和上下文认真分析判断句意和功能,特别注意各种副词、连词以及标点符号的使用和位置。

第一篇

原文

The impact of rising market power on the responsiveness of inflation to economic conditions—the so-called Phillips curve, which has flattened over the past two decades (Chapter 3 of the April 2013 WEO and Chapter 3 of the October 2016 WEO)—is less clear and depends on how firms (re)set prices, among other factors. On one hand, greater market power could weaken firms' incentives to keep prices close to those of their competitors for fear of losing market share; they might then be more inclined to adjust their prices after a shock, in which case inflation would become more responsive to economic conditions.

请自行翻译后查看后文的分析点评

分析点评

The impact of rising market power on the responsiveness of inflation to economic conditions—the so-called Phillips curve, which has flattened over the past two decades (Chapter 3 of the April 2013 WEO and Chapter 3 of the October 2016 WEO)—is less clear and depends on how firms (re)set prices, among other factors. On one hand, greater market power could weaken firms' incentives to keep prices close to those of their competitors for fear of losing market share; they might then be more inclined to adjust their prices after a shock, in which case inflation would become more responsive to economic conditions.

批 注

① "所谓（的）"后面紧跟的专有名词或引述内容通常需要加引号。
②③ 按照《世界经济展望》中文本的惯例，章次应为"三"而非"3"。
④ 漏译。
⑤ 注意"prices"前的"their"，此处需译出。

市场势力上升对经济状况反应的影响——所谓的菲利普斯曲线①，在过去二十年中已经趋于平缓（2013年4月《世界经济展望》第3章②和2016年10月《世界经济展望》第3章③）——不再那么明确，取决于公司如何（重新）定价以及其他因素。一方面，市场势力的上升可能会使企业由于担心丧失市场份额而不愿使其价格接近于其竞争者；他们可能④更倾向于在经受经济冲击后调整价格⑤，在这种情况下，通货膨胀对经济状况的反应力加强。

通货膨胀对于经济状况的灵敏性可以所谓的"菲利普斯曲线"来表示，该曲线在过去二十年已经趋于平缓（2013年4月《世界经济展望》第三章和2016年10月《世界经济展望》第三章）；市场支配力增长对这种灵敏性产生的影响不再那么明确，并且取决于企业如何（重新）定价等因素。一方面，市场支配力的增长可能会弱化企业因担心丧失市场份额而维持自身价格与竞争者价格接近的动力；这些企业此后可能更倾向于在经受冲击后调整自身价格，在这种情况下，通货膨胀对于经济状况的灵敏性将会提高。

点评

1. 翻译本段开头部分，关键在于理解"Phillips curve"。经济学的相关解释是："菲利普斯曲线是用来表示失业与通货膨胀之间交替关系的曲线，由新西兰经济学家威廉·菲利普斯于1958年在《1861—1957年英国失业和货币工资变动率之间的关系》一文中最先提出。"因此，这个专有名词对应的不是"The impact of rising market power"，而是"the responsiveness of inflation to economic

conditions"。译文在这个点上理解有误。此外，本段最后一句中的"inflation would become more responsive to economic conditions"也可印证上述理解。

2. 译者将"the responsiveness of inflation to economic conditions"译为"经济状况反应"，明显漏了"inflation to"。

3. 括号中"Chapter 3 of the April 2013 WEO and Chapter 3 of the October 2016 WEO"旨在注明"the responsiveness of inflation to economic conditions—the so-called Phillips curve, which has flattened over the past two decades"的出处，应紧跟在这一内容之后。

4. 根据国际货币基金组织术语表，"market power"应译作"市场力量"；此外，本文对"market power"并无贬低之意，而"力量"相对于"势力"而言较为中性，所以用"力量"更为妥当。根据此处的背景内容，也可使用"市场支配力"。

5. 译者对本段第二句的理解存在偏差。对"weaken firms' incentives to keep prices close to those of their competitors for fear of losing market share"的正确理解应当是：……导致企业不再积极地将自身价格保持在与竞争对手接近的水平，而企业之所以维持相近价格，是由于害怕损失市场份额。另外，可以从逻辑角度分析：随着自身市场支配力的增长，企业便不再那么担心损失市场份额，也就无须时时保持价格接近于同类竞争者的价格。

6. 在国际货币基金组织术语表中，"responsive"译作"反应灵敏的"，"responsiveness"译作"灵敏性"。本段中的这两个词完全可以采用该组织的惯用译法。

Measuring market power is challenging. This chapter considers two main alternatives. The first, and most common, is the ability of firms to charge prices that exceed their marginal cost of production. Under this definition, a firm's market power can be measured through its markup, defined as the ratio of price to marginal cost. This is the main measure used throughout the chapter. A second possible definition is the ability of firms to obtain extraordinary profits—so-called economic rents. A frequently used indicator here is an (operational) profitability measure, such as the ratio of operating earnings to sales; this is an empirical measure of the Lerner index, which also relates closely to a firm's markup.

参考译文

衡量市场支配力这一工作不乏挑战性。本章考虑了两种主要的（市场支配力）定义。第一种也是最常见的定义是企业收取高于其边际生产成本的价格的能力。根据这一定义，企业的市场支配力可以通过其加价率，即价格与边际成本的比率来衡量。这是本章使用的主要衡量标准。第二种可能的定义是企业获取超额利润（所谓的"经济租金"）的能力。这里经常使用的指标是（运营）盈利能力衡量标准，例如，营业收入与销售额的比率；这是勒纳指数的一个实证指标，也与企业的加价率密切相关。

第二篇

原文

Other factors may have also played some role, however—possibly magnifying the impact of technological changes. Winner-takes-most outcomes and the associated increase in winners' market power may be more likely when competition policy fails to adapt or becomes less stringent, for example, when it comes to merger enforcement or exclusionary conduct by dominant firms. Over the broad sample of firms analyzed in this chapter, the evidence shows that mergers and acquisitions have been followed by significantly higher markups (Box 2.2). That said, whether the loss to consumers from such increases has been typically more than offset by gains from cost and price reductions due to economies of scale and scope, or by other efficiency gains, is an open question that warrants investigation.

请自行翻译后查看后文的分析点评

分析点评

Other factors may have also played some role, however—possibly magnifying the impact of technological changes. Winner-takes-most outcomes and the associated increase in winners' market power may be more likely when competition policy fails to adapt or becomes less stringent, for example, when it comes to merger enforcement or exclusionary conduct by dominant firms. Over the broad sample of firms analyzed in this chapter, the evidence shows that mergers and acquisitions have been followed by significantly higher markups (Box 2.2). That said, whether the loss to consumers from such increases has been typically more than offset by gains from cost and price reductions due to economies of scale and scope, or by other efficiency gains, is an open question that warrants investigation.

翻译稿

其他因素也可能起到一定作用，但可能会放大技术变革的影响。当竞争政策无法适应现状或开始放宽时，例如，涉及主导公司的兼并或排他行为，可能更

批注

① 注意原文的时态是现在完成时。

有可能出现赢者通吃的局面以及获胜者市场势力的上升[①][②] 在本章分析的广泛公司样本中，证据表明，兼并和收购之后加价率明显提高（专栏2.2）。也就是说，消费者由于这种加价率提高而蒙受的损失是否往往会被由规模经济和范围经济带来的成本和价格降低或其他效率提升所抵消，这是一个值得研究的争议问题。

然而，其他因素可能也起到了一定作用，可能放大了技术变革的影响。当涉及诸如兼并执法或主导企业的排他行为等的竞争政策无法适应或开始放宽时，也许更有可能出现"赢者通吃"的结果以及赢者市场支配力的相应增长。在本章分析的广泛企业样本中，有证据表明，兼并和收购之后加价率明显上升（专栏2.2）。即便如此，规模经济和范围经济引起的成本和价格降低所产生的收益或者其他效率增益是否通常在抵消消费者因加价率上升而蒙受的损失之后还有结余，这仍然是一个值得研究的待决问题。

1. 翻译稿将"merger enforcement"一词误解为"兼并"，实际上它是指公司兼并领域的执法。注意，"enforcement"尤其在法律领域比较多用于表示"执法（行为）"。

2. 关于"Winner-takes-most"，MBA智库百科对"Winner-takes-most（赢者通吃）"的解释是：市场竞争最后胜利者获得所有的或绝大部分的市场份额，而失败者往往被淘汰出市场而无法生存。赢家获取全部，败者一无所有。如果遇到此类将特定领域的专用表述/行话移用于其他领域或场合的情况，通常应当在译文中以引号标注。

3. 在理解"whether the loss to consumers from such increases has been typically more than offset by gains from cost and price reductions due to economies of scale and scope, or by other efficiency gains"这一部分时，应当首先抓住句子的核心主干，即"A be more than offset by B"。这个短语的意思是B抵消A绰绰有余。而译者的理解正好与之相反。注意相似短语"A more than offset B"，其意思是A抵消B绰绰有余。例如，"The international food price increases more than offset the hoped-for benefits of the original price insulation policies."是指国际粮食价格的上涨绰绰有余地抵消了原先价格绝缘政策的期望收益。

4. 最后一行中的"open question"意指尚未盖棺定论的问题、尚无定论的问题，因此应当翻译为"待决问题"或"未决问题"，而不是"争议问题"。

补充练习

By reducing investment, rising markups can generate economic slack that may offset their immediate inflationary effect and may also imply a trade-off for monetary policy. These issues are explored through an estimated dynamic stochastic general equilibrium model of the euro area and the United States (see Online Annex 2.3C for

---

批 注

① 漏译。

② 注意中英文标点符号的切换。

details). The model is calibrated to match the within-firm component of the observed trend in markups since 2000 in each of the two areas documented in the section titled "The Rise of Corporate Market Power". Considering only the within-firm rise in markups, rather than the total increase, aligns more closely with the model's setup and focus on rising market power within firms. Rising markups are modeled as a decline in the substitutability between the goods and services produced by different firms (Jones and Philippon 2016; Eggertsson, Robbins, and Wold 2018).

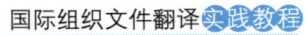

加价率上升会导致投资减少，从而引起经济萧条，这可能抵消其立竿见影的通货膨胀效应，也可能意味着货币政策需要权衡取舍。围绕这些问题的探讨采用了欧元区和美国的估计动态随机一般均衡模型（详见在线附件2.3C）。该模型经过校准，可以匹配"企业市场支配力的增长"一节所载观测到的上述两个地区自2000年以来加价率增长趋势的企业内部成分。仅考虑企业内部加价率上升而非总体上升的做法更契合该模型的建立及其对于企业内部市场支配力增长的关注。加价率的上升被建模为不同企业生产的货物和服务之间的可替代性的下降（Jones 和 Philippon，2016 年；Eggertsson、Robbins 和 Wold，2018 年）。

第三篇

The destination-based version of these taxes—which tax corporate income based on the location of final consumption, rather than the origin of profits—has the further advantage of being able to withstand profit shifting by multinational firms (Auerbach and others 2017). In this way, it also helps level the playing field between large firms—which are typically better equipped to shift profits across jurisdictions—and their smaller, current, or potential competitors.

请自行翻译后查看后文的分析点评

分析点评

The destination-based version of these taxes—which tax corporate income based on the location of final consumption, rather than the origin of profits—has the further advantage of being able to withstand profit shifting by multinational firms (Auerbach and others 2017). In this way, it also helps level the playing field between large firms—which are typically better equipped to shift profits across jurisdictions—and their smaller, current, or potential competitors.

翻译稿

基于特定地点的税收制度——企业所得税基于最终消费地而非利润来源地——[1]在承受跨国公司利润转移方面具有更多优势（Auerbach 等，2017）。通过这种方式[2]，还有助于平衡大公司——这些公司通常能够更加便利地在司法管辖区之间转移利润——以及其较规模小[3]的、当前的或潜在的竞争对手之间的竞争环境。

审校稿

基于目的地的税收（基于最终消费所在地、而非利润来源地征收企业所得税）还具有另一项优势：不受跨国公司转移利润行为的影响（Auerbach 等人，2017 年）。在这方面，它还有助于在大型企业（通常更有能力在不同司法管辖区之间转移利润）和它们的现有或未来的小型竞争者之间创建一个公平的竞争环境。

批注

① 相比用破折号进行夹注，在译文里将这部分说明内容放入括号的做法能够更好地保持句子的整体性。

② 此处应结合上下文确定应当表述为"通过某种方式""在某个方面"还是"这样一来"。

③ 注意中文语序。

点评

1. 本段开头的"destination-based"在税收中是指基于目的地的税收方式/原则。在对特定领域术语进行翻译时，必须准确查阅对应的表述。

2. 翻译稿对"has the further advantage of being able to withstand profit shifting by multinational firms"的理解有问题。首先，"the further advantage"是单数，应当是指"另一项优势"；其次，"advantage of being able to"是指具备能够如何如何的一种优势；最后，"withstand profit shifting"是指经受得起利润转移的影响。

3. 原文中"are...better equipped to"意思是具备更大的能力、更有能力做某事。翻译稿使用的"能够更加便利地"在一定程度上偏离了原文，严格来说不妥。

4. 翻译稿最后一句的关键在于对"level the playing field between"的理解。与此相关的一个短语是"level playing field"（其中"level"为形容词，表示"同等的"），《柯林斯在线词典》对该短语的解释是：a situation in which none of the competing parties has an advantage at the outset of a competitive activity。上述原文短语中的"level"是动词，表示"使同等"，该短语是对"level playing ground"的变形活用，应当翻译为"在……和……之间创建一个公平的竞争环境"，而非"平衡……之间的竞争环境"。

补充练习

The drivers of the relationship between rising concentration (or markups) and increasing corporate saving are not yet fully understood. One possible factor, explored in Dao and others (forthcoming), is the trend decline in global real interest rates (and corporate tax rates) over the past couple of decades. Given that larger firms are less financially constrained and able to leverage more, lower interest rates benefit them disproportionately. As a result, they are better able to exploit opportunities to invest in high-return projects (because, for example, of network effects or increasing returns to scale). When liquidity is constrained and firms must put away investment funds for future projects, larger firms save disproportionately more for these high-return projects.

集中程度（或加价率）上升与企业储蓄增加之间关系的驱动因素尚未完全被人所理解。Dao 等人（即将发表）探讨的一个可能因素是过去几十年内全球实际利率（和企业税率）的趋势下降。鉴于较大企业在财务方面受到的限制较少且能够获得更多贷款，较低的利率对其特别有利。因此，这些企业更能利用机会以投资高收益项目（例如，由于网络效应或规模收益递增）。当流动性受到限制、企业必须为未来项目而储存投资资金时，较大企业为这些高收益项目进行的储蓄更多。

第四篇

原文

Model simulations suggest that the trend rise in markups may have raised inflation somewhat, produced some slack, and slightly reduced natural interest rates in advanced economies, starting from at least the early 2000s. Under rising markups, inflation is higher and potential output growth is lower, and so the natural interest rate—the interest rate that arises absent wage and price rigidities—is also lower than it would be under stable markups. For the euro area and the United States as a group, the output gap might have been about 0.3 percentage point wider, inflation about 0.2 percentage point higher, and the natural interest rate about 10 basis points lower by 2015 than if markups had stayed at their 2000 level—all else equal; that is, abstracting from the impact of the 2008 financial crisis (Figure 2.9). The focus of the model-based analysis on weaker investment is qualitatively—and quantitatively—consistent with the empirical results, which highlight higher markups' harm on investment and their broadly neutral effect on innovation.

请自行翻译后查看后文的分析点评

分析点评

Model simulations suggest that the trend rise in markups may have raised inflation somewhat, produced some slack, and slightly reduced natural interest rates in advanced economies, starting from at least the early 2000s. Under rising markups, inflation is higher and potential output growth is lower, and so the natural interest rate—the interest rate that arises absent wage and price rigidities—is also lower than it would be under stable markups. For the euro area and the United States as a group, the output gap might have been about 0.3 percentage point wider, inflation about 0.2 percentage point higher, and the natural interest rate about 10 basis points lower by 2015 than if markups had stayed at their 2000 level—all else equal; that is, abstracting from the impact of the 2008 financial crisis (Figure 2.9). The focus of the model-based analysis on weaker investment is qualitatively—and quantitatively—consistent with the empirical results, which highlight higher markups' harm on investment and their broadly neutral effect on innovation.

模型模拟表明，<u>从至少</u>①21世纪初开始，加价率的趋势性增长可能在某种程度上导致了通货膨胀上升，导致发达经济体的自然利率产生一些松弛且略有下降的趋势。在加价率增长的情况下，通货膨胀率上升，潜在产出增长率降低，因此自然利率——<u>即</u>②工资和价格刚性所产生的利率——也低于加价率稳定情况下的自然利率。将欧元区和美国作为一个整体，如果加价率保持2000年的水平——而所有其他条件相同，那么到2015年，与实际水平相比，产出缺口可能<u>会扩大</u>③0.3个百分点左右，通货膨胀率<u>会高</u>④0.2个百分点左右，自然利率<u>会低</u>⑤10个基点；也就是说，<u>会从</u>⑥2008年金融危机的影响中抽离出来（图2.9）。关于投资弱化的模型分析焦点与强调<u>加价率</u>⑦不利于投资并对创新存在广泛中立影响的实证结果在定性和定量方面存在一致性。

模型模拟表明，至少从21世纪头十年初开始，加价率的趋势上升在某种程度上可能已经导致了通货膨胀率的上升，造成了某种程度的萧条，以及小幅降低了发达经济体的自然利率。在加价率上升的情况下，通货膨胀率上升，潜在产出增长率下降，因此自然利率——不含工资和价格刚性的利率——低于加价率稳定情况下的自然利率。针对欧元区和美国这个组，如果加价率保持在2000年的水平，而所有其他条件相同，那么到2015年，产出缺口可能扩大了0.3个百分点左右，通货膨胀率可能提高了0.2个百分点左右，自然利率可能降低了大约10个基点；也就是说，从2008年金融危机的影响中抽离出来（图2.9）。关于投资减弱的模型分析的焦点在性质和数量方面与强调加价率上升不利于投资并会对创新产生大致中性的影响的实证结果一致。

1. 关于"the early (1980s, 1990s, 2000s, ...)"，应处理为"20世纪80年代初""20世纪90年代初""21世纪头十年初"；尤其要注意最后一个，翻译时容易因中文表述不便而像译者那样简化为"21世纪初"，此举不可取。

批　注

① 应从中文语序角度考虑，调整"至少"的位置。
② 此处破折号表示说明，紧跟其后的内容前面无须加"即"。
③ 注意时态。原文表示在设想的状况下2015年（过去时间）某些经济指标的可能水平，译文表述应有别于对未来的预期。
④ 同本页批注③。
⑤ 同本页批注③。
⑥ 同本页批注③。
⑦ 漏译。

2. 翻译稿对"produced some slack, and slightly reduced natural interest rates in advanced economies"中"slack"一词的理解出现问题，因此导致全句结构错误。"slack"作为形容词时，意思为"松弛的""萧条的""懈怠的""缓慢的"等；而作为名词时，意思是"（绳索的）松弛部分""富余部分""懈怠""萧条"等。原文中的"slack"不应作形容词理解，一是因为该词一般不用于描述"natural interest rate"；二是因为其后加了逗号，表明该词与后面的内容关系并不紧密。"produced some slack"与"slightly reduced natural interest rates in advanced economies"是并列的两种情形。

3. 翻译稿在处理"the interest rate that arises absent wage and price rigidities"时，似乎把"absent"看成了"from"，所以将这部分译为"工资和价格刚性所产生的利率"。实际上这部分应为"排除了／不含工资和价格刚性的利率"。

4. "For the euro area and the United States as a group"不能译为"将欧元区和美国作为一个整体"，该句是指欧元区和美国属于同一个对照组。需要注意的是，在此类研究分析中，"group"通常译为"组"。

5. 最后一句中的"broadly neutral effect"是指"大致中性的影响"，而不是"广泛中立的影响"。首先看"neutral"："影响"一般是"有利""有害"或者"无利也无害"即"中性"的；而"中立"一般形容人的立场或态度。其次看"broadly"：在这里是用于形容"neutral"的副词，应当理解为程度，即"大体上""大致上"，而非"广泛"。由此例可见，在遇到词语义项较多时，应当结合文件性质和上下文进行比较和选择。

补充练习

After remaining largely stable for decades, the share of national income paid to labor has fallen since the 1980s across many advanced economies, by an average of about 2 percentage points (Chapter 3 of the April 2017 WEO). The four most widely studied explanations for this decline are technological change, including the associated decline in the relative price of capital; globalization and offshoring; measurement difficulties associated with the rise of intangible capital or increased depreciation of physical capital; and weaker worker bargaining power. In particular, Chapter 3 of the April 2017 WEO highlights the role of technology and globalization in reducing labor shares in advanced and emerging market and developing economies. A fifth possible driver, which has gained recent attention, could be increased corporate market power and the associated rise in economic rents accruing to firm owners (Barkai 2017; De Loecker, Eeckhout, and Unger 2018; Eggertsson, Robbins, and Wold 2018).

参考译文

在维持大致稳定几十年之后，自20世纪80年代以来，许多发达经济体的国民收入中向劳动力支付的比重下降，下降幅度平均约为2个百分点（2017年4月

《世界经济展望》第三章）。造成这一下降的因素中，研究范围最广的四个因素是：技术变革，包括与之相关的相对资本价格的下降；全球化和离岸外包；与无形资本增加或有形资本折旧增加有关的计量困难；工人议价能力的削弱。特别是，2017年4月《世界经济展望》第三章强调，在发达经济体以及新兴市场和发展中经济体中，技术和全球化在降低劳动力比重方面发挥了作用。最近受到关注的第五个可能的驱动因素是企业市场支配力的增长以及企业所有者经济租金的相应上涨（Barkai，2017年；De Loecker、Eeckhout 和 Unger，2018年；Eggertsson、Robbins 和 Wold，2018年）。

第五篇

原文

A key contributor almost everywhere is the increase in markups charged by a small fraction of firms. Most of these firms are rather small, but the larger ones in the group account for the vast majority of the group's total revenue. High-markup firms also perform better than others—their productivity is higher and they are more likely to invest in intangible assets, such as patents and software. In the United States, these firms also gained market share during 2000—2015, contributing to the larger increase in aggregate markups compared with other countries—and consistent with a (productivity-enhancing) growth of high-productivity, high-markup firms at the expense of those with low productivity and low markups.

请自行翻译后查看后文的分析点评

分析点评

A key contributor almost everywhere is the increase in markups charged by a small fraction of firms. Most of these firms are rather small, but the larger ones in the group account for the vast majority of the group's total revenue. High-markup firms also perform better than others—their productivity is higher and they are more likely to invest in intangible assets, such as patents and software. In the United States, these firms also gained market share during 2000—2015, contributing to the larger increase in aggregate markups compared with other countries—and consistent with a (productivity-enhancing) growth of high-productivity, high-markup firms at the expense of those with low productivity and low markups.

批 注

① "公司"占"总收入"的绝大部分？中文表述逻辑有问题。

② "表现"不如"绩效"准确和专业。

在几乎所有领域，加价率上升的关键贡献者都是一小部分公司。这些公司大多为小公司，但其中规模较大的公司占群体总收入[①]的绝大部分。加价率较高的公司其表现[②]优于其他公司——这些公司的生产率更高，更有可能投资于无形资产，如专利和软件。在美国，这些公司在2000—2015年期间也获得了更多市场份额，这使美国总加价率与其他国家相比上升幅度较大——并且与高生产率、高增长率公司的（有助于提高生产力的）增长相一致，以低生产率和低加价的公司为代价。

几乎在所有地方，做出关键贡献的都是一小部分企业加价率的上升。这些企业大多为小企业，但其中规模较大的企业的收入占这一群体总收入的绝大部分。加价率较高的企业绩效也优于其他企业——生产率更高，也更有可能投资于无形资产，例如专利和软件。在美国，这些企业在2000年至2015年期间还获得了更大的市场份额，这使美国总加价率的升幅高于其他国家——并且与高生产率、高加价率企业（有助于提高生产率）的增长以牺牲低生产率、低加价率企业为代价的情况相符。

1. 第一句的译文有两个问题：第一，"everywhere"应当理解为"在所有地方"还是"在所有领域"？本段后半部分是关于美国与其他国家的比较，而不是不同领域或部门之间的比较，由此可以判断，第一句是对世界各地，而非不同领域情况的总结；第二，"A key contributor"是"a small fraction of firms"还是"the increase in markups"。根据原文的逻辑可以判断是"the increase in markups"。翻译稿将这个宾语改换成了"一小部分公司"，虽然中文表述和大致意思没有问题，但是从准确性角度来说，两种译法仍然是有差异的。

2. 理解和翻译最后一句后半部分的关键在于弄清楚"consistent with"的对象是"a (productivity-enhancing) growth"还是"a (productivity-enhancing) growth...at the expense of..."。从翻译稿的表述"……这使美国总加价率……与高生产率、高增长率公司的（有助于提高生产力的）增长相一致"可见，译者认为"consistent with"的对象仅仅是"a (productivity-enhancing) growth"。而事实上，其对象应当是"a (productivity-enhancing) growth...at the expense of..."。无论是从句子结构（没有任何标点符号分隔）还是从内容逻辑角度看，"at the expense of those with low productivity and low markups"都是针对"a (productivity-enhancing) growth"而言的。因此，"以牺牲低生产率、低加价率企业为代价"必须紧跟"增长"这一中心词，将它们糅合在一起加以理解。

补充练习

Increasing use of renewable energy sources could help curb carbon emissions substantially—a necessary step to slow the pace of climate change, which threatens the economic future of countries across the globe (Chapter 3 of the October 2017 World Economic Outlook). Once considered uneconomical, in recent years, the cost of installing low-carbon electric generation capacity has declined dramatically for some renewable energy sources. Between 2009 and 2017, prices of solar photovoltaics and onshore wind turbines fell most rapidly, dropping by 76 percent and 34 percent, respectively—making these energy sources competitive alternatives to fossil fuels and more traditional low-carbon sources (Figure 3.1.1).

参考译文

气候变化威胁着全球各国未来的经济；而增加可再生能源的使用有助于大幅限制碳排放，这是减缓气候变化速度的必要步骤（2017年10月《世界经济展望》第三章）。某些可再生能源的低碳电力装机容量安装成本曾经被认为不够经济，不过近年来已大幅降低。在2009年至2017年间，太阳能光伏和陆上风力发电机价格下降幅度最大——降幅分别达到76%和34%，因此已成为化石燃料和较为传统的低碳能源的竞争性替代品（图3.1.1）。

第六篇

原文

The upshot of the analysis is that higher markups have been associated with somewhat lower investment and capital in advanced economies over the past two decades. This has been mostly driven by the small fraction of firms whose markups increased sharply. Higher markups in advanced economies may have also entailed mild adverse spillovers to emerging markets. Together with the mixed impact of higher markups on innovation—which the previous analysis suggests may be negligible so far, but would turn increasingly negative with increased market power of high-markup firms—these macroeconomic implications of rising market power should be a cause for policy concern.

请自行翻译后查看后文的分析点评

分析点评

The upshot of the analysis is that higher markups have been associated with somewhat lower investment and capital in advanced economies over the past two decades. This has been mostly driven by the small fraction of firms whose markups increased sharply. Higher markups in advanced economies may have also entailed mild adverse spillovers to emerging markets. Together with the mixed impact of higher markups on innovation—which the previous analysis suggests may be negligible so far, but would turn increasingly negative with increased market power of high-markup firms—these macroeconomic implications of rising market power should be a cause for policy concern.

批 注

① 漏译 "somewhat lower"。
② 注意 "may have also entailed" 采用的是现在完成时。
③ "higher-markups" 指 "高加价率"。
④ "成为一项政策关切" 在可读性方面不如 "引起政策关注"。

翻译稿

分析结果认为，在过去二十年中，较高的加价率与发达经济体的投资和资本水平相关。这主要由加价率急剧上升的一小部分公司所推动。发达经济体的加价率上升可能也会对新兴市场产生轻微的不利溢出效应。再加上高加价率对创新的综合作用——上文的分析表明到目前为止该影响可能微不足道，但随着高市值公司市场势力的上升其负面影响会加剧——市场势力上升的宏观经济影响应该成为一项政策关切④。

审校稿

分析要点在于，在过去二十年中，发达经济体加价率的上升与其投资和资本水平略有下降密切相关。这主要是源于一小部分企业加价率急剧上升。发达经济体的加价率上升可能还对新兴市场产生了轻微的不利溢出效应。连同加价率上升对创新的综合影响（上文的分析认为该影响迄今为止或许还微不足道，但随着高加价率企业市场支配力的增长，这种影响会变得越来越趋于负面），市场支配力增长的这些宏观经济影响应当引起政策关注。

点评

1. 第一句中 "in advanced economies" 的限定范围需要根据意思进行判定。其限定的对象应当是 "higher markups have been associated with somewhat lower investment and capital"。除了根据这句话本身判定以外，第三句开头的主语 "Higher markups in advanced economies" 也可辅助印证对第一句的上述理解。

2. 这段话中出现了四个形容词比较级，分别为 "higher" "lower" "Higher" 和 "higher"。通常，形容词的比较级只需在形容词前面添加 "更""较" 即可，但是应当注意，出于中文表达的灵活和顺畅性，形容词的比较级有时候适宜转译为相应的动词（比如，本段中四个词分别可以考虑译为 "上升""下降""上升""上升"），以反映出情况的变化趋势。

3. 最后一句话中理解和翻译 "but would turn increasingly negative" 的关键是找准其主语—— "which"，这个 "which" 指代的是 "the mixed impact of higher markups on innovation"，那么将这部分内容补充完整后就是 "but the mixed impact of higher markups on innovation would turn increasingly negative"。翻译稿的表述是 "（上文的分析表明到目前为止该影响可能微不足道，）但随着高市值公司市场势力的上升其负面影响会加剧"。按照中文逻辑推断，这里的 "其" 指代的是括号中前半句里的"该影响",这样一来后半句的完整表述就成了"该影响的负面影响会加剧",这样做逻辑有问题。考虑到原文说的是"the mixed impact"会变得越来越"negative"。因此,将其改述为"这种影响会变得越来越趋于负面"更加适宜。从根本上说,这里的表述问题实际上是厘清句子结构的问题。

补充练习

The mergers and acquisitions data are collected by Zephyr and come from governmental regulatory filings, media reports, and reporting arrangements with investment banks. Therefore, the resulting data set on mergers and acquisitions theoretically includes data for the universe of mergers and acquisitions transactions. One shortcoming is the underreporting of deal values, which are missing for about one-half of reported transactions. Hence, while some descriptive statistics are included using existing deal values—bearing in mind the underreporting issue—the main empirical analysis in this box abstracts from using deal values.

参考译文

兼并和收购数据由 Zephyr 收集,来自政府监管文件、媒体报道以及与投资银行的报告安排。因此,由此产生的兼并和收购数据集在理论上包括全部兼并和收购交易的数据。其缺点之一是交易价值的漏报——大约一半的报告交易缺失交易价值。因此,一些描述性的统计数据是利用现有交易价值得出的(考虑到漏报问题),而本专栏中主要的实证分析是在使用交易价值的过程中提炼出来的。

第七篇

原文

To address the risk that the relationship between mergers and acquisitions and markups may be obscured by confounding factors, the analysis controls for firm and country-industry-year (four-digit NACE (Nomenclature statistique des activités économiques dans les Communauté européenne)) fixed effects, as well as for the firm's size (operating revenue), efficiency (total factor productivity), and profitability (earned income before interest and taxes divided by total assets). Standard errors are clustered at the firm level. The results show a sizable and statistically significant association between mergers and acquisitions and the subsequent change in a firm's markup, on the order of 1.1 percentage points, on average, and 1.2 percentage points for horizontal mergers and acquisitions (Figure 2.2.2, rows 1 and 2).

请自行翻译后查看后文的分析点评

分析点评

To address the risk that the relationship between mergers and acquisitions and markups may be obscured by confounding factors, the analysis controls for firm and country-industry-year (four-digit NACE (Nomenclature statistique des activites economiques dans les Communauté européenne)) fixed effects, as well as for the firm's size (operating revenue), efficiency (total factor productivity), and profitability (earned income before interest and taxes divided by total assets). Standard errors are clustered at the firm level. The results show a sizable and statistically significant association between mergers and acquisitions and the subsequent change in a firm's markup, on the order of 1.1 percentage points, on average, and 1.2 percentage points for horizontal mergers and acquisitions (Figure 2.2.2, rows 1 and 2).

为了解决①综合性因素可能会掩盖兼并与收购和加价率②之间关系的风险，分析以企业和国家－行业－年度【四位数NACE（欧共体经济活动统计分类体系）】固定效应，以及公司规模（营业收入）、效率（全要素生产率）和利润率③（利息和税前收入除以总资产）进行控制。标准误差集中在公司层面。结果显示，兼并和收购之间存在相当大的、在统计上具有重要性的关联，公司加价率的后续变化平均为1.1个百分点，横向兼并收购为1.2个百分点（图2.2.2，第1、2行④）。

为了消除干扰因素可能会掩盖兼并和收购与加价率之间的关系这一风险，本分析剔除了企业固定效应和国家－行业－年度（四位数NACE（欧共体经济活动统计分类体系））固定效应，以及企业规模（营业收入）、效率（全要素生产率）和盈利能力（息税前收入除以总资产）。标准误差集中在企业层面。结果显示，并购与随后企业加价率的变化之间在统计上存在相当大的显著关联性，平均大约为1.1个百分点；如果是横向兼并和收购，大约为1.2个百分点（图2.2.2，第1行和第2行）。

1. 第一句话中的"control for"是一个常见的统计术语，其具体含义为"In statistics, controlling for a variable is the attempt to reduce the effect of confounding variables in an observational study or experiment. It means that when looking at the effect of one variable, the effects of all other variable predictors are taken into account, either by making the other variables take on a fixed value (in an experiment) or by including them in

---

批 注

① "解决"与"风险"搭配欠妥，应改用"消除""化解"等其他动词。

② "兼并"和"收购"在这里是并存关系，而且可以视为一体，应用"和"连接；而"兼并和收购"和"加价率"之间存在一定的对立关系，应用"与"连接。译文的表达正好相反。

③ 国际货币基金组织术语表中使用的是"盈利能力"。如果需要反映具体数据及其变化，使用"利润率"则更加贴切。

④ 在出版物中，应当注意表述的完整性和正式性。

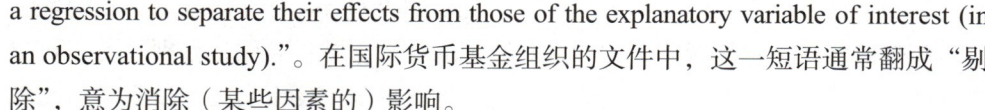

a regression to separate their effects from those of the explanatory variable of interest (in an observational study)."。在国际货币基金组织的文件中,这一短语通常翻成"剔除",意为消除(某些因素的)影响。

2. 翻译稿对第三句话中的"a sizable and statistically significant association between mergers and acquisitions and the subsequent change in a firm's markup"理解有误,将其翻译为"兼并和收购之间存在……关联,公司加价率的后续变化……"。实际上,此处的"兼并"和"收购"可以视为一体,即平时常说的"并购"。句中所谓的"关联"应当是"mergers and acquisitions"和"the subsequent change in a firm's markup"之间的。

3. "statistically significant"在国际货币基金组织常用的译文是"统计显著的",在此处可以灵活表述为"在统计上具有显著性的",或者"具有统计显著性的"。

4. 翻译稿漏译第三句话最后一部分中的"on the order"。《柯林斯在线词典》对这个短语的解释是"somewhat resembling; similar to"或者"approximately; roughly"。在这里可以翻译为"大约"。

5. 将"1.2 percentage points for horizontal mergers and acquisitions"翻译为"横向兼并收购为 1.2 个百分点"是不准确的,并且容易引起歧义。这个分句要表达的意思是:在横向兼并和收购的情况下,变化幅度是 1.2 个百分点。因此,在承前省略的情况下,应当翻成"如果是横向兼并和收购,大约为 1.2 个百分点"。

In a counterfactual exercise that attempts to control for unobserved factors that could drive a firm to seek a merger or acquisition and also increase its markups, the same regression estimation is performed using a sample of mergers and acquisitions deals that were announced but then aborted. This set of announced acquirers with ultimately withdrawn deals should share similar characteristics, observed and unobserved, with acquirers in completed deals. The result yields a (statistically insignificant) negative relationship between markups and the (counterfactual) post–mergers and acquisitions period, controlling for the same variables and including the same set of fixed effects as before. The sample size is much smaller for this set of counterfactual mergers and acquisitions, and there could be specific reasons behind the failure of these announced mergers and acquisitions that also negatively affect markup rates. Bearing these caveats in mind, the results suggest that when mergers and acquisitions are not completed, the markups of aspiring acquirers do not increase following the mergers and acquisitions announcement, while they do for firms that succeed in completing the deals.

参考译文

在一个试图剔除未观测到,但可能推动企业寻求兼并或收购并提高其加价率的因素的反事实模拟中,采用已公布但随后中止的兼并和收购交易样本进行了同样的回归估计。这组已公布但最终撤销了交易的收购者与已完成交易的收购者应具有相似的特征，包括观测到的和未观测到的特征。结果表明，在剔除了相同变量并纳入了与上文相同的固定效应组之后，加价率与（反事实的）后兼并和收购期之间存在着（无统计显著性的）负相关性。对于这一组反事实的兼并和收购而言，样本规模小得多，而且这些已公布的兼并和收购失败的某些具体原因也会对加价率产生负面影响。考虑到这些限制因素，结果表明，在兼并和收购没有完成的情况下，意图收购者的加价率在兼并和收购公布之后不会上升，而那些成功完成交易的企业的加价率却会上升。

第八篇

原文

In the emerging market and developing economy group, core inflation remains contained at about 2 percent in China, where domestic demand has slowed in response to financial regulatory tightening. In India, core inflation (excluding all food and energy items) has risen to about 6 percent as a result of a narrowing output gap and pass-through effects from higher energy prices and exchange rate depreciation. Core inflation has declined in Brazil and Mexico (to about 2½ percent and 3½ percent, respectively), reflecting moderations in activity and improved anchoring of expectations. In Russia, core inflation dropped this year (averaging less than 2 percent until May, and rising slightly in June), consistent with moderately tight monetary policy, declining inflation expectations, and low exchange rate pass-through.

请自行翻译后查看后文的分析点评

分析点评

In the emerging market and developing economy group, core inflation remains contained at about 2 percent in China, where domestic demand has slowed in response to financial regulatory tightening. In India, core inflation (excluding all food and energy items) has risen to about 6 percent as a result of a narrowing output gap and pass-through effects from higher energy prices and exchange rate depreciation. Core inflation has declined in Brazil and Mexico (to about 2½ percent and 3½ percent, respectively), reflecting moderations in activity and improved anchoring of expectations. In Russia, core inflation dropped this year (averaging less than 2 percent until May, and rising slightly in June), consistent with moderately tight monetary policy, declining inflation expectations, and low exchange rate pass-through.

翻 译 稿

在新兴市场和发展中经济体集团中，中国的国内需求因金融监管收紧而出现放缓迹象，核心通货膨胀仍维持在 2% 的水平上。因产出缺口收窄以及能源价格上涨和汇率贬值而产生的传导效应，印度的核心通货膨胀（不包括食品和能源项目）已升至约 6%。在巴西和墨西哥，核心通货膨胀均有下滑（分别降低约 2.5% 和 3.5%），原因是经济活动放缓以及预期固化的改善。在俄罗斯，核心通货膨胀本年度内出现下滑（截至 5 月平均不足 2%，在 6 月稍有上升），印证了适度紧缩的货币政策、持续下降的通胀预期以及较低的汇率传导效应④ 所发挥的作用。

批 注

① 漏译"about"。
② 一般而言，"经济"多用"下滑"，"率"多用"下降""降低"。
③ 此为专业术语。
④ 此为专业术语。

审 校 稿

在新兴市场和发展中经济体组中，中国的国内需求增长因金融监管收紧而放缓，其核心通货膨胀率仍控制在大约 2% 的水平。因产出缺口收窄以及能源价格上涨和汇率贬值而产生的传导效应，印度的核心通货膨胀率（不包括任何食品和能源项）已升至约 6%。巴西和墨西哥的核心通货膨胀率有所下降（分别降至约 2.5% 和 3.5%），原因是经济活动放缓以及锚定预期状况的改善。在俄罗斯，核心通货膨胀率在本年度内出现下降（截至 5 月平均不足 2%，在 6 月稍有上升），印证了适度紧缩的货币政策、持续下降的通货膨胀预期以及较低的汇率传导效应所发挥的作用。

点 评

1. 本段四次出现"core inflation"一语，该术语意思为"核心通货膨胀"。然而，在经济与金融类文件中，它有时泛指核心通货膨胀状况，也可以具体指核心通货膨胀率，翻译时必须根据上下文判断其真实含义。在涉及特定百分比数值或者上升／下降的情形时，应当将该术语理解为"核心通货膨胀率"，本段中的"core inflation"即属于这种情况——分别"remains contained about 2 percent""has risen to about 6 percent""has declined"和"dropped"。因此，四处均应当译为"核心通货膨胀率"。

2. 第一句的翻译存在若干问题：第一，将"remains contained at"译为"仍维持在"不妥，因为"contained"一词意思侧重于"受控制""被阻止"等角度，而非"得到支撑""获得维持"等角度。因此，译为"仍控制在"更为贴切；第二，将"domestic demand has slowed"直译为"国内需求……放缓"有误，因为从中文角度看，"需求"与"放缓"并不搭配，进而根据句子意思判断可知，原文实际上说的是"国内需求增长……放缓"；第三，将开头部分的"the emerging market and developing economy group"译为"新兴市场和发展中经济体集团"不当，因为此处的"group"并不指类似于"Group of Seven（七国集团）""Group of Twenty（二十国集团）"的固有组织团体，而只是一种分组或者分类，因此宜使用"组"而不是"集团"。

3. 第三句的翻译存在两个问题：第一，对"has declined...(to about 2½ percent and 3½ percent, respectively)"翻译错误，译为"均有下滑（分别降低约 2.5% 和 3.5%）"，而"has declined...to"意指"下降至"，因此译文应当为"有所下降（分别降至约 2.5% 和 3.5%）"；第二，没有弄清"anchoring of expectations"这一术语的意思，误用了"预期固化"这一表述。该短语的意思是"锚定通胀预期"或者"对通胀预期的锚定"。需要注意的是，"anchor"一词在此类文件中较多用"锚/锚定"的说法，与之相关的是"anchoring effect（锚定效应）"。锚定效应是指"当人们需要对某个事件做定量估测时，会将某些特定数值作为起始值，起始值像锚一样制约着估测值。在作决策的时候，会不自觉地给予最初获得的信息过多的重视"。有经济学家称："如果能良好地锚定住对通胀的预期，任何导致通胀的冲击（不管它是来自需求侧、能源价格还是汇率波动）对于通胀预期的影响都会更小，实际的通胀趋势也会更小。因而，这些冲击只会对通胀造成短暂的波澜。"基于这一背景知识，可以确定，上述短语应翻译为"锚定预期"。

补充练习

As discussed in previous WEOs, various factors could trigger a sudden change in global financial conditions. Signs of firmer-than-expected inflation in the United States (for example, as capacity constraints become more binding) could lead to a shift in market expectations of US interest rate hikes, which are currently well below those assumed in the WEO baseline forecast. A negative shock could trigger a sudden deterioration of risk appetite, which in turn could lead to disruptive portfolio adjustments, accelerate and broaden the reversal of capital flows from emerging markets, and lead to further US dollar appreciation, straining economies with high leverage, fixed exchange rates, or balance sheet mismatches. Rising trade tensions and political and policy uncertainty could also make market participants abruptly reassess fundamentals and risks. The recent turmoil in Turkey, exacerbated by political tensions with the United States against the backdrop of deteriorating fundamentals, including a belated monetary policy response to increasing inflation, exemplifies the increased salience of this risk for other vulnerable emerging markets.

正如前面几期《世界经济展望》所述，导致全球金融条件突然变化的因素多种多样。美国通货膨胀高于预期的迹象（例如，因为产能限制变得更具约束力）可能导致市场对美国加息的预期发生转变，而美国目前的加息远低于《世界经济展望》基线预测中假设的水平。一项负面冲击可能引起风险偏好的突然恶化，进而可导致破坏性的证券投资调整，加快和扩大来自新兴市场的资本流动的逆转，并导致美元进一步升值,令那些杠杆率较高、汇率固定或资产负债表不匹配的经济体承受压力。贸易紧张局势加剧以及政治和政策的不确定性也可能使市场参与者突然重新评估基本面和风险。在基本面持续恶化(包括货币政策未能对不断上升的通货膨胀及时采取应对措施)的背景下,土耳其近期形势动荡,与美国之间的政治紧张关系更令局势雪上加霜,例证了这种风险对于其他脆弱的新兴市场而言越来越突出。

第九篇

原文

The baseline forecast incorporates the impact of tariffs that had been announced by the United States as of mid-September, namely a 10 percent tariff on all aluminum imports, a 25 percent tariff on all steel imports, a 25 percent tariff on $50 billion of imports from China imposed in July and August, and a 10 percent tariff on an additional $200 billion of imports from China imposed in late September, rising to 25 percent by year end, as well as the retaliatory measures taken by trading partners. The forecast assumes that part of the negative effect of these trade measures will be offset by policy stimulus from China (and possibly other economies as well). The forecast does not incorporate the impact of further tariffs on Chinese and other imports threatened by the United States, but not yet implemented, due to uncertainty about their exact magnitude, timing, and potential retaliatory response. Scenario Box 1 discusses the potential economic consequences of further escalation in trade tensions and rising trade barriers.

请自行翻译后查看后文的分析点评

分析点评

The baseline forecast incorporates the impact of tariffs that had been announced by the United States as of mid-September, namely a 10 percent tariff on all aluminum imports, a 25 percent tariff on all steel imports, a 25 percent tariff on $50 billion of imports from China imposed in July and August, and a 10 percent tariff on an additional $200 billion of imports from China imposed in late September, rising to 25 percent by year end, as well as the retaliatory measures taken by trading partners. The forecast assumes that part of the negative effect of these trade measures will be offset by policy stimulus from China (and possibly other economies as well). The forecast does not incorporate the impact of further tariffs on Chinese and other imports threatened by the United States, but not yet implemented, due to uncertainty about their exact magnitude, timing, and potential retaliatory response. Scenario Box 1 discusses the potential economic consequences of further escalation in trade tensions and rising trade barriers.

翻 译 稿

基线预测考虑了美国截至 9 月中旬已宣布采取的关税措施的影响，即对所有铝制品进口加征 10% 关税、对所有钢铁进口加征 25% 关税、从 7 月和 8 月开始分两次对来自中国价值 500 亿美元的进口商品加征 25% 关税、从 9 月下旬开始对来自中国价值 2 000 亿美元的额外进口商品加征 10% 关税（将于今年年末升至 25%），其中包括贸易伙伴所采取的报复性措施的影响。本预测假定这些贸易措施的部分负面效应将为中国（也可能包括其他经济体）所采取的政策刺激措施所抵消。本预测并不包含美国威胁但仍未实施对中国和其他进口商品进一步加征关税的影响，因为关于其具体力度、时机和潜在报复性措施仍存在不确定性。情景专栏③1 讨论了贸易紧张情势进一步升级和贸易壁垒增多可能产生的经济后果。

批 注

① 征收关税的对象是进口的货物/服务，因此，这里使用"进口铝制品"的表述比"铝制品进口"更为适当。

② 此处使用"另外"较"额外"更为妥当。

③ 此为专用表述。

审 校 稿

基线预测考虑了美国截至 9 月中旬已宣布采取的关税措施（即，对所有进口铝制品加征 10% 的关税、对所有进口钢铁加征 25% 的关税、7 月和 8 月对来自中国的价值 500 亿美元的进口商品加征 25% 的关税、9 月下旬对来自中国的另外价值 2 000 亿美元的进口商品加征 10% 的关税并于今年年末将这一税率提高至 25%）的影响，以及贸易伙伴所采取的报复性措施。本预测假设这些贸易措施的部分负面效应将被中国（也可能还有其他经济体）所采取的政策刺激措施抵消。本预测并不包含美国威胁将对来自中国的和其他的进口商品进一步加征、但未实际加征的关税的影响，因为其确切力度、时机和潜在的报复性应对措施还不确定。情景专栏 1 讨论了贸易紧张局势进一步升级和贸易壁垒升高可能产生的经济后果。

点 评

1. 第一句翻译的主要问题在于最后一个分句"as well as the retaliatory measures taken by trading partners"。译者将"as well as"翻译为"其中包括"，明显对原文理解有误。应当注意，这句话的主干是"The baseline forecast incorporates the impact of tariffs..., as well as the retaliatory measures..."。其中"as well as"意为"（既）……又""以及"，连接前后两个并列的同等成分，语意重点在前一部分而非后一部分。这句话里，并列的同等成分是"the impact of tariffs that had been announced by the United States as of mid-September"和"the retaliatory measures taken by trading partners"。因此，翻译稿将对应的后一部分翻为"贸易伙伴所采取的报复性措施的影响"，也存在一定程度上的偏差。

2. 第一句话的另一个问题是"namely a 10 percent tariff on all aluminum imports, a 25 percent tariff on all steel imports, a 25 percent tariff on $50 billion

of imports from China imposed in July and August, and a 10 percent tariff on an additional \$200 billion of imports from China imposed in late September, rising to 25 percent by year end"这部分插入内容的位置和处理办法。这部分是对"tariffs that had been announced by the United States as of mid-September"的具体说明,包含四项关税措施。翻译稿将相应部分翻译为"美国截至 9 月中旬已宣布采取的关税措施的影响,即……",导致在中文读者看来,"namely...rising to 25 percent by year end"是"the impact of tariffs that had been announced by the United States as of mid-September"。可行的解决办法是将插入内容的译文置于"关税措施"之后。

3. 第一句话的第三个问题是对时间介词的理解有误。"in July and August"和"in late September"分别意指"(在)7 月和 8 月"以及"(在)9 月下旬",而不是"从 7 月和 8 月开始"或"从 9 月下旬开始"。

4. 第二句和第三句中均出现了表述不明确的问题。第二句话中,将"...from China (and possibly other economies as well)"翻译为"中国(也可能包括其他经济体)";第三句话中,将"...the impact of further tariffs on Chinese and other imports..."翻译为"对中国和其他进口商品进一步加征关税的影响",这两处翻译均不明确,从中文角度说,逻辑关系混乱。前一处原文意思是:除了中国以外,可能还有其他经济体(采取了政策刺激措施);其中,"other economies"与"China"是并列关系。使用的"包括"一词不当。后一处原文意思是:对来自中国的进口商品和其他的进口商品进一步加征的……关税的影响,其中,"Chinese"与"other"并列作为"imports"的定语。采用省略式的译法将其翻成"对中国和其他进口商品",逻辑关系不清晰,容易导致误解和歧义。

5. 第三句话中还要注意最后的"response"一词。相对于"measure""action"等措辞来说,"response"不单单是指措施或行动,它还包含具体针对某种(类)在先行动或措施而相应采取某种(类)行动或措施的意思。翻译时需要注意领会并表达出不同措辞之间的细微差别。

补充练习

At the same time, rising trade tensions and policy uncertainty—discussed in more detail below—raise concerns about global economic prospects. These factors could lead firms to postpone or forgo capital spending and hence slow down growth in investment and demand. This slowdown would also weaken trade growth, as capital and intermediate goods account for an important share of global trade. As mentioned earlier, high-frequency data point to a slowdown in global trade and industrial production, somewhat weaker manufacturing purchasing managers' indices, and especially weaker export orders, but the extent to which these factors have affected capital spending and trade are still unclear. Consistent with signs of slower production of capital goods, the forecast for fixed investment growth in 2018 was revised downward in advanced economies by about 0.4 percentage point relative to the April 2018 WEO, particularly in advanced Asia and the United Kingdom. This downward revision was accompanied by downward revisions to export growth (by over 1 percentage point) and especially import growth (by 1.4 percentage point). The forecast for investment and trade growth in 2019 is also weaker. For emerging market and developing economies, trade growth was revised down modestly for 2018 and more substantially for 2019. The forecast for investment growth for 2018—19 is weaker than in April, despite higher capital spending in India, on account of contracting investment in economies under stress, such as Argentina and Turkey, which is also reflected in a downward revision for import growth, particularly for 2019.

同时，贸易紧张局势加剧以及政策不确定性升高（详见下文讨论）也加重了对全球经济前景的担忧情绪。这些因素可导致企业推迟或放弃资本支出，并因此减慢投资和需求增长的速度。因为资本和中间产品在全球贸易中占很大比例，贸易增长也会因此趋于疲软。如上所述，高频数据表明全球贸易和工业生产减速、制造业采购经理人指数略显疲软、特别是出口订单表现乏力，但这些因素在多大程度上影响了资本支出和贸易仍不明朗。根据资本货物生产放缓的迹象，对发达经济体（特别是针对亚洲发达经济体及英国）2018年固定投资增长率的预测相对于2018年4月《世界经济展望》的数据下调了约0.4个百分点。在下调固定投资增长率的同时，出口增长率和进口增长率、特别是进口增长率也被下调，分别下调超过1个百分点和1.4个百分点。对2019年投资和贸易增长率的预测水平同样继续走低。对于新兴市场和发展中经济体，2018年的贸易增长率预测小幅下调，2019年预测的下调幅度更大。尽管印度的资本支出升高，但考虑到阿根廷和土耳其等陷入财务困境的经济体持续收缩投资（也反映在进口增长率的向下调整、特别是针对2019年的向下调整中），预测的2018—2019年投资增长率低于4月份的预测值。

原文

As discussed in the 2018 *External Sector Report*, widening external imbalances in some large economies, such as the United States—where the fiscal expansion will likely increase the country's current account deficit—could further fuel protectionist sentiments. The proliferation of trade actions and threats, and the ongoing renegotiations of major free trade agreements, such as NAFTA and the economic arrangements between the United Kingdom and the rest of the European Union, have created pervasive uncertainty about future trade costs. An intensification of trade tensions and the associated further rise in policy uncertainty could dent business and financial market sentiment, trigger financial market volatility, and slow investment and trade. An increase in trade barriers would disrupt global supply chains, which have become an integral part of production processes in the past decades, and slow the spread of new technologies, ultimately lowering global productivity and welfare. It would also make tradable consumer goods less affordable, harming low-income households disproportionately. In addition to their negative effects on domestic and global growth, protectionist policies would likely have very limited effect on external imbalances, as discussed in the 2018 *External Sector Report*.

请自行翻译后查看后文的分析点评

分析点评

As discussed in the 2018 *External Sector Report*, widening external imbalances in some large economies, such as the United States—where the fiscal expansion will likely increase the country's current account deficit—could further fuel protectionist sentiments. The proliferation of trade actions and threats, and the ongoing renegotiations of major free trade agreements, such as NAFTA and the economic arrangements between the United Kingdom and the rest of the European Union, have created pervasive uncertainty about future trade costs. An intensification of trade tensions and the associated further rise in policy uncertainty could dent business and financial market sentiment, trigger financial market volatility, and slow investment and trade. An increase in trade barriers would disrupt global supply chains, which have become an integral part of production processes in the past decades, and slow the spread of new technologies, ultimately lowering global productivity and welfare. It would also make tradable consumer goods less affordable, harming low-income households disproportionately. In addition to their negative effects on domestic and global growth, protectionist policies would likely have very limited effect on external imbalances, as discussed in the 2018 *External Sector Report*.

正如2018年《对外部门报告》所述，美国等一些大型经济体对外不平衡幅度持续扩大，加上财政扩张政策将可能增加其经常账户逆差①，保护主义情绪可能会进一步加剧。铺天盖地②的贸易行动和威胁，加上主要自由贸易协定正在进行的重新谈判，例如《北美自由贸易协定》以及英国与欧盟其他国家之间的经济安排，已给未来的贸易成本带来广泛的不确定性。贸易紧张情势加剧以及因此进一步升高的政策不确定性可能伤及③企业和金融市场情绪，引发金融市场波动，

批 注

① 注意"current account deficit"中的"deficit"应译为"逆差"。

② 原文为"proliferation"译为"铺天盖地"明显有夸大之嫌，相比而言，"不断扩散"较为合适。

③ "影响"情绪比"伤及"情绪更为适当。

并导致投资和贸易放缓。贸易壁垒增多可能会破坏全球供应链，伤及过去数十年所建立的生产流程根本，并会降低新技术传播的速度，最终降低全球生产率及福利。它还会使贸易消费品的价格不再那么低廉，给低收入住户造成不成比例的伤害。保护主义政策会对国内和全球增长带来负面效应，但正如2018年《对外部门报告》所述，其减缓外部不平衡的作用极其有限。

正如2018年《对外部门报告》所述，美国等一些大型经济体的对外不平衡状况持续加剧，加上财政扩张可能增加其经常账户逆差，保护主义情绪可能会进一步上升。贸易行动和威胁不断扩散，主要自由贸易协定（例如《北美自由贸易协定》以及英国与欧洲联盟其他国家之间的经济安排）又正在进行重新谈判，这些已经给未来的贸易成本带来广泛的不确定性。贸易紧张局势的加剧以及相关政策不确定性的进一步升高，可能影响企业和金融市场情绪，引发金融市场波动，并导致投资和贸易放缓。贸易壁垒升高可能会破坏全球供应链——过去数十年生产流程的必要组成部分，并降低新技术传播的速度，最终降低全球生产率及福利。它还会使贸易消费品的价格不再低廉，从而过度损害低收入家庭的利益。保护主义政策会对国内和全球增长带来负面效应。除此以外，正如2018年《对外部门报告》所述，其在对外不平衡方面的作用极其有限。

1. 这段译文最主要的问题在于对"An increase in trade barriers would disrupt global supply chains, which have become an integral part of production processes in the past decades, and slow the spread of new technologies, ultimately lowering global productivity and welfare."中"which have become an integral part of production processes in the past decades"部分的理解和表述。很显然，这是一个非限定性定语从句，"which"指代的是"global supply chains"。译为"破坏全球供应链，伤及过去数十年所建立的生产流程根本"，其中存在两个错误点：第一，将"integral part"译为"根本"有误。"integral"意指"构成整体所必不可少的"。因此，"根本"这一表达偏离了原意，而"必要组成部分"更为恰当；第二，这个分句的表达没有体现出与其所限定的部分，也就是"全球供应链"之间的关系。中文读者会误认为"破坏全球供应链"与"伤及过去数十年所建立的生产流程根本"是纯粹的并列关系，表达的是两层独立的意思。可行的修改是在"全球供应链"后加破折号予以说明。

2. 最后一句话"In addition to their negative effects on domestic and global growth, protectionist policies would likely have very limited effect on external imbalances, as discussed in the 2018 External Sector Report."的翻译稿也存在比较明显的问题。第一，将其中的"In addition to"错误地翻译为了"但"。除了这一短语本身的译文与原文意思不符以外，错误使用"但"还导致整个句子的意思出现偏差，令中文读者误以为后面部分是对前面部分意思的转折；第二，"(protectionist policies) would likely have very limited effect on external imbalances"

的译文"其减缓外部不平衡的作用极其有限"将原文"have...effect on"具体化为"减缓……的作用"。为忠实表达原文意思，建议仍然采用"在……方面的作用"；第三，"external imbalance"应按照国际货币基金组织术语表中的对应表述"对外不平衡""国际收支失衡"进行翻译。

3. "disproportionately"一词在经济与金融领域的翻译中经常出现。这个词语的意思是"不成比例地"。然而在许多情况下，这一表述并不能清晰，甚至不能顺畅地表达出原文的意思。有鉴于此，译者有必要具体分析上下文内容，通过语意把握其具体所指，以便在翻译时准确表达其含义。众所周知，消费品价格升高对低收入家庭的影响是最大的；由此可以判断，贸易壁垒升高导致贸易消费品价格上涨，由此对低收入家庭产生"不成比例"的损害，实际上是指低收入家庭比一般家庭受损害的程度更深，即"过度"。

4. 第二句话中"such as NAFTA and the economic arrangements between the United Kingdom and the rest of the European Union"是主句的插入部分，举例说明了"major free trade agreements"。而译者将其翻译为"加上主要自由贸易协定正在进行的重新谈判，例如《北美自由贸易协定》以及英国与欧盟其他国家之间的经济安排"，内容虽然没有错误，但是位置/次序不对。这一插入语应当紧跟在"major free trade agreements"之后。另外，为了避免插入语内容过长导致读者对主句的理解受到影响，采取将其置于括号之中的处理办法较为妥当。

Most nonfood commodities have registered price increases since mid-2017. Most notable has been the increase in oil prices—about $30 a barrel, or 70 percent, since June 2017. Some of this increase is expected to dissipate over the medium term because of higher US shale production and OPEC+ supply. Nonetheless, as shown in the Commodities Special Feature, oil futures curves are notably higher than a year ago. The improved outlook for oil prices contributes to revisions to growth prospects for fuel exporters and importers—with a more notable impact on the exporters, given the implied magnitude of the changes in disposable income (Figure 1.9). A comparison of forecast revisions between the April 2018 WEO and the current report shows an upward revision of about 0.1 and 0.3 percentage point for 2018 and 2019, respectively, for a group of fuel exporters, excluding countries whose prospects are heavily conditioned by domestic strife, geopolitical tensions, or outright macroeconomic collapse. In contrast, growth prospects for the same period have been revised downward by about 0.1–0.3 percentage point for the rest of the world, a group dominated by fuel importers (Figure 1.9, panel 3).

自2017年中期以来，大多数非粮食大宗商品的价格均出现上涨。其中最显著的是石油价格的上涨——自2017年6月以来每桶上涨约30美元，涨幅70%。中期内，因为美国页岩油产量和"欧佩克+"供应量的增加，部分价格上涨预计难以持久。尽管如此，正如"大宗商品专题"所示，石油期货曲线明显高于一年前的水平。考虑到推定的可支配收入变化幅度，石油价格前景变好推动了对燃料出口国和进口国的增长前景做出修正，其中出口国受到的影响更为明显（图1.9）。通过比较2018年4月《世界经济展望》与本期报告的预测修正可发现，燃料出口国组2018年和2019年预测数据分别约有0.1和0.3个百分点的向上调整，但其中不包括那些前景受国内冲突、地缘政治紧张局势或宏观经济直接崩溃状况严重影响的国家。相比之下，其他国家，即主要为燃料进口国的小组，同一时期的增长前景已向下调整了约0.1至0.3个百分点（图1.9，小图3）。

背景介绍

以下六篇材料选自国际货币基金组织出版物《2014年政府财政统计手册》（第一章：导言；第二章：机构单位和部门；第三章：经济流量、存量头寸和会计规则；第四章：政府财政统计分析框架）。

《政府财政统计手册》是国际货币基金组织在政府财政统计方面的国际标准，提供了各种概念、分类和定义，帮助编制人员编制和报告"适用"于政策分析的财政统计数据，旨在为以一种可靠且透明的方式编制财政统计数据提供基础，进而为财政分析和政策决策提供支持。它是国际经济统计标准架构中的一个重要支柱。目前，全世界有140多个国家都在使用《政府财政统计手册》，使不同时期不同国家的财政统计数据具有了可比性。

在翻译此类文件时，除具备经济金融背景知识以外，还要掌握相当的统计分析专业知识，此外，特别需要注意对不同项目和数值之间关系的理解和准确表达。此外，该手册侧重于概念的定义和分类，编制和分发政府财政统计的概念性指导准则，翻译时必须对各种术语、关键词、易混淆概念、定义表述和说明等保持高度敏感性。

第十一篇

原文

Contractual agreements—The existence of a contractual agreement between a government and an NPI may allow the government to determine key aspects of the

NPI's general policy or program. As long as the NPI is ultimately able to determine its policy or program to a significant extent, such as by being able to fail to comply with the contractual agreement and accept the consequences, to change its constitution, or to dissolve itself without requiring government approval other than that required under the general regulations, then it would not be considered controlled by government.

请自行翻译后查看后文的分析点评

分析点评

Contractual agreements—The existence of a contractual agreement between a government and an NPI may allow the government to determine key aspects of the NPI's general policy or program. As long as the NPI is ultimately able to determine its policy or program to a significant extent, such as by being able to fail to comply with the contractual agreement and accept the consequences, to change its constitution, or to dissolve itself without requiring government approval other than that required under the general regulations, then it would not be considered controlled by government.

翻译稿

合同安排——政府可凭借其与非营利机构之间的合同约定，决定相关非营利机构①一般性政策或计划的重要方面。只要非营利机构对其政策或计划的最终决定权达到一个显著的程度，比如能够违反合同约定并承担相应后果，能够在不违反一般法规要求的情况下，无须征得政府同意即可修订自己的章程或宣布解散，则就②不应视其受政府控制。

审校稿

合同约定——政府与非营利机构之间存在着的某种合同约定规定政府可以决定该非营利机构一般性政策或计划的重要方面。只要该非营利机构最终能够在很大程度上决定其政策或计划，比如，能够违反这种合同约定并承担相应后果，能够修改自己的章程，或者能够不征得政府同意即宣布解散（除了一般法规要求征得政府同意的情况以外），即不应视为受政府控制。

点评

1. 对"As long as the NPI is ultimately able to determine its policy or program to a significant extent,"的翻译存在两个问题：第一，"ultimately able to determine"不宜理解为"最终决定权"，而应当按原文表述翻译为"最终能够……决定"；第二，"to a significant extent"译为"达到一个显著的程度"与前文的"决定"不搭配，翻成"在很大/较大程度上"更为妥当。

2. 最后一句话中的"such as by being able to fail to comply with the contractual

批 注

① 原文为"the NPI"，前文出现过，译为"非营利机构"，所以这里应当相应译为"该非营利机构"，以免产生歧义。

② 中文重复累赘。

agreement and accept the consequences, to change its constitution, or to dissolve itself without requiring government approval other than that required under the general regulations..."包含"by being able"引导的三个并列成分："to fail to comply with the contractual agreement and accept the consequences""to change its constitution"和"to dissolve itself without requiring government approval other than that required under the general regulations"。其中，"without requiring government approval other than that required under the general regulations"仅针对"to dissolve itself"，翻译稿对此显然存在误判，将其限定范围扩大到包括"to change its constitution"。

3. 此外，"other than that required under the general regulations"中"that required under the general regulations"省略的内容较多，它的完整意思是"一般法规要求征得政府同意（之后方可宣布解散）的情况"。译者将"other than that required under the general regulations"内容提前，并翻译为"在不违反一般法规要求的情况下"，将其特指的内容泛化，没有准确表达出原文的意思。

补充练习

Nonlife insurance premiums and claims are also treated as transfers in GFS. This type of premium entitles the units making the payment to benefits only if one of the events specified in the insurance contract occurs. That is, one unit pays a second unit for accepting the risk that a specified event may occur to the first unit. These transactions are considered transfers because in the nature of the insurance business, they distribute income between policyholders to those who claim, as opposed to all policyholders who contribute. There is uncertainty whether the contributing unit will receive any benefits and, if it does receive benefits, they may bear no relation to the amount of the premiums previously paid. Nonlife insurance includes social security schemes and employer social insurance schemes for government employees that do not provide retirement benefits. Thus, social security contributions receivable and social security benefits payable by government units, which are not for employment-related pensions, are treated as transfers in GFS.

在政府财政统计中，非人寿险保险保费和赔偿也被当作转移处理。缴纳这类保险费后，缴费单位仅在保险合同规定的事件之一发生时才有权获得赔偿。也就是说，一个单位向另一个单位支付款项，以作为后者承担前者可能遭遇规定事件的风险的代价。这些交易被视为转移，因为就保险业的性质而言，它们是向投保人中的索赔者，而不是全体缴费者分配收益。缴费单位能否得到任何赔付，这一点存在不确定性，如果得到了赔付，赔付金额也可能与它们之前缴纳的保费数额无关。非人寿保险包括不提供退休福利的政府雇员社会保障计划和雇主社会保险计划。因此，政府单位应收社会保障缴款和应付社会保障福利，如果不用作与就业有关的养老金,那么在政府财政统计中应作为转移处理。

第十二篇

原文

Some countries may be able, at least initially, to compile only a part of the integrated GFS framework. It is not feasible to lay down general priorities for data collection when economic circumstances may vary widely from one country to another. In practice, priorities usually are best established by national authorities that are familiar with the situation, needs, and challenges of their countries.

It is recognized that the implementation of the fully integrated GFS framework presented in this Manual will take some time. In particular, many countries will need to revise their underlying accounting systems to accommodate the accrual basis of reporting and fully reflect the revised classifications of the GFS framework.

请自行翻译后查看后文的分析点评

分析点评

第 1 段

Some countries may be able, at least initially, to compile only a part of the integrated GFS framework. It is not feasible to lay down general priorities for data collection when economic circumstances may vary widely from one country to another. In practice, priorities usually are best established by national authorities that are familiar with the situation, needs, and challenges of their countries.

刚开始实施时,有些国家只能编制集成政府财政统计框架①内容的一部分。各国经济情况千差万别,要为数据收集规定一般性②优先次序,实不可行。在实施过程中,因各国管理当局熟悉自己国家的情况、需要和挑战,由其确定优先次序往往最合适不过。

至少在最初的时候,一些国家可能只能编制统一政府财政统计框架内容的一部分。在各国经济情况可能大不相同时,制定统一的数据收集重点并不可行。实

批 注

① 注意,"integrated"虽然有"集成"的意思,但"集成"多用于科技领域;此处应翻译为"统一""综合"等。

② 从意思角度看,"一般性"亦可;不过考虑到与"各国情况各异"相对,采用"统一"更为合适。

际上，重点通常最好由熟悉各自国家的情况、需要和挑战的各国当局来确定。

1. 这两段的翻译存在较为严重的漏译，虽然漏译的部分并非关键性内容或者大段文字，但影响了译文的准确性，对于作为国际标准的《政府财政统计手册》来说，准确性至关重要。这一段中漏译的是第一句中的"may""at least"和第二句中的"may"，依次应分别译为"可能""至少"和"可能"。

2. "Priority"一词本身既有"优先次序"的意思，又有"优先事项""优先权"/"优先性"的意思。本段中的"priorities"使用了复数形式，首先可以排除"优先权"/"优先性"的义项，然后从句子意思的角度出发，可以判断其意为"（收集数据的）优先事项/重点"，而不是某种"先后次序"。

3. 这一段最后一句"In practice, priorities usually are best established by national authorities that are familiar with the situation, needs, and challenges of their countries."的翻译出现两个问题：第一，"In practice"译为"在实施过程中"，不符合原文意思；第二，"that are familiar with the situation, needs, and challenges of their countries"这个限定性定语从句与主句并不存在明确的因果关系，不应当翻译为"因各国管理当局熟悉自己国家的情况、需要和挑战，……"。

第 2 段

It is recognized that the implementation of the fully integrated GFS framework presented in this Manual will take some time. In particular, many countries will need to revise their underlying accounting systems to accommodate the accrual basis of reporting and fully reflect the revised classifications of the GFS framework.

要实施本《手册》所述全面集成的政府财政统计框架，必定需要一段时间。特别是，为适应报告的权责发生制，并充分反映政府财政统计框架经修订的分类，许多国家将需要修订其基础会计制度。

我们承认，实施本《手册》介绍的完全统一的政府财政统计框架需要一些时间。特别是，许多国家需要修改其基本会计制度，以便适应报告的权责发生制，并充分反映修订后的政府财政统计框架分类。

1. 这一段漏译开头的"It is recognized"，其中"It"是形式主语，真正主语是"that"引导的主语从句，可译为"公认""人们认为""我们承认"等。

2. 这一段最后一句"In particular, many countries will need to revise their underlying accounting systems to accommodate the accrual basis of reporting and fully reflect the revised classifications of the GFS framework."的翻译稿也存在两个问题：第一，"the revised classifications of the GFS framework"翻译为"政府财政统

计框架经修订的分类"不符合中文表述的习惯；第二，不宜将"to accommodate the accrual basis of reporting and fully reflect the revised classifications of the GFS framework"部分的译文提至"will need to revise their underlying accounting systems"的译文之前——提前是为了表示强调，然而结合前一句的核心意思"实施……需要一些时间"来看，这一句的重点强调的应当是"许多国家需要修改其基本会计制度"。

In the due-for-payment basis of recording, flows that give rise to cash payments are recorded at the latest times they can be paid without incurring additional charges or penalties or, if sooner, when the cash payment is made. The period of time (if any) between the moment a payment becomes due and the moment it is actually made is bridged by recording other accounts receivable/payable, just as with the accrual basis. If a payment is made before it is due, then no receivable is necessary. Although due-for-payment recording furnishes a more comprehensive description of monetary flows than cash accounting, recording is limited to monetary flows and therefore does not capture all economic events.

参考译文

在记录的支付到期制下，产生现金支付的流量在不发生额外费用或罚款的付款最后时刻得到记录；如在此之前完成了现金支付，则在现金支付发生时记录。在支付到期时与实际支付时之间的间隔时期（如有）内记录其他应收/应付账款，这和权责发生制的做法一样。如果一笔付款在到期前支付，则不必记录应收账款。虽然支付到期制记录方式提供了比收付实现制更全面的关于货币流量的描述，但是记录仅限于货币流量，所以不反映所有经济事件。

第十三篇

原文

Internal or intra-unit transactions take place when a single unit acts in two different capacities, and it is analytically useful to record this act as a transaction. The choice of which internal actions to treat as transactions is subjective to the purpose of recording these actions. GFS follows the 2008 SNA by treating consumption of fixed capital as an internal transaction to allow the calculation of the operating costs of government.

Similarly, the transfer of materials and supplies from inventories to use of goods and services and other internal changes in inventories are treated as internal transactions (see paragraph 8.46–8.47).

请自行翻译后查看后文的分析点评

分析点评

Internal or intra-unit transactions take place when a single unit acts in two different capacities, and it is analytically useful to record this act as a transaction. The choice of which internal actions to treat as transactions is subjective to the purpose of recording these actions. GFS follows the 2008 SNA by treating consumption of fixed capital as an internal transaction to allow the calculation of the operating costs of government. Similarly, the transfer of materials and supplies from inventories to use of goods and services and other internal changes in inventories are treated as internal transactions (see paragraph 8.46–8.47).

【翻译稿】

内部或单位内交易发生在一个单位以两种身份开展活动时，而且将这种活动记录为交易有助于分析。选择将哪些内部活动当作交易处理，取决于记录这些活动的目的。政府财政统计沿用《2008 年国民账户体系》的做法，将固定资产② 消耗作为内部交易处理，以便计算政府的运行成本。同样③，库存物资和供应品向库存中商品和服务的使用和其他内部变化转移，被当作内部交易处理（见第 8.46～8.47 段）。

批 注

① "action" 一般译为"行动"。
② 注意 "fixed capital" 为"固定资本"。
③ 从准确性角度看，"similarly" 应译为"与此类似""与之相似"等。

【审校稿】

当一个单位以两种不同身份行事，而且为了便于分析将这种行为记录为交易时，就出现了内部或单位内交易。选择将哪些内部行动视为交易，这取决于记录这些行动的目的。政府财政统计沿用《2008 年国民账户体系》的做法，将固定资本消耗视为内部交易，以便计算政府的运作成本。与此类似，库存物资和供应品向货物和服务的使用转移以及库存的其他内部变化，也被视为内部交易（见第 8.46～8.47 段）。

【点评】

1. 原文第一句话"Internal or intra-unit transactions take place when a single unit acts in two different capacities, and it is analytically useful to record this act as a transaction."中，"when"引导的是"a single unit acts in two different capacities"和"and it is analytically useful to record this act as a transaction"，且引导的这两个分句为并列关系，意思是：在单位以两种不同身份行事而且将其行为记录为交易有助分析的情况下。翻译稿错误理解了这两个分句的关系，导致译文出现偏差。

2. 对于原文最后一句话中"the transfer of materials and supplies from inventories to use of goods and services and other internal changes in inventories are treated as internal transactions"部分，翻译稿理解有误，认为"treated as internal transactions"的主语是"the transfer of materials and supplies"和"the transfer of other internal changes"。事实上，这部分的主语应当是"the transfer of materials and supplies"和"other internal changes in inventories"，另外，"from inventories to use of goods and services"旨在描述"transfer"的对象和方向。

Payments in kind other than remuneration in kind occur when any of a wide variety of payments is made in the form of goods and services rather than money. A payment to settle a liability can be made in the form of goods, services, or noncash assets rather than money. For example, a government unit may agree to settle a claim for past-due taxes if the tax-payer transfers ownership of land or fixed assets to the government, or inheritance taxes may be payable by making donations of paintings or other valuables to government.

当多种类型的支付中有任何一种是采取货物和服务而非货币的形式时，就出现了实物报酬之外的实物支付。为清结负债而进行的支付可以采取货物、服务或非现金资产等非货币形式。例如，如果纳税人向政府转移土地或固定资产所有权，那么政府单位可同意了结对逾期未缴税款的追索，或者可以通过向政府捐赠画作或其他贵重物品的方式支付遗产税。

第十四篇

Government usually comprises two or more institutional units, and there normally is one unit that controls the other units. The controlling unit most likely includes the legislature, head of state, and judiciary. In contrast to corporations (see Paragraph 2.107), one government unit controls another government unit by appointing its managers and/or determining the laws and regulations that provide its finance rather than through equity ownership. Generally, government units do not issue shares. SPEs, wealth funds, or other entities of government that are legally constituted as corporations but do not satisfy the statistical definition of a corporation should be classified as government units in one of the subsectors of the general government. As a result, a liability for equity and investment fund shares could appear in the consolidated general government's balance sheet (see Paragraphs 2.137 and 2.152−2.155).

请自行翻译后查看后文的分析点评

分析点评

Government usually comprises two or more institutional units, and there normally is one unit that controls the other units. The controlling unit most likely includes the legislature, head of state, and judiciary. In contrast to corporations (see Paragraph 2.107), one government unit controls another government unit by appointing its managers and/or determining the laws and regulations that provide its finance rather than through equity ownership. Generally, government units do not issue shares. SPEs, wealth funds, or other entities of government that are legally constituted as corporations but do not satisfy the statistical definition of a corporation should be classified as government units in one of the subsectors of the general government. As a result, a liability for equity and investment fund shares could appear in the consolidated general government's balance sheet (see Paragraphs 2.137 and 2.152−2.155).

政府通常包括两个或两个以上的机构单位，且往往有一个控制其他单位的单位。处于控制地位的单位最可能包括立法机构、国家首脑和司法机构。不同于公司（见第 2.107 段），一个政府单位通过任命另一政府单位的管理人员和 / 或决定为另一政府单位提供资金的法律和法规来控制另一政府单位，而不是通过股权拥有。一般来说，政府单位并不发行股票。特殊目的实体、财富基金或其他政府实体作为公司依法组成但不满足①统计意义上的公司定义的，应被归类为政府单位，并纳入广义政府的一个子部门。因此，股权和投资基金份额的负债可出现在合并的广义政府资产负债表中（见第 2.137 段和第 2.152 ～ 2.155 段）。

批 注

① 与"定义"不搭配。

政府通常包括两个或两个以上的机构单位，且往往是一个单位控制着其他单位。处于控制地位的单位极有可能是立法机构、国家元首和司法机构。与公司（见第 2.107 段）不同，一个政府单位通过任命另一政府单位的管理人员和 / 或决定为另一政府单位提供资金的法律和法规（而不是通过拥有股权）来控制该另一政府单位。一般来说，政府单位并不发行股票。特殊目的实体、财富基金或其他政府实体虽然依法成立为公司，但不符合统计意义上的公司定义，应被归类为广义政府中某一子部门下的政府单位。因此，股权和投资基金份额的负债可出现在合并的广义政府资产负债表中（见第 2.137 段和第 2.152～2.155 段）。

1. 原文第二句中的"most likely includes"，翻译稿处理为"最可能包括"。这一译法有两个问题：一、"most"在此并无比较的意味，只是表明某种可能性"很大"，因此"most likely"较宜译为"极有可能""很有可能"等；二、"includes"在这里表示列举，"有""是"比"包括"更为恰当。

2. 翻译稿对原文第三句末尾的"rather than through equity ownership"理解正确，但译文的位置不妥。这句话在否定"through equity ownership"的同时，相应肯定了"by appointing its managers and/or determining the laws and regulations that provide its finance"，因此，前者的译文宜紧跟后者的译文，可以采用双破折号夹注的形式，或者放入括号作为补充说明的形式，防止割裂句子的整体意思。

3. 倒数第二句中"that are legally constituted as corporations"的译文"作为公司依法组成"表述存在逻辑问题。这部分的意思是"（相关实体）依法组建为公司法人形式"。类似于"作为公司依法组成"等的表述有颠倒因果之嫌，应予避免。

4. 将"should be classified as government units in one of the subsectors of the general government"译为"应被归类为政府单位，并纳入广义政府的一个子部门"并不妥当，其准确含义是"应被归类为广义政府中某一子部门下的政府单位"。将其一分为二并在"be classified（归类）"之外增译"纳入"之举属于画蛇添足，导致意思偏差。

The remainder of this chapter defines the concept of residence to delineate an economy, and describes institutional units and the types of institutional units that exist in macroeconomic statistics before defining the institutional sectors. The chapter applies these concepts to delineate the general government sector and the public sector. Finally, a decision tree to assist with the classification of public sector entities and the application of sector classification principles to some examples are discussed.

参考译文

本章的其余部分定义了用以划定经济体界限的所在地的概念，并描述了各机构单位以及宏观经济统计中存在的机构单位类型，之后定义了各机构部门。本章运用这些概念界定了广义政府部门和公共部门的范围。最后，本章讨论了辅助公共部门实体分类的决策树以及部门分类原则在一些示例中的应用。

第十五篇

原文

When a unit sells an item and does not expect to receive payment, or the corresponding payment is not due for an unusually long time, the value of the principal (recorded in other accounts payable/receivable) is reduced by an amount that reflects the time to maturity using an appropriate discount rate, such as the contractual rate for similar debt instruments. If payment is not due for an unusually long period of time, this reduction is by partitioning the market price of the item purchased, which equals the reduced principal amount, and accrued interest, the assumption being that the amount to be paid includes an allowance for interest. If payment is not expected for an unusually long period of time, such as due to the circumstances of the debtor, a reduction in the principal to be paid is recorded through a valuation change in other accounts payable/receivable, with interest accruing on the reduced principal amount, reflecting the time delay in payment. In both the circumstances described in this paragraph, interest should accrue until payment is made, at the rate used to discount the principal.

请自行翻译后查看后文的分析点评

分析点评

When a unit sells an item and does not expect to receive payment, or the corresponding payment is not due for an unusually long time, the value of the principal (recorded in other accounts payable/receivable) is reduced by an amount that reflects the time to maturity using an appropriate discount rate, such as the contractual rate for similar debt instruments. If payment is not due for an unusually long period of time, this reduction is by partitioning the market price of the item purchased, which equals the reduced principal amount, and accrued interest, the assumption being that the amount to be paid includes an allowance for interest. If payment is not expected for an unusually long period of time, such as due to the circumstances of the debtor, a reduction in the principal to be paid is recorded through a valuation change in other accounts payable/receivable, with interest accruing on the reduced principal amount, reflecting the time delay in payment. In both the circumstances described in this paragraph, interest should accrue until payment is made, at the rate used to discount the principal.

当一个单位出售一个项目单①不②期望收到支付款，或者相应支付款的到期时间特别长，本金价值（记录在其他应付/应收账款中）利用适当折现率③减去反映到期时间的数额，例如利用相似债务工具的合同折现率。如果支付到期时间特别长，这种扣减是通过对所购项目的市场价格进行分割④，扣减额等于减去的本金数额和应计利息，同时假定有待支付的额包括利息减让。如果预计在一个特别长的时间内不会收到支付，例如由于债务人的情况，有待支付的本金的减少额将通过其他应付/应收账款的定值⑤变化入账，而利息将基于减少后的本金产生，以此反映支付延迟的时间。在本段所述的两种情况下，利息应当持续累积直至进行支付，利率为本金贴现率。

当一个单位出售一个项目但未期望收到支付款，或者相应支付的到期时间特别长，本金价值（记录在其他应付/应收账款中）将有所降低，减少的金额使用适当贴现率（例如，与之类似的债务工具的合同利率）反映了距离到期的时间。如果支付到期时间特别长，那么这种减少将通过分割所购项目的市场价格（其金额等于减少后的本金数额）和应计利息的方式实现——假定有待支付的金额包含利息减免。如果预计在特别长的时间内不会收到支付款（例如，由于债务人的境况），那么有待支付的本金的减少额将通过其他应付/应收账款的计值变化入账，而利息将基于减少后的本金产生，以此反映支付延迟的时间。在本段所述的两种情况下，利息均应持续累积直至进行支付，利率为本金贴现率。

1. 对 "...the value of the principal...is reduced by an amount that reflects the time to maturity using an appropriate discount rate, such as the contractual rate for similar debt instruments." 的翻译存在严重理解错误。这句话的结构可以拆分为三个部分：第一，句子主干是 "the value of the principal...is reduced by an amount..."，意思是本金价值将减少一定数额；第二，"that reflects the time to maturity using an appropriate discount rate" 是对 "an amount" 的限定，意思是（减少的这一数额）"使用适当贴现率反映了距离到期的时间"；第三，"such as the contractual rate for similar debt instruments" 是对 "an appropriate discount rate" 的补充举例，相应译文应紧跟 "适当贴现率"。

2. 译文对 "...partitioning the market price of the item purchased, which equals the reduced principal amount, and accrued interest, the assumption being that the amount to be paid includes an allowance for interest" 的结构划分有误。该句主干应为 "partitioning the market price of the item purchased...and accrued interest..."。其中，"which equals the reduced principal amount" 限定了 "the market price of the item purchased"，而 "the assumption being that the amount to be paid includes an allowance for interest" 则是对整句内容设置的前提条件。

3. 倒数第二句中的 "such as due to the circumstances of the debtor" 显然是插

批 注

① "单"为错别字，应为"但"。
② 相比"未"而言，"不"体现的主观性较强。
③ 国际货币基金组织常将其译作"贴现率"。
④ 中文表述不完整，至少应补充完整为"通过……分割的方式进行/实现/做出"。
⑤ 根据国际货币基金组织术语表，"valuation"有"计值""定值""估价"等意思，此处"计值"比"定值"更妥帖。

入语，属于对"payment is not expected for an unusually long period of time"原因的补充说明，与句子核心意思关联不紧密。如果按照翻译稿的做法直接以逗号隔开，可能会产生误解；而将其放入括号并紧跟所补充的内容，则可以避免上述问题。

补充练习

Golden shares and options—A government may own a "golden share", particularly in a corporation that has been privatized. In some cases, this share gives the government some residual rights to protect the interests of the public by, for example, preventing the company selling off some categories of assets or appointing a special director who has strong powers in certain circumstances. A golden share is not of itself indicative of control. If, however, the powers covered by the golden share do confer on the government the ability to determine the general corporate policy of the entity in particular circumstances and those circumstances currently existed, then the entity should be in the public sector from the date in question. The existence of a share purchase option available to a government unit or a public corporation in certain circumstances may also be similar in concept to the golden share arrangement discussed earlier. It is necessary to consider whether, if the circumstance in which the option may be exercised exists, the volume of shares that may be purchased under the option and the consequences of such exercise mean that the government has "the ability to determine the general corporate policy of the entity" by exercising that option. An entity's status in general should be based on the government's existing ability to determine corporate policy exercised under normal conditions rather than in exceptional economic or other circumstances, such as wars, civil disorders, or natural disasters.

参考译文

黄金股和期权——政府可能拥有公司的"黄金股"，尤其是在经过私有化的公司。在某些情况下，黄金股给予政府一些剩余权利以保护公共利益，例如，阻止公司变卖某些类别的资产或者任命在某些情形下具有很大权力的特别董事。黄金股本身并非控制权的标志。但如果黄金股包含的权力确实赋予政府在特定情形下决定相关实体的一般性公司政策的能力，而且这些特定情形已经出现，那么该实体就应从相关日期开始归入公共部门。政府单位或公共公司在某些情形下拥有购买公司股份的期权，这在概念上与上述黄金股的安排可能有相似之处。有必要考虑，如果行使期权的条件得到满足，期权所允许购买的股份数量和行使期权的后果是否意味着政府通过行使期权而具有了"决定相关实体的一般性公司政策的能力"。一般而言，一个实体的地位应根据政府在通常情况（而非战争、动乱或自然灾害等特殊经济或其他情形）下决定公司政策的既有能力而定。

第十六篇

原文

While some nonmarket transactions, such as grants in kind, have no market price, other nonmarket transactions may take place at implied prices that include some element of grant or concession so that those prices also are not market prices (see Paragraphs 3.10–3.11). Examples of such transactions could include negotiated exchanges of goods between governments and governments' concessional lending. While there is no precise definition of concessional loans, it is generally accepted that they occur when units lend to other units and the contractual interest rate is intentionally set below the market interest rate that would otherwise apply. The degree of concessionality can be enhanced with grace periods (see Paragraph 6.69), frequencies of payments, and a maturity period favorable to the debtor. Since the terms of a concessional loan are more favorable to the debtor than market conditions would otherwise permit, concessional loans effectively include a transfer from the creditor to the debtor. However, except for the case of concessional lending to government employees (see Paragraph 6.17 and Chapter 6, Footnote 11) and concessional lending by central banks (see Box 6.2), the means of incorporating the impact of concessional lending into GFS have not been fully developed. Accordingly, until the appropriate treatment of concessional debt is resolved, information on concessional debt should be provided as supplementary information (see Paragraph 7.246).

请自行翻译后查看后文的分析点评

分析点评

While some nonmarket transactions, such as grants in kind, have no market price, other non-market transactions may take place at implied prices that include some element of grant or concession so that those prices also are not market prices (see Paragraphs 3.10–3.11). Examples of such transactions could include negotiated exchanges of goods between governments and governments' concessional lending. While there is no precise definition of concessional loans, it is generally accepted that they occur when units lend to other units and the contractual interest rate is intentionally set below the market interest rate that would otherwise apply. The degree of concessionality can be enhanced with grace periods (see Paragraph 6.69), frequencies of payments, and a maturity period favorable to the debtor. Since the terms of a concessional loan are more favorable to the debtor than market conditions would otherwise permit, concessional loans effectively include a transfer from the creditor to the debtor. However, except for the case of concessional lending to government employees (see Paragraph 6.17 and Chapter 6, footnote 11) and concessional lending by central banks (see Box 6.2), the means of incorporating the impact of concessional lending into GFS have not been fully developed. Accordingly, until the appropriate treatment of concessional debt is resolved, information on concessional debt should be provided as supplementary information (see Paragraph 7.246).

虽然有一些非市场交易，例如实物赠予①，没有市场价格，其他非市场交易可能以隐含价格发生，这些价格包含赠予或优惠，因此这些价格也不是市场价格（见第 3.10～3.11 段）。这类交易的实例可能包括政府之间经过商洽②的商品交换和政府的优惠贷款。虽然优惠贷款没有精确定义，但是一般认为它们发生在一些单位借给其他单位款项、③而且故意将利息率④设定在其他情况下适用的市场利息率之下时。优惠程度有可能因宽限期（见第 6.69 段）、支付频率和有利于债务人的到期时间⑤而提高。因为优惠贷款的条款比市场条件允许的条款更有利于债务人，优惠贷款实际上包含从债权人到债务人的转移，给予政府雇员的优惠贷款除外（见第 6.17 段和第六章脚注 11）和中央银行发放的优惠贷款（见方框 6.2）除外，将优惠贷款的影响纳入《政府财政统计》的方法，尚不完备。因此，在对优惠贷款⑥的恰当处理问题解决之前，应当将优惠贷款⑦的有关资料作为补充资料予以提供（见第 7.246 段）。

批 注

① 插入的补充举例，可置于括号内作为补充说明。
② 政府之间就商品交换的商洽宜用"谈判"。
③ 顿号用于分隔并列的事，通常是单字、词语或短句。短语内部的关系可用在并列词组之间。
④ 漏译"contractual"。
⑤ 原文"a maturity period"意为"偿还期限"（一段时间）而非"到期时间"（特定时刻）。
⑥ 原文为"concessional debt"，应表述为"优惠债务"。
⑦ 同本页批注⑥。

虽然一些非市场交易（例如，实物赠予）没有市场价格，但是其他非市场交易可能存在隐含价格，这些价格包含某种赠予或优惠的因素，因此也不是市场价格（见第 3.10～3.11 段）。这类交易的实例可能包括政府之间经过谈判的商品交换和政府的优惠贷款。虽然没有关于优惠贷款的精确定义，但是一般认为它们发生在一些单位向另一些单位借出款项且故意将合同利率设定得低于本应适用的市场利率时。优惠程度有可能因宽限期（见第 6.69 段）、支付频率和偿还期限有利于债务人而加大。因为优惠贷款的条款比市场环境允许的条款更有利于债务人，所以优惠贷款实际上包含一项从债权人到债务人的转移。然而，除了给予政府雇员的优惠贷款（见第 6.17 段和第六章，脚注 11）和中央银行发放的优惠贷款（见专栏 6.2），将优惠贷款的影响纳入政府财政统计的方法尚不完备。因此，在恰当处理优惠债务这个问题解决之前，应当将关于优惠债务的信息作为补充资料予以提供（见第 7.246 段）。

1. 译文两次出现关联词使用不完整的问题：一次出现在第一句，"虽然……，其他非市场交易可能以隐含价格发生……"中逗号后缺少"但是"；另一次出现在第五句,"因为……,优惠贷款实际上包含从债权人到债务人的转移……"中逗号后缺少"所以"。此外,翻译稿还漏译一个表转折关系的连词:原文第六句开头的"However"。翻译中应注意勿漏翻表示词与词、词组与词组或句子与句子之间某种逻辑关系的虚词,特别是中文里成对使用的关联词,以免影响译文的阅读和理解。

2. 翻译稿对"some element of grant or concession"的内容进行了删减处理,译为"赠予或优惠"。如非必需,不建议采用这种做法,而应当译为"某种赠予或优惠(的)因素"。

3. 将"the market interest rate that would otherwise apply"译为"设定在其他情况下适用的市场利息率之下",属于理解有误。原文中的"otherwise"意为"否则",而不是"在其他方面"。因此,这一短语的意思是:在不另行设定合同利率的情况下,原本应当适用的市场利率;放在整个句子中,可以简化表述为"低于本应适用的市场利率"。

4. 翻译稿在将"However, except for the case of concessional lending to government employees (see Paragraph 6.17 and Chapter 6, Footnote 11) and concessional lending by central banks (see Box 6.2), the means of incorporating the impact of concessional lending into GFS have not been fully developed."与前一句话合并翻译时出现了句式杂糅和意思错误的问题。这句话的译文"……,给予政府雇员的优惠贷款除外(见第 6.17 段和第六章脚注 11)和中央银行发放的优惠贷款(见方框 6.2)除外,将优惠贷款的影响纳入《政府财政统计》的方法,尚不完备。"会让读者认为两个"除外"是针对其前面的内容而言,而"将优惠贷款……尚不完备"是单独的意思。事实上,两个"除外"是针对"将优惠贷款……尚不完备"而言的。

补充练习

　　In some cases, actual exchange values may not represent market prices. Examples are transactions involving transfer prices between affiliated units, manipulative agreements with third parties, and certain noncommercial transactions. Prices may be under-or over-invoiced, in which case an assessment of a market-equivalent price needs to be made. Although, conceptually, adjustment should be made when actual exchange values do not represent market prices, this may not be practical in many cases. In some cases, transfer pricing may be motivated by income distribution or equity buildups or withdrawals. Replacing book values with market-value equivalents is desirable in principle, when the distortions are large and when the availability of data (such as adjustments by customs or tax officials or from partner economies) makes it feasible to do so. Selection of the best market-value equivalents to replace book values is an exercise calling for cautious and informed judgment. In many cases, compilers may have no choice other than to accept valuations based on explicit costs incurred in production or any other values assigned by the unit.

  在某些情况下，实际交换价值可能不代表市场价格。例如，涉及附属单位之间转让价格的交易、与第三方之间的操纵性协议，以及某些非商业交易。价格可能低于或高于发票价格，在此情况下，需要评估市场价格的对等值。虽然在概念上，当实际交换价值不代表市场价格时，就应当做出调整，但是在很多情况下，这也许并不切实可行。在某些情况下，转移定价可能是因收入分配或者股权积累或撤回而发生。在扭曲状况严重而数据可用性（例如，海关或税务官员的调整或来自伙伴经济体的调整）允许的条件下，原则上可以用市场价值的对等值代替账面价值。选取最佳的市场价值的对等值替代账面价值，这是一项需要进行谨慎的知情判断的工作。在许多情况下，编制者可能没有其他选择，只能接受以生产中产生的显性成本或单位指定的任何其他价值为基础进行计值。

  以下四篇材料选自国际货币基金组织2019年出版物《中国债券市场的未来》（第一章：中国债券市场：特征、前景与改革；第六章：国债期货；第十五章：离岸人民币点心债券；第十六章：中国的离岸公司美元债券）。

  《中国债券市场的未来》是一份多专题论文汇编，其作者来自国际货币基金组织、中国人民银行、中国证券监督管理委员会、财政部和中央国债登记结算有限公司以及私人部门和学术界，体现了国际货币基金组织与中国相关部门之间的密切合作。该出版物立足于中国四十年来金融体系的发展状况，概述了债券市场的独特发展状况和制度架构，分析了中国债券市场的各个组成部分，还涵盖了债券期货、资产支持证券和离岸债券市场，并明确了改革的关键领域。此外，它还就如何取消隐性担保、加强金融稳定和增强沟通提出了建议。

  该出版物面向中国相关部门的专业人员（例如，中国人民银行、证监会、银保监会等机构的相关工作人员），以中国国情，尤其是中国债券市场状况为主要内容，常常涉及中国证券领域的国家政策、法律法规、专业论著以及研究结论。翻译此类文件，译者必须具备基本的证券投资知识、熟悉证券行业术语，并且了解中国乃至国际相关制度、做法以及合作情况，才能正确地理解原文内容。术语和资料多来自国际货币基金组织，以及中国人民银行、证监会、银保监会、各商业银行、证券交易所的网站和资料。

第十七篇

原文

Given that capital account liberalization represents a regime change that relaxed restrictions on Chinese firms' access to overseas financing, the question that arises is whether the surge in China's offshore corporate bond issuance is associated with carry trades, similar to developments in other emerging market economies, or whether it is driven by policy changes that resulted in more liberalized capital accounts. In the latter case, it could make the traditional functions of offshore debt markets—namely, trade financing and precautionary borrowing for future financing needs—more accessible to Chinese nonfinancial corporations.

请自行翻译后查看后文的分析点评

分析点评

Given that capital account liberalization represents a regime change that relaxed restrictions on Chinese firms' access to overseas financing, the question that arises is whether the surge in China's offshore corporate bond issuance is associated with carry trades, similar to developments in other emerging market economies, or whether it is driven by policy changes that resulted in more liberalized capital accounts. In the latter case, it could make the traditional functions of offshore debt markets—namely, trade financing and precautionary borrowing for future financing needs—more accessible to Chinese nonfinancial corporations.

翻译稿

考虑到资本账户自由化代表①着对国内公司海外融资放松管制的一种政策②变化，其中存在的问题在于中国离岸公司债券发行激增是否与套利交易有关，与其他新兴市场经济体类似，或者这是否是由导致③资本账户进一步自由化④的政策变化驱动。在后一种情况下，这可以使离岸债务市场的传统功能——即为满足未来融资需求而进行的贸易融资和预防性借款——更容易被中国非金融公司所接受。

审校稿

考虑到资本账户放开意味着对中国公司海外融资渠道放松管制的制度变更，于是产生了这样一个问题：中国离岸公司债券发行的激增是否会像其他新兴市场经济体的发展状况那样与套利交易有关，抑或它是否由推动资本账户进一步放开的政策变革所驱动。在后一种情况下，这可促进中国非金融公司享受离岸债务市

批注

① 此处用"代表"不妥。
② 注意原文措辞为"regime"（制度、政权），并非"policy"。
③ 注意词语的褒贬含义，"导致"的结果一般是不良的。
④ 使用"放开"亦可。

场的传统功能——贸易融资和为满足未来融资需求而进行的预防性借款。

1. 原文第一句中的"access to"漏译，此处这一短语应译为"渠道"。原文最后一句出现了"make (A) more accessible to (B)"，意为"使 A 更容易为 B 所获取 / 进入 / 访问"，或者"使 B 更容易获取 / 进入 / 访问 A"。将其译为"使……更容易被……接受"，属于用词错误。在经济与金融类文件翻译中，经常会遇到"access"一词，在表述的时候往往难以处理。这个词常见的译法有：获取、获得、渠道、机会，应视情况选择使用。

2. 对"...namely, trade financing and precautionary borrowing for future financing needs"中"for future financing needs..."的限定范围判断失误。根据相关内容，"for future financing needs"实际上仅限定"precautionary borrowing"，因此，"namely"引导的部分应译为"贸易融资和为满足未来融资需求而进行的预防性借款"。

3. 对原文第一句中"...whether the surge in China's offshore corporate bond issuance is associated with carry trades, similar to developments in other emerging market economies, ..."的翻译处理欠妥。原文的意思是"the surge in China's offshore corporate bond issuance is associated with carry trades"这种状况与"developments in other emerging market economies"相似。如果按照翻译稿的表述"中国离岸公司债券发行激增是否与套利交易有关，与其他新兴市场经济体类似"会导致读者认为"与其他新兴市场经济体类似"是与"与套利交易有关"并列的另一内容。为避免这种歧义，应当将"similar to developments in other emerging market economies"插入前面的相应位置，译为"……中国离岸公司债券发行的激增是否会像其他新兴市场经济体的发展状况那样与套利交易有关，……"。

补充练习

China is among the major contributors to this growing offshore corporate bond market. By 2016, Chinese nonfinancial corporations had issued about US$500 billion in offshore markets—about 20 percent of total emerging market economies' corporate bonds—from nearly zero in the mid-2000s. At the outset, this development reflected the liberalization of China's capital account in the past decade, including the easing of restrictions on corporations to tap into offshore financial markets (TANG and ZHU, 2016). More specifically, the National Development and Reform Commission, the regulator for China's onshore enterprise bond market (see Chapter 1), implemented a policy in September 2015 to replace the previous case-by-case approval system for corporate offshore bond issuance with a predeal filing system. In 2016, the People's Bank of China also introduced a macroprudential assessment framework for cross-border financing to replace the previous ad hoc system of case-by-case approval and quota allocations. This new framework is designed to manage risks associated with capital flows by influencing the overall volume and composition of capital flows in a countercyclical manner through the use of prudential parameters, including one on excess leverage (IMF, 2018b). It can be used to target single, multiple, or all financial or nonfinancial institutions in terms of overseas financing. "In 2017, the Ministry of Finance issued the first sovereign dollar bonds in over a decade, partly to serve as a benchmark for the nation's surging dollar corporate bonds."

中国是离岸公司债券市场不断发展的主要贡献者之一。到 2016 年，中国的非金融公司已经在离岸市场上发行了约 5 000 亿美元债券——约占新兴市场经济体公司债券发行总量的 20%，而在 21 世纪头十年中期，这一发行量还几乎为零。起初，这一发展反映了过去十年中国资本账户放开的过程，包括放宽对公司进入离岸金融市场的限制（TANG 和 ZHU，2016）。更具体地说，中国国家发展和改革委员会，即中国在岸企业债券市场的监管者（见第一章），于 2015 年 9 月实施了一项政策，该政策以交易前备案登记制取代了此前离岸公司债券发行的逐案审批制。2016 年，中国人民银行还引入了针对跨境融资的宏观审慎评估框架，取代了此前的临时逐案审批制和定额分配制。这个新框架旨在运用审慎参数（包括关于过度杠杆化的参数）、以反周期方式影响资本流动的总量和构成，从而管理资本流动的相关风险（基金组织，2018b）。这一框架可用于进行海外融资的单一、多个或全部金融或非金融机构。"2017 年，财政部发行了十多年以来第一笔美元主权债券，一定程度上是为了给不断增长的中国企业的美元公司债券立下基准。"

原文

Policy bank bonds (part of financial bonds) play an important part in China's bond market. Since investors assume that they are backed by the government and, hence, are risk free, they are also used as benchmarks for the pricing of other securities. Unlike sovereign bonds, policy bank bonds are not tax exempt. The first policy bank bonds were issued in 1994 by the China Development Bank and now include those issued by the Export-Import Bank and the China Agricultural Development Bank.

The size of the market is similar to that of the sovereign bond market, but it turns out that policy bonds are actually more liquid. Possibly reflecting higher market trading, policy bank bonds tend to be more responsive to changes in macroeconomic fundamentals, as proxied by industrial production, as well as monetary policy signals (7-day repo rate). This reinforces the view that improving trading liquidity will be key to boosting the information efficiency and policy transmission mechanism of the China government bond market.

请自行翻译后查看后文的分析点评

分析点评

第 1 段

Policy bank bonds (part of financial bonds) play an important part in China's bond market. Since investors assume that they are backed by the government and, hence, are risk free, they are also used as benchmarks for the pricing of other securities. Unlike sovereign bonds, policy bank bonds are not tax exempt. The first policy bank bonds were issued in 1994 by the China Development Bank and now include those issued by the Export-Import Bank and the China Agricultural Development Bank.

政策性银行债券（金融债券的一部分）在中国债券市场发挥着重要作用。由于投资者假定它们由政府支持，因而无风险，因此它们也被用作其他证券定价的基准。不同于主权债券，① 政策性银行债券不免税。1994 年，中国国家开发银行首次发行政策性银行债券，现在政策性银行债券包括由中国进出口银行和中国农业发展银行发行的债券。

批 注

① 不符合中文表达习惯。

政策性银行债券（金融债券的一部分）在中国债券市场上发挥着重要作用。投资者假定它们由于获得政府支持而不存在风险，因此它们也被用作其他证券定价的基准。政策性银行债券不免税，这一点不同于主权债券。1994 年，中国国家开发银行首次发行政策性银行债券，如今政策性银行债券包括由中国进出口银行和中国农业发展银行发行的债券。

点评

这一段的主要难点在 "Since investors assume that they are backed by the government and, hence, are risk free, they are also used as benchmarks for the pricing of other securities." 这句。该句存在两重因果关系：一、因为 "investors assume...", 所以 "they are also used as"; 二、因为 "...they are backed by...", 所以 "...hence, are risk free..."。第二重因果关系是第一重因果关系中 "assume" 的内容。

第 2 段

The size of the market is similar to that of the sovereign bond market, but it turns out that policy bonds are actually more liquid. Possibly reflecting higher market trading, policy bank bonds tend to be more responsive to changes in macroeconomic fundamentals, as proxied by industrial production, as well as monetary policy signals (7-day repo rate). This reinforces the view that improving trading liquidity will be key to boosting the information efficiency and policy transmission mechanism of the China government bond market.

市场规模与主权债券市场相仿，但事实证明，政策性债券实际上流动性更强。政策性银行债券可能反映较高的市场交易①，受到工业生产和货币政策信号（7天回购利率）推动，往往对宏观经济基本面的变化反应更为灵敏。这进一步表明，改善②交易流动性将是提高中国政府债券市场信息效率和政策传导机制的关键。

批 注

① 形容词与中心语不搭配。这里的"market trading"实指"市场交易量"。

② 此处"improve"可以用"改善"；需要注意的是，它也可以翻译为"提高""提升""增强""改进""完善"等，勿千篇一律用"改善"。

政策性银行债券市场规模与主权债券市场规模相仿，但事实证明，政策性债券实际上流动性更强。政策性银行债券可能反映了更高的市场交易量，因此它对宏观经济基本面（以工业生产为代理变量）的变化以及货币政策信号（7天回购利率）往往反应更为灵敏。这进一步证实了提升交易流动性将成为提高中国国债市场信息效率和政策传导机制的关键这一看法。

1. 这一段的重点在"...policy bank bonds tend to be more responsive to changes in macroeconomic fundamentals, as proxied by industrial production, as well as monetary policy signals (7-day repo rate)."这部分的结构。其中，"tend to be more responsive to"的对象是"changes in macroeconomic fundamentals"和"monetary policy signals"，而"as proxied by industrial production"是对"macroeconomic fundamentals"的补充说明。注意"proxied by"意指"以……为代理变量"，不是"受……推动"。翻译稿显然混淆了句子结构。

2. 翻译稿对本段第一句开头部分"The size of the market is similar to that of the sovereign bond market..."采用了对照原文直译的做法，译为"市场规模与主权债券市场相仿"，这里有两个问题。第一，在一段的开头使用"市场规模"这一措辞，指代不明；第二，漏译了"that of"，导致中文表述中"市场规模"与"主权债券市场"两者不具有可比性。针对前者，应当根据前一段的内容将"市场规模"补充完整，译为"政策性银行债券市场规模"；针对后者，应当在"主权债券市场"后增加"规模"。

补充练习

China's local government bond market—regulated by the Ministry of Finance—developed almost overnight and now exceeds the size of sovereign bonds (Chapter 5). Before 2015, local governments were largely prohibited from borrowing. Instead, and especially since the large stimulus program following the global financial crisis, they have relied on off–balance sheet activities through LGFVs, effectively circumventing borrowing constraints. To reduce reliance on LGFVs and minimize financial sector risks, local governments can issue bonds subject to an annual ceiling set by the National People's Congress, a strategy introduced under the motto "opening the front door" while "closing the back door". To facilitate the transition, the government announced a large-scale debt-swap program, reaching RMB 15 trillion (23 percent of GDP in 2017), making China's local government bond market one of the largest in the world.

参考译文

由财政部监管的中国地方政府债券市场几乎是在一夜之间发展起来的，如今其规模已超过主权债券市场（第五章）。2015年以前，地方政府基本上被禁止举债。然而，尤其是自全球金融危机后出台大规模刺激计划以来，它们一直依赖地方政府融资平台的表外业务，有效地规避了借贷约束。为了减少对地方政府融资平台的依赖以及将金融部门风险降至最低，地方政府可以在全国人民代表大会规定的年度上限以内发行债券，这项策略采用了"开前门"和"堵后门"的思路。为了促进转型，政府宣布了一项达15万亿元人民币（占2017年GDP的23%）的大规模债务置换计划，使中国的地方政府债券市场成为世界最大的债券市场之一。

第十九篇

原文

Moreover, China has continued to advance bond market opening in recent years. International investors are now able to access the bond market through the Qualified Foreign Institutional Investor/Renminbi Qualified Institutional Investor (QFII/RQFII) regime, as People's Bank of China–approved foreign institutional investors in the China Interbank Bond Market or through Bond Connect. By the end of August 2018, Treasury bonds held by foreign institutions reached RMB 1 034.3 billion, up RMB 427.8 billion from the end of 2017, an increase of 71 percent. Such a large jump surpassed that of any other type of investor. Despite their active participation in the cash market, however, foreign institutions cannot yet access the Treasury futures market. This situation entails a potential risk that foreign institutions' capital flows into or out of the bond market due to lack of hedging tools may adversely impact the exchange rate. It is therefore imperative to open China's Treasury futures market to foreign investors, which would help improve the investment environment in the cash market and enhance interest-rate and exchange-rate stability.

请自行翻译后查看后文的分析点评

分析点评

Moreover, China has continued to advance bond market opening in recent years. International investors are now able to access the bond market through the Qualified Foreign Institutional Investor/Renminbi Qualified Institutional Investor (QFII/RQFII) regime, as People's Bank of China–approved foreign institutional investors in the China Interbank Bond Market or through Bond Connect. By the end of August 2018, Treasury bonds held by foreign institutions reached RMB 1 034.3 billion, up RMB 427.8 billion from the end of 2017, an increase of 71 percent. Such a large jump surpassed that of any other type of investor. Despite their active participation in the cash market, however, foreign institutions cannot yet access the Treasury futures market. This situation entails a potential risk that foreign institutions' capital flows into or out of the bond market due to lack of hedging tools may adversely impact the exchange rate. It is therefore imperative to open China's Treasury futures market to foreign investors, which would help improve the investment environment in the cash market and enhance interest-rate and exchange-rate stability.

翻译稿

此外，近年来中国继续推进债券市场开放。国际投资者现在可以通过合格境外机构投资者／人民币合格境外机构投资者（QFII／RQFII）制度进入债券市场，上述投资者为中国人民银行在中国银行间债券市场或通过债券通批准的外国机构投资者。截至 2018 年 8 月底，外资机构持有的国债达到 10 343 亿元，比 2017 年年末增加 4 278 亿元，增长 71%。如此大的跳跃式发展幅度超过了任何其他类型的投资者。然而，尽管外资机构积极参与现货市场，但目前还无法进入国债期货市场。由于缺乏对冲工具，外资机构资金流入或流出债券市场的潜在风险可能会对汇率产生不利影响。因此，必须向外国投资者开放中国国债期货市场，这将有助于改善现货市场的投资环境，提高利率和汇率稳定性。

批 注

① 凡涉及款项金额之处必须注明币种；除非上下文已做出说明。
② 同本页批注①。

审校稿

此外，近年来中国继续推进债券市场的开放。国际投资者现在可以通过合格境外机构投资者/人民币合格境外机构投资者（QFII/RQFII）制度、以经中国人民银行批准的中国银行间债券市场外国机构投资者身份，或者通过"债券通"进入债券市场。截至2018年8月底，外国机构持有的国债达10 343亿元人民币，比2017年年末增加了4 278亿元人民币，增长率为71%。如此大的飞跃式发展超过了任何其他类型投资者的投资。然而，尽管外国机构积极参与现货市场，但它们目前还无法进入国债期货市场。这种情况可能导致外国机构资本因缺乏对冲工具而流入或流出债券市场，这可能对汇率产生不利影响。因此，向外国投资者开放中国国债期货市场势在必行，这将有助于改善现货市场的投资环境，加强利率和汇率稳定性。

1. 翻译稿对第二句最后一部分"as People's Bank of China–approved foreign institutional investors in the China Interbank Bond Market or through Bond Connect"的处理方式有误。这句话中有两个补充说明部分：一个是"through the Qualified Foreign Institutional Investor/Renminbi Qualified Institutional Investor (QFII/RQFII) regime"，另一个是"as People's Bank of China–approved foreign institutional investors in the China Interbank Bond Market or through Bond Connect"。前者说明的是"International investors are now able to access the bond market"的途径/渠道，后者说明的是"International investors"以何种身份"access the bond market"。后者应当与前者一样，插入句子主干之中，而非作为并行的另一个分句。

2. 原文倒数第二句"This situation entails a potential risk that foreign institutions' capital flows into or out of the bond market due to lack of hedging tools may adversely impact the exchange rate."的翻译稿存在若干问题：一、其中的"This situation entails"漏译，导致这句话与上文之间的内在联系消失不见；二、"potential risk"不宜译为"潜在风险"，这一短语在这里的意思是"某种可能性"；三、"由于缺乏对冲工具，外资机构资金流入或流出债券市场的潜在风险可能会对汇率产生不利影响"这一表述导致了原文因果关系的扭曲。原文中，"lack of hedging tools"导致的是"foreign institutions' capital flows into or out of the bond market"；这种因"lack of hedging tools"导致的"foreign institutions' capital flows..."可能会"adversely impact the exchange rate"；"foreign institutions' capital flows...may adversely impact the exchange rate"是"a potential risk"；这种"potential risk"是"This situation"带来的。

补充练习

Going forward, further advances in the Treasury futures market will not only allow investors to better hedge risk, but will also strengthen the underlying cash market. In particular, introducing more diversified products, such as longer-term Treasury bond futures and Treasury futures options with different terms, would meet the market's diversified risk management needs and strengthen the bond yield curve. Another area for reform is improving investor composition. Further financial sector liberalization needs to go hand in hand with the ability of institutions and investors to hedge risks. Because about 70 percent of Treasury bonds are held by commercial banks, allowing them to participate in the Treasury futures market will contribute to better interest rate risk management and, in turn, increase cash market liquidity. The same is true of foreign investors, who increasingly have access to the domestic bond market through the different quota schemes and China's Interbank Bond Market through Bond Connect but have not been able to participate in the Treasury futures market. In addition, to better meet investors' diversified needs for hedging and strategy-based trading—and based on international experience—China could consider providing alternative trading, in addition to its current auction-based system, such as block trade, exchange for physicals, exchange for swap, and exchange for risk.

未来国债期货市场的进一步发展不仅有利于投资者更好地对冲风险，还可以巩固潜在的现货市场。特别是，更多元化产品（例如长期国债期货和不同期限的国债期货期权）的引入将满足市场多元化的风险管理需求，改善债券收益率曲线。另一个改革领域为改善投资者构成。金融部门的进一步放开需要辅以机构和投资者对冲风险的能力。由于约70%的国债由商业银行持有，因此，允许它们参与国债期货市场将有助于优化利率风险管理，继而增加现货市场的流动性。外国投资者也是如此，它们越来越多地通过各种配额计划进入国内债券市场，以及通过"债券通"进入中国银行间债券市场，但未能参与国债期货市场。此外，为了更好地满足投资者对于对冲和策略性交易的多样化需求，基于国际经验，中国除了采用目前以拍卖为基础的制度以外，可以考虑提供替代交易方式，例如大宗交易、期货转现货、期货转掉期和期货转风险。

To overcome the currency mismatch between the source and use of funds, some dim sum bond issuers may swap renminbi into US dollars in the offshore market to fund their overseas investment. Mainland issuers that receive US dollar revenues generated from their overseas investments may swap the US dollar proceeds into renminbi to pay off the mature dim sum bonds. This suggests that the renminbi exchange rate and hedging cost play a role, as they would affect overall funding costs. Historically, appreciation of the renminbi effective exchange rate has tended to support external financing using dim sum bonds, while depreciation has discouraged issuance activities. Apart from exchange rate considerations, hedging costs may also influence issuance of dim sum bonds if the issuers plan to swap back their US dollar proceeds from overseas investment to settle renminbi bond payments at maturity. This suggests that a weaker renminbi forward rate may increase such incentives, which can be shown from the positive correlation between net issuance of dim sum bonds and changes in the one-year offshore renminbi forward rate, which is a proxy of hedging costs.

请自行翻译后查看后文的分析点评

分析点评

To overcome the currency mismatch between the source and use of funds, some dim sum bond issuers may swap renminbi into US dollars in the offshore market to fund their overseas investment. Mainland issuers that receive US dollar revenues generated from their overseas investments may swap the US dollar proceeds into renminbi to pay off the mature dim sum bonds. This suggests that the renminbi exchange rate and hedging cost play a role, as they would affect overall funding costs. Historically, appreciation of the renminbi effective exchange rate has tended to support external financing using dim sum bonds, while depreciation has discouraged issuance activities. Apart from exchange rate considerations, hedging costs may also influence issuance of dim sum bonds if the issuers plan to swap back their US dollar proceeds from overseas investment to settle renminbi bond payments at maturity. This suggests that a weaker renminbi forward rate may increase such incentives, which can be shown from the positive correlation between net issuance of dim sum bonds and changes in the one-year offshore renminbi forward rate, which is a proxy of hedging costs.

翻译稿

为避免资金来源和用途之间的币不匹配，一些点心债券发行人可能会在离岸市场中进行人民币和美元的互换交易，以向境外投资提供资金。中国大陆发行人收到境外投资产生的美元收入时，可进行美元和人民币的互换交易，以偿还到期的点心债券。这表明人民币汇率和对冲成本也影响债券发行，因为它们会影响总体资金成本。历史趋势表明，人民币有效汇率升值往往支持点心债券外部融资①，而贬值②则减弱发行活跃度。除了汇率方面的考虑因素，如果发行人计划将境外投资产生的美元收入换回人民币以偿还到期债券③，则对冲成本也可能影响点心债券的发行。这表明较低的人民币远期汇率可能增加发债积极性，正如点心

批 注

① 原文中的"using"一词不可省略。
② 此处宜补译为"人民币有效汇率贬值"，以明确主语。
③ 漏译"RMB"。

债券净发行额与一年期离岸人民币远期汇率的变化之间的正相关系数所表明的那样。此处该远期汇率被用于替代对冲成本。

为避免资金来源和用途之间的币种错配，一些点心债券发行人可能会在离岸市场中进行以人民币兑美元的交易，为海外投资提供资金。中国大陆发行人收到海外投资产生的美元收入时，可将美元收益兑换为人民币，以偿还到期的点心债券。这表明人民币汇率和对冲成本有可能影响债券发行，因为它们会改变总体融资成本。一直以来，人民币有效汇率升值往往支持使用点心债券进行境外融资，而人民币有效汇率贬值则抑制发行活动。除了汇率方面的考虑，如果发行人计划将海外投资产生的美元收益兑换为人民币以支付到期的人民币债券，则对冲成本也可能影响点心债券的发行。这表明人民币远期汇率下降可能会提高发债的积极性，这可能会体现在点心债券净发行量与一年期离岸人民币远期汇率（对冲成本的一个指标）变动之间存在的正相关的关系上。

1. 原文中重要的金融术语"currency mismatch"意思是"币种错配""货币错配"。虽然目前还没有一致公认的定义，但具体含义大同小异。戈德斯坦和特纳（2005年）对货币错配所下的定义是：由于一个权益实体（包括主权国家、银行、非金融企业和家庭）的收支活动使用了不同的货币计值，其资产和负债的币种结构不同，导致其净值或净收入（或者兼而有之）对汇率的变化非常敏感，即出现了所谓的货币错配。从存量的角度看，货币错配指的是资产负债表（即净值）对汇率变动的敏感性；从流量的角度看，货币错配则是指损益表（净收入）对汇率变动的敏感性。

2. 原文中的"funding costs"应当译为"融资成本"。"funding"一词基本上应翻为"融资""供资"等，不过在某些（很少）情况下，根据上下文意思或者中文表述需要，也会翻译为"资金"。本段中此处"资金成本"不妥。

3. 原文第二句中"...may swap the US dollar proceeds into renminbi..."被译为"可进行美元和人民币的互换交易"。这一表述除了漏翻"proceeds"以外，模糊了兑换的方向，应当准确地将其译为"将美元收益兑换为人民币"。

4. 第四句开头的"Historically"并非"历史趋势表明"，而是意指"从历史的角度来看""有史以来""一直以来"。

5. 原文最后一句的翻译稿主要存在两个问题：一、对用于修饰"the one-year offshore renminbi forward rate"这部分的"which is a proxy of hedging costs"理解错误并且处理不当。其中"proxy"意指"代理变量"，可引申为"指标"，并非"替代"之意。另外，将这一部分独立成一个句子的做法导致了整个句子意思松散；二、"a weaker renminbi forward rate may increase such incentives"宜译为"人民币远期汇率下降可能会提高发债的积极性"，"下降"和"提高"均为一个动态过程，能够清晰而准确地反映"人民币远期汇率"变动与"发债的积极性"变化之间的关系。

补充练习

To explain issuance activity in the offshore renminbi bond market, the net issuance of dim sum bonds is used to examine its dynamics with different driving factors. One motive for enterprises to raise offshore renminbi funds is to finance their direct investment overseas or in China. Past development shows that net issuance of dim sum bonds has stronger co-movement with China's ODI than inward FDI. This echoes the fact that China's mainland firms have been more active than foreign companies in raising renminbi funds in the dim sum bond market. Given that a significant portion of ODI conducted by mainland firms is in the form of outbound merger and acquisitions, which are usually settled in US dollars or other foreign currencies, the use of renminbi would be more common in developing economies with closer economic ties with China, as they can use renminbi to settle imports of goods and services from China. This can be seen from the rapid expansion in China's ODI settling in renminbi from RMB 27 billion in 2011 to RMB 1 062 billion in 2016, before easing to RMB 457 billion in 2017.

参考译文

为解释离岸人民币债券市场的发行活动，我们使用点心债券净发行量来研究发行活动在不同驱动因素作用下的变动情况。企业筹集离岸人民币资金的动机之一是为其在海外或中国的直接投资提供资金。过去的发展状况显示，点心债券的净发行量与中国的对外直接投资之间的联动性大于其与境内的外商直接投资之间的联动性。这与中国大陆公司比外国公司更积极地通过点心债券市场筹集人民币资金的事实相呼应。考虑到中国大陆公司开展的对外直接投资中有很大一部分为海外并购，而此类交易常以美元或其他外币结算，因此，较常使用人民币的是那些与中国经济联系更紧密的发展中经济体，因为它们可使用人民币来支付从中国进口的货物和服务。这一点可见于中国以人民币结算的对外直接投资金额曾经从2011年的270亿元人民币快速增至2016年的1.062万亿元人民币（后于2017年减少至4 570亿元人民币）的情况。

背景介绍

本篇材料选自国际货币基金组织2019年第四条磋商讨论工作人员总结声明。

根据《国际货币基金组织协定》第四条，基金组织通常每年与成员国进行双边讨论，由一个工作人员小组（代表团）访问成员国，收集经济和金融信息并与该国官员讨论经济发展情况和政策。工作人员会就此准备一份报告，以此作为执董会讨论的基础。这就是所谓的"第四条磋商"。

第四章 经济与金融

除与其他类别文件同样需要具备经济与金融方面的背景知识，同样要求严格遵照术语进行翻译以外，此类文件自身具有一定的系统性，可参考国际货币基金组织代表团以往与中国政府以及与其他国家政府的第四条磋商文件中的相关表述和格式。

第二十一篇

原文

Although growth is expected to bottom out later this year, the recovery is likely to be gradual, and the output gap remaining negative over the medium term. Growth is expected to fall to [0.3] percent in 2019 and rise only to [1.5] percent in 2020 with a recovery of private consumption, well below potential growth of about 2½ percent. With increased trade barriers and disruptions to global supply chains as a persistent drag on trade-related activities, growth is expected to recover toward its potential rate at a slower pace than in previous recoveries. The slowing economy is expected to shed jobs, thus raising unemployment, though the flexible labor market should allow for a significant share of laid-off workers to be absorbed by other services sectors. With an estimated negative output gap of about [2½] percent of GDP, inflation is projected to fall to about 2½ percent in 2020 as food prices stabilize.

Given the urgent need to increase housing supply, additional spending on housing and related infrastructure developments is warranted. Bringing forward planned spending on infrastructure projects and scaling it up after the above targeted transfers are unwound would not only expedite the supply of land and housing but would avoid an early withdraw of fiscal impulse needed to close the negative output gap over the medium term. Cumulative increase in spending of 3½ ppt of GDP over the next five years would increase real GDP by about 2¼ ppt during this period.

请自行翻译后查看后文的分析点评

分析点评

第 1 段

Although growth is expected to bottom out later this year, the recovery is likely to be gradual, and the output gap remaining negative over the medium term. Growth is expected to fall to [0.3] percent in 2019 and rise only to [1.5] percent in 2020 with a recovery of private consumption, well below potential growth of about 2½ percent. With increased trade barriers and disruptions to global supply chains as a persistent drag on trade-related activities, growth is expected to recover toward its potential rate at a slower pace than in previous recoveries. The slowing economy is expected to shed jobs, thus raising unemployment, though the flexible labor market should allow for a significant share of laid-off workers to be absorbed by other services sectors. With an estimated negative output gap of about [2½] percent of GDP, inflation is projected to fall to about 2½ percent in 2020 as food prices stabilize.

批 注

① 词义不准确。
② 理解错误。
③ 表述有待改进。

尽管经济增长预计在今年晚些时候将触底，但复苏可能趋于平缓①，中期内产出缺口仍为负值。随着私人消费的复苏，预计 2019 年的增长率将跌至 [0.3%]，2020 年将只增加到 [1.5%]② 远低于约 2.5% 的潜在增长率。随着贸易壁垒的增加和全球供应链的中断对贸易相关活动的持续拖累，经济增长预计将以较以往复苏更慢的速度③ 向潜在增长率趋近。经济放缓预计将导致就业岗位减少，从而使失业率增加，尽管灵活的劳动力市场应允许大量下岗工人被其他服务部门吸收。据估计，负产出缺口约为 GDP 的 [2.5%]，随着食品价格的稳定，通货膨胀预计将在 2020 年降至 2.5% 左右。

尽管经济增长预计在今年晚些时候将触底，但复苏可能是渐进的，中期内产出缺口仍为负值。预计 2019 年的增长率将跌至 [0.3]%；随着私人消费的复苏，2020 年的增速将仅上升到 [1.5]%，远低于约 2.5% 的潜在增长率。随着贸易壁垒的增加和全球供应链的中断对贸易相关活动的持续拖累，经济增长预计将以低于之前的复苏速度向潜在增长率回升。经济放缓预计将导致就业岗位减少，从而使失业率增加，尽管灵活的劳动力市场应允许大量下岗工人被其他服务业部门吸收。在估计负产出缺口约为 GDP 的 [2.5]% 的情况下，随着食品价格企稳，通货膨胀预计将在 2020 年降至 2.5% 左右。

1. "Gradual" 一词有"逐渐的、渐进的、平缓的"意思。如果只从字面意思判断，复苏既可以是渐进的，也可以是平缓的，具体选择哪个词义需要结合上下文的逻辑关系做出判断。前半句说的是"尽管经济增长预计在今年晚些时候将触底"，指明了一种不利情况，后半句在逻辑上应该转而指向一种有利情况。翻译稿的"平缓"是一个中性词，无法体现这种逻辑关系，而"渐进"有一种持续转好的意思，相比"平缓"，更加贴切。因此，修改后的译文使用了"渐进"一词。

2. 原文中有一个介词结构"with a recovery of private consumption"，表示一种伴随状态。翻译稿将这个结构看作是修饰整个句子，理解有误。根据就近原则，"with a recovery of private consumption" 应该仅修饰"rise only to [1.5] percent in 2020"。除了从语法结构上进行判断之外，还可以从语义上判断。前半句提到

"预计 2019 年的增长率将跌至 [0.3]%",如果按照原译文的译法,既然私人消费已经复苏,增长率就不应该再下降,那么将"随着私人消费的复苏"放在整个句子的前面,在逻辑上就说不通。因此,原译文对这个结构的理解错误。

第 2 段

Given the urgent need to increase housing supply, additional spending on housing and related infrastructure developments is warranted. Bringing forward planned spending on infrastructure projects and scaling it up after the above targeted transfers are unwound would not only expedite the supply of land and housing but would avoid an early withdraw of fiscal impulse needed to close the negative output gap over the medium term. Cumulative increase in spending of 3½ ppt of GDP over the next five years would increase real GDP by about 2¼ ppt during this period.

鉴于增加住房供应的迫切需要,有必要在住房和相关基础设施建设上增加支出。增加计划用于基础设施项目的支出①,并在上述有针对性的转移完成后②扩大支出规模,不仅会加快土地和住房供应,还会避免过早削减在中期内缩小负产出缺口所需的财政动力。未来五年内,支出累计增长将占 GDP 的 3.5%③,从而使同一时期的实际 GDP 增加 2.25%④左右。

批 注

① 理解错误。
② 句子结构理解错误。
③④ ppt 是指百分点,而不是百分比。

鉴于增加住房供应的迫切需要,有必要在住房和相关基础设施建设上增加支出。在上述有针对性的转移支付完成后,提前规划用于基础设施项目的支出,并扩大支出规模,不仅会加快土地和住房供应,还会避免过早取消在中期内缩小负产出缺口所需的财政刺激。未来五年内,若支出累计增长 GDP 的 3.5 个百分点,那么这一时期的实际 GDP 将增加 2.25 个百分点左右。

1. 翻译稿理解有误。"Bringing forward"是"提前"而不是"增加"的意思,因此,"Bringing forward planned spending on infrastructure projects"是指提前规划用于基础设施项目的支出而不是增加计划用于基础设施项目的支出。

2. 这句话的重点在于"after the above targeted transfers are unwound"是紧跟在"scaling it up"之后还是跟在"Bringing forward planned spending on infrastructure projects and scaling it up"的后面。在这里,应该结合上文做出判断。第一句指出,需要在住房和相关基础设施建设上增加支出。第二句紧接着说在增加支出之后,应该采取何种措施。从逻辑上看,"after the above targeted transfers are unwound"放在整个句子的前面没有问题。另外,仅就本句而言,提前规划支出和扩大支出规模应该是在转移支付完成后进行。综上所述,"after the above targeted transfers are unwound"应跟在"Bringing forward planned spending on infrastructure projects and scaling it up"之后。翻译稿对这部分的句子结构分析错误,导致译文错误。

补充练习

Greater countercyclical fiscal policy would help the economy navigate through negative shocks while maintaining long-term sustainability. With a comfortable level of fiscal reserves, there is scope for near-term support to the slowing economy. The authorities need to balance near-term demand needs against longer-term weakening of the structural fiscal position arising from rapid population aging and corresponding increase in social expenditure. This can be achieved by aligning short-term measures with long-term goals and shifting spending forward (e.g., on identified infrastructure projects) in a manner that helps ensure long-term sustainability.

In the near term, there is room to increase spending to cope with cyclical downturn and address structural challenges of insufficient housing and high inequality. In addition to one-off relief measures included in the 2019/2020 budget, the authorities have announced new fiscal stimulus to help the slowing economy, including support for the SMEs, further tax relief, extra social security payments, and subsidies for households. Staff welcome the announced measures. Staff project continued fiscal surplus of about [1] percent of GDP over the medium term and recommend an additional comprehensive fiscal package. Spending increases of around 1¼–1½ percent of GDP per year (7 ppt of GDP in total over 2020—2024), relative to the projected baseline, would help close the negative output gap over the medium term with a drawdown of fiscal reserves of less than 5 ppt of GDP.

参考译文

加强逆周期财政政策将有助于经济抵御负面冲击，同时也有助于保持其长期可持续性。由于财政储备水平适宜，为经济增长放缓提供短期的财政支持仍有空间。当局需要在人口快速老龄化和社会支出相应增加导致结构性财政状况长期疲弱的情况下平衡各种近期需求。这可以通过协调短期措施与长期目标以及以有助于确保长期可持续性的方式前移支出（例如，就已经确定的基础设施项目）来实现。

从近期来看，仍有增加支出的空间以应对周期性经济下滑，解决住房不足和不平等严重的结构性挑战。除了在 2019/2020 年度预算中纳入一次性减免措施之外，当局还宣布了新的财政刺激措施来帮助增长放缓的经济，其中包括为中小型企业提供支持、进一步减税、提供额外的社会保障支出（支付）和家庭补贴。工作人员欢迎已宣布的措施。工作人员预计，在中期内，财政盈余将继续保持在 GDP 的 [1]% 左右，并建议额外采取全面的一揽子财政措施。相对于预测的基线，每年的支出增长大约将占 GDP 的 1.25% 至 1.5%（2020—2024 年，总共为 GDP 的 7 个百分点），这将有助于在中期内缩小负产出缺口，使财政储备的减少不超过 GDP 的 5 个百分点。

背景介绍

本篇材料选自国际货币基金组织执行董事会文件"基金组织参与社会支出的战略"的执行摘要部分。

该文件提出了国际货币基金组织应该何时和如何参与国家层面社会支出的战略，并介绍了相关背景以及所涉资源和风险问题。以该文件为代表的执董会文件在形式上并无特殊之处，大多是按照"导言—正文—结论"的大致结构编制；在语言上，用词平实客观，逻辑严密，专业性强，经济、金融、税务等领域的术语出现频率高，这对翻译提出了一定挑战。

在翻译时，除按一般的翻译原则处理译文外，译者在遇到涉及经济、金融、税务等专业知识之处时，还务必要耐心、细致地查阅往年相关文件资料，切勿敷衍了事，以保证译文的准确性。

第二十二篇

原文

1. The strategy would support a more effective IMF engagement. It is informed by additional background analyses, internal and external consultations, and the 2017 IEO Report:

...

1.1 Engagement would be guided by an assessment of the macro-criticality of a specific social spending issue and consideration of that issue in a program context, and by the existence of in-house expertise. The key channels through which social spending can become macro-critical are fiscal sustainability, spending adequacy, and spending efficiency. The strategy encourages early engagement with the authorities and envisages that staff continues developing policy advice on sustainable financing of social spending and increases the focus on the quality of such spending for improving social outcomes, drawing on the expertise of IDIs.

1.2 Advice on the use of targeted and universal transfers would be discussed in the context of the effectiveness of the social safety net. The appropriate design depends on countries' social and political preferences and should be consistent with their fiscal and administrative constraints.

...

2. Implementation of the strategy will require granular and gradually evolving guidance to Fund staff. A Staff Guidance Note, to be completed by end—2020, will detail

the already significant existing support and initiatives for strengthening this support, including further tools for country teams and improved knowledge management. It will aim to help country teams in prioritizing when and how extensively to engage on different social spending issues. The Note will be updated as needed to reflect the evolving nature of social spending issues, and as the Fund acquires more experience. In the interim, country teams would continue their already extensive engagement on social spending drawing on existing resources.

请自行翻译后查看后文的分析点评

分析点评

第 1 段

The strategy would support a more effective IMF engagement. It is informed by additional background analyses, internal and external consultations, and the 2017 IEO Report：

战略① 将支持基金组织更有效的参与。本文件② 的信息来源包括进一步的背景分析、内部和外部磋商，以及 2017 年独立评估办公室报告：

本战略将助力基金组织提高参与实效。本战略的参考信息来源包括进一步的背景分析、内部和外部磋商，以及 2017 年独立评估办公室报告：

表述不明确。首先，文件标题为"基金组织参与社会支出的战略"，所以通篇论述的也是这个战略，所以可直接将"The strategy"明确为"本战略"。后面的"It"同样是指这项战略，指明了在编制本战略时所参考的信息，可以明确为"本战略的参考信息来源包括……"

第 1.1 段

Engagement would be guided by an assessment of the macro-criticality of a specific social spending issue and consideration of that issue in a program context, and by the existence of in-house expertise. The key channels through which social spending can become macro-critical are fiscal sustainability, spending adequacy, and spending efficiency. The strategy encourages early engagement with the authorities and envisages that staff continues developing policy advice on sustainable financing of social spending and increases the focus on the quality of such spending for improving social outcomes, drawing on the expertise of international development institutions (IDIs).

批 注

① 注意原文中的定冠词表示特指。

② 对原文中的"It"具体指代理解错误。

第四章 经济与金融

参与将<u>以评估具体社会支出问题的宏观重要性和在规划背景下审议该问题，以及存在内部专门知识为指导</u>①。社会支出成为宏观重要性问题的关键渠道是财政可持续性、支出充足性和支出效率。战略鼓励尽早与当局合作，<u>设想</u>②工作人员继续就社会支出的可持续融资问题制定政策建议，并<u>利用国际发展机构的专门知识，加强对此类支出在改善社会成果的质量方面的关注</u>③。

参与将以具体社会支出问题宏观重要性评估和计划背景下对该问题的审议，以及现有内部专门知识为指导。社会支出成为重大宏观问题的关键渠道是财政可持续性、支出充足性和支出效率。本战略鼓励及早与当局接触，并提出了两个设想，一是工作人员继续就社会支出的可持续融资问题制定政策建议；二是工作人员加大对社会支出质量的重视，利用国际发展机构（IDI）的专门知识，改善社会成果。

批 注

① 以 A、B、C 为指导，A、B、C 应统一为名词短语。
② 理解无误，但表述有待改进。
③ 逻辑处理错误。

1. 关于"Engagement would be guided by"一句，原文的意思是以评估（结果）、审议（结果）和现有知识为指导，但翻译稿却统一处理为动名词结构，形式上不妥当，意思上也与原文存在一定背离；统一处理为名词短语后，所有问题随之解决。

2. "Envisages that"一句较长，可尝试拆分为短句。翻译稿对此句的处理紧贴原文，行文较长。不妨拆分为短句，将结构调整为"提出了两个设想，一是……；二是……"，逻辑更清晰，意思更明确，可读性更强。

第 1.2 段

Advice on the use of targeted and universal transfers would be discussed in the context of the effectiveness of the social safety net. The appropriate design depends on countries' social and political preferences and should be consistent with their fiscal and administrative constraints.

将在社会保障体系有效性<u>的范围内</u>④讨论关于使用有针对性和普适性转移的建议。适当的设计取决于各国的社会和政治偏好，并<u>应符合其财政和行政制约因素</u>⑤。

关于使用有针对性的普遍转移的建议将结合社会保障体系的有效性加以讨论。相应设计取决于各国的社会和政治偏好，但不应该超出各国财政和行政所能承受的限度。

批 注

④ 理解无误，但表述有待改进。
⑤ 机械直译不可取。

1. "Advice on...would be discussed in the context of..."一句，是典型的英文被

271

动句。在翻译时,要么尽量译为中文主动句;要么寻找英文句中的逻辑主语作为译文的主语。原译文显得突兀。按原文顺序处理为主动句,反而效果更好。另外,"in the context of"在此表示"在……范围之内",译者理解无误,但将表述调整为"结合……",更加符合汉语习惯,读来更舒服。

2. 关于"should be consistent with their fiscal and administrative constraints",原译文过于机械僵硬。实际意思就是各国在进行设计时要考虑到本国财政和行政因素,量力而行,也即"不应该超出各国财政和行政所能承受的限度"。

第 2 段

Implementation of the strategy will require granular and gradually evolving guidance to Fund staff. A Staff Guidance Note, to be completed by end—2020, will detail the already significant existing support and initiatives for strengthening this support, including further tools for country teams and improved knowledge management. It will aim to help country teams in prioritizing when and how extensively to engage on different social spending issues. The Note will be updated as needed to reflect the evolving nature of social spending issues, and as the Fund acquires more experience. In the interim, country teams would continue their already extensive engagement on social spending drawing on existing resources.

执行战略将需要对基金组织工作人员提供详细和逐步演变①的指导。将于 2020 年年底前完成②一份工作人员指导说明,其中将详细说明为加强这种支持而已经存在的重大支持和倡议③,包括为国家工作队提供更多工具和改进知识管理。它④的目的是帮助国家工作队确定何时以及如何广泛地参与不同的社会支出问题的优先次序。该指导说明将根据需要并随着基金组织获得更多的经验进行更新⑤,以反映社会支出问题不断演变的性质。在此期间,国家工作队将继续利用现有资源广泛参与社会支出。

批 注

① "逐步演变的指导"表述不当。
② 注意被动句的处理。
③ 太过拘泥于原文,以致译文不到位。
④ 尽量少用"它",而要具体化。
⑤ 应尝试拆分为短句。

在执行战略期间,必须向基金组织工作人员提供详细且循序渐进的指导。《工作人员指导说明》将于 2020 年年底前完成,其中将详细介绍现有的重大支持和为强化现有支持而拟采取的举措,包括为国家工作队提供更多工具和改进知识管理。《指导说明》旨在帮助国家工作队确定何时以及如何广泛参与不同社会支出问题的优先次序。随着基金组织经验的不断积累,还应视需要对《指导说明》进行更新,以反映社会支出问题不断演变的性质。在此期间,国家工作队将继续利用现有资源,一如既往地广泛参与社会支出。

整体来说,译者对原文意思整体理解正确,但落实到译文上,小问题较多,细究下来,译者如能在翻译完毕之后,抛开原文,仔细审读一遍,大多数问题可以避免。

1. 表述僵化。关于"Implementation of the strategy will require...gradually evolving guidance"这句,翻译稿中的"执行战略将需要"和"逐步演变的指导"都是机械直译,读起来十分别扭,修改过后,就自然顺畅多了。

2. 被动句处理欠佳。关于"A Staff Guidance Note, to be completed by end—2020, will detail",其处理技巧同前段点评2。

3. "Including"一句处理得当,译者将"further"和"improved"两个形容词作动词化处理,效果佳。

4. 应尽量避免用"它"。根据上下文,"It"是指《指导说明》,在译文中应具体化,而非用"它"代替,这种不加细究的"省事"之举也让译文效果打了折扣。

5. "The Note will be updated as...and as..."被无端复杂化。这句原文结构清晰,逻辑明确。前半部分:《指导说明》应视需要进行更新,以反映……;后半部分:《指导说明》应随着基金组织经验的不断积累进行更新,再根据汉语习惯稍作调整、整合即可。

Interest in social spending issues has intensified over the last decade. This reflects concerns about rising inequality and the need to support vulnerable groups, especially in the aftermath of the global financial crisis. There is also a global commitment to continue support for inclusive growth, as expressed in the 2030 Sustainable Development Goals (SDGs). And ongoing demographic, technological, and climate developments will pose new challenges. Social spending is viewed as a key policy lever for addressing these issues.

The Fund has concomitantly increased its work on social spending. Analytical work has cast new light on the relationship between inequality and growth, the important role social spending plays in promoting sustained and inclusive growth, and the resource requirements for achieving the SDGs in education and health. The growing emphasis on inclusive growth is also reflected in operational activities, including the use of social spending "floors" in IMF-supported programs. There has been enhanced engagement on inequality issues in surveillance, as well as increased technical assistance to expand fiscal space for social spending.

【参考译文】

过去十年来,社会支出问题所受关注程度日增。这反映出两点,一是日益加剧的不平等引发关切,二是必须向弱势群体提供支助,特别是在全球金融危机过后。全球各方还承诺继续支持《2030年可持续发展目标》(SDG)中提出的包容性增长。当前持续的人口、技术和气候发展态势将带来新的挑战。社会支出被视为解决这些问题的一个关键政策杠杆。

与此同时，基金组织在社会支出方面的工作也有增加。基金组织的分析工作进一步阐明了不平等与增长之间的关系、社会支出在促进持续和包容性增长方面的重要作用以及实现教育和卫生领域可持续发展目标所需的资源。对包容性增长的日益重视还反映在其业务活动当中，包括在基金组织资助规划中使用社会支出"最低标准"。基金组织加强了对不平等问题监督工作的参与，并加大了技术援助力度，以扩大社会支出的财政空间。

背景介绍

以下两篇材料来自联合国国际贸易法委员会（贸易法委员会）：前一篇为贸易法委员会秘书长在第三十三届会议上所做报告；后一篇选自贸易法委员会秘书处向贸易法委员会提交的问题说明。

联合国国际贸易法委员会于1966年由联合国大会设立（1966年12月17日 第2205（XXI）号决议）。作为联合国系统在国际贸易法领域的核心法律机构，其基本任务是促进国际贸易法的逐步协调和统一。自设立以来，该委员会编写了种类繁多的公约、示范法和其他文书。贸易法委员会文件所涉主题广泛、专业，多涉及国际贸易以及贸易仲裁术语。要求译者具备相关的专业素养并积累背景知识和术语。在翻译此类文件时，必须以联合国专业词汇为准，在此基础上补充以贸易领域相关背景词汇，紧扣题材和上下文把握句段主旨并厘清结构关系，准确而流畅地进行表达。

第二十三篇

原文

The rationale for handling an unsolicited proposal without using a competitive selection procedure is to provide an incentive for the private sector to identify new or unanticipated infrastructure needs or to formulate innovative proposals for meeting those needs.

Competent suppliers and contractors are sometimes reluctant to participate in procurement proceedings for high-value contracts, where the cost of preparing the submission may be high, if the competitive field is too large and where they run the risk of having to compete with submissions presented by unqualified suppliers or contractors.

请自行翻译后查看后文的分析点评

 分析点评

第1段

The rationale for handling an unsolicited proposal without using a competitive selection procedure is to provide an incentive for the private sector to identify new or unanticipated infrastructure needs or to formulate innovative proposals for meeting those needs.

不利用竞争性筛选程序处理非邀约投标书①的理由是，鼓励私营部门确定新的或未预料到的基础设施需要，或拟订满足这些需要的创新建议②。

不利用竞争性筛选程序处理未经征求而提交的建议书，理由是激励私营部门查明新的或未预料到的基础设施需要，或拟订满足这些需要的创新性建议书。

批 注

① 注意根据背景选取用词。
② 注意用词准确性。

1. 这是联合国维也纳办事处的一份稿件，内容涉及私人融资基础设施项目，这里的"unsolicited proposal"在经贸领域可以泛指"非邀约投标书"或"非应标建议书"，但在本文中，根据上下文判断，并不涉及邀约或应标，基本上用的是"unsolicited"的本意"未经征求的，未经所求的"，指未经征求意见就提交，故应翻译为"未经征求而提交的建议书"。

2. 此处需要注意的还有另一个词"proposal"，该词在联合国文件中属于高频词，用途非常广泛，在不同类型的文件中词义各不相同，即我们常说的一词多义，需要区别斟酌。最常见的用法是"提议、建议""提案""建议书"。此处使用"建议书"是由上下文和题材决定的。

3. 关于词语搭配。根据上下文判断，此处涉及的显然是正式的文件，故而使用"建议书"，而不是"建议"。另外，"创新建议"从搭配上看稍微欠妥，指的是这份建议书具有创新特点，虽然从字面上也可以理解其含义，但更宜将其翻译为"创新性建议书"。

第2段

Competent suppliers and contractors are sometimes reluctant to participate in procurement proceedings for high-value contracts, where the cost of preparing the submission may be high, if the competitive field is too large and where they run the risk of having to compete with submissions presented by unqualified suppliers or contractors.

有能力的供应商和承包商有时不愿参加高价值合同的采购程序，因为竞争领域过宽③会导致编写提交书的成本较高，而且它们可能不得不与不合格的供应商

批 注

③ 此译文有望文生义之嫌。

或承包商递交的提交书相竞争。

审校稿

有能力的供应商和承包商有时不愿参加高价值合同的采购程序，因为参与竞争的投标人过多会导致编写提交书的成本较高，而且它们可能不得不与不合格的供应商或承包商递交的提交书相竞争。

点评

1. "Competent"在联合国文件中经常出现，有多重含义，"胜任的、有能力的、能干的、足够的"等。这里用的是"有能力的"，比较容易理解。联合国文件中该词还有一个较常用的含义是"主管的"，例如"Encourages the competent authorities of the nuclear-weapon-free zone treaties to provide assistance to the States parties and signatories to those treaties so as to facilitate the accomplishment of the goals of the treaties."（"鼓励无核武器区条约主管机构协助条约缔约国和签署国实现这些条约的目标"。）具体含义须依据上下文判定。

2. 词义的引申和变通。"Submission"一词在联合国文件中有多种含义"划界案[海洋法]、仲裁、协议书、呈件、服从、提交"等。此处指的是提交的文件，并非协议书之类，故而选其引申义"提交书"。

3. 翻译的原则是信、达、雅。就是说翻译的时候语意出来还不够，还必须准确、讲透，让读者能够理解其背后的含义。"Competitive field is too large"原译为"竞争领域过宽"，这显然有点望文生义，让读者感到难以理解何为"过宽"。这里讲的是采购过程中供应商和承包商参与合同竞标，那么显然是讲它们在同一竞争平台展开竞争，"competitive field"也可以理解为"竞技场"，故而这里可以译为"参与投标的人过多"，使读者能够一眼就看明白。

补充练习

1. The procuring entity may suffer losses if suppliers or contractors withdraw their submissions or if a procurement contract with the supplier or contractor whose submission had been accepted is not concluded due to fault on the part of that supplier or contractor (e.g., the costs of new procurement proceedings and losses due to delays in procurement). Article 16 authorizes the procuring entity to require suppliers or contractors participating in the procurement proceedings to post a tender security so as to cover such potential losses and to discourage them from defaulting.

参考译文

如果供应商或承包商撤回提交书，或者如果由于提交书已获接受的供应商或承包商的过失而未与该供应商或承包商订立采购合同，则采购实体可能遭受损失（例如，重新进行采购程序的费用和采购推迟造成的损失）。第16条授权采购实体要求参与采购程序的供应商或承包商交存一笔投标担保金，以便弥补此类潜在损失并阻止它们违约。

2. The purpose of the article is to set out requirements as regards tender securities as defined in article 2 (t), in particular as to their acceptability by the procuring entity, the conditions that must be present for the procuring entity to be able to claim the amount of the tender security, and the conditions under which the procuring entity must return or procure the return of the security document.

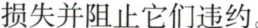

本条的目的是载列关于第 2 条 (t) 项所定义的投标担保的要求，特别是投标担保可否为采购实体接受、采购实体必须具备什么条件才能对投标担保的金额提出主张，以及采购实体在什么条件下必须退还或者促成退还担保文书。

第二十四篇

Independence and impartiality of the adjudicator are key elements of any system of justice, meant to ensure fair trial and compliance with due process requirements. The Working Group emphasized that sufficient guarantees of independence and impartiality on the part of arbitrators is essential in ISDS (A/CN.9/935, para. 47).

A widely held view in the Working Group was that, in order to be considered effective, the ISDS framework should not only ensure actual impartiality and independence of arbitrators and decision makers, but also the appearance of those qualities. The view was expressed that efforts should therefore include both elements (A/CN.9/935, para. 53).

The most widespread conception of independence and impartiality is that they are distinct, but closely related, concepts. While independence usually relates to the lack of a business, financial, or personal relationship between an arbitrator and a party to the arbitration, impartiality means the absence of bias or predisposition of the arbitrator or decision maker towards a party. Lack of independence usually derives from problematic relations between an arbitrator and a party or its counsel and lack of impartiality would arise, for instance, if an arbitrator appears to have pre-judged some matters.

The requirements of independence and impartiality apply to any judicial or judicial-like dispute settlement process.

分析点评

第 1 段

Independence and impartiality of the adjudicator are key elements of any system of justice, meant to ensure fair trial and compliance with due process requirements. The Working Group emphasized that sufficient guarantees of independence and impartiality on the part of arbitrators is essential in ISDS (A/CN.9/935, para. 47).

裁决人的独立性和公正性是任何司法系统的关键要素，这是为了确保审判公允和遵守正当程序要求。工作组强调在 ISDS 中仲裁员的独立性和公正性必须有充分保障①（A/CN.9/935，第 47 段）。

批 注

① 句子重心偏移。

审裁人的独立性和公正性是一切司法系统的关键要素，旨在确保审判公正和正当程序要求得到遵守。工作组强调，在投资人与国家间争议解决中，务必充分保障仲裁员的独立性和公正性（A/CN.9/935，第 47 段）。

1. 术语处理不准确。在此语境下，"adjudicator" 应译为"审裁人"。另外，"ISDS" 应该译出中文。译者如不确定，可通过两种方式进行查询，一是联合国多语言专业术语数据库（UNTERM Portal）；二是根据文中所附相关文号，在 ODS 系统查阅文件中的对应翻译。

2. 句子结构不对称，见 "ensure fair trial and compliance with due process requirements"。翻译稿中的"审判公允"和"遵守正当程序要求"有失对称，将后者改为"正当程序要求得到遵守"即可解决。

3. 主语拆分不当，削弱译文节奏感，见段末 that 引导的宾语从句。该从句中的主语是 "sufficient guarantees of independence and impartiality on the part of arbitrators"，翻译稿将 "of" 前后部分一拆为二，致使译文不够紧凑，在审校稿中，整个主语有机地结合在一起，谓语 "is essential" 译文前置，处理为"工作组强调……务必充分保障仲裁员的独立性和公正性"，效果要好得多。

第 2 段

A widely held view in the Working Group was that, in order to be considered effective, the ISDS framework should not only ensure actual impartiality and independence of arbitrators and decision makers, but also the appearance of those qualities. The view was expressed that efforts should therefore include both elements (A/CN.9/935, para. 53).

工作组中一种普遍的观点是^①，ISDS 框架不仅应当确保仲裁员和决策人实际具备公正性和独立性，还应当确保他们显现出这些素质，这样这一框架才能被视为有效。现已表达出的一种观点是^②，所做努力因此应当包括这两个要素（A/CN.9/935，第 53 段）。

批 注

① 中文表述略显拗口。
② 可将被动句化为主动句。

工作组成员普遍认为，投资人与国家间争议解决框架不仅应当确保仲裁员和裁定人切实具备公正性和独立性，还应当确保他们体现出这两项素质，这样这一框架才能被视为有效。因此有观点认为，所做努力应当包括这两个要素（A/CN.9/935，第 53 段）。

1. 术语处理不准确。在此语境下，"decision maker" 应译为"裁定人"。具体见第 1 段点评 1。

2. 被动句处理技巧有待加强。"A widely held view in the Working Group was that..." 和 "The view was expressed that" 两个都是典型的英文被动句，其翻译技巧 a 是尽量译为中文主动句；寻找英文句中的逻辑主语作为译文的主语。对于前一句，翻译稿显然正确地采用了技巧 b，只是表述有待完善。对于后者，则应使用技巧 a，按照中文表达习惯处理为"有观点认为"。

第 3 段

The most widespread conception of independence and impartiality is that they are distinct, but closely related, concepts. While independence usually relates to the lack of a business, financial, or personal relationship between an arbitrator and a party to the arbitration, impartiality means the absence of bias or predisposition of the arbitrator or decision maker towards a party. Lack of independence usually derives from problematic relations between an arbitrator and a party or its counsel and lack of impartiality would arise, for instance, if an arbitrator appears to have pre-judged some matters.

对于独立性和公正性最普遍持有的看法^③是它们^④是两个不同但关系密切的概念。独立性通常是关于仲裁员与仲裁当事人之间没有生意、财务或人际方面的交往，而公正性则意味着仲裁员或裁定人对一方当事人没有偏颇或倾向性。缺乏独立性通常产生于仲裁员和当事人或其顾问之间有毛病的交往^⑤如果，举例来说，仲裁员显得^⑥对某些事项已经预先做出判断，就会产生缺乏公正性的局面。

批 注

③ 表述欠妥。
④ 避免用它/它们。
⑤ 表述欠妥。
⑥ 表述欠妥。

关于独立性和公正性，目前最为普遍的看法是，这两个概念截然不同但又密切相关。独立性通常是指仲裁员与仲裁当事方之间不存在任何业务、经济或人际

往来，而公正性则意味着仲裁员或裁定人对当事方不抱有偏见或其他倾向。缺乏独立性通常是因为仲裁员与当事方或其律师之间的关系存在问题，而缺乏公正性则是由于仲裁员貌似对某些事项已经预先做出判断等。

1. 学习化长句为短句，见第一句。相比翻译稿，审校稿多用了一个逗号，就使整个句子的结构和节奏得到改善。

2. 尽量少用甚至不用"它/它们"，见"they are distinct, but closely related, concepts"一句。翻译稿也对，但审校稿效果更好一些。

3. 译完后，要自我审读。如能做到这一点，像"有毛病的交往"和"显得已经预先做出判断"这样不地道的中文表述大多可以避免。

第 4 段

The requirements of independence and impartiality apply to any judicial or judicial-like dispute settlement process.

独立性和公正性要求适用于任何司法或类似司法的①议解决程序。

独立性和公正性要求适用于任何司法或类司法性质的争议解决程序。

此段只有一句，结构简单，也无生僻词汇。译文对"judicial-like"一词的处理不够准确，将"类似司法的"改为"类司法性质的"更显专业。

① 表述欠准确。

补充练习

At its 35th session, the Working Group suggested that the Secretariat (i) prepare a list of the concerns about investor-State dispute settlement (ISDS) raised during its thirty-fourth and 35th sessions; (ii) set out a possible framework for its future deliberations; and (iii) consider the provision of further information to assist States with respect to the scope of some concerns (A/CN.9/935, para. 99).

As is the case for other documents provided to the Working Group, this Note was prepared with reference to a broad range of published information on the topic.

While this Note provides information to assist the Working Group in its consideration of certain concerns in ISDS and the desirability of reforms, it does not seek to express a view on the issues raised, which is a matter for the Working Group to consider.

参考译文

工作组第三十五届会议建议秘书处（一）拟定一份清单，列明在工作组第三十四届和第三十五届会议上提出的有关投资人与国家间争议解决的关切；（二）为工作组今后的审议工作确立一个可行的框架；以及（三）考虑就某些关切的范围向各国提供对其有助益的进一步信息（A/CN.9/935，第99段）。

一如之前提交工作组的其他文件，本说明是参照已经发布的有关该专题的各类资料编写而成。

本说明旨在提供信息，帮助工作组审议投资人与国家间争议解决中某些令人关切的问题和改革的可取性，但并不试图就已经提出的各项问题发表意见，这些问题应留待工作组审议。

背景介绍

本篇材料选自经合组织报告，主题为公共企业和私营企业之间的公平竞争环境。

经合组织是由38个市场经济国家组成的政府间国际经济组织，其宗旨是促进成员国经济和社会的发展，推动世界经济增长。与世界银行和国际货币基金组织不同，经合组织并不提供基金援助，而是旨在为各国政府制定经济政策提供一个进行讨论和思考的场所。

这份报告从宏观角度阐述了如何维持公共企业与私营企业之间的公平竞争环境，专业词汇较多，表述较为灵活，而且个别句式复杂，套有多个非谓语成分，处理起来有难度。

在翻译这类篇章时，切忌过于贴合原文，要先结合前后语境"捏准"词义，再理清逻辑关系，弄清楚各个非谓语修饰的成分，最后适当调整句子语序，以流畅连贯的中文进行表述。

第二十五篇

原文

Different jurisdictions address aspects or elements of competitive neutrality in diverse ways through competition, public procurement, tax and regulatory policies or a combination of these policies. Some countries may have made a selective commitment to competitive neutrality, in other words they may not address all the building blocks. While this may often be a second best option, it still may suit the jurisdiction depending on the national context, the extent and nature of public policy functions imposed on SOEs, and the regulatory capacity to enforce and advocate competitive neutrality.

The most effective way of obtaining competitive neutrality is arguably to establish an encompassing policy framework, including suitable complaints handling, enforcement and implementation mechanisms and in consistency with international commitments. Although few countries have done this, the approaches of Australia or the EU are notable examples. Some north European economies have addressed competitive neutrality, by introducing competition law based approaches in parallel with an overall restructuring of the SOE sector to ensure full incorporation of public businesses, including by municipalities and other sub-national levels of government.

请自行翻译后查看后文的分析点评

分析点评

第 1 段

Different jurisdictions address aspects or elements of competitive neutrality in diverse ways through competition, public procurement, tax and regulatory policies or a combination of these policies. Some countries may have made a selective commitment to competitive neutrality, in other words they may not address all the building blocks. While this may often be a second best option, it still may suit the jurisdiction depending on the national context, the extent and nature of public policy functions imposed on SOEs, and the regulatory capacity to enforce and advocate competitive neutrality.

批 注

① 不符合中文表达习惯。
② 误译。
③ 搭配不当，"职能"通常与"范围"而不是"力度"搭配。
④ 用词不当。

不同的司法管辖区通过竞争、公共采购、税收和监管政策或这些政策的结合以多种方式处理竞争中立的各个方面或各种要素。一些国家可能对竞争中立做出一种有选择性的承诺，换句话说，它们可能不会关注竞争中立的所有构成要素。尽管这可能是一个次最佳选择①，它仍可根据具体国情、该国针对国有企业的公共政策②的实施力度③和性质，以及执行和宣传竞争中立的监管能力来适应④具体的司法辖区。

不同的管辖区通过竞争、公共采购、税收和监管政策或这些政策的组合以多种方式处理竞争中立的各个方面或各种要素。一些国家可能对竞争中立做出了选

282

择性承诺,换句话说,它们可能不会关注竞争中立的所有构成要素。尽管这通常只是次优选择,但综合考虑各国具体国情、该国给予国有企业的公共政策职能的范围和性质,以及实施和倡导竞争中立的监管能力,这种选择仍然可能是适合某特定辖区的方案。

1. "A second best option"从字面意思上看是"次最佳选择",但这并不符合中文表达习惯,在翻译的过程中要灵活选词,做到准确、可读,可改成"次优选择"更为妥当。

2. "suit"一词有多个意思,比如"适合""符合""适应",这句话的意思是选择最适合某个管辖区的方案,所以用"适合"比"适应"更恰当。

3. 虽然"extent"也有力度的意思,但在这里修饰的是职能,所以不是指"力度",而是"范围"。

4. 原文是"public policy functions"而不是"public policy",译为"公共政策"属于误译。

第2段

The most effective way of obtaining competitive neutrality is arguably to establish an encompassing policy framework, including suitable complaints handling, enforcement and implementation mechanisms and in consistency with international commitments. Although few countries have done this, the approaches of Australia or the EU are notable examples. Some north European economies have addressed competitive neutrality, by introducing competition law based approaches in parallel with an overall restructuring of the SOE sector to ensure full incorporation of public businesses, including by municipalities and other sub-national levels of government.

可以说,获得竞争中立最有效的方法是建立一个包容性政策框架,包括适当的投诉处理、执行和实施机制,并与国际承诺保持一致。虽然鲜少由国家采取这种做法,澳大利亚或欧盟的做法仍是值得注意的范例。一些北欧经济体在对国有企业部门进行整体重组的同时①引进基于竞争法的手段,确保市政府和其他次国家级②政府充分纳入公共企业,以处理竞争中立的问题③。

可以说,获得竞争中立最有效的方法是建立一个包容性政策框架,其中包含适当的投诉处理、执行和实施机制,并与国际承诺保持一致。虽然鲜有国家采取这种做法,但澳大利亚或欧盟的方法仍是值得注意的范例。北欧的一些经济体在引进基于竞争法的方法的同时,对国有企业部门进行全面重组,确保市政府和其他地区级政府等充分纳入公共企业,从而解决了竞争中立问题。

批 注

① 两个动作有主次之分,这里显然没有体现这种区别。
② 语意模糊。
③ 逻辑不明。

1. "by"后面跟的是手段或者途径,最终是为了解决某个问题或是达到某种效果。"以"仅仅表示目的,并没有充分体现上下文的这种逻辑关系,所以此处用"从而"更好。

2. "in parallel with"在本句中是指同时采取两项举措,但两个动作有主次之分,根据原文,重心应该在"重组"上,而翻译稿并没有体现这种关系。

3. "sub-national levels"从字面来看是说在国家以下的各级,但国家以下其实是指地区,翻译稿中的"次国家"语意不明,可读性差,改成"地区级"更明确。

The report is separated into three parts. Part A provides a conceptual framework, definitions and economic arguments underpinning the paper. Part B of the report covers each of the eight "building blocks" of competitive neutrality. Part C highlights different national approaches, including the placement of competitive neutrality commitments in legislation and within the national administration.

The report serves as a catalogue of options for ensuring a level playing field between public and private business. It is outcomes based, in that it recognizes there are usually several ways in which competitive neutrality can be achieved in practice. For this reason, the report provides a large number of examples of competitive neutrality related experiences from OECD and other economies. These experiences are drawn from a questionnaire-based exercise highlighting national practices and actual cases where issues have arisen. The report is further supported by a synthesis of existing OECD instruments, good practices and related guidance with a bearing on the topic.

参考译文

本报告分为三部分。第一部分列举了为本报告提供支撑的概念框架、定义和经济论据。第二部分阐述了竞争中立的所有八大"基石"。第三部分强调了各国解决竞争中立问题的不同方法,包括在立法和国家行政体系中引入竞争中立承诺。

本报告列举了确保为公共企业和私营企业营造一个公平竞争环境的可选方案。这份报告以结果为导向,因为它认可竞争中立在实践中通常可以通过几种方式实现。为此,本报告提供了大量范例,介绍经合组织和其他经济体在竞争中立方面的经验。这些经验通过调查问卷获得,重点强调了各国的实际做法以及出现问题的真实案例。经合组织有关本专题的现有政策工具、良好实践和相关指南为本报告提供了进一步支持。

本章词汇

7-day repo rate　7天回购利率
accounting system　会计制度
accounts receivable/payable　应收/应付账款
accrual basis　权责发生制
accrued interest　应计利息
actual rate of return　实际回报率
advance　预付款；短期贷款；垫款
affiliated enterprise　关联企业；联营企业
amount outstanding　未偿还额；余额
anchoring of expectations　锚定预期
back-up line　备用额度
balance of payments deficit　国际收支逆差
balance sheet　资产负债表
bank cash ratio　银行现金比率
bank run　银行挤兑；挤提
bargaining power　议价能力；讨价还价的能力
baseline forecast　基线预测
basis points (BPS)　基点
basket peg　钉住一篮子货币
benchmark　基准（数字、指标）
beneficial ownership　实际所有权
Bond Connect　"债券通"
book value　账面价值、发票价格
borderline case　边缘情况；模棱两可的情况
break-even point　保本点；盈亏临界点；收支平衡点
capital account liberalization　资本账户自由化；资本账户放开
capital adequacy rules　资本充足率规则
carry trade　套利交易
cash market　现货市场
China Interbank Bond Market　中国银行间债券市场
closing asset/liabilities　期末资产/负债
concessional lending/loan　优惠贷款
consumer price index (CPI)　消费者价格指数
contractionary policy　紧缩政策
core inflation　核心通货膨胀；根本性通货膨胀
countercyclical action　反周期行动
counterfactual　反事实
credit default swap　信用违约掉期
crowding-in/crowding-out effect　挤进/挤出效应
currency mismatch　货币错配；币种错配
currency union　货币联盟
current account　经常账户；经常项目
cyclical unemployment　周期性失业
debt amortization　分期偿还；摊还
debt refinancing　债务再融资
debt-servicing capacity　偿债能力
debt-swap program　债务置换计划
deep-discount bond　高折扣债券
dim sum bond　点心债券
discount rate　贴现率
disposable income　可支配收入
due-for-payment basis of recording　记录的支付到期制
dynamic stochastic general equilibrium model　动态随机一般均衡模型
economic rent　经济租金
economies of scale　规模经济
embedded derivative　嵌入式衍生产品
empirical analysis　实证分析
exchange rate pass-through　汇率传导效应
exchange value　交换价值
explicit cost　显性成本
external financing　外部融资；境外融资
external imbalance　对外不平衡；国际收支失衡
extraordinary profit　超额利润
fair value　公允价值
financial contagion　金融波及效应
financial inclusion　普惠金融；金融包容性
financial intermediaries　金融中介机构
financial soundness　金融稳健性
fixed effect　固定效应
floating interest rate　浮动利率
foreign direct investment (FDI)　外国直接投资

foreign exchange position   外汇头寸
fundamentals   （经济）基本面
general government   广义政府
Gini coefficient   基尼系数
golden share   黄金股
Government Finance Statistics (GFS)   政府财政统计
grace period   宽限期
gross domestic product (GDP)   国内生产总值
gross national income (GNI)   国民总收入
gross national product (GNP)   国民生产总值
hedging   对冲
higher-middle-income country   中等偏高收入国家
hostile takeover   恶意收购
illiquidity   缺乏流动性
implicit guarantee   隐含担保
imported unemployment   输入性失业
incomplete market   不完全市场
institutional investor   机构投资者
intangible assets   无形资产
intermediate goods   中间产品
international monetary system   国际货币体系
labor force participation   劳动力参与（率）
labor market rigidity   劳动力市场刚性
labor productivity   劳动生产率
Lerner index   勒纳指数
leveraged buyout   杠杆收购（公司）
liquid asset ratio   流动性-资产比率
loan loss provision   贷款损失准备金
Local Government Financing Vehicles (LGFV)   地方政府融资平台
lower-middle-income country   中等偏低收入国家
macroprudential assessment   宏观审慎评估
marginal cost   边际成本
marginal rate of tax   边际（税）率
market power   市场力量
marketable goods   适销产品；可销售产品
markup   加价率
maturity mismatch   期限不匹配
merger and acquisition   兼并和收购（并购）
misallocation of resources   资源配置不当

monetary easing   放松银根；放松货币政策
monetary tightening   紧缩银根
monetary transmission   货币传导
natural interest rate   自然利率
nominal effective exchange rate index   名义有效汇率指数
nonfactor input   非要素投入
nonnegotiable security   不可转让的证券
nonprofit institution (NPI)   非营利机构
notional government bond   名义政府债券
offshore market   离岸市场
offshoring   离岸外包、境外外包
one-year offshore renminbi forward rate   一年期离岸人民币远期汇率
opening asset/liability   期初资产/负债
option   期权
Outbound Direct Investment (ODI)   对外直接投资
output gap   产出缺口
outstanding bond   已发行尚未偿还的债券
over-the-counter (OTC) financial derivative   场外交易的金融衍生产品
paid-up capital   实缴资本
pegged exchange rate regime   钉住汇率制度
percentage point   百分点
Phillips curve   菲利普斯曲线
physical capital   有形资本
policy interest rate   政策利率
policy transmission   政策传导
policyholder   投保人
portfolio investment   证券投资、组合投资
positive correlation   正相关
precautionary borrowing   预防性借款
price rigidities   价格刚性
principal   本金
proceeds   收益、收入
profit shifting   利润转移
profitability   盈利能力
Qualified Foreign Institutional Investor (QFII)   合格境外机构投资者
quantitative easing (QE)   量化放松的货币政策

quota scheme　配额计划
rate tiering　分档次的利率；利率分级
real interest rate　实际利率
real purchasing power　实际购买力
regression　回归
regulatory arbitrage　监管制度套利；利用监管制度的差异来谋取利益
Renminbi Qualified Institutional Investor (RQFII)　人民币合格境外机构投资者
required reserve ratio　法定准备金比率
responsiveness　灵敏性
retail financial market　零售金融市场
retaliatory measure　报复性措施
return on equity (ROE)　股本回报率
reversal of capital flows　资本流动的逆转
risk appetite　风险偏好
risk-on/risk-off period　追逐/趋避风险的时期
risk-weighted asset (RWA)　风险加权资产
securitized mortgage loan　证券化的抵押贷款
sensitivity stress test　敏感性压力测试
settlement day　交割日；结算日
shadow banking　影子银行业
Short-Term Liquidity Facility (SLF)　短期流动性贷款机制
social security contribution　社会保障缴款
sovereign bond　主权债券
special drawing right (SDR)　特别提款权
special purpose entity (SPE)　特殊目的实体
spillover　溢出效应
spot market　即期市场；现货市场
standard error　标准误差
start-up　新创办的企业
statistically significant　统计显著的；在统计上具有显著性
stock buyback　股票回购
stocks and flows　存量与流量
structural unemployment　结构性失业
swap　掉期
tariff rate quota system　关税税率配额制度
tax concession　税收优惠；税收减免
tax credit　税收抵免
tax threshold　税款起征点
taxes on income, profits, and capital gains　所得税、利润税及资本利得税
total factor productivity (TFP)　全要素生产率
trade-off　取舍；得失权衡
transfer price　转让价格
transfer pricing　转移定价；转让价格；调拨定价
Treasury futures market　国债期货市场
underlying asset　对应资产
unfunded liabilities　无资金准备的负债
upward/downward revision　向上/向下调整
velocity of circulation　（货币）流通速度
wealth fund　财富基金
yield curve　收益率曲线

第五章

环境与发展

本章导言

如今，生态环境问题变得日益严峻，全球变暖、臭氧层消失，人类或将面对"最寂静的春天"。尽管蕾切尔·卡森（海洋生物学家）在《寂静的春天》这本书中对人类生境的预言充满悲观色彩，但这种呐喊逐渐唤醒了公众，环境与发展日益受到重视。为保护环境，维护生物多样性，在联合国环境规划署的推动下，包括各国政府在内的各方都采取了积极举措，相继签署了《人类环境宣言》和《生物多样性保护公约》，让生态环境保护的理念越来越深入人心。

环境与发展密切相关，对发展有着深远的影响。近年来，联合国相关文件日益增多，涉及范围广泛，通过翻译与学习此类文件，也可深入了解当今环境问题以及环境给发展带来的诸多挑战。

联合国环境与发展类文件在联合国文件中自成体系，此类文件通常由环境规划署及其下属机构、多边基金执行委员会、人居署等机构或其相关小组起草编写。本章所选十三篇文章，涵盖了项目提案、人居署报告、统计委员会报告、工作方案和预算、决策者摘要、风险管理评价等方面。通过这些文件，大致可以了解联合国环境与发展类文件的特点和风格，也可以了解当今社会面临的环境与发展问题。

处理此类文件时，应注意以下几点。

一、词汇处理技巧——熟词新译

联合国文件的行文用词自成一体，许多时候都有独特的要求，且各部门各机构可能还有自己的特殊要求，需区别对待，切忌"望文生义"，以免一不小心落入误区。例如，第一篇第 1 段中的 "UN-Habitat Assembly" 一词，很容易译为"人居署大会"，但实际上应译为"人居大会"，这是联合国内罗毕办事处的特殊要求。再如，在第四篇第 2 段 "In December 2018, the General Assembly adopted Resolution 73/239 by which it established a new governance structure for UN-Habitat, consisting of the universal UN-Habitat Assembly..."， "General Assembly" 在绝大多数联合国文件中都翻译为"大会"，但在这里为了区别于人居大会，译为"联大"，即"联合国大会"。

二、句子翻译技巧

（1）注意逻辑关系切割

环境与发展类稿件的一个特点是有的句式结构过长，层层相套，这就要求厘清逻辑关系，例如：

➢ 第一篇第 1 段 "The present document sets out the proposed work programme...which is based..." 一句是典型的环环相扣结构（详见正文分析）。

➢ 第十篇第 2 段第 1 句 "The report includes a discussion of an increased focus and illustrates the need to develop a common position on this important and emerging field of statistics" 含有两个谓语动词，句子较长，应进行逻辑关系分析，根据需要调整句子语序，使其符合汉语表达习惯（详见正文分析）。

（2）掌握、查找背景知识

要想译文准确到位，译者必须了解背景知识，否则容易踏入误区。此类背景知识，可查阅环境规划署、人居署、生物多样性公约和多边基金执行委员会的官方网站。例如：

第六篇第 3 段 "UN-Habitat will work with governments for access to climate and environmental resources for urban action, channelled through facilities developed under UN frameworks such as the Green Climate Fund, the Global Environment Facility and the Adaptation Fund." 应具体查清"frameworks"到底指什么，与后面的"Fund"和"Facility"是什么关系，才能精确翻译出来，不致犯错。

（3）注意"度"的把握

环境与发展领域所涉及的文件多为正式会议文件，不可太过自由发挥。

三、语篇分析

（1）注意字词含义与语境含义统一。译文避免机械，兼顾上下文，契合句子当前语境。

（2）注意全文前后连贯性，避免顾此失彼。例如：

➢ 第十三篇第 1 段 "...the quantity of C8 species (including PFOA) within C6 technologies can be present at greater concentrations,..." 一句中 "quantity" 和 "concentration" 翻译稿处理为"现有研究证明利用 C6 技术制造的 C8 类物质（包括全氟辛酸）数量可能以更高浓度存在"，此处显然"数量"无法以"浓度"形式存在，遇到这种情况，就要适当考虑变通。

➢ 第一篇第 2 段 "It was an inspiring visit, and I left convinced of the relevance of our work." 一句翻译稿处理为"这是一次鼓舞人心的访问，我离开时确信我们工作的相关性"，这种直译的处理方式不可取，没有显示前后两句之间的关系。稍加推敲，即可得知这是在说"访问令人满意，因此让人相信所做的工作是有价值、有意义的"。

对译者而言，在翻译联合国环境与发展类文件时，首先，要严格遵循此类文件的特定要求，特别是对于某些特定词汇、术语等，不可按照一般性文件处理。其次，对于专业性要求高的一类文件，除了需要具有扎实的语言基本功外，还需要适当查阅、浏览和参考此类文件，学习其表达方式，想方设法使译文更加地道、更加专业、更加"内行"，这方面需要日积月累，勤学苦练，方显专业特色。

背景介绍

以下第一篇至第八篇材料均选自联合国人类住区规划署《2020年工作方案和预算》。这份文件是联合国人类住区规划署执行局执行主任根据《联合国人类住区规划署2020—2023年战略计划》，就2020年联合国人类住区规划署工作方案及联合国生境和人类住区基金会预算提出的一份报告。联合国人类住区规划署（人居署），总部设在联合国内罗毕办事处，其宗旨是促进社会和环境可持续人类住区发展，达到为所有人提供合适居所的目标。通过支持城市发展和规划，推动经济增长和社会发展，减少贫困和不平等。这类文件通常为年度或双年度报告，一般分为两部分：一是任务规定和背景、近期事态发展、战略和外部因素、总体所需财政和人力资源、基金会未指定用途的资源、决策机关等。二是工作方案，分为4个次级方案，主要涉及城乡空间不平等与贫困现象，促进城市共同繁荣，强化气候行动，改善城市环境，有效预防、应对城市危机。

此类文件的特点是篇幅较长，内容广泛，语言较平实，句式结构规整，由于是方案和预算，必然涉及预算方面的许多术语，中间往往穿插许多表格和图。翻译过程中，要注意以下几点。①术语要前后统一，特别是专业词汇要统一；②遵循此类文件以往的翻译惯例，特别是某些标题的翻译，要尽量统一；③用词尽量简洁、精确、到位。

第一篇

原文

The present document sets out the proposed work programme of the United Nations Habitat and Human Settlements Foundation for the year 2020, which is based on the four-years strategic plan 2020—2023 as approved pursuant to Resolution 1/1 adopted by the first session of the UN-Habitat Assembly on United Nations Human Settlements Programme Strategic Plan for the period 2020—2023. The work programme was prepared in accordance with the support guide issued on 31 December 2019 by the Programme Planning and Budget Division of the Office of Programme Planning, Budget and Accounts of the Secretariat.

Ultimately, our mandate is about improving the lives of people. It is about transforming places and communities, to improve the quality of life for all. When I visited the informal settlements of Mathare in Nairobi in March 2018, I spent time with some of the young men and women there. They shared with me their concerns, their aspirations, and their experiences. It was an inspiring visit, and I left convinced of the relevance of our work. At UN-Habitat, we strive for "a better quality of life for all in an urbanizing world" by improving housing and urban services, creating safe public spaces for everyone, fostering entrepreneurship, generating social cohesion and empowering the most vulnerable members of our communities, conscious of the millions of households living in the urban slums. I left Mathare more committed than ever, that UN-Habitat should leave no place and no one behind.

请自行翻译后查看后文的分析点评

分析点评

第 1 段

The present document sets out the proposed work programme of the United Nations Habitat and Human Settlements Foundation for the year 2020, which is based on the four-years strategic plan 2020—2023 as approved pursuant to Resolution 1/1 adopted by the first session of the UN-Habitat Assembly on United Nations Human Settlements Programme Strategic Plan for the period 2020—2023. The work programme was prepared in accordance with the support guide issued on 31 December 2019 by the Programme Planning and Budget Division of the Office of Programme Planning, Budget and Accounts of the Secretariat.

本文件列出了联合国生境和人类住区基金会 2020 年拟议工作方案，其依据是根据人居署大会①第一届会议通过的关于联合国人类住区规划署 2020—2023 年战略计划的第 1/1 号决议核准的 2020—2023 年四年战略计划②。工作方案是根据秘书处方案规划、预算和账户厅方案规划和预算司 2019 年 12 月 31 日发布的支助指南编制的。

批 注

① 专门术语翻译不符合联合国要求。

② 译文定语过长，难以理解。

本文件阐述了联合国生境和人类住区基金会 2020 年拟议工作方案。它以 2020—2023 年四年战略计划为基础，而战略计划则根据人居大会第一届会议通过的关于联合国人类住区规划署 2020—2023 年战略计划的第 1/1 号决议获得核准。工作方案是根据联合国秘书处方案规划、预算和账户厅方案规划和预算司 2019 年 12 月 31 日发布的支助指南编制的。

1. "proposed work programme" 也有写作 "proposed programme of work"，通常译为"拟议工作方案"。"proposed" 作形容词用，联合国常译为"拟议"，例如，"proposed programme budget" 译为"拟议方案预算"，"proposed strategic

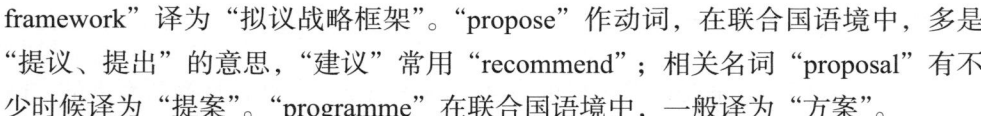

framework"译为"拟议战略框架"。"propose"作动词,在联合国语境中,多是"提议、提出"的意思,"建议"常用"recommend";相关名词"proposal"有不少时候译为"提案"。"programme"在联合国语境中,一般译为"方案"。

2. United Nations Habitat and Human Settlements Foundation:是一个基金会的专门名称。

3. UN-Habitat Assembly:译为"人居大会",不译"人居署大会",这是联合国内罗毕办事处的特别要求。

4. 第1句"The present document sets out the proposed work programme…"带有一个"which"引导的非限制性定语从句,非限制性定语从句中又有"as approved"引导的定语短语,"as approved"定语短语中又有"adopted"引导的定语,定语层层相叠,宛如俄罗斯套娃。如果都按英文句法译为定语,放在所修饰的名词前,译文将非常晦涩难懂。翻译稿的问题就在这里。审校稿为了简单易懂,进行了拆分处理。另外,这一句中还有两点要厘清。一是"which",它指谁,是指"the present document",还是指"the proposed work programme"?假如是指"the proposed work programme",行不行呢?那就是说,方案"based on the four-years strategic plan…",可第2句却说,方案是"was prepared in accordance with the support guide…",这不是矛盾吗?因此,"which"应指"the present document"。二是"as approved"中的"as"可视为关系代词,在此相当于"that"或"which"。"as approved"就相当于"that or which was approved"。"as"一词用法既多且繁,翻译时要结合语境,多用心揣摩。

5. Programme Planning and Budget Division:方案规划和预算司,是方案规划、预算和账户厅的下级单位。

6. Office of Programme Planning, Budget and Accounts:方案规划、预算和账户厅,本属于管理部(Department of Management),自2019年1月1日起,改为"方案规划、财务和预算厅"(Office of Programme Planning, Finance and Budget),归"管理战略、政策和合规部"(Department of Management Strategy, Policy and Compliance)管。

第2段

Ultimately, our mandate is about improving the lives of people. It is about transforming places and communities, to improve the quality of life for all. When I visited the informal settlements of Mathare in Nairobi in March 2018, I spent time with some of the young men and women there. They shared with me their concerns, their aspirations, and their experiences. It was an inspiring visit, and I left convinced of the relevance of our work. At UN-Habitat, we strive for "a better quality of life for all in an urbanizing world" by improving housing and urban services, creating safe public spaces for everyone, fostering entrepreneurship, generating social cohesion and empowering the most vulnerable members of our communities, conscious of the millions of households living in the urban slums. I left Mathare more committed than ever, that UN-Habitat should leave no place and no one behind.

批注

① 照搬英汉词典释义，太死板。

 翻译稿

最终，我们的使命是改善人民的生活，改变地方和社区，提高所有人的生活质量。2018年3月，当我访问内罗毕的马沙尔非正式定居点时，我与那里的一些年轻男女一起度过了一段时间。他们与我分享了他们的关切、愿望和经历。这是一次鼓舞人心的访问，我离开时确信我们工作的相关性①。在人居署，我们通过改善住房和城市服务、为每个人创造安全的公共空间、培养创业精神、产生社会凝聚力和增强我们社区最弱势成员的权能，努力提高"城市化世界中所有人更高的生活质量"，同时意识到生活在城市贫民窟的数百万家庭。离开马萨雷时我比以往任何时候都更加坚定，人居署不应该落下任何地方和任何人。

 审校稿

归根结底，我们的任务是改善人民的生活，是改造地方和社区，从而提高所有人的生活质量。2018年3月，我走访内罗毕的马塔雷非正规住区时，同那里的一些男女青年进行了交谈。他们向我谈起了他们的关切、愿望和经历。这是一次鼓舞人心的访问，我离开时深信我们的工作是有意义的。在人居署，我们力争"在世界城市化进程中提高所有人的生活质量"，改善住房和城市服务，为每个人创造安全的公共空间，培养创业精神，形成社会凝聚力，增强我们社区中最脆弱成员的权能，同时也意识到有数以百万计的家庭生活在城市贫民窟中。我离开马塔雷时，比以往任何时候更坚信，人居署不应让任何一个地方和任何一个人掉队。

 点评

1. "mandate"，联合国一般译为"任务"或"授权任务"，不译为"使命"。再如，enlargement of mandate，扩大任务；thematic mandate，专题任务；negotiation mandate，谈判任务；有时又译为"授权"，如 legislative mandate，立法授权或法定任务。audit mandate，审计授权或审计任务。

2. "informal settlement" 译为"非正规住区"，"formal settlement" 则译为"正规住区"。

3. "concerns"：联合国一般译为"关切"。再如，gender-sensitive concerns，对性别问题有敏感认识的关切。

4. "relevance"：一般英汉词典有"相关（性）"这一释义，但上海译文出版社的《英汉大词典》中，也有"重大关系；意义；实用性"等释义。《麦克米伦高阶英汉双解词典》的释义为"the quality of being connected with and important to something else"。所以应当视上下文，灵活翻译。

5. 第6句"At UN-Habitat, we strive for...by..."，句子很长，却不难理解。介词"by"表方式，遇到此类句子，通常都照翻译稿那样翻译。这样译没什么不对，但有时就显得太拘泥于英文语法，按照审校稿顺译，则显得更自然。

此句的"conscious of the millions of households living in the urban slums"是并列句子，表示"意识到……"，译为中文时可适当加上辅助词，这里处理为"同时也意识到……"，使整个短语更加层次分明，句子一下子泾渭分明，逻辑清楚。

6. 第 7 句中，"leave behind" 是成语，有"留下"的释义，但这里是"落下"的意思。"leave no one behind" 在联合国文件中反复出现，几乎成了联合国的标语，联合国纽约总部已经把它收入词库，译为"不让任何一个人掉队"，以利统一，免得译得五花八门。因此，就将 "leave no place and no one behind" 译为了 "不让任何一个地方和任何一个人掉队"。

补充练习

From 2016 to 2018, UN-Habitat, through the Global Land Tool Network, the World Bank and FAO facilitated the establishment of the Arab Land Governance Initiative, which serves as a platform for land actors and stakeholders in the region to collaborate and build capacity for developing and implementing innovative and inclusive solutions to address these land related challenges.

参考译文

从 2016 年至 2018 年，人居署通过全球土地工具网络、世界银行和粮农组织促进订立了阿拉伯土地治理倡议，该倡议充当一个平台，供该地区土地行为体和利益攸关方开展协作和能力建设，以便制订和执行具有包容性的创新型解决方案来应对这些与土地有关的挑战。

第二篇

原文

By 2050, the world's urban population is expected to nearly double, making urbanization one of the most significant trends of the twenty first century. Urbanization is growing at a fast pace, with 90 per cent of urban growth taking place in less developed regions, where it is mostly unplanned, and capacities and resources are most constrained. Unplanned urban growth fuels expansion of informal settlements or slums that are a visible symptom of urban poverty and inequality. Housing remains largely unaffordable in both the developing and some developed countries and globally, over 1.6 billion people live in inadequate housing, with 1 billion living in slums. About 1.2 billion people lack access to clean drinking water world-wide, and 2.5 billion lack access to safe sanitation. Fewer than 35 per cent of cities in developing countries have their waste water treated. Slum dwellers lack land tenure rights and decent livelihoods and experience social exclusion and marginalization. All these forms of exclusion disproportionately affect women, youth, older persons, migrants, and other marginalised groups. In some parts of the world, urban areas are increasingly becoming epicentres of crises, insecurity and violence, sometimes contributing to displacement and forced migration. Globally, there are currently 763 million internal migrants and 224 million international migrants, and most of these live in urban areas, often under difficult conditions. Cities also account for about 60 to 80 per cent of global energy consumption, 70 per cent of global carbon emissions, as well as over 70 per cent of resource use. The urban poor suffer the worst consequences of climate change related disasters, natural and human-made crises and conflicts. While urbanization brings along challenges, it also presents huge opportunities that bring benefits to all levels of human settlements.

UN-Habitat's support aimed at developing the capacity of Governments to formulate and implement policies for sustainable development is also provided through the implementation of the regular programme of technical cooperation and Development Account projects.

请自行翻译后查看后文的分析点评

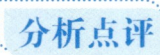

第1段

By 2050, the world's urban population is expected to nearly double, making urbanization one of the most significant trends of the twenty first century. Urbanization is growing at a fast pace, with 90 per cent of urban growth taking place in less developed regions, where it is mostly unplanned, and capacities and resources are most constrained. Unplanned urban growth fuels expansion of informal settlements or slums that are a visible symptom of urban poverty and inequality. Housing remains largely unaffordable in both the developing and some developed countries and globally, over 1.6 billion people live in inadequate housing, with 1 billion living in slums. About 1.2 billion people lack access to clean drinking water world-wide, and 2.5 billion lack access to safe sanitation. Fewer than 35 per cent of cities in developing countries have their waste water treated. Slum dwellers lack land tenure rights and decent livelihoods and experience social exclusion and marginalization. All these forms of exclusion disproportionately affect women, youth, older persons, migrants, and other marginalised groups. In some parts of the world, urban areas are increasingly becoming epicentres of crises, insecurity and violence, sometimes contributing to displacement and forced migration. Globally, there are currently 763 million internal migrants and 224 million international migrants, and most of these live in urban areas, often under difficult conditions. Cities also account for about 60 to 80 per cent of global energy consumption, 70 per cent of global carbon emissions, as well as over 70 per cent of resource use. The urban poor suffer the worst consequences of climate change related disasters, natural and human-made crises and conflicts. While urbanization brings along challenges, it also presents huge opportunities that bring benefits to all levels of human settlements.

到 2050 年时，世界城市人口预计将增加近一倍，使城市化成为 21 世纪最重大的趋势之一。城市化在显著①发展，90% 的城市增长发生在较不发达区域，大都无规划，能力和资源受限制程度最大。无计划和无序②的城市扩展加剧了非正规住区或贫民窟的涌现③，凸显了④城市的贫穷和不平等现象。在发展中国家和一些发达国家中，住房在很大程度上仍然负担不起；全球有 16 亿人缺少足够的住房，有 10 亿人居住在贫民窟中。约有 12 亿人没有清洁的饮用水，25 亿人没有安全的卫生设施。发展中国家中只有不到 35% 的城市对废水进行处理。贫民窟居民缺乏土地保有权和体面的生计，遭受社会排斥并处于社会的边缘。所有这些形式的排斥尤其影响到妇女、青年、老年人、移民和其他边缘化群体。在世界一些地区，城区正日益频现⑤危机、不安全和暴力，有时导致⑥流离失所和被迫迁移。在全球范围内，目前有 7.63 亿境内移民和 2.24 亿国际移民，他们大都生活在城市地区，生活条件往往很差。城市还消耗了全球 60% 至 80% 的能源，排放了全球 70% 的碳，使用了 70% 以上的资源⑦。城市贫民承受气候变化引起的灾害、自然和人为危机以及冲突的最严重后果。虽然城市化带来了挑战，但也带来了巨大的机会，可能对所有层面的人类住区产生好处。

批 注

① 笔误。
② 多余的增译。
③ 不确。
④ 精彩。
⑤ 翻译不准确。
⑥ 不确。
⑦ 妙译。

到 2050 年时，世界城市人口预计将增加近一倍，使城市化成为 21 世纪最重大的趋势之一。城市化在快速发展，90% 的城市增长发生在较不发达区域，大都漫无计划，能力和资源也受到极大的限制。无计划的城市增长加剧了非正规住区或贫民窟的扩张，凸显了城市的贫穷和不平等现象。在发展中国家和一些发达国家中，住房在很大程度上仍然让人负担不起；全球有 16 亿多人缺少适足住房，有 10 亿人居住在贫民窟中。世界各地约有 12 亿人用不上清洁的饮用水，25 亿人缺乏安全的卫生设施。发展中国家中只有不到 35% 的城市对废水进行处理。贫民窟居民缺乏土地保有权和体面的生计，遭受社会排斥，处于社会边缘。所有这些形式的排斥尤其影响到妇女、青年、老年人、移民和其他边缘群体。在世界一些地区，城市地区正日益成为危机、不安全和暴力中心，有时也助长了流离失所和被迫迁移。在全球范围内，目前有 7.63 亿境内移民和 2.24 亿国际移民，他们大都生活在城市地区，往往生活条件艰苦。城市还消耗了全球大约 60% 至 80% 的能源，排放了全球 70% 的二氧化碳，使用了 70% 以上的资源。城市贫民承受气候变化相关灾害、自然和人为危机以及冲突的最严重后果。城市化尽管带来了种种挑战，但也创造了巨大的机遇，令各层次的人类住区受益。

1. "Urbanization is growing at a fast pace":把"at a fast pace"译为"显著",显然不妥,可能是无心之错。"at a fast pace"字面意思"以很快的速度",也就是"迅速、快速"之义。

2. "Unplanned urban growth fuels expansion of informal settlements or slums that are a visible symptom of urban poverty and inequality."一句,译文既有不足,也有可叹赏之处。①"unplanned",无计划,当然就是随意,随意就是不讲次序,不讲次序当然就是"无序",所以增译"无序",实属叠床架屋,没有必要。②把"expansion"译为"涌现",既离字面意思很远,又不见巧妙;译为"扩张"就行了。③"a visible symptom of..."字面意思当然是"……一个的明显症状",译为"凸显了"则大显译者的笔力,可喜。

3. "land tenure rights":专门术语,意为"土地保有权"。

4. "marginalised groups"是联合国常用词汇,纽约总部译为"边缘群体"。同样,"forced migration"也是联合国常用词汇,有"被迫移民、强迫移民或强迫迁移"等译法。

5. "...urban areas are increasingly becoming epicentres of crises, insecurity and violence, sometimes contributing to displacement..."一句,译文有两个问题。①"epicentre"本义是"震中",与"hypocenter"(震源)有关,引申或比喻义是"the central point of something, typically a difficult or unpleasant situation"(《新牛津词典》),即"中心、集中点"。转译为动词"日益频现",无法很好体现"聚集之地"或"渊薮"之意,所以不可取。②"contributing to"是"助长",为次要原因,译为"导致",就变成了主要原因,甚至唯一原因,所以不准确。

6. "Cities also account for about 60 to 80 per cent of global energy consumption, 70 per cent of global carbon emissions, as well as over 70 per cent of resource use."一句,动词短语"account for"带三个名词短语或者说宾语(global energy consumption、global carbon emissions 和 resource use),正是英文的本色。"account for",在本文中是"引起,对……负责"的意思,直译的话,就会显得乏力。译文舍去英文谓语动词之形而存其义,把三个名词短语译为动宾,将英文一主一谓三宾译为中文的一主三谓三宾,尽显中文风采。

7. "all levels of human settlements"译为"所有层面……",不如译"各层次",也就说人类住区是有层次之分的,有正规住区,也有非正规住区。

第 2 段

UN-Habitat's support aimed at developing the capacity of Governments to formulate and implement policies for sustainable development is also provided through the implementation of the regular programme of technical cooperation and Development Account projects.

人居署旨在发展各国政府制定和执行可持续发展政策的能力的支助也是通过

执行技术合作经常方案和发展账户项目提供的[1]。

① 句式结构太长。

审校稿

人居署也通过执行技术合作经常方案和发展账户项目提供支助，意在提高各国政府制定和执行可持续发展政策的能力。

点评

1. "formulate"，《韦氏大学英语词典》的解释是"1c：DEVISE"，给出的例子是"*formulate* a policy"，联合国常译为"拟订、制订"，如 formulate concrete recommendations 拟订具体建议，formulate a draft strategy 拟订战略草案，formulate targeted policies and concrete strategies 拟订目标明确的政策和具体战略，formulate legislation and policy directives 拟订立法和政策指示，formulate provisions/principles 拟订规定/原则等。

2. "Development Account"：发展账户。它是联合国秘书处的一个能力发展方案，旨在增强发展中国家在联合国发展议程优先领域的能力。

3. 整段就一句话，是个被动句，成分不算太复杂：主语是"UN-Habitat's support"（人居署的支助），"aimed at developing the capacity of Governments to formulate and implement policies for sustainable development"过去分词作定语，"is also provided..."是谓语部分，"through the implementation...projects"为方式状语。翻译稿照英文语法结构顺序，形神兼备，既准确传达了原文意思，又很好地保留了原文形式，唯一美中不足的可能是句式结构太长。审校稿提供另一翻译方式：按照中文习惯行文，回避太长的定语，少用被动式，译得准确，又通顺。

补充练习

UN-Habitat, through its normative work that includes various knowledge building activities, new research and capacity building, will set standards, proposes norms and principles and shares good practices. It also monitors global progress and supports intergovernmental, regional, national and subnational bodies in their formulation of policies related to sustainable cities and human settlements. In doing this, UN-Habitat builds on its past experience of evidence-based normative work. Examples of its normative work include: global flagship reports (the Global Report on Human Settlements and the State of the World's Cities Report, now combined into the periodic World Cities Report); Global Urban Indicators Database; tools for improving access to land and security of tenure developed in collaboration with the Global Land Tool Network (GLTN); and International Guidelines on Decentralization and Access to Basic Services for All.

人居署通过其规范性工作,包括各种知识生成活动、新的研究和能力建设,将制定标准,提出规范和原则,分享良好做法。它还监测全球进展情况,支持政府间、区域、国家和国家以下各级机构制定与可持续城市和人类住区有关的政策。在开展这种工作时,人居署以既往开展循证规范性工作的经验为基础。人居署规范性工作的实例包括:全球旗舰报告(《全球人类住区报告》和《世界城市状况报告》,两者已合并为定期出版的《世界城市状况报告》);全球城市指标数据库;与全球土地工具网络合作开发的、用于改善获得土地机会和保障土地保有权的工具;《关于权力下放和为所有人提供基本服务的国际准则》。

第三篇

原文

The objectives of the subprogrammes are also aligned with the outcomes of the United Nations Conferences on Human Settlements and on Housing and Sustainable Urban Development, particularly the outcome of the Third Conference adopted by the General Assembly through Resolution 71/235 and the New Urban Agenda adopted through Resolution 71/256. The objectives of the subprogrammes are also aligned with transformative agendas, including the Addis Ababa Action Agenda of the Third International Conference on Financing for Development, the Sendai Framework for Disaster Risk Reduction 2015—2030, the Paris Agreement under the United Nations Framework Convention on Climate Change, the outcome of the 2016 high-level plenary meeting of the General Assembly on addressing large movements of refugees and migrants entitled "New York Declaration for Refugees and Migrants" and the 2018 Global Compact on Safe, Orderly and Regular Migration.

In May 2018, UN-Habitat presented to the General Assembly the first of five quadrennial reports on the implementation of the New Urban Agenda. The report, prepared in consultation with 23 United Nations entities, the 5 regional economic and social commissions, and 30 partners, provided qualitative and quantitative analysis of the progress made on implementation of the New Urban Agenda. It recommended steps to ensure the successful production of subsequent reports until 2036.

请自行翻译后查看后文的分析点评

分析点评

第 1 段

The objectives of the subprogrammes are also aligned with the outcomes of the United Nations Conferences on Human Settlements and on Housing and Sustainable Urban Development, particularly the outcome of the Third Conference adopted by the General Assembly through Resolution 71/235 and the New Urban Agenda adopted through Resolution 71/256. The objectives of the subprogrammes are also aligned with transformative agendas, including the Addis Ababa Action Agenda of the Third International Conference on Financing for Development, the Sendai Framework for Disaster Risk Reduction 2015—2030, the Paris Agreement under the United Nations Framework Convention on Climate Change, the outcome of the 2016 high-level plenary meeting of the General Assembly on addressing large movements of refugees and migrants entitled "New York Declaration for Refugees and Migrants" and the 2018 Global Compact for Safe, Orderly and Regular Migration.

次级方案的目标还与以下文件保持一致：联合国人类住区会议和住房与城市可持续发展大会成果，特别是大会第 71/235 号决议通过的第三次会议的成果①和第 71/256 号决议通过《新城市议程》。次级方案的目标还与转型议程保持一致，包括第三次发展筹资问题国际会议的《亚的斯亚贝巴行动议程》《2015—2030 年仙台减少灾害风险框架》《巴黎协定》②和题为"关于难民和移民的纽约宣言"的联大 2016 年关于大量难民和移民流动问题的大会高级别全体会议的成果③以及 2018 年《安全、有序和正常移民全球契约》。

批 注

① 增译不当。
② 漏译 "under the United Nations Framework Convention on Climate Change"。
③ 语序不佳。

次级方案的目标也符合联合国人类住区会议与住房和城市可持续发展大会成果，特别是联大第 71/235 号决议通过的第三次会议的成果和第 71/256 号决议通过的《新城市议程》。次级方案的目标还契合转型议程，包括《第三次发展筹资问题国际会议亚的斯亚贝巴行动议程》《2015—2030 年仙台减少灾害风险框架》《联合国气候变化框架公约》下的《巴黎协定》和联大 2016 年解决难民和移民大规模流动问题高级别全体会议题为"《关于难民和移民的纽约宣言》"的成果以及 2018 年《安全、有序和正常移民全球契约》。

这一段翻译有两个难点，一是"The objectives of the subprogrammes are also aligned with the outcomes of..."中"aligned with"的译法；二是专有名称多。译好前者需要翻译技巧；处理后者，需要专业背景知识。

1. "align"源于古法文，该法文又来自拉丁文，本义是"into line"，所以 Random

House Kernerman Webster's College Dictionary 对"align"的解释就是"1. to arrange in a straight line; adjust according to a line; 2. to bring into a line or alignment"。英汉词典解释一般都是"排成直线，使成一条直线"，把 align with something 解释为"与……成一条直线"或"与……一致"。多数译者没有深入开动脑筋，也就盲从英汉词典的释义。"be aligned with"，"与……一致"，其实也就是"符合、契合、吻合"的意思。审校稿把"be aligned with"译为"符合"和"契合"，既简洁，又使译文顺畅。

2. "United Nations Conferences on Human Settlements and on Housing and Sustainable Urban Development"，要注意"Conferences"用的是复数，分别指"United Nations Conferences on Human Settlements"即"联合国人类住区会议"和 United Nations Conference on Housing and Sustainable Urban Development，即"联合国住房和城市可持续发展大会"，不可误解。

"联合国人类住区会议"召开过两次，第一次于 1976 年 5 月 31 日至 6 月 11 日在加拿大温哥华举行，简称"人居一"，第二次于 1996 年 6 月 3 日至 14 日在土耳其伊斯坦布尔举行，简称"人居二"。"联合国住房和城市可持续发展大会"于 2016 年 10 月 17 日至 20 日在厄瓜多尔首都基多举行，简称"人居三"。

3.《巴黎协定》后面漏译了"under the United Nations Framework Convention on Climate Change"，细致不出疏漏是翻译的第一要则。

4. "the outcome...New York Declaration for Refugees"是讲，大会（General Assembly）2016 年举行了一次"high-level plenary meeting...on addressing large movements of refugees and migrants"，会议的成果（"outcome"）entitled "New York Declaration for Refugees"。

第 2 段

In May 2018, UN-Habitat presented to the General Assembly the first of five quadrennial reports on the implementation of the New Urban Agenda. The report, prepared in consultation with 23 United Nations entities, the 5 regional economic and social commissions, and 30 partners, provided qualitative and quantitative analysis of the progress made on implementation of the New Urban Agenda. It recommended steps to ensure the successful production of subsequent reports until 2036.

批 注

① 句子不佳。
② 漏译"economic and social"。
③ 漏译"of the New Urban Agenda"。

翻译稿

2018 年 5 月向大会提交了关于《新城市议程》执行情况的四年期报告，这是五份此类四年期报告中的第一份。本报告由人居署与 23 个联合国实体、5 个区域委员会和 30 个伙伴协商编写，对执行进展③进行了定性和定量分析，并提出了采取哪些步骤来确保顺利编写后续报告，直至 2036 年。

审校稿

2018 年 5 月，人居署向联大提交了关于《新城市议程》执行情况的第一份 4 年期报告，总共要提交 5 份。本报告由人居署与 23 个联合国实体、5 个区域经济和社会委员会和30个伙伴协商编写，对《新城市议程》的执行进展进行了定性和定量分析，建议采取步骤，确保至2036年前顺利编写后续报告。

1. 第1句"...UN-Habitat presented to the General Assembly the first of five quadrennial reports on the implementation of the New Urban Agenda"，翻译稿想打破英文语法的束缚，终究没能彻底跳出来。审校稿以翻译稿为基础，会其意，舍其形，把"5份"拎出，增译"总共要提交"几个字，既准确传达原文意思，又是地道的中文。

2. 第2句"The report...provided qualitative and quantitative analysis of the progress made on implementation of the New Urban Agenda"，译文有两处问题。

一是"5 regional economic and social commissions"译为"5个区域委员会"，漏译了定语"economic and social"，不应该。这5个区域委员会都由经济及社会理事会（Economic and Social Council）设立，它们分别是亚洲及太平洋经济社会委员会（Economic and Social Commission for Asia and the Pacific），简称亚太经社会（ESCAP）；西亚经济社会委员会(Economic and Social Commission for Western Asia)，简称西亚经社会（ESCWA）；拉丁美洲和加勒比经济委员会（Economic Commission for Latin America and the Caribbean），简称拉加经委会（ECLAC）；欧洲经济委员会（Economic Commission for Europe），简称欧洲经委会（ECE）及非洲经济委员会（Economic Commission for Africa），简称非洲经委会（ECA）。二是"progress made on implementation of the New Urban Agenda"省略了"the New Urban Agenda"，虽然从上下文可以理解，但还是以不省为好，因为不省读起来更明白，也不显得啰唆。

3. 第3句"It recommended steps to ensure the successful production of subsequent reports until 2036"，既可以如翻译稿处理的那样，与上句合并，一句讲两件事。也可以依照原文形式，分译为两句，一句讲一件事，更加分明。

另外，把"recommended steps"译为"提出了采取哪些步骤"，既啰唆，又没有必要；"直至2036年"也有失严谨，不如审校稿译得明确。

补充练习

The mandates of UN-Habitat guide the subprogrammes in producing their respective deliverables, which contribute to the attainment of each subprogramme's objective. The objectives of the subprogrammes are aligned with the Organization's purpose "to achieve international cooperation in solving international problems of an economic, social, cultural or humanitarian character, and in promoting and encouraging respect for human rights and for fundamental freedoms for all without distinction as to race, sex, language, or religion", as stipulated in article 1 of the Charter of the United Nations. In the context of the 2030 Agenda for Sustainable Development, the four purposes stipulated in Article 1 of the Charter are embodied by the Sustainable Development Goals.

人居署的任务规定指导各次级方案制订各自的交付成果，这有助于实现各次级方案的目标。次级方案的目标符合联合国的宗旨，即"促成国际合作，以解决属于经济、社会、文化及人类福利性质之国际问题，且不分种族、性别、语言或宗教，增进并激励对于全体人类之人权及基本自由之尊重"，详见《联合国宪章》第一条的规定。在《2030年可持续发展议程》的背景下，《宪章》第一条规定的四项宗旨均体现在可持续发展目标中。

第四篇

原文

The ninth session of The World Urban Forum, the largest global forum on sustainable urbanization and human settlements representing national, regional and local governments, civil society, parliamentarians, local communities, the private sector, multilateral organizations, academicians, researchers, and a wide range of stakeholders, took place in Kuala Lumpur, Malaysia, in February 2018. The participants shared knowledge and experiences on sustainable urbanization and human settlements and encouraged localisation and scaling up of the implementation of the New Urban Agenda as an accelerator for achieving the Sustainable Development Goals. The outcome document, the Kuala Lumpur Declaration on Cities 2030, called attention to persistent challenges faced by cities and human settlements. It called for urgent action be taken to address these challenges, highlighted the transformative power of cities and the genuine aspiration to leave no one and no place behind. It made actionable recommendations, including adoption of specific collaborative governance mechanisms and innovative solutions.

In December 2018, the General Assembly adopted Resolution 73/239 by which it established a new governance structure for UN-Habitat, consisting of the universal UN-Habitat Assembly, a 36-member Executive Board and a Committee of Permanent Representatives.

请自行翻译后查看后文的分析点评

第五章 环境与发展

第1段

The ninth session of The World Urban Forum, the largest global forum on sustainable urbanization and human settlements representing national, regional and local governments, civil society, parliamentarians, local communities, the private sector, multilateral organizations, academicians, researchers, and a wide range of stakeholders, took place in Kuala Lumpur, Malaysia, in February 2018. The participants shared knowledge and experiences on sustainable urbanization and human settlements and encouraged localisation and scaling up of the implementation of the New Urban Agenda as an accelerator for achieving the Sustainable Development Goals. The outcome document, the Kuala Lumpur Declaration on Cities 2030, called attention to persistent challenges faced by cities and human settlements. It called for urgent action be taken to address these challenges, highlighted the transformative power of cities and the genuine aspiration to leave no one and no place behind. It made actionable recommendations, including adoption of specific collaborative governance mechanisms and innovative solutions.

　　世界城市论坛是代表国家、区域和地方政府、民间社会、议员、地方社区、私营部门、多边组织、学者、研究人员和广泛利益攸关方的最大的可持续城市化和人类住区全球论坛①，第九届会议于2018年2月在马来西亚吉隆坡举行。与会者分享了关于可持续城市化和人类住区的知识和经验②，并鼓励将《新城市议程》的实施本地化和扩大规模，作为实现可持续发展目标的加速器③。成果文件《2030年吉隆坡城市宣言》呼吁关注城市和人类住区面临的持续挑战。它呼吁采取紧急行动应对这些挑战，强调城市的变革力量和不让任何人和任何地方掉队的真诚愿望。它提出了可行的建议，包括采用具体的合作治理机制和创新解决方案。

批　注

① 拆得不错，还可以再拆。
② 不确，但似乎"合情合理"。
③ 也可以转译。

　　世界城市论坛是全球最大的可持续城市化和人类住区论坛，代表各个国家、区域和地方政府、民间社会、议员、地方社区、私营部门、多边组织、学者、研究人员和广泛的利益攸关方，第九届会议于2018年2月在吉隆坡举行。参加论坛者分享了可持续城市化和人类住区的知识和体验，并鼓励《新城市议程》执行工作本地化、扩大化，以此加快实现可持续发展目标。成果文件《2030年城市吉隆坡宣言》提请注意城市和人类住区所面临的持续挑战；呼吁紧急采取行动应对这些挑战，强调城市的变革力量以及不让任何一个人和任何一个地方掉队的愿望。成果文件还提出了可行建议，包括采用具体的合作治理机制和创新解决办法。

1. 第 1 句"The ninth session of The World Urban Forum...took place in Kuala Lumpur, Malaysia, in February 2018"的主干是"第九届会议于 2018 年 2 月在马来西亚吉隆坡举行"。"The World Urban Forum"作为定语，修饰"The ninth session"；"the largest global forum on sustainable urbanization and human settlements"既是"The World Urban Forum"的同位语，本身又有很长的定语"representing national, regional and local governments...and a wide range of stakeholders"。这种先确立一个重点，紧接着"展开论述"，然后再回到重点的句法，在英文中司空见惯；中文则少见这一习惯。翻译时可将定语"The World Urban Forum"拎出，译为主语，将定语"representing..."这一动宾词群译为谓语，然后接英文主干句子，从容译来，非常自然；如果再加以拆分，如审校稿那样处理，则更加妥当。

2. 第 2 句"The participants shared knowledge and experiences...as an accelerator for achieving the Sustainable Development Goals"，在翻译时有两点须稍加注意。

（1）"experience"用的是复数：依英英词典解释，作"经验"解，是不可数名词，当作单数；复数，则表示"体验"。按常理讲，"share knowledge and experience"一般都是"分享知识，交流经验"，当然"交流体验"，或"交流心得体会"也可以。

（2）"as an accelerator for..."：英文所取这一形象，在中文中也很容易理解，原译既译出英文的意思，又保留英文的形式，形神兼备，很好。不过，因为"accelerator"取象并不新颖生动，所以也可以舍其形，取其意，译为"加速"；把这个名词转为动词有一个特别的好处，可以避开在中文里并不常用、但在英文中是套语的"as..."结构，体现中文多动词的特点。

3. "actionable"这个词，用得比较晦涩，比较高深。在常见的英语词典中，仅给出"可起诉的"（giving sb a valid reason to bring a case in a court of law）这一个义项，放在本段文字中不合适，因为成果文件不可能"提出了可起诉的建议"，这显然违背逻辑。

然而，如翻译稿，译为"可行的建议"，符合上下文意，有没有根据呢？有。《韦氏大学英语词典》给出了两种解释"① subject to or affording ground for an action or suit at law；② capable of being acted on"，翻译稿取第 2 个义项。《新牛津英语词典》的第 2 个义项是"able to be done or acted on; having practical value"，解释更加明白易懂。

第 2 段

In December 2018, the General Assembly adopted Resolution 73/239 by which it established a new governance structure for UN-Habitat, consisting of the universal UN-Habitat Assembly, a 36-member Executive Board and a Committee of Permanent Representatives.

联大2018年12月通过了第73/239号决议，建立了人居署，这是一个<u>由人居大会</u>①、一个有36名成员的执行局和常驻代表委员会组成的新的治理结构。

批 注

① 不恰当省略"universal"。

2018年12月，联大通过了第73/239号决议，为人居署确立了新的治理结构，设有全体参与的人居大会、一个由36名成员组成的执行局和一个常驻代表委员会。

点评

1. "General Assembly"是指联合国主要的审议、政策制定和代表机关，因为是在人居署语境中，为了区别于人居大会，译为"联大"，即"联合国大会"。另外，在国际原子能机构的文本中，也译为联大。

2. 第1句"...adopted Resolution 73/239 by which it established..."中的"by which"，意思是要"根据该决议"，如死扣翻译，不省略的话，当译为"……通过了第73/239号决议，根据该决议联大为人居署确立……"这样处理，并没有使文意更加清晰，反而显得啰唆；反而是省去不译，来得简洁明白。

3. "consist of"英汉词典上给出意思就是"由……组成"。这样解释没错，翻译中这么用也对，但有时显得太死板。灵活变通一下，译为"新的治理结构，设有……"也可以。

4. "the universal UN-Habitat Assembly"，这里有两点要注意，一是UN-Habitat Assembly译为"人居大会"；二是"universal"不可省，它在此表示强调，是指人居署全体成员参与的人居大会，是与执行局的"36名成员"和一个委员会的成员"常驻代表"相对而言的。

Through General Assembly Resolution 73/307, the Governing Council was dissolved as a subsidiary organ of the General Assembly and replaced with a universal UN-Habitat Assembly which meets every four years for five days and is responsible for approving UN-Habitat's strategic plan. The General Assembly also established a 36-member Executive Board whose members are elected by the UN-Habitat Assembly. The Executive Board strengthens oversight over UN-Habitat's operations and also enhances accountability, transparency, efficiency and effectiveness of the Programme. It oversees preparation of the draft Strategic Plan before its approval by the UN-Habitat Assembly and is also responsible for the review and approval of the Annual Work Programme and Budget. In addition, the Executive Board has the responsibility of reviewing financial rules and regulations and matters associated with running of the Programme.

联大第73/307号决议，解散了作为联大附属机关的理事会，代之以一个全体参与的人居大会。人居大会每四年举行一次会议，为期五天，负责核准人居署的战略计划。联大还设立了一个执行局，共有36名成员，均由人居大会选举产生。执行局强化对人居署业务的监督，并增强人居署的问责制、透明度、效率和效力。它监督战略计划草案在送交人居大会核准之前的编制工作，也负责审查和核准年度工作方案和预算。此外，执行局还负责审查财务细则和条例以及与方案运作有关的事项。

Pursuant to Rule 5 (c) of the rules of procedure, the functions of the Executive Board include among others the approval and oversight of the annual wok programme and budget and the resource mobilization strategy in accordance with the strategic plans and political guidelines provided by the UN-Habitat Assembly. The Executive Board agreed during that meeting to resume its first meeting at a later date in November 2019 and decided to defer consideration of the UN-Habitat work programme and budget for the year 2020 to its resumed meeting. The resumed meeting will take place from 19 to 20 November 2019 at the headquarters of UN-Habitat in Nairobi.

In subprogramme 2, entitled "enhanced shared prosperity of cities and regions", UN-Habitat will leverage its knowledge and expertise. The expanded focus on connectivity and regional planning is determined by several studies that have demonstrated the strong connection between urban and regional planning and the promotion of shared prosperity. Working with strategic partners, such as the Organization for Economic Cooperation and Development, the World Bank and others, UN-Habitat will support government authorities at different levels to develop policies, frameworks and actions to boost the productivity of cities and regions through an integrated territorial development approach. Working with the International Labour Organization, the United Nations Industrial Development Organization, the Food and Agriculture Organization of the United Nations, the International Fund for Agricultural Development, the International Organization for Migration and other organizations, UN-Habitat will promote inclusive and sustainable economic growth, employment and decent work for all, in particular women and youth through specific policies and actions.

请自行翻译后查看后文的分析点评

分析点评

第 1 段

Pursuant to Rule 5 (c) of the rules of procedure, the functions of the Executive Board include among others the approval and oversight of the annual wok programme and budget and the resource mobilization strategy in accordance with the strategic plans and political guidelines provided by the UN-Habitat Assembly. The Executive Board agreed during that meeting to resume its first meeting at a later date in November 2019 and decided to defer consideration of the UN-Habitat work programme and budget for the year 2020 to its resumed meeting. The resumed meeting will take place from 19 to 20 November 2019 at the headquarters of UN-Habitat in Nairobi.

翻译稿

根据议事规则第 5（c）条，执行局的职能包括根据人居署大会①提供的战略计划和政治准则，批准和监督年度工作方案和预算以及资源调动战略。执行局在该次会议上同意在 2019 年 11 月晚些时候恢复②第一次会议，并决定将对人居署 2020 年工作方案和预算的审议推迟到续会。续会将于 2019 年 11 月 19 日至 20 日在内罗毕人居署总部举行。

批注

① 未查专业词汇。
② 未顾及下文。

审校稿

根据议事规则第 5（c）条，执行局的职能包括根据人居大会提供的战略计划和政治准则，批准和监督年度工作方案和预算以及资源调动战略等。执行局在该次会议上同意在 2019 年 11 月晚些时候召开第一次会议续会，并决定将对人居署 2020 年工作方案和预算的审议推迟到续会。续会将于 2019 年 11 月 19 日至 20 日在内罗毕人居署总部举行。

点评

1. "rules of procedure"：在大会、安理会、经社理事会等机构，该短语都译为"议事规则"；在法院，如国际刑事法院，该短语则译为"程序规则"。不可混淆。

2. "Executive Board"译法比较复杂，共有三种。①世卫组织译为"执行委员会"；②开发署、环境署、教科文组织、儿基会、粮食署、人居署均译为"执行局"；③货币基金组织、世界银行等译为"执行董事会"。

3. "among others"联合国文件通常译为"除其他外"，当然也可以译为"等"或"等等"，放在最后。译文略去未译，无关宏旨，但按联合国的一向严谨的传统，以译出为佳。

4. "resume"为及物动词，此处意思是"to return to or begin again after interruption"（《韦氏词典》）。把"resume its first meeting"译为"恢复第一次会议"，大致不错，但不如译为"召开第一次会议续会"，这样可以让中文读者更清楚地理解下文两个"resumed meeting"（续会）的所指。

第 2 段

In subprogramme 2, entitled "enhanced shared prosperity of cities and regions", UN-Habitat will leverage its knowledge and expertise. The expanded focus on connectivity and regional planning is determined by several studies that have demonstrated the strong connection between urban and regional planning and the promotion of shared prosperity. Working with strategic partners, such as the Organization for Economic Cooperation and Development, the World Bank and others, UN-Habitat will support government authorities at different levels to develop policies, frameworks and actions to boost the productivity of cities and regions through an integrated territorial development approach. Working with the International Labour Organization, the United Nations Industrial Development Organization, the Food and Agriculture Organization of the United Nations, the International Fund for Agricultural Development, the International Organization for Migration and other organizations, UN-Habitat will promote inclusive and sustainable economic growth, employment and decent work for all, in particular women and youth through specific policies and actions.

批 注

① 努力就合中文，但还有改进余地。
② 需要调整和增译。

在题为"加强城市和区域的共同繁荣"的次级方案 2 中，人居署将利用其知识和专长。几项研究表明，城市和区域规划与促进共同繁荣之间有着密切的联系，这些研究确定了对连通性和区域规划的更大关注。①人居署将与经济合作与发展组织、世界银行等战略伙伴合作，支持各级政府当局制定政策、框架和行动，通过综合领土发展办法提高城市和区域的生产力。人居署将与国际劳工组织、联合国工业发展组织、联合国粮食及农业组织、国际农业发展基金、国际移民组织和其他组织合作，通过具体政策和行动，促进包容性和可持续的经济增长、就业和人人有体面工作，特别是妇女和青年②。

在题为"加强城市和区域的共同繁荣"的次级方案 2 中，人居署将充分利用其知识和专长。有几项研究表明，城市和区域规划与促进共同繁荣之间有着密切的联系，这决定了连通性和区域规划更加值得关注。人居署将与经济合作与发展组织、世界银行等战略伙伴合作，支持各级政府当局制定政策、框架和行动，通过综合领土发展办法提高城市和区域的生产力。人居署将与国际劳工组织、联合国工业发展组织、联合国粮食及农业组织、国际农业发展基金、国际移民组织和其他组织合作，通过具体政策和行动，促进包容性的可持续经济增长和就业，让人人都有体面工作，特别是妇女和青年有体面工作。

1. "leverage"：作动词，《牛津高阶英汉双解词典》《麦克米伦词典》等尚未收入；《柯林斯学习词典》解释的是金融方面的用法；《朗文当代高级词典》有两个义项，第一项与金融有关，第二项是"to spread or use resources (=money, skills, buildings etc. that an organization has available), ideas etc. again in several different ways or in different parts of a company, system etc."，好像还是与金钱脱不了关系；《韦氏词典》中该词动词形式的第 2 个义项"to use for gain: EXPLOIT"，似乎有点贬义；《美国传统词典》等美国的其他大学词典，也没有此处所要的释义；只有《新牛津英语词典》的解释"use (something) to maximum advantage"，"充分利用"，最合适。

2. 第 2 句"The expanded focus on connectivity and regional planning is determined by several studies...of shared prosperity"是英文惯用的被动句，为就合"主谓"结构，把非主要动词"expand"变为"expanded"，当形容词用。若照原文语法结构译为中文"对连通性和区域规划的扩大的侧重是由……决定的"，不仅词语搭配成问题，整个句子也疲弱无力，因为违背了中文多动词的习惯。翻译稿看到了这一点，跳出英文语法，但改得不够彻底。审校稿按照句子逻辑，重铸新句，读来更自然。

3. 最后一句"...promote inclusive and sustainable economic growth, employment and decent work for all, in particular women and youth..."，谓语动词"promote"带有三个宾语，译文也亦步亦趋，显得行文不协调，在原文中，"inclusive and sustainable economic growth""employment"和"decent work for all"属同类，都是名词性词语，译文则不然，"包容性和可持续的经济增长和就业"固然是名词性词语，"人人有体面工作"却是句子；还有，"特别是妇女和青年"也翻译不当，按英文逻辑，当译为"人人，特别是妇女和青年，有体面工作"。

The findings of the evaluation and self-evaluations referenced in paragraph 40 above have been taken into account for the programme plan for 2020. For example, an evaluation of the Global Water Operators' Partnerships Alliance recommended that a Global Water Operators' Partnerships Alliance Strategy for 2018—2022 be developed, a task force set up subsequently developed a new strategy for its future work. The ongoing organizational reform and governance reform of UN-Habitat aimed at making the Programme fit for purpose are a response to evaluation recommendations to strengthen accountability, effectiveness and efficiency.

参考译文

2020 年方案计划已经考虑到了上文第 40 段中所述评价和自我评价的结果。例如，全球水运营商伙伴关系联盟的评价建议制定一项《全球水运营商伙伴关系联盟 2018—2022 年战略》，随后设立的一个工作队为该联盟未来的工作制定了一项新战略。人居署正在进行组织改革和治理改革，旨在使人居署能够堪当其任，是对关于加强问责制、提升效力和效率的评价建议的回应。

第六篇

原文

In exercising its focal point role, it will collaborate with a number of other United Nations coordination bodies, such as UN-Water, UN-Energy and Sustainable Energy for All, and United Nations entities, such as the United Nations Development Programme, the United Nations Entity for Gender Equality and the Empowerment of Women (UN-Women), the United Nations Children's Fund, the United Nations Educational, Scientific and Cultural Organization, as well as a large number of non-governmental partners and stakeholders and the private sector.

UN-Habitat will partner with other UN agencies where opportunities for synergy exist. A partnership with UN Environment Programme, who have expertise in air quality monitoring and ecosystem-based approaches to adaptation will complement UN-Habitat's expertise in city and metropolitan-level planning processes to support local governments develop improved local-level clean air and climate action plans. UN-Habitat will also partner with the Secretariat of the United Nations Framework Convention on Climate Change to enhance awareness of issues relating to cities and human settlements and for the dissemination of knowledge and international best practices to support implementation of urban climate action strategies.

UN-Habitat will work with governments for access to climate and environmental resources for urban action, channelled through facilities developed under UN frameworks such as the Green Climate Fund, the Global Environment Facility and the Adaptation Fund.

请自行翻译后查看后文的分析点评

分析点评

第 1 段

In exercising its focal point role, it will collaborate with a number of other United Nations coordination bodies, such as UN-Water, UN-Energy and Sustainable Energy for All, and United Nations entities, such as the United Nations Development

Programme, the United Nations Entity for Gender Equality and the Empowerment of Women (UN-Women), the United Nations Children's Fund, the United Nations Educational, Scientific and Cultural Organization, as well as a large number of non-governmental partners and stakeholders and the private sector.

在发挥其协调中心作用时，它将与若干其他联合国协调机构合作，如联合国水机制、联合国能源机制和人人享有可持续能源机制，以及联合国各实体，如联合国开发计划署、联合国促进性别平等和增强妇女权能署（妇女署）、联合国儿童基金会、联合国教育、科学及文化组织，以及大量非政府伙伴和利益攸关方和私营部门。

在发挥其协调中心作用时，它将与下列诸方合作：其他若干联合国协调机构，如联合国水机制、联合国能源机制和人人享有可持续能源；联合国各实体，如联合国开发计划署、联合国促进性别平等和增强妇女权能署（妇女署）、联合国儿童基金会、联合国教育、科学及文化组织；以及许多非政府伙伴和利益攸关方及私营部门。

英文"collaborate with"后接多个宾语（ABC），眉目清楚；中文若译为"与……合作"，则难以为继，结果只有两种：①"与A合作"，不管BC；②"与A、B以及C合作"，相隔又太远，所以须依照中文习惯做特殊处理，如审校稿那样"与下列诸方合作"，再列出ABC，则条理分明。

当然，也可以译为"它发挥了协作中心作用，协作单位计有其他若干联合国协调机构……"。

第2段

UN-Habitat will partner with other UN agencies where opportunities for synergy exist. A partnership with UN Environment Programme, who have expertise in air quality monitoring and ecosystem-based approaches to adaptation will complement UN-Habitat's expertise in city and metropolitan-level planning processes to support local governments develop improved local-level clean air and climate action plans. UN-Habitat will also partner with the Secretariat of the United Nations Framework Convention on Climate Change to enhance awareness of issues relating to cities and human settlements and for the dissemination of knowledge and international best practices to support implementation of urban climate action strategies.

人居署将与存在协同机会的②其他联合国机构合作。与在空气质量监测和基于生态系统的适应方法方面具有专长③的联合国环境规划署建立伙伴关系，将补

批 注

① 位置不当。

② 理解有误。
③ 可更简洁。

批 注

① 变译。
② 啰唆。
③ 有误。

充人居署在城市和都市一级规划进程中的专长，以支持地方政府制定改进的① 地方一级② 清洁空气和气候行动计划。人居署还将与《联合国气候变化框架公约》秘书处③ 合作，提高对城市和人类住区相关问题的认识，传播知识和国际最佳做法，以支持实施城市气候行动战略。

审校稿

如果有协同增效机会，人居署将与联合国其他机构结伴合作。联合国环境规划署擅长空气质量监测和采取以生态系统为本的适应方法，与联合国环境规划署建立伙伴关系，将补充完善人居署在城市和都市一级规划进程方面的专长，以支持地方政府制定更完善的地方清洁空气和气候行动计划。人居署还将与联合国气候变化框架公约秘书处合作，提高对城市和人类住区相关问题的认识，传播知识和国际最佳做法，以支持实施城市气候行动战略。

点评

1. 在第 1 句中，"...where opportunities for synergy exist"，从语法角度看，是有歧义的，既可理解为"agencies"的定语，又可视为表示条件的状语。究竟哪种理解正确？这就得深入理解"synergy"的含义，《牛津高阶英汉双解词典》给出的解释是"the extra energy, power, success, etc. that is achieved by two or more people or companies working together, instead of on their own"，意思是说两个或多个人或公司合作可取得额外的成功等，所以"where"当是连词，表示在有协同增效机会的情况下，就与其他联合国机构协作，以取得格外的效果或成功。翻译稿的理解不合逻辑。

2. 第 2 句"A partnership with UN Environment Programme, who have expertise in air quality monitoring and ecosystem-based approaches to adaptation will complement UN-Habitat's expertise...improved local-level...plans"，有三点需要注意。

（1）对于"who"（严格来讲，应当用"which"或"that"）引导的非限定性定语从句，可以如翻译稿处理的那样，将其直接译为定语；如果把"UN Environment Programme"拎出来，立为主语，把"who"非限制性定语从句译为谓语，然后再说与环境署建立伙伴关系如何如何，则简洁明了。

（2）"have expertise in..."可照字面直译，也可以转译为动词"擅长、专擅、长于"。

（3）"local-level"是英文的是"官样文章"，不一定都要译为"地方一级"，有时去掉"一级"，也不妨碍中文的理解。

3. 第 3 句"UN-Habitat will also partner with the Secretariat of...to enhance awareness of issues relating to cities and human settlements and for the dissemination of knowledge..."有两处需要妥善处理。

（1）Secretariat of the United Nations Framework Convention on Climate Change："United Nations Framework Convention on Climate Change"作为专有名称，单独使用，一般都要加书名号，译为《联合国气候变化框架公约》；与其

他成分一起使用时，则不一定，如此处，《公约》是"Secretariat"的定语，按联合国惯例，译为"联合国气候变化框架公约秘书处"，不加书名号。另外，"Conference of the Parties to the *United Nations Framework Convention on Climate Change*"，译为"联合国气候变化框架公约缔约方会议"，其中的《公约》也不加书名号。

（2）本句有两个目的状语，一个是"enhance..."，另一个用"for"引导的介词短语。

第 3 段

UN-Habitat will work with governments for access to climate and environmental resources for urban action, channelled through facilities developed under UN frameworks such as the Green Climate Fund, the Global Environment Facility and the Adaptation Fund.

人居署将与各国政府合作，通过在绿色气候基金、全球环境基金和适应基金等联合国框架①下开发的设施，为城市行动获取气候和环境资源。

人居署将与各国政府合作，为城市行动获取气候和环境资源，通过在联合国框架下建立的绿色气候基金、全球环境基金和适应基金等机构予以输送。

此段就一句话，结构不复杂，可如果缺乏背景知识，也会译错，翻译稿就是如此。

此句有一个歧义成分，即"such as"后面的三个基金到底是谁的同位语，是"facilities"的，还是"frameworks"的？

此处仅靠词义辨析或者句子结构分析是不足以厘清的，译者应积极查询文字涉及的背景知识。经查，Global Environment Facility, Green Climate Fund 和 Adaptation Fund 均为基金，属于实体机构，也即是 facility，不是 frameworks。

批 注

① 理解有误。

补充练习

In 2020, UN-Habitat will expand partnerships in the region, particularly with donors, academia and the private sector through expert group meetings. It will also undertake capacity building workshops, awareness raising and, production of technical materials. UN-Habitat will provide technical advisory services at country level for implementation of inclusive, gender responsive land tools. Experiences and lessons from Iraq pilot project will be shared with stakeholders in the region to inform the replication in other countries. This will build harmonisation and coherence of approaches by different development actors towards addressing land challenges in the region.

参考译文

2020年，人居署将通过专家组会议扩大在该地区的伙伴关系，特别是与捐助者、学术界和私营部门的伙伴关系。它还将举办能力建设讲习班，开展提高认识活动，编写技术材料。人居署将在国家一级提供技术咨询服务以便采用具有包容性、促进性别平等的土地工具。将与该地区的利益攸关方分享伊拉克试点项目的经验教训，为在其他国家推广提供参照。这将使不同发展行为体处理该地区土地挑战问题采用协调一致的方法。

第七篇

原文

UN-Habitat's operational work comprising varied forms of technical assistance will draw on the Programme's unique and specialised technical cooperation expertise to execute human settlements programmes and projects that provide valuable tailored support to Member States in implementing policies, strategies, best practices, norms and standards.

This will build upon UN-Habitat's experience of implementing programmes and projects at local, national and regional levels that have a demonstrable impact on the lives of beneficiaries. Over the years, the programme has developed a wide range of diverse projects, largely focused on integrated programming for sustainable urbanisation, but also includes crisis response through to post-disaster and post conflict reconstruction and rehabilitation.

In its catalytic role, UN-Habitat will carry out advocacy, communication and outreach activities and mobilise public and political support, in addition to increasing its collaborative interventions at all levels, also with a view to sharing best practices. UN-Habitat will make maximum use of advocacy and knowledge platforms including the World Urban Forum (which now also serves as one of the platforms on the reporting processes of the New Urban Agenda), World Cities Day and World Habitat Day, as well as the World Cities Report. As the United Nations system-wide focal point on sustainable urbanization and human settlements, UN-Habitat will monitor and report on global conditions and trends and lead and coordinate implementation of the New Urban Agenda in the UN system, in collaboration with other UN agencies. It will rely on the use of innovative and smart solutions, as well as robust data and analysis generated through tools such the Global Urban Observatory and the City Prosperity Index to support the global monitoring of the SDGs related to urban development.

请自行翻译后查看后文的分析点评

分析点评

第 1 段

UN-Habitat's operational work comprising varied forms of technical assistance will draw on the Programme's unique and specialised technical cooperation expertise to execute human settlements programmes and projects that provide valuable tailored support to Member States in implementing policies, strategies, best practices, norms and standards.

人居署的业务工作包括各种形式的技术援助，它将利用人居署特有的、专业化的技术合作专长来执行人类住区方案和项目，在执行政策、战略、最佳做法、规范和标准方面为会员国提供有价值的量身定制的[①]支持。

人居署的业务工作包括各种形式的技术援助，它将利用人居署特有的、专业化的技术合作专长来执行人类住区方案和项目，在执行政策、战略、最佳做法、规范和标准方面为会员国提供量身定制的宝贵支持。

原文有双重结构，即定语中还有定语，总的来说，翻译稿处理得不错，只有一处可再加推敲。"valuable tailored support" 顺译为"有价值的量身定制的支持"，固然不算错误，而译为"量身定制的宝贵支持"，似乎更佳。名词前有多个形容词时，英文有英文的顺序，中文有中文的顺序，二者不一定相同，要有意识地根据中文顺序加以调整。

另外，在联合国文件中，"best practices"和"norms"通常译为"最佳做法"和"规范"。"norms"也有译为"准则"的时候，如 norms of conduct（行为准则）。这里译为"规范"，很好。

第 2 段

This will build upon UN-Habitat's experience of implementing programmes and projects at local, national and regional levels that have a demonstrable impact on the lives of beneficiaries. Over the years, the programme has developed a wide range of diverse projects, largely focused on integrated programming for sustainable

批 注

① 措辞欠佳。

urbanisation, but also includes crisis response through to post-disaster and post conflict reconstruction and rehabilitation.

批 注

① 增译过度。
② 理解有误。

这将建立在人居署在地方、国家和区域各级执行对受益者生活产生明显影响的方案和项目方面拥有丰富经验①的基础之上。多年来，人居署制定了多种不同项目，主要侧重于编制可持续城市化综合方案，但也包括通过开展灾后和冲突后重建和恢复工作来应对②危机。

这将建立在人居署在地方、国家和区域各级执行对受益者生活有明显影响的方案和项目方面取得的经验的基础之上。多年来，人居署制定了多种不同项目，主要侧重于编制可持续城市化综合方案，但也包括应对危机，直至灾后和冲突后重建与恢复。

1. 第 1 句 "This will build upon UN-Habitat's experience...beneficiaries"，原译是常规译法，没有大错，基本可用，审校通常也就不改了；只是在"经验"前面增译"丰富"二字，可以不必。

若求译文美上加美，本句也可译为"人居署在地方、国家和区域各级执行对受益者生活有明显影响的方案和项目，积累了经验，为上述吸收工作奠定了基础。"

2. 在第 2 句的"...includes crisis response through to post-disaster and post conflict reconstruction and rehabilitation"中，through 是副词，起强调作用，是"直达"的意思，若译为"includes [from] crisis response (through) to post-disaster and post conflict reconstruction and rehabilitation"就不会引起误解了，但文件起草人选择不把"from"写出来。译者把"through"错误地理解为介词，又置"to"于不顾，于是发生错误。

第 3 段

In its catalytic role, UN-Habitat will carry out advocacy, communication and outreach activities and mobilise public and political support, in addition to increasing its collaborative interventions at all levels, also with a view to sharing best practices. UN-Habitat will make maximum use of advocacy and knowledge platforms including the World Urban Forum (which now also serves as one of the platforms on the reporting processes of the New Urban Agenda), World Cities Day and World Habitat Day, as well as the World Cities Report. As the United Nations system-wide focal point on sustainable urbanization and human settlements, UN-Habitat will monitor and report on global conditions and trends and lead and coordinate implementation of the New Urban Agenda in the UN system, in collaboration with other UN agencies. It will rely on the use of innovative and smart solutions, as well as robust data and analysis generated through tools such the Global Urban Observatory and the City Prosperity Index to support the global monitoring of the SDGs related to urban development.

  人居署将起推动作用，开展宣传、沟通和外联活动，争取①公众和政治支持，在各级增加协作措施②。人居署将最大限度地利用各主要宣传和知识平台，其中包括世界城市论坛（该论坛现在也是《新城市议程》提交报告工作③的一个平台）、世界城市日和世界人居日以及《世界城市报告》。作为联合国全系统可持续城市化和人类住区问题的协调中心，人居署将与联合国其他实体协作，监测和报告全球状况和趋势，在联合国系统内主导和协调《新城市议程》的执行工作。它将依靠创新型智能解决方案以及全球城市观测站和城市繁荣指数等工具生成的强大数据和分析，来支持在全球对涉及城市发展的可持续发展目标开展监测。

批 注

① 用本义也可以。
② 省略有点过。
③ 理解偏差。

  人居署将起到推动作用，开展宣传、沟通和外联活动，调动公众和政治支持，此外也加强各级协作干预，以期分享最佳做法。人居署将最大限度地利用各宣传和知识平台，其中包括世界城市论坛（该论坛现在也是《新城市议程》报告进程的一个平台）、世界城市日和世界人居日以及《世界城市状况报告》。作为联合国全系统可持续城市化和人类住区问题的协调中心，人居署将与联合国其他机构协作，监测和报告全球状况和趋势，在联合国系统内主导和协调《新城市议程》的执行工作。它将依靠创新型智能解决方案以及全球城市观测站和城市繁荣指数等工具生成的强大数据和分析结果，来支持在全球对涉及城市发展的可持续发展目标进行监测。

点 评

  1. "advocacy"，联合国常常译为"宣传"，"Advocacy Section"译为"宣传科"。"outreach activities"译为"外联活动"。"mobilise"也可译为"调动"。

  2. "collaborative interventions"意为"协作干预"，与"协作措施"不同。

  3. "in addition to"，一般译法都放在句首，译"除……以外"；当然也可以顺译，译为"此外还"，原译省去，不好。另外，原译也漏译了"also with a view to sharing best practices"。

  4. 最后一句"It will rely on the use of innovative and smart solutions…urban development"，译者省去"the use of"不译，倒是不错，非但不影响中文的意思，反倒使中文更简洁。

  The challenge was to achieve better coordination between the recovery and rehabilitation efforts by humanitarian and development agencies in Mosul, in a way which takes into account both the immediate and long-term development priorities of the returnees in the delivery of humanitarian, development and peacebuilding initiatives.

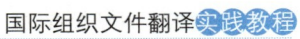

所面临的挑战是在摩苏尔人道主义和发展机构的各种恢复和重建努力之间实现更好的协调，在执行人道主义、发展及建设和平倡议方面考虑到回返者的当前和长期发展重点。

第八篇

It [UN-Habitat] collaborates closely with UNEP on Greener Cities Partnership and environmental sustainability in urban development. In this regard, within the context of its normative role, UN-Habitat will continue working closely with DESA and the Regional Economic Commissions as a knowledge platform and the first global port of call for data and knowledge on cities, towns and rural settlements in all regions and countries of the world.

Total projected revenue for 2020 amounts to US$20.8 million of which US$19.4 million is projected to come from voluntary contributions from Member States. The foundation will charge the project portfolio a programme support rate of 13% in cost recovery which is projected to receive US$1.3 million in 2020 based on programme support revenue projected at US$10.0 million.

The Committee of Permanent Representatives will convene in Nairobi twice every four years, once prior to the UN-Habitat Assembly, to prepare for that meeting and the second time, for a high-level mid-term review meeting.

分析点评

第 1 段

It [UN-Habitat] collaborates closely with UNEP on Greener Cities Partnership and environmental sustainability in urban development. In this regard, within the context of its normative role, UN-Habitat will continue working closely with DESA and the Regional Economic Commissions as a knowledge platform and the first global port of call for data and knowledge on cities, towns and rural settlements in all regions and countries of the world.

它［人居署］与环境署密切合作，发展绿色城市伙伴关系和处理城市发展过程中的环境可持续性①问题。在这方面，人居署将根据它的②规范作用，继续与联合国秘书处经济和社会事务部③及各区域委员会密切合作，起一个知识平台的作用，成为获取世界所有区域和国家的城市、城镇和农村住区数据和知识的全球首选机构④。

批 注

① 顺译增译。
② 可改进。
③ 不符合联合国翻译要求。
④ 有所欠缺。

它［人居署］与环境署密切合作，发展绿色城市伙伴关系，处理城市发展过程中的环境可持续性问题。在这方面，人居署将根据其规范作用，继续与经社部及各区域委员会密切合作，充当知识平台，成为获取世界所有区域和国家的城市、城镇和农村住区数据和知识的全球首选访问机构。

1. 第 1 句 "It collaborates closely with UNEP on Greener Cities Partnership and environmental sustainability in urban development" 译得实在可喜可贺。

按常规翻译，死跟英文结构译，译文为"它（人居署）就绿色城市伙伴关系和城市发展中的环境可持续性问题与环境署密切合作。"

或者："它（人居署）在绿色城市伙伴关系和城市发展中的环境可持续性方面与环境署密切合作。"

这样译，虽然中文也可以接受，但究竟不地道。翻译稿深入揣摩英文介词"on"的精蕴，采取顺译方法，该去掉的时候去掉，去掉"on"，该增译的时候增译，如"城市发展"后增译"过程"，"可持续性"后增译"问题"，自然而顺畅。

2. "within the context of its normative role"，译为"根据它的规范作用"，很不错；译为"根据其规范作用"，更佳。"within the context of" 字面意思是"在……背景/语境下"，其实就是"在……范围内""以……为限"，所以本句也可以译为"以发挥其规范作用为限"。

3. 第 2 句的"DESA"，译为"联合国秘书处经济和社会事务部"，意思虽然没错，却不合联合国惯例。按惯例，全称译全称，简称译简称。

United Nations Department of Economic and Social Affairs：联合国经济和社会事务部。

Department of Economic and Social Affairs：经济和社会事务部。

DESA：经社部。

英文用简称，译文也要用中文简称，英文简称没有对应中文简称的，可沿用英文简称；没有中文简称的，才可以用全称。

4. "port of call"：《朗文高级英汉双解字典》的解释是 "(*informal*) one of a series of places that you visit"，审校稿使用了其比喻义。翻译稿把"first global

port of call"译为"全球首选机构",意思不够周全;译为"全球首选访问机构",方妥当。

第 2 段

Total projected revenue for 2020 amounts to US$20.8 million of which US$19.4 million is projected to come from voluntary contributions from Member States. The foundation will charge the project portfolio a programme support rate of 13% in cost recovery which is projected to receive US$1.3 million in 2020 based on programme support revenue projected at US$10.0 million.

2020 年预计总收入为 2 080 万美元,其中 1 940 万美元预计来自会员国的自愿捐款。基金会将向项目组合收取 13% 的费用回收方案支助率①,根据预计 1 000 万美元的方案支助收入,预计 2020 年将收到 130 万美元。

2020 年预计总收入为 2 080 万美元,其中 1 940 万美元预计来自会员国的自愿捐款。基金会将向项目组合收取 13% 的方案支助费,以回收成本。按方案支助收入预计 1 000 万美元算,预计 2020 年将收到 130 万美元方案支助费。

第 2 句 "The foundation will charge the project portfolio a programme support rate of 13% in cost recovery which is projected...million."略显复杂。有 3 个专门术语:"project portfolio"项目组合,"programme support"方案支助,"cost recovery"成本回收、费用回收。

翻译稿有三处不妥。

一是"rate",虽然有时译为"率",如"exchange rate"(汇率);"interest rate"(利率),此处却是:"[C] a fixed amount of money that is charged or paid for sth 价格;费用"(《牛津高阶英汉双解词典》),所以译为"率"逻辑不通。

二是翻译稿没有透彻理解"in cost recovery"中介词"in"的意思:《韦氏大学英语词典》给出的第 4 个义项是:"used as a function word to indicate purpose",举例"said in reply";《美国传统词典》的解释更加明白易懂:"11. With the aim or purpose of",所举的例子是"followed in pursuit"。所以,"in cost recovery"意思就是"为了收回成本"。

三是理解关系代词"which"是指"programme support rate",而翻译稿却没有准确把握这一点。

只有准确理解这三点,再依中文习惯加以调整,才可译出明白通顺的中文。

第 3 段

The Committee of Permanent Representatives will convene in Nairobi twice every four years, once prior to the UN-Habitat Assembly, to prepare for that meeting and the

批 注

① 取义不准确。

second time, for a high-level mid-term review meeting.

翻译稿

常驻代表委员会将每四年在内罗毕举行①两次会议，一次在人居大会召开前举行②，以便为会议③作准备，第二次④为高级别中期审查会议⑤。

审校稿

常驻代表委员会将每四年在内罗毕召开两次会议，一次在人居大会之前，为该会议做准备，另一次为高级别中期审查会议做准备。

点评

1. "convene"，本为"召集"，或"召开"，演绎为"举行"虽然意思不错，用原意更好。

2. "召开前举行"增译太多，没有必要，有损行文简洁。

3. "that meeting"指人居大会会议，"that"不可略去不译。

4. "the second time"：英文在此以"once"对"the second time"，中文讲两次的话，则常以"一次"对"另一次"。

5. "for a high-level mid-term review meeting"之前，为了行文简洁，承前省略了"to prepare"，所以"为高级别中期审查会议"之后，宜增译"做准备"，令语意完整，且与前文对称。

批注

① 改变了原文措辞。
② 增译没有必要，且啰唆。
③ 省略不当。
④ 未注意中文习惯。
⑤ 该增译未增译。

补充练习

The Strategic and Knowledge Division (i) provides overall strategic guidance to senior management and the rest of the organization; (ii) leads strategic initiatives, including the development, implementation and monitoring of the strategic plan and flagship programmes; (iii) coordinates corporate/programme monitoring, including preparation of corporate reports on the implementation of the strategic plan; also leads mainstreaming of results-based management; (iv) provides strategic direction and manage the implementation of the UN-Habitat communications and advocacy strategy aligning all platforms including print, digital and social media to ensure greater awareness, effectiveness and clarity about UN-Habitat's role especially with regards to its mandate, the New Urban Agenda and the SDGs; (v) coordinates resource mobilization initiatives as well as development of strategic partnerships, including private sector engagement; (vi) advises the ED on innovation trends and opportunities; (vii) provides overall strategic guidance and coordination on flagship reports and global urban data; and (viii) leads the positioning of UN-Habitat as a global centre of excellence and innovation on sustainable urban solutions.

参考译文

战略和知识司①向高级管理层和本组织其他部门提供总体战略指导；②领导战略举措，包括战略计划和旗舰方案的制订、实施和监测；③协调机构/方案监测，包括编写关于战略计划执行情况的机构报告；还带头将成果管理制纳入主流；④提供战略指导并管理人居署交流和宣传战略的实施，协调所有平台，包括印刷、数字和社交媒体，确保加深认识，提高效力，更清楚人居署的作用，特别是在人居署的任务、《新城市议程》和可持续发展目标方面；⑤协调资源调动举措，协调发展战略伙伴关系，包括私营部门的参与；⑥就创新趋势和机会为执行主任出谋划策；⑦就旗舰报告和全球城市数据提供总体战略指导和协调；⑧领导人居署的定位工作，把人居署定位为可持续城市解决方案全球卓越和创新中心。

背景介绍

联合国大会2016年7月一致通过决议，将2016年至2025年定为"第三个非洲工业发展十年"，以促进非洲工业化、实现非洲大陆经济结构转型并消除极端贫困。本篇选自《第三个非洲工业发展十年》报告。

本篇探讨非洲工业、贸易、能源、环境与气候变化、信通技术等领域的发展现状，"第三个十年"主要优先事项的落实进展情况，以及与此相关的合作、资源调动、妇女和青年等的参与情况。这类文件的特点是涉及非洲多个国家、多个机构、多个领域，内容多种多样，从字里行间可以一窥非洲发展面貌。文风朴实，难度较低，有时涉及技术和贸易等领域的专业术语。翻译时需注意了解文化背景，特别是时代背景，要特别留意一些非洲国家特有的机构的译法。

第九篇

原文

In the coming decades, Africa will be the youngest and most populous continent in the world, with a working-age population expected to grow by around 70 per cent to 450 million by 2035. Policymakers acknowledge that the continent's economies require a systematic structural transformation from resource-based to more diversified economies, specifically by increasing the shares of manufacturing and agro-related industry in national investment, output and trade. Future industrial development in African countries will require a workforce that is able to take advantage of new technologies and innovations, yet currently below 25 per cent of students in Africa graduate in science, technology, engineering and mathematics. Technological innovation is vital to addressing both low structural transformation and the lack of inclusive development on the African continent.

The fourth industrial revolution is rapidly altering the traditional labour intensive path to industrialization. The slow rate of digitalization in Africa requires urgent attention. It is debatable whether Africa currently has the legal framework and enabling environment for digital trade and other activities related to digital technology to flourish in the future AfCFTA market. Only 1 per cent of all funding provided under Aid for Trade is currently allocated to information and communications technology solutions and multilateral development banks are investing a mere 1 per cent of their total spending on information and communications technology projects. It is crucial that African countries put in place policies to adapt to the digital future in order to attract production to Africa and at the same time avoid the reshoring of manufacturing tasks from Africa to other emerging economies.

请自行翻译后查看后文的分析点评

分析点评

第1段

In the coming decades, Africa will be the youngest and most populous continent in the world, with a working-age population expected to grow by around 70 per cent to 450 million by 2035. Policymakers acknowledge that the continent's economies require a systematic structural transformation from resource-based to more diversified economies, specifically by increasing the shares of manufacturing and agro-related industry in national investment, output and trade. Future industrial development in African countries will require a workforce that is able to take advantage of new technologies and innovations, yet currently below 25 per cent of students in Africa graduate in science, technology, engineering and mathematics. Technological innovation is vital to addressing both low structural transformation and the lack of inclusive development on the African continent.

在未来的几十年中，非洲将成为世界上最年轻、人口最多的大陆，到2035年，工作年龄人口预计将增长约70%，达到4.5亿。政策制定者承认，非洲大陆的经济需要从以资源为基础向更多样化的经济体发展①，特别是通过增加制造业和与农业相关的产业在国家投资、产出和贸易中的份额。非洲国家未来的工业发展将

批 注

① 漏译。

批 注

① 内容重点错误。

需要一支能够利用新技术和创新的劳动力,但目前非洲不到25%的学生毕业于科学、技术、工程和数学专业①。技术创新对于解决非洲大陆结构转型低和缺乏包容性发展至关重要。

未来几十年,非洲将成为世界上最年轻的、人口最多的大陆。预计到2035年,非洲劳动年龄人口将增长约70%,达到4.5亿人。政策制定者承认,非洲大陆各经济体需要有计划有步骤地进行结构转型,从资源型经济体转型为更具多样性的经济体,特别是通过扩大制造业和农业相关产业在国家投资、产出和贸易中的份额。未来,非洲国家要想实现工业发展,就必须具备一支能够利用新技术和创新的劳动力,然而,目前非洲科学、技术、工程和数学领域的毕业生占比尚且不足25%。技术创新对于解决非洲大陆结构转型水平低和包容性发展缺失两大挑战至关重要。

1. "working-age population"在联合国文件中经常出现,"工作年龄人口"和"劳动年龄人口"都是获得认可的译法。

2. 翻译稿漏译"a systematic structural transformation",漏译造成表达上中心词混乱的错误。此外,审校稿没有将"systematic"和"structural"处理为两个并列的形容词,而是将"systematic"转化为副词来形容"transformation"的进行过程。

3. "目标"+require+"行为"这样的搭配在联合国文件中也经常出现,除译为"需要"之外,在前后两部分内容较长或较为复杂的情况下,也可拆分成"要想……就需要/必须……"或类似形式的两个小句。

4. 显而易见,这句话的重点在于"少于25%",翻译稿沿用原文的语序,乍一看没有任何错误,然而,由于两种语言在表达习惯上的差异——英文常在句首或在主句中点明核心,而中文多在最后才敲定、推导出主旨——审校稿中将"少于25%"置于句尾,更加有力。

第2段

The fourth industrial revolution is rapidly altering the traditional labour intensive path to industrialization. The slow rate of digitalization in Africa requires urgent attention. It is debatable whether Africa currently has the legal framework and enabling environment for digital trade and other activities related to digital technology to flourish in the future AfCFTA market. Only 1 per cent of all funding provided under Aid for Trade is currently allocated to information and communications technology solutions and multilateral development banks are investing a mere 1 per cent of their total spending on information and communications technology projects. It is crucial that African countries put in place policies to adapt to the digital future in order to attract production to Africa and at the same time avoid the reshoring of manufacturing tasks from Africa to other emerging economies.

第四次工业革命正在迅速改变传统的劳动密集型工业化道路。非洲数字化速度缓慢，需要紧急关注[①]。非洲目前是否拥有法律框架和数字贸易以及与数字技术有关的其他活动的有利环境，在未来的非洲自由贸易区市场上是否繁荣尚有争议[②]。目前，在贸易援助项下提供的所有资金中，只有1%用于信息和通信技术解决方案，多边开发银行仅将其总支出的1%用于信息和通信技术项目。非洲国家制定政策以适应数字未来至关重要，以吸引生产到非洲，同时避免将制造任务从非洲转移到其他新兴经济体。

第四次工业革命正在迅速颠覆传统的劳动密集型工业化道路。而非洲数字化却进展缓慢，亟须关注。非洲目前是否已然具备数字贸易和其他数字技术相关活动在未来的非洲大陆自贸区市场中蓬勃发展所需的法律框架和有利环境，这一点尚有待商榷。目前，在"促贸援助倡议"下提供的所有资金中只有1%用于信息和通信技术解决方案，而且多边开发银行用于信息和通信技术项目的支出仅占其总支出的1%。非洲国家务必要制定适应数字化未来的政策，以便将生产引至非洲，同时避免将制造业任务从非洲转移到其他新兴经济体。

批 注

① 能否在中文里找到更加恰当的表述方式？
② 常见的并列项和修饰对象混乱问题。

点评

1. 将"alter"译为"改变"没有任何错误，但审校稿的译法更胜一筹，生动直观地强调了"改变"的程度和规模，是不拘泥于词典标准解释的灵活做法。同理，在没有具体数据出现的情况下，审校稿的优点在于将"rate"一词活译为"进展"，而没有死板地译为"速度"。

2. 翻译稿和审校稿对本段第二句的处理也有所不同，审校稿在英语原文的基础上，补充了一个连接词"而"，使其与第一句之间的衔接更加流畅，明示了第二句与第一句之间的承接关系，指出非洲在数字化方面的进展落后于全球普遍趋势。

3. 译者在翻译过程中应当有意识地积累一些中英文中可以对应的短语或搭配，例如，"require urgent..."这一搭配，在中文中就有"亟须"一词与之恰当对应，从而避免出现类似于翻译稿中"需要紧急……"这样的机械翻译。

4. 本段第三句容易出现长句翻译中并列项和修饰对象混乱的问题："legal framework"与"enabling environment"并列，用于说明其作用对象的是"for"后面并列的"digital trade"与"other activities"（related to digital technology 仅修饰 other activities），而"to flourish in the future AfCFTA market"在逻辑上的主语是"digital trade"和"other activities"。

ITC, the Department for International Development of the United Kingdom of Great Britain and Northern Ireland, the China Council for the Promotion of International Trade and the China-Africa Development Fund are partners in a project to increase investment and local development in agroprocessing and light manufacturing in Ethiopia, Kenya, Mozambique and Zambia. The Partnership for Investment and Growth in Africa is aimed at boosting manufacturing and create jobs by increasing foreign direct investment. In Ethiopia, ITC is facilitating a $2 billion investment project to set-up a paper mill and a furniture industry park using domestic bamboo supplies.

In March 2019, in Vienna, UNIDO convened the first meeting of focal points representing the key institutions involved in the implementation of the Third Decade. Participants held consultations and exchanged information on, inter alia, areas for development and implementation of joint programmes, a coordination mechanism for the effective implementation of Third Decade activities and a resource mobilization strategy. The meeting stressed the importance of the road map for the implementation of the Third Decade as a blueprint for guiding concerted international action in support of the industrialization of African countries consistent with General Assembly Resolution 70/293.

参考译文

　　国际贸易中心、大不列颠及北爱尔兰联合王国国际发展部、中国国际贸易促进委员会和中非发展基金合作实施了一个项目，助力埃塞俄比亚、肯尼亚、莫桑比克和赞比亚农业加工和轻工制造业获得更多投资，实现更好发展。"非洲投资与增长伙伴关系"旨在通过增加外国直接投资来促进制造业发展和创造就业机会。在埃塞俄比亚，国际贸易中心正在推动一个价值20亿美元的投资项目，即利用国内竹材供应建立造纸厂和家具工业园。

　　在"第三个非洲工业发展十年"的框架内，工发组织于2019年3月召集参与实施"第三个非洲工业发展十年"的主要机构的协调中心举行了第一次会议。会议在维也纳举行，旨在提供一个平台，供与会者就制定和执行联合方案、有效落实"第三个十年"活动的协调机制、资源调动战略等问题展开磋商和信息交流。会议强调了"第三个十年"实施路线图的重要性，认为这是根据大会第70/293号决议指导国家社会协调一致行动以支持非洲国家工业化的蓝图。

背景介绍

　　本篇选自灾害统计报告，编写机构是联合国统计委员会的秘书处（经济和社会事务部统计司）。联合国统计委员会是联合国经社理事会的职能委员会，是负责国际统计工作的最高决策委员会，主要工作是制定和推广国际统计标准、统计指标和统计方法，就有关统计资料的收集、分析和发布等问题提出指导意见，提高各国统计数据的可比性。该委员会的文件通常涉及就联合国各领域开展的统计工作，对此类统计的需求、今后行动等，文风朴实，表达上遵循一般性联合国文件体例，大部分简洁明快，少部分涉及专业统计词汇。翻译时需要紧扣原文，掌握统计领域的专业词汇，统筹把握全文。

第十篇

原文

The present report, which was prepared by the Statistics Division of the Department of Economic and Social Affairs of the Secretariat, in its capacity as secretariat of the Statistical Commission, in collaboration with the Economic and Social Commission for Asia and the Pacific, the Economic Commission for Europe, the Economic Commission for Latin America and the Caribbean and the United Nations Office for Disaster Risk Reduction, and in accordance with Economic and Social Council Decision 2018/227 and past practices, contains a discussion of disaster-related statistics and highlights the growing relevance and greater focus of statistics relating to both hazardous events and disasters, given the importance of the Sendai Framework for Disaster Risk Reduction 2015—2030.

The report includes a discussion of an increased focus and illustrates the need to develop a common position on this important and emerging field of statistics. It elaborates on the growing data demands and needs for disaster-related statistics, and the report takes stock of the current situation of activities around the world, with an emphasis on the constraints that developing countries face.

The report contains a summary of the work of the main international and regional organizations that are active in statistics relating to hazardous events and disasters and demonstrates that there is already considerable complementarity, coordination and cooperation taking place on this topic under the purview of the Statistical Commission. In this regard, ways to continue to build and strengthen a common statistical framework and a network of experts among the multiple disciplines and areas of expertise involved are also explored in the report. The Statistical Commission is invited to express its views on the report and discuss the way forward.

请自行翻译后查看后文的分析点评

分析点评

第1段

The present report, which was prepared by the Statistics Division of the Department of Economic and Social Affairs of the Secretariat, in its capacity as secretariat of the Statistical Commission, in collaboration with the Economic and Social Commission for Asia and the Pacific, the Economic Commission for Europe, the Economic Commission for Latin America and the Caribbean and the United Nations Office for Disaster Risk Reduction, and in accordance with Economic and Social Council Decision 2018/227 and past practices, contains a discussion of disaster-related statistics and highlights the growing relevance and greater focus of statistics relating to both hazardous events and disasters, given the importance of the Sendai Framework for Disaster Risk Reduction 2015—2030.

经济和社会事务部统计司作为统计委员会秘书处，按照经济及社会理事会第2018/227号决定和以往惯例，协同亚洲及太平洋经济社会委员会、欧洲经济委员会、拉丁美洲和加勒比经济委员会及联合国减少灾害风险办公室编写了本报告。同时①考虑到《2015—2030年仙台减少灾害风险框架》的重要性，本报告对灾害统计进行了讨论②，强调了与危险事件和灾害有关的统计数据日益重要，并且得到越来越多的关注。

批　注

① 原文无此意。
② 复杂冗余。

经济和社会事务部统计司作为统计委员会秘书处，按照经济及社会理事会第2018/227号决定和以往惯例，协同亚洲及太平洋经济社会委员会、欧洲经济委员会、拉丁美洲和加勒比经济委员会及联合国减少灾害风险办公室编写了本报告。考虑到《2015—2030年仙台减少灾害风险框架》的重要性，本报告讨论了灾害统计，并强调与危险事件和灾害有关的统计数据日益重要，并受到越来越多的关注。

点评

1. 从"which was prepared by..."到"...past practices"都是描述"the present report"的定语从句，多达76个单词。如果限定性定语从句的结构较为复杂，意义较为繁杂，通常需要在译文中间调整语序，如果仍然按照原文的语序，会显得定语过于冗长，影响语义表达。

因此，需要将较长的定语从句与先行词，按照语义逻辑单独成句，让先行词出现在新句中适当的位置。在本例中，主语是"经济和社会事务部统计司"，谓语是"编写"，先行词"本报告"根据逻辑在单独成句的新句中作为宾语出现，补充其他状语从句，即可保证译文清晰明了。

2. 联合国总部的机构的独特翻译:"department"多译为"部","division"多译为"司",但也有特例,在进行联合国文件翻译时,需要小心查证各级机构、部门的正规译法。

3. 短语"in its capacity as"经常出现在联合国文件当中,此时"capacity"的意思不是"能力",而是"职位、职责"。

4. 鉴于定语从句已经单独成句,可以在新句后使用句号,提高中文译文的明晰度,所以翻译稿中补译的"同时"逻辑不明,多此一举,可删除。

第 2 段

The report includes a discussion of an increased focus and illustrates the need to develop a common position on this important and emerging field of statistics. It elaborates on the growing data demands and needs for disaster-related statistics, and the report takes stock of the current situation of activities around the world, with an emphasis on the constraints that developing countries face.

这一新兴的统计领域十分重要,因此,本报告讨论了对这一事项越来越多的关注,并且阐明需要就此事项建立共同立场。本报告详细阐述了对灾害统计的数据需求和需要越来越多,并总结了在全球范围内所开展活动的当前状况①,其中以发展中国家面临的制约因素为重点②。

批 注

① 注意保持简洁。
② 同本页批注①。

人们日益关注新出现的这一重要统计领域,有必要就此事项建立共同立场,本报告讨论和阐明了这一点。本报告详细阐述了对灾害统计的数据需求和需要越来越多,并总结了在全球范围内所开展活动的现状,其中重点关注发展中国家面临的制约因素。

1. 第 2 段第 1 句是十分典型的根据中文的因果逻辑关系进行语序调整的译法。原句的逻辑划分如下:

	A	B	C	D
(1)	The report	includes a discussion of	an increased focus	on this important and emerging field of statistics.
(2)		illustrates	the need to develop a common position	

句中有两个谓语动词,分别是"includes"和"illustrates",语义上呈并列关系,因此全句本质上是两个主语相同的句子的并列。

第(1)句中的逻辑关系是,先出现了"this important and emerging field of statistics",然后人群中出现"an increased focus",之后本报告讨论了这种关注。

第(2)句中的逻辑关系是,先出现了"this important and emerging field of statistics",说明存在"the need to develop a common position",之后本报告阐释

了这种需求。在翻译时，为了符合中文"流水短句""前因后果"的习惯形式，必须对这三个部分的顺序进行调整，然后将可以合并的部分进行合并和简化，融合成一个句子。审校稿实际采用的顺序为：C1-D，C2-D，A-(B1+B2)。

2. 第一句中的 an increased focus 需要根据中文的习惯表达方式补译一个无特指的主语，即"人们"。

第 3 段

The report contains a summary of the work of the main international and regional organizations that are active in statistics relating to hazardous events and disasters and demonstrates that there is already considerable complementarity, coordination and cooperation taking place on this topic under the purview of the Statistical Commission. In this regard, ways to continue to build and strengthen a common statistical framework and a network of experts among the multiple disciplines and areas of expertise involved are also explored in the report. The Statistical Commission is invited to express its views on the report and discuss the way forward.

批 注

① 应追求简洁，使文本的逻辑更加清晰易懂，中文应尽量减少连接词。
② 做出补充？做出协调？做出合作？
③ 句意理解错误。

本报告总结了活跃在与危险事件和灾害有关的统计领域内①的主要国际和区域组织所开展的工作，并且表明，在委员会的职权范围内，已经就此专题做出了重要的补充、协调与合作②。在这方面，本报告还探讨了如何继续建立和强化共同的统计框架，以及为参与③其中的来自各个学科和专门知识领域的专家建立和强化专家网络。请统计委员会发表关于该报告的意见并讨论下一步行动。

本报告总结了活跃在危险事件和灾害相关统计领域的主要国际和区域组织所开展的工作，并且表明，在委员会的职权范围内，已经就这个专题做了重要补充，并开展协调与合作。在这方面，本报告还探讨了如何继续建立和强化共同的统计框架以及多种学科和专门知识领域的专家网络。请统计委员会就本报告发表意见并讨论下一步行动。

"名词 + be + taking place"的意思很明显，表示这个名词所指的动作或行为正在发生。但是在译文中，考虑到搭配问题以及中文的表达习惯，不建议直接翻译。例如，在本段中，绝不可译为"关于这一专题的补充、协调与合作正在发生"，正确的做法是，在表示动作或行为的名词之前，搭配适当的动词，以保证译文的通顺流畅。

翻译稿已经考虑到了第一层，但在选取动词时仍有欠缺，必要时不必拘泥于原文，可仅使用一个动词统领所有并列的名词，也可以进行拆分。

补充练习

At its forty-ninth session, the Statistical Commission, in its Decision 49/113, welcomed a greater focus on disaster-related statistics, given the importance of the Sendai Framework, and decided to include in the agenda for its fiftieth session a separate item on this topic, building on existing work in this emerging area. The present report contains a discussion of an increased focus on disaster-related statistics, including statistics relating to hazardous events and disasters; elaborates on the growing data demands and needs; and takes stock of the current situation of activities around the world, with an emphasis on the constraints that developing countries face. The report provides a summary of the work of the main international and regional organizations that are active in this emerging area of statistics and demonstrates that there is already considerable complementarity, coordination and cooperation taking place on this topic under the purview of the Commission. In this regard, ways to continue to build and strengthen a common statistical framework and a network of experts among the multiple disciplines and areas of expertise involved are also explored in the report. The Commission is invited to express its views on the report and discuss the way forward.

统计委员会在其第四十九届会议上，考虑到《仙台框架》的重要性，在其第49/113号决定中欢迎各方加强对灾害相关统计的关注，并且决定，根据在这一新兴领域开展的现有工作，将这一主题作为独立项目纳入第五十届会议的议程。本报告讨论了各方对灾害相关统计越来越多的关注，包括与危险事件和灾害相关的统计数据，详细阐述了日益增加的数据需求和需要，并总结了在全世界范围内所开展活动的现状，其中重点关注发展中国家面临的制约因素。本报告总结了活跃在这一新兴统计领域内的主要国际和区域组织所开展的工作，并且表明，在委员会的职权范围内，已经就此主题做出了重要补充，并就此开展协调与合作。在这方面，本报告还探讨了如何继续建立和强化共同的统计框架，以及为涉及多个学科和专门知识领域的专家网络。请统计委员会就该报告发表意见并讨论下一步行动。

背景介绍

本篇选自生物多样性和生态系统服务政府间科学—政策平台编写的《美洲生物多样性和生态系统服务区域和次区域评估的决策者摘要》，旨在从粮食、水、能源、生境多个维度如实、客观地介绍美洲生物多样性和生态系统的评估结果并提供相应解释。

生物多样性和生态系统服务政府间科学—政策平台（以下简称"平台"）由

两个进程整合形成，一是千年生态系统评估（MA）（2001—2005）后续行动，二是生物多样性科学知识国际机制（IMoSEB），目的是在生物多样性领域建立一个政府间科学机制，加强该领域的科学与政策之间的沟通和联系，促进与生物多样性有关的各项工作的协同和互补。

本篇为偏说明介绍性的文章，文风平实，结构严谨，句式以非灵主语为主，用词简单但有专业引申含义。因此，在翻译本文段落时，要注意以下几点。

（1）具有全文语境思维，注意在谈及同一主题、同一主体的问题上是否存在前后呼应的地方，理解背景信息。

（2）在切分长难句时，除要考虑语法结构之外，还要根据语境分清句子的真正主语和侧重点，充分体现句子的隐藏含义。

（3）个别词汇要结合上下文，译出其具体的语义。

第十一篇

原文

Energy security: Cultivated biofuels and hydropower has increased in all the subregions of the Americas. Nevertheless, at the local level, bioenergy production may compete with food production and natural vegetation and may have consequences for different components of biodiversity and livelihood. Increases in hydropower production alter watersheds, with consequences for aquatic biodiversity, displacement of people, and alternative uses of land that is inundated or otherwise altered and for uses of water needed by hydropower facilities.

Many aspects of quality of life are improving at regional and subregional scales. However, this comes at the cost of the majority of countries in the Americas using nature more intensively than the global average and exceeding nature's ability to renew the contributions it makes to quality of life. The 13% of the global human population residing in the Americas produces 22.8% of the global ecological footprint, with North America accounting for 63% of that proportion. Moreover, the distribution of benefits from the use of many nature's contributions to people is uneven among people and cultures in the Americas, such that nature-based securities face threats or show declines.

Human induced climate change is becoming an increasingly more important direct driver, amplifying the impacts of other drivers (i.e. habitat degradation, pollution, invasive species and overexploitation) through changes in temperature, precipitation and frequency of extreme events and other variables.

请自行翻译后查看后文的分析点评

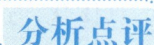 分析点评

第1段

Energy security: cultivated biofuels and hydropower has increased in all the subregions of the Americas. Nevertheless, at the local level, bioenergy production may compete with food production and natural vegetation and may have consequences for different components of biodiversity and livelihood. Increases in hydropower production alter watersheds, with consequences for aquatic biodiversity, displacement of people, and alternative uses of land that is inundated or otherwise altered and for uses of water needed by hydropower facilities.

 翻译稿

能源安全：在美洲所有次区域，开发的①生物燃料和水电能源均有所增加。然而，在地方一级，生物能源生产会与粮食生产和自然植被争夺资源，并可能对生物多样性和生计的不同方面②产生影响。水力发电的增多改变了流域形态，并对水生生物多样性，被迫迁移者的生活，以其他方式使用被淹没的或通过其他方式改变的土地或使用水电设施所需的水源产生了影响。

批 注

① "Cultivated" 为错译。
② 此处的用词不够严谨、精确。

 审校稿

能源安全：在美洲所有次区域，栽培生物制燃料和水电均有所增加。然而，在地方一级，生物能源的生产可能同粮食生产和自然植被发生竞争，并可能对生物多样性和生计的不同组成部分产生影响。水力发电的增加改变了流域，影响水生生物多样性，造成人口迁徙，改变被淹没土地的用途，或为了提供水电设施所需用水而以其他方式改变土地的用途。

 点评

1. 用词与化境问题。翻译稿在用词上存在两个问题，第一是只考虑了词汇本身意义，而没有根据文件的具体语境，即所涉及的生物多样性主题酌情进行化境。以"cultivated biofuels"为例，译文没能深入思考这个词在具体语境中的含义。"cultivated"搭配"land"等词有开发的含义，但是与生物燃料搭配应当理解为与"种植、栽培、养育"有关的含义。因此，翻译为栽培生物制燃料更贴切、更符合语境。第二个问题是选词不够准确。翻译稿中的"components"翻译为了"方面"，实际上"components"本身就是组成部分的意思，并且"方面"与"组成部分"是两个不同概念，不能等而化一，在选词时要尽可能准确、严谨。

2. 长句切分与具体化问题。在后半句话中，"with consequences for"是一个难点，翻译稿对这个结构的理解是有问题的，将"with consequences for"与 for 后面的所有内容连在一起，直译为对"水生生物多样性，被迫迁移者的生活……使用水电设施所需的水源"产生了影响，实际上在此处需要对"with consequences

for"进行灵活处理,根据搭配的不同宾语将这种"consequences"具体化,这句需要用到一个常用的翻译技巧,即词性转换。具体来说,"displacement of people",人口迁徙,那么搭配"with consequences for",就可以具体处理为"造成人口迁徙",将名词转化为动词,同理在处理"alternative uses of land"时,可以补充一个动词,译为改变了土地的用途。因此在理解和切分句子结构时,具体的语境能为我们提供另一种处理思路。

第 2 段

Many aspects of quality of life are improving at regional and subregional scales. However, this comes at the cost of the majority of countries in the Americas using nature more intensively than the global average and exceeding nature's ability to renew the contributions it makes to quality of life. The 13% of the global human population residing in the Americas produces 22.8% of the global ecological footprint, with North America accounting for 63% of that proportion. Moreover, the distribution of benefits from the use of many nature's contributions to people is uneven among people and cultures in the Americas, such that nature-based securities face threats or show declines.

在区域和次区域各级①,生活质量的许多方面都在改进。然而,这造成的代价是美洲大部分国家的自然利用程度②远重于全球平均水平,超出了自然恢复为改善生活质量所做贡献的能力。全球人口的 13% 住在美洲,产生了全球生态足迹的 22.8%,北美占这一比重的 63%。此外,在美洲,不同民族和不同文化分配到的从利用自然对人类的贡献中得到的利益是不均衡的,以至于自然提供安全保障面临威胁或呈现减少之势。

批 注

① Scales 此处翻译不准确。
② 此处不符合汉语表达。

在区域和次区域层面,生活质量的许多方面都在得到改进。然而,代价是美洲大部分国家利用自然程度远远超出全球平均水平,导致自然没有能力恢复,难以继续为改善生活质量做出贡献。全球人口的 13% 住在美洲,产生了全球生态足迹的 22.8%,其中 63% 来自北美洲。此外,美洲的不同民族和不同文化从自然所做的贡献中分享到的利益并不均衡,以致自然提供的安全保障面临威胁或呈现减少的趋势。

点 评

1. 逻辑不通顺是这一段的主要问题。一方面体现在措辞上,不符合汉语表达规范,如"using nature more intensively"译为了"自然利用程度",而正确的译法应当是"利用自然的程度",汉语多倾向于动态表达,以动词为核心,在翻译时应当注意表达贴合目的语。另一方面是表现为定语的位置问题,"the distribution of benefits from the use of many nature's contributions to people is uneven among people and cultures in the Americas",翻译稿对"from"引导的定语位置理解有误,将"distribution of benefits"与"from"后面的成分切分开,没有考虑到这两部分的修饰关系,导致译文不顺,可读性低。流畅的译文首先建立在对句子结构的正确理解和切分之上,其次要在表达上尽可能符合目的语的习惯与规范。

2. "scales"翻译得不准确。"scales"可根据语境酌情翻译为各级、方面、维度、层面,但在本段语境中,区域和次区域表示的是"面积、区域"这种横向概念,指的是"美洲这一大片区域"而不是"中央—地方"这种垂直概念,因而翻译为"层面"更准确。

第3段

Human induced climate change is becoming an increasingly more important direct driver, amplifying the impacts of other drivers (i.e. habitat degradation, pollution, invasive species and overexploitation) through changes in temperature, precipitation and frequency of extreme events and other variables.

人类引起的气候变化正在成为一种越来越重要的直接驱动因素,它通过引起气温、降水和极端气候事件的频率及其他变量的变化①扩大了②其他驱动因素的影响(例如,生境退化、污染、入侵物种和过度开发)。

人类引起的气候变化正在成为一种越来越重要的直接驱动因素,它通过改变气温、降水、发生极端事件的频率以及其他变量,放大了其他驱动因素的影响(例如,生境退化、污染、入侵物种和过度开发)。

批注

① 表达不够简洁。
② "Amplify"翻译得不够精确。

1. 对"amplify"的选词不够精确,"放大了"比"扩大了"好在对侧重点的理解更准确,"放大"是程度上的加强,"扩大"则是范围上的扩张,结合语境来说,"放大"比"扩大"更好。

2. 标点符号的运用。在遇到过长的句子时,可以酌情使用逗号,将"through"前后的两个分句拆开,显得主次有别,更清晰直观。

3. 表达简洁性。在翻译稿中"through changes in"直译为"通过引起……的变化",这样表达也不错,但关键是"changes in"后面跟的定语过长,导致译文未免有些冗长。可尝试将"changes in"变成动词形式,译为"改变气温、降水……"能加强表达的简洁性。

补充练习

Intensified, high-input agricultural production contributes to food and energy security, but has produced elevated nutrient loadings, pesticide residues and other agro-chemicals into ecosystems, threatening water security, biodiversity and health in all subregions.

Despite abundance, freshwater supplies can be locally scarce. This uneven availability, combined with inadequate distribution and waste treatment infrastructure, make water security a problem for over half the America's population, reducing access to sufficient quality, quantity and reliability of freshwater, with impacts on human health.

集约化和高产量的农业生产有助于保障粮食和能源供应，但增加了生态系统中的营养素载量、农药残留物和其他农用化学品，威胁到所有次区域的水安全、生物多样性和健康。

尽管淡水总量丰富，但局部淡水供应可能会不足。由于淡水供应不均衡，加之水分配和废水处理基础设施不足，美洲有一半以上的人口面临水安全问题，质量稳定、数量充足、安全可靠的淡水供应减少，进而影响到人类的健康。

背景介绍

本篇选自人居署住房问题报告。从格式体例上分析，报告中包括文本、框文、图表等多块内容，分成各个小专题加以论述。此类报告多为各个国家提交的材料汇编，涉及各国在人居、城市发展、地方经济、国家政策等领域的情况，因此在涉及具体区域有关住房问题的政策、国情概况时，应当适当查阅该国的法律条文、政策规章并加以理解。另外，由于研究类报告会大量引用专业学者的观点，所以在表述方面，被动句式、非灵主语句式以及插入式表达也比较多，会对我们理解文本造成干扰，因此需要尽可能找出引用学者的权威出处来源，并结合其在文中引入的位置以及原文语境的核心思想加以综合理解。

第十二篇

In general, there has been a concentration of populations of lower socioeconomic and educational levels in peripheral areas (ECLAC, 2014a). However, contradictory trends have been observed in the past decade in terms of residential segregation, particularly driven by social diversification and improved economic conditions in peripheral areas of cities. This is partly because people with higher income levels have moved to these areas in a context of population growth in peripheral areas. However, the movement of higher income groups to peripheral areas does not automatically give rise to improved social integration. In the context of closed condominiums and the privatization of services, high-income communities can live segregated within low-income areas, partly driven by the perception of insecurity and reinforced by public space privatization (Caldeira, 2000). In the Caribbean, data are not always available to analyse changes in socioeconomic residential patterns. However, in some cases a higher concentration of low incomes may be observed in central urban areas (Barbados, Draft Habitat Ⅲ National Report, 2015).

Many countries have learned from the weaknesses of the predominant models of recent decades, based on a concept of housing as a good provided by markets (the "saving, bonus and credit" model). Policies and programmes have been developed that recognize the right to the city and the social function of property and consider social housing to be a comprehensive social inclusion and protection mechanism (Bonomo and others, 2015), recognizing the impacts of access to housing for well-being, quality of life, adaptability to changing circumstances, access to economic opportunities and vulnerability to natural disasters, among others (Bouillon, 2012). Strategies begin to go beyond the production and financing of formal housing, encompassing regulations and instruments for the production of affordable land and more comprehensive solutions for public housing investments (Bonomo and others, 2015).

请自行翻译后查看后文的分析点评

分析点评

第 1 段

In general, there has been a concentration of populations of lower socioeconomic and educational levels in peripheral areas. However, contradictory trends have been observed in the past decade in terms of residential segregation, particularly driven by social diversification and improved economic conditions in peripheral areas of cities. This is partly because people with higher income levels have moved to these areas in a context of population growth in peripheral areas. However, the movement of higher income groups to peripheral areas does not automatically give rise to improved social integration. In the context of closed condominiums and the privatization of services, high-income communities can live segregated within low-income areas, partly driven by the perception of insecurity and reinforced by public space privatization. In the Caribbean, data are not always available to analyse changes in socioeconomic residential patterns. However, in some cases a higher concentration of low incomes may be observed in central urban areas.

批注

① 逻辑关系不明确。
② 理解不准确。

一般而言，城市周边地区集中的人口的经济社会和教育水平较低。然而，过去几十年，出现了一种居住分离的矛盾趋势，特别是在社会多元化以及城市周边地区经济条件有所改善的带动下。部分原因是，在这些地区出现人口增长以前，高收入群体已经搬过去了。①然而，高收入群体向周边地区移动并不能自发促进社会隔离改善。在共管公寓封闭化和服务私有化的情况下，高收入群体会与低收入群体隔开居住，部分原因在于他们有不安全感，并进一步受到公共空间私有化的影响。②加勒比并不总能提供用于分析社会经济居住模式变化的数据。不过，在一些情况下，城市中心地区会出现低收入群体高度集中的现象。

一般而言，经济社会水平和教育水平较低的人聚集在城市周边地区。然而，过去几十年，居住隔离呈现出各种相互矛盾的趋势，特别是在社会多元化以及城市周边地区经济条件有所改善的推动下。部分原因是，周边地区的人口出现增长，收入水平较高的群体搬进来。然而，高收入群体流向周边地区并不能自动增进社会融合。由于公寓是封闭式的和服务私有化，高收入群体可以在与外界隔离的情况下生活在低收入地区，部分原因是他们感到不安全，这种不安全感因公共空间私有化而加剧。加勒比并不总能提供用于分析社会经济居住模式变化的数据。不过，在一些情况下，城市中心地区会出现低收入群体高度集中的现象。

1. 对"in the context of"的理解与处理，见"This is partly because people with higher income...in a context of population growth in peripheral areas."以及"In the context of closed condominiums"。翻译稿对这两处采用了直译的方法，分别处理为"在……以前"和"在……的情况下"，单从词汇本意来看，似乎没有什么问题，但从更细微的逻辑关系上来看，似乎偏离了原文本身。"在这些地区出现人口增长以前，高收入群体已经搬过去了"体现了一种时间先后关系，即"高收入群体先搬过去，之后出现人口增长"，而实际上此处"人口增长"是"高收入人群搬入"的一种背景，没有很明显的逻辑关系，因此翻译稿相当于强加了一种逻辑关系。而对于第二处，根据"high-income communities can live segregated within low-income areas"可以判断出，"in the context"所引导的"closed condominiums and the privatization"是出现这一结果的原因，而翻译稿没有体现出这一因果关系。总结之，在处理"in the context of"时，需要在理解前后逻辑关系的基础上灵活处理，不能强化或弱化文本本身的逻辑关系。

2. 见"...insecurity and reinforced by public space privatization"一句。在翻译稿中，这句话的处理方式为"部分原因在于他们有不安全感，并进一步受到公共空间私有化的影响"，乍看似乎不影响理解，但是细究来看，"进一步受到……影响"的主语似乎不明确，既可以理解成"他们"，也可以理解成"他们的不安全感"，从而造成了歧义，并且翻译为"进一步受到……影响"与"reinforced"一词的本义"加强"也存在一定差距，既然涉及加强，那必定是原先就存在的事项，在此基础上才会"加强"，根据这一分析，可以推断出"加强"的主语是不安全感，所以审校稿采用增译的技巧，将此处翻译为"部分原因是他们感到不安全，这种不安全感因公共空间私有化而加剧"比较妥当。

第 2 段

Many countries have learned from the weaknesses of the predominant models of recent decades, based on a concept of housing as a good provided by markets (the "saving, bonus and credit" model). Policies and programmes have been developed that recognize the right to the city and the social function of property and consider social housing to be a comprehensive social inclusion and protection mechanism, recognizing the impacts of access to housing for well-being, quality of life, adaptability to changing circumstances, access to economic opportunities and vulnerability to natural disasters, among others. Strategies begin to go beyond the production and financing of formal housing, encompassing regulations and instruments for the production of affordable land and more comprehensive solutions for public housing investments.

在了解住房系市场所供商品的概念后，许多国家已经认识到近几十年来实行的主导模式（即"储蓄、补贴和信贷"模式）的缺陷。政策和方案的制定承认了城市权以及房地产的社会功能，并将社会住房视为一种综合性社会包容与保护机制，同时，还承认了获得住房对福利、生活质量、适应环境变化能力、获得经济机会以及减少易受自然灾害影响等方面的影响。在战略方面，开始突破正规住房的提供与筹资层面，囊括了提供可负担土地的规定和工具以及更全面的公共住房投资解决方案。

批 注

① 忽略了时态。

近几十年来的主要模式（即"储蓄、补贴和信贷"模式）是建立在住房是市场提供的商品这一概念上的，许多国家已经吸取了这一模式不足之处的经验教训。已经制定了政策和方案以便承认城市权利以及房地产的社会功能，将社会住房视为一种综合性的社会包容与保护机制，并承认获取住房对福利、生活质量、适应环境变化能力、获得经济机会以及易受自然灾害影响程度产生的影响。各项战略开始不局限于正规住房的建造与筹资，还包括提供可负担土地的条例和工具以及更加全面的公共住房投资解决方案。

1. 见"Policies and programmes have been developed that recognize the right to"一句。注意此处是一个现在完成时的被动语态，在翻译时要体现出这一点，译为"已经制定了政策和方案"比"政策和方案的制定"更精准。

2. 翻译技巧锤炼。见"Many countries have learned from the weaknesses..."这句，通过对比翻译稿和审校稿，可以发现它们体现了两种不同的思路。一种是顺着原文的句法结构来组织语言；另一种是跳出句法结构，按照先讲背景后评述，先摆事实再具体说明的思路来组织。从可读性和行文条理性看，处理成"近几十年来的主要模式（即'储蓄、补贴和信贷'模式）是建立在住房是市场提供的商品这一概念上的"这种译法更清楚，先对这一模式做出客观的陈述，再提出主观性的做法，这种译法可以在翻译类似文本时予以借鉴、使用。

3. 词的处理。就"Strategies begin to go beyond the production and financing of formal housing, encompassing regulations and instruments for the production of affordable land and more comprehensive solutions for public housing investments"一句中"go beyond"和"production"的译法而言，这两个词的含义比较抽象，在处理时可以不拘泥于词语本身的含义，采用反译法，将"go beyond"处理成"不局限于"，而对于"production"，可以采用化境法，将该词具体处理成与住房相关的含义，所以处理成"建造"比"提供"更贴切。

补充练习

The overlapping of rights, especially territorial rights (tenure of land and natural resources), is not a minor issue, especially in countries with high indigenous participation in small cities (Belize, Bolivia, Brazil, Ecuador, El Salvador, Guatemala, Honduras and Paraguay).

If the region is to address the structural challenge of historically low tax revenues and low investment in infrastructure, urban financing must be strengthened to ensure sustainable urban development. Urban financing is based on two main sources that will require institutional strengthening: firstly, on self-financing through higher taxing power and instruments to recover value generated by urban development; and secondly, on external sources through public-private partnerships (although contract renegotiation can pose major challenges), models based on regulated assets, private investment and international cooperation, among others. Given the high regional vulnerability, the various sources of climate finance are an additional focus and emphasize the need to strengthen capacities to generate quality projects, particularly in the most vulnerable subregions.

权利重叠，特别是领土权利（土地和自然资源保有权）的重叠是一个不可小觑的问题，特别是在土著人口高度集中在小城市的国家（伯利兹、玻利瓦尔、巴西、厄瓜多尔、萨尔多瓦、危地马拉、洪都拉斯和巴拉圭）。

该区域要想应对税收历来很少和基础设施投资少这一结构性挑战，就必须加强城市融资，以确保可持续的城市发展。城市融资依靠两个需要加强机构建设的主要来源：第一，自筹资金，通过加强征税能力和手段来回收城市发展产生的价值；第二，通过公私伙伴关系获取（尽管重新谈判合同可能是一个主要挑战）外部资金，具体模式包括管制资产、私人投资和国际合作。鉴于该区域境况非常脆弱，要另外重点关注各种来源的气候融资，强调需要加强打造优质项目的能力，尤其是在最脆弱的次区域。

背景介绍

本篇选自持久性有机污染物审查委员会《全氟辛酸、其盐类及其相关化合物风险管理评价增编草案》，其中援引了该委员会编写的《风险管理评价》的重要详细内容，供委员会第十四次会议开展知情讨论。《风险管理评价》是体例类文件，此类文件一般介绍某一化学品的方方面面，如特性、用途、优缺点、影响、管控措施、替代品等等，其特点是具有极强的专业性，经常会出现大量名称非常长的化学品，甚至有各种化学分子结构。有时句式结构很长，环环相扣，逻辑关系复杂。翻译时首先要注意此类专业术语，要熟悉、了解和掌握此类化学品名称的处理方法。其次应尽可能化长句为短句，使其深入浅出，而不致太过复杂。

第十三篇

原文

Fluorinated fire-fighting foams have been used as an effective means of fighting Class B (oil) fires, with a preference in the past for C8 technologies developed by ECF (Swedish Chemicals Agency, 2015). This included PFOS, which is now a POP under the Stockholm Convention, and PFOA, primarily used as the ammonium salt (APFO). Where human health and environmental concerns over C8 perfluorinated compounds exist, industry moved to shorter chain C6 technologies developed through telomerisation (Swedish Chemicals Agency, 2015). While C6 fluorotelomers are not manufactured using PFOA, final goods can contain PFOA as an unintentional by-product. The Swedish Chemicals Agency (2015) and Seow (2013) suggest that this is typically a trace residue but also highlight studies exist demonstrating that the quantity of C8 species (including PFOA) within C6 technologies can be present at greater concentrations, potentially up to 50:50% wt/wt and can contain PFOA precursors such as acrylamide-based fluorosurfactant (CAS No: 70969-47-0).

请自行翻译后查看后文的分析点评

分析点评

Fluorinated fire-fighting foams have been used as an effective means of fighting Class B (oil) fires, with a preference in the past for C8 technologies developed by ECF (Swedish Chemicals Agency, 2015). This included PFOS, which is now a POP under the Stockholm Convention, and PFOA, primarily used as the ammonium salt (APFO). Where human health and environmental concerns over C8 perfluorinated compounds exist, industry moved to shorter chain C6 technologies developed through telomerisation (Swedish Chemicals Agency, 2015). While C6 fluorotelomers are not manufactured using PFOA, final goods can contain PFOA as an unintentional by-product. The Swedish Chemicals Agency (2015) and Seow (2013) suggest that this is typically a trace residue but also highlight studies exist demonstrating that the quantity of C8 species (including PFOA) within C6 technologies can be present at greater concentrations, potentially up to 50:50% wt/wt and can contain PFOA precursors such as acrylamide-based fluorosurfactant (CAS No: 70969-47-0).

批 注

① 表述不准确。
② 专有名词译法错误。
③ 可读性有待提高。
④ 表述不到位。
⑤ 过于贴近原文。

氟化消防泡沫一直被用作一种应对B级（石油）火灾①的有效手段，过去偏向于使用通过电化氟化法开发的C8技术（瑞典化学品管理局，2015年）。这包括全氟辛烷磺酸，现已列为《斯德哥尔摩公约》之下的一种持续性有机污染物②，以及主要作为铵盐（全氟辛酸铵）使用的全氟辛酸。在C8全氟化合物存在人体健康和环境关切的情况下，业界转向使用通过调聚法开发的短链C6技术（瑞士化学品管理局，2015年）。尽管C6基含氟调聚物在制造时没有使用全氟辛酸③，但最终产品可能包含一种作为无意副产品④的全氟辛酸。瑞典化学品管理局（2015年）和Seow（2013年）指出，这是一种典型的痕量残余，但也强调，现有研究证明利用C6技术制造的C8类物质（包括全氟辛酸）数量⑤可能以更高浓度存在，最高有可能达到50:50%重量比，并可能包含全氟辛酸前体，例如基于丙烯酰胺的含氟表面活性剂（化学文摘社编号：70969-47-0）。

氟化消防泡沫一直被用作一种扑救B类（石油）火灾的有效手段，过去偏向于使用通过电化氟化法开发的C8技术（瑞典化学品管理局，2015）。这包括全氟辛烷磺酸，现已列为《斯德哥尔摩公约》下的一种持久性有机污染物，以及主要作为铵盐（全氟辛酸铵）使用的全氟辛酸。对于C8全氟化合物给人体健康和环境所造成影响引发的关切，业界转向使用通过调聚法开发的短链C6技术（瑞士化学品管理局，2015）。尽管在制造C6含氟调聚物的过程中没有使用全氟辛酸，但最终产品可能包含一种无意中出现的副产品——全氟辛酸。瑞典化学品管理局（2015）和Seow（2013）指出，这是一种典型的痕量残余，但也强调，现有研究证明利用C6技术制造氟化消防泡沫的过程中仍然会产生C8类物质（包括全氟辛酸）而且 C8 类物质的含量仍然较高，重量比最高可达 50∶50%，并可能包含全氟辛酸前体，例如基于丙烯酰胺的含氟表面活性剂（化学文摘社编号：70969-47-0）。

点评

1. 翻译稿将"fighting Class B (oil) fires"译作"应对 B 级（石油）火灾"，如果只读译文，这种表述似乎没有问题，但原文使用的是"fight"一词而不是"respond"或"react"，"应对"一词没有体现原意，不够准确。"fight a fire"有救火、灭火的意思，所以修改后的译文将"应对"改为"扑救"。

2. "POP"是"Persistent Organic Pollutant"的简写，属于专有词汇，译作"持久性有机污染物"，而不是"持续性有机污染物"。

3. 翻译稿将"While C6 fluorotelomers are not manufactured using PFOA"译作"尽管 C6 基含氟调聚物在制造时没有使用全氟辛酸"，不是通畅的中文，可改为"尽管在制造 C6 含氟调聚物的过程中没有使用全氟辛酸"。

4. 翻译稿将"unintentional by-product"译作"无意副产品"，完全按照英文结构对译过来，让人摸不着头脑，这种译法既不属于联合国词汇中的专有译法，意思也不明确。可以适当使用"增译"技巧，对内容进行扩展，使译文表述更到位。

5. "...the quantity of C8 species (including PFOA) within C6 technologies can be present at greater concentrations"译为"利用 C6 技术制造的 C8 类物质（包括全氟辛酸）数量可能以更高浓度存在"，但这种表述非常不符合中文表达习惯，因为"数量"无法以"浓度"形式存在。实际上，尽管原文同时出现了"quantity"和"concentration"，但这句话整体是指 C8 类物质的浓度会更高。另外，"within C6 technologies"是指用 C6 技术生产氟化消防泡沫，而"C8 species"则是这一过程中的副产品。因此，在翻译时，要避免不作甄别地完全贴合原文，而忽略原文真正的含义。只有在理解原文意思的基础上，才有可能找到最贴切的表述。

补充练习

Military.com (2017) (quoted within IPEN, 2018) provides details of discussions held in the US senate regarding around 400 military facilities where PFOS and PFOA based fire-fighting foams had been previously used and lost to the environment causing ground contamination such as that Fairchild Air Force base. Total estimated remediation costs for ground contamination are cited within the article as being as high as USD$2 billion dollars.

Klein (2013) provides examples of a number of cases of groundwater contamination at facilities (military, airports and petroleum refineries) where perfluoroalkyl-containing (chiefly PFOS) fire-fighting foams have been used for training or real cases of fire. In particularly Klein refers to a case study at US military fire training grounds where PFOS had been previously used, and even 10–15 years after the use had ceased monitoring found that groundwater would still contain high concentrations of fluorotelomer (14.6mg/L fluorotelomer sulfonate). Another case study at Jersey Airport, Jersey Island, report that the use of PFOS-based AFFF on fire training grounds contaminated the island's aquifer and drinking water.

Military.com（2017）（引自消除持久性有机污染物联盟，2018）提供了在美国参议院开展讨论的详情，讨论的内容是在约 400 处军事设施中，先前使用过并向环境排放了基于全氟辛烷磺酸和全氟辛酸的消防泡沫，从而造成地面污染的情况（例如费尔柴尔德空军基地）。根据文内引用的资料，地面污染恢复总成本估计高达 20 亿美元。

Klein（2013）提供的实例表明，在各种设施（军事设施、机场和炼油厂）使用含有全氟烷基（主要是全氟辛烷磺酸）的消防泡沫进行消防训练或应对实发火灾后，地下水受到了污染，这种情况已出现若干起。Klein 特别提到了在先前使用过全氟辛烷磺酸的美国军事消防训练场开展的一项案例研究，在训练场停用全氟辛烷磺酸 10 至 15 年后进行监测，竟仍发现地下水含有高浓度的含氟调聚物（氟调聚磺酸盐 14.6mg/L）。另一项在泽西岛的泽西机场开展的案例研究报告称，在消防训练场使用含全氟辛烷磺酸的水成膜泡沫对该岛的含水层和饮用水造成了污染。

本章词汇

actionable 可行的
adaptation 适应
Addis Ababa Action Agenda of the Third International Conference on Financing for Development 第三次发展筹资问题国际会议亚的斯亚贝巴行动议程
agency support costs 项目资助费用
alternative technology 替代技术
alternatives to be phased in 采用替代品
among others 除其他外、等、等等
Article 5 country 第 5 条国家
best practices 最佳做法
biodiversity 生物多样性
blowing agent 发泡剂
"bottom up" survey "自下而上"式调查
by-product 副产品
carbon emission 碳排放
certification system 资格认定制度
co-financing 共同出资
controlled substances 受控物质
conversion/convert 转型；技术转换；改造
cost recovery 成本回收、费用回收
cost-effectiveness threshold 成本效益阈值
counterpart funding 配套资金
decent work 体面工作
desk study 案头研究
displacement 流离失所
dissemination 传播
documentation 文件，文献，单据
domestic refrigeration 家用制冷
door-to-door survey 入户调查
ecological footprint 生态足迹
economies in transition 转型期经济体
enabling environment 有利环境
epicentre 震中、中心
Executive Board 执行局、执行委员会、执行董事会
expertise 专长、专门知识

first/second/third...tranche 第一/二/三……次付款
flagship reports 旗舰报告
forced migration 被迫移民、强迫迁移
freeze 冻结
fund disbursement 资金发放
Global Environment Facility 全球环境基金
Harmonized System of Customs Codes 海关编号协调制度
HCFC phase-out management plan preparation activities 氟氯烃淘汰管理计划编制活动
HCFC phase-out management plan 氟氯烃淘汰管理计划
HCFC consuming manufacturing sector 使用氟氯烃的制造行业
incremental operating costs 增支经营成本
informal settlement 非正规居住地、非正规住区、非正式安置点（难民安置）
input 投入
institutional strengthening 体制强化，机构建设
International Organization for Migration 国际移民组织
invasive species 入侵物种
land tenure 土地保有权、土地保有制度
lead implementing agency 牵头执行机构
leverage 充分利用
licensing and quota system for HCFC imports and exports 氟氯烃进出口许可证和配额制度
list of banned substances 禁用物质清单
localisation 本地化
low-global warming potential (GWP) refrigerants 低全球升温潜能值制冷剂
low-GWP alternative 低全球升温潜能值制冷剂替代品
low-volume consuming (LVC) and non-LVC country 低消费量和非低消费量国家
marginalised groups 边缘群体
mobile air-conditioner 移动空调

national ozone unit　国家臭氧机构
New Urban Agenda　新城市议程
non-refillable cylinder　非可重复充灌气缸
ODP（Ozone Depletion Potential）　消耗臭氧潜能值
ODS alternatives　消耗臭氧层物质替代品
ODS　消耗臭氧层物质
ODS-based equipment　使用消耗臭氧层物质的设备
ozone protection　臭氧保护
Permanent Representative　常驻代表
phase-down　逐步减少
progress report　进度报告
project evaluation sheet　项目评价表
project proposal　项目提案
quadrennial report　四年期报告
recovery and reclamation project　回收和再生项目
refrigerant　制冷剂
refrigeration and air-conditioning (RAC)　制冷和空调
rehabilitation　康复、恢复
replacement technology　替代技术
residential air-conditioning　住宅空调
retrofit　改型
rules of procedure　议事规则
sales tax　销售税
Senior Monitoring and Evaluation Officer　高级监测和评价干事
servicing sector　维修行业
social exclusion　社会排斥
stakeholder　利益攸关方
stand-alone commercial refrigeration　独立商业制冷
starting point with annual reduction target　年度削减目标起始点
subprogramme　次级方案
subsidized loan　贴息贷款
Sustainable Development Goals　可持续发展目标
systems houses　配方厂家
terms of reference　职权范围，工作范围
"top down" survey　"自上而下"式调查
top-up　充灌
tranche implementation plan　付款执行计划
United Nations Habitat and Human Settlements Foundation　联合国生境和人类住区基金会
urbanisation　城市化
valid permit　有效许可证
verification report　核查报告
voluntary contributions　自愿捐款
workshop　讲习班
World Urban Forum　世界城市论坛

第六章

人文与社会

本章导言

文化多样性已经成为全世界认可的价值取向，作为这种价值取向的主要推手，以联合国教育、科学及文化组织（教科文组织）为代表的联合国各机构一直在国际舞台上宣传、倡导、促进文化多样性，紧紧围绕文化人权、文化自觉、文化保护、文化制度建设等议题，深入扎根于各国国情及各社区、各群体、各阶层背景，在相关公约机制下落实了诸多举措，为文化这种无形存在赋予了各种有形载体。因此，人文与社会类文本作为一种独特的官方叙事文本，有诸多值得深入领会和挖掘的"宝藏"资源，不仅在翻译技巧、体例规范等层面值得我们借鉴，更有助于初学者积累文化常识，培养文体敏感度，拓宽翻译思路。

联合国人文社科类文件是人文社科类文件的一个特殊类别，一方面，具有此类文件的普遍特点（内容包罗万象，涉及文史哲、艺术、社会心理、语言媒体、教育生活等多个领域；风格多样多元、表达自由灵活、颇有形散神聚特色，需注意"意合"与"形合"的区别；依托社会、文化语境，有广阔的语义场，同时语篇内逻辑性较强，译者需熟悉文本主题及其所涉各方面背景）。另一方面，它们又是联合国的官方文件，语言风格、行文体例方面又有其独到之处。与其他市场主体或个人创作的人文类文本不同的是，联合国人文类文件由活跃在文化领域的国际组织或机构撰写，例如教科文组织，其语言逻辑建立在国际治理思维的基础上，将文化及其"周边"活动置于全球及地方社会背景下予以解读和研究，那么在处理这类文件时，要求译者具有文化决策意识，站在治理者的角度去思考行文逻辑；另一方面，此类文件的措辞具有强烈的官方色彩，具有规整的行文体例，即使是文学色彩较强的非会议类稿件，首要的要求依然是忠实于原文的风格和内容，虽然可以拥有适度的灵活与自由，但不能以辞害意，译文应当逻辑严谨，朴实流畅。

国际组织在教育、科学和文化领域的职责通常涉及以下方面。

（1）开展前瞻性研究：研究明天的世界需要什么样的教育、科学、文化和传播。

（2）发展、传播和交流知识：开展研究、培训和教学。

（3）制定准则：起草和通过国际文件和法律建议。

（4）提供知识和技术：以"技术合作"的形式为会员国（或成员国）提供制定发展政策和发展计划所需的知识和技术。

（5）交流专门化信息。

按照上述职能，国际组织的相关文件大概可分为三类。

第一类，正式的报告文件，包括但不限于根据各公约撰写的监测报告、综述报告、调研报告（见本章第四篇和第五篇）。此类文件最为正式，应特别注意译名规范及专业术语查询问题，并且此类文件对治理思维逻辑的要求最高。

第二类，杂志风格的出版物，例如联合国教科文组织的《信使》（*Courier*）（见本章第七篇至第十篇）。此类文件最为灵活，涵盖领域、主题最为广泛，特别是涉及年度新兴、热点文化事件，一般以专辑形式呈现。对于这类文件，除具备社科类稿件的通用技能外，在查询背景资料时，应尽可能以联合国官方网站（包括新闻网站、教科文组织官网以及公约网站）为准，在措辞上不要过于拘泥于字面表述，应考虑字面背后的理念和思想，并结合杂志体的语言特色，带着"文化自觉和文化多样性意识"处理原文。

第三类，文件介于两者之间，包括研究报告（本章第六篇）、非政府组织向经社理事会提交的工作报告（本章第一篇至第三篇）等，前者是介于报告与叙述之间的文体，要求译者在掌握报告规范的基础上融入叙事视角，后者则有固定的行文体例，相应地有较固定的中文表达。这两类文本都映射了广泛的社会文化背景，后者还会呈现明显的地方文化背景，译者在翻译过程中，需要多方查证，追本溯源。

本章所选十一篇文章，涵盖了上述各类文件，旨在为大家系统了解联合国人文社科类文件翻译提供较为全面的视角。

评价联合国人文社科文件翻译的质量时，通常遵循以下标准。

（1）严谨、准确地传达原文信息，避免带入个人主观视角，确保政治上的严谨。

（2）表达流畅、语言简练，可读性强，给读者以"易读、享读、想读"的体验。

（3）原文中遣词造句的精妙之处应尽量予以体现，具有与原文相对应的文采。

（4）对于新闻体风格的文本，例如《信使》，应体现"新闻体"的风格。

为达到上述标准，应重点掌握如下语言技巧。

1. 在术语规范上

在术语规范上，要注意专门机构（非政府组织）的名称，如第一篇第1段中的"Triglav Circle"，需首选参考最具权威性的来源，如联合国词汇库UNTERM，其次可参考该组织或其所在国政府的官方网站，慎用非官方信息源；另外还要注意专门机构对词汇的特殊要求，如在大多数联合国文件中，"programme"翻译为"方案"，但在教科文组织的文件中，则通常翻译为"计划"。再如，"bi-annual"一词在除教科文组织以外的联合国机构中一般译为"两年期"，但教科文组织的固定译法为"双年度"。词汇严谨是联合国所有类别文件翻译的基础，内容相对活泼灵动的社科类文件也不例外，在不能判断出词汇对于特定组织是否有特殊词义和用法的情况下，务必首先诉诸联合国系统的词汇库、官网资源、作准文件。

2. 在翻译技巧上

在翻译技巧上，相比其他类别的文件，社科类文件中的句间逻辑关系较为"跳脱"，翻译时不一定以词、段或整句为单位进行处理，通常需要运用以下翻译技巧。

（1）在词汇层面

① 化抽象为具体，如第十一篇第2段中"related to"一词，在文章所选例文中，不仅限于"有关""关于""就……"，根据文本特色及语境，可灵活处理为"匹配"，更有助于读者理解；再如第三篇第2段中"input"一词，如直译为"投入"，则与语境相脱离，应本着化境的理念，将该词内涵具体化。

② 常见词变通处理，如第二篇第 2 段中"outreach"一词，在联合国正式文件中，以"外联"含义出现频率较多，但也可在这层含义之上引申为"拓展"；再如第十一篇第 1 段中"episode"一词，如仅从字面意思考虑，不结合文章主题"游戏"这一背景，则导致表达缺乏"代入感"。

③ 词性转换，如第二篇第 3 段中"be integral to"译为"成为"，处理成动词形态后，使得语言精练度有一定提升。

（2）在句法层面

① 长句简化为短句，如第四篇第 1 段中"there are two major developments that provide a new context for..."，如遵守原文句法，则会产生长句，不符合汉语表达习惯，不妨采用汉语结构"一是，二是"，简化为短句；再如第七篇第 1 段中"Spanish galleons made the crossing from Manila—their holds filled with porcelain, spices..."一句，对于这种结构复杂、插入成分较多的长句，可将"长句拆短"作为思考的切入点。

② 厘清句子重心和论述重点，如第一篇第 2 段中"while"引导的句子，要根据语境理清前后主次、调整重点，勿受原文语法前后顺序的束缚。

③ 增译，将原文中隐藏的逻辑关系译出，如第一篇第 3 段中"a notion of harmony synonymous with wisdom and happiness in integrated societies"一句，通过增译动词"提出"，可使原本模糊的逻辑关系"现身"，也增加了可读性；再如，第十篇第 1 段中对"radio"一词内涵的增补，更能贴合整篇文章的主题，起到画龙点睛的作用。

④ 调整语序，断句切分，如第十篇第 2 段中"Proclaimed in 2011, the Day reminds us of the crucial..."，通过调整语序，有助于凸显句间逻辑关系，使整句话显得主从层次分明、重点突出；以及第十一篇第 3 段中"a group of students aged 14 to 16 was involved in a three-day workshop that foresaw both theoretical and practical activities to reflect on the specific topic"一句，重点要掌握句子在何处进行拆分，选择不同拆分点会影响对原文的理解以及表达的流畅性。

⑤ 表达简洁性，见第八篇第 1 段中"...the temple's inner sanctuary..."一句，无须重复已有的含义，在形式上简洁更有助于提升表达层次感；再如第一篇第 1 段中"convened in Copenhagen in March 1995..."一句，对于插入成分，如处理成定语则会导致句子过长、重点不突出，不妨以加括号形式提高表达的简洁性。

⑥ 表达书面化，如"He for She Campaign"一词，原文表达过于简洁直白，出于文体考虑，应进行书面化加工，处理成符合组织、官方文件特色的译名。

3. 在译文风格上

（1）在直译与意译之间寻找平衡，突出画面感，如第四篇第 2 段中"presents a summary of activities..."一句，原文本身就使用了具有修辞特色的句子，要凸显出这种特色，就不可过于死板。

（2）转换视角，如第十篇第 2 段中"Organization has relied on this key medium to help"一句，应体会选择不同主语作为句子起点对语意传达、重心表述的影响，以及影响的深度。

（3）在翻译与编译之间寻找平衡，如第七篇第 3 段中"the Concepción broke up on the reefs of..."一句，翻译稿的处理已超出了"风格"的范畴，加入了过多个人理解，这种"加戏"行为不符合上文所述的风格体色彩。我们所说的风格，一定是在理解原文基础上，将原文的风格，如新闻传记特色、故事特色，以精妙的语言组织方式显现出来，而非过多体现译者自身的文风。

联合国人文社科类文件是一类特色鲜明的官方文件，对译者文字功底有很高要求。译者既要遵循既定规范，又须酌情跳出条框；既要严格把握词汇、句段、语篇的特点，又要能在一定程度上跳出原文的束缚，寻求最合乎作者意图的"对等"。译者要掌握好灵活度，培养对文化意识、国际组织专有词汇的敏感度，带着"全球文化观"的思维去领悟文字的灵魂。

背景介绍

以下三篇材料均为经济及社会理事会非政府组织委员会的报告。非政府组织委员会是经社理事会下属的常设委员会，是联合国系统内唯一负责审议非政府组织申请经社理事会咨商地位、讨论制定非政府组织行为规范等问题的机构。根据理事会第1996/31号决议，具有咨商地位（包括一般和特别咨商地位）的非政府组织每四年应经秘书长要求，向非政府组织委员会提出简要工作报告，具体说明该组织对联合国工作的支助情况，文件名通常为"新收到的非政府组织所提经济及社会理事会咨商地位申请书"，通常分为7个部分："①咨商地位（一般或者特别咨商地位）；②简介（位置、性质、分支机构及工作人员情况）；③目标和宗旨；④重大变化；⑤对联合国工作的贡献；⑥参加联合国会议的情况；⑦与联合国各机构的合作以及为支持千年发展目标所采取的举措"。在翻译时，不可擅自调换顺序。

提交此类文件的非政府组织来自不同国家，涉及多个国家的不同社会文化背景，因此译者应广泛查阅各种背景资料，包括所涉组织官方网站、国家背景概括，综合处理信息；此外，这些组织的编写人也并非均以英语为母语，导致此类文件的语法可能有错漏之处，其句子表述较为零散，甚至有可能逻辑关系模糊不明晰，译者应注意将不符合语法规范、零散的分句组合成前后连贯、有条理的译文。具体详见篇章中的详细分析。

The Triglav Circle was created in preparation for the United Nations World Summit for Social Development, convened in Copenhagen in March 1995.

The Circle strives for more humane progress while preserving the noble and diversified heritage of humanity and the integrity of the natural environment. It seeks to define and promote the common good of humankind through reflection, research and dialogue. It shares these goals with the United Nations. It carries out its work through seminars, research and collaboration with national and international institutions. Its members are from different parts of the world and different walks of life.

The Triglav Circle participated regularly in the annual meetings of the Commission for Social Development in New York. On 2 February 2012, at the fiftieth session of the Commission, the Cricle made a statement on the theme of eradication of poverty, emphasizing the critical need to examine wealth and ethics in the world economy. On 2 February 2011, at the forty-ninth session of the Commission, the Circle made a statement on the indivisibility of humanity, of community, of the person and of human rights for a good society. On 5 February 2010, at the forty-eighth session of the Commission, the Circle made a statement on policies for social integration and declared that love as conceived by Locke should be fundamental for regulating human society. On 5 February 2009, at the forty-seventh session of the Commission, the Circle made a statement on experiences in social integration, a notion of harmony synonymous with wisdom and happiness in integrated societies.

请自行翻译后查看后文的分析点评

分析点评

第 1 段

The Triglav Circle was created in preparation for the United Nations World Summit for Social Development, convened in Copenhagen in March 1995.

创建特里格拉夫之圈^①是为 1995 年 3 月在哥本哈根举行的联合国社会发展问题世界首脑会议作准备。

特里格拉夫组织系于联合国社会发展问题世界首脑会议（1995 年 3 月，哥本哈根）筹备期间创建，旨在为会议的召开作准备。

（1）非政府组织名称的翻译问题，见"Triglav Circle"一词。经社理事会有关 NGO 的文件，无论是咨商地位申请，还是书面陈述，抑或是四年期报告，都普遍涉及 NGO 名称的翻译问题。一般的处理流程是，① 查联合国多语言专业术语数据库（UNTERM）以及待译文件随附的参考文件（以 UNTERM 为准），② 如查无结果，再通过互联网参鉴或直接采用历史文件或联合国官网、外交部等政府机构的网站、人民日报或新华社等权威来源的译法，③ 若第 ② 步仍查无结果，再结合文件所载内容以及网上所载的其他背景信息，按照组织名全称进行翻译。对于"Triglav Circle"，经查联合国词汇库 UNTERM，发现该词已有商定译法"特里格拉夫组织"，译者切勿自行翻译。

（2）译文句子结构拘泥于原文，见"was created in preparation for..."，译文理解和表述正确，但称不上"好"。在介绍一个组织时，中文中往往会采用"本 / 该组织于 ××（时间）在 ××（地点）创建，致力于 / 旨在……"的句式。因此，译

批　注

① 名称错译。

者在吃透原文意思后，可进行调整，呈现高质量的译文。此外，对于"convened in Copenhagen in March 1995"一句的处理，审校稿借用括号的形式，较之翻译稿，简洁性和可读性均有提升。

第 2 段

The Circle strives for more humane progress while preserving the noble and diversified heritage of humanity and the integrity of the natural environment. It seeks to define and promote the common good of humankind through reflection, research and dialogue. It shares these goals with the United Nations. It carries out its work through seminars, research and collaboration with national and international institutions. Its members are from different parts of the world and different walks of life.

该组织①追求更仁慈的发展②，同时保护人类宝贵的多样化财产，维护自然环境的完整性。它③寻求通过反思、研究和对话确定并推动人类的共同利益，并与联合国共同实现这些目标④。它与国家和国际机构一道，通过研讨会、研究和合作开展工作。其成员来自世界各地和各行各业。

批 注
① 人称不对。
② 搭配不当，用词欠妥。
③ 是指谁？应具体化。
④ 错译。

本组织在努力保护宝贵而多样化的人类遗产、维护自然环境完整性的同时，力求实现更具人性化的进步。本组织寻求通过反思、研究和对话来确定并推动人类的共同利益，这些目标与联合国一脉相承。本组织通过与国内和国际机构一道举办研讨会、开展研究和共同合作的方式开展工作。当前，本组织的成员遍及世界各地，遍布各行各业。

1. NGO 的译名规范问题，见 "The Circle"。译者处理为"该组织"，但正确的做法是译为"本组织"，因为按照规定，此类报告由各 NGO 自身撰写，通过秘书长向理事会及其附属机构分发，所以应使用第一人称。相关详细信息，请查阅经社理事会第 1996/31 号决议第五编第 36、37 段。

2. 译文句子重心偏移，见 "while"。这是一个极为常见的连词，其意为 "during/at the time when sth else is happening"，英语句式 "A while B" 所强调的重点在于 "while" 前面的事件 A 上，因此在汉语中要转换为"在 B 的同时，（做/进行）A"，以体现原文的重心所在。

3. 见两处 "It" 以及 "Its members"，首先，避免用"它"，而是应根据上下文确定其逻辑主语，另外"其成员"为第三人称，结合本段点评 1，应统一具体化为"本组织"。

4. 错译问题，见 "shares these goals with the United Nations"，在此，"share" 应取 "have the same feelings, ideas, experiences, etc. as sb else" 之意，如理解成 "to

do something together with..."则会导致原文本意偏离,即"作为联合国的合作伙伴,共同实现目标",也会导致论述重点出现偏离,因为此处强调的是该NGO的目标与联合国宗旨的一致性,因此译为"共同实现目标"并不妥当。

第3段

The Triglav Circle participated regularly in the annual meetings of the Commission for Social Development in New York. On 2 February 2012, at the fiftieth session of the Commission, the Cricle made a statement on the theme of eradication of poverty, emphasizing the critical need to examine wealth and ethics in the world economy. On 2 February 2011, at the forty-ninth session of the Commission, the Circle made a statement on the indivisibility of humanity, of community, of the person and of human rights for a good society. On 5 February 2010, at the forty-eighth session of the Commission, the Circle made a statement on policies for social integration and declared that love as conceived by Locke should be fundamental for regulating human society. On 5 February 2009, at the forty-seventh session of the Commission, the Circle made a statement on experiences in social integration, a notion of harmony synonymous with wisdom and happiness in integrated societies.

特里格拉夫之圈定期出席在纽约举行的社会发展委员会年度会议。在2012年2月2日举行的委员会第五十届会议上①,该组织做了有关消除贫穷主题的声明②,强调了审视世界经济的财富和道德的迫切需要。在委员会2011年2月2日举行的第四十九届会议上,该组织做了关于一个良好社会中人类、社区、个人和人权的不可分割性的声明。在委员会2010年2月5日举行的第四十八届会议上,该组织做了关于实现社会融合的相关政策的声明,并宣称正如洛克所秉持的观点:爱应该成为调节人类社会的根本手段。在委员会2009年2月5日举行的第四十七届会议上,该组织做了关于社会融合方面经验的声明,和谐观就是指融合社会的智慧与幸福③。

批 注

① 时间混淆,后三句存在相同错误。
② 错译。
③ 突兀,与前一句是何关系?

特里格拉夫组织定期出席在纽约举行的社会发展委员会年度会议。2012年2月2日,本组织在该委员会第五十届会议上,作了主题为消除贫穷的陈述,强调了审视世界经济中的财富和道德的迫切必要性。2011年2月2日,本组织在该委员会第四十九届会议上,就人类、社区、个人和人权之于良好社会的不可分割性作了陈述。2010年2月5日,本组织在该委员会第四十八届会议上,就促进社会融合的政策作了陈述,并宣称,应该以洛克提出的"爱"之论为基础,去规范人类社会。2009年2月5日,本组织在该委员会第四十七届会议上,就社会融合方面的经验作了陈述,提出社会融合是一种和谐观,是共融社会中智慧和幸福的代名词。

点评

1. 背景知识问题。第一，见"On 2 February 2012, at the fiftieth session of the Commission, the Cricle made a statement on"一句，译者混淆了社会发展委员会年度会议的时间与 NGO 的陈述时间。社会发展委员会年度会议一般于每年 2 月份在纽约举行，会期较长，持续数天，译者如能事先了解这一背景知识，就可以免去此误。第二，在本段中出现四次的"made a statement on"一词，在涉及经社理事会的文件中，"statement"不译为"发言"或"声明"，而当译为"陈述"，这与经社理事会的职能有关。根据理事会第 1996/31 号决议，具有咨商地位（包括一般和特别咨商地位）的非政府组织可指派授权代表以观察员身份列席理事会及其附属机构的公开会议，经批准，还可在会上作口头陈述。鉴于该背景知识，"statement"应当理解为"陈述"，更多相关信息，见经社理事会第 1996/31 号决议第四编第 29 和 32 段。

2. 增译逻辑关系。见"a notion of harmony synonymous with wisdom and happiness in integrated societies"一句。结合前文，可判断此句为 NGO 陈述中提出的观点，但从翻译稿中难以看出此句译文与前文之间的这种逻辑关系，因此审校稿中增译"提出"二字，明确了这种逻辑关系。

补充练习

1. The Network of Non-Governmental Organizations of Trinidad and Tobago for the Advancement of Women is a comprehensive national "umbrella" organization. The Network is committed to the aims of the Convention on the Elimination of all Forms of Discrimination against Women. Therefore, the Network supports and acts as the advocate for all women's organizations in the country. The Network builds on sharing and inclusivity.

参考译文

特立尼达和多巴哥提高妇女地位非政府组织网络是一家综合性的国家"伞式"组织。本网络致力于实现《消除对妇女一切形式歧视公约》的各项目标。因此，本网络为国内所有妇女组织提供支持并为之谋利益。本网络以共享和包容为立足点。

2. The Network successfully works towards ensuring gender equality, promotes women's human rights and promotes women's empowerment nationally, regionally and globally. While maintaining the highest ethical and professional standards, its mission is to provide effective representation and advocacy and to promote and enhance the quality of life for women and girls in Trinidad and Tobago.

本网络在国内、区域和全球三级努力确保性别平等，促进妇女人权，增强妇女权能，工作卓有成效。本网络在维持最高道德和职业标准的同时，还肩负着在特立尼达和多巴哥做出有力表态、大力宣传以及促进和提高妇女和女童生活质量的使命。

3. As of September 2011, the Network has been granted an annual subvention to cover 60 per cent of its recurrent expenditure by the Government of Trinidad and Tobago. This has allowed the Network of NGOs to have two full-time and one part-time staff members; previously, the Network functioned entirely with volunteers and part-time workers.

截至 2011 年 9 月，特立尼达和多巴哥政府每年都向本网络提供拨款，让本网络 60% 的经常性支出有了着落。得益于此，本网络现已成功招募到两名全职和一名兼职工作人员；在此之前，本网络的运作完全依靠志愿者和兼职人员。

We believe, as stated on the Beijing Declaration and Platform for Action, the creation of an educational and social environment, in which women and men, girls and boys, are treated equally and encouraged to achieve their full potential, respecting their freedom of thought, conscience, religion and belief, and where educational resources promote non-stereotypical images of women and men, would be effective in the elimination of the causes of discrimination against women and inequalities between women and men.

Women also have the right to the enjoyment of the highest attainable standard of physical and mental health. The enjoyment of this right is vital to their well-being and their ability to participate in all areas of public and private life. We believe in focusing on addressing risky behaviour in girls and boys through healthy lifestyle promotion to take care of women and their physical and mental health. Our healthy Lifestyle Promotion program helps girls and women to make wise decisions. The program incorporates life skill training, life counselling, training of trainers, peer-to-peer outreach (ripple program), and mass campaign.

Today's girl children are tomorrow's women. This generation of leaders must accept and promote a world in which every child is free from injustice, oppression and inequality and free to develop her own potential. The principle of holistic youth development program must therefore be integral to the process.

请自行翻译后查看后文的分析点评

分析点评

第1段

We believe, as stated on the Beijing Declaration and Platform for Action, the creation of an educational and social environment, in which women and men, girls and boys, are treated equally and encouraged to achieve their full potential, respecting their freedom of thought, conscience, religion and belief, and where educational resources promote non-stereotypical images of women and men, would be effective in the elimination of the causes of discrimination against women and inequalities between women and men.

翻译稿

我们相信，正如《北京宣言》和《行动纲要》所述，创造一种教育和社会环境，其中使① 妇女和男子、女孩和男孩受到平等待遇② 并鼓励他们发挥充分潜力，尊重他们思想、意识、宗教和信仰的自由，并在这种环境下，使教育资源用于促进男女非陈规定型的形象，这将可有效消除对妇女歧视③ 和男女不平等的根源。

批 注

① 注意逻辑关系处理。
② 注意搭配。
③ 适当加词。

审校稿

我们相信，正如《北京宣言》和《行动纲要》所指出的，创造一种教育和社会环境——在这种环境中，妇女和男子、女孩和男孩获得平等待遇，受到鼓励充分发挥各自的潜力，思想、意识、宗教和信仰自由亦得到尊重；将教育资源用于宣传非陈规定型的男女形象，从而有效消除导致歧视妇女和男女不平等现象的根源。

点评

1. 逻辑关系处理。此段文字简明扼要，一目了然，讲的是《北京宣言》和《行动纲要》要求创造一种环境，在这种环境中期冀形成蓝图和景象。显而易见，前面的"in which"和后面的"where"都是用来修饰"environment"，所以在处理的时候直接合并即可。原译从理解上并无太大问题，只是前者"使……"，后面"并在这种环境下"，显得不够紧凑。故而可以适当作变通处理。

2. 搭配问题。此段文字中讲的是这种环境中期待的景象，上下转承要顺其自然，符合汉语表达习惯。"in which women and men, girls and boys, are treated equally"一句中原译文处理为"其中使妇女和男子、女孩和男孩受到平等待遇"，在表达上稍微欠妥。汉语中，"待遇"通常搭配的是"得到""获得"等，而不是"受到"，虽然于大意上无错，但稍显别扭，而调整一下语序和搭配，译文则显得更为地道。

3. 适当增减词。适当地添加词是常用的翻译技巧。本段内容涉及增词译法，在原文的基础上添加必要的单词、词组、分句或完整句，使译文在语法、语言形式上符合目的语习惯并在文化背景、词语联想方面与原文保持一致，在内容、形式和精神三方面实现译文与原文的对等。原文中"would be effective in the elimination of the causes of discrimination against women and inequalities between women and men"一句，翻译稿中译为"这将可有效消除对妇女歧视和男女不平等的根源"，此处"消除"搭配的是"对妇女歧视"和"男女不平等的根源"，"消除"是动作，那么搭配的应当是名词。我们通常讲消除一种现象，而不能直接是动作消除行为，故而可通过增译"现象"一词，将这两处并列成分处理为"导致歧视妇女和男女不平等现象的根源"，不仅更加符合汉语表达习惯，也更具有可读性。

4. 具体词义表达方法。"stereotypical"是"stereotype"的形容词。在联合国文件中，特别是妇女类文件中出现的频率很高，翻译时通常有几种固定译法，即"陈规定型的看法""定型观念""成见""陈规定性观念"等。比如，"Acknowledging the importance of taking measures to raise awareness of the rights of persons with disabilities in order to eliminate discrimination, stereotypes, prejudices and other barriers which constitute a major impediment to their full, equal and effective participation in society and the economy, as well as in political and public life"（承认必须采取措施提高对残疾人权利的认识，以便消除歧视，定型观念，偏见和严重阻碍他们充分、平等和有效参与社会、经济及政治和公共生活的其他障碍）。而在此段内容中则采用的是其形容词形式，可依照上下文翻译。

5. 专有名词处理。"Beijing Declaration and Platform for Action"乍一看以为是一体的，也很好理解，很容易望文生义，将其处理为一个专有名词。实际上，此处是两个名词《北京宣言》和《行动纲要》（1995年第四次妇女大会通过），必要时可查阅其出台背景和时间。在联合国文件中，此类形式很多见，唯一的办法是多查勤查，确定其真正的含义和用法，不可自行处理。

第2段

Women also have the right to the enjoyment of the highest attainable standard of physical and mental health. The enjoyment of this right is vital to their well-being and their ability to participate in all areas of public and private life. We believe in focusing on addressing risky behaviour in girls and boys through healthy lifestyle promotion to take care of women and their physical and mental health. Our healthy Lifestyle Promotion program helps girls and women to make wise decisions. The program incorporates life skill training, life counselling, training of trainers, peer-to-peer outreach (ripple program), and mass campaign.

批 注

① 注意敏感词。
② 切忌硬伤。
③ 需遵循惯例。

妇女同样有权享有可达到的最高标准的身体和心理健康①。这一权利的享有对于她们的福祉和她们参与公共和私人生活所有领域的能力至关重要。我们认为应当通过促进健康生活方式，关怀妇女及其身体和心理健康，着重解决女童和男童的风险行为②。我们的健康生活方式促进方案帮助女童和妇女作出明智的决定。方案③纳入了生活技能培训、生活咨询、培训员的培训、点对点的拓展（涟漪方案）以及群众运动。

妇女同样有权享有可达到的最高标准的身心健康。享有这一权利对于妇女的福祉及其参与公共和私人生活所有领域的能力而言至关重要。我们认为，应当通过促进健康生活方式，关怀妇女及其身心健康，借此重点解决女童和男童群体中的危险行为。我们的促进健康生活方式方案帮助女童和妇女做出明智的决定。该方案纳入了生活技能培训、生活咨询、培训员训练、点对点拓展（涟漪方案）及群众运动等。

1. 对词汇保持敏感。在联合国文件中，一些非首字母大写的词组或句子都有类似于专有名词的固定译法，开始接触联合国文件时，往往会忽视而自行翻译。本文中"enjoyment of the highest attainable standard of physical and mental health"一句从UNTERM中可以找到固定译法，对于此类词，一方面是积累，见到了立刻知道需查阅；另一方面将其部分或全部输入UNTERM去查，往往就会查找到标准译法或参考译法。此处在联合国词汇里可以查找到"right of everyone to the enjoyment of the highest attainable standard of physical and mental health"，对应的是"人人享有能达到的最高标准身心健康的权利"，故可完全参照翻译。

2. 表达要严谨。翻译过程中须随时谨记避免硬伤，遇到拿不准的或无对应表述（词义空缺）的情况下，尽量细化处理，勿拘泥于该词表面含义，给读者留下不专业的印象。本文中"risky behaviour"其实很简单，但原译处理成了"风险行为"，显然不够严谨。语境中涉及的是"女童和男童"群体中的行为，理应搭配"危险行为"。

3. 注意某些词的特定含义。在联合国文件中，"incorporate"和"outreach"通常都有其规定的译法，"incorporate"通常翻译为"纳入"，遇特殊情况可适当变通。而"outreach"通常翻译为"外联"，例如"The conditions needed to implement the plan will be created by six performance enablers: monitoring and knowledge; innovation; advocacy; communication and outreach"（将通过以下六个提高业绩因素为执行计划创造必要的条件：监测和知识；创新；宣传、沟通和外联），根据上下文可以适当变通，此处根据上下文处理为"拓展"。"peer"则有多种译法，

"同伴、同行"等,须根据上下文判断;"peer-to-peer"则可以翻译为"对等""端对端"等。

第3段

Today's girl children are tomorrow's women. This generation of leaders must accept and promote a world in which every child is free from injustice, oppression and inequality and free to develop her own potential. The principle of holistic youth development program must therefore be integral to the process.

今天的女童是明天的妇女。当代领导人必须接受并促进我们的世界,使其中每位儿童都免受不公正、压迫和不平等,并且能够自由发展她自己的潜力①。因此,以整体的青年发展方案为原则必须是②这一进程中不可分割的组成部分。

今天的女童即是明天的妇女。当代领导人必须接受并推动建立一个每名儿童都免遭不公正、压迫或不平等,并且能够自由发展其自身潜力的世界。因此,以综合性青年发展方案为原则必须成为这一进程中不可分割的组成部分。

批 注

① 注意紧凑性。
② 注意词性转换。

1. 行文紧凑性问题。原译文总体理解到位,但在表达上稍显松散,"世界"与后面的修饰内容相隔较远,容易产生歧义。在句式结构并非很长的情况下,应尽量使其紧凑连贯,一目了然,故而审校稿将其处理为"推动建立……的世界"比较可取。类似的用法还有"including…",尽可能以紧凑原则为主,避免过于松散。当然,如后面定语部分过长,则可考虑拆分。

2. 注意词性转换问题。在翻译的过程中,还可掌握词性转换这一翻译技巧,如名词变动词,形容词变动词等,此处审校稿对于"The principle of holistic youth development program must therefore be integral to the process"一句中"be integral to"处理为"成为",变为动词后一下子为句子点亮了色彩,使其更加生动鲜明。

3. "holistic"一词在联合国文件中出现的频率也很高,通常处理为"整体的""全面的""综合的"等,如"holistic approach"(整体方法)、"holistic tourism"(综合旅游)等。

补充练习

1. Women play an important role in development, but they are often excluded from development policies and particularly from the macroeconomic system. This trend demonstrates the need to improve policies in order to support the empowerment of African women, including both those in Africa and those who live abroad, who are made even more vulnerable by migration.

妇女在发展中发挥着重要作用，但她们常常被排除在发展政策之外，尤其是被排除在宏观经济体系之外。这个趋势表明，有必要完善政策以支持增强非洲妇女的权能，包括生活在非洲和国外的妇女——她们在移徙后更容易受到伤害。

2. Women's empowerment presents both an opportunity and a challenge for the post-2015 agenda. The growth rate in Africa, although impressive, does not benefit the majority of the population, and particularly not women. This highlights the pressing need for industrialization and for the inclusion of women in the industrialization process. To achieve inclusive growth, women must both benefit from the rewards of growth and participate in the processes that stimulate it. In order to make women's empowerment a reality, women must be given the means to access the macroeconomy through the promotion of socio-economic resilience and the diversification and greater accessibility of sources of finance, with a view to sustainable human and economic development.

对2015年后议程而言，增强妇女权能既是机会也是挑战。非洲的发展速度虽然令人印象深刻，但并未使大部分人口，特别是使妇女受益。这一点凸显了对工业化以及将妇女纳入工业化进程的迫切需要。为实现包容性增长，妇女必须从增长收益中受益并参与促进发展的进程。为使增强妇女权能成为现实，必须通过促进社会经济复原力以及提供更多样化的资金来源及更好的获取途径，为妇女提供参与宏观经济的手段，以期实现人类和经济的可持续发展。

One of the organization's main activities during the reporting period has been the annual HIV/AIDS sensitisation campaign. Activities included HIV/AIDS screening with the support of private health facilitators who also conducted counselling. Workshops also addressed prevention and reduction of stigmatisation of people infected and affected by the disease.

Women's Action Group (WAG) contributes through implementation of its programmes, mainly on sexual and reproductive health and rights, gender based violence, and HIV/AIDS. WAG is implementing the He for She Campaign, initiated by the United Nations Entity for Gender Equality and the Empowerment of Women (UN Women), through which WAG is mobilising men to stand up in support of women's rights. WAG collaborated with other organizations in preparing the Zimbabwe Civil Society shadow report to Committee on the Elimination of all Forms of Discrimination against Women in 2012. WAG played a critical role in ensuring that the new constitution of Zimbabwe included gender equality and women's rights provisions in collaboration with the Group of 20, 2009—2013. In the area of HIV/AIDS, WAG continues to advocate for female condoms and to ensure women's access anti-retroviral therapy. WAG provided inputs in the formulation of the Zimbabwe HIV and AIDS Strategy for 2011—2015.

请自行翻译后查看后文的分析点评

分析点评

第 1 段

One of the organization's main activities during the reporting period has been the annual HIV/AIDS sensitisation campaign. Activities included HIV/AIDS screening with the support of private health facilitators who also conducted counselling. Workshops also addressed prevention and reduction of stigmatisation of people infected and affected by the disease.

在报告所涉期间①，本组织的主要活动之一是每年开展艾滋病毒/艾滋病宣传活动。活动包括在私人健康促进者的支持下进行艾滋病毒/艾滋病筛查，这些引导人也提供辅导。研讨会②还讨论了如何预防和减少对受感染者和受影响者的侮辱。

批 注

① 固定译法。
② 固定译法。

在报告所述期间，本组织的主要活动之一是每年开展艾滋病毒/艾滋病宣传活动。活动包括在私人健康引导人的支持下进行艾滋病毒/艾滋病筛查，这些引导人也提供咨询。讲习班还讨论了如何预防和减少对艾滋病感染者和受其影响者的侮辱问题。

1. 固定译法。在翻译联合国文件翻译时，需注意遵循其固定译法。此类固定译法涉及决议、决定、公约、议定书以及许多术语，此外还有特定机构文件的特定要求。这里"during the reporting period"和"workshop"即属于固定译法，通常不会翻译成其他含义。"during the reporting period"在此类非政府组织文件中规定要求翻译为"在报告所述期间"。而"workshop"多译为"讲习班",与"seminar"即"研讨会"做出区分。

2. 细节判断问题。在UNTERM里,"facilitator"可翻译为"协助者(指那些为海盗活动提供各种服务和便利并从中受益者,在安理会决议中也可译为"协助者)""调解人(国、方、者)""主持人(会议或工作)""促进者"等,但在社科类文件中,不可过于拘泥于上述含义。本段原译文将其处理为"健康促进者"显然过于贴字面含义,审校稿根据上下文语境以将其翻译为"引导人"要更为妥帖,符合常规表述。

3. "sensitisation"与"stigmatisation"的辨析。"sensitisation"有"对……敏感之意",例如"gender sensitization training"(使对性别问题敏感的培训),同时还有"提高认识敏感性"的含义,即引申出"宣传",因此本文使用该层含义。"stigmatisation"等同于"stigmatization",UNTERM里提供的译法是"污名化",例如"Reported cases of women and girls with disabilities who are survivors of gender-based violence not being able to gain access to justice owing to multiple barriers, such as stigmatization of victims, fear of reprisals and difficulties in producing evidence"(据报告,作为性别暴力行为幸存者的残疾妇女和女童由于对受害者的污名化、害怕报复和难以出示证据等多重障碍无法获得司法保护)。根据上下文,也可将其处理为"羞辱""侮辱"等。

第2段

Women's Action Group (WAG) contributes through implementation of its programmes, mainly on sexual and reproductive health and rights, gender based violence, and HIV/AIDS. WAG is implementing the He for She Campaign, initiated by the United Nations Entity for Gender Equality and the Empowerment of Women (UN Women), through which WAG is mobilising men to stand up in support of women's rights. WAG collaborated with other organizations in preparing the Zimbabwe Civil Society shadow report to Committee on the Elimination of all Forms of Discrimination against Women in 2012. WAG played a critical role in ensuring that the new constitution of Zimbabwe included gender equality and women's rights provisions in collaboration with the Group of 20, 2009—2013. In the area of HIV/AIDS, WAG continues to advocate for female condoms and to ensure women's access anti-retroviral therapy. WAG provided inputs in the formulation of the Zimbabwe HIV and AIDS Strategy for 2011—2015.

翻译稿

本组织通过实施自身关于性健康和生殖健康及权利、基于性别的暴力和艾滋病毒/艾滋病的方案作出贡献。本组织正在开展由联合国促进性别平等和增强妇女权能署(妇女署)发起的"①"运动,借助该运动,本组织动员男子站起来支持妇女的权利。2012年,本组织与其他组织合作编写了提交给消除对

批注

① 注意查阅和参考资料。

妇女一切形式歧视委员会的津巴布韦民间社会非正式报告。2009—2013 年，本组织与 20 国集团协作，为确保在津巴布韦新宪法中纳入关于性别平等和妇女权利的条款方面发挥了关键作用。在艾滋病毒／艾滋病领域，本组织继续倡导使用女用安全套，并确保妇女获得抗逆转录病毒治疗。本组织为制定 2011—2015 年津巴布韦艾滋病毒和艾滋病战略提供了投入①。

批 注

① 注意灵活处理。

本组织通过实施自身主要关于性健康和生殖健康及权利、性别暴力和艾滋病毒／艾滋病的方案做出贡献。本组织正在开展由联合国促进性别平等和增强妇女权能署（妇女署）发起的"男性促进女性权利"运动，借助该运动，本组织动员男性站起来支持妇女的权利。2012 年，本组织与其他组织合作编写了向消除对妇女一切形式歧视委员会提交的津巴布韦民间社会影子报告。2009 至 2013 年间，本组织与 20 国集团协作，在确保在津巴布韦新宪法中纳入关于性别平等和妇女权利的条款方面发挥了关键作用。在艾滋病毒／艾滋病领域，本组织继续倡导使用女用安全套，并确保妇女获得抗逆转录病毒治疗。本组织为制定《2011—2015 年津巴布韦艾滋病毒和艾滋病战略》建言献策。

1. 背景资料查询问题。本段中"He for She Campaign"乍一看很简单，但翻译起来却颇费功夫，翻译稿直白地将其处理为"他为了她运动"，虽然也能理解，但表达不够书面，显得不太严谨考究。实际上这项运动是妇女署发起的一项影响广泛的运动，旨在让男性促进女性的权利，并且从 UNTERM 上就可以准确找到"男性促进女性权利运动"这一提法。

2. 词汇由虚化实法。见"input"一词。"input"在联合国会议文件中多处理成"投入"，此处如采用直译法，则有些抽象，读起来稍显生硬，对于一项政策，不妨将其具体含义还原，处理为"建言献策"。在其他类稿件中，也可根据上下文将其处理成"投入、协助、参与"等。

3. 机构专有词汇问题。在许多联合国文件中，"programme"翻译为"方案"，但在教科文组织文件中，则通常翻译为"计划"。"gender based violence"一般可翻译为"性别暴力"，区别于"sexual violence"（性暴力）。"shadow report"一般可以翻译为"影子报告"，"alternative report"则通常翻译为"非正式报告"或"补充报告"。

补充练习

1. The organization supported the primary education of 1 000 children of widows living under poverty below 15 years of age and the higher education for 50 young widows under the age of 25. It also assisted in providing funds from the local government for capacity building and skills development trainings in 60 single women

groups from 60 districts. Spaces for single women were built in 16 districts to provide different skill development training and legal counselling.

本组织为1 000名贫困寡妇所生15岁以下的子女提供接受初等教育支持，为50名年龄在25岁以下的青年寡妇提供高等教育支持。本组织还利用地方政府提供的资金，协助60个地区的60名单身女性群体进行能力建设并开展技能培训。在16个地区建立了单身女性专属空间，以开展技能培训和提供法律咨询。

2. The Women's International Zionist Organization (WIZO) is committed to increase equality in all fields and on all levels of society. Through its many projects, WIZO enables every member of society receiving its services, to obtain the tools and skills they need to achieve equal opportunities to better their lives, thus helping to reduce gaps and differences. These projects include providing equal education; eliminating illiteracy and computer ignorance amongst adults; combatting violence against women, children and youth; and advancing the status of women in legislation and through practical measures.

国际犹太复国主义妇女组织致力于促进在社会各个领域和各个层面实现平等。本组织通过开展多个项目，使每位社会成员获得本组织所提供的各项服务，以掌握必要的工具和技能，获得改善生活的平等机会，从而有助于消除差距和减少分歧。这些项目包括提供平等教育；成人识字和计算机扫盲；打击暴力侵害妇女、儿童和青年的行为以及通过立法和切实措施提高妇女地位。

背景介绍

以下两篇均摘自教科文组织保护和促进文化表现形式多样性政府间委员会四年度定期报告。文化多样性是人文社科领域的一项关键议题，也是教科文组织的一个重要工作领域，教科文组织根据《保护和促进文化表现形式多样性公约》开展相关工作。通过定期报告机制和监测机制，对各国就文化多样性领域采取的政策措施及其落实情况进行监督。因此，此类报告具有如下特点：以报告内容综述形式呈现，在特殊用法、组句以及常规体例上有既定特点，特别是长句较多，修饰成分冗杂，在将源语转换成目的语时易受原文结构和语言组织形式的干扰，译者须掌握"化长句为短句、适当打破原文结构"这一重要翻译技巧，同时应对教科文组织官方文件的文风形成大致认识，调动在文化决策方面的常识以及对治理问题的敏感度，以便按照文字背后的语境逻辑灵活地进行双语转换。

第四篇

Since the fifth ordinary session of the Conference of Parties, there are two major developments that provide a new context for the Convention and reporting on the Secretariat's workplan of activities and expected results, namely, the creation of a new framework to monitor the implementation of the Convention and the adoption of the UN 2030 Agenda for Sustainable Development (hereinafter "the 2030 Agenda").

Accordingly, this report presents a summary of activities undertaken by the Secretariat in line with the Convention's monitoring framework made up of four overarching goals, namely to: support sustainable systems of governance for culture (Goal 1); achieve a balanced flow of cultural goods and services and increase the mobility of artists and cultural professionals (Goal 2); integrate culture in sustainable development frameworks (Goal 3); and promote human rights and fundamental freedoms (Goal 4). This framework enables synergies between the Secretariat's reporting on results (through this report) and Parties reporting on results through the quadrennial periodic reports, to the extent possible and relevant. The objective is to eventually provide a more coherent picture of the implementation of the Convention at both the global and country levels.

请自行翻译后查看后文的分析点评

第 1 段

Since the fifth ordinary session of the Conference of Parties, there are two major developments that provide a new context for the Convention and reporting on the Secretariat's workplan of activities and expected results, namely, the creation of a new framework to monitor the implementation of the Convention and the adoption of the UN 2030 Agenda for Sustainable Development (hereinafter "the 2030 Agenda").

翻译稿

自缔约方大会第五次常会①以来，有两项重大进展为《公约》和秘书处提出活动工作计划和预期成果报告提供了新的背景，即②创建了一个监测《公约》实施情况的新框架和通过了《联合国 2030 年可持续发展议程》（以下简称《2030 年议程》）。

批 注

① 有固定译法。
② 尝试拆分为短句。

自缔约方大会第五次例会以来，取得了两项重大进展，一是创建了一个监测《公约》实施情况的新框架；二是通过了《联合国2030年可持续发展议程》（以下简称"《2030年议程》"），为《公约》和报告秘书处活动工作计划和预期成果提供了新的背景。

1. 有关会议的固定译法问题。联合国文件中涉及的会议较多，一般情况下，"ordinary session"译为"例会"，"regular session"译为"常会"。

2. 学习掌握"化长句为短句、适当打破原文结构、视需要增/略译"的翻译技巧。翻译稿按照原文"there are two major developments that provide a new context for..., namely, ..."的结构作顺译处理，并没有错误，但如能适当打破原文结构，采用总分句式，用逗号拆分长句为短句，改为"取得了两项重大进展，一是……；二是……，为……"，效果更好。

第2段

Accordingly, this report presents a summary of activities undertaken by the Secretariat in line with the Convention's monitoring framework made up of four overarching goals, namely to: support sustainable systems of governance for culture (Goal 1); achieve a balanced flow of cultural goods and services and increase the mobility of artists and cultural professionals (Goal 2); integrate culture in sustainable development frameworks (Goal 3); and promote human rights and fundamental freedoms (Goal 4). This framework enables synergies between the Secretariat's reporting on results (through this report) and Parties reporting on results through the quadrennial periodic reports, to the extent possible and relevant. The objective is to eventually provide a more coherent picture of the implementation of the Convention at both the global and country levels.

批 注

① 是否为上段提到的新框架？
② 意义偏离。
③ 原文有画面感，译文是否也应予以体现？

因此，本报告介绍了秘书处根据<u>《公约》监测框架</u>①开展活动的概况，该框架共由四个总体目标组成，分别是：为可持续的文化治理制度提供支持（目标1）；实现文化产品和服务的平衡流动，提高艺术家和文化专业人员的流动性（目标2）；将文化纳入可持续发展框架（目标3）；促进人权和基本自由（目标4）。通过这一框架，可使秘书处（通过本报告进行）的结果汇报与各缔约方通过四年度定期报告进行的结果汇报尽量<u>在相关问题上</u>②实现协同增效。最终的目的是<u>更加连贯地描述</u>③《公约》在全球和国家两级的实施情况。

因此，本报告简要介绍了秘书处根据该《公约》监测框架开展的各项活动，该框架共由四个总体目标组成，分别是：支持可持续的文化治理体系（目标1）；

实现文化产品和服务的均衡流通，提高艺术家和文化专业人员的流动性（目标2）；将文化纳入可持续发展框架（目标3）；增进人权和基本自由（目标4）。该框架有助于在秘书处（通过本报告进行）的成果报告与缔约方（通过四年度定期报告进行）的成果报告之间实现最大限度的关联协同。最终目的是更加清楚地呈现《公约》在全球和国家两个层面的实施情况。

点评

译者对整段的理解到位，但存在以下几个小问题。

1. 应贯彻"吃透原意、地道表述"原则。翻译稿采用直译手法处理段首句"presents a summary of activities…"，译文略显死板；在处理段末句中的"provide a more coherent picture of…"时，又放弃沿用有画面感的原文风格，采用直白的"描述"一词，使原文本身的修辞效果大打折扣。译文虽然清楚地表达了原文之意，但文笔晦涩，影响读者理解。相比之下，审校稿中的译文更加为读者考虑，表意清楚。

2. 应准确把握上下文逻辑关系。从本段句首的"accordingly"一词判断，第2行中的"monitoring framework"就是第一段中提到的"new framework"，明确这一点后，审校稿在"《公约》监测框架"前面增译了"该"一词，译为"该《监测框架》"，做到了前后呼应，使上下逻辑关系一目了然。

3. 难词处理问题。关于"to the extent possible and relevant"，这是本段的处理难点。根据《牛津高阶英汉双解词典》，"to...extent" is used to show how far sth is true or how great an effect it has；"relevant" has the meaning of "closely connected with the subject you are discussing or the situation you are thinking about"，在本句中，"to the extent possible and relevant"可理解为"as long as these synergies are possible and relevant to Secretariat's reporting and Parties' reporting"，也即在秘书处报告与缔约国报告之间实现最大限度的关联协同，而非"在相关问题上协同增效"，这也是与最后一句所述最终目的相呼应的。

补充练习

1. The Convention delineates a system of governance for culture as one that meets people's demands and needs and is transparent in decision making processes; participatory by engaging civil society in policy design and implementation; and informed through the regular collection of evidence that can support policy making decisions. In order to achieve this goal, cultural policies and measures are to be implemented in accordance with Articles 5, 6, 7 and 11 of the Convention.The implementation of this goal can provide evidence in the monitoring of SDG 16, target 16.7 to "ensure responsive, inclusive, participatory and representative decision making at all levels".

按照《公约》的规定，文化治理体系应符合人的需求和需要，其决策进程应当做到公开透明；必须让民间社会广泛参与制定和实施各项政策；应定期收集可为决策决定提供支持的证据，以做到充分知情。为实现这一目标，文化政策和措施须按照《公约》第五、六、七和十一条的规定予以实施。落实这一目标可为监测可持续发展目标 16 的具体目标 16.7 "确保各级的决策反应迅速，具有包容性、参与性和代表性"提供证据。

2. Findings from the 2015 Global Report show that new cultural policy strategies have been adopted aimed at strengthening the value chain of creation, production, distribution and access to diverse cultural goods and services. Yet, it also reports a lack of evaluation and monitoring mechanisms making it difficult to determine how transparency in decision-making will be achieved. It signals that the role of civil society as "cultural watchdog" remains underdeveloped and that platforms for dialogue between governments and civil society do not exist or are fragile. Lastly, it highlights the lack of reliable information and data resources necessary for informed policy making.

《2015 年全球报告》的调查结果显示，新的文化政策战略已经通过，目的是加强由创造、制作、传播和获取环节构成的多样化文化产品和服务价值链。但报告也指出，评估和监测机制缺失，导致难以确定如何才能实现决策的公开透明。报告还表明，民间社会作为"文化监督者"的作用依然没有得到充分发挥，政府与民间社会之间的对话平台要么不存在，要么脆弱不堪。最后，报告强调指出，缺乏做出充分知情决策所需的可靠信息和数据资源。

The reporting and monitoring mechanisms of the Convention have demonstrated their potential as strategic tools to support participatory, transparent and informed policymaking. Indeed, they offer an opportunity to better understand the state of the creative sectors, establish benchmarks, identify priority areas for future action and share innovative policy practices nationally and internationally. These mechanisms are thus framing policy making on the diversity of cultural expressions as well as new visions and strategies, contributing to re-shape cultural policies around the world.

The reporting cycle, in particular, is contributing to the establishment of inclusive policy dialogue platforms between governmental and civil society actors, involving cultural and media professionals, and new coordination mechanisms among various government ministries responsible for issues such as trade, employment, social affairs, ICT, development, or international cooperation.

Both the Global Report and the capacity-building programme have also offered a unique opportunity to raise awareness on key and emerging themes related to the promotion of the diversity of cultural expressions in the digital age, namely, artistic freedom, media pluralism, and gender equality. Thanks to the attention brought forth by the launch of the Global Report in December 2015, these issues have been central to many public events, debates, round tables and conferences at the international and national levels. The national reporting processes have also promoted further information sharing and transparency for policy making and empowered civil society actors to have open dialogue with governments for the first time. Lastly, the Global Report has also played a catalyst role to include artistic freedom in UNESCO's draft Programme and Budget for the years 2018—2021 (39C/5).

请自行翻译后查看后文的分析点评

第 1 段

The reporting and monitoring mechanisms of the Convention have demonstrated their potential as strategic tools to support participatory, transparent and informed policymaking. Indeed, they offer an opportunity to better understand the state of the creative sectors, establish benchmarks, identify priority areas for future action and share innovative policy practices nationally and internationally. These mechanisms are thus framing policy making on the diversity of cultural expressions as well as new visions and strategies, contributing to re-shape cultural policies around the world.

《公约》的报告和监测机制已经证明了它们作为战略工具用于支持参与性、透明和知情决策的潜力。事实上，它们提供了一个机会，以更好地了解创意部门的现状，建立基准，确定今后行动的优先领域，并在国家和国际范围内分享创新性政策做法①。因此，这些机制构成了制定关于文化表现形式多样性以及新的愿景和战略的政策基础，有助于在世界范围内重塑文化政策。

批 注

① 对词汇的理解有问题。

《公约》的报告和监测机制已经证明它们作为支持参与性、透明和知情决策

的战略工具的潜力。实际上,它们为更好地了解创意部门的现状、建立基准、确定今后行动的优先领域以及在国内和国际层面分享创新性政策实践提供了一个机会。因此,这些机制正在构建关于文化表现形式多样性的决策以及新的愿景和战略,有助于在全世界重塑文化政策。

1. 词汇理解问题。见"share innovative policy practices nationally and internationally…"一句。翻译稿和审校稿的处理分别是"在国家和国际范围内分享"和"在国内和国际层面分享"。这个点看似无足轻重,实际很考验译者的功力。在原文表述较为模糊的情况下,要选择"范围"还是"层面",就要细细体味文字背后的用意,同时要有在处理国际组织文件上积累的敏感性。"范围",强调的是一种广度,而"层面"强调的是层级,实际上"国家和国际"就已经体现出广度,但当一国制定出政策后,不仅要在国家级别,如在各部委、各行政区进行分享宣传,还应当拿到国际层级,在联合国等实体国际组织进行分享交流,因此在此处译为"层级"更合情合理。

2. 断句问题。见"Indeed, they offer an opportunity to better understand…"一句。翻译稿的译法,即在"opportunity"之后断句,将"to better…"译成整句话的目的状语,这种译法也不为错,但在联合国文件中,应当采用更为严谨的译法,将"to better understand…"提前,作为"opportunity"的目的状语,即为"更好地理解""提供了一个机会",并且这种译法也使目的状语与"opportunity"的关系更紧凑。此类句式在联合国文件中很常见,初学者在遇到类似句式时,要注意采用更严谨的译法。

第 2 段

The reporting cycle, in particular, is contributing to the establishment of inclusive policy dialogue platforms between governmental and civil society actors, involving cultural and media professionals, and new coordination mechanisms among various government ministries responsible for issues such as trade, employment, social affairs, ICT, development, or international cooperation.

特别是,报告周期正在促进政府行为体与涉及文化和媒体专业人士的民间社会行为体开展包容性政策对话①,以及促进在负责贸易、就业、社会问题、ICT、发展或国际合作等问题的各政府部委之间形成新的协调机制。

报告周期尤其推动建立了政府与包括文化和媒体专业人士在内的民间社会行为者之间的包容性政策对话平台;并在负责贸易、就业、社会事务、信通技术、发展或国际合作等问题的各政府部委之间建立了新的协调机制。

① 表达不严谨。

1. 时态问题。见 "The reporting cycle, in particular, is contributing to..." 一句。我们可以看出，这句话原文时态很明显是现在进行时，而审校稿却处理成过去时态，其中原因何在？实际上，如果单看本段（在文中第 25 段），按照原文处理成进行时态完全没有问题，可如果结合整篇文件来看，处理成进行时则不妥。此处，需要补充文件第 23 段一句话 "The reporting and monitoring mechanisms of the Convention have demonstrated their potential as strategic tools to support participatory, transparent and informed policymaking"，这句话提示我们"报告周期机制"实际上已经建立并已在发挥成效了，而在本段则是对其成效的进一步解释，即一方面推动建立了对话平台，另一方面建立了新的协调机制。另外，再结合 23 和 24 段段首的时态（分别是 "have demonstrated" 和 "have adopted legislation"），均使用完成时，那么可提示我们，此处的行为亦完成。因此，一定要树立全局意识，立足于整篇文件，如发现存在疑点的段落，应查看前后段落，找到提示和依据。

2. 表达不严谨问题。同见此句。翻译稿对原文的理解存在偏差。很明显，翻译稿没有将"平台"一词译出，并不是漏译，而是有意为之。可以看出，译者对这句话的理解是，报告周期在直接促进政府与相关行为体开展对话，有意强调"政府"与"行为体"对话这一层含义，因此舍去了"平台"一词。然而，我们要注意，贯穿联合国文件翻译的一个重要原则是严谨，过于灵活的译法并不可取。实际上，报告周期促进、推动的是 "establishment of inclusive policy dialogue platforms"，可理解为一种平台（机制），即报告周期推动建立一种平台，而这种平台是"政府"和"相关方"的对话平台，因此重点在于建立平台，而非直接推动开展对话。如此分析来看，翻译稿表述偏离本义，表述不严谨。

第 3 段

Both the Global Report and the capacity-building programme have also offered a unique opportunity to raise awareness on key and emerging themes related to the promotion of the diversity of cultural expressions in the digital age, namely, artistic freedom, media pluralism, and gender equality. Thanks to the attention brought forth by the launch of the Global Report in December 2015, these issues have been central to many public events, debates, round tables and conferences at the international and national levels. The national reporting processes have also promoted further information sharing and transparency for policy making and empowered civil society actors to have open dialogue with governments for the first time. Lastly, the Global Report has also played a catalyst role to include artistic freedom in UNESCO's draft Programme and Budget for the years 2018—2021 (39C/5).

《全球报告》和能力建设计划均提供了一个独特的机会，以提高对在数字时代（即艺术自由、媒体多元化和性别平等）与促进文化表现形式有关的关键主题

批 注

① 拆分与合并。
② 表达不通顺。

和新主题的认识。2015年12月发布的《全球报告》引起了关注，这些问题进而成了许多国际和国家公共活动、辩论、圆桌会议和会议的中心问题。国家报告进程还促进了进一步的信息共享和决策的透明度，并增强了民间社会行为体的权能，使之第一次与政府进行公开对话。最后，《全球报告》还在将艺术自由纳入教科文组织2018—2021年方案和预算草案（39C/5）方面起到了促进作用②。

《全球报告》和能力建设计划均为在数字时代提高对促进文化表现形式多样性相关主要新兴主题（即艺术自由、媒体多元化和性别平等）的认识提供了一个独特的机会。由于2015年12月发行的《全球报告》引起的关注，这些问题已成为许多国际和国内公共活动、辩论、圆桌会议和会议的中心议题。国家报告进程还促进了进一步的信息共享和决策透明度，并增强了民间社会行为方的权能，使之首次能够与政府进行公开对话。最后，在将艺术自由纳入教科文组织《2018—2021年计划和预算草案》（39C/5）方面，《全球报告》也发挥了促进作用。

1. 拆译与合译问题。见"key and emerging themes"。对于此处的译法，翻译稿和审校稿显然对"themes"的理解是不同的，前者理解的是两类主题，"关键主题"和"新兴主题"，而后者采用合译方式，省略了连接词"and"，译为"主要新兴主题"。显然，如按照翻译稿的理解，原文应当是"key themes and emerging themes"，而不是key and emerging themes。

2. 句子表达通顺问题。见"Lastly, the Global Report has also played a catalyst role to include"一句。翻译稿为直译，读起来未免拗口，不够通顺，主要原因是将"include in..."" 在……方面"这一状语成分插入句中，作为主干显得主句过长，且会干扰这句话的真正主干"played a catalyst role"，因此为通顺起见，不妨采用拆译法，将"在……方面"单独提出、另起一句，即处理成"在将艺术自由纳入教科文组织《2018—2021年计划和预算草案》方面"，然后再单独处理主干句，即"《全球报告》也发挥了促进作用"。结合上一段点评，此处要总结的是，合译和拆译是处理联合国文件的一类常用技巧，其用途主要在于化繁为简，合译是在去除不必要的虚词之后将修饰词合并，起到加强句子紧凑度的作用；拆译是为了将冗杂的长句变成短句，将状语成分与主干相分离，起到主次分明，加强句子层次感和逻辑性的效果。

补充练习

1. Coinciding with the 10th anniversary of the Convention, the publication of the first Global Report in December 2015 provided Parties and non-governmental stakeholders with an opportunity to critically review the achievements and guide the implementation of the Convention over the next decade.

正值《公约》十周年之际，2015 年 12 月发布的第一版《全球报告》为缔约方和非政府利益攸关方审视已经取得的成就及指导今后十年《公约》的实施提供了一个机会。

2. The second edition of the Global Report will be published in December 2017 and launched during the eleventh session of the Committee. It will strike out in several new directions by implementing a number of the 33 core indicators and related means of verification introduced in the first edition. It will assess the impact of newly reported policies and measures and provide evidence towards how they contribute to implement several SDGs and targets, as well as address the difficulties encountered in their implementation. In addition, it will contain analytical reflections on recent and emerging trends and developments in the cultural field that will be brought to the attention of Parties.

第二版《全球报告》将于 2017 年 12 月公布，并在委员会第十一次例会期间发行。通过执行第一版引入的 33 个核心指标和相关核查手段，报告将出现几个新的方向。它将对新报告的政策和措施的影响进行评估，就它们如何促进执行若干可持续发展目标和具体目标提供证据，并且解决在这些目标执行过程中遇到的困难。此外，还将对文化领域内近期出现的新趋势和发展进行分析和思考，以提请缔约方注意。

背景介绍

本篇来自联合国教科文组织《全球教科书和课程摸底调查》，其内容涉及大屠杀警示教育的国际现状。教科文组织和格奥尔格·埃克特研究所在2014年编写的这份报告旨在补充关于大屠杀警示教育的现有报告，介绍世界各国课程和教科书中关于大屠杀事件的描述，这是迄今为止尚无人涉足的教育领域。作为教科文组织的一类通用文件，《摸底调查》属于研究报告，相比正式会议文件和综述报告（上文第四篇和第五篇），有其自身独有特点：在内容上，夹叙夹议，并非对事实（此处即指大屠杀警示教育现状）进行主观描述，而是采用一种客观的叙述视角，对具有代表性的具体概念和事件进行描述；这就决定了在遣词和行文的组织上，会使用典型的报告类文件中不经常出现的句式，如疑问句、短句、散句。此外，报告中经常出现的一些词汇，如"address"等常见词的含义，也不能局限于在官方报告中出现时通常具备的含义，译者应根据具体语境予以理解。本篇所选文件的风格介乎于正式报告（第一篇至第五篇）与更为自由的杂志体文件（第七篇至第十篇）之间，综合体现了联合国文件的"报告风格"与"叙述风格"，值得深入揣摩研究。

第六篇

Is teaching about the Holocaust explicitly addressed in curricula, in what terms is the Holocaust defined, and in which contexts is it dealt with? The Holocaust is stipulated in the history curricula of approximately half of the countries investigated, with varying contexts and terminologies. The event is presented most frequently in the context of the Second World War, but also features in the context of lessons about human rights violations. It is generally referred to with the term "Holocaust", while fewer curricula use the term "Shoah" or else both terms in conjunction. In some cases, curricula forego both the terms "Holocaust" and "Shoah", preferring to describe the event with alternative terms such as "extermination" or "genocide of the Jews", with indirect references to the event (with terms such as "concentration camp" or "Final Solution"), or by combining terms which clearly indicate teaching about the Holocaust (such as "destruction" and "Jews", or "genocide" and "National Socialism").

In some curricula, only Jews are named explicitly as victims, while references to Sinti and Roma, people with disabilities, political opponents, homosexuals or other socially marginalised groups are infrequent. Most curricula do not specify the victim groups to be discussed in teaching. Moreover, while a quarter of all curricula contain no reference to the Holocaust, they instead discuss the purpose of the subject and methods to be used in its teaching, or else they explicitly refer to its historical contexts such as the Second World War and/or National Socialism, such that one may assume that the topic is part of teaching in the subject although it is not explicitly named. The study also points out semantic variations arising from the various languages whose vocabularies do not permit the direct adoption of the customary terms "Holocaust" or "Shoah".

请自行翻译后查看后文的分析点评

第 1 段

Is teaching about the Holocaust explicitly addressed in curricula, in what terms is the Holocaust defined, and in which contexts is it dealt with? The Holocaust is stipulated in the history curricula of approximately half of the countries investigated, with varying contexts and terminologies. The event is presented most frequently in the context of the Second World War, but also features in the context of lessons about human rights violations. It is generally referred to with the term "Holocaust", while fewer curricula use the term "Shoah" or else both terms in conjunction. In some cases, curricula forego both the terms "Holocaust" and "Shoah", preferring to describe the event with alternative terms such as "extermination" or "genocide of the Jews", with indirect references to the event or by combining terms which clearly indicate teaching about the Holocaust.

课程中是否明确述及①关于大屠杀的教学内容，从哪些方面对大屠杀进行定义②，以及在何种背景下对其进行处理③？在接受调查的国家中，约有一半国家的历史课程对大屠杀作了规定④，但背景和术语有所差别。在第二次世界大战背景下对这一事件进行描述的情况最常见⑤，而且当涉及从侵犯人权中吸取教训⑥时，该事件也会成为重要内容。通常使用"大屠杀"这一术语来指称该事件，而较少的课程使用"浩劫"这一术语或将两个术语结合使用。在某些情况下，课程会放弃使用"大屠杀"和"浩劫"这两个术语，而是偏向于使用"灭杀"或"犹太人的种族灭绝"等替代术语、间接指称该事件，或通过将明确表明大屠杀教学内容的术语相结合来描述该事件。

批 注

① 不够贴切。
② 理解有误。
③ 语义错误。
④ 不合逻辑。
⑤ 被原文"牵着走"。
⑥ 理解有误，表述完全错误。

课程是否明确涉及关于大屠杀的教学内容，是如何定义大屠杀的，在何种背景下论及大屠杀事件？在调查的国家中，约有一半国家的历史课明确规定必须讲述大屠杀事件，但采用的背景和术语各不相同。最常见的做法是将大屠杀事件置于第二次世界大战的背景下，但也会出现在关于侵犯人权的课程当中。通常采用"大屠杀"来指代这一事件，少数课程会使用"浩劫"一词，或是同时使用这两个术语。在某些情况下，课程不使用"大屠杀"和"浩劫"等词，而是倾向于采用"灭绝"或"针对犹太人的种族灭绝"等替代术语来描述这一事件，间接提及事件本身，或是将明确指代大屠杀教学内容的术语结合起来。

1. 选词问题。第一，见"address"一词。"address"的词义有很多，用作动词时，"述及""涉及"都较为常见。结合背景来看，翻译稿处理成"述及"，不够准确，因为课程不是仅仅是对"大屠杀"相关内容进行介绍，还包括其他内容。换言之，"大屠杀"相关内容是课程的一部分，用"涉及"更贴切。与"address"类似的是"dealt with"一词，结合文本背景来看，"dealt with"显然不是"处理"的意思，因为"Holocaust"的出现有其特殊的背景，这里是说在怎样的背景下谈及大屠杀事件，所以应当译为"谈及"。第二，见"in what terms"一词；原文中的"in what terms"不是指"从哪些方面"，而是如何进行定义，因为原文强调的只是"Holocaust"的定义，而不是"Holocaust"的定义包含哪些方面。翻译稿对原句理解不到位，导致被原文"牵着走"，被束缚于"in what terms"的字面意思。

2. 语句理解问题。 前文问及"在何种背景下论及大屠杀事件",这里给出了答案。翻译稿对这句话的理解并不到位,所以在表述上也无法体现原文真正的含义。原文是说这些课程最常采用的做法是在第二次世界大战背景下论及大屠杀事件。单看原译文,很容易造成误解,让人误以为对这些事件的描述是在第二次世界大战背景下发生的。不是"在第二次世界大战背景下对这一事件进行描述",而是"将大屠杀事件置于第二次世界大战的背景下"。因此,审校稿对其作了修改。

3. 歧义词问题。 这句话中容易造成歧义的词是"lessons",这个词既有"教训"的含义,也有"课程"的含义,而且这两种含义都较为常见。如何判断词义,仍需联系上下文并按照一定的逻辑进行推断。翻译稿选用词义的是"教训",乍一看,"从侵犯人权中吸取教训"似乎也讲得通,但上下文并没有提及"教训"一类,通篇只是在客观阐述事实,其侧重点并不在"教训"上。实际上,这句话仍在说明在何种背景下论及"大屠杀",除了在第二次世界大战背景下,还会在与侵犯人权相关的课程中提及。因此,在处理歧义词时,要结合所在句、段的语境并注意原文论述重点。

第 2 段

In some curricula, only Jews are named explicitly as victims, while references to Sinti and Roma, people with disabilities, political opponents, homosexuals or other socially marginalised groups are infrequent. Most curricula do not specify the victim groups to be discussed in teaching. Moreover, while a quarter of all curricula contain no reference to the Holocaust, they instead discuss the purpose of the subject and methods to be used in its teaching, or else they explicitly refer to its historical contexts such as the Second World War and/or National Socialism, such that one may assume that the topic is part of teaching in the subject although it is not explicitly named. The study also points out semantic variations arising from the various languages whose vocabularies do not permit the direct adoption of the customary terms "Holocaust" or "Shoah".

在一些课程中,只有犹太人被明确称为①受害者,而很少提及辛提人和罗姆人、残疾人、政敌、同性恋者或其他社会边缘群体②。多数课程没有具体说明在教学过程中将被讨论的受害者群体。此外,虽然在所有课程中有四分之一没有提及大屠杀,但这些课程讨论了开设该科目的意图以及在教学过程中将会使用的方法,或者明确提及了该事件的历史背景,例如第二次世界大战和(或)国家社会主义,这会使人们认为这一主题是该科目教学内容的一部分,尽管并没有提及该事件。本研究还指出了源于不同语言的语义变化,这些语言的词汇使得无法直接使用惯常术语"大屠杀"或"浩劫"③。

在一些课程中,只有犹太人被明确列为受害者,很少提及辛提人和罗姆人、

批 注

① 不准确。
② 表述有误。
③ 理解有误。

残疾人、政敌、同性恋或其他社会边缘化群体。大多数课程没有具体说明将在教学过程中讨论的受害者群体。此外，有四分之一的课程没有提及大屠杀事件，但讨论了开设科目的意图以及教学中使用的方法，或是明确提及第二次世界大战和（或）纳粹等历史背景，由此可以认为这一主题是相关科目教学内容的一部分，尽管没有明确提及。研究报告还指出了源自不同语言的语义变化，这些语言因词汇限制，无法直接采用"大屠杀"或"浩劫"等惯常用语。

1. 用词准确问题。第一，原文中的"name as"不是最常见的"称为"这个意思。这句话是说犹太人被称为受害者，而是被列为受害者。原译文词义不够准确；第二，原文中"socially marginalised groups"有固定的译法，即"社会边缘化群体"，在有固定译法的情况下应当首先采用固定译法。

2. 表达问题，被英文"牵着"走。"whose vocabularies do not permit"是说这些语言受到词汇限制。在翻译过程中，尤其是社科类文章的翻译，译者需要结合上下文仔细揣摩，理解真正的含义，而不要一味地在形式上贴近原文。

1. The curricula analysis is based on 272 curricula from 135 (out of a potential total of 195) countries which were valid at the time of the study from 2013 to 2014. The primary aim thereof is to provide a comprehensive overview of the countries in which the Holocaust features or does not feature in history or social studies education. And since it strives to offer a broad overview in as many countries as possible and represent all continents, the analysis is confined to general information concerning (a) whether the Holocaust is taught, (b) where, in relation to other historical events, such teaching is stipulated, (c) in what terms it is stipulated, and (where available) (d) any information about the objectives ascribed to teaching about the Holocaust.

【参考译文】

课程分析的依据是135个国家（共有195个国家）在2013至2014年研究期间开设的272门课程。课程分析的主要目的是全面概述大屠杀事件成为（或没有成为）该国历史或社会学教育重要内容的国家。这项分析力图涉及尽可能多的国家，提供普遍概况，并且体现出各大洲的情况，为此，分析对象仅限于以下几方面的基本信息：（a）大屠杀是否属于教学内容；（b）相对于其他历史事件，有哪些国家对这方面的教学做出规定；（c）规定的具体内容是什么；以及（如果有的话）（d）关于大屠杀教学相关目标的任何信息。

2. The textbook analysis draws on 89 textbooks published in 26 countries since 2000. The selection of 26 countries on whose textbooks we conducted close analysis was made on the basis of hypotheses designed to ensure that the study

covers a wide range of different historiographical forms which lend themselves to infra- and international comparison. The selection of countries highlights a wide range of characteristic approaches to the Holocaust in various parts of the world. The criteria for selection were (a) geographical (to provide a broad overview of various regions of the world), (b) based on historical and political issues (countries involved or not involved in the event, in which mass violence or genocide has taken place, and former members of the Warsaw Pact or the Soviet Union), and (c) pragmatic (determined by the accessibility of curricula and textbooks and language expertise). This approach seeks to highlight common features, divergent differences and overlaps in order to enable educational policymakers to learn from challenges which are faced in other countries.

参考译文

教科书分析的依据是2000年以来26个国家出版的89本教科书。我们选择深入分析这26个国家的教科书，根据的是这样一条假设——确保此次研究广泛涵盖适于开展国内及国际对比的多种不同的史学形式。选择这些国家，凸显出世界各国针对大屠杀事件采取了多种多样且各具特点的处理方法。选择标准是：（a）地理标准（以便提供关于世界各地多个地区的普遍概况）；（b）基于历史和政治问题（参与或未参与这一事件的国家，曾经发生过大规模暴力行为或种族灭绝的国家，《华沙条约》或前苏联的成员国）；以及（c）实用标准（取决于能否获取课程和教科书以及语言专长）。这种方法力图强调共同特点、扩散性差异和重叠部分，目的是让教育决策者能够从其他国家面临的挑战中有所收获。

背景介绍

以下四篇（第七篇至第十篇）均选自教科文组织《信使》杂志。

《信使》杂志分为六大板块（社论、广角、影像、观点、嘉宾、时事），所选文章主题分别涉及自然遗产、文化遗产、人物传记和媒体媒介，既有描述具体事件的"故事体"，亦有抒发个人观点的"散文体"，充分体现了杂志类文本的特有风格。

第七篇以史上几大著名沉船事件为线索，引出水下遗产主题，行文上偏新闻体，按照背景、事实、评述的顺序铺陈展开，特别是组句方式极为灵活，需要跳出句与句之间的藩篱，以语篇为单位处理文本。

第八篇选新闻体风格更为鲜明，从个人视角讲述故事，以点带面引出人类文化遗产"阿布辛贝神庙"这一宏大主题，语言极为精妙细腻，译者应深入打磨自身的文字表达能力。

第九篇是一份笔记摘录，以联合国教科文组织《信使》杂志发刊七十周年为背景，向创刊人桑迪·科夫勒(1916—2002)致敬，邀请他的孙女奥雷利娅·多斯（Aurélia Dausse）分享她对祖父的记忆。该篇具有传记性质，语言较为灵活，许多表达甚至口语化。在翻译时，既要把握这种灵活的表达方式，又要避免因为过于贴近原文而导致译文难以理解。

第十篇是一则抒情类小品文，就联合国电台从传统到现代的蜕变进程抒发感想，属于典型的评述体。在翻译时，要注意明确文章的中心思想和基调，再以此为基础选词造句，既不可拘泥于字面含义，也不可过度代入个人感情，任意发挥。

第七篇

It was access to the riches of Asia that originally motivated the Spanish exploration of the Pacific. Chinese merchants, meanwhile, were in search of silver extracted from the mines of the New World. From the sixteenth century onwards, trade between them became a very lucrative business. It is in this context that the sea-route between the port of Manila, in the Spanish Philippines, and Acapulco, the main port on the Pacific coast of New Spain, was opened. Once or twice a year, Spanish galleons made the crossing from Manila—their holds filled with porcelain, spices, silk, gold, lacquerware and medicinal plants, mostly from China and Japan. The goods, unloaded in Acapulco, were then transported by land to Veracruz, and finally conveyed to Spain by sea.

As the number of crossings was limited, the galleons were designed with a large capacity—they could carry over 1 000 passengers and up to 2 000 barrels. It took no less than four months to complete this risky voyage. Battles and storms claimed many of these gigantic vessels between the mid-sixteenth century and 1815, when the Mexican War of Independence began. No fewer than forty wrecks now lie in the waters of the Philippines archipelago, and along the North American coast.

The most impressive galleon of her time, the Concepción broke up on the reefs of Saipan (Philippines) following an argument among the crew during a storm. Stranded on the island, the sailors were attacked by indigenous peoples. Only six of the castaways survived.

请自行翻译后查看后文的分析点评

分析点评

第1段

It was access to the riches of Asia that originally motivated the Spanish exploration of the Pacific. Chinese merchants, meanwhile, were in search of silver extracted from the mines of the New World. From the sixteenth century onwards, trade between them became a very lucrative business. It is in this context that the sea-route between the port of Manila, in the Spanish Philippines, and Acapulco, the main port on the Pacific coast of New Spain, was opened. Once or twice a year, Spanish galleons made the crossing from Manila—their holds filled with porcelain, spices, silk, gold, lacquerware and medicinal plants, mostly from China and Japan. The goods, unloaded in Acapulco, were then transported by land to Veracruz, and finally conveyed to Spain by sea.

翻译稿

16世纪，富饶的东方世界打开了西班牙人探索太平洋的初心，与此同时，新大陆的矿产也引发了中国商人开采白银的好奇心，故而两国因贸易结缘，将海运打造成了一门极其有利可图的生意①。基于这一背景，西班牙王室开通了西属菲律宾马尼拉港与新西班牙太平洋沿岸大港阿卡普尔科之间的海上航线。为横渡太平洋，西班牙帆船队每年从马尼拉出发一到两次——归来时，船舱装满各种瓷器、香料、丝绸、黄金、漆器和药用植物，其中大部分来自中国和日本。货物先在阿卡普尔科卸下，然后经陆路运至韦拉克鲁斯，最后经海路运往西班牙②。

审校稿

回望16世纪，攫取亚洲财富的野心驱使西班牙人踏上太平洋探险之路，与此同时，中国商人竞相追逐从新大陆矿藏中开采出的白银。自那时起，两国开始互通贸易，"其利百倍"。正是在这一大背景之下，西属菲律宾马尼拉港（Manila）与新西班牙太平洋沿岸大港阿卡普尔科（Acapulco）之间的海上航线应运打通。西班牙大帆船队每年定期航行一次或两次，满载主要来自中国和日本的各种瓷器、香料、丝绸、黄金、漆器和药用植物，从马尼拉出发，横跨太平洋，中途先在阿卡普尔科卸货，然后经陆路将货物转运至韦拉克鲁斯（Veracruz），最后再经海路运抵西班牙。

点评

1. 理解问题。见"From the sixteenth century onwards, trade between them became a very lucrative business."一句。翻译稿将这句话处理为"故而两国因贸易结缘，将海运打造成了一门极其有利可图的生意"，如果单看译文，似乎逻辑通顺，也颇有文采，但结合原文来看，可发现增补了太多原文本不存在的内容，如"将其打造成一门""结缘"，难免有追求文采而忽略忠实之嫌；此外，"trade between them became very lucrative"，是客观陈述事实，特别是"became"

批 注

① 理解不准。
② 组句问题。

表明一种状态,并不一定是两国刻意为之,因此应按照审校稿处理,译为"其利百倍"。

2. 句间组句问题。见两个长句"Spanish galleons made the crossing from Manila—their holds filled with porcelain, spices..."。原文用句号隔开的两个句子,在翻译时,不必完全将其作为两个独立的完整句来处理,应当跳出思维局限,将两个句子以及句子间逻辑厘清,确定是将两个句子分开处理还是合译合适。对于本句,可以看出其原文的逻辑关系不是很明朗,先以"Spanish galleons"开头,然后又转而叙述"The goods, unloaded in Acapulco",转换了主语和语气,实际上这两句结合起来描述的是整个返航流程,先满载货物,然后出发,卸货等。如果按照我们常识理解,应当将这两个单独的句子结合起来组织语言,按照空间先后顺序调整句子顺序,因此句间组句也是一个需要加以注意的策略。

第 2 段

As the number of crossings was limited, the galleons were designed with a large capacity—they could carry over 1 000 passengers and up to 2 000 barrels. It took no less than four months to complete this risky voyage. Battles and storms claimed many of these gigantic vessels between the mid-sixteenth century and 1815, when the Mexican War of Independence began. No fewer than forty wrecks now lie in the waters of the Philippines archipelago, and along the North American coast.

鉴于渡口①数量有限,西班牙探险者对帆船进行了大体量设计——最多可运载 1 000 多名乘客和 2 000 桶原油。完成一次冒险航行②至少要花四个月时间。在 16 世纪中期到 1815 年墨西哥独立战争爆发之间,频繁的战争和风暴使无数艘巨帆香消玉殒。如今,至少有 40 艘沉船仍葬身于菲律宾群岛水域及北美海岸。

批 注

① 一词多义问题。
② 使用"拆译法"。

为解决每年航行次数有限的问题,海运所用大帆船均为专门设计,运载量惊人——最多可容纳 1 000 多名乘客和 2 000 桶原油。一次航行至少要花费四个月时间,而且风险重重。自 16 世纪中期到 1815 年墨西哥独立战争爆发,无数巨帆在战争和风暴中殒没。如今,在菲律宾群岛水域和北美海岸之下依然散落着 40 多艘失事船只的残骸。

1. 词汇理解问题。见"number of crossings..."一句。"crossing"本身有多重含义,既有"渡口、交叉口"含义,也有"横渡、横越、横跨"含义。无论选哪一种,似乎都与本文语境很贴近,所以在选词上须更加谨慎。在此处,我们需要理解的是,到底是渡口有限还是航行次数有限会对帆船设计产生实际影响,如果是前者,其对帆船设计会产生一定影响,但不是主导性因素,因为可通过绕行解决这一问题；而如果是航行次数问题，那么一定会对帆船的容载量有要求，即进行大体量设计的必要原因，因此应当选"航行次数"。

2. 拆译法。见"risky voyage"。翻译稿将"risky voyage"处理成"冒险航行"也不算错，但是相比审校稿在文采上略显逊色。审校稿将"risky"作为定语拆分出来单独组句，相比翻译稿的处理，更凸显了航行的难度，并且拆译出来，也缩短了原句长度，采用四字格形式，增强了其可读性，在文采上也更符合汉语表达。

第 3 段

The most impressive galleon of her time, the Concepción broke up on the reefs of Saipan (Philippines) following an argument among the crew during a storm. Stranded on the island, the sailors were attacked by indigenous peoples. Only six of the castaways survived.

作为17世纪最瞩目的大帆船，康塞普西翁号以一次海难退场，在一场风暴中，② 船员们发生争执，随后船只在塞班岛（菲律宾海域）触礁失事，只有六名水手幸存。这几名落难者被困在岛上，遭到土著人袭击。

当彼之时，康塞普西翁号可谓独领风骚，后不幸遭遇海上风暴，加之船员们争执不下，在塞班岛（菲律宾）触礁失事。船上人员皆被困在岛上，又遭到土著人袭击，最终只有六名水手幸存。

1. 选词问题。见"impressive"一词。"impressive"就其本义，可理解为"瞩目、印象深刻、刻骨铭心"，如翻译稿所采用的用法，似乎也不为错，但如果不把"impressive"当作定语来处理即"瞩目的大帆船"，而是处理成谓语，那么会有更为可取的表达，如审校稿的处理方式，译为"独领风骚"，更体现了康塞普西翁号的独特、与众不同之处，也是对"impressive"一词最大程度的美化。

2. 重复问题。见"the Concepción broke up on the reefs of..."一句。翻译稿在处理这句话时，可能出于文采、可读性考虑，将"storm"重复了一次，先总体上表明"以海难退场"，再作具体描述，"在一场风暴中"，从逻辑上讲，也讲得通，但是这种处理方式更接近于"编译"，而非"翻译"，包括在句首增加的"17世纪"，也有编译之嫌，虽然《信使》相对于其他会议类文件偏文学性，但不能将此与"编辑、编译"对等，带入过多个人理解；研究审校稿，我们会发现其可取之处在于，不仅四字短句与长句相结合，还以适当的逻辑词连接，如"当彼之时""后不幸""加之"，使得前后逻辑顺序明晰，读起来错落有致，值得我们借鉴学习。

批 注

① 选词问题。
② 重复问题。

 补充练习

1. For a long time, this submerged heritage was not subject to any particular protection. But in 2001, UNESCO Member States, concerned by the destruction of submerged sites—particularly with the development of technologies that facilitated access to the sea bed—adopted the Convention on the Protection of the Underwater Cultural Heritage. This makes it possible to protect and promote these archaeological sites, which include ancient shipwrecks, decorated caves and sunken cities.

参考译文

长期以来，诸如此类的水下遗产迟迟未受到任何特殊保护。直到2001年，联合国教科文组织会员国出于对水下遗址屡遭破坏的关切——特别是随着海床勘探技术的发展——通过了《保护水下文化遗产公约》。从此，保护和宣传古代沉船残骸、彩绘洞穴和沉没之城等考古遗址从不可能变为可能。

2. Commissioned by the Spanish crown to explore the Californian coast in search of harbours and watering points, the ship sank after a storm. It was not until 1941 that archaeologists found part of the cargo.

 参考译文

圣奥古斯丁号受西班牙王室委托，前往加利福尼亚海岸寻找港口和水源，后于一场风暴中沉没。直到1941年，考古学家才发现从船上遗落的部分货物。

第八篇

 原文

I still have a particularly vivid memory of the issues dedicated to the Nubia campaign. I was a high school student back then, and knew nothing about the Abu Simbel temple. In the Courier issue of February 1960, Save the Treasures of Nubia, I learnt that the construction of the Aswan Dam across the Nile in Egypt would flood 3 000-year-old monuments. This was at the end of the 1950s, and UNESCO mobilized the whole world to save them. The Organization garnered tremendous international support to undertake the monumental effort of entirely dismantling the majestic Abu Simbel temple and rebuilding it in another location, several metres higher—so that twice a year, the rays of the sun would penetrate the temple's inner sanctuary, just as they did in its original location.

Impressed by the four colossi of Rameses Ⅱ, I read, in an article entitled Abu Simbel, Now or Never (Courier, October 1961), this detailed explanation by Peter Ritchie-Calder, the famous British scientific writer: "A narrow passage leads to the inner sanctuary where are seated the statues of the three gods to whom the temple is dedicated, and Rameses himself. And here is seen the purposeful ingenuity of the architects and engineers. Like skilful stage-lighters, they contrived that the rising sun would penetrate 200 feet into the heart of the mountain, to illumine the faces of only three of the immortals. The fourth, the god of the Underworld, Ptah, on the extreme left remained eternally in darkness. This essential feature of Abu Simbel was one of the things taken into account in deciding how the temple should be finally preserved from the rising waters of the High Dam."

请在自行翻译后查看后文的分析点评

分析点评

第1段

I still have a particularly vivid memory of the issues dedicated to the Nubia campaign. I was a high school student back then, and knew nothing about the Abu Simbel temple. In the Courier issue of February 1960, Save the Treasures of Nubia, I learnt that the construction of the Aswan Dam across the Nile in Egypt would flood 3 000-year-old monuments. This was at the end of the 1950s, and UNESCO mobilized the whole world to save them. The Organization garnered tremendous international support to undertake the monumental effort of entirely dismantling the majestic Abu Simbel temple and rebuilding it in another location, several metres higher—so that twice a year, the rays of the sun would penetrate the temple's inner sanctuary, just as they did in its original location.

翻译稿

我对专门讲述努比亚运动的那几期杂志仍记忆犹新。当时我还是一名高中生，对阿布辛贝神庙一无所知。在1960年2月的那期《信使》——"拯救努比亚的瑰宝"——中，我了解到在埃及建造的横跨尼罗河的阿斯旺水坝将淹没有着3 000年历史的遗迹。这件事发生在20世纪50年代末，教科文组织动员全世界拯救这些遗迹。教科文组织获得了巨大的国际支持，付出了艰辛努力，终将雄伟的阿布辛贝神庙拆除，并在另一个地点完成重建，新址比原址高出了几十米②，所以太阳光束每年可射入神庙内部的神殿③两次，

批 注

① 主语变更问题。
② 理解错误。
③ 略显啰唆。

就像在原址上那样。

审校稿

我对专门讲述努比亚运动的那几期杂志仍记忆犹新。当时我还是一名高中生，对阿布辛贝神庙一无所知。在1960年2月的那期《信使》——"拯救努比亚的瑰宝"——中，我了解到在埃及尼罗河上建造阿斯旺水坝将淹没已有3 000年历史的遗迹。这件事发生在20世纪50年代末，联合国教科文组织动员全世界拯救这些遗迹。联合国教科文组织获得了巨大的国际支持，付出了艰辛努力，终将雄伟的阿布辛贝神庙拆除，并在另一个地点完成重建，高出了几米，使太阳光束每年可射入神庙内殿两次，就像在原址上那样。

点评

1. 主语变更问题。见原文中的"...construction of the Aswan Dam across the Nile in Egypt..."一句，主语是"construction"，而不是"Aswan Dam"。原译文将此译成"在埃及建造的横跨尼罗河的阿斯旺水坝"，变换了主语，导致前后不连贯，而且连用几个"的"，使译文可读性变差。因此，应当按照审校稿的处理方式，将动词用作主语，处理成"在埃及尼罗河上建造阿斯旺水坝"，使表达更加简略精当。

2. 表达不准问题。原文是"several metres higher"，也就是"几米"而不是"几十米"，尤其是结合背景知识，对于水利建筑工程而言，"几米"和"几十米"差距非常大，必须予以谨慎表述。第二点是过度"增译"问题。原文中没有出现"新址""旧址"的字样，翻译稿增译这些词是没有必要的，完全可以接着前面的语句继续叙述，且不会造成中文语义上的中断。

3. 表述简洁问题。见"...the temple's inner sanctuary..."一句，从字面意思来看，正如原译文所说，是"神庙内部的神殿"，但这种表述略显啰唆，已经是神庙了，没有必要再重复"神殿"。另外，跳出表述简洁这一点，根据背景知识和生活常识，也可以将"the temple's inner sanctuary"理解为神庙内殿。

第 2 段

Impressed by the four colossi of Rameses II, I read, in an article entitled Abu Simbel, Now or Never (Courier, October 1961), this detailed explanation by Peter Ritchie-Calder, the famous British scientific writer: "A narrow passage leads to the inner sanctuary where are seated the statues of the three gods to whom the temple is dedicated, and Rameses himself. And here is seen the purposeful ingenuity of the architects and engineers. Like skilful stage-lighters, they contrived that the rising sun would penetrate 200 feet into the heart of the mountain, to illumine the faces of only three of the immortals. The fourth, the god of the Underworld, Ptah, on the extreme left remained eternally in darkness. This essential feature of Abu Simbel was one of the things taken into account in deciding how the temple should be finally preserved from the rising waters of the High Dam."

翻 译 稿

拉美西斯二世时期的四尊神像给我留下了深刻印象,我在一篇题为《阿布辛贝,现在还是永不》的文章(《信使》,1961年10月)中读到了英国著名科学作家彼得·里奇-卡尔德的详细说明:"一条狭窄的走廊直通神殿内部,里面坐落着三尊神像,这座神庙就是为他们而建①,除此之外还有拉美西斯二世自己②的雕像。在这里能看到建筑师和工程师们为了明确的目的所发挥的聪明才智③。与技能高超的舞台灯光师一样,他们将神庙设计④为能使旭日的金光穿过200英尺的庙廊直抵岩洞尽头⑤,只照亮其中三座神像的面庞。最左边的第四座神像——冥界之神则永远留在黑暗中。在决定如何保护这座神庙最终不被水位不断上涨的高坝淹没时,阿布辛贝神庙的这个基本特点也是考虑因素之一。"

批 注

① 可读性不强。
② 用词不准确。
③ 可读性差。
④ 可以使用更有文采的表述。
⑤ 略显啰唆。

审 校 稿

拉美西斯二世时期的四尊神像给我留下了深刻印象,我在一篇题为《阿布辛贝,现在还是永不》的文章(《信使》,1961年10月)中读到了英国著名科学作家彼得·里奇-卡尔德(Peter Ritchie-Calder)的详细说明:"一条狭窄的走廊直通内殿,里面坐落着三尊主奉神像,还有拉美西斯二世本人的雕像。在这里可以看出建筑师和工程师们成竹在胸,匠心独运。像技能高超的舞台灯光师一样,他们巧加设计,使旭日的金光穿过200英尺照进大山中央,只照亮其中三座神像的面庞,而最左边的第四座神像——冥界之神卜塔则永远留在黑暗中。在决定如何保护这座神庙最终不被因修建高坝而不断上涨的河水淹没时,阿布辛贝神庙的这个基本特点也是考虑因素之一。"

点 评

1. 表达简洁和专业问题。在"statues of the three gods to whom the temple is dedicated"这一句中,比较难处理的是"dedicated"一词。翻译稿先说神像,后面又列分句,解释了这座神庙是专门为这些神像建立的。从意思上来说,似乎没有问题,但考虑到这类社科文章的可读性要求,可以选择更简洁的表述。另外,因涉及宗教术语,在处理一些词汇时可以往这一专业领域靠拢,可按照审校稿的处理方法,将此处"dedicated"处理成"主奉"。第二处见"heart of the mountain"一词,该词即指"大山中央"。原译文中的"直抵岩洞尽头"添加的成分太多,略显啰唆,没有必要。

2. 书面语与口语表述。见"himself"一词,该词确有"自己"的意思,但在这里并不恰当。"自己的雕像"过于口语化,可以选择更贴切的表达,即"本人"。

3. 灵活译法。翻译稿对"purposeful ingenuity of the architects and engineers"的处理略显生硬,几乎是按照英文对译过来的,缺少美感,可读性也较差。在处理社科类文章时,必要时可选择灵活的表述,尤其是《信使》这类文学色彩较强的文本,在准确无误的基础上,应将语言的神韵表达出来,可按照审校稿的处理方式,对"purposeful ingenuity"进行艺术拔高,处理成"成竹在胸,匠心独运"。同理,对于"contrive"一词也可以作灵活处理,以体现出建筑师和工程师们高超的技艺，审校稿改成"巧加设计"，为文字赋予了更多美感。

4. 逻辑问题。"how the temple should be...waters of the high dam"一句中，应该是修建高坝后，水位上涨，造成神庙被淹没，而不是高坝淹没了神庙。

1. But five years later, the magazine reappeared. The first issue of the revived Courier, was published in April 2017, with the motto: "Several Voices, One World". Now a quarterly, it continues to enrich the collection. You can access the entire collection, from 1948 to the present, in the digital archives. Most of the archives are available in English, Spanish and French, but issues from the last few years can be found in many more languages on the journal's website. It is worth the detour. I recommend it. Reading the Courier, you will discover a serious vision of the major current issues facing humanity. Its massive ambition—it is one of the greatest past and current merits of UNESCO—is to promote links between various forms of thought, different ways of looking at problems, and a call to humankind.

然而，五年之后，这本杂志再次面世。第一期复刊后的《信使》于2017年4月出版，其格言是："多种声音，一个世界"。如今的《信使》是一本季刊，它继续充实了之前的合集。你可以在数字档案馆获阅从1948年至今的整个合集。档案馆中的大多数文件有英文本、西班牙文本和法文本，但关于最近几年各期，可以在《信使》网站上找到许多其他语种的版本。它值得我们费一点周章。我推荐这本杂志。你在阅读《信使》时会发现一种关于人类当前面临的主要问题的严肃见解。它的宏伟目标（这是联合国教科文组织过去和现在最伟大的价值之一）是加强不同形式的思想之间的联系，促进以不同方式看待问题，以及加强对人类的呼吁。

2. To reiterate what I have already stated, the journal's major contribution is the promotion of a culture which encompasses both a diversity of opinions and respect. This is the culture—and I say this with the utmost sincerity, recalling my family background—I acquired by reading the Courier with passion and enthusiasm. I was a young boy who was eager to learn, and through its pages, I found a source to do so. This is why I write these lines.

我想重申我已经说过的内容，这本杂志的主要贡献在于促进一种既能包容不同观点又能给予尊重的文化。这种文化 —— 回想起我的家庭背景，我带着最大的诚意说这句话 —— 是我如痴如醉阅读《信使》了解到的文化。当时我还是一个少年，渴望学习，通过这本杂志，找到了学习的源泉。这就是我为何写下这些文字。

3. The importance of UNESCO and its Courier in today's world, and tomorrow's, is all the more important, as the fundamental principles of the Organization's Constitution are being put to the test by those who promote "the mutual incomprehension between peoples" and contradict these principles "by exploiting ignorance and prejudice". Let us not forget this.

在当今世界和以后的世界，联合国教科文组织及其刊物《信使》越来越重要，因为联合国教科文组织《组织法》中的基本原则正在受到那些推崇"人们之间的相互不理解"及"利用无知和偏见"来反驳这些原则的人们的检验。我们不要忘记这一点。

第九篇

Back in New York, Sandy became a part-time columnist for the newspaper America, and learned the techniques of printmaking. At the same time, he attended seminars by the French anthropologist, Claude Lévi-Strauss, at the New School for Social Research. Lévi-Strauss had also left France just before the Occupation and the two men became friends.

Several years later, they would meet up again in Paris, one as Editor-in-Chief of the Courier, the other as one of the authors of the first UNESCO Statement on Race (1950), and the author of Race and History (1952), one of the great classics of anti-racist literature. Koffler would regularly invite Lévi-Strauss to contribute to the Courier during the 1950s, so that many of the fundamental articles on anthropology were first published in the Courier, before being reprinted in books.

The climate of war motivated Sandy to sign up and work for the US Army's Psychological Warfare Branch (PWB). He trained at the Office of War Information (OWI), a US government information agency, which wanted to use modern mass-propaganda methods to disseminate pacifist ideas. He was sent to Rabat (Morocco) aboard an American (naval cargo) Liberty Ship, which was delivering supplies to the Allied Forces during the Battle of the Atlantic. There, he worked as a correspondent and information director for Voice of America radio, developing a round-the-clock programme of world news broadcasts. In 1944, he wrote in his diary: "I can't tell you how much I love this work, I find it useful and feel it's worth it."

请自行翻译后查看后文的分析点评

分析点评

第 1 段

Back in New York, Sandy became a part-time columnist for the newspaper America, and learned the techniques of printmaking. At the same time, he attended seminars by the French anthropologist, Claude Lévi-Strauss, at the New School for Social Research. Lévi-Strauss had also left France just before the Occupation and the two men became friends.

回到纽约之后，桑迪成了美国报纸①的兼职专栏作家，并学习了版画制作技巧。与此同时，他参加了法国人类学家克劳德·列维·斯特劳斯②在纽约新社会研究院举办的讲习班。列维·斯特劳斯也是就在纳粹要占领法国之前离开了，他们二人成了朋友。

批 注

① 理解问题。
② 人名翻译问题。

回到纽约之后，桑迪成了报纸《美国》的兼职专栏作家，并学习了版画制作技巧。与此同时，他参加了法国人类学家克劳德·列维·斯特劳斯（Claude Lévi-Strauss）在纽约新社会研究院举办的讲习班。列维·斯特劳斯也是就在纳粹要占领法国之前离开了，他们二人成了朋友。

1. 理解问题。原文中是"newspaper America"，而不是"American newspaper"。这里的"America"指的是报刊的名称，即名为《美国》的报纸，翻译稿将此处译成"美国报纸"，显然将"America"和"American"混淆了。

2. 人名翻译问题。在《信使》杂志中，所有出现的人名都需要翻译。在第一次出现时，要在中文后面保留人名的英文，放在括号里。这段中的人名"克劳德·列维·斯特劳斯"是全文第一次出现，所以正确的格式应该是"克劳德·列维·斯特劳斯（Claude Lévi-Strauss）"。

第 2 段

Several years later, they would meet up again in Paris, one as Editor-in-Chief of the Courier, the other as one of the authors of the first UNESCO Statement on Race (1950), and the author of Race and History (1952), one of the great classics of anti-racist literature. Koffler would regularly invite Lévi-Strauss to contribute to the Courier during the 1950s, so that many of the fundamental articles on anthropology were first published in the Courier, before being reprinted in books.

批 注

① 漏译；中文不够地道。
② 语气不连贯。
③ 表述不合乎中文习惯。

翻译稿

几年后，他们在巴黎再次相遇，其中一人成了《信使》的主编，另一人成了《种族与历史》（1952年）的作者，这本书是关于反种族主义的伟大经典著作之一。在1950年代，科夫勒定期邀请列维·斯特劳斯向《信使》投稿。因此，许多关于人类学的基本文章在被重新印刷成册之前最先在《信使》上发表。

审校稿

几年后，他们在巴黎再次相遇。一人成了《信使》的主编，另一人参与了第一份《联合国教科文组织种族问题声明》（1950年）的起草，撰写了《种族与历史》（1952年），一本关于反种族主义的伟大经典著作。20世纪50年代，科夫勒定期邀请克劳德·列维·斯特劳斯向《信使》投稿。因此，许多关于人类学的基本文章在被重新印刷成册之前最先在《信使》上发表。

点 评

1. 漏译问题。翻译稿遗漏了"authors of the first UNESCO Statement on Race (1950)"。"UNESCO Statement on Race"是《联合国教科文组织种族问题声明》，"authors of statement"说明这份声明的起草者有很多，如果单纯译成作者，略显生硬，而且也没有体现出"one of"的意思，所以应按照审校稿的方法处理，将此译为"参与……的起草"。第二个遗漏点是"the author of Race and History"。从结构上来看，"the author of Race and History"与前面的"authors of the first UNESCO Statement on Race (1950)"类似，但不同的是，"Race and History"是一本书，而"UNESCO Statement on Race"是一份声明，所以在处理"author"的译法时，需要灵活处理。对于声明而言，"起草"可与之搭配，但对于一本书，如果还译成起草，就会显得搭配不当，所以这里将其处理成"撰写"。而翻译稿按照英文对译过来，处理成"作者"，从意思上来说不能算错，但"成为……的作者"不符合中文的表达习惯，所以应该避免过于贴近原文而导致译文的可读性变差。

2. 语序表述问题。见"one of the great classics of anti-racist literature"一句。从语法上来说，"one of the great classics of anti-racist literature"是"Race and History"的同位语，其修饰对象是前面提到的著作。翻译稿的处理方法是，先提及作者，然后又变换主语，提及这本书，导致语气不连贯，缺乏可读性，而审校稿先提到这部著作，紧接着补充说明，使前后主次分明，语气连贯，符合中文表达习惯。

3. 表达规范问题。在联合国稿件中，无论是正式的会议文件，还是相对灵活的出版物稿件，都应注意数字日期的规范表述，因此，按照汉语习惯，"1950s"应译为"20世纪50年代"。

第3段

The climate of war motivated Sandy to sign up and work for the US Army's Psychological Warfare Branch (PWB). He trained at the Office of War Information (OWI), a US government information agency, which wanted to use modern mass-propaganda methods to disseminate pacifist ideas. He was sent to Rabat (Morocco) aboard an American (naval cargo) Liberty Ship, which was delivering supplies to the Allied Forces during the Battle of the Atlantic. There, he worked as a correspondent and information director for Voice of America radio, developing a round-the-clock programme of world news broadcasts. In 1944, he wrote in his diary: "I can't tell you how much I love this work, I find it useful and feel it's worth it."

战争的氛围促使桑迪与美国陆军心理作战部签约并为其工作。他在战争情报局，美国政府的一个情报机构①接受培训，这个机构想要利用现代大众宣传方法传播和平主义思想。他被派往拉巴特（摩洛哥），登上了一艘在大西洋海战期间负责向同盟军输送物资的美国（海上货物）自由号船只。他在那里作为无线电台"美国之音"的通讯记者和信息主管开展工作②，并开发了一档24小时播报世界新闻的栏目。1944年，他在日记中写道："简直无法言说我有多热爱这份工作，我认为它很有用并且觉得它很有价值。"

批 注

① 语气中断，不符合中文表达习惯。
② 表述不准确，过于贴近原文。

战争的氛围促使桑迪与美国陆军心理战部签约并为其工作。他在美国政府的一个情报机构——战争情报局接受培训，这个机构想要利用现代大众宣传方法传播和平主义思想。他被派往拉巴特（摩洛哥），登上了一艘在大西洋海战期间负责向同盟军输送物资的美国（海上货物）自由号轮船。他在那里担当无线电广播"美国之音"的通讯记者和信息主管，并开发了一档24小时播报世界新闻的节目。1944年，他在日记中写道："简直无法言说我有多热爱这份工作，我认为它很有用并且觉得它很有价值。"

1. 表达于贴近原文。见"There, he worked as a correspondent and information director..."一句。翻译稿在翻译"work as"这个短语时，过于贴近原文，"作为……开展工作"几乎是按照英文对译过来的，这种译法不符合中文表达习惯，可读性较差。这句话的意思是说担任通讯记者，而"开展工作"已经隐含其中，完全没有必要再重复说明。

2. 语气中断问题。见"He trained at the Office of War Information (OWI), a US government..."一句。原文中的"US government information agency"是"Office of War Information"的同位语。翻译稿按照原文语序，将"美国政府的一个情报机构"放在"战争情报局"之后，这种处理方式导致语气中断，不连贯。此处可以灵活处理，先说后面的"US government information agency"，再提及"Office

of War Information",这种先总括再举例的表述方式符合中文表达习惯,能够避免语气中断。

1. For Sandy, multiplying the number of language versions of the Courier was a way of building bridges between men. This is what he said in Madras (now Chennai), India, at the launch of the Tamil edition: "In the past, nations were self-centred. In the past twenty years, we have witnessed an astounding phenomenon of countries looking far beyond all borders to the horizons, to every corner of the globe, to work together for peace and understanding. This is the message that UNESCO and all the United Nations family is trying to achieve. This afternoon, I had the privilege to see the Chief Minister [of Tamil Nadu state]. He informed me that Madras is prepared to go ahead and has given us the green light for the production of a Tamil edition of the Courier. As the Editor-in-Chief of the Courier, my blood tingled when he said that, because this is an achievement."

在桑迪看来,增加《信使》的语言版本数量是在人们之间搭建桥梁的一种方式。他在泰米尔语版发行时于印度马德拉斯(如今的金奈)所言如下:"从前,各个民族都以自我为中心。在过去 20 年里,我们亲眼看见了一种令人震惊的现象,各国纷纷突破边界,眺望远方的地平线,遥望世界的各个角落,共同合作以求和平与理解。这是联合国教科文组织和联合国大家庭一直试图实现的宗旨。今天下午,我有幸见到 [泰米尔纳德邦] 首席部长。他告诉我,马德拉斯已做好前行准备,已经为《信使》泰米尔语版的编制打开了绿灯。作为《信使》的主编,闻听他此言,我热血沸腾,因为这是一项功绩。"

2. Sandy Koffler was indisputably a great professional, gifted with solid interpersonal skills. A close friend of leading figures who have marked the twentieth century—such as the Swiss ethnologist Alfred Métraux and the American engineer and painter, Frank Malina, both colleagues at UNESCO—he was much appreciated by the first seven Directors-General of the Organization. One of them, René Maheu (1961—1974) would say of him that his "talent was never separated from his convictions".

毋庸置疑,桑迪·科夫勒是一位伟大的专业人员,天生拥有出色的人际交往能力。身为 20 世纪标志性领军人物 [例如瑞士人种学家阿尔弗雷德·梅特罗(Alfred Métraux)和美国工程师兼画家弗兰克·马林纳(Frank Malina)],他们都是桑迪在教科文组织的同事的亲密朋友,他深受教科文组织头七位总干事的赏识。其中一位总干事勒内·马厄(René Maheu)(1961 年至 1974 年任职)对他的评价是他"有才华，有信念"。

3. Determined and charismatic, a tireless worker in the service of UNESCO's ideals of peace, always watchful to remain politically neutral, even as international tensions mounted during the Cold War, Sandy Koffler had an inflexible character: "He never accepted orders, even from the highest diplomatic and political American officials; he was intransigent, and unshakeable; and that posed some problems for him," said Pauline Koffler, his second wife.

桑迪·科夫勒意志坚定、魅力非凡，孜孜不倦地为实现教科文组织的和平理想而奋斗。他始终非常警惕，以保持政治立场中立，即使是在冷战时期国际局势紧张的情况下亦然。他生性刚强。"他从不接受命令，哪怕是美国最高外交官员和政治官员下达的命令；他从不妥协，坚定不移；这给他带来了一些麻烦，"他的第二任妻子玻琳·科夫勒（Pauline Koffler）如是说。

原文

Is radio out of date? Is it time to bury this medium that entered our homes nearly a century ago? Far from it. Certainly, the transistor of yesteryear has lived its life. Linear listening, ear glued to the radio receiver, has had its day. Radio has begun its digital transformation. Today, listeners are just as likely, if not more so, to tune in on their mobile phones or computers. A major factor in reinventing the medium has been the production of podcasts—programmes available on demand. Radio can sometimes even be watched, when programmes are filmed and posted online. The listener has evolved too. Once passive behind their devices, they can now take part in broadcasts, and even help shape programmes, by voicing their opinions on social media.

So it is a very different but thriving medium that we now celebrate on 13 February each year, on World Radio Day. Proclaimed in 2011, the Day reminds us of the crucial role this medium plays—reaching the widest audience in the world, in the most isolated areas or in emergency situations. Since UNESCO's creation, the Organization has relied on this key medium to help fulfil its mandate to foster freedom of expression and the free flow of ideas throughout the world.

It is important that radio reflects the audiences it serves more accurately, because diversity in radio is the key to fair and independent information. It is also a means of giving a voice to the variety of cultures and opinions that form the basis for critical thinking. In spite of the evolution of radio in recent years, it remains that irreplaceable voice which populates our solitude and seems to speak to us alone—even though it addresses the multitude. In a world invaded by screens, "paradoxically, one advantage of radio is that it is not accompanied by the image", noted the UNESCO Courier in the editorial of its February 1997 issue devoted to radio.

请自行翻译后查看后文的分析点评

分析点评

第 1 段

Is radio out of date? Is it time to bury this medium that entered our homes nearly a century ago? Far from it. Certainly, the transistor of yesteryear has lived its life. Linear listening, ear glued to the radio receiver, has had its day. Radio has begun its digital transformation. Today, listeners are just as likely, if not more so, to tune in on their mobile phones or computers. A major factor in reinventing the medium has been the production of podcasts—programmes available on demand. Radio can sometimes even be watched, when programmes are filmed and posted online. The listener has evolved too. Once passive behind their devices, they can now take part in broadcasts, and even help shape programmes, by voicing their opinions on social media.

批 注
① 用词不准。
② 自由发挥过度。
③ 理解问题。

广播^①过时了吗？是该将这个近一个世纪前进入千家万户的媒体埋葬了吗？答案远非如此。当然，老古董晶体管已经寿终正寝。接入天线，用耳朵紧贴着听收音机的日子也一去不复返了。广播已开始数字化转型^②。今天，听众也有可能，甚至更有可能打开手机或电脑收听广播。媒体重塑的一个主要因素是播客的制作——按需制作节目^③。有些广播在节目录制完并在网上发布后，甚至可以"收看"。听众也实现了进化，过去他们被动地躲在个人设备背后，而现在，他们不仅可以参与广播互动，甚至可通过在社交媒体上发表意见，协助节目制作。

电台广播过时了吗？是到了将这个近一个世纪前传入千家万户的媒体淘汰的时候了吗？事实远非如此。当然，过去的晶体管收音机已经寿终正寝。耳朵紧贴收音机的线性收听模式也一去不复返。电台广播开始了数字化转型过程。今天，听众即便不是完全可以、也有可能可以打开手机或计算机收听广播。彻底改造媒体的一个重大因素是播客的制作——按需提供节目。有时候，在广播节目拍摄结束并发布到网上后，甚至可以"收看"电台广播。听众也与时俱进了。过去，观

众只能被动地待在设备后面,而现在,他们不仅可以参与广播,甚至可以在社交媒体上发表意见,从而帮助打造节目。

1. 用词不准问题。见"radio"一词。翻译稿将"radio"处理成了"广播",而审校稿处理为"电台广播",相比之下,之所以要增补"电台"一词,从理论上来说,一方面是出于对联合国固定词汇用法的考虑;另一方面是对原文整体语境的考虑。就第一方面而言,"radio"在术语库中的常规表达包括"无线电""广播电台",特别是"radio section"译为广播电台科,并且"UNRadio"一般也称为"联合国电台",所以增译"电台"符合常规表达习惯;就第二方面的语境而言,结合"Radio can sometimes even be watched, when programmes are filmed and posted online"该句,可发现"radio"不仅仅是以听觉形式存在的广播,还可以是可供收看的媒体形式,因此也包含了"电台"这层含义。因此,增译合情合理。

2. 理解问题。见"Today, listeners are just as likely, if not more so, to tune in on..."一句。译文将这句话译为"听众也有可能,甚至更有可能打开手机或电脑收听广播",显然是对"as just as likely, if not more so"这一结构理解有误,正确的处理方式应当是先译"if not more",再译前面的"are just as likely",也即按照审校稿的处理方式,译为"听众即便不是完全可以、也有可能可以打开手机或电脑收听广播"。

3. 过度发挥与灵活处理。见"the transistor of yesteryear has lived its life" "Linear listening, ear glued to the radio"以及"The listener has evolved too"这几处。之所以将这几处结合起来对比,是为了强调过度发挥与灵活处理之间的区别,我们可以看出翻译稿的不成熟之处在于对应当灵活处理的地方过于贴近原文,而有些地方又发挥过度。先看"The listener has evolved too"这句。将"evolve"译为"进化"显然是对原文理解有问题,导致在转化成汉语时过度贴合字面含义,实际上"evolve"此处的深刻内涵并非"进化",而是一种改进,或者进步,当译为"与时俱进";再看"the transistor of yesteryear has lived its life"以及"Linear listening, ear glued to the radio"这两处,通过对比翻译稿与审校稿,我们可发现译者刻意增加了许多内容,如"老古董""接入天线"。单从原文中的"yesteryear"和"linear",我们无法推出这些"非文本含义",可能是译者出于文法文采考虑增加了这些表达,就联合国稿件的翻译标准而言,这些处理未免有过渡发挥之嫌。因此,我们得出的结论是,是过度发挥还是灵活处理,根本在于对原文理解透彻,所谓的灵活,不是在脱离原文之上发挥,而是在基于原文内涵之上将其"隐身"现形。

第2段

So it is a very different but thriving medium that we now celebrate on 13 February each year, on World Radio Day. Proclaimed in 2011, the Day reminds us of the crucial role this medium plays—reaching the widest audience in the world, in the most isolated areas or in emergency situations. Since UNESCO's creation, the Organization has relied on this key medium to help fulfil its mandate to foster freedom of expression and the free flow of ideas throughout the world.

批 注

① 组句、断句问题。
② 理解问题。

因此，广播作为一种媒体，不仅独具特色，而且欣欣向荣，以至于我们在每年的 2 月 13 日当天都会庆祝世界无线电日。这个在 2011 年宣布的节日旨在提醒我们，① 广播作为一种媒体所发挥的关键作用——覆盖全球最广泛的受众，触及最偏远的地区，或第一时间播报紧急情况。自联合国教科文组织成立以来②，这一关键载体始终在为该组织履行其在全世界促进言论自由和思想自由流动的使命提供可靠支持。

因此，电台广播这种媒体与众不同而又欣欣向荣，每年 2 月 13 日世界无线电日我们都会为此庆祝。2011 年宣布 2 月 13 日为世界无线电日，目的就是提醒我们这种媒体所发挥的关键作用——最广泛地覆盖全球受众，包括最偏远地区或处于紧急状况的受众。联合国教科文组织自成立以来，一直倚赖这一重要媒体履行其在全世界促进言论自由和思想自由流动的使命。

1. 理解问题。见 "in the most isolated areas or in emergency situations…" 一句。翻译稿将该这一成分单独处理成了整句，并补充了自己理解的含义，从而将该句译成了"触及最偏远的地区，或第一时间播报紧急情况"。从语法上来看，"in the most isolated areas or in emergency situations" 并不是一个独立的句子，而是 "reaching the widest audience in the world" 的补充状语，其修饰的对象应当是 "widest audience"，如此来看，译为"触及地区，播报紧急情况"偏离了原文结构，属于错译，可按照审校稿的处理方式，译为"包括最偏远地区或处于紧急状况的受众"，将修饰对象进行还原。

2. 断句组句问题。见 "Proclaimed in 2011, the Day reminds us of the crucial role this medium plays—reaching the widest audience…" 一句。通过对比翻译稿和审校稿，我们可发现，翻译稿中的句子过长，并且完全按照英文的句法结构来组句，其结果一是可读性不够，二是句子没有主次轻重。遇到这种情况，比较理想的翻译策略是，将英文长句拆分成两个短句，分开来译，先译事实，即"2011 年宣布 2 月 13 日为世界无线电日"，再译其目的和初衷，即"目的就是提醒我们……"。

3. 视角转换问题。见 "Organization has relied on this key medium to help" 一句。翻译稿和审校稿分别采用了两种不同的翻译策略，一种是以媒体 "medium" 为视角，另一种是以"联合国"为视角，由于选用的主语不同，导致句子的论述重点、侧重点略有差异，但从通顺性、可读性上看并无影响，因此这两种视角均可接受，而且"视角转换"作为一种技巧，可供模仿学习。

第 3 段

It is important that radio reflects the audiences it serves more accurately, because diversity in radio is the key to fair and independent information. It is also a means of giving a voice to the variety of cultures and opinions that form the basis for critical thinking. In spite of the evolution of radio in recent years, it remains that irreplaceable voice which populates our solitude and seems to speak to us alone—even though it addresses the multitude. In a world invaded by screens, "paradoxically, one advantage of radio is that it is not accompanied by the image", noted the UNESCO Courier in the editorial of its February 1997 issue devoted to radio.

广播必须更准确地代表①其服务的受众，因为广播的多样性是获得公正、独立的信息的关键。广播也是一种为各种文化和观点传声的手段，正是这些不同的文化和观点为进行批判性思考提供了依据。尽管广播在近年来实现了转型，但仍作为一种无可取代的声音存在，尽管它面向大众，却填满了每个孤独的灵魂，仿佛只与个人窃窃私语。联合国教科文组织《信使》杂志1997年2月广播专辑的社论中提到，在一个充满银幕②的世界中，③"自相矛盾的是，没有图像恰好成了广播的一个优点。"

批 注

① 选词问题。
② 选词问题。
③ 表述不准问题。

电台广播必须更准确地反映其所服务的听众，因为广播领域的多样性是实现信息公平独立的关键。广播也是让各种文化和观点各抒己见的手段，正是这些不同的文化和观点为批判性的思考提供了依据。尽管电台广播近年来有所发展，但它仍然是那个可以排解我们的孤独、虽然面向大众却仿佛只与我们单独对话的无可取代的声音。联合国教科文组织《信使》1997年2月刊中关于电台广播的专题社论指出，在一个被各色屏幕霸占的世界中，"电台广播的优势之一正是它没有图像，这听起来颇有些自相矛盾。"

1. 表述不准问题。见"in the editorial of its February 1997 issue devoted to radio"一句。翻译稿将"editorial"与"issue"割裂理解，将"issue"作为一个单独的成分来理解，最终译成了"广播专辑"，实际上"issue devoted to"所修饰的对象正是"editorial"，因此作为"editorial"的修饰语，应将其译为"专题"，也即"专题社论"。

2. 选词问题。见"reflects"和"invade"两词。翻译稿之所以会出现错误，主要原因在于对有多重含义或语意较广的词理解不当。对于第一种，"reflect"既可以理解为"代表"，也可以理解为"反映、体现"，但作为"代表"，更多用于政治背景，并且结合后一句语境"because diversity in radio is the key to fair and independent information"，涉及多元性、多样性问题，应当理解为受众、观众的多元化，那么将"reflects"译为"反映"也就不难理解了；对于"invade"，其本意有"侵占、侵略"含义，翻译稿采用了被动转主动的译法，译为"充满银屏"，这种表述在汉语中很少见。而如果将"invade"一词的含义加以引申,在"侵占、侵略"的基础上进一步扩充,理解为"霸屏",就更符合我们日常表达习惯了。

补充练习

1. The Organization provided programmes to radio stations around the world, supporting radio information campaigns—such as the 2016 information campaign on the Zika virus in Latin America and the Caribbean—something it continues to do today. UNESCO offers training in radio broadcasting and reporting, as it has done for young Syrian refugees in Lebanon since 2014. It also supports the creation of community radio stations, or those broadcasting in the aftermath of natural disasters.

参考译文

联合国教科文组织向世界各地的广播电台提供节目以支持电台广播信息宣传运动。例如,2016年拉丁美洲和加勒比关于寨卡病毒的信息宣传运动;这项工作今天仍在继续。该组织提供无线电广播和报道方面的培训,就像其自2014年以来一直在为黎巴嫩境内的叙利亚青年难民提供的那种培训。它还支持建立社区广播电台,或在自然灾害后进行广播的广播电台。

2. The lack of statistics in many countries makes it impossible to draw a global map of diversity in radio. But the data that does exist, speaks for itself. In France in 2018, women accounted for thirty-seven per cent (Conseil supérieur de l'audiovisuel (CSA), 2019) of radio broadcasters. They constituted twenty-three per cent of political guests, and thirty-seven of experts on radio. In the United Kingdom, while fifty-one per cent of radio staff were women, only thirty-six per cent held positions of responsibility (Ofcom, 2019). Another example: in the United States, in 2017, only eleven per cent of radio newsroom staff were from minority backgrounds (The Radio and Television Digital News Association (RTDNA) and Hofstra University Newsroom Survey, 2018).

参考译文

由于多个国家缺乏统计数据,无法绘制电台广播领域多样性的全球地图。不过,现有的数据足以说明问题。2018年,法国女主播在电台主播中占37%(法国高等视听委员会(CSA),2019年)。女性政治嘉宾和女性广播电台专家的占比分别为23%和37%。在联合王国,虽然电台的女工作人员占51%,但是担任责任职务的女工作人员只占36%(英国通信管理局,2019年)。另一个例子是:2017年,美国电台新闻编辑部只有11%的工作人员具有少数民族背景(广播电视数字新闻协会(RTDNA)和霍夫斯特拉大学新闻编辑部调查,2018年)。

背景介绍

本篇选自世界知识产权组织关于各国家知识产权局游戏产权开发宣传材料汇编。版权与文化创意是近年来人文社科领域的热点话题。作为联合国保护知识产权的专门机构,为保护文学和艺术表现形式(图书、电影、音乐、建筑、艺术)等各项文化权利,世界知识产权组织开展了全方位工作,促进版权保护的商业化和市场化。各国知识产权局每年都会向产权组织提交相关材料,由产权组织予以汇编。此类文件无论在行文还是在表达措辞上都与正式的官方会议文件有明显区分:一、无固定体例、常规表述要求,"书面化"色彩不强;二、长短句频繁切换组合,主语、主被动视角变化灵活;三、广泛涉及版权领域知识,但非专业术语,而是与版权有关的各种知识,这要求我们跳出正式文件框架,灵活调动各领域知识,让看似口语化的表达保持规范的同时,尽可能在可读性上多下功夫,通过使用"化境"等翻译方法,将读者真实地带入原文语境中。

第十一篇

True Hunters is a "serious game" that aims to sensitize teenagers aged 14 to 16 to Intellectual Property (IP) and its related issues, highlighting the value of authentic and original products and showing counterfeiting and piracy risks in daily life. This particular target was chosen because in recent years the younger generation has been more exposed to the issues related to IP and counterfeiting because of an increase in their purchasing power and the wide use of the new communication technologies. The first episode of True Hunters is freely available online (http://truehunters.eu/en/), in both English and Italian language. Stakeholders (high school leaders and teachers) who are interested in using True Hunters can also find online the project handbook, an e-book which has the aim of facilitating the use of this serious game and its potential adaptation.

Each character's role and personality led the development of his or her graphic design. Even if the group wears the same uniform that identifies them as a part of the True Hunters team, each character has been designed to be easily recognizable by the players and has been characterized using specific visual shapes and colors. Moreover, each one of them has a unique feature related to his or her role and expertise: Els has her holographic tablet to manage the missions, Kris has a mechanical arm built by himself, Byte has a portable holographic device and

Max has a robot called RICE (Robotic Investigative Cute Entity) that helps him analyzing evidence.

Moreover, a group of students aged 14 to 16 was involved in a three-day workshop that foresaw both theoretical and practical activities to reflect on the specific topic and guide them in the creation of two narrative scenarios for True Hunters. The last day, they were able to write two synopses and one of them was used as the starting point to write one of the episodes of the serious game.

请自行翻译后查看后文的分析点评

分析点评

第 1 段

True Hunters is a "serious game" that aims to sensitize teenagers aged 14 to 16 to Intellectual Property (IP) and its related issues, highlighting the value of authentic and original products and showing counterfeiting and piracy risks in daily life. This particular target was chosen because in recent years the younger generation has been more exposed to the issues related to IP and counterfeiting because of an increase in their purchasing power and the wide use of the new communication technologies. The first episode of True Hunters is freely available online (http://truehunters.eu/en/), in both English and Italian language. Stakeholders (high school leaders and teachers) who are interested in using True Hunters can also find online the project handbook, an e-book which has the aim of facilitating the use of this serious game and its potential adaptation.

《真实捕手》是一款"严肃游戏",旨在提高14至16岁的青少年对知识产权及其相关问题的认识,突出真品和原创产品的价值,并反映日常生活中存在的假冒和盗版风险。选择这一代青少年作为特定目标群体的原因在于,近些年,由于其购买力的提高和新通信技术的广泛使用,他们更易面临知识产权和假冒的相关问题。① 关于《真实捕手》第一章的英文和意文版本,可从 http://truehunters.eu/en/ 网站免费获取。对使用《真实捕手》感兴趣的利益攸关方(中学领导和教师)还可在线获取项目手册,这本电子书旨在为这一严肃游戏及其可能改编材料的使用提供便利。②

"寻找真相"是一款"严肃的游戏",旨在提高14至16岁青少年对知识产权和相关问题的敏感认识,强调正品和原创产品的价值,并体现日常生活中的假冒和盗版风险。之所以专门针对青少年,原因在于近年来青少年的购买力提高,并

批 注

① 表达不流畅。
② 表达过于机械。

且他们广泛使用新通信技术,因此更容易遭遇知识产权和假冒的相关问题。"寻找真相"的第一幕有英文和意大利文版本,可从http://truehunters.eu/en/网站免费获取。为方便游戏玩家,并为可能的改进提供便利,"寻找真相"游戏配备了一份电子版的项目手册,有兴趣的利益攸关方(中学领导和教师)可从网站获取该手册。

1. 用词不准、过于死板问题。见"authentic"和"episode"二词。在译文中,这三个词分别译成了"真品"和"第一章"。翻译稿对这几个词的驾驭不够灵活,这或是对背景知识不了解,或是过于拘泥于这些词汇在联合国正式文件中的固定译法。就本文而言,作为一份宣传材料,特别是涉及开发一款游戏产品,其文风是比较灵活的,在翻译时不能局限于词汇字面意思,而应当将其与游戏、游戏版权等专业背景联系起来。对于"authentic",如从版权的角度考虑,可以译为"正版的",从而与盗版、非正版产品形成对比。对于"episode",如果放在一份正式文件中,译成"第一章""第一回"是没有问题的,但如果放在介绍游戏的非正式文体中,应当将其化境,结合游戏术语背景,将其译为"第一幕"。

2. 表达不流畅问题。见"This particular target was chosen because in recent years the younger generation"一句。译文的问题如下。首先,过于贴合英文的句法组织语言,所以成文不流畅,不符合汉语的表达习惯。应当调整句子的逻辑顺序,让"青少年"成为句子主语,即可顺利连带出来"购买力提高""广泛使用新通信技术""更容易遭遇知识产权和假冒问题"三个动作。其次,对于"more exposed to the issues"的处理不当,也导致整句话读起来不够流畅。在本段语境中,知识产权和假冒问题是一种具体、切实存在的问题,译为"遭遇"比"面临"更恰当。

3. 灵活处理。见"Stakeholders (high school leaders and teachers) who are interested in using True Hunters..."一句。通过对比翻译稿和审校稿,我们可发现,审校稿的高明之处在于,一是对抽象的词汇进行具体化境,如对"facilitating the use of this serious game and its potential adaptation"的处理,分别译为"为方便游戏玩家"和"为可能的改进提供便利",使其内涵更加具体;二是调整了这句话的语序,即将"an e-book which has the aim of facilitating the"提前,将主句置后,先说明"真正的猎手"游戏配备手册的目的,再说明其下载方式。

第 2 段

Each character's role and personality led the development of his or her graphic design. Even if the group wears the same uniform that identifies them as a part of the True Hunters team, each character has been designed to be easily recognizable by the players and has been characterized using specific visual shapes and colors. Moreover, each one of them has a unique feature related to his or her role and expertise: Els has her holographic tablet to manage the missions, Kris has a mechanical arm built by himself, Byte has a portable holographic device and Max has a robot called RICE (Robotic Investigative Cute Entity) that helps him analyzing evidence.

批 注

① 表达过于抽象。
② 人名处理有问题。

根据每个角色的职责和个性，设计了各自的平面造型。即使给整个团队穿的是标志真实捕手团队身份的统一制服，但对每个角色做了易于玩家分辨的造型设计，并用特定的视觉形态和颜色加以区分。此外，每名队员都具有与其职责和专长有关的独有特性。①Els 有一台管理任务的手写板，Kris② 有一只自行设计的机械臂，Byte 有一部便携式手写设备，而 Max 有一个帮助他分析证据的机器人 RICE（机器人型调查迷你实体）。

按照每位角色的职责和个性为其设计了各自的平面造型。虽然所有成员穿的都是"真正的猎手"小组的统一制服，但每个角色又有特定的外貌和颜色区分，在造型上容易被游戏玩家识别。此外，每名成员都有与各自的职责和专长匹配的特点。埃尔斯有一块任务管理全息平板，克瑞斯有一只自己设计的机械臂，贝斯有一台便携式全息设备，而麦克斯有一个机器人莱斯（可爱型调查机器人），可帮助他分析证据。

1. 表达/用词问题。见"each one of them has a unique feature related to his or her role and expertise"一句和"Max has a robot called RICE (Robotic Investigative Cute Entity) that helps him analyzing evidence"一句。翻译稿将这两句话分别处理成"每名队员都具有与其职责和专长有关的独有特性"和"Max 有一个帮助他分析证据的机器人 RICE（机器人型调查迷你实体）"。单从表面意思来看，并无可读性问题，也符合语法规则，但如果结合前后文语境，则会对理解造成干扰，因为"有关的独特特性"和"迷你实体"实在太过于抽象。审校稿提供了更为贴合文意的表达。在第一处，将"related to"的含义进一步具体化，译为"匹配"，这样就能对"unique feature"有更为直观的认识。在第二处，同理，也可以将这个"entity"具体还原成"机器人"。

2. 灵活处理问题。见"each character has been designed to be easily recognizable by the players and has been characterized using specific visual shapes and colors"一句。对比翻译稿和审校稿，发现这句话的前后顺序有了调整。就英文并列句而言，本身并没有绝对的主次、前后顺序之别，因此不能先入为主，认为并列词前后连接的两个分句是顺序是不可逆的。但在此处，之所以要做顺序上的调整，是因为其中隐含了一种逻辑顺序，即因为每个角色有特定的外貌和颜色区分，所以容易被识别出。为突出这种逻辑关系，需要调整前后语序。另见文中"group"一词。翻译稿将"group"译成了整个团队，而在审校稿中的译法为"所有成员"，在此处，需要转换一下思维，思考"group"强调的是集体概念还是个体概念，这里强调的是团队中的每个人员、所有人,那么就应当是一种个体概念,如此一来,可将"group"译成"所有成员"。

3. 规范问题。在一般情况下,英文人名均须译成中文,除非有特别规定。而且,作为一份介绍游戏的材料,一般而言游戏所涉及的方方面面都应当进行汉化处理,因此要将人名译成中文。

第3段

Moreover, a group of students aged 14 to 16 was involved in a three-day workshop that foresaw both theoretical and practical activities to reflect on the specific topic and guide them in the creation of two narrative scenarios for True Hunters. The last day, they were able to write two synopses and one of them was used as the starting point to write one of the episodes of the serious game.

此外,<u>一组14至16岁的学生参与了为期三天的讲习班,该讲习班预先提供了理论和实践活动,以就具体专题进行思考</u>①,并指导学生为《真实捕手》创造两种故事情节。在最后一天,<u>他们能够写出两种梗概,其中一个学生的梗概被用作编写严肃游戏其中一章的基础</u>②。

批 注

① 句子切分问题。
② 理解问题。

此外,一组14至16岁的学生参与了为期三天的讲习班,该讲习班预先设想了体现这一具体专题的理论与实践活动,并指导学生们为"寻找真相"游戏编写两个故事情节。在讲习班的最后一天,学生们都能写出两份提纲,以其中一份提纲为基础编写了一幕游戏场景。

1. 理解问题。见"they were able to write two synopses and one of them was used as the starting point to..."一句。翻译稿对"one of them..."的理解存在问题,将其理解成学生个人,而其实指代的是"two synopses",也就是其中一份提纲。就语境角度而言,作为一个讲习班,是为了让每个学生都能接受指导,写出提纲,以其中一份作为基础,从这一点上也应将其理解成"提纲"。

2. 断句切分问题。见"a group of students aged 14 to 16 was involved in a three-day workshop that foresaw both theoretical and practical activities to reflect on the specific topic"一句。翻译稿在处理这句话时,出现一个严重的错误,在"to"之后作了不当切分,将"to reflect"译为"involved in a three-day workshop that foresaw both theoretical and practical activities"的不定状语,从而将其含义译成了"思考"。实际上,"to reflect"修饰的是"theoretical and practical activities"而不是整句话,并且,处理成"就具体专题进行思考"与"理论和实践活动"之间并无具体关联。

补充练习

1. The choice of developing a serious game to talk about counterfeiting was made in light of the advantages offered by this kind of solution to engage youngsters. Serious games, in particular, allow stimulating identification and active participation. The player has to immerse himself in the game context and make decisions in the first person. In this way learning occurs through experience and the player has the chance to see the immediate consequences of a specific decisional process. The player is prompted to find out further information to progress in the game and achieve a final goal.

严肃游戏能吸引青少年参与,正是考虑到这种解决方案具有的优势,才选择开发一款严肃的游戏讨论假冒问题。特别是,严肃游戏能够唤起认同感,促进积极参与。玩家必须融入游戏场景并以主角的身份做出决定。玩家可以通过这种方式从游戏体验中学到知识,并有机会看到某个具体决策过程的直接后果。这促使玩家在游戏中找到通关的进一步信息,实现最终目标。

2. The story of the serious game takes place in the year 2610, a future where piracy and counterfeiting are overflowing, with devastating consequences for economic, political and social conditions. To counteract this threat, an international special unit has been created: the True Hunters. This special unit is composed of four lead members, each one representing a subject matter expert associated with a specific topic in order to highlight a particular aspect of IP.

游戏背景设置在 2610 年,在未来的那一年,盗版和假冒泛滥,带来了经济、政治和社会方面的灾难性后果。为应对这一威胁,成立了"真正的猎手"国际特别股。该机构由四名领导成员组成,他们都是某个方面的专家,各自负责具体的专题,以突显知识产权的具体方面。

本章词汇

target　目标群体
IP and counterfeiting　知识产权和假冒
workshop　讲习班
narrative scenarios　故事情节
identification　认同感
monitoring mechanisms　监测机制
informed policymaking　知情决策
establish benchmarks　建立基准
cultural expressions　文化表现形式
reporting cycle　报告周期
national reporting processes　国家报告进程
information sharing　信息共享
expected result　预期成果
ordinary session　例会
overarching goal　总体目标
synergy　协同增效，协同效应
mainstreaming　主流化
networking　建立联系，联谊，建立关系网，联网
preferential treatment　优惠待遇
sector-specific strategy　部门特定战略
visibility　知名度，影响力
common good of humankind　人类的共同利益
integrated society　共融社会
social integration　社会融合
geographic representation　地域代表性
network of cells　基层组织网络
speaking notes　发言稿
racial profiling　种族特征分析
data capture　数据采集
subscriptions　租位
convention　惯例表示法
anecdotal evidence　传闻证据
retreat　务虚会
demographic　人口统计
motive　动议
point of order　程序
emergency management　应急管理

malfunction　故障
global profile　全球普及面
fair value　公允价值
extra　增刊
expand access to　扩大了获取……的机会
summary　概述；摘要
executive summary　提要（教科文）
oblige　责成
references　提法
indigenous territories　土著领地
culturally relevant manner　文化适宜
end-of-life　报废时影响
concluding meeting　总结/闭幕会议
point of order　程序
voting pattern　表决方式
affiliate, and candidate countries　联系国候补成员国
may wish to　谨建议，不妨
letter dated　信件
is transmitting　谨转递
kindly noted that　恳请注意
before submission to the Governing Council　在呈交理事会前
outstanding recommendations　所载但未落实的建议
briefing　情况通报会
text of the draft principles　原则草案案文
resolution　决议
decision　决定
omnibus decision　总括决定
living document　动态文件
established format of the meetings had　固定的会议形式
draw up the plan　拟定规划
institutional settings　机构设置
by majority of　超过半数
observer constituencies　观察员界别
draft articles　条款草案
articles/guidelines/regulations　条款、准则、规范

和原则

moot point　这一点尚待讨论
narrative sections　叙述性章节
observations on　评述
preliminary list　暂定项目表
initiate the Settlement　草签
attend meeting physically　前往现场
general session　全体会议
substantive comments　实质性评论
voting member　执行官员
hosting firm　托管公司
staggered three-year term　交错任期制
one alternative　候补
non-voting liaison　不具表决权的联络人
take voice of　代表××的意见
petition for formal constituency recognition　请求获得正式选区组织资格
post structure　员额结构
Professional salaries　专业人员薪金
net Professional salaries　专业薪金净额
General Service salaries　一般事务薪金
common staff costs　共同人事费
public officers　公职人员
cross-border movement　跨境流动
customer due diligence　对客户的尽职调查
correspondent banking　代理行
politically exposed persons　政治公众人物
institutional framework　体制框架
rules of procedure　程序规则
urban legislation, land and governance　城市立法、土地和治理
urban planning and design　城市规划和设计
urban economy and municipal finance　城市经济和市级财政
urban basic services　城市基本服务
housing and slum upgrading　住房和贫民窟改造
risk reduction, rehabilitation and urban resilience　减少风险、恢复和城市复原力
urban research and capacity development　城市研究和能力发展

results-based management　成果管理制
pension system registrations　养老金系统登记
significant disparities　显著不均
care services　护理服务
improve the accessibility of existing housing　改善现有住房的无障碍程度
carers　照料者
tenure of land and natural resources　土地和自然资源保有权
undocumented migrants　无证移民
structured national urban policy　层次分明的国家城市政策
peri-urban land policies　城市周边土地政策
outskirts of cities　城市郊区
abandonment of social housing　弃置
high rates of uninhabited houses　住房空置率
collective construction of housing　集体建设住房
comprehensive neighborhood recovery　居民区全面恢复
rezoning processes　实施重新区划程序
urban components　城区
social production of habitat　社会建设生境；社会合建住房
diversifying housing supply and rental policies　实行住房供应和租赁政策多样化
high-density complexes　高密度楼群
mitigating and controlling the degradation of existing and future housing stock　减缓和控制现有和未来住房存量减少
obsolescence and deterioration process　废弃和老化
rezoning processes　实施重新区划
institutional strengthening　体制强化活动
underlying data　基本数据
cross subnational borders　跨越次国家边界
provides amenity value　发挥景观价值
Treasurer　财务主任
fast-start contributions　快速启动捐款
level　额度
conversion　改造
against　参照

compliance　履约
contributions against pledges　认捐捐款
internet access　互联网接入设备
National and International Applications　国内国际申请
publicly available and subscription-based databases and facilities　公开可用的订阅数据库和设备
competent authority for other receiving offices　其他受理局的主管单位
official copies　官方复制品
patent clearance　清查
physical copies　有形复制品
protection systems for geographical indications　地理标志保护体系
TCE　传统文化表现形式

misappropriation　盗用
the most interested party　最相关当事方
baseline of the contributions　缴费基线
types of contributions　缴款方式
non-registered forms of trademarks　非注册商标形式
self-financed　资金自筹
International Registry　国际注册部
substantive patent law　实体专利法
various jurisdictions　不同管辖区域
the protection and enforcement of patent rights　专利权的保护和执行
patent landscape　专利态势
biosimilars　非专利药
title to intellectual property　知识产权的所有权

第七章

卫生与健康

本章导言

2020年新型冠状病毒COVID-19全球大流行，作为联合国系统内卫生的指导和协调机构，世界卫生组织（世卫组织）针对疫情编写了各类文件，包括技术指南、科学简报、常见问题问答等。包括COVID-19病毒在内的突发卫生事件仅仅是全球卫生治理领域的一个专题，在联合国讨论的卫生专题还涵盖：常见传染病、重大疾病、基本药物药品与物质滥用、烟草与吸烟问题、涉及妇女身心健康的避孕与计划生育、卫生、妊娠助产问题、关乎儿童权利的营养与发育、卫生、视听恢复问题，甚至还涉及与气候变化和千年发展目标有关的气候和流行病症问题、与食品、饮水安全和环境清洁有关的食源性疾病问题。此外，围绕这些卫生健康问题所开展的卫生筹资、卫生人力、卫生设施部署等也是世卫组织卫生大会和执行委员会所负责的事项。

除世卫组织外，联合国大会每年届会期间也会召开涉及卫生专题的高级别会议，如"第73届联合国大会防治结核病问题高级别会议"，并在大会报告中概述特定议题下的卫生活动和卫生事件。联合国还专门设立麻醉药品委员会和国际麻醉品管制局，负责汇编涉及麻醉药品等重要危险物质的管理、管制、科学研究、监测和运销情况的专门技术文件。

卫生与健康所涉专题广泛，内容庞杂，不仅涉及各种医药化学品专门知识，而且涉及主管机构的具体职能。因此联合国卫生与健康领域的文件并非常见的医药文件，为体现其特点，本篇选取了较具代表性的文件类别。从文体上区分，包括：世卫组织的专门领域报告（第一篇至第七篇）和专门委员会文件（第九篇至第十一篇）、综合报告（第八篇）及卫生会议文件（第十二篇）；从内容上分，覆盖了：烟草与健康（第一篇、第二篇）、新冠病毒防治（第七篇）、视力问题（第三篇、第四篇）、营养（第五篇）和肠道感染（第六篇）问题以及麻醉药品药物管制和运销专题（第九篇至第十一篇），目的是让大家较为全面地了解健康卫生领域的联合国文件相关风格。

总体而言，该领域文件具有以下特点。

（1）术语、专业名词多，需从多种来源寻求其权威性作准版本。

（2）句型结构复杂，尤其体现在破折号、非灵主语、被动句的使用方面。

（3）语篇前后联系紧密，尤其在近义词和同位语的方面。

这些特点要求我们在翻译时，要做到以下几点。

（1）验证术语的权威性，具备"自疑"意识，如第五篇第一段中的"double burden of malnutrition"，可能很难想到该词是一个有固定译法的术语，在直译不通、意思不明的情况下就需要从联合国相关术语库以及医学词典、科普网站、文献等来源寻求"解药"。

（2）掌握破折号成分的处理技巧，如第六篇第一段中"National Institute for Communicable Diseases, South Africa, gave a presentation on whole genome sequencing (WGS)—paving the way forward globally to better understand food systems"，对于破折号连接的成分是否应放入括号，需分析其与主句之间的关系，考虑到处理为非核心限定成分是否会影响整句话的主次重点和流畅性。

（3）掌握非灵主语的处理技巧，如第七篇第二段中"Through MDA, all individuals in a targeted population are given antimalarial medicines—often at repeated intervals"一句，对于这种无主语句，要通过结合语境，分析出其真正的主语，并酌情进行补充。

（4）注意近义词或同义词的翻译，注意区分其核心意义和附加意义在中文语境中是否完全相同，以及不予以区别化处理是否合适，如第四篇第一段中与视力有关的各种近义词："ability to see""vision""sense"以及第五篇第二段中"undernutrition"与"malnutrition"。

（5）在处理同位语时，应分析出内容与先行词之间的实质关系，并按照汉语的思维整理成逻辑清晰、表意分明的句式。如第八篇第二段中"Following a request from a Board member that..."这一句（详见下文分析）。

另外，该领域文件的体例也值得我们注意，不仅有多级标题和目录，而且涉及与化学品、药物有关的多种缩略语和分子式，要保持前后统一，且化学式的书写规则应准确无误。简而言之，卫生健康领域文件突出体现了专业性、学术权威性和体例规范性，同时要注意健康也是一项重要人权，在思考相关的背景语意时，应考虑卫生与人权的话语关联以及政策制定者的人道主义思维。

背景介绍

以下七篇（第一篇至第七篇）涉及世界卫生组织主管领域的相关报告。第一篇和第二篇涉及烟草与健康问题；第三篇和第四篇选自《世界听力报告》；第五篇选自营养不良问题相关报告；第六篇选自关于肠道感染的报告；第七篇选自有关COVID-19防治的问答指南。除第七篇外，其余六篇均为报告，其中第一篇和第二篇为管制情况报告，第三篇至第六篇为全球情况问题概述报告。在这些报告中，既有对各国各自开始的活动概述，也有对世界卫生组织在烟草框架公约下开展的全方位活动的介绍，既有科学性的实验论证（烟草制品检测报告），也有针对烟草广告宣传提出的建议和指导，这就要求译者在翻译时尤其注意论述的视角。这些报告文件均由具有医学专业背景的工作人员编写，专业性较强，涉及不同的卫生领域，对于意义较为模糊或有多重意义的词汇和术语，译者应结合全球公共卫生背景知识妥善处理。

第一篇

原文

In addition, there will be some analytical requirements for tobacco products testing that have no counterpart in analysis used in other testing programmes. The most obvious example of this is the need for the equipment and controlled temperature and humidity facilities required for the smoking of combusted conventional tobacco products. Existing laboratory management may hesitate to acquire these new capabilities. This should be discussed beforehand and an estimated timeline and plan clarified to prevent misunderstandings in the future.

At that time, the laboratory already had a dedicated staff with 10 years of experience in using advanced analytical instrumentation applied to biomonitoring to evaluate exposure to users and non-users of tobacco products. Laboratory buildings were already in place with required environmental control and an uninterrupted power supply. In addition, service contracts for the equipment were in place with replacement parts on site to enable quick repairs. The laboratory already had an extensive quality control programme and statistical and IT support. Finally, there was a strong support structure in place that was not dependent on quick results but understood the need for a strategic approach.

Several staff from the NCEH laboratory visited the private commercial tobacco analysis laboratory, Labstat Incorporated, in Kitchener, Canada. The staff graciously explained all of the requirements (environmental controls, equipment, staff, etc.) needed to outfit a successful tobacco testing laboratory. This allowed the staff of the NCEH laboratory to understand what other requirements were necessary to successfully develop the laboratory capabilities to test tobacco products.

请自行翻译后查看后文的分析点评

第 1 段

In addition, there will be some analytical requirements for tobacco products testing that have no counterpart in analysis used in other testing programmes. The most obvious example of this is the need for the equipment and controlled temperature and humidity facilities required for the smoking of combusted conventional tobacco products. Existing laboratory management may hesitate to acquire these new capabilities. This should be discussed beforehand and an estimated timeline and plan clarified to prevent misunderstandings in the future.

批 注

① 理解有误。
② 用词不准。

此外，烟草制品检测中的某些分析要求在其他检测规划所采用的分析中没有对应要求。最明显的一个例子是，需要具备专业的设备，并且要控制燃烧类传统烟草制品所需抽吸设施的温度和湿度。① 实验室现任管理人员可能对掌握这些新技能有所顾虑。对此，应当事先进行讨论，并对预计的时间线② 和计划做好解释，以防止日后产生误解。

此外，烟草制品检测的某些分析要求并不适用于其他检测规划采用的分析。最明显的例子是，前者需要有相关设备及温湿度可控设施以便检测传统烟草制品点燃后的出烟情况。实验室现任管理人员可能对掌握这些新技能有所顾虑。对此，应当事先进行讨论，并澄清预计的时限和计划，以防日后产生误解。

点评

1. 理解断句问题。见 "The most obvious example of this is the need for the equipment…" 一句。翻译稿中的一个很明显错误在于断句位置有问题，译者在处理长句时过于贴合语法结构，在 "that" "and" 等句法逻辑词前后断句，导致对整句话的理解存在偏差，实际上从语法角度考虑，"equipment" 和 "facility" 都是 "smoking of combusted conventional tobacco products" 所修饰的对象，另外从语义上理解，设备和设施也应当是并列的，所以在处理有共同修饰语的长句时，在断句上务必谨慎。

2. 用词不准问题。见"timeline and plan"一句。"timeline"在联合国术语库中有"时间线、时间表"的含义，但并非在所有语境中都要使用"时间线"这一含义，特别是在本句话中，"timeline"与"plan"并列，而"plan"本身就有"计划、时间线"的含义，因此"timeline"应理解为"时限"。

第 2 段

At that time, the laboratory already had a dedicated staff with 10 years of experience in using advanced analytical instrumentation applied to biomonitoring to evaluate exposure to users and non-users of tobacco products. Laboratory buildings were already in place with required environmental control and an uninterrupted power supply. In addition, service contracts for the equipment were in place with replacement parts on site to enable quick repairs. The laboratory already had an extensive quality control programme and statistical and IT support. Finally, there was a strong support structure in place that was not dependent on quick results but understood the need for a strategic approach.

当时，实验室已经具备了专业的实验人员，他们在使用先进的分析仪器进行生物监测以评估烟草制品对使用者和非使用者的暴露程度①方面拥有 10 年的经验。实验室的大楼已经建好，需要对环境进行控制并保证不间断供电。此外，也签订了设备服务②合同，可以当场更换部件，以便快速维修。实验室也具备了全方位的质控程序以及统计和 IT 支持。最后，实验室还有一个强有力的支持架构，一方面不依赖于快速取得成果；另一方面对采用战略方法的需求予以理解。

批 注

① 词汇理解问题。
② 用词不准问题。

审 校 稿

当时，实验室已经具备了专门的实验人员，他们在使用先进的分析仪器进行生物监测以评估使用者和非使用者接触烟草制品的程度方面拥有 10 年的经验。实验室的大楼已经建好，具备要求的控制环境和不间断供电的条件。此外，也签订了设备维护合同，可以当场更换部件，以便快速维修。实验室也配备了全方位的质量控制程序以及统计和信息技术支持。最后，实验室还有一个强有力的支持架构，它不依赖于快速取得成果，但了解采用战略方法的必要性。

1. 词汇理解问题。见"exposure to users and non-users of tobacco products"一词。"exposure to"常见含义有"暴露、风险、显露"等，正是因为这个词本身含义比较模糊，在使用时就应当根据语境意思加以具体化，例如，在环境文件中，"exposure to"常译为"照射量"，而在货币基金文件中则有"承受风险"的含义，同样，在世卫组织文件中，涉及烟草制品时，特别是其主语是"user"，则采用"接触"更为合适，而不是"暴露"。

2. 用词不准问题。见"service contracts for the equipment..."一句。"service contract"在很多语境下译为"服务合同"没有什么问题，但在本句语境中，搭配的对象是"equipment"，就需要结合该术语做出适当调整，即处理成"设备维护合同"更贴合语境含义。总而言之，上述几处错误的共同点在于在处理词汇时不够严谨，没有结合机构文件特点和语境进行灵活处理。

第3段

Several staff from the NCEH laboratory visited the private commercial tobacco analysis laboratory, Labstat Incorporated, in Kitchener, Canada. The staff graciously explained all of the requirements (environmental controls, equipment, staff, etc.) needed to outfit a successful tobacco testing laboratory. This allowed the staff of the NCEH laboratory to understand what other requirements were necessary to successfully develop the laboratory capabilities to test tobacco products.

国家环境卫生中心实验室的几名工作人员考察了位于加拿大基奇纳的私营商业烟草制品分析实验室——Labstat 公司。工作人员耐心地解释了使烟草检测实验室达到完美配置标准所需满足的所有要求（环境控制、设备、人员等）①。这使国家环境卫生中心实验室的工作人员对就烟草制品检测实验室进行能力建设所需具备的其他要求有了一定理解②。

批 注

① 用词和语序不当。
② 语序不当。

国家环境卫生中心实验室的几名工作人员考察了位于加拿大基奇纳的私营商业烟草分析实验室——Labstat 公司。工作人员耐心地解释了为配置一个合格的、优秀的烟草检测实验室所需满足的所有要求（环境控制、设备、人员等）。这使国家环境卫生中心实验室的工作人员能够了解到成功实现/具备实验室检测烟草制品的检测能力还需要哪些要求。

点 评

1. 两处均为译文重心问题。见"outfit a successful tobacco testing laboratory"和"This allowed the staff of the NCEH laboratory to understand what other requirements were necessary to"两句。对比翻译稿和审校稿时会发现，这两稿在理解层面都讲得通，但是语序是不一样的，更具体来说，落脚点是不同的，翻译稿的处理方法是将重心放在了"配置标准"和"形成理解"上。如仔细揣摩原文，不难发现，"配置"和"理解"都是围绕"requirements（要求）"而言的，也就是说"要求"才是核心词、落脚点，这样理解的话，审校稿的处理方式更为合理。在第一处中，"成功配置实验室"相比"实验室达到完美配置标准"更简洁，有助于将整句话重点聚焦到后面的"要求"上；"能够了解"相较于"对……有一定了解",也更能将读者的注意力集中到"要求"上。

2. 词义选择。"successful"本意是"成功的",但用在尚未建成运转的实验上不太妥当,可译为"优秀的"或"合格的"。"develop"本意为"开发、建立",但因为实验要达到某些要求,才能"具备"或"实现"相应的检测能力,所以"具备"或"实现"的意思在此处更为妥帖。

1. A good example of a laboratory that uses pre-existing government laboratory capabilities is the Cigarette Testing Laboratory (CTL) in Singapore. The CTL, together with the Pharmaceutical Laboratory and Cosmetics Laboratory, make up the Pharmaceutical Division at the Health Sciences Authority of Singapore. Established in the late 1980s, the CTL was tasked to test for tar and nicotine in mainstream cigarette smoke in support of tobacco regulatory compliance. It later expanded its scope to deal with toxicants beyond tar and nicotine by utilizing existing analytical facilities in the pharmaceutical and cosmetics laboratories. This approach allowed the laboratory to expand its capabilities at marginal additional cost.

新加坡的卷烟检测实验室(CTL)就是一个利用政府现有实验室能力的实验室范例。卷烟检测实验室与医药实验室和化妆品实验室共同组成了新加坡卫生科学局药学部。卷烟检测实验室成立于20世纪80年代末,其任务是检测主流卷烟烟雾中的焦油和尼古丁含量,以检验烟草制品是否合规。随后,实验室通过利用医药实验室和化妆品实验室中的现有分析设施,将其检测范围扩大到焦油和尼古丁以外的毒物。通过这种方法,实验室只额外花费了少量经费就解决了其功能扩展问题。

2. This space-requirement description is only an estimate based on what is typically expected for testing needs. A programme not intending to carry out as many analyses would need less space and a programme that intends to perform more analyses would need more. It is highly recommended that, before programmes make final space decisions, they visit a currently operating tobacco testing laboratory to better understand the anticipated requirements.

这些占地需求描述仅仅是根据对检测需求的常规预期得出的估计数。未打算开展大量分析的规划对空间的需求较少,而计划开展更多分析的规划则需要更大空间。强烈建议工作人员在就规划的空间需求做出最终决定之前,前往正在运行的烟草检测实验室进行实地考察,以更好地理解预期要求。

第二篇

原文

Media depictions of tobacco use beyond traditionally paid mass media advertisements have been documented and assessed for their potential to increase youth tobacco uptake and normalize tobacco use. Entertainment media content such as movies, music videos, online videos, television programmes, streaming services, social media posts, video games and mobile phone applications have all been shown to depict and promote tobacco use and tobacco products in ways that may encourage youth smoking uptake. As the majority of this entertainment media content is consumed/viewed through mobile devices and the Internet, it transcends conventional geographical and digital borders. This cross-border digital media consumption provides new and emerging channels through which the tobacco industry can circumvent controls on tobacco advertising or marketing.

While continued monitoring of tobacco depictions in entertainment media is both useful and necessary to understanding patterns of youth exposure, the collected body of evidence clearly shows that media tobacco depictions increase youth tobacco uptake. Therefore, policies that reduce youth exposure to entertainment media depictions are required. In order to keep up with these technological advancements and assist Parties with effective policy action, it is necessary to provide further advice to Parties on this topic, possibly through an addendum to the existing Article 13 Implementation guidelines.

Article 13 Implementation guidelines were developed in light of the primary available means, at the time, for TAPS. Since the guidelines were adopted, there has been a notable expansion in cross-border digital entertainment media, including wide Internet access, social media, smartphones, and access to free digital video, films and games. There is significant potential for these forms of digital media to be used now for TAPS. Digital media has vast reach, especially for young people. This means that the current Article 13 implementation guidelines no longer comprehensively cover the available means for TAPS.

请自行翻译后查看后文的分析点评

分析点评

第 1 段

Media depictions of tobacco use beyond traditionally paid mass media advertisements have been documented and assessed for their potential to increase youth tobacco uptake and normalize tobacco use. Entertainment media content such as movies, music videos, online videos, television programmes, streaming services, social media posts, video games and mobile phone applications have all been shown to depict and promote tobacco use and tobacco products in ways that may encourage youth smoking uptake. As the majority of this entertainment media content is consumed/viewed through mobile devices and the Internet, it transcends conventional geographical and digital borders. This cross-border digital media consumption provides new and emerging channels through which the tobacco industry can circumvent controls on tobacco advertising or marketing.

有记录显示，媒体对烟草使用的描述超出了传统付费大众媒体的广告范围，并且对于媒体在促进青年养成吸烟习惯以及使烟草使用正常化①的潜在可能，也进行了评估。娱乐媒体内容，如电影、音乐视频、网络视频、电视节目、流服务、社交媒体帖子、视频游戏和移动手机应用软件都显示存在以鼓励青年养成吸烟习惯的方式描述②烟草使用和促销烟草产品的内容。由于大部分此类娱乐媒体内容通过移动设备和互联网消费/浏览，因此它超出了传统的地理和数字边界。这种跨国界数字媒体消费为烟草行业绕开就烟草广告或营销施加的控制提供了新的新兴渠道。

批 注

① 理解不透彻。
② 表达过于贴近字面。

有记录显示，媒体对烟草使用的描述超出传统付费大众媒体的广告范围，并对这种描述增加青年吸烟和养成烟草使用习惯的可能性进行了评估。电影、音乐视频、网络视频、电视节目、流服务、社交媒体帖子、视频游戏和手机应用软件等娱乐媒体内容都有可能鼓励青年吸烟、推动烟草使用和促销烟草产品的描述。由于大部分此类娱乐媒体内容都是通过移动设备和互联网消费/浏览的，因此，它超出了传统的地理和数字边界。这种跨国界数字媒体消费为烟草行业规避烟草广告或营销控制提供了新渠道。

1. 词汇理解不透彻。见"increase youth tobacco uptake and normalize tobacco use"一词。先不看原文，只读翻译稿，"促进青年养成吸烟习惯"和"使烟草使用正常化"在内容上有所交叉，似乎表达的是一种含义，令人略有不解。在翻译如"normalize""regulate""formulate"等抽象含义的词汇时，需保持一定灵活性，结合语境进行归化处理。通过深入分析原文，可得知"increase uptake"与"normalize"存在一种递进关系，即先增多，再逐渐形成一种固定的习惯。具备这一理解后，即可将"normalize"往"习惯养成"这层含义上靠拢，处理成"养成烟草使用习惯"。另一个需要注意的点是，"tobacco use"在世卫组织稿件中如没有特别具体语境含义，一般作中性词处理，即译为"烟草使用"。

2. 表达过于贴近字面直译。见"mobile phone applications have all been shown to depict and promote tobacco use and tobacco products in ways"一句。翻译稿的问题在于对文中结构"have been shown...in ways that..."的处理过于机械，为了保留原文的"形式"而舍弃表意，没有突出这句话表达的重点。实际上"in ways that"后接的"may encourage youth smoking uptake"是对"depict and promote tobacco use and tobacco products"的修饰，因此被修饰的对象，即"关于××的描述"（或描述的内容）才应当是论述重点。如依照翻译稿，"以鼓励青年养成吸烟习惯的方式描述……"似乎将重点转到了"描述方式"上，这不符合原文表达。在涉及"形合"与"意合"问题时，应当全面考虑各方面因素。

第 2 段

While continued monitoring of tobacco depictions in entertainment media is both useful and necessary to understanding patterns of youth exposure, the collected body of evidence clearly shows that media tobacco depictions increase youth tobacco uptake. Therefore, policies that reduce youth exposure to entertainment media depictions are required. In order to keep up with these technological advancements and assist Parties with effective policy action, it is necessary to provide further advice to Parties on this topic, possibly through an addendum to the existing Article 13 Implementation guidelines.

尽管持续监测烟草在娱乐媒体中的描述对了解青少年接触模式既有用又有必要，但所收集的证据清楚地表明，媒体对烟草的描述促进了青年吸烟习惯的养成。因此，需要制定减少青少年接触娱乐媒体描述的政策。为了与这些技术进步保持一致并协助缔约方采取有效的政策行动，<u>有必要为缔约方提供关于该主题的更多建议，有可能通过为现行第 13 条实施准则编写一项增编实现</u>。[①]

① 表述问题。

尽管持续监测烟草在娱乐媒体中的描述对了解青年接触烟草的方式是有用的，也是必要的，但收集的大量证据明确表明，媒体对烟草的描述增加了青年对烟草的使用。因此，需要制定关于减少青年接触娱乐媒体描述的政策。为了跟上这些技术进步和协助缔约方采取有效的政策行动，有必要就这一主题向缔约方提供进一步的建议，通过为现行第 13 条实施准则编写一份增编可能是一种办法。

点评

1. 词汇增补问题。见"patterns of youth exposure"一词。值得注意的一点是，在卫生类稿件中，如"tobacco""drug"这样的主题词在原文中经常出现，所以有些地方会有所省略，这就需要在译成汉语时酌情增补必要的关键词。文中"youth exposure"显然是对"youth exposure to tobacco"的省略，如直译为"青少年接触模式"，则不够具体、精准，应当通过增补必要词汇，将其扩充为"青少年接触烟草方式"。

2. 表述问题。见"it is necessary to provide further advice to Parties on this topic, possibly through an addendum to..."一句。通过对比翻译稿与审校稿，可发现两者看似在内容准确度上并无区别，只是表述方式不同。但在翻译实践中，表述方式也属于准确度的范畴。在信息内容准确无误的基础上，应当寻求最符合原文精神内涵、论述重点的表述方式，并且表达视角也可以看出译者对文字理解的深度。就前半句而言，显然"topic"相比"Parties"更重要，处理成"就这一主题向缔约方提供"比"向缔约方提供关于该主题"更得当；对于"possibly through an addendum to"，其强调的重点是"一种可能方式"，将落脚点处理成名词形式的"一种办法"更合适，即译为"通过为现行第 13 条实施准则编写一份增编可能是一种办法"。

第 3 段

Article 13 Implementation guidelines were developed in light of the primary available means, at the time, for TAPS. Since the guidelines were adopted, there has been a notable expansion in cross-border digital entertainment media, including wide Internet access, social media, smartphones, and access to free digital video, films and games. There is significant potential for these forms of digital media to be used now for TAPS. Digital media has vast reach, especially for young people. This means that the current Article 13 implementation guidelines no longer comprehensively cover the available means for TAPS.

第 13 条实施准则是根据跨国界烟草广告、促销和赞助的主要可用手段制定的。自通过《准则》以来，跨国界数字娱乐媒体的覆盖范围显著扩大，包括大范围的互联网接入、社交媒体、智能手机以及获取免费数字视频、电影和游戏。如今，这些形式的数字媒体在服务于烟草广告、促销和赞助方面有巨大潜力。数字媒体的覆盖面巨大，特别是对年轻人有吸引力。这意味着现行的第 13 条实施准则不再全面覆盖烟草广告、促销和赞助的可用手段。

批 注

① 注意"access"的不同含义。

第 13 条实施准则是按当时的跨国界烟草广告、促销和赞助主要可用手段制定的。自通过该准则以来，跨国界数字娱乐媒体的覆盖范围显著扩大，包括广泛接入互联网、社交媒体和智能手机以及大范围获取免费数字视频、电影和游戏。现在，这些形式的数字媒体极有可能用于烟草广告、促销和赞助。数字媒体覆盖面广，特别是针对年轻人。这意味着现行的第 13 条实施准则已不再全面覆盖各种可用的烟草广告、促销和赞助手段。

1. 表述统一问题。见"including wide Internet access, social media, smartphones, and access to free digital video, films and games"一句。单看翻译稿，其问题在于，对"access to free"的理解过于直接、表面，"access"一词的含义很丰富，结合

不同主体有不同译法，不仅仅限于"获取"这一种，还可以灵活处理为"提供、问世、出现"。

2. 在第一句话的结尾处，access 一词出现两次。该词的主语不同，在翻译该词时也应有适当的调整，不能千人一面。"wide Internet access" 译为"广泛接入互联网"，那么"and access to free digital video, films and games" 就可以译为"大范围获取免费数字视频、电影和游戏"，这样显得译文更加灵活，结构也更加对称。

3. 前后呼应问题。见句首的"primary available means"与句尾的"available means for TAPS"。此处应注意前后呼应与对应问题，如本段前后都出现了"means"一词，但其搭配的对象不同，这表明原文中的"means"一词有各自的侧重点，在翻译时要进行对比、区分。对于第一处，可直接译为"主要可用手段"，而对于第二处"available means"，如果按照翻译稿直接译为"可用手段"，似乎与"primary available means"相比没有做出区分。如果结合语境中的"comprehensively cover"，或许可将其理解为"全部、各种可用手段"，这便与句首的"主要可用手段"形成对比，构成前后对照，这是一种基于语篇的翻译策略。在其他类似的语段中，如涉及一词在语段前后反复出现，不妨从这一角度来思考。

补充练习

1. The Expert Group considered the relationship between tobacco marketing and smoking behaviour, noting that this has been extensively researched. The accumulated evidence base shows a strong causal relationship between tobacco promotion and increased tobacco use. Young people are particularly vulnerable to the influential affects of media depictions of tobacco use. Reducing youth exposure to depictions of tobacco use embedded in entertainment media is essential to successful tobacco use prevention.

参考译文

专家小组审议了烟草营销与吸烟行为之间的关系，指出已对这种关系进行了广泛研究。积累的证据基础显示，烟草促销与烟草用量增加之间存在明显的因果关系。青年特别容易受到媒体对烟草使用描述的影响。减少青年接触娱乐媒体中植入的烟草使用描述对成功预防烟草使用至关重要。

2. Parties are urged to develop legislation or administrative measures to reduce tobacco depictions in entrainment media such as requiring tobacco industry disclosure of all expenditures associated with TAPS, requiring health and content warnings on material that depicts tobacco, banning tobacco branding from all entertainment media, requiring that any tobacco products shown must include required health warnings and

other regulatory requirements relating to packaging (such as plain packaging), and requiring age ratings on entertainment media including music videos and video games. Further, Parties are urged to prohibit tax concessions or subsidies for films that include tobacco promotions.

敦促缔约方采取立法或行政措施，减少烟草在娱乐媒体中的描述，例如要求烟草行业披露与烟草广告、促销和赞助有关的所有支出，要求在描述烟草的材料上印制健康和成分警语，禁止所有娱乐媒体推广烟草品牌，要求展示的所有烟草产品必须包括健康警告，符合与包装（如无装饰包装）有关的其他监管规定，并要求对包括音乐视频和视频游戏在内的娱乐媒体进行年龄分级。此外，敦促缔约方禁止对含有烟草促销内容的电影进行税收减免或提供补贴。

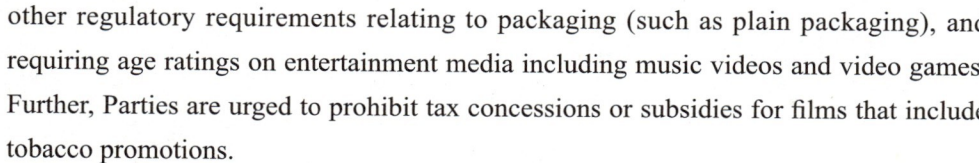

Eye conditions that can cause vision impairment and blindness—such as cataract, trachoma and refractive error—are, for good reasons, the main focus of prevention and other eye care strategies; nevertheless, the importance of eye conditions that do not typically cause vision impairment—such as dry eye and conjunctivitis—must not be overlooked. These conditions are frequently among the leading reasons for presentation to eye care services all countries.

Eye conditions are remarkably common. Those who live long enough will experience at least one eye condition during their lifetime. Globally, at least 2.2 billion people have a vision impairment or blindness, of whom at least 1 billion have a vision impairment that could have been prevented or has yet to be addressed. More reliable data on the met and unmet eye care needs, however, are required for planning. Also, the burden of eye conditions and vision impairment is not borne equally. The burden tends to be greater in low- and middle-income countries and underserved populations, such as women, migrants, indigenous peoples, persons with certain kinds of disability, and in rural communities. Population growth and ageing, along with behavioural and lifestyle changes, and urbanization, will dramatically increase the number of people with eye conditions, vision impairment and blindness in the coming decades.

请自行翻译后查看后文的分析点评

分析点评

第 1 段

Eye conditions that can cause vision impairment and blindness—such as cataract, trachoma and refractive error—are, for good reasons, the main focus of prevention and other eye care strategies; nevertheless, the importance of eye conditions that do not typically cause vision impairment—such as dry eye and conjunctivitis—must not be overlooked. These conditions are frequently among the leading reasons for presentation to eye care services all countries.

批 注

① 注意习惯用法。
② 调序。

有充分理由认为，可导致视力损伤和失明①的眼部疾病（如白内障、沙眼和屈光不正）是预防和其他眼部护理战略的主要重点②；然而，不能忽视通常不会导致视力损害的眼部状况的重要性，如干眼症和结膜炎。这些情况经常是所有国家提供眼睛护理服务的主要原因。

有充分的理由将可能导致视力损害和盲症的眼疾（例如白内障、沙眼和屈光不正）作为预防和其他眼保健战略的重点；不过，绝不能忽视通常不会引起视力损伤的眼疾（如干眼症和结膜炎）的重要性。这些眼疾常常是所有国家提供眼保健服务的主要原因。

1. 世卫组织的稿件有其独特的要求，很多时候，其词汇自成一体。在这段选取的内容中，"blindness"我们一般可泛指"失明"，但在这类文件中，通常统称为"盲症"。

2. 语序的调整问题。在句子的表达中，由于英中两种语言的独特特点，决定了英文中经常使用名词，而在中文中则习惯使用动词结构来表达，比如文中 "Eye conditions that can cause vision impairment and blindness—such as cataract, trachoma and refractive error—are, for good reasons, the main focus of prevention and other eye care strategies" 是典型的英式结构 "是……的主要重点"，在处理时，应尽可能遵循汉语习惯，将语序适当调整，变为 "有充分的理由……将……作为……"。

3. 小词的处理。对于 "conditions" 一词，如果稍不留神，就可能按照习惯译法翻译成 "条件、情况、状况" 等，若考虑到本材料涉及卫生与健康问题，显然应将其译为 "疾病"。词虽小但意义重大，不可掉以轻心。

第 2 段

Eye conditions are remarkably common. Those who live long enough will experience at least one eye condition during their lifetime. Globally, at least 2.2 billion people have a vision impairment or blindness, of whom at least 1 billion have a vision impairment that could have been prevented or has yet to be addressed. More reliable data on the met and unmet eye care needs, however, are required for planning. Also, the burden of eye conditions and vision impairment is not borne equally. The burden tends to be greater in low- and middle-income countries and underserved populations, such as women, migrants, indigenous peoples, persons with certain kinds of disability, and in rural communities. Population growth and ageing, along with behavioural and lifestyle changes, and urbanization, will dramatically increase the number of people with eye conditions, vision impairment and blindness in the coming decades.

翻译稿

眼疾非常普遍。寿命足够长的人一生中至少会经历①一次眼部疾病。在全球范围内，至少有 22 亿人患有视力障碍或失明，其中至少有 10 亿人患有本可以预防或尚未解决的视力障碍②。然而，规划③需要更可靠的关于满足和未满足的眼部护理需求的数据。此外，眼疾和视力障碍的负担也不平等。低收入和中等收入国家以及服务不足的人口，如妇女、移民、土著人民、某些类型的残疾人和农村社区的负担往往更大。人口增长和老龄化，加上行为和生活方式的改变，以及城市化，将在未来几十年中大幅增加患有眼病、视力障碍和失明的人数。

批 注

① 不够准确。
② 理解不到位。
③ 适当增词。

审校稿

眼疾现象非常普遍。寿命足够长的人在一生当中至少会患上一种眼疾。全球至少有 22 亿人患有视力损害或盲症，其中至少有 10 亿人的视力损害本可以预防或尚有治愈的可能。但是，制定规划需要有更可靠的关于已满足和未满足的眼保健需求的数据。另外，眼疾和视力损害的负担也分布不均。中低收入国家和未得到充分服务的民众，例如妇女、移民、土著人民、某些类型的残疾人以及农村社区的民众往往负担更重。人口增长和老龄化以及行为与生活方式改变和城市化，将在今后几十年里使眼疾、视力损害和盲症患者人数急剧增长。

点评

1. 多数时候，很容易在一些小词上犯错，上文和此处的"experience"就是实例。我们经常会谈到"经历生活、经历……事件"，但如果后面是疾病，显然应该指的是"患上疾病"，不可翻译为"经历"。

2. 虚拟语气结构中，"a vision impairment that could have been prevented or has yet to be addressed"，前面"could have been prevented"指"本可以预防"，而后面的"has yet to be addressed"，翻译稿将其按照原来的结构处理，显然不到位，这里指的是"尚有治愈的可能"，这是更深一层的含义。

3. 适当增词。"More reliable data on the met and unmet eye care needs, however, are required for planning"一句是典型的倒序结构，翻译时除了调整语序外，对于

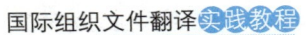

"planning"还有必要增加"制定"一词，使其更加明确到位。

4. "underserved"在联合国文件翻译中通常译为"得不到充分服务的"，这一点也要适当考虑到。"vision impairment"则参考世卫组织以往文件翻译为"视力损害"。

补充练习

1. The health and social harm caused by the illicit use of psychoactive drugs is enormous. The harm includes direct damage to the physical and mental health of users and dramatically reduces the length and quality of their lives. Drug use harms families and communities through crimes against property and people. It contributes to traffic and domestic injuries, child abuse, gender-based sexual violence and other forms of violence. Members of the Assembly know the global statistics quite well. They do not need to be reminded. Nonetheless, let me share the fact that an estimated 27 million people have drug-use disorders. More than 400 000 of them die each year. Injection-drug use accounts for an estimated 30 per cent of new HIV infections outside sub-Saharan Africa. Injection-drug use contributes significantly to epidemics of hepatitis B and hepatitis C in all regions of the world. About 10 million people who inject drugs now are infected with hepatitis C. Do members of the Assembly know how expensive it is to treat hepatitis C? It is very expensive; even the richest countries in the world cannot afford it.

非法使用精神刺激药物对健康和社会带来的危害极大。这种危害包括直接损害使用者的身心健康，严重缩短他们的寿命，降低生活质量。吸毒带来侵害财产和人的犯罪，危害家庭和社区。吸毒造成交通和家庭伤害、虐待儿童、基于性别的性暴力和其他形式的暴力。大会成员清楚地了解了这方面的全球数据，不需要再提醒。然而，让我分享一个事实：世界上约有2 700万人有吸毒病症；每年有40多万人死亡。据估计，在撒哈拉以南非洲地区之外，新增艾滋病毒感染者30%是因为注射吸毒造成的。世界所有地区乙型肝炎和丙型肝炎流行，注射吸毒是重要因素。现在约有1 000万注射吸毒者感染有丙型肝炎。大会成员们是否知道，治疗丙型肝炎有多昂贵？非常昂贵，即使世界上最富有的国家都无法承担。

2. In addition to having major security implications, the enormous profits generated through drug trafficking and its linkage with other forms of organized crime—corruption, money laundering and terrorism—constitute a threat to State authority, impede the economic development of societies and undermine the rule of law. Overdose, addiction and the spread of HIV and hepatitis also demonstrate why the drug problem presents a risk to the health and well-being of people worldwide. It is therefore evident that a

more effective response to this phenomenon calls for a holistic and integrated approach that encompasses the entire nexus of human rights, safety, security and sustainable development. The 2030 Agenda for Sustainable Development (Resolution 70/1)—more specifically its Goals 3 and 16—provides an opportunity to reinvigorate our efforts in order to come closer to a healthier, safer and more prosperous future for all.

参考译文

除了具有重大安全影响之外，毒品贩运产生的巨大利润，以及它与其他形式的有组织犯罪——腐败、洗钱和恐怖主义——的关联，对国家权力机构构成威胁，阻碍社会的经济发展，并且破坏法治。吸毒过量、成瘾、艾滋病毒和肝炎传播也显示出，毒品问题为何会对全世界人民的健康与福祉构成风险。因此，要想更加有效地应对这一现象，显然必须采取一种全面综合的方法，其中包含了人权、安全、安保和可持续发展的整体联系。《2030年可持续发展议程》（第70/1号决议）——更具体地说是目标3和16——提供了一个机会，借此可以重振我们的各项努力，迈向所有人更加健康、安全和繁荣的未来。

第四篇

原文

In a global society built on the ability to see, vision plays a critical role in every facet and stage of life. Vision is the most dominant of the five senses and plays a crucial role in every facet of our lives. It is integral to interpersonal and social interactions in face-to-face communication where information is conveyed through non-verbal cues such as gestures and facial expressions.

Globally, societies are built on the ability to see. Towns and cities, economies, education systems, sports, media and many other aspects of contemporary life are organized around sight. Thus, vision contributes towards everyday activities and enables people to prosper at every stage of life.

From the moment of birth, vision is critical to child development. For infants, visually recognizing and responding to parents, family members, and caregivers facilitates cognitive and social development and the growth of motor skills, coordination and balance.

From early childhood to adolescence, vision enables ready access to educational materials and is pivotal to educational attainment. Vision supports the development of social skills to foster friendships, strengthen self-esteem and maintain well-being.

It is also important for participation in sports and social activities that are essential to physical development, mental and physical health, personal identity and socialization.

In adulthood, vision facilitates participation in the workforce, contributing to economic benefits and a sense of identity. It also contributes towards the enjoyment of many other areas of life that are often designed around the ability to see, such as sports or cultural activities.

Later in life, vision helps with maintaining social contact and independence and facilitates the management of other health conditions. Vision also helps to sustain mental health and levels of well-being, both of which are higher among those with good vision.

请自行翻译后查看后文的分析点评

分析点评

第 1 段

In a global society built on the ability to see, vision plays a critical role in every facet and stage of life. Vision is the most dominant of the five senses and plays a crucial role in every facet of our lives. It is integral to interpersonal and social interactions in face-to-face communication where information is conveyed through non-verbal cues such as gestures and facial expressions.

在一个以视力为根基的全球社会里，视觉在生活的各个方面和生命的每个阶段都起着至关重要的作用。视觉是五种感官中最主要的感官[①]，在我们生活的各个方面都起着至关重要的作用。在信息通过非语言提示[②]（例如手势和面部表情）传递的情况下，视觉是面对面交流中人际交往和社会互动的组成部分。

批 注

① 概念有误。
② 选词可更精练。意译更有助于理解。

在一个以视力为根基的全球社会里，视觉在生活的各个方面和生命的每个阶段都起着至关重要的作用。在人的五感中，视觉是最重要的一种感觉，它在人们生活的各个方面起着至关重要的作用。在利用非言语的手段（例如手势和表情）面对面传递信息的场合，视觉对于人际交往和社会互动是不可或缺的。

1. 本篇选自世界卫生组织关于眼部疾病的一份报告。本篇有多处要注意辨别词汇的细微差别。预览本篇全文，可以发现文中出现多个与视力有关的近义词和表达。包括 "ability to see" "vision" "sight" 和 "sense"。作者使用这些词，是为了让表达形式更丰富，还是因为这些词的确含义不同？它们能否彼此替代？

对应的中文译词是什么？中文译词能否体现这些英文词之间的区别？在动手翻译之前，首先要分辨和理解原文的意图，回答这些问题。

2. 见第一句和第二句。在第一句中，ability to see 译作"视力"，即"看的能力"；紧随着的 vision 一词，是否也译为"视力"？在第二句中提到"Vision is the most dominant of the five senses"，可见 vision 是指"sense"，也即一种感觉。前后对照，vision 应译为"视觉"。尤其要注意的是，人有五官，五官所感为五感。视觉为五感之一，不是五官之一。

3. 本段中，"non-verbal"译为"非言语"比译作"非语言"更贴切，更强调一种不需要通过发声说话来进行沟通的交际手段，例如"手势"和"表情"。

第 2 段

Globally, societies are built on the ability to see. Towns and cities, economies, education systems, sports, media and many other aspects of contemporary life are organized around sight. Thus, vision contributes towards everyday activities and enables people to prosper at every stage of life.

全球社会①都以视力为基础。城镇、经济、教育系统、体育运动、媒体和当代生活的许多其他方面，都是围绕着视觉安排的。因此，视觉有助于日常活动②，使人们能够在人生的每个阶段获得成功。

从全球来看，各个社会都以视力为基础。城镇、经济、教育系统、体育运动、媒体以及当代生活的许多其他方面，都围绕着视觉来安排布置。因此，视觉有助于人们开展日常活动，让人在人生每个阶段顺遂成功。

1. 本句中"globally, societies…"与上一句的"global society"之间有单复数的区别。两者强调的重点不一样。统一处理为"全球社会"不妥。

2. 处理"Thus, vision contributes towards everyday activities…"一句时，加入"人们"一词不仅可厘清上半句的逻辑关系，还可与下半句形成呼应，这是深刻理解原文之后的增译。

第 3 段

From the moment of birth, vision is critical to child development. For infants, visually recognizing and responding to parents, family members, and caregivers facilitates cognitive and social development and the growth of motor skills, coordination and balance.

从出生那一刻起③，视觉对于儿童发育便至关重要。对婴儿而言，通过视觉

批 注

① 英文中的复数形式未得到体现。
② 逻辑不通。

批 注

③ 注意与第 4 段和第 5 段的内容呼应。

批 注

① 注意一词多译的好处。

辨认自己的父母、家庭成员和照护者并与其进行回应，有助于^①认知和社会发展以及活动、协调和平衡能力的提高。

从出生的那一刻，视觉对于儿童发育便至关重要。婴儿通过视觉辨认和回应父母、家庭成员与照护者，这有助于婴儿的认知和社会发展，能促进提高其活动、协调和平衡能力。

1. 本句中的"From the moment of birth"与第 4 至 6 段句首的"From early childhood to adolescence""In adulthood"和"Later in life"共同描述了整个人生阶段。译文中也应体现这种时期上的连续性。请注意后续各段中的对应译文。

2. 本句中将"facilitate"译为"有助于"和"促进"这两个词义相近的词，能顺利衔接后面的"development"和"growth"，是灵活的意译手段。

第 4 段

From early childhood to adolescence, vision enables ready access to educational materials and is pivotal to educational attainment. Vision supports the development of social skills to foster friendships, strengthen self-esteem and maintain well-being. It is also important for participation in sports and social activities that are essential to physical development, mental and physical health, personal identity and socialization.

批 注

② 不贴切。
③ 不准确。
④ 是因果关系吗？逻辑不通。

从幼儿期到青春期，视觉使人能够随时随地^②获得学习材料，而且对于受教育水平^③也至关重要。视觉有助于社交技能的发展，可增进友谊、增强自尊心并保持幸福感。视觉对于参加体育运动和社交活动也很重要，因为^④这两种活动对于身体发育、身心健康、个人认同和社会化至关重要。

从幼儿到青少年时期，人们借助视觉可以很方便地阅读教育材料，视觉对教育成果至关重要。视觉有助于发展社交技能增进友谊，强化自尊，保持幸福感。视觉对开展体育运动和社交活动非常重要，而这二者对人们锻炼身体，保持身心健康，实现自我认同和社会化而言是不可或缺的。

1. 本句中"access"一词，一般理解为"获得、获取"，词义含混，在翻译时通常要根据上下文来固定其确切的含义。本句中将该词与"视觉"和"教育材料"联系起来理解，可意译为"阅读教育材料"。类似例子还有"broaden the access to education"，可译为"扩大受教育的途径"。

2. 第二句中的 that 从句，处理为表示"原因"的从句并不妥当，逻辑不清。

处理为递进关系更能体现原文的意图。

第 5 段

In adulthood, vision facilitates participation in the workforce, contributing to economic benefits and a sense of identity. It also contributes towards the enjoyment of many other areas of life that are often designed around the ability to see, such as sports or cultural activities.

成年之后，视觉有助于人们加入劳动队伍，创造经济利益并获得认同感。视觉还有助于享受许多其他通常围绕着视力设计的生活领域①，例如体育运动或文化活动。

成年之后，视觉有助于人们加入劳动队伍，创造经济利益，实现身份认同。视觉还有助于人们享受生活的许多其他方面，例如体育运动或文化活动等需要视力的活动。

第二句中的"that are often designed around the ability to see"，翻译稿采用直译手法，略显生硬难懂。在保证准确的前提下，译"意"而不是译"词"，换一种表述方式，更有利于实现沟通传达的目的。

第 6 段

Later in life, vision helps with maintaining social contact and independence and facilitates the management of other health conditions. Vision also helps to sustain mental health and levels of well-being, both of which are higher among those with good vision.

到了生命后期，视觉帮助维护社交联系和独立性，并有助于控制其他病症②。视力③还有助于维护精神健康和幸福感，视力良好者这两项水平都更高。

人到晚年，视觉能帮助维持社会联系，保持个人独立，方便管理其他健康事宜。此外，视觉还有助于保持人的健康精神和幸福感，视觉良好的人精神更健康，幸福感更强。

"vision"一词之前一直译为"视觉"。译文需保持前后一致，这也是联合国文件翻译标准中的"一致性"标准的要求。

批 注

① 直译的动宾搭配生硬。

批 注

② 理解不到位。
③ 与前文不一致。

补充练习

1. In a world built on the ability to see, vision, the most dominant of our senses, is vital at every turn of our lives. The newborn depends on vision to recognize and bond with its mother; the toddler, to master balance and learn to walk; the schoolboy, to walk to school, read and learn; the young woman to participate in the workforce; and the older woman, to maintain her independence.

参考译文

在一个以视力为基础的世界里，视觉是我们最主要的感觉，在我们生命的每个阶段都起着至关重要的作用。新生儿依靠视觉辨认母亲，并建立亲子关系；幼儿依靠视觉掌握平衡，学会走路；小学生依靠视觉上学、读书和学习；年轻妇女依靠视觉参加劳动；老年妇女依靠视觉保持独立。

2. While some eye conditions cause vision impairment, many do not and yet can still lead to personal and financial hardships because of the treatment needs associated to them. Vision impairment occurs when an eye condition affects the visual system and one or more of its vision functions. A person who wears spectacles or contact lenses to compensate for their vision impairment, still has a vision impairment.

参考译文

一些眼疾会导致视力损害，还有一些眼疾并不会损害视力，但相关的治疗需求却可能导致个人遇到困难，包括经济困难。当眼疾影响到视觉系统及一种或多种视觉功能时，就会出现视力损害。为弥补受损的视力而佩戴眼镜或隐形眼镜的人仍然有视力损害。

第五篇

原文

The double burden of malnutrition is growing among individuals, households, communities and nations, disproportionately affecting the poorest and most vulnerable. From 126 low- and middle-income countries studied, 48 faced the double burden of malnutrition in the 2010s—with their population facing simultaneous wasting, stunting, thinness and obesity. This change is driven by a new nutrition reality, characterised by a transformation in the way people grow, live, work, eat, move and age, alongside shifts in our global food systems, from production to marketing, purchasing and consumption.

Undernutrition and overweight/obesity promote themselves and each other, as well as their adverse health effects across the life-course and generations. This is driven through interconnected biological pathways, along with broader societal and ecological factors within the new nutrition reality. Interventions and programmes that seek to address undernutrition and overweight/obesity must do so simultaneously, with a life-course and multi-generational approach.

Current approaches to address and measure malnutrition in all its form are inadequate and new economic modelling tools are required to accurately estimate the economic impact of the double burden of malnutrition. Double-duty actions may be more economically effective to address malnutrition in its multiple forms than interventions and programmes that focus on undernutrition or overnutrition separately.

请自行翻译后查看后文的分析点评

分析点评

第 1 段

The double burden of malnutrition is growing among individuals, households, communities and nations, disproportionately affecting the poorest and most vulnerable. From 126 low- and middle-income countries studied, 48 faced the double burden of malnutrition in the 2010s—with their population facing simultaneous wasting, stunting, thinness and obesity. This change is driven by a new nutrition reality, characterised by a transformation in the way people grow, live, work, eat, move and age, alongside shifts in our global food systems, from production to marketing, purchasing and consumption.

营养不良的双重负担[①]在个人、家庭、社区和国家中日益增加，对最贫穷和最弱势群体的影响格外严重。在研究的 126 个中低收入国家中，有 48 个国家在 21 世纪 10 年代面临营养不良的双重负担（它们的人口同时面临[②]虚弱、发育迟缓、消瘦和肥胖问题）。这种变化是因为一种新的营养现实而产生的，其特征是人们生长、生活、工作、饮食、行动和衰老方式在转变，而且我们的全球粮食体系也在发生从生产向营销、采购和消费的转变。

个人、家庭、社区和国家的双重营养不良问题日益严重，最贫穷和最弱势群体受到的影响格外严重。在研究所涉的 126 个中低收入国家中，48 个国家在 21 世纪 10 年代出现双重营养不良问题——这些国家的人口在身体虚弱、消瘦和发育迟缓的同时又面临肥胖问题。一种新的营养现状推动发生这种改变，表现为

批 注

① 与既有译法不符。
② 标点符号不必改换。

人们的身体生长、生活、工作、饮食、行动和衰老的方式发生变化，同时全球食物体系也随之改变，从生产转向营销、采购和消费。

1. 遇到专有名词如何处理？最重要的是具备"自疑"态度和"查询"意识。首先结合上下文，质疑自己的译出语是否到位，其次利用联合国词汇库和其他可靠搜索资源，寻找佐证。以本段第一句中的"double burden of malnutrition"为例，通过结合上下文，发现本段第二句中提及"...facing simultaneous wasting, stunting, thinness and obesity"，可以看出"double burden"的本意是指一方面瘦弱一方面肥胖，是营养欠佳的双重表现。因此，译作"双重营养不良"。接下来，搜索该词是否为通用词，发现权威科普网站均采用该词，表明该词已具有普遍性。最终确定该词译为"双重营养不良"。

2. 使用破折号和括号，都有解释说明的作用。为保持形式上的统一，除非影响到意思表达的完整和通顺，否则无须将原文中的破折号改为括号，反之亦然。

3. 见第三句中的"global food systems"。"food"一词，在联合国文件语境下，有"食物、食品"和"粮食"双重含义，例如"food safety"译为"食物安全"或者"食品安全"，"food security"译为"粮食安全"。一般而言，"食物"的覆盖范畴大于"粮食"，具体采纳哪个词义，要根据上下文仔细斟酌。这也是联合国文件翻译"准确性"标准提出的要求。

第 2 段

Undernutrition and overweight/obesity promote themselves and each other, as well as their adverse health effects across the life-course and generations. This is driven through interconnected biological pathways, along with broader societal and ecological factors within the new nutrition reality. Interventions and programmes that seek to address undernutrition and overweight/obesity must do so simultaneously, with a life-course and multi-generational approach.

营养不足和超重/肥胖本身相互促进[①]，并且对一生的健康产生不利影响，而且会代际传递。这是因为相互关联的生物途径以及新的营养现实中更广泛的社会和生态因素造成的。旨在解决营养不足和超重/肥胖问题的干预措施和规划必须同时进行，必须采取关注一生和多代的办法。

营养不足和超重/肥胖不仅自我恶化，而且互为推动，二者对健康的负面影响贯穿人的一生，在代际之间传递。这是相互关联的生物途径与新的营养现实中更广泛的社会和生态因素共同造成的。旨在解决营养不足和超重/肥胖问题的干预措施和规划必须同时进行，并采取关注人的一生和多个世代的办法予以实施。

① 有漏译。

1. 注意区分"undernutrition"与"malnutrition",前者为"营养不足",后者为营养方面出了问题,是"营养不良",二者的外延不同,不可混用。译词的一个原则是,原文中有区别的词,译文中也应当体现这种区别,不能大而化之,一带而过。

2. 见最后一句中的"with a life-course and multi-generational approach"。这是一个补充性的信息,补充说明前文所述相关干预措施的实施方式。翻译稿将其译为"必须采取……办法",处理为并列关系,与原文的语法逻辑相悖。

第 3 段

Current approaches to address and measure malnutrition in all its form are inadequate and new economic modelling tools are required to accurately estimate the economic impact of the double burden of malnutrition. Double-duty actions may be more economically effective to address malnutrition in its multiple forms than interventions and programmes that focus on undernutrition or overnutrition separately.

目前处理和衡量各种形式营养不良的方法不够充分,需要有新的经济建模工具来准确估计营养不良的双重负担对经济的影响。两用行动① 在应对多种形式的营养不良问题方面可能比单独关注营养不足或营养过剩的干预措施和规划更具经济效益。

批 注

① 是否有固定译法?如果没有,应遵循怎样的翻译原则?

目前处理和衡量各种形式营养不良的方法不够充分,需要有新的经济建模工具来准确估计双重营养不良对经济的影响。在应对多种形式的营养不良方面,双重责任行动可能比单独关注营养不足或营养过剩的干预措施和规划更具经济效益。

见最后一句的"double-duty actions"一词。"double-duty"与"double burden"是对应的,要解决双重问题,当然需要承担其双重责任。翻译稿译为"两用"一词,一方面容易被误解为"两种用途";另一方面也没有体现这种对应关系。译词的第二个原则是,顾及上下文,根据该词出现的具体情境推敲最贴切的译法。

补充练习

1. Renowned global health and development academics and practitioners authored The Lancet Series on the Double Burden of Malnutrition.

全球卫生与发展领域著名学者和从业人员为《柳叶刀》杂志撰写关于双重营养不良问题的系列文章。

2. The world is facing a new nutrition reality. Being undernourished or overweight are no longer separate public health issues.

世界正面临一个新的营养现实。营养不足或营养过剩不再是彼此不相关的公共卫生问题。

3. The double burden of malnutrition is growing and disproportionally affecting the poorest and most vulnerable populations.

双重营养不良情形正日益增加，对最贫穷和最弱势人口造成的影响格外严重。

4. Both extremes of malnutrition also impact individuals throughout their lifetime and can be passed to the next generation.

这两种极端的营养不良情况也会影响人的一生，还有可能继续影响下一代。

第六篇

Juno Thomas, Centre for Enteric Diseases, National Institute for Communicable Diseases, South Africa, gave a presentation on whole genome sequencing (WGS)—paving the way forward globally to better understand food systems. She presented this as a revolution in public health microbiology, one with immense power in field applications and research—some readily realized, and yet more untapped. Whole genome sequencing represents a potent tool for: phylogenetic, epidemiologic surveillance; transmission studies; food testing and monitoring; outbreak and trace-back investigations; source tracking and attribution; and root-cause analysis.

As a single workflow, it has the potential to replace many phenotypic and genotypic methodologies currently used in a typical microbiology laboratory. Isolate preparation is identical for all bacterial pathogens, and the "wet laboratory" components (DNA extraction, library preparation and sequencing reactions) are quick and easy to perform. With the cost of WGS declining, it is fast becoming a cost-effective technology for food-borne pathogen speciation and subtyping. Complementary epidemiologic and WGS datasets provide the ultimate tool for delineating outbreak events, whether localized or transcontinental.

The use of WGS during the listeriosis outbreak in South Africa in 2017–18 was invaluable in guiding the successful outbreak investigation and eventual source identification. This was a landmark event for both the country and the African continent, proving that even resource-limited countries can ably implement this technology and gain tremendous benefit. The single greatest challenge for less-developed countries to use the WGS for public health purposes is the availability of basic epidemiology, surveillance and food monitoring and testing infrastructure.

请自行翻译后查看后文的分析点评

第1段

Juno Thomas, Centre for Enteric Diseases, National Institute for Communicable Diseases, South Africa, gave a presentation on whole genome sequencing (WGS)—paving the way forward globally to better understand food systems. She presented this as a revolution in public health microbiology, one with immense power in field applications and research—some readily realized, and yet more untapped. Whole genome sequencing represents a potent tool for: phylogenetic, epidemiologic surveillance; transmission studies; food testing and monitoring; outbreak and trace-back investigations; source tracking and attribution; and root-cause analysis.

翻译稿

南非国家传染病研究所肠道疾病中心的 Juno Thomas 就全基因组测序——为更好地了解食品系统在全球铺平道路做了专题介绍。她认为这①是公共卫生微生物学的一场革命，在实地应用和研究中具有巨大的力量——有些已经很容易实现，但还没有得到充分利用②。全基因组测序是以下方面的有力工具：系统发育、流行病学监控；传播研究；食品检测和监测；疫情暴发和追溯调查；源跟踪和归因；以及根源分析。

批注

① 指代不明。
② "有些"是指什么？是指"全基因组测序"还是指"实地的应用和研究"？

南非国家传染病研究所肠道疾病中心的 Juno Thomas 做专题介绍，题为全基因组测序——在全球范围内为更好地了解食品系统铺平道路。她认为全基因组测序是公共卫生微生物学的一场革命，它能在实地应用和研究中发挥巨大作用——该技术已迅速运用于一些应用和研究领域，但在其他很多领域并未得到推广。全基因组测序是以下方面的有力工具：系统发育、流行病学监控；传播研究；食品检测和监测；疫情暴发和追溯调查；源跟踪和归因；以及根源分析。

本段的难点主要在第二句。首先，this 所指代的对象是谁？在翻译指代词时，应尽量转变为其指代的名词，以免误解。将 this 的指代对象"全基因组测序"译出，可与后面的"one with..."形成明确的对应关系，从而明确句意。其次，这一句中的"one with immense power in field applications and research"，翻译稿中译为"在实地应用和研究中具有巨大的力量"，是典型的直译法，如果采用意译，可以译为"在实地应用和研究中发挥巨大作用"，二者的意思差别并不大，但意译更容易理解，在这种情况下，选择意译更为妥当，因为翻译的主要任务是实现沟通。最后，如何理解这句中的"some readily realized, and yet more untapped"？英文喜用破折号，对前面的内容作补充说明，那么到底是补充说明前面的哪个部分，有时候并非一目了然，翻译时必须仔细辨别，一要靠语法分析，二要靠逻辑分析，三要靠联系上下文。此处的关键是"some"一词，联系上句中的"this..., one..."，一为复数，一为单数，可见两者并非都是指"全基因组测序"，这里的"some"是指"applications and research"，应理解为"有些应用领域已经采用全基因测序这种技术手段"。

第 2 段

As a single workflow, it has the potential to replace many phenotypic and genotypic methodologies currently used in a typical microbiology laboratory. Isolate preparation is identical for all bacterial pathogens, and the "wet laboratory" components (DNA extraction, library preparation and sequencing reactions) are quick and easy to perform. With the cost of WGS declining, it is fast becoming a cost-effective technology for food-borne pathogen speciation and subtyping. Complementary epidemiologic and WGS datasets provide the ultimate tool for delineating outbreak events, whether localized or transcontinental.

作为单一的工作流程①，全基因组测序有可能取代目前在普通微生物实验室中使用的许多表型和基因型分析法。所有细菌病原体的隔离制备都是相同的，并且"湿实验室"组件（DNA 提取、文库制备和测序反应）快速且易于执行②。

批 注

① 此处有隐含的因果关系。
② 有语病。

随着全基因组测序成本下降,它已迅速成为一种具有成本效益的技术,用于食源性病原体类型形成和分亚型。相互补充的提供了描述本地①或跨大陆疫情暴发事件的终极工具。

批　注

① 表述不到位。

全基因组测序是单一的工作流程,因而有可能取代目前在普通微生物实验室中使用的许多表型和基因型分析法。在该流程中,所有细菌病原体的分离制备都是相同的,并且"湿实验室"的各个组件(DNA 提取、文库构建和测序反应)都能迅速且简便地投入使用。随着全基因组测序的成本下降,它已迅速成为一种经济有效的划分食源性病原型别和亚型的工具。流行病学和全基因组测序数据集互为补充,为描述局部性或跨大陆的疫情暴发事件提供了终极工具。

1. 本段第一句"As..., it has the potential to..."中,"as"引导一个原因状语从句,虽然语气并不如"because"那样强烈,不一定要译为"因为……,所以……",但前后之间的因果关系,必须得到体现,否则不能解释全基因组测序法为何有可能替代其他分析方法。审校稿用"因而"一词,较好地点明了这种弱因果关系。

2. 本段第二句,翻译稿将"components...are quick and easy to perform"处理为"组件快速且易于执行",这是一处明显的语病,不符合中文表达逻辑。译者在翻译过程中,应保持"回头看"的良好习惯,当翻译速度过快,过于顺利时,可有意识地暂停下来,回头审视已完成的工作,往往就能发现浮光掠影之间被忽略的问题。

3. 本段涉及较多专业词汇,如"phenotypic",也有常见词的特殊用法,比如"isolate preparation"。前者属于生僻词,译者一般不熟悉,反而比较警惕,会去积极查询词义,而后者由于常见,一些粗心的译者就按照常见词义处理,造成错误。在处理涉及科技科学类的联合国文件时,译者反而要更加重视常见词在专门领域的特殊译法,保持警惕,不能想当然。

4. 本段最后一句中的"localized"一词,单独出现时,译为"本地的"并无不妥,但该句中该词与"transcontinental"并列,所以译为"局部性的",更能体现这种疫情影响地域方面的对比。

第 3 段

The use of WGS during the listeriosis outbreak in South Africa in 2017-18 was invaluable in guiding the successful outbreak investigation and eventual source identification. This was a landmark event for both the country and the African continent, proving that even resource-limited countries can ably implement this technology and gain tremendous benefit. The single greatest challenge for less-developed countries to use the WGS for public health purposes is the availability of basic epidemiology, surveillance and food monitoring and testing infrastructure.

批注

① "具有里程碑意义的事件"更好。
② 选词不妥。
③ 意义不明。

在2017—2018年南非暴发李斯特菌病期间，使用全基因组测序对于指导成功调查疫情和最终识别病源极具价值。这对于该国和非洲大陆而言都是里程碑事件①，证明即使是资源有限的国家也可以得力地②采用此项技术并获得巨大惠益。对于欠发达国家而言，将全基因组测序用于公共卫生用途最大的挑战在于流行病学基础知识、监控以及食品监测和检测基础设施的可用性③。

2017—2018年李斯特菌病在南非暴发期间，用全基因组测序对于指导成功调查疫情和最终识别病源极具价值。这对于南非和非洲大陆而言都是里程碑式的事件，证明即使资源有限的国家也可以很好地采用此项技术并获得巨大惠益。对于欠发达国家而言，将全基因组测序用于公共卫生用途取决于基础流行病学、监控以及食品监测与检测基础设施是否可用，这是最大的一项挑战。

1. 本段难点集中体现在词汇上。"landmark event"，要么译为"里程碑式的事件"，要么译为"具有里程碑意义的事件"。

2. "ably implement"可有多重译法，但中文需通顺，译为"得力地采用"显然不妥。

3. "availability"一词本身就是抽象概括的词，如果译作"可用性"，就是一种万金油式的模糊译法，并未将其确切的含义译出。应结合上下文明确其含义，不能满足于字面翻译，让读者觉得似是而非。

补充练习

Steven Musser, Deputy Director, Center of Scientific Operations, Food and Drug Administration, the United States of America, introduced novel analytical methods and models for enhanced food safety. He noted that food can be adulterated by a wide variety of chemical and microbiological contaminants, which may occur at any point in the distribution chain. Therefore, regulators, public health officials and the food industry must continually invest in new food-testing technologies that lead to innovative approaches to rapidly and accurately identify and characterize the hazard. The innovative methods go beyond food laboratories and include field test kits, smartphones and other handheld detection technologies. The application of many novel analytical methods, including WGS, is expanding and becoming more accessible, both from a field-technological standpoint, but also economically. New tools have the potential to be more accurate and more rapid, improving surveillance and monitoring systems, and permitting increased levels of food traceability.

美利坚合众国食品和药品管理局科学运作中心副主任 Steven Musser 介绍了增强食品安全的新型分析方法和模型。他指出,食品中可能会掺杂各种化学和微生物污染物,这些污染物可能出现在分销链的任何一个环节。因此,监管者、公共卫生官员和食品行业必须不断投资于新的食品测试技术,以便开发出创新方法快速并准确地识别危害并确定其特征。创新方法不仅限于食品实验室,还包括现场测试用品包、智能手机和其他手持式检测技术。无论是从现场技术角度还是从经济角度来看,包括全基因组测序在内的许多新型分析方法的应用正在扩展,并且越来越容易获得。新工具有可能更加准确且更加迅速,可以改善监控和监测系统,并有助于提高食品的可追溯水平。

How many malaria-affected countries have reported cases of COVID-19? Malaria-endemic countries in all WHO have regions have reported cases of COVID-19. In the WHO African Region, which carries more than 90% of the global malaria burden, 37 countries had reported cases of the disease as of 25 March; of these, 10 countries reported local transmission of the disease. The latest situation reports on the COVID-19 pandemic are available on the WHO website.

What about WHO-recommended preventive therapies be maintained in sub-Saharan Africa? Yes, delivery of intermittent preventive treatment in pregnancy (IPTp), seasonal malaria chemoprevention (SMC), and intermittent preventive treatment in infants (IPTi) should be maintained provided that best practices for protecting health workers—and other front-line workers—from COVID-19 are followed. Ensuring access to these and other core malaria prevention tools saves lives and is an important strategy for reducing the strain on health systems in the context of the COVID-19 response.

Mass drug administration (MDA) is a WHO-recommended approach for rapidly reducing malaria mortality and morbidity during epidemics and in complex emergency settings. Through MDA, all individuals in a targeted population are given antimalarial medicines—often at repeated intervals—regardless of whether or not they show symptoms of the disease.

请自行翻译后查看后文的分析点评

第1段

How many malaria-affected countries have reported cases of COVID-19? Malaria-endemic countries in all WHO have regions have reported cases of COVID-19. In the WHO African Region, which carries more than 90% of the global malaria burden, 37 countries had reported cases of the disease as of 25 March; of these, 10 countries reported local transmission of the disease. The latest situation reports on the COVID-19 pandemic are available on the WHO website.

批 注

① 过于重复。

有多少个受疟疾影响国家报告了COVID-19病例？ 世卫组织所有区域的疟疾流行国家都报告了COVID-19病例。世卫组织非洲区域的疟疾负担占全球负担的90%以上，截至3月25日，<u>该区域有37个国家报告了这种疾病的病例；其中有10个国家报告该病存在本地传播</u>。^① 关于COVID-19大流行的最新状况报告可从世卫组织网站获取。

有多少个受疟疾影响国家报告了COVID-19病例？ 世卫组织各区域的疟疾流行国家都报告了COVID-19病例。世卫组织非洲区域占到了全球疟疾负担的90%以上，截至3月25日，该区域有37个国家报告了COVID-19病例；其中有10个国家报告存在本地传播。关于COVID-19大流行的最新状况报告可从世卫组织网站获取。

1. 增减问题。见"37 countries had reported cases of the disease as of 25 March; of these, 10 countries reported local transmission of the disease"一句。翻译稿对这句话的处理大体是没问题的，但细究来看，在表达上有些重复，特别是"这种疾病"重复了两遍。最为关键的一点是，这句话的上一句先提到了"COVID-19"又提到了"malaria"，如果不将"the disease"指代的具体疾病还原，会导致理解问题，因此应当先采用增补译法，增补出"the disease"对应的"COVID-19"。如此一来，对于后半句中的"transmission of the disease"则可以省略"疾病"，直接译为"报告存在本地传播"即可。

2. 表达简洁问题。见"carries more than 90% of the global malaria burden"一句。与上一句类似，翻译稿的处理方式也可接受，但如果追求准确基础上的更简洁表达，无妨按照审校稿的方式作一些调整，无须将"非洲区域的疟疾负担"译出，直接简化为"非洲区域"，不影响理解，也更简洁。

第2段

What about WHO-recommended preventive therapies be maintained in sub-

Saharan Africa? Yes, delivery of intermittent preventive treatment in pregnancy (IPTp), seasonal malaria chemoprevention (SMC), and intermittent preventive treatment in infants (IPTi) should be maintained provided that best practices for protecting health workers—and other front-line workers—from COVID-19 are followed. Ensuring access to these and other core malaria prevention tools saves lives and is an important strategy for reducing the strain on health systems in the context of the COVID-19 response.

继续在撒哈拉以南非洲实施世卫组织推荐的预防性治疗吗？是的，① 应继续实施怀孕期间间歇性预防治疗、季节性疟疾化学预防和婴儿间歇性预防性治疗，前提是采取最佳做法保护卫生工作者及其他一线工作人员免受 COVID-19 感染。确保获得这些工具和疟疾预防的其他核心工具 ② 挽救了生命，是在应对 COVID-19 背景下减轻卫生系统所承受压力的重要战略。

批 注

① 问题与回答对应。
② 代词理解问题。

世卫组织推荐的预防性治疗是否应继续在撒哈拉以南非洲实施？是的，怀孕期间间歇性预防治疗、季节性疟疾化学预防和婴儿间歇性预防性治疗应继续实施，前提是采取最佳做法保护卫生工作者及其他一线工作人员免受 COVID-19 感染。确保获得这些措施并采用其他关键的疟疾预防工具挽救了生命，是在应对 COVID-19 背景下减轻卫生系统压力的一项重要战略。

1. 对应问题。见本段问题"What about WHO-recommended preventive therapies be maintained in sub-Saharan Africa?"与回答"yes..."。如翻译稿中的回答为"是"，但在问题部分并没有相对应形式的问句，并且以"继续"作为问句开头，显得句子头轻脚重，主次不分明。应当按照审校稿的方式，将"预防性治疗"作为句子主语，并采用"是否"结构，以符合汉语表达习惯。

2. 代词理解问题。见"Ensuring access to these and other core malaria prevention tools saves lives"一句。文中出现的"these"以及相并列的"other core malaria prevention tools"很容易使人误以为"these"也指代工具，但前文并未提到相关工具，而是提到"应继续采取……措施"。因此，不能按照译稿将"these"处理成工具，而应当处理成"措施"，并搭配相应的动词，即"获得这些措施并采用其他关键的疟疾预防工具"。

3. 对于"core"一词，也应当根据语境含义作灵活处理，此处译为"关键"比"核心"更妥当，"核心"的搭配对象一般多为抽象事物如"核心价值"，"关键"则涵盖具体事物。

第 3 段

Mass drug administration (MDA) is a WHO-recommended approach for rapidly reducing malaria mortality and morbidity during epidemics and in complex emergency settings. Through MDA, all individuals in a targeted population are given antimalarial medicines—often at repeated intervals—regardless of whether or not they show symptoms of the disease.

批 注

① 断句问题。

大型服药活动是世卫组织推荐的办法，用于在流行期间和复杂的紧急情况下迅速降低疟疾死亡率和发病率。^①通过大型服药活动，目标人群中的所有个体，无论是否显示出这种疾病症状，都会得到抗疟疾药物——通常要重复服用。

群体性服药是世卫组织推荐的一种在流行期间和复杂紧急情况下迅速降低疟疾死亡率和发病率的办法。通过大型服药活动，可为目标群体中的所有个体，无论是否显示出这种疾病症状，提供抗疟疾药物——通常要重复间隔服用。

1. 断句问题。见"Mass drug administration (MDA) is a WHO-recommended approach for..."一句。这句话字数较多，结构较复杂，按照翻译稿采用切分方式处理能够增加可读性。不过，此句话的落脚点是"方法"，"for"之后引导的"rapidly reducing malaria mortality and morbidity during epidemics and in complex emergency settings"是对这一方法的修饰，限定了该方法的使用范围，因此按照限制修饰关系及其与修饰对象的紧密程度，采用合译法更为恰当，更能突出主次轻重关系。

2. 主体问题。见"Through MDA, all individuals in a targeted population are given antimalarial medicines—often at repeated intervals"一句。这是一个典型的非灵主语句，其语言组织上为被动结构，按照翻译稿的处理方式，将被动句转换成主动句，将"individuals"处理成主语作为一种翻译方法也可接受，此处，审校稿采用的另一种方法也值得借鉴。依照审校稿的思路，群体性服药显然是政府或相关主管机构组织的，也即隐藏的主语是"政府机构"，通过开展这一活动，为"目标群体中的所有个体"提供药品，这样不仅将被动语态转换为主动语态符合汉语表达习惯，而且暗示了句子真正的主体（主语），在理解上也更深刻。

补充练习

1. In recent weeks, the COVID-19 pandemic has tested the resilience of robust health systems around the world. Recognizing the heavy toll that malaria exacts on vulnerable populations in countries with fragile health systems, WHO underlines the critical importance of sustaining efforts to prevent, detect and treat malaria. In all regions, protective measures should be utilized to minimize the risk of COVID-19 transmission between patients, communities and health providers. WHO has developed detailed guidance for health workers in the context of the COVID-19 outbreak

response, as well as operational guidance for safely maintaining essential health services.

最近几周，COVID-19 大流行考验了全世界强大的卫生系统的韧性。世卫组织认识到疟疾给卫生系统脆弱国家的弱势民众带来了沉重负担，强调持续努力预防、发现和治疗疟疾的至关重要性。所有区域都应采取保护措施，以最大限度降低患者、社区和卫生服务提供者之间传播 COVID-19 的风险。世卫组织在应对 COVID-19 疫情暴发背景下制定了详细的卫生工作者指南，并为继续安全地提供基本卫生服务制定了业务指南。

2. WHO strongly encourages countries not to suspend the planning for—or implementation of—vector control activities, including ITN campaigns, while ensuring these services are delivered using best practices to protect health workers and communities from COVID-19 infection. Modifications of planned distribution strategies may be needed to minimize exposure to the coronavirus.

世卫组织大力鼓励各国不要暂停规划或实施病媒控制活动，包括驱虫蚊帐分发运动，同时确保提供这些服务时采用保护卫生工作者和社区免受 COVID-19 感染的最佳作法。可能需要修改已规划的分发战略，以最大限度减少接触冠状病毒。

背景介绍

本篇选自世卫组织总干事提交给第七十三届世界卫生大会的综合报告。与前几篇专业报告相比，综合报告在论述深度上较为有限，但往往涉及多个领域。按照惯例，总干事将按照会议议程，逐项汇编各议程项目下开展的活动，汇总成一份综合报告提交世卫大会审议，以便世卫大会了解目前各个事项的进程。因此，报告一定会提及多份权威性文件，这些文件或者是决议决定，或者是科学报告，或者是概要介绍。因此，翻译时要首先注意查证权威性文件的标题、正文以及脚注，核对正在处理的原文与该权威性文件的内容是否一致，如果不一致，应予以标注；如果一致，还应查询是否有权威译本，如有，应遵循权威译本。从报告的行文风格而言，因其中所引述的权威文件来自不同领域，风格各异，翻译时一方面要注意贴近相关文件的各自特色；另一方面要注意保持总体行文风格的统一，以简洁简练，准确达意为首要标准，做到不仅"达意"，还能"传情"。除此之外，此类文件中多见标题、目录、文件名称，其英文特色是浓缩、确切和简练，在翻译时要体现这种特点，切勿啰唆冗述。

第八篇

Consolidated Report by the Director-General

PILLAR 1: ONE BILLION MORE PEOPLE BENEFITTING FROM UNIVERSAL HEALTH COVERAGE

11. Review of and update on matters considered by the Executive Board

11.2 Follow-up to the high-level meetings of the United Nations General Assembly on health-related issues

• Political declaration of the third high-level meeting of the General Assembly on the prevention and control of non-communicable diseases

At its 146th session, the Executive Board noted the reports in documents EB146/7 and EB146/7 Add.1. In its decision EB146(14) on accelerating action to reduce the harmful use of alcohol, it requested the Director-General (1) to develop an action plan (2022—2030) to effectively implement the global strategy for consideration by the Seventy-fifth World Health Assembly, through the Board at its 150th session, in 2022; (2) to develop a technical report on cross-border marketing and advertising before the 150th session of the Board; (3) to adequately resource the work; and (4) to review the global strategy to reduce the harmful use of alcohol and report to the Board at its 166th session, in 2030, for further action.

Following a request from a Board member that the Secretariat demonstrate how WHO's engagement with private sector entities for the prevention and control of noncommunicable diseases provides a clear benefit to public health, the Secretariat indicated that it would respond when transmitting the reports in documents EB146/7 and EB146/7 Add.1 to the Seventy-third World Health Assembly. That response is contained in a new annex to document EB146/7, Annex 5, which is appended below.

请自行翻译后查看后文的分析点评

分析点评

第 1 段

Consolidated Report by the Director-General

总干事编写的① 综合报告

批 注

① 冗余。

总干事综合报告

此段为文件的标题，英文力求精简，中文相应地也无须冗述。在翻译过程中，应重视原文的目的和行文特色，不能仅以"传意"为唯一目标，否则将导致译文的风格偏离原文。

第 2 段

PILLAR 1: ONE BILLION MORE PEOPLE BENEFITTING FROM UNIVERSAL HEALTH COVERAGE

　　11. Review of and update on matters considered by the Executive Board

　　11.2 Follow-up to the high-level meetings of the United Nations General Assembly on health- related issues

　　· **Political declaration of the third high-level meeting of the General Assembly on the prevention and control of non-communicable diseases**

　　支柱 1：超过①10 亿人受益于全民健康覆盖

　　11. 经执行委员会审议的事项回顾与进展

　　11.2 联合国大会卫生相关问题高级别会议的后续②

　　●《大会第三次预防和控制非传染性疾病问题高层③会议政治宣言》

批 注

① 错误理解"more"一词。

② 指代不明。

③ 该词的英文有固定含义，不能随心自行翻译。

　　支柱 1：全民健康覆盖受益人口新增 10 亿人

　　11. 执行委员会审议的事项回顾与进展

　　11.2 联合国大会卫生相关问题高级别会议的后续行动

　　●《大会第三次预防和控制非传染性疾病问题高级别会议政治宣言》

　　1. 本段为正文的标题。翻译时同样要秉持简略、精练的原则，在确保意思正确的前提下，尽量少用字词。例如"审查和更新经执行委员会审议的事项"一句，其中的"经"一字即可不用。这种精简文字的习惯看似吹毛求疵，但对于译员淬炼流畅明晰的文风是大有裨益的。

　　2. 本段出现多个联合国文件的标题常见词，这些词均有其固定含义。

　　（1）"pillar"译为"支柱"，指某组织的主要部门、某项工作的主要内容或某个目标的主要分项。例如"Pillar Ⅳ"为"第四支柱部门"，"A pillar"为"支柱 A"，"development pillar"为"发展支柱"。

　　（2）"review"译为"审议、审评、审查"，不译为"回顾"。

　　（3）"update"在标题中出现时，通常译为"更新"，在正文中出现时，译为

"最新情况"。

（4）"follow-up"是指后续开展的工作，翻译时应根据其出现的背景，酌情译为"后续机制""后续行动"或"后续程序"，如果翻译时间有限，不足以浏览全文掌握背景，通常可译为"后续行动"。

（5）"high-level"通常译为"高级别"，例如"high-level political forum on sustainable development"为"可持续发展高级别政治论坛"，"High-level Meeting on Scaling Up Nutrition"为"增强营养问题高级别会议"。

（6）"Executive Board"一词在不同机构有不同译法，翻译时必须查明该词出自哪个组织机构。例如在 WHO，该词译为"执行委员会"，而在 IMF 和 World Bank，则译为"执行董事会"，在 UNDP、UNFPA 和 UNESCO 又译为"执行局"。专有名词首先查询其来源和出处，不能望文生义，这是做联合国文件的一项基本原则。

第 3 段

At its 146th session, the Executive Board noted the reports in documents EB146/7 and EB146/7 Add.1. In its decision EB146(14) on accelerating action to reduce the harmful use of alcohol, it requested the Director-General (1) to develop an action plan (2022—2030) to effectively implement the global strategy for consideration by the Seventy-fifth World Health Assembly, through the Board at its 150th session, in 2022; (2) to develop a technical report on cross-border marketing and advertising before the 150th session of the Board; (3) to adequately resource the work; and (4) to review the global strategy to reduce the harmful use of alcohol and report to the Board at its 166th session, in 2030, for further action.

批 注

① 不符合联合国文件的固定译法。
② 问题同上。
③ 涉及数字时，原文用英文的，译文用中文；原文用阿拉伯数字的，译文对应使用阿拉伯数字。

执行委员会在第 146 届会议上注意到第 EB146/7 和 EB146/7 Add.1 号文件所载的报告。执委会在其关于加紧行动以减少酒精有害使用的第 EB146(14) 号决定②中，要求总干事：（1）制订有效实施全球战略的行动计划（2022—2030 年），并通过 2022 年执委会第 150 届会议提交第七十五届世界卫生大会审议；（2）在执委会第 150 届会议之前，编写一份关于跨境营销和广告活动的技术报告；（3）为工作提供充足的资源；（4）审查《减少有害使用酒精全球战略》，并向 2030 年执委会第 166 届会议报告情况，以采取进一步行动。

执行委员会在第 146 届会议上注意到 EB146/7 和 EB146/7 Add.1 号文件所载的报告。执委会在其关于加紧行动减少酒精有害使用的 EB146(14) 号决定中，要求总干事：（1）制订一项旨在有效实施全球战略的行动计划（2022—2030 年），并在执委会 2022 年第 150 届会议上由执委会提交给第七十五届世界卫生大会审议；（2）在执委会第 150 届会议之前，编写一份关于跨境营销和广告活动的技术报告；（3）为工作提供充足的资源；（4）审查《减少有害使用酒精全球战略》，并在 2030 年执委会第 166 届会议上向执委会报告情况，以采取进一步行动。

1. 公开媒体上经常出现"A 号令""B 级指示"，而不是"第 A 号令"或"第 B 级指示"。这是一个约定俗成的惯例，联合国文件的编号也同样遵循。凡以字母开头的文件编号，均不能冠以"第"字。因此"documents EB146/7 and EB146/7 Add.1"应当译为"EB146/7 和 EB146/7 Add.1 号文件"，"decision EB146(14)"应当译为"EB146(14) 号决定"。

2. 见"to develop an action plan (2022—2030) to effectively implement the global strategy"一句。翻译稿将其译为"制订有效实施全球战略的行动计划（2022—2030 年）"，审校稿将其译为"制订一项旨在有效实施全球战略的行动计划（2022—2030 年）"，哪种译法更好呢？首先，两者都是正确的译法，都不影响读者的理解，这是前提。但优秀的译员不应仅局限于"准"，在时间允许的情况下，文件翻译也要追求"好"。在原文中，"to"表示目的，表明制定该行动计划是为了落实全球战略，审校稿用"旨在"一词，清楚地体现了这种目的，逻辑关系更为清晰，更易于读者理解，因而也就略胜翻译稿一筹。

第 4 段

Following a request from a Board member that the Secretariat demonstrate how WHO's engagement with private sector entities for the prevention and control of noncommunicable diseases provides a clear benefit to public health, the Secretariat indicated that it would respond when transmitting the reports in documents EB146/7 and EB146/7 Add.1 to the Seventy-third World Health Assembly. That response is contained in a new annex to document EB146/7, Annex 5, which is appended below.

根据执委会委员①提出的要求，即②秘书处须证明世卫组织与私营部门实体交往促进预防和控制非传染性疾病如何显示明确有益于③公共卫生，秘书处表示，它将在向第七十三届世界卫生大会转递文件 EB146 和 EB146/7 Add.1④所载的报告时做出答复。该答复载于文件 EB146/7 的新附件即附件 5 中，并附于下文。

根据一名执委会委员提出的要求，秘书处须证明世卫组织与私营部门实体在预防和控制非传染性疾病方面的合作如何明确地有益于公共卫生。秘书处表示将在向第七十三届世界卫生大会转递 EB146/7 和 EB146/7 Add.1 号文件所载报告时做出答复。该答复载于 EB146/7 号文件的新附件，也即下文所示附件 5。

批 注

① 单复数不明。容易误解。
② "根据……要求，即……"，不符合中文的逻辑。
③ 名词做动词化处理，是顺应中文表达习惯的较好处理方法，如删除前面的"显示"一词，将更加通顺简洁。
④ 格式不对。参见第 1 段的点评 1。

点评

1. "Following a request from a Board member that..." 一句，that 引导的是同位语从句，其先行词为 request。在处理同位语从句时，我们通常会将"that"一词译为"也即/即"，以体现从句的内容与先行词之间的关系。但在翻译本句时，该方式并不适用，因为在中文的逻辑中，提出要求后就应当去履行，而不是对该要求做出解释。英汉语言的思维方式不同，导致表达方式存在很大差异，英文中成立的逻辑，译为中文就变为缺乏逻辑联系，反之亦成立。这一点值得所有翻译工作者时刻警惕。

2. 注意"transmitting"一词，该词译为"转递"，注意不要译为"提交"。

3. 原文最后一句，which 一词的先行词容易在"response"和"annex"之间混淆，这属于仅依靠语法分析无法辨明的情况，此时应积极寻找上下文，根据背景做出正确判断。翻译稿将该句译为"该答复载于文件 EB146/7 的新附件即附件 5 中，并附于下文"，看似下文所附的是"该答复"，但通过查看该文件全文，发现下文所附的是"Annex 5"，可见在翻译过程中要有全局观，不能孤立地处理词、句和段落。审校稿改译为"也即下文所示附件 5"。

补充练习

PILLAR 3: ONE BILLION MORE PEOPLE ENJOYING BETTER HEALTH AND WELL-BEING

15. Review of and update on matters considered by the Executive Board

15.1 Decade of Healthy Ageing: development of a proposal for a Decade of Healthy Ageing 2020—2030

4. At its 146th session, the Board noted the report in document EB146/23 on the development of a proposal for a Decade of Healthy Ageing 2020—2030. The Board also adopted decision EB146(13). In response to comments made during the discussions, the Secretariat has updated paragraphs 24 and 27 of document EB146/23, which are reproduced in full below.

Activities

24. The activities will:

• take place at the local, national, regional and global levels, with a focus on improving the lives of older people, their families and their communities;

• tackle the current challenges that older people face, while anticipating the future for those who will journey into older age;

• take a life course approach, which recognizes the importance of multisectoral actions that focus on a healthy start to life, in each life stage and also target the needs of people at critical periods throughout their life, but focuses on the second half of life, given the unique issues that arise in older age, and the limited attention this period has received compared with other age groups;

参考译文

支柱 3：健康和福祉得到改善的人口新增 10 亿人

15. 经执行委员会审议的事项回顾与进展

15.1 健康老龄化行动十年：拟定有关 2020—2030 年健康老龄化行动十年的建议

4. 执委会第 146 届会议注意到关于拟定有关 2020—2030 年健康老龄化行动十年的建议的 EB146/23 号文件。执委会还通过了 EB146(13) 号决定。根据讨论期间提出的意见，秘书处更新了文件 EB146/23 第 24 段和第 27 段，全文转载如下。

活动

24. 这些活动将：

● 在地方、国家、区域和全球各级开展，重点是改善老年人、其家庭和社区的生活；

● 应对老年人当前面临的挑战，并预测那些将步入老年的人的未来；

● 采取生命历程办法。该办法认识到多部门行动的重要性，这些行动不仅重视开启每个生命阶段的健康生活，还侧重于人们一生中各个关键时期的需求，但以生命后半程为重点，因为老年阶段会遇到特殊的问题，而且与其他年龄段相比，这一时期受到的关注有限；

背景介绍

以下三篇材料均涉及卫生领域的重要主题之一，即麻醉药品管制，其中第九篇和第十篇选自麻醉药品委员会编写的文件，第十一篇选自国际麻醉药品管制局编写的报告。

麻醉药品委员会是联合国经社理事会下设的一个职司委员会，是联合国麻醉药品管制领域的决策机构；而国际麻醉药品管制局是独立的准司法监督机构，于 1968 年按照《1961 年麻醉品单一公约》设立。前者的主要职能包括：协助联合国经社理事会制定国际管制和禁止麻醉药品滥用和非法贩运的政策和措施；草拟必要的国际公约，并执行有关公约授予的其他职能；后者主要负责确保医疗和科研用途的药品供应充足、确保药物不会从合法来源流入非法渠道、监测各国政府对可能用于非法生产毒品的化学品的管制情况，并协助防止化学品转移到非法途径。

与两大机构的职能相对应，三篇材料在内容主题上分别涉及精神药物药性评估、麻醉品管制以及非法毒品药品贩运管制。此类文本的语言措辞较为平实，但因涉及大量化学品专用术语，应将准确性和严谨性作为首要考虑因素。首先，应从《麻醉品公约》以及麻醉品管制清单、目录中寻找最准确译名，同时还应注意译名的前后沿袭性；其次，还可从各国家药品监管局规范文件、国际化学药品学术刊物中查阅相关译法。对于涉及毒品贩运管制的文件，在确保毒品名准确无误的前提下，还应结合各国国情、地理概况以及管制公约（《联合国禁止非法贩运麻醉药品和精神药物公约》）和各国刑法或专门法中有关走私、贩运、运输、制造毒品罪名的规定。

第九篇

原文

Actual abuse and/or evidence of likelihood to produce abuse

While some preclinical research using self-administration and conditioned place preference models has shown reinforcing effects of pregabalin, taken as a whole, the results from such research are contradictory and inconclusive.

In clinical trials, patients have reported euphoria, although tolerance develops rapidly to this effect. Human laboratory research is very limited and only a relatively low dose of pregabalin has been tested in a general population sample; the results indicated low abuse liability. However, a higher dose of pregabalin administered to users of alcohol or sedative/hypnotic drugs was rated similar to diazepam, indicative of abuse liability.

Pregabalin is more likely to be abused by individuals who are using other psychoactive drugs (especially opioids), with significant potential of adverse effects among these subpopulations. The adverse effects of pregabalin include dizziness, blurred vision, impaired coordination, impaired attention, somnolence, confusion and impaired thinking. Other reported harms associated with non-medical use of pregabalin include suicidal ideation and impaired driving. Users of pregabalin in a number of countries have sought treatment for dependence on the drug. While pregabalin has been cited as the main cause of death in over 30 documented overdose fatalities, there are very few cases of fatal intoxications resulting from pregabalin use alone and the vast majority of instances involve other central nervous system depressants such as opioids and benzodiazepines.

请自行翻译后查看后文的分析点评

分析点评

第1段

Actual abuse and/or evidence of likelihood to produce abuse

While some preclinical research using self-administration and conditioned place preference models has shown reinforcing effects of pregabalin, taken as a whole, the results from such research are contradictory and inconclusive.

实际滥用和/或可能产生滥用的证据

虽然一些使用自身给药和条件性位置偏爱模型的临床前研究显示了普瑞巴林的强化效应①，但从整体来看，这些研究的结果是矛盾和不确定的。

实际滥用和（或）可能产生滥用的证据

虽然一些使用自身给药和条件位置偏爱模型的临床前研究显示了普瑞巴林的强化效果，但从整体来看，这些研究的结果是互相矛盾和没有定论的。

1. "and/or"在中文中多改写为"和（或）"的形式。

2. 注意常见词在专业文本中的译法，比如"administration"常见的意思为"行政、管理"，但在卫生领域，该词指"（药物的）施用"。

3. 在翻译时，需要固定搭配的专业词组保持敏感度，并反复查证，才能确保将专业度较高的文本尽可能准确地翻译出来，比如文中"conditioned place preference"就是一个固定词组，并且已经有通行的标准译法，不能随意地调整语序和选择译法。

4. 近义词的选择。翻译稿中的"效应"多指物理或化学作用所产生的结果，也常用于社会科学方面的规律；而审校稿中的"效果"指由某种力量、因素或行为产生的结果。经过推敲，此处选用"效果"更为适当。

5. "inconclusive"在翻译稿中译为"不确定"，这在一定程度上会引发歧义，是指"结果不确定"，还是"虽然得出了结果，但无法从这些结果中推导出结论"？根据上下文，语义应当理解为后者。

第 2 段

In clinical trials, patients have reported euphoria, although tolerance develops rapidly to this effect. Human laboratory research is very limited and only a relatively low dose of pregabalin has been tested in a general population sample; the results indicated low abuse liability. However, a higher dose of pregabalin administered to users of alcohol or sedative/hypnotic drugs was rated similar to diazepam, indicative of abuse liability.

在临床试验中，患者报告了欣快感，尽管耐受性迅速发展到这种效果②。人体实验室研究非常有限，在一般人群样本中仅测试了相对较低剂量的普瑞巴林；测试结果表明滥用可能性较低。然而，对酒精或镇静/催眠药物使用者施用的更

批 注

① 用词不够准确。

批 注

② 表达不清。

高剂量普瑞巴林被认为类似于地西泮，存在滥用可能。

在临床试验中，患者报告了欣快效果，不过很快就对这种效果产生了耐受性。人体实验室研究非常有限，仅在一般人群样本中测试了相对较低剂量的普瑞巴林；测试结果表明其滥用可能性较低。然而，对酒精或镇静/催眠药物使用者施用的更高剂量普瑞巴林所导致的滥用水平与地西泮类似，因此存在滥用可能。

1. 虽然"euphoria"的标准译法是"欣快感"，但结合后半句的"this effect"，适当调整为"欣快效果"使行文更加流畅。

2. "耐受性迅速发展到这种效果"显然过于直译，读者难以理解译文，应转化成符合中文习惯的表达方式。

第3段

Pregabalin is more likely to be abused by individuals who are using other psychoactive drugs (especially opioids), with significant potential of adverse effects among these subpopulations. The adverse effects of pregabalin include dizziness, blurred vision, impaired coordination, impaired attention, somnolence, confusion and impaired thinking. Other reported harms associated with non-medical use of pregabalin include suicidal ideation and impaired driving. Users of pregabalin in a number of countries have sought treatment for dependence on the drug. While pregabalin has been cited as the main cause of death in over 30 documented overdose fatalities, there are very few cases of fatal intoxications resulting from pregabalin use alone and the vast majority of instances involve other central nervous system depressants such as opioids and benzodiazepines.

批 注

① 是否强调"个人"？
② 修饰内容错误。
③ 搭配不当。

普瑞巴林更有可能被使用其他精神活性药物（尤其是阿片剂）的个体[①]滥用，在这些亚群体中存在发生显著[②]不良反应的可能。普瑞巴林的不良反应包括头晕、视力模糊、协调障碍、注意力受损、嗜睡、意识模糊和思维受损。其他报告的与普瑞巴林非医疗使用有关的危害包括自杀意念和不清醒驾驶。在许多国家，使用普瑞巴林的人已经寻求治疗对药物的依赖。虽然普瑞巴林已被列为30多例记录在案的过量使用普瑞巴林造成死亡的主要死因[③]，但仅使用普瑞巴林造成的致命性中毒案例却很少，绝大多数案例都涉及其他中枢神经系统镇静剂，例如类阿片和苯二氮䓬类药物。

普瑞巴林更有可能被使用其他精神活性药物（尤其是类阿片）的人滥用，并且极有可能在这些亚群体中造成不良效果。普瑞巴林的不良效果包括头晕、视力

模糊、协调障碍、注意力受损、嗜睡、意识错乱和思维受损。其他报告的与普瑞巴林非医疗使用有关的危害包括自杀意念和不清醒驾驶。在许多国家,使用普瑞巴林的人已经寻求治疗对药物的依赖。虽然普瑞巴林已被列为30多例记录在案的因服用过量造成死亡事件的主要原因,但因仅使用普瑞巴林而造成的致命性中毒事件却很少,绝大多数死亡都同时涉及其他中枢神经系统镇静剂,例如类阿片和苯二氮䓬类药物。

1. "opioid"的标准译法为"类阿片",它是一个广义词,更常用于指具有如同吗啡特性但化学结构可能与吗啡不同的天然和合成药物。而翻译稿中"阿片剂"的英文是"opiate"。在专业度较强的文本中,切忌得过且过,造成原文与译文出现语义偏差等实质性错误。下文"benzodiazepine"同理。

2. "individual"就是指"人",在英文中经常出现,在没有特别指向"个体"时,译为"人"更加通顺。

3. "significant"修饰的是"potential"而不是"adverse effects",翻译稿中出现了马虎导致的错误。

4. 仔细查看后我们会发现,翻译稿中,"记录在案的"这一修饰语并没有恰当的中心词。因此,审校稿中,根据语义补充出了"事件"这一中心词,使句子的结构更加完整,组成"记录在案的(……死亡)事件"。在修饰成分比较复杂的情况下,要注意句子结构是否完整,避免出现翻译稿中的这种情况。

1. *Actual abuse and/or evidence of likelihood of abuse*

Consistent with its opioid mechanism of action, human brain imaging has shown that tramadol activates brain reward pathways associated with abuse. While reports from people who have been administered tramadol in controlled settings have shown that it is identified as opioid-like, and tramadol has reinforcing effects in experienced opioid users, these effects may be weaker than those produced by opioids such as morphine and may be partially offset by the unpleasant effects of tramadol such as sweating, tremors, agitation, anxiety and insomnia.

参考译文

实际滥用和(或)滥用可能性证据

与其类阿片药物作用机制一致,人脑成像显示,曲马多会激活与滥用有关的大脑奖赏通路。虽然在受控环境中使用曲马多的人报告曲马多被识别为类阿片样药物,但在曾使用过类阿片药物的人中,曲马多具有增强效果,这些效果可能比吗啡等类阿片药物产生的效果弱,而且可能被曲马多产生的出汗、震颤、焦虑不安、焦虑和失眠等不愉快效果部分抵消。

2. Abuse, dependence and overdose from tramadol have emerged as serious public health concerns in countries across several regions. Epidemiological studies in the past have reported a lower tendency for tramadol misuse when compared with other opioids, but more recent information indicates a growing number of people abusing tramadol, particularly in a number of Middle Eastern and African countries. The sources of tramadol include diverted medicines as well as falsified medicines containing high doses of tramadol. Seizures of illicitly trafficked tramadol, particularly in African countries, have risen dramatically in recent years.

在若干区域的各个国家内，滥用、依赖和过量使用曲马多已成为严重的公共健康问题。过去的流行病学研究表明，与其他类阿片药物相比，曲马多不当使用趋势较弱，但最近的更多信息表明，滥用曲马多的人越来越多，特别是在中东和非洲某些国家。曲马多的来源包括移作他用的药物以及含有高剂量曲马多的伪造药品。近年来，非法贩运的曲马多的缉获量急剧增加，特别是在非洲国家。

3. The oral route of administration has been the predominant mode of tramadol abuse as it results in a greater opioid effect compared with other routes. It is unlikely that tramadol will be injected to any significant extent. Abuse of tramadol is likely to be influenced by genetic factors; some people will experience a much stronger opioid effect following tramadol administration compared with others. The genotype associated with a stronger opioid effect following tramadol administration occurs at different rates in populations across different parts of the world.

口服给药途径一直是滥用曲马多的主要方式，因为与其他途径相比，它会产生更强的类阿片药物效果。曲马多不太可能进行大量注射。曲马多滥用可能受遗传因素的影响；在施用曲马多后，有些人会比其他人出现更强的类阿片药物效果。与施用曲马多后出现较强的类阿片药物效果有关的基因型，在世界各地不同人群中的发生概率并不相同。

Furthermore, in accordance with article 3 of the 1961 Convention, the Commission will have before it for consideration a recommendation by WHO to add to Schedule Ⅲ of that Convention preparations containing *delta*-9-tetrahydrocannabinol (dronabinol), produced either by chemical synthesis or as preparations of cannabis that are compounded as pharmaceutical preparations with one or more other ingredients and in such a way that *delta*-9-tetrahydrocannabinol (dronabinol) cannot be recovered by readily available means or in a yield that would constitute a risk to public health.

Whether or not it wishes to add THC (isomers of *delta*-9-tetrahydrocannabinol) to Schedule Ⅰ of the 1961 Convention, subject to the Commission's adoption of the recommendation to add dronabinol and its stereoisomers to Schedule Ⅰ of the 1961 Convention and whether or not it wishes to delete THC (isomers of *delta*-9-tetrahydrocannabinol) from Schedule Ⅰ of the 1971 Convention, subject to the adoption of the recommendation to add THC (isomers of *delta*-9-tetrahydrocannabinol) to Schedule Ⅰ of the 1961 Convention.

请自行翻译后查看后文的分析点评

分析点评

第1段

Furthermore, in accordance with Article 3 of the 1961 Convention, the Commission will have before it for consideration a recommendation by WHO to add to Schedule Ⅲ of that Convention preparations containing *delta*-9-tetrahydrocannabinol (dronabinol), produced either by chemical synthesis or as preparations of cannabis that are compounded as pharmaceutical preparations with one or more other ingredients and in such a way that *delta*-9-tetrahydrocannabinol (dronabinol) cannot be recovered by readily available means or in a yield that would constitute a risk to public health.

另外，根据《1961年公约》第三条，委员会将收到并审议世卫组织提出的如下建议：① 含有 δ-9-四氢大麻酚（屈大麻酚）的制剂，即通过化学合成的制剂，或者作为大麻制剂，作为与其他一种或多种成分混合形成的药物制剂，其制备方式② 使 δ-9-四氢大麻酚（屈大麻酚）无法通过既有方式回收，或产量会对公众健康构成威胁的制剂，应加入《1961年公约》附表三。

另外，根据《1961年公约》第三条，麻委会将收到并审议世卫组织提出的如下建议：含有 δ-9-四氢大麻酚（屈大麻酚）的制剂，即化学合成的制剂，或者作为药物制剂与另外一种或多种成分混合而成的大麻制剂，其制备方式使

批 注

① 这是常见的处理方式。
② 注意切割句式结构，理解有误。

δ-9-四氢大麻酚（屈大麻酚）无法通过既有手段还原，或还原产量会对公众健康构成威胁的，应加入《1961 年公约》附表三。

本段只有一句话，需要切割句式结构。此处先是提出一项建议，然后具体展开建议的内容，"the Commission will have before it for consideration a recommendation by WHO"，其中的 "...have before it for consideration a recommendation by..." 在联合国文件中常见，通常可处理为"……将收到并审议世卫组织提出的如下建议：……"。当然，如果建议的内容短小，也可考虑直接处理为一句话即可。

第 2 段

Whether or not it wishes to add THC (isomers of *delta*-9-tetrahydrocannabinol) to Schedule Ⅰ of the 1961 Convention, subject to the Commission's adoption of the recommendation to add dronabinol and its stereoisomers to Schedule I of the 1961 Convention and whether or not it wishes to delete THC (isomers of *delta*-9-tetrahydrocannabinol) from Schedule Ⅰ of the 1971 Convention, subject to the adoption of the recommendation to add THC (isomers of *delta*-9-tetrahydrocannabinol) to Schedule Ⅰ of the 1961 Convention.

是否希望将四氢大麻酚（δ-9-四氢大麻酚的异构体）加入《1961 年公约》附表一，但须经① 委员会通过将屈大麻酚及其立体异构体加入《1961 年公约》附表一的建议，以及是否希望将四氢大麻酚（δ-9-四氢大麻酚的异构体）自《1971 年公约》附表一中删去，但须经委员会通过将四氢大麻酚（δ-9-四氢大麻酚的异构体）加入《1961 年公约》附表一的建议。

① 注意结构处理。

在麻委会通过将屈大麻酚及其立体异构体加入《1961 年公约》附表一的建议的前提下，是否要将四氢大麻酚（δ-9-四氢大麻酚的异构体）加入《1961 年公约》附表一，以及在麻委会通过将四氢大麻酚（δ-9-四氢大麻酚的异构体）加入《1961 年公约》附表一建议的前提下，是否要将四氢大麻酚（δ-9-四氢大麻酚的异构体）自《1971 年公约》附表一中删去。

1. "subject to" 在英文句式结构中经常出现，有"使服从；使遭受；受……管制；以……为条件"等含义，这类句式有时候后面跟着的内容很长，处理的时候注意切割拆分。

2. 此段翻译稿大意理解尚可，但读起来拗口，句子有点头轻脚重，重心偏离，也不符合中文的表达习惯。可将 "subject to" 引申为"在……的前提下"，这样处理后，结构重心提前，让读者一眼可以看得明白。

补充练习

1. There is no evidence that any of these listed isomers are being abused or are likely to be abused so as to constitute a public health or social problem. However, the Committee noted the potential difficulty of differentiating these six isomers (listed in Schedule Ⅰ of the 1971 Convention) from Δ_9-THC (listed in Schedule Ⅱ of the 1971 Convention) using standard methods of chemical analysis, due to their chemical similarities. The Committee further noted that this is an important factor to consider in the scheduling of these isomers.

没有证据表明这些所列的任何异构体正在或可能被滥用,从而构成公共卫生问题或社会问题。然而,专家委员会指出,(列于《1971年公约》附表一的)这六种异构体与(列于《1971年公约》附表二的)δ-9-四氢大麻酚由于其化学相似性,可能难以使用标准化学分析方法区分开来。专家委员会进一步指出,这是将这些异构体列管时要考虑的一项重要因素。

2. The Committee recommended that tetrahydrocannabinol (understood to refer to the six isomers currently listed in Schedule Ⅰ of the 1971 Convention) be deleted from the 1971 Convention, subject to the Commission's adoption of the recommendation to add tetrahydrocannabinol to Schedule Ⅰ of the 1961 Convention.

专家委员会建议将四氢大麻酚(理解为指目前列于《1971年公约》附表一的六种异构体)从《1971年公约》中删去,但须麻委会通过关于将四氢大麻酚列入《1961年公约》附表一的建议。

原文

There has been an increase in the production of cannabis resin in Afghanistan. The country was identified as the source of seized cannabis resin in 19 per cent of countries that reported the sources of seized cannabis resin in the period 2012—2016, in particular countries in Central Asia, the Southern Caucasus and Europe. In 2017, Afghanistan also continued to see increases in methamphetamine seizures, in addition to detecting new clandestine laboratories manufacturing that substance on its territory.

On 8 March 2018, the Security Council adopted resolution 2405 (2018), extending the mandate of UNAMA until 17 March 2019. In the same resolution, the Council expressed its deep concern about the significant increase in the illicit cultivation and production of and trade and trafficking in drugs in Afghanistan, which significantly contributed to the financial resources of the Taliban and its associates and could also benefit Al-Qaida and ISIL and its affiliates, and encouraged the Government of Afghanistan, supported by the international community and regional partners, to intensify its efforts to address drug production and trafficking with a balanced and integrated approach, in accordance with the principle of common and shared responsibility.

The main trafficking route for opiates originating in Afghanistan remains the Balkan route, accounting for 37 per cent of global heroin seizures in 2016, which runs through the Islamic Republic of Iran, Turkey and the Balkan countries to destination markets in Western and Central Europe. Authorities in Turkey believe that significant increases in heroin seizures, coupled with an increase in acetic anhydride seizures on its territory, may indicate that increased amounts of heroin could have been entering European drug markets in the period 2017—2018.

请自行翻译后查看后文的分析点评

分析点评

第 1 段

There has been an increase in the production of cannabis resin in Afghanistan. The country was identified as the source of seized cannabis resin in 19 per cent of countries that reported the sources of seized cannabis resin in the period 2012—2016, in particular countries in Central Asia, the Southern Caucasus and Europe. In 2017, Afghanistan also continued to see increases in methamphetamine seizures, in addition to detecting new clandestine laboratories manufacturing that substance on its territory.

阿富汗的大麻脂产量有所增加。2012 至 2016 年期间，多个国家报告了被缴获① 大麻脂的来源地，特别是中亚、高加索和欧洲的国家，其中 19% 的国家认定阿富汗是被缴获的大麻脂的来源地。2017 年，阿富汗除侦破境内制造甲基苯丙胺的新秘密窝点② 外，缴获该种物质的数量也持续增加。

批 注
① 尽量少用被动。
② 特定译法。

阿汗的大麻脂产量有所增加。2012 至 2016 年期间，多个国家报告了缉获的大麻脂的来源地，特别是中亚、南高加索和欧洲的国家，其中 19% 的国家认定

阿富汗是缉获的大麻脂的来源地。2017年，阿富汗除侦破境内制造甲基苯丙胺的新秘密制药厂外，该物质的缉获量也持续增加。

1. 英语和汉语区别明显，在句式结构上，英文用被动句、被动词的频率很高，而中文则相对用得少，在翻译时应尽量少用被动结构和表达方式。这里翻译稿将"seized"一词处理为"被缴获"，但此处的原文指的是一种主动行为，无须使用被动表达。另外，"seize"一词在相关文件中通常译为"缉获"。

2. 特词特译。联合国文件常常对一些词有自己独特的译法，翻译的时候在不影响句意通顺表达的情况下应严格按照其特有要求翻译。比如"laboratory"一词，这个词的译法几经变化，最开始处理为"窝点"，后来改为"制备点"，新近改为"制药厂"，而不是我们常见的"实验室"。

第 2 段

On 8 March 2018, the Security Council adopted Resolution 2405 (2018), extending the mandate of UNAMA until 17 March 2019. In the same resolution, the Council expressed its deep concern about the significant increase in the illicit cultivation and production of and trade and trafficking in drugs in Afghanistan, which significantly contributed to the financial resources of the Taliban and its associates and could also benefit Al-Qaida and ISIL and its affiliates, and encouraged the Government of Afghanistan, supported by the international community and regional partners, to intensify its efforts to address drug production and trafficking with a balanced and integrated approach, in accordance with the principle of common and shared responsibility.

安全理事会于2018年3月8日通过了<u>第 2405 (2018) 号决议</u>①，将联合国阿富汗援助团（联阿援助团）的任务期限延至2019年3月17日。在这项决议中，对于阿富汗非法药品的种植、生产、贸易和贩运大幅增加，使塔利班及其附庸的财政资源大幅增加，而且可能使基地组织和伊拉克和黎凡特伊斯兰国（伊黎伊斯兰国）（达伊沙）附庸受益的局面，<u>安理会表示深为关切</u>②并鼓励阿富汗政府在国际社会和区域伙伴的支持下，根据共同和分担的责任原则，加紧努力，以均衡和综合方式取缔毒品生产和贩运活动。

批 注

① 未引用决议用语。
② 句子头重脚轻。

安全理事会于2018年3月8日通过了第2405（2018）号决议，将联合国阿富汗援助团（联阿援助团）的任务期限延至2019年3月17日。在这项决议中，安理会表示深为关切阿富汗非法药品的种植、生产、贸易和贩运大幅增加，使塔利班及其附庸者的财政资源大幅增加，而且可能使基地组织和伊拉克和黎凡特伊斯兰国（伊黎伊斯兰国）（达伊沙）及其附庸者受益，安理会还鼓励阿富汗政府在国际社会和区域伙伴的支持下，根据共同和分担的责任原则，在解决阿富汗的

毒品问题方面加紧努力，以均衡和综合方式取缔毒品生产和贩运活动。

1. 联合国文件中经常会引用决议、决定、公约等的内容，有的是直接引用，有的是间接引用。对于加引号的引用或者未加引号但内容完全一样的引用，应查找相关内容的定本。对于未加引号且内容不完全一致的引用，原则上有参考的必须参考，无参考的情况下可自行翻译。此处引用的决议内容糅合了原决议的几部分内容，但大体一致，故应该采用原决议用语。

2. "drug"一词的用法。"drug"可以翻译为"药品、毒品、药物"等，在《毒品问题报告》中，在大多数情况下使用"毒品"都没问题。而在联合国麻醉品管制局文件中，指向特别明确时要考虑使用"药物"。

3. "trafficking""associate"和"principle of common and shared responsibility"这些词也要重视，不确定时需要查阅相关词汇，特别是"principle of common and shared responsibility"一定要按照术语表翻译。

第 3 段

The main trafficking route for opiates originating in Afghanistan remains the Balkan route, accounting for 37 per cent of global heroin seizures in 2016, which runs through the Islamic Republic of Iran, Turkey and the Balkan countries to destination markets in Western and Central Europe. Authorities in Turkey believe that significant increases in heroin seizures, coupled with an increase in acetic anhydride seizures on its territory, may indicate that increased amounts of heroin could have been entering European drug markets in the period 2017—2018.

批　注

① 词义变化。
② 不准确。

巴尔干路线仍然是原产于阿富汗的鸦片剂①的主要贩运路线。2016年，在这条路线缴获的海洛因数量占全世界海洛因缴获量的37%。这条路线途经伊朗伊斯兰共和国、土耳其和巴尔干国家，到达西欧和中欧的目的地市场。土耳其当局②认为，海洛因缴获量显著增加，加上本国境内醋酸酐缴获量的增加，可能表明，在2017—2018年，可能有更多的海洛因进入欧洲毒品市场。

巴尔干路线仍然是原产于阿富汗的阿片剂的主要贩运路线。2016年，在这条路线缉获的海洛因数量占全世界海洛因缉获量的37%。这条路线途经伊朗伊斯兰共和国、土耳其和巴尔干国家，到达西欧和中欧的目的地市场。土耳其主管部门认为，海洛因缉获量显著增加，加上本国境内醋酸酐缉获量增加，可能表明，在2017—2018年，可能有更多的海洛因进入欧洲毒品市场。

1. 词义变化。词的翻译常常会发生演变，翻译的时候通常要尽量采用最新的权威译法。比如"opium"一词指的是阿片（学名）；鸦片（引用《1961年公约》时使用）。在缉毒方面有时会有"鸦片糊""鸦片膏"等说法。"opioid"可译为"阿片类药物"或者"类阿片药物"，前者是指吗啡、海洛因等使用植物萃取制成的药物，后者是指药效类似的各种化学合成类药物。还有就是"khat"指的是恰特草（《精神药品品种目录》（2013年版），中国国家食品药品监督管理总局、公安部、国家卫生和计划生育委员会于2013年11月11日发布）。"opiates""opioids"指的是类阿片剂、类阿片药物。在本文中，"opiates"在文件中出现，采用"阿片剂"的用法。

2. 关于"authority"或"authorities"一般的译法有"机关、部门、人员、当局"等，我们经常见到的"national authority (authorities)、competent authority (authorities)、competent authority (authorities)"，通常对应的译法有"主管机关、主管部门、主管人员（指人的时候）"，而不会用"当局"。

3. "acetic anhydride"可译为"乙酸酐"（中文正式化学名称）或"醋酸酐"（《1988年公约》中的译法），此处沿用该公约中的译法。

1. The so-called "Balkan route", which passes through the Islamic Republic of Iran, Turkey and the Balkan countries towards destination markets in Western and Central Europe, remains the main path for trafficking in opiates originating in Afghanistan. Countries along the Balkan route account for about 37 per cent of global heroin seizures. At the same time, in 2017, Afghan opiates continued to be trafficked via a sub-branch of the Balkan route passing from the Islamic Republic of Iran to the countries of the Southern Caucasus and then onward to Ukraine via the Black Sea into Eastern Europe.

参考译文

所谓的"巴尔干路线"经由伊朗伊斯兰共和国、土耳其和巴尔干国家输往西欧和中欧的目的地市场，它仍然是贩运原产于阿富汗的阿片剂的主要路径。巴尔干路线沿线国家的海洛因缉获量约占全世界海洛因缉获量的37%。与此同时，2017年，阿富汗的阿片剂继续经巴尔干路线的一条支线，途经伊朗伊斯兰共和国被贩运到南高加索国家，然后继续取道黑海被贩运到乌克兰，进而被贩运到东欧。

2. Instability and armed conflicts across the Middle East continued to facilitate trafficking in narcotic drugs and psychotropic substances in the subregion. Counterfeit "captagon" has become a drug of choice in war zones in the Middle East and potentially serves as a source of income for terrorist and insurgency groups. Lebanon continues to

be a source of cannabis resin seized globally, and its production continued to increase. There are indications that Iraq is also gaining importance for illicit drug cultivation and production, including heroin manufacture and opium poppy and cannabis plant cultivation. In addition, drug trafficking and abuse in the Basra region of Iraq, which borders Iran (Islamic Republic of) and Kuwait, has seen substantial increases in recent years. Many countries in the Middle East also continued to observe trafficking and abuse of the prescription drug tramadol, a synthetic opioid not under international control, and there are indications that terrorist groups may also be involved in its trafficking in that subregion.

中东的动荡局势和武装冲突继续助长了该次区域麻醉药品和精神药物的贩运活动。假"芬乃他林"已经成为中东交战地区的一种选择药物，有可能被恐怖主义集团和叛乱团体作为一项收入来源。黎巴嫩依然是全球缴获的大麻脂的来源地，其产量继续增加。种种迹象表明，因非法药物种植和生产，包括制造海洛因以及种植罂粟和大麻植物，伊拉克也变得重要起来。此外，在与伊朗伊斯兰共和国和科威特接壤的伊拉克巴士拉地区，贩运毒品和滥用药物的现象近年来大幅增多。许多中东国家还继续注意到贩运和滥用处方药曲马多的现象，这是一种不受国际管制的合成类阿片，还有迹象表明恐怖主义团体也可能参与该次区域贩运曲马多的活动。

背景介绍

本篇选自联合国大会第七十四届会议有关卫生与健康领域的正式文件。卫生健康是大会每年常设议程项目，其内容不仅涉及医疗、药品等狭义的健康卫生领域专题，还涉及环境卫生、个人清洁等与人类生存有关的更为宽泛的主题。此外，联合国大会作为探讨人权问题的最高级别国际论坛，承担着特殊使命，在讨论健康、卫生领域的问题时，也会广泛触及各类群体在卫生健康领域的相关权利，如儿童的身心健康权（如材料节选部分涉及的根除脊髓灰质炎活动、麻疹疫苗接种、儿童色情制品管制）、妇女健康权利（如针对艾滋病毒抗体呈阳性孕妇的抗逆转录病毒疗法、产科瘘、贫血症）以及残疾人和残疾儿童享有的各项权利问题。因此，在翻译此类文件时，除应具备卫生科学领域的通识外，还应掌握卫生健康与人权、人道以及可持续发展之间的叙事关系，在组织语言时有意地使用"人权"滤镜，可酌情参考《2030年可持续发展议程》《儿童权利公约》和《消除对妇女一切形式歧视公约》中的相关表述。

Eradication of polio remains a global priority. In 2016, the smallest number of children in history were paralysed by the disease, with 37 cases occurring in small geographical areas of Afghanistan, Nigeria and Pakistan. In 2016, over 17 000 community-based vaccinators were deployed to the highest-risk areas in Pakistan, resulting in the highest immunization coverage figures in those areas in the country's history, with the proportion of children missed in national campaigns falling from 25 per cent in 2014 to 5 per cent by the end of 2016. In response to the first detection of polio in two years in Nigeria, UNICEF, WHO and partners supported the Government of Nigeria in large-scale emergency immunization activities across the Lake Chad region, immunizing 116 million children, with special emphasis on children in high-risk areas.

Ending open defecation, which was still practised by 1 billion people in 2016, and achieving universal access to basic sanitation by 2030 will require a substantial acceleration in progress, particularly in rural areas, where 9 out of 10 people who practise open defecation live. This is largely centred in Central and Southern Asia, Eastern and Southeast Asia and sub-Saharan Africa. In 2016, it was estimated that girls and women collectively spend 97 billion hours annually securing a safe place to defecate. Fetching water is another challenge, especially for children and women, who globally spend a cumulative 73 billion hours fetching water annually. While hygiene behaviours have improved, the proportion of people with hand-washing facilities consisting of soap and water at home needs to be increased.

As reported in 2015, the under-five mortality rate and the absolute number of under-five deaths per year have fallen by more than half since 1990. This means that an average of 19 000 young lives have been saved every day. The average annual rate of reduction in under-five mortality more than doubled, from 1.8 per cent in 1990 to 3.9 per cent in 2016. This has saved the lives of 122 million children below age 5 since 1990. The maternal mortality ratio declined less rapidly, but still substantially, decreasing from 385 deaths per 100 000 live births in 1990 to 216 in 2016.

请自行翻译后查看后文的分析点评

分析点评

第 1 段

Eradication of polio remains a global priority. In 2016, the smallest number of children in history were paralysed by the disease, with 37 cases occurring in small geographical areas of Afghanistan, Nigeria and Pakistan. In 2016, over 17 000 community-based vaccinators were deployed to the highest-risk areas in Pakistan, resulting in the highest immunization coverage figures in those areas in the country's history, with the proportion of children missed in national campaigns falling from 25 per cent in 2014 to 5 per cent by the end of 2016. In response to the first detection of polio in two years in Nigeria, UNICEF, WHO and partners supported the Government of Nigeria in large-scale emergency immunization activities across the Lake Chad region, immunizing 116 million children, with special emphasis on children in high-risk areas.

批注
① 因理解不准确导致的错译。
② 错译。

根除脊髓灰质炎仍是一个全球优先事项。2016 年，患有麻痹的儿童人数^①跌至历史最低，阿富汗、尼日利亚和巴基斯坦三国小片地区出现 37 例病例。2016 年，在巴基斯坦的脊髓灰质炎高发集中区安排了 17 000 多名疫苗接种员，使该国这些地区的免疫覆盖率达到历史最高水平，在全国性运动中流产的儿童比例从 2014 年的 25% 降至年末的 5%^②。为应对两年前在尼日利亚发现的第一例脊髓灰质炎病例，儿基会、世卫组织和各伙伴支持尼日利亚政府在乍得湖区域开展了大规模的应急免疫接种活动，为 1.16 亿名儿童，特别是高危区的儿童接种了疫苗。

根除脊髓灰质炎仍是一个全球优先事项。2016 年，因脊髓灰质炎而瘫痪的儿童人数跌至历史最低，在阿富汗、尼日利亚和巴基斯坦三国很小的地区出现了 37 例病例。2016 年，在巴基斯坦的脊髓灰质炎高发集中区雇用了 17 000 多名疫苗接种员，使该国这些地区的免疫覆盖率达到历史最高水平，错过全国疫苗接种运动的儿童比例从 2014 年的 25% 降至 2016 年年底的 5%。为应对两年内在尼日利亚首次发现脊髓灰质炎病例，儿基会、世卫组织和各伙伴支持尼日利亚政府在乍得湖区域开展了大规模的应急免疫接种活动，为 1.16 亿名儿童，特别是高危区的儿童接种了疫苗。

1. 因理解不准确导致的错译，见"children in history were paralysed by the disease"和"proportion of children missed in..."两处表达。翻译稿分别将这两处处理成"患有麻痹的儿童人数"和"在全国性运动中流产的儿童"，显然这是对一些卫生术语理解不全面、用法不熟悉造成的。对于第一处，翻译稿想当然地认为"paralysed"是"polio"的同义表述，实际上这里隐含了一种逻辑关系，即"paralysed"是"polio"的结果而不是其本身，即"因病致瘫"。要注意避免因对词汇隐含逻辑关系理解不透彻所产生的错译。

2. 第二处错译是由对语境分析不透彻所致。诚然，"missed in"有丢失、失去含义，并且可引申为"流产"，但是在本段语境中，没有其他相关词语可与之对应，唯独有一个"national campaigns"一词，如果我们结合后一句的"in large-scale emergency immunization activities"，便可得知此处的"national campaigns"指的就是这种大规模接种活动，再将"missed in"与该语境进行结合，便不难得出"错过运动"这层含义。在处理一些含义较为宽泛的词汇时，要对语境做全面、细致的分析，一是找到准确的同义表述，二是找到呼应词、对应词。

3. 常见词汇的特殊用法问题。见"deployed to the highest-risk areas in Pakistan"一句中"deployed"一词。"deploy"其本身有"部署、安排、安置"含义，指一种从上到下的总体安置、资源配置，但在卫生健康领域，尤其是涉及人力、物资的调配问题时，就需要做灵活处理。在本段中，"deployed"的对象专指医护人员，并且是为此次"national campaign"临时调配的，那么应当将这层细微含义表达出来，即当译为"雇佣"。在类似的卫生领域，"deploy"还可酌情译为"响应"等其他含义，如"When the Ebola outbreak was confirmed in late March 2014, Rob was part of the first clinical response team to deploy to Guinea"一句的适当译法为"2014年3月埃博拉疫情得到确认时，Rob加入首个临床响应团队前往几内亚"。

第2段

Ending open defecation, which was still practised by 1 billion people in 2016, and achieving universal access to basic sanitation by 2030 will require a substantial acceleration in progress, particularly in rural areas, where 9 out of 10 people who practise open defecation live. This is largely centred in Central and Southern Asia, Eastern and Southeast Asia and sub-Saharan Africa. In 2016, it was estimated that girls and women collectively spend 97 billion hours annually securing a safe place to defecate. Fetching water is another challenge, especially for children and women, who globally spend a cumulative 73 billion hours fetching water annually. While hygiene behaviours have improved, the proportion of people with hand-washing facilities consisting of soap and water at home needs to be increased.

2016年，仍有10亿人随地便溺，实现到2030年普遍获得基本环境卫生的目标仍需要大幅加快这方面的进展，特别是在农村地区，因为90%的随地便溺者生活在农村。这部分人口主要集中在中亚和南亚、东亚和东南亚和撒哈拉以南的非洲。2016年，据估计，女童和妇女每年为确保找到安全便溺地点共要付出970亿小时。取水是另一个挑战，特别是对儿童和妇女而言，每年，全球各地

批 注

① 漏译。

的儿童和妇女在取水上要累计付出 730 亿小时。尽管个人卫生习惯有所提高，但一定比例的人口仅使用肥皂和清水这些洗手设施的事实仍是一个挑战。

2016 年，仍有 10 亿人随地便溺。结束随地便溺，到 2030 年实现普遍用上基本卫生设施，仍需要大幅加快这方面的进展，特别是在农村地区，因为农村 90% 的人随地便溺。这部分人口主要集中在中亚和南亚、东亚和东南亚及撒哈拉以南的非洲。2016 年，据估计，女童和妇女每年为找到安全便溺地点共要付出 970 亿小时。取水是另一个挑战，特别是对儿童和妇女而言，每年，全球各地的儿童和妇女在取水上要累计付出 730 亿小时。尽管个人卫生行为有所改进，但拥有肥皂和清水之类洗手设施的人所占比例仍需要扩大。

漏译问题。见"Ending open defecation...and achieving universal access to basic sanitation"一句。首先翻译稿值得肯定的一点是，对原文语序做了重新调整，按照先事实再陈述的逻辑顺序先译"which"引导的定语从句再译主句，这种译法值得借鉴。然而，译者在翻译过程中遗漏了重要信息"Ending open defecation"，虽然"实现到 2030 年普遍获得基本环境卫生的目标"包含"结束随地便溺"这层含义，但既然原文中单独提出了，就不能省略此处含义。

第 3 段

As reported in 2015, the under-five mortality rate and the absolute number of under-five deaths per year have fallen by more than half since 1990. This means that an average of 19 000 young lives have been saved every day. The average annual rate of reduction in under-five mortality more than doubled, from 1.8 per cent in 1990 to 3.9 per cent in 2016. This has saved the lives of 122 million children below age 5 since 1990. The maternal mortality ratio declined less rapidly, but still substantially, decreasing from 385 deaths per 100 000 live births in 1990 to 216 in 2016.

正如 2015 年报告所称，自 1990 年以来，5 岁以下儿童死亡率和每年死亡的 5 岁以下儿童绝对数已下降一半以上。这意味着每天平均有 19 000 个小生命得到拯救。1990 年，5 岁以下儿童死亡率年均下降率为 1.8%，此后这一速率增加了一倍，[1] 到 2016 年达到 3.9%。自 1990 年以来，这方面的加速拯救了 1.22 亿名 5 岁以下儿童的生命。孕产妇死亡率的下降速度略慢，但仍有大幅下降，从 1990 年每 100 000 例活产死亡 385 人下降至 2015 年每 100 000 例活产死亡 216 人。

正如 2015 年报告所称，自 1990 年以来，5 岁以下儿童死亡率和 5 岁以下儿童每年死亡的绝对数已下降一半以上。这意味着每天平均有 19 000 个小生命得到拯救。5 岁以下儿童死亡率年均下降速度加快了一倍多，从 1990 年的 1.8%

① 表达不具体。

增加到 2016 年的 3.9%。自 1990 年以来，死亡率下降拯救了 1.22 亿名 5 岁以下儿童的生命。孕产妇死亡率的下降速度较慢，但仍有大幅下降，从 1990 年每 100 000 例活产死亡 385 人下降至 2016 年每 100 000 例活产死亡 216 人。

1. 表达不具体。见"The average annual rate of reduction in under-five mortality more than..."一句。翻译稿将这句处理成"1990 年，5 岁以下儿童死亡率年均下降率为 1.8%，此后这一速率增加了一倍"，这种表述过于贴近原文字面含义，脱离了汉语中关于"速度"的常规表达，特别是"速率增加一倍"机械地贴合原文，应当将其理解成"下降速度"；另外的问题是，在卫生类稿件中常常出现的关于速度、数字的描述上，一般要先言明结论，再列举数字，即先言明下降程度，再说明具体下降数值，从这一角度来看，也应当按照审校稿的方式，对"下降率为 1.8%"与"这一速率增加了……"的前后顺序做出调整。

2. 指示代词还原问题。见"This has saved the lives of 122 million children below age 5"一句。此处要强调的一点是，在出现"this""that"等指示代词的情况下，如果有明确的对应指代，应当将其还原。译文中"这方面的加速"实际上就是"死亡率"，如不加以还原，则导致前后含义不连贯，甚至会产生歧义。

1. A child's chance to survive and thrive was much greater in 2016 than it was when the global community adopted the Millennium Development Goals in 2000. There continues to be clear evidence of significant progress made in child survival, nutrition and primary school enrolment and in reduction of mother-to-child transmission of HIV, among other areas. The absolute number of children dying before their fifth birthday has fallen by more than half, from 12.7 million in 1990 to about 5.9 million in 2015.

参 考 译 文

与 2000 年全球社会通过千年发展目标时比，2016 年儿童的生存和成长机会已大大增加。有明确的证据表明，在儿童生存、营养、小学入学以及减少幼儿经母体感染艾滋病等领域取得了重大进展。5 岁前死亡的儿童绝对数下降了一半以上，从 1990 年的 1 270 万人降至 2015 年的 590 万人左右。

2. In Ethiopia, young people, in collaboration with religious and community leaders, have actively participated in large-scale community dialogue and social mobilization efforts, resulting in 20 districts publicly declaring the abandonment of female genital mutilation/cutting. In Madagascar, 550 young volunteers and peer educators were trained in the use of the communication for humanitarian action toolkit and engaged approximately 22 500 people in villages affected by floods on issues

of sanitation and hygiene, nutrition and health through group theatre, quizzes and community radio.

参考译文

在埃塞俄比亚,年轻人与宗教领袖和社区领袖合作,积极参与了大规模的社区对话和社会动员工作,促使20个地区公开宣布放弃切割女性生殖器的做法。在马达加斯加,550名年轻志愿者和同伴教育者接受了使用人道主义行动通信工具包的培训,还通过小组演出、知识竞赛和社区广播吸引了大约22 500名受洪水影响的村民参与讨论环境卫生和个人卫生、营养和保健问题培训。

本章词汇

analytical requirements　分析要求
counterpart　对手/对应方
controlled temperature and humidity facilities　温湿度可控设施
dedicated staff　专门的人员
exposure　接触
on site　在现场/当场
tar and nicotine　焦油和尼古丁
toxicants　毒物
(to) circumvent controls　规避管控
youth exposure to...　青年接触……
plain packaging　无装饰包装
tax concessions　税收减免
eye conditions　眼疾
vision impairment　视力损害
blindness　盲症
psychoactive drugs　精神刺激药物
domestic injuries　家庭伤害
child abuse　虐待儿童
gender-based sexual violence　基于性别的性暴力
(to) inject drugs　注射吸毒
overdose　吸毒过量
addiction　成瘾
undernutrition　营养不足
malnutrition　营养不良
overweight/obesity　超重/肥胖
double-duty actions　双重责任行动
most vulnerable population　最弱势人口
whole genome sequencing　全基因组测序
source tracking and attribution　源跟踪和归因
library preparation　文库制备
sequencing reactions　测序反应
food-borne　食源性

pathogen speciation and subtyping　病原型别和亚型
cost-effective　成本收益高的
basic epidemiology　基础流行病学
surveillance　监控
food monitoring and testing　食品监测和检测
global malaria burden　全球疟疾负担
pandemic　大流行病
intermittent preventive treatment　间歇性预防治疗
seasonal malaria chemoprevention　季节性疟疾化学预防
mass drug administration　群体性服药
vector control　病媒控制
ITN (insecticide-treated mosquito nets)　驱虫蚊帐
consolidated report　综合报告
consolidated budget　合并预算/汇总预算
private sector entities　私营部门实体
euphoria　欣快感/欣快效果
tolerance　耐受性
human laboratory research　人体实验室研究
opioids　类阿片
opiate　阿片剂
opium　阿片
fatal intoxications　致命性中毒事件
preparations　制剂
ingredients　药物成分
stereoisomers　立体异构体
cannabis resin　大麻脂
laboratory　制备点/制药厂
vaccinators　疫苗接种员
immunization coverage　免疫覆盖范围
emergency immunization　应急免疫接种
maternal mortality ratio　儿童死亡率
chance to survive and thrive　生存和成长机会

第八章 科学与技术

本章导言

　　人工智能、大数据、机器学习，这些概念已成为人们耳熟能详的流行术语。但科技作为一把双刃剑，在涉及教育、人居环境、国际和平与安全等关乎人人利益的问题上既给全球社会带来了变革与机遇，又带来了冲击与挑战。高科技是全球治理的一个最新高地，联合国尤为重视科学技术在应对和解决全球事务中的应用，正逐步依托云计算、数据库等新技术建立统一、同步的办公系统，为推进全球事务提供便利。

　　围绕科学与技术这一永恒主题，联合国系统各机构在各自主管领域推出了多种促进科技创新、加强科技监管、规范科技资助活动的举措。在科学与教育领域，联合国教科文组织推出了涉及数学、物理、化学等领域的国际基础科学计划以及加强学生多方面科技素养的远程学习和在线教育方案；在科学与环境领域，联合国环境规划署及其下属组织机构就危害生命健康、大气污染、生物多样性的有害物品管制推出了鼓励性的技术供资支持及惩罚性的监管措施；在科学与国际和平安全领域，针对全面禁核和外太空安全，相关公约机构和委员会针对该领域专门技术使用编写了示范案文和规范准则。此外，科学技术还涉及其他领域，如世界知识产权组织在专利发明领域所进行的技术创新——专利文献神经机器翻译工具；如国际货币基金组织力推的沙箱监管机制。以这些活动为载体，各机构编写的科技题材文件也呈现出一种交叉性特征，即科学科技与治理监管、规范标准制定、资金分配、支助与宣传相结合。

　　这也决定了联合国科学与技术类文件与科普类文件是有区别的，前者一般具有以下特征。

　　（1）内容更充实、丰富，不仅限于对某项或某几类科学原理的技术性描述，还包括叙述性概述以及依托技术原理编写的技术规范、法律文本。

　　（2）广泛援引决议决定、公约、法律文书。

　　（3）与项目管理、治理、人权人道等国际主题相结合，以全球化视角为立足点，对技术的应用进行讨论，高瞻远瞩，具有科技人文色彩。

　　与此同时，联合国科学与技术类稿件也兼具科技文体特征，如长句、复杂句较多、被动结构突出、大量使用抽象名词和介词等。

本章选取了三种具有代表性的科学技术类文件。

第一类：科技新闻体文件。如第一篇所选材料，侧重于从通识角度介绍热点话题，此类文件技术难度最低，但对译者的文字功底要求较高。

第二类：技术工作文件、项目提案和案头研究报告。如第二篇至第四篇，此类材料充分体现了科学技术与其他领域的交汇色彩，涉及项目申报、活动资助以及化学品管制等主题。

第三类：专业性技术报告。如第五篇至第八篇，其中第五篇所涉专业知识及术语最为复杂，需参考学术性文献；此外，这几篇都涉及外太空安全，对译者的科技素养以及政治敏锐性都提出了一定要求。

因此，在处理联合国科学与技术类稿件时，应在熟悉科技类文体特征的基础上，灵活应用如下翻译技巧。

一、词汇层面

（1）注意介词的灵活转化，例如第二篇第1段"Assuming that PFOA and PFOA-related compounds are used at..."一句。对于有多个介词的成分，应根据句式特征，分析出前后修饰关系以及句子核心论述点，重组逻辑关系。

（2）注意模糊词的具体化。例如对第二篇第2段中的"fight"、第三篇第3段中"based"以及第五篇第8段中"documentation"的处理应避免仅考虑词汇的常用含义，应通过查阅通用词典（《牛津英汉双解百科词典》）以及其他科技术语词典，厘清词汇的多重含义。同样，还应注意，有些词汇在既定领域或某类技术文件中有固定的含义，例如（第四篇第2段中）"approach""phase-down"以及（第六篇第3段中）"space"等。

（3）巧用造词技巧。例如第七篇第2段中出现的"Moon-based"这种科技类合成词，我们可借鉴"space-based"表述来造出一个新词，同时也可将思维发散开来，如对"-borne"结构，还可联想到在其他领域（如卫生）的用法来造词。

二、句法层面

（1）注意语句论述的重心及落脚点。例如第一篇第2段中"In the new version, a tiny camera (which costs less than $1.50) fitted on the bionic hand..."一句，根据前后语境，选择一个合适的主语作为句子的起点，对整句话内涵的传达和表意尤为重要。

（2）对省略、简化的表达进行补充。例如第二篇第1段中"11 890 gallons of PFOA-related"一句，如不补充必要成分，会使原本理解起来就比较困难的句子更为晦涩难懂。

（3）注意语态处理。例如第三篇第3段中"126 Customs and enforcement officers were trained...and...were provided"，应选择适当的被动句处理技巧。

（4）掌握长句、定语的拆分技巧。例如第四篇第2段中"In response to..., the Senior Monitoring and Evaluation Officer has submitted..., based on..."一句，可先从语法角度分析出状语从句的一般结构，然后按照前后因果逻辑顺序处理；再如第八篇第3段中"conclusively necessary to be factored into, the concept of ensuring the long-term sustainability of outer space activities"一句，采用拆译法一方面可将重要的核心成分提出，起到提携作用；另一方面读起来也更加层次分明。

三、语篇与文体层面

（1）注意研究技术类文件的编写结构。例如第四篇第 2 段中 "some questions in the terms of reference had not been answered fully" 一句，如不清楚文件由哪几部分组成，每一部分分别讨论的事项，则在处理单句时容易忽视整份文件的主题，而局限于其字面含义。

（2）注意避免硬译。例如第五篇第 9 段中 "Confirm that equipment items, core and auxiliary, required only for the techniques listed in Part Ⅱ, Subparagraphs 69(f)-(g)" 一句，虽然技术类文本的语法特征较为"显性"，但不意味着完全按照其句法结构对照译出就达到此类文件的翻译标准，应当在对语法解码的基础上将其隐含的逻辑关系流畅地表达出来。

（3）注意科技文体也有"感情"。例如第七篇第 1 段中 "beneficiary" 一词的使用显然是运用了修辞技巧，那么就应当将其真正的指代意义还原出来。

总而言之，科学与技术专题是联合国文件中对译者综合能力要求较高的一类材料，通过学习此类文件的翻译技巧，不仅可掌握科普类文体的通用翻译技巧（如专有名词、专有术语、长难句的处理），还有助于提高参阅专业文献的技能，加强跨领域活用背景知识的悟性，积淀科技素养。

背景介绍

本篇材料选自联合国教科文组织《信使》杂志科技专栏，是一篇探讨最新科技热点的新闻体稿件，旨在通过个人叙事视角，贴近事实地讲述人工智能在追查犯罪、医疗卫生领域的应用及其对日常生活的切实改观。本篇材料以实情实例为基础，在内容上涉及人工智能、机器学习等前沿科学概念，同时其文体属于杂志体，虽有一些科技术语，但专业难度较低，是大众较为常见的科技材料，特别是在词汇、句式和文风上兼具社科领域特点，要求译者在基本准确掌握科技行话的同时提高表达的逻辑性和流畅性，熟悉英汉科技类文体在重点信息组织、表达重心上的差异。

第一篇

原文

The question already being raised is: isn't there a risk that data available to AI will be used to confirm preconceived ideas and prejudices? Racial profiling, censorship, prediction of the criminal personality, etc.—these discriminatory criteria are already being used by machines that are taught to analyse patterns of behaviour. The more complex the technological development becomes, the more complex are the ethical questions it raises. The development of killer robots is a striking example of this.

The usual process requires the user to see the object, physically stimulate the muscles in the arm and trigger a movement in the prosthetic limb. In the new version, a tiny camera (which costs less than $1.50) fitted on the bionic hand takes a picture of an object in front of it, assesses its shape and size, and triggers a series of smooth movements to pick up the object—in a matter of seconds. "Responsiveness has been one of the main barriers to artificial limbs. Controlling them takes practice, concentration and time," explains Nazarpour. "Prosthetic limbs have changed very little in the past 100 years—the design is much better and the materials are lighter in weight and more durable, but they still work in the same way," he adds.

Nazarpour, who has focused his research on improving prosthetics since 1999, grew up in Iran dreaming of becoming a medical doctor. The doctor's research is motivated by the potential of prosthetics to restore function to individuals with sensorimotor deficits, by transforming thought into action and sensation into perception.

请自行翻译后查看后文的分析点评

分析点评

第 1 段

The question already being raised is: isn't there a risk that data available to AI will be used to confirm preconceived ideas and prejudices? Racial profiling, censorship, prediction of the criminal personality, etc.—these discriminatory criteria are already being used by machines that are taught to analyse patterns of behaviour. The more complex the technological development becomes, the more complex are the ethical questions it raises. The development of killer robots is a striking example of this.

我们要回答的问题是：用人工智能领域的现有数据来证实成见和偏见是否存在风险？① 对于种族定性②、审查、预测犯罪人格等——这些歧视性标准，机器已经学会用它们来分析行为模式。技术发展越复杂，提出的伦理问题越复杂。杀手机器人的发展就是这方面的一个显著例子。

批 注

① 对问句理解有误。
② 对词汇理解有误。

我们要回答的问题是：用人工智能领域现有的数据来证实成见和偏见，难道不会有风险吗？机器已经学会了用种族特征分析、审查和犯罪人格预测等歧视性标准来分析行为模式，并正在将它们投入使用。技术发展越复杂，提出的伦理问题也就越复杂。杀手机器人的成功开发就是这方面的一个显著例子。

1. 理解疑问句。见"isn't there a risk...ideas and prejudices"一句。在处理这个疑问句时，翻译稿采用的是直译法，将原文逐句对照译为"用人工智能领域的现有数据来证实成见和偏见是否存在风险"。乍看之下好像无不当之处，但是仔细推敲的确存在问题。首先，从语法意义上说，"isn't there"引导的句子是一个反义疑问句，相比"is there"引导的句子，有一种反问的色彩，有必要将这层语法含义转换成汉语中的对应句式。其次，不符合文本文风。本文是一篇科技类的小品文，介绍了人工智能技术在解决人权领域问题方面的应用，尤其是开篇以一个问句形式提出问题，那么其意图就是向受众提出问题，引起受众思考，如果译成一个简单的疑问句，则过于平淡无奇，而使用反问句式，如审校稿所用的"难道不会有风险？"更能引起读者思考和共鸣，也为开篇增加了一丝文学色彩。所以，虽然本文选自科技题材，但作为一篇社科类出版物，要考虑受众的接受度，细细推敲文字背后的深层含义，才能让译文更有感染力。

2. 词汇理解问题。见"racial profiling"一词。翻译稿将该词译成了"种族定性",可见译者查阅了联合国术语词汇库,在人权类文件中"racial profiling"的固定译法就是"种族定性"。但是,在此处要注意并非术语库中的所有词汇在所有文件中都可以固定套用,还要结合文本的文体特征以及具体语境加以灵活使用。"profiling"一词本义有"简介、分析"的含义,而结合文本语境,"profiling"与"censorship"和"prediction"是并列出现的,因此不妨考虑其与后面两个词汇的联系,那么作为连贯的一系列动作,可以是先对种族进行分析,然后再进行审查和预测,因此"racial profiling"可以译为"种族特征分析"。同理,对于在联合国维也纳办事处涉及毒品问题的文件中出现的"forensic profiling"一词,则可以译为"法医特征分析"。

3. 句式调整与拆分问题。见"Racial profiling, censorship…these discriminatory criteria are already being used…analyse patterns of behaviour."一句。可以看出,原文的这句话很长,并且前后出现了主语的转换,从"标准"转化成了"机器学习"。对于这种结构较复杂、较长的句子,要用到切分技巧。在切分句子时,应把握两个原则:一是尽可能不影响原文句子含义,不仅仅是句子表层含义,还有深层的,如句子重心、侧重点尽量不要偏移;二是尽可能使用一个主语,不要出现太多主语。研究翻译稿,可以看出译者有切分意识,但是对这个技巧的使用尚不熟练。译者的问题在于,一是将"对于种族定性、审查、预测犯罪人格等——这些歧视性标准"提前,作为一个单独的成分,而后半句的主语又变成了"机器",使句子前后逻辑不够连贯;二是拆分出现了漏译,"being used by machines"和"are taught to"是两个动作,主语都是机器,而译者将这两个动作合并,译成了"已经学会用它们来"这是不准确的,应当按照审校稿的思路,将这个动作按照逻辑顺序逐一译出,即"机器已经学会了……""并正在将它们投入使用"。

第 2 段

The usual process requires the user to see the object, physically stimulate the muscles in the arm and trigger a movement in the prosthetic limb. In the new version, a tiny camera (which costs less than $1.50) fitted on the bionic hand takes a picture of an object in front of it, assesses its shape and size, and triggers a series of smooth movements to pick up the object—in a matter of seconds. "Responsiveness has been one of the main barriers to artificial limbs. Controlling them takes practice, concentration and time," explains Nazarpour. "Prosthetic limbs have changed very little in the past 100 years—the design is much better and the materials are lighter in weight and more durable, but they still work in the same way," he adds.

翻译稿

在一般过程中,使用者要先看到物体,以获得对手臂肌肉的生理刺激[①],再触发假肢运动。在新版本中,仿生手在几秒之内,即通过内置微型摄像头(成本不超过 1.50 美元)采集前方物体图像,评估其形状和大小,从而触发一系列拾

批 注

① 翻译重点出现偏移。

取物体的流畅动作。"反应能力是人工假肢的主要障碍之一。掌握它的动作方法需要练习、专注力和时间,"纳扎普尔解释说。"在过去100年里,假肢基本没怎么发生变化——设计更精细,材料的重量更轻、更耐用,但仍以同样的原理工作,"他补充说。

在通常的过程中,使用者先要看到物体,然后从生理上刺激手臂肌肉,接着才触发假肢运动。新版的仿生手内置微型摄像头(成本不超过1.50美元),它能采集前方物品的图像,评估其形状和大小,然后触发拾取物品的一系列流畅动作,这一切只需要几秒钟的时间。"反应能力是人工假肢的主要障碍之一。要掌握它的动作方法,需要大量练习,保持专注,并投入时间",纳扎普尔(Nazarpour)解释说。"在过去100年里,假肢基本没有发生什么变化,只不过是设计更精细,材料更轻、更耐用,但工作原理却是一样的,"他补充说。

1. 表达的重点不同。见"physically stimulate the muscles"。翻译稿是"获得对手臂肌肉的生理刺激",可以看出译者有翻译转化意识,对原文有一定推敲,但是这种处理方式导致这个词汇的落脚点、重心变成了"生理刺激",而结合后文的一系列动作,不难看出如果将这个词处理成一个动词结构,即"生理上刺激",即可与后面的"触发假肢"形成一系列连贯动作。这样对重心的把握更为精确。

2. 主语重心问题。见"In the new version, a tiny camera (which costs less than $1.50) fitted on the bionic hand..."一句。通过语法结构判断,可以看出句子的主语是"tiny camera",但是整段论述的主语是"bionic hand",对于这种转换主语、句子与段落不一致的情况,需要确定合适的主语作为句子的起点。翻译稿中仍沿用"仿生手"为主语,译成了"通过内置微型摄像头采集前方物体图像",乍看似乎没有问题,但是细究发现,"采集图像"的主语实际是"摄像头",而不是"仿生手通过摄像头",因此翻译稿的处理是有问题的。参考审校稿的译法"新版的仿生手内置微型摄像头","摄像头……"这样巧妙地在保留整段论述主语的前提下引出句子的小主语,将这种不一致化而为一,可供我们参考借鉴。

3. 增译问题。见"Controlling them takes practice, concentration and time."一句。翻译稿处理"需要练习、专注力和时间"也不为错,但是与审校稿"需要大量练习,保持专注,并投入时间相比"还不够好。此处为什么要增译,一是为了呼应原文的"掌握动作方法",增译动词"保持、投入"更能体现动作连贯性,与前文相呼应;二是出于表达美感考虑,增译动词使句子更整齐,体现了节奏韵律感。

第3段

Nazarpour, who has focused his research on improving prosthetics since 1999, grew up in Iran dreaming of becoming a medical doctor. The doctor's research is motivated by the potential of prosthetics to restore function to individuals with sensorimotor deficits, by transforming thought into action and sensation into perception.

批 注

① 句子过长，可读性差。

在伊朗长大梦想成为医师的纳扎普尔从 1999 年开始一直在专门从事假肢改良方面的研究。① 作为一名医生，他的研究受到了假肢潜力的启发，即通过将想法变成行动，将感觉转为知觉，使感觉运动能力缺陷者恢复功能。

纳扎普尔在伊朗长大，从小就梦想成为一名医生。从 1999 年起，他开始潜心研究如何改良假肢。假肢可以帮助在感觉运动方面存在缺陷的人士恢复功能，也就是将想法变成感觉，再将感觉转化为知觉，这一点激发了他的研究兴趣。

点 评

1. "individuals with sensorimotor deficits" 可译为"感觉运动能力缺陷者"，也可意译为"在感觉运动方面存在缺陷的人士"。

2. 表达问题。见 "who has focused his research on..." 一句。翻译稿处理得过长，将全部信息量浓缩在一句话，使读者找不到这句话的论述重点，可读性较差。对于这种从句嵌套从句、信息量较大的长句，可以根据信息关联度进行合并同类项，先介绍大概背景，再一步步往论述主题推进，即可参考审校稿采用的拆译法，将这句话的信息拆分成两部分，分别是"在伊朗长大、想成为医生"和"1999 年开始专门研究"，这样更易于读者接受。

1. The technological aspects of AI are fascinating, but some fear that AI may eventually eclipse human intelligence. Even if we accept the idea that AI will help the advance of humanity, we must anticipate the dangers if humans lose control of the technology, and be aware of its ethical implications.

参 考 译 文

人工智能技术的方方面面令人着迷，但有些人担心人工智能最终可能会碾压人类智慧。即便我们可以接受人工智能有助于人类进步的观点，我们也必须预见到如果人类失去对该技术的掌控将会带来危险，并认识到它的伦理影响。

2. One pervasive concern that is examined from different perspectives across the book is whether humans deliberately entrust their decision-making powers to the

AI. Is the AI a substitute for humans? What are the potential measures to safeguard us from the abuse of AI? These questions are discussed in addition to the points of view developed by Netexplo, by comparing different scenarios.

本书从不同视角讨论了人们普遍关切的问题，即人类是否有意地将他们的决策权交给人工智能。人工智能是不是人类的替代品？可以采取哪些措施来防止人工智能遭到滥用？除了 Netexplo 提出的观点之外，还通过对比不同情境，对这些问题进行了讨论。

背景介绍

以下三篇材料均选自环境署相关委员会（持久性有机污染物审查委员会、执行蒙特利尔议定书多边基金执行委员会）的技术类文件。从题材上细分，分别为技术工作文件、项目提案和案头研究报告。

技术工作文件旨在对某一技术领域（如化学品管制）进行相关风险评估，内容包括其缔约方向委员会提交的评估材料及委员会就此给出的审查建议，因此往往会涉及管制物品及相关技术的现状、应用情况、适用对象、前景、风险危害等专业知识，需要译者对科学技术所涉行业领域、原理、数字单位等方面有一定敏锐性。其特点主要体现在，一是有大量专业性化学品、化合物名称。在翻译时，须查阅《斯德哥尔摩公约》《鹿特丹公约》和《巴塞尔公约》等公约及相关管制清单所载的准确术语。二是多介词、多被动句，且主被动句切换频繁，须找准句子的侧重点和落脚点以及各修饰成分之间的关系，在厘清句子关系的基础上自然地进行主被动转换。

对于项目提案和案头研究报告，要将术语置于材料的背景知识及组织结构中加以理解。执行蒙特利尔议定书多边基金系根据《蒙特利尔议定书》缔约方第二次会议（1990年6月，伦敦）的一项决定设立，并于1991年开始运作，致力于扭转地球臭氧层恶化趋势，其主要目标是为《蒙特利尔议定书》缔约国中消耗臭氧层物质（ODS）氯氟烃（CFC）和哈龙人均年度消费水平低于0.3千克的发展中国家提供援助，助其遵守《议定书》控制措施。目前，《蒙特利尔议定书》的197个缔约方中有147个满足这些标准。它们被称为第5条国家。第5条国家为开展与淘汰消耗臭氧层物质有关的工作，可向基金秘书处提交项目提案，申请供资，由后者核准并供资。此类提案在形式上由三部分组成：项目评价表、项目说明（涉及之前的供款申请/付款执行情况、相关行业的转换和淘汰情况、政府的监管情况等）以及秘书处的评论和建议。其特点是专业性强、技术术语多且某些术语有固定译法。

第二篇

原文

Assuming that PFOA and PFOA-related compounds are used at between 0.1–1% wt/wt in fire-fighting concentrates. 11 890 gallons of PFOA-related = 1.18–11.79–1 million US gallons of concentrate. 23 600 US gallons of PFOA-related = 2.36–23.59–2 million US gallons of concentrate.

According to the Fire-fighting Foam Coalition (FFFC) AFFF agents containing fluorotelomer-based fluorosurfactants are the most effective foam agents currently available to fight flammable liquid fires in military, industrial, aviation and municipal applications. Test data provided by the United States Naval Research Laboratories (NRL, 2016) showed that, in pool fire tests, an AFFF agent achieved extinguishment in 18 seconds compared to 40 seconds for the fluorine-free foam. However, an alternate study from 2004 (Lerner, 2018) with the US Navy commented that based on testing of AFFF based foams from 3M and fluorine-free alternatives that similar rates were achieved for putting out fires. The fluorine-free alternative put out fires within 39 seconds, while AFFF ranged from 25 to 36 seconds.

请自行翻译后查看后文的分析点评

分析点评

第 1 段

Assuming that PFOA and PFOA-related compounds are used at between 0.1–1% wt/wt in fire-fighting concentrates. 11 890 gallons of PFOA-related = 1.18–11.79–1 million US gallons of concentrate. 23 600 US gallons of PFOA-related = 2.36–23.59–2 million US gallons of concentrate.

翻译稿

假设使用在消防浓缩物中的浓度介于 0.1% 至 1% 重量比之间的全氟辛酸和全氟辛酸相关化合物①。11 890 加仑的全氟辛酸②=118 万至 1 179 万美国加仑浓度。23 600 美国加仑的全氟辛酸 = 236 万 -2 359 万 -200 万美国加仑③浓度。

审校稿

假设全氟辛酸和全氟辛酸相关化合物在消防浓缩物中的使用浓度介于 0.1% 至 1%（重量比）之间。11 890 加仑的全氟辛酸相关化合物 = 118 万 –1 179 万 –100 万

批 注
① 理解有问题。
② 漏译。
③ 专业术语翻译错误。

美制加仑浓缩物。23 600 美制加仑的全氟辛酸相关化合物 = 236 万 - 2 359 万 - 200 万美制加仑浓缩物。

1. 见"US gallons"一词，对科技术语的翻译务必要精准，尽可能从专业术语词典中找到相关依据。

2. 见"11 890 gallons of PFOA-related"一词，对于原文省略、简化的表达，在翻译时要尽可能将其原型补充完整，即按照"PFOA-related compounds"加以处理，翻译成"11 890 加仑的全氟辛酸相关化合物"。

3. 见"Assuming that PFOA and PFOA-related compounds are used at…"一句。这句话的难点在于介词较多，导致介词连接的多个成分之间的修饰关系不够明朗，再加上处理为被动句，难以判断主语及主语的位置。在处理此类多介词、多被动结构的科技文本时，一个原则是找准句子的侧重点，以此来重组逻辑关系。可以看出，这句话的重点在于"are used at between 0.1 – 1% wt/wt"，侧重点在于全氟辛酸和全氟辛酸相关化合物的使用，并且通过后面的公式也可做出这一判断。如果按照翻译稿的译法，这句话的落脚点就放在了"全氟辛酸和全氟辛酸相关化合物"上面，而非其使用浓度，这就偏离了原文的主旨。

第 2 段

According to the Fire-fighting Foam Coalition (FFFC) AFFF agents containing fluorotelomer-based fluorosurfactants are the most effective foam agents currently available to fight flammable liquid fires in military, industrial, aviation and municipal applications. Test data provided by the United States Naval Research Laboratories (NRL, 2016) showed that, in pool fire tests, an AFFF agent achieved extinguishment in 18 seconds compared to 40 seconds for the fluorine-free foam. However, an alternate study from 2004 (Lerner, 2018) with the US Navy commented that based on testing of AFFF based foams from 3M and fluorine-free alternatives that similar rates were achieved for putting out fires. The fluorine-free alternative put out fires within 39 seconds, while AFFF ranged from 25 to 36 seconds.

据消防泡沫联盟称，含有基于含氟调聚物的含氟表面活性剂的水成膜泡沫灭火剂是目前在应对军事、工业、航空和市政基础设施中易燃液体火灾①的最有效的泡沫灭火剂。美国海军研究实验室（NRL，2016）提供的数据显示，在油池火灾测验中，水成膜泡沫灭火剂的灭火速度为 18 秒，相比之下，无氟泡沫为 40 秒。不过，与美国海军实验室从 2014 年起开展的另一项替代品研究评论（Lerner，2018）称②，根据对 3M 公司的水成膜泡沫及无氟替代品所做的一项测验显示，两者的灭火速率相当。无氟替代品在 39 秒内灭火，而水成膜泡沫的灭火时间在 25 ~ 36 秒。

批 注

① 表达不准确。

② 注意圆括号的位置。

据消防泡沫联盟称，含有基于含氟调聚物的含氟表面活性剂的水成膜泡沫灭火剂是目前在军事、工业、航空和市政应用中扑救易燃液体火灾的最有效的泡沫灭火剂。美国海军研究实验室（2016）提供的测试数据显示，在油槽火灾测试中，水成膜泡沫灭火剂的灭火速度为18秒，而无氟泡沫为40秒。不过，从2004年起与美国海军实验室开展的另一项研究（Lerner，2018）评论指出，对3M公司的水成膜泡沫和无氟替代品进行的一项测试显示，两者的灭火速率相当。无氟替代品在39秒内灭火，而水成膜泡沫的灭火时间在25秒至36秒之间。

1. 见"However, an alternate study from 2004 (Lerner, 2018) with"一句。要注意括号内成分的位置，翻译稿在处理这一细节时忽视了括号所修饰的对象，将其放在了"commented"之后，处理为研究"评论（Lerner，2018）称"，正确的处理方式为"一项研究（Lerner，2018）评论称"。

2. 见"are the most effective foam agents currently available to fight flammable liquid fires in military"一句。翻译稿出现两个错误，其一，对"fight"一词的翻译不够贴合语境，应当结合其搭配对象"fires"，将"扑灭、扑救"这层含义译出，译成"应对"过于含糊；其二：对"fight flammable liquid fires in military, industrial, aviation and municipal applications"的成分切分有误，"military, industrial, aviation and municipal applications"并不是"火灾"的修饰语，去掉插入成分"to fight flammable liquid fires"，应当紧跟"most effective foam agents currently available"这句。此外，在处理科技类文本时，应当对某项技术、发明的适用对象、应用范围、应用前景及推广等这些背景信息有一定的敏锐性。在此处，很明显"军事、工业、航空和市政"是应用范围，"易燃液体火灾"是适用对象，将应用范围与应用对象相混淆，也不符合正确认知。

补充练习

1. In foam degradation tests, fluorine-free foam degraded after 1–2 minutes, while the AFFF lasted 35 minutes before it has been degraded. The FFFC does not support the opinion that AFFF agents are no longer needed and recommends the use of AFFF only in specific circumstances where a significant flammable liquid hazard occurs and that all available measures to minimize emissions to the lowest possible level should be implemented when using AFFF agents (FFFC, 2017).

在泡沫降解测试中，无氟泡沫在1～2分钟后降解，而水成膜泡沫在降解前持续了35分钟。消防泡沫联盟不支持已不再需要水成膜泡沫灭火剂的观点，并建议仅在发生重大可燃液体危险的特定情况下使用水成膜泡沫，并且在使用

水成膜泡沫灭火剂时应采取所有可行措施尽量降低排放水平（消防泡沫联盟，2017）。

2. The Institute for Fire and Disaster Control Heyrothsberge in Germany tested six fluorine free alcohol resistant firefighting foams and one PFAS containing foam for their ability to extinguish fires of five different polar liquids. The authors conclude that there are fluorine-free foams available which show a similar performance compared with PFAS containing foams (see Keutel and Koch, 2016).

德国 Heyrothsberge 消防和灾难控制研究所测试了六种无氟耐酒精消防泡沫和一种含有全氟和多氟烷基化合物的泡沫，以了解其扑灭五种不同极性液体火灾的能力。作者的结论是，有的无氟泡沫的性能与含有全氟和多氟烷基化合物的泡沫相似（见 Keutel 和 Koch，2016）。

On behalf of the Government of Mongolia, UNEP as the lead implementing agency, has submitted to the 77th meeting a request for funding for the third tranche of stage I of the HCFC phase-out management plan (HPMP), at the amount of US $69 000, plus agency support costs of US $8 970 for UNEP only. The submission includes a progress report on the implementation of the second tranche, the verification report on HCFC consumption and the tranche implementation plan for 2017 to 2019.

The verification report confirmed that the Government is implementing a licensing and quota system for HCFC imports and exports, and that the total consumption of HCFC for 2015 was 0.64 ODP tonnes, which is below the allowable level of consumption under the Montreal Protocol and the Agreement with the Executive Committee.

The Government of Mongolia continues to implement ozone regulations; HC-290, HFC-32, R-152a and R-477-based equipment is exempted from sales tax to encourage the use of low-global warming potential (GWP) refrigerants; a ban on new production of HCFC-22-based XPS foam is in place since 2013, inclusion of HCFC-141b in the list of banned substances in 2014; 126 Customs and enforcement officers were trained on control of import and export of ODS and two sets of ODS identifiers were provided; and the certification system for refrigeration and air-conditioning (RAC) servicing technicians was developed.

请自行翻译后查看后文的分析点评

分析点评

第 1 段

On behalf of the Government of Mongolia, UNEP as the lead implementing agency, has submitted to the 77th meeting a request for funding for the third tranche of stage Ⅰ of the HCFC phase-out management plan (HPMP), at the amount of US$69 000, plus agency support costs of US$8 970 for UNEP only. The submission includes a progress report on the implementation of the second tranche, the verification report on HCFC consumption and the tranche implementation plan for 2017 to 2019.

环境署作为牵头执行机构，代表蒙古政府向第七十七次会议提交了一份关于为氟氯烃淘汰管理计划第一阶段第三批款项供资①的请求②，金额为 69 000 美元，外加一笔机构资助费用 8 970 美元，仅供环境规划署使用。所提交的申请包括一份关于第二批款项执行情况的进度报告③、关于氟氯烃消费的核查报告和 2017 年至 2019 年款项执行计划。

批 注

① 有固定译法。
② 有固定译法。
③ 有待简炼和完善。

环境署作为牵头执行机构，代表蒙古国政府向第七十七次会议提交了氟氯烃淘汰管理计划第一阶段第三次付款供资申请，金额为 69 000 美元，外加仅供环境规划署使用的机构资助费用 8 970 美元。所提交的申请材料包括第二次付款执行进度报告、氟氯烃消费核查报告和 2017 至 2019 年付款执行计划。

点评

1. 注意术语的固定译法。见"request"和"tranche"，前者较为常见，意为"asking for sth formally and politely"，翻译稿处理为"请求"，在此应为"申请"，"tranche"意为"a portion of sth, esp money"，一般情况下，按翻译稿处理本来并无不妥，但在此类文体中固定处理为"（第 × 次付款）"。另外，关于"submission"一词，该词在联合国文件中经常出现，其译法也有规律可循：①表示动作，可直接处理为"提交"；②指提交的对象——"提交的材料"，在此段中，是指"提交的申请材料"，另外，在人权类文件，经常会看到"(joint) submission ××"一般译为"（联署）材料 ××"。

2. 某些名称表述欠简练，见"a request for funding for..." "a progress report on..." 以及 "the verification report on..."，相比之下，审校稿中的表述更为简洁，也更符合中文表达习惯。

第 2 段

The verification report confirmed that the Government is implementing a licensing and quota system for HCFC imports and exports, and that the total consumption of HCFC for 2015 was 0.64 ODP tonnes, which is below the allowable level of consumption under the Montreal Protocol and the Agreement with the Executive Committee.

核查报告确认，政府①正在实施氟氯烃进出口许可及配额制度②，而且 2015 年氟氯烃总消费量为 0.64 ODP 吨，低于《蒙特利尔议定书》和该国与执行委员会所签协定下的允许消费量。

批 注

① 需要具体化。
② 有固定表述。

核查报告确认，该国政府正在实施氟氯烃进出口许可证和配额制度，而且该国 2015 年氟氯烃总消费量为 0.64 ODP 吨，低于《蒙特利尔议定书》和该国与执行委员会所签协定规定的允许消费量。

1. "licensing and quota system for HCFC imports and exports" 有固定译法。
2. 主体欠具体化，见 "the Government is implementing a..., and that the total consumption of HCFC..."。翻译稿或是因为太过严谨，担心译错，直译为"政府正在实施……而且 2015 年氟氯烃总消费量……"但如果单看此段译文，会让人不禁疑惑究竟是"哪个国家的政府/消费量"。文件开头明确交代这是蒙古国提交的提案，不涉及任何其他国家，而且上下文中也多次明确提到"Government of Mongolia"。因此，完全可以大胆地译明"蒙古国政府"和"蒙古国消费量"，或者取折中译法，处理为"该国政府"和"该国消费量"。

第 3 段

The Government of Mongolia continues to implement ozone regulations; HC-290, HFC-32, R-152a and R-477-based equipment is exempted from sales tax to encourage the use of low-global warming potential (GWP) refrigerants; a ban on new production of HCFC-22-based XPS foam is in place since 2013, inclusion of HCFC-141b in the list of banned substances in 2014; 126 Customs and enforcement officers were trained on control of import and export of ODS and two sets of ODS identifiers were provided; and the certification system for refrigeration and air-conditioning (RAC) servicing technicians was developed.

批注

① 直译，导致译文意思欠明确。全段同。
② 语态上与前后文不一致。
③ 理解偏差。

蒙古国政府继续执行臭氧规定；对基于①HC-290、HFC-32、R-152a 和 R-477 的设备免征销售税，以鼓励使用低全球升温潜能值制冷剂；自 2013 年起禁止再度生产基于 HCFC-22 的挤塑聚苯乙烯泡沫塑料，并于 2014 年将 HCFC-141b 纳入禁用物质清单；126 名海关和执法人员接受了②消耗臭氧层物质进出口管制培训，并配备了两套消耗臭氧层物质识别器，以及开发了③制冷和空调维修技术人员资格认证系统。

蒙古国政府继续执行臭氧条例；对使用 HC-290、HFC-32、R-152a 和 R-477 的设备免征销售税，以鼓励使用低全球升温潜能值制冷剂；自 2013 年起禁止再度生产使用 HCFC22 的挤塑聚苯乙烯泡沫塑料，并于 2014 年将 HCFC-141b 列入禁用物质清单；对 126 名海关和执法人员进行了消耗臭氧层物质进出口管制培训，并为其配备了两套消耗臭氧层物质识别器，以及确立了制冷和空调维修技术人员资格认定制度。

1. 见两处"-based"，翻译稿中直译为"基于"，有不求甚解之嫌，处理为"使用（物质名称）的"更为准确。

2. 语态与前后文不一致以及被动句的处理问题。见"126 Customs and enforcement officers were trained...and...were provided"，典型的英文被动句。英文被动句的翻译技巧是：a. 尽量译为中文主动句；b. 寻找英文句子中的逻辑主语作为译文的主语。翻译稿采用了技巧 a，单看此句，不失为好译文，但放在整段文字中来看，技巧 b 更好，因为全段说的是政府采取的措施，政府为全段的主语，处理为"对……进行了……培训，并为其配备了……"更为妥当。

1. As of mid-2013, the two enterprises (Bilguun Trade LLC and New Warm LLC) discontinued the use of HCFC-22 for XPS foam production and phased out 9.9 mt (0.54 ODP tonnes).

参考译文

截至 2013 年中期，有两家企业（Bilguun Trade 有限责任公司和 New Warm 有限责任公司）停止将 HCFC-22 用于挤塑聚苯乙烯泡沫塑料生产，并逐步淘汰了 9.9 公吨（0.54 ODP 吨）。

2. In April 2014, the two enterprises selected HFC-152a as the replacement technology due to safety issues associated with the use of hydrocarbons (HC) on

XPS boards (while HFC-152a is mildly flammable, it has low fire-generating and combustion qualities compared with HC and has also a low-GWP (i.e., GWP of 124)), and better options for the beneficiaries and their resulting products for market penetration. A technical assistance was carried out in September 2016 to verify that safety measures are in place, and to confirm the destruction of the old equipment. The project will be completed by December 2016, verification of the final conversion of these two enterprises is ongoing, and a final report should be ready by January 2017.

2014年4月，这两家企业选择使用HFC-152a作为替代技术（HFC-152a虽轻度易燃，但和碳氢化合物相比，具有不易起火燃烧的特点，且其全球变暖潜能值低（全球变暖潜能值为124)），原因有两个：一是在挤塑聚苯乙烯板材上使用碳氢化合物存在安全隐患；二是这两家受益企业有更好的技术选择，而且利用这些技术生产的产品更具市场渗透力。2016年9月进行了技术援助，以核查是否已采取安全措施，并确认旧设备确已销毁。该项目将于2016年12月之前完成，对这两家企业最终转型情况的核查工作正在稳步推进，最后报告应于2017年1月之前编制完毕。

At its 82nd meeting, the Executive Committee considered the desk study for the evaluation of HCFC phase-out management plan preparation activities to assist with the implementation of the Kigali Amendment submitted by the Senior Monitoring and Evaluation Officer.

During the discussions, some members indicated that some questions in the terms of reference had not been answered fully. Specific examples included....One member also highlighted the lack of information in the desk study on how to ensure compliance with the rapidly approaching HFC-23 phase-down target. The Senior Monitoring and Evaluation Officer explained that some of the questions in the terms of reference had remained unanswered because the information was not available. Some members added that even though the report contained some gaps, the desk study provided a number of useful insights and suggestions that the Secretariat would be able to consider when developing draft guidelines for the preparation of HFC phase-down plans.

In light of the different opinions on whether the desk study should be revised and resubmitted to the 83rd meeting, and following further discussions, the Executive

Committee took note that an extension of the desk study had been included in the monitoring and evaluation work programme for the year 2019.

In response to concerns expressed by some members regarding incomplete answers to some questions in the terms of reference, the Senior Monitoring and Evaluation Officer has submitted to the 83rd meeting a revised desk study for the evaluation of HCFC phase-out management plan preparation activities to assist with the implementation of the Kigali Amendment, based on the desk study submitted to the 82nd meeting. Changes made to the document submitted to the 82nd meeting are shown in bold text below.

请自行翻译后查看后文的分析点评

分析点评

第 1 段

At its 82nd meeting, the Executive Committee considered the Desk study for the evaluation of HCFC phase-out management plan preparation activities to assist with the implementation of the Kigali Amendment submitted by the Senior Monitoring and Evaluation Officer(UNEP/OzL.Pro/ExCom/82/12).

批 注
① 此处特别注意"Desk Study（案头研究）"的全称。
② 擅自增减内容，属于错译。
③ 主谓搭配不符合中文习惯。

翻译稿

在第八十二次会议上，执行委员会审议了高级监测和评估干事提交的评估为协助执行《基加利修正案》而进行的氟氯烃淘汰管理计划编制活动①的修订版②案头研究③。

审校稿

执行委员会在第八十二次会议上审议了高级监测和评价干事提交的关于为协助执行《基加利修正案》而进行的评价氟氯烃淘汰管理计划编制活动的案头研究报告。

点评

1. 学会利用既有资料查阅所涉背景知识：案头研究的标题相对较长，在不了解背景信息的情况下，着实不好处理。译者应学会利用原文中提供的线索"顺藤摸瓜"：一、诚如导言部分所述，原文抬头部分已注明案头研究是环境署执行蒙特利尔议定书多边基金执行委员会第八十三次会议讨论的一份文件，即第八十三次会议议程上的一个项目，因此可登录多边基金网站查阅会议议程的英文本，同时也可查阅到中文本（http://www.multilateralfund.org/83/pages/English.aspx）；二、利用原文中既已给出的文号"UNEP/OzL.Pro/ExCom/82/12"，在多边基金网站第八十二次会议部分查阅该文件的英文版，或中文版，以便了解背景信息，以更好地进行翻译。在此，采用第一种方法，可查到中英两种文本，一般可直接采用中文本所载译文，如存在错误，可再结合文件所载具体信息进行调整。

2. 酌情增／减译与切勿妄自增／减译，见"Desk study for...of the Kigali Amendment"这一长标题。其中同时存在妄自增译和未能酌情增译的问题：①翻译稿中的"修订版"三个字毫无根据，怀疑译者是受文件标题中"Revised Desk Study..."的影响，对原文审视不够仔细之故；②"Desk study"被处理为"案头研究"，但就该短语而言并无不妥，但放置整句中即为"会议审议了……干事提交的……案头研究"，不符合中文表达习惯，应酌情增译"报告"二字。

第 2 段

During the discussions, some members indicated that some questions in the terms of reference had not been answered fully. Specific examples included....One member also highlighted the lack of information in the desk study on how to ensure compliance with the rapidly approaching HFC-23 phase-down target. The Senior Monitoring and Evaluation Officer explained that some of the questions in the terms of reference had remained unanswered because the information was not available. Some members added that even though the report contained some gaps, the desk study provided a number of useful insights and suggestions that the Secretariat would be able to consider when developing draft guidelines for the preparation of HFC phase-down plans.

讨论期间，几个成员表示，与工作范围有关的一些问题尚未得到充分回答①。具体的例子包括……一位成员还强调说，案头研究报告未说明如何确保遵守快速处理减少 HFC-23 的目标②。高级监测和评估干事解释说，由于未获得相关信息，才一直未回答与工作范围有关的一些问题。几个成员补充说，即便报告存在一些漏洞③，该案头研究也为秘书处提供了一些有用的见解和建议，供其在制定关于编制氢氟碳化物减少计划的准则草案时纳入考虑范围。

批 注

① 未明确研究报告的结构和逻辑。
② 理解错误＋术语问题。
③ 未结合上下文。

讨论期间，一些委员指出，案头研究工作范围对某些问题未做充分回答，具体包括……。一位委员还强调指出，案头研究未说明如何确保快速实现三氟甲烷（HFC-23）逐步减少的目标。高级监测和评价干事解释称，之所以未对工作范围内的某些问题做出充分回答，是因为没有相关的信息。还有几名委员补充指出，报告虽存在一些空白，但案头研究提出了很多有益的见解和建议，可供秘书处在编制氢氟碳化物逐步削减计划编制准则草案时考虑。

1. 整体来看，翻译稿未能宏观把握文件框架，厘清内容逻辑。上段交代，执委会审议了案头研究报告，本段则是说明执委会委员对研究报告的评论意见以及报告提交人高级监测和评估干事针对委员评论意见做出的解释和答复。

2. 见"some questions in the terms of reference had not been answered fully"一句，翻译稿未能查阅背景文件。经查可发现，案头研究由目标、研究方法、工作范围以及所评估的各个组成部分组成，执委会讨论是分部分进行，某些委员会认为"工作范围"部分对某些问题未做充分回答。此外，这一结构特点在下文中亦有明确体现，详见第 4 段及其后各段。

3. 见"how to ensure compliance with the rapidly approaching HFC-23 phase-down target"，其中存在理解错误及术语翻译不当的问题。在此，"approach"应取"to come near to sb./sth. in distance or time"而非"to start dealing with a problem, task, etc. in a particular way"之意。"phase-down"是专有名词，固定译法为"逐步削减 / 减少"。

第 3 段

In light of the different opinions on whether the desk study should be revised and resubmitted to the 83rd meeting, and following further discussions, the Executive Committee took note that an extension of the desk study had been included in the monitoring and evaluation work programme for the year 2019.

鉴于关于是否①应修订案头研究并重新提交给第八十三次会议存在不同意见，②执行委员会指出，2019 年的监测和评估工作计划包括对案头研究的延期。

鉴于在是否应修订案头研究报告并重新提交第八十三次会议的问题上存在意见分歧，经进一步讨论后，执行委员会注意到，2019 年监测和评价工作方案中已包括该项案头研究的延期。

1. 见"In light of the different opinions on whether..."，译文不符合中文习惯。
2. 见"following further discussions"，存在漏译。

第 4 段

In response to concerns expressed by some members regarding incomplete answers to some questions in the terms of reference, the Senior Monitoring and Evaluation Officer has submitted to the 83rd meeting a revised desk study for the evaluation of HCFC phase-out management plan preparation activities to assist with the implementation of the Kigali Amendment, based on the desk study submitted to the 82nd meeting. Changes made to the document submitted to the 82nd meeting are shown in bold text below.

批 注

① "鉴于关于是否……存在不同意见"这句译文通顺吗？
② 漏译。

为了回应几个成员就一些工作范围问题的不完整答复表示的关切，高级监测和评估干事已根据提交第 82 次会议的案头研究报告，向第 83 次会议提交了一份评估为协助执行《基加利修正案》而进行的氟氯烃淘汰管理计划编制活动的修订版案头研究报告①。下文粗体文本显示了对提交至第 82 次会议的文件所做的改动②。

批 注

① 理解错误。
② 表述不符合中文习惯。

为回应几名委员就案头研究工作范围未对某些问题做出充分回答表达的关切，高级监测和评价干事对提交第八十二次会议的案头研究报告做了修订，向第八十三次会议提交了关于为协助执行《基加利修正案》而进行的评价氟氯烃淘汰管理计划编制活动的订正案头研究报告。对提交第八十二次会议的文件所做改动，下文中一律用黑体显示。

1. 见 "In response to..., the Senior Monitoring and Evaluation Officer has submitted..., based on..."，此句很长，但结构清晰，翻译稿存在理解错误和表述不到位的问题。前半句 "In response to..., " 为状语从句，交代原因，详见第 2 段点评 2。关于中间的主句 "the Senior Monitoring and Evaluation Officer has submitted...,"难点在于案头研究标题的处理，见第 1 段点评 1。关于后半句 "based on"，翻译稿的译法较为笼统，结合上文第 1 和 2 段，以及此段最后一句，可进一步具体化，增译为"对提交第八十二次会议的案头研究报告做了修订"。

2. 见 "Changes made to the document submitted to the 82nd meeting are shown in bold text below" 一句，翻译稿表达出了原文的基本意思，但修改后的表述更符合中文习惯，意思也更加明确。

1. In September 2007, the Ninetieth Meeting of the Parties to the Montreal Protocol agreed to accelerate the phase-out of the production and consumption of HCFCs through Decision XIX/6. Subsequently, the Executive Committee approved, at its 54th meeting, the draft guidelines for the preparation of HCFC phase-out management plans (HPMPs) covering three aspects: timing and approach, policy issues related to HPMPs and a draft format for the HPMPs (Decision 54/39).

参考译文

2007 年 9 月，《蒙特利尔议定书》缔约方第九十次会议在第 XIX/6 号决定中同意加快停止氟氯烃的生产和消费。随后，执行委员会在第五十四次会议上核准了氟氯烃淘汰管理计划编制准则草案，草案内容涵盖三个方面：时间和方法；与

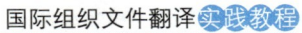

氟氯烃淘汰管理计划有关的政策问题，以及氟氯烃淘汰管理计划格式草案（第54/39号决定）。

2. The guidelines discussed the need to approve HPMPs early to meet the freeze in 2013 and the 10 per cent reduction from the HCFC baseline out in 2015. The main policy issue discussed was the need to establish an ODS import/export licensing system which also covered HCFCs. This would be a requirement for the approval of HPMP funding. The draft format for HPMPs requires a description of existing legislation, regulations and policy in place and how it operates. It also requires a description of the quota system, bans on imports of ODS-based equipment and ODS refrigerants in place or proposed, and any other Government initiatives related to HCFC phase out.

参考译文

该准则所做论述指出，必须及早核准氟氯烃淘汰管理计划，以便在2013年实现冻结，并在2015年实现在氟氯烃基准基础上削减10%的目标。准则所讨论的主要政策问题是有必要建立一项延及氟氯烃的消耗臭氧层物质进出口许可证制度。这是核准氟氯烃淘汰管理计划供资请求的一个必要前提。氟氯烃淘汰管理计划格式草案要求说明现有法律法规、规章和政策以及计划运作方式，另外还要求说明配额制度、现已或拟议出台的关于使用消耗臭氧层物质的设备和消耗臭氧层物质制冷剂的进口禁令以及与淘汰氟氯烃有关的任何其他政府举措。

背景介绍

本篇选自全面禁止核试验条约组织筹备委员会现场视察作业手册草案修订示范案文。全面禁止核试验条约组织筹备委员会是为促成全面禁止核试验条约在全球范围内生效所设立的专门委员会，主要任务是推广条约并建立核查制度，确保条约生效时的可操作性。为促进每次核爆炸都记录在案，围绕该制度建立了三个支柱，分别为国际监测系统、现场观察以及海啸预警和环境。这三种机制都有既定程序和规范，本篇所选示范案文就是对现场观察活动各程序所做的规则描述，由总则、秘书处技术支持、实习协调与支持、行动指南、视察技术、保密原则、技术执行程序、参考文献等部分组成，其中述及的视察技术有定位、目测观察、地震勘察、样板分析等，专业性较强，多引自科学专著和学术论文，需译者广泛查阅各种背景资料，同时，与科普类文本不同的是，作为一种技术规范文件，不仅在于对具体技术的原理进行解释和描述，更在于对技术的使用、执行程序、步骤及其依据文本（如《议定书》）进行规范性解读，因此在表述上兼具法律性文本的特征，严谨、条理清晰，尤其强调主体以及前后因果逻辑，对细节的处理要求较高，译者需在厘清前后关系的情况下对常见词如"documentation"等进行解释。

第五篇

原文

Personnel acting on behalf of the TS to crew or service a non-scheduled aircraft fulfil only the same role as the crew of a scheduled commercial aircraft and do not participate in inspection activities unless listed in the inspection mandate as an inspector or inspection assistant.

The time of arrival of the IT at the POE is the time at which the ITL hands the inspection mandate to the ISP representative in accordance with Part Ⅱ, Paragraph 52, of the Protocol.

The IT and the ISP discuss and agree on how to proceed in parallel with the three following groups of issues: IIP, equipment checking and supportive POE activities such as administrative and logistical discussions. Equipment checking is likely to be an intensive task and should be started as early as possible.

The ITL and ISP each nominate points of contact as necessary for coordination purposes (see 4.10.2).

The ITL gives further explanations of the mandate and the IIP and, if requested, provides the ISP with a copy of all information and data and documentation in its possession related to the inspection, subject to the privileges and immunities of the IT.

This includes the IA file and the triggering event file. Copies of confidentiality undertaking documents will be provided in accordance with Paragraph 10.2.5.

To facilitate the checking procedures, preparations are made in accordance with Part Ⅱ, Paragraph 38, of the Protocol and Sections 3.3 and 3.12 of this manual. Part Ⅱ, Subparagraphs 27(d) and (g), of the Protocol are also relevant in this regard.

Documentation prepared in accordance with Paragraph 3.12.2 is handed to the ISP. The IT assists the ISP with the review of these documents at the start of equipment checking at the POE, and subsequently following the arrival of any shipment of approved equipment.

Confirm that equipment items, core and auxiliary, required only for the techniques listed in Part Ⅱ, Subparagraphs 69(f)–(g), of the Protocol have been grouped separately and labelled to make clear that they are for use during different inspection periods as indicated by the mandate.

The checking process should be duly recorded, if the IT or the ISP so wishes.

In the event that TIDs are damaged and/or show signs of interference following the transport of equipment while in ISP territory, the ISP and the IT may carry out checks to confirm that the equipment has not been damaged or altered and still functions according to specification.

请自行翻译后查看后文的分析点评

分析点评

第 1 段

Personnel acting on behalf of the TS to crew or service a non-scheduled aircraft fulfil only the same role as the crew of a scheduled commercial aircraft and do not participate in inspection activities unless listed in the inspection mandate as an inspector or inspection assistant.

翻译稿

技术秘书处派出的非定班飞机机组或服务人员，只履行商业班机机组人员的职责，不参加视察活动，作为视察员或视察助理列入视察任务授权者除外。

审校稿

以技术秘书处名义（或代表技术秘书处）在非定期航班担任机组或服务人员的，只履行定期商业航班机组人员的职责，不参加视察活动，作为视察员或视察助理列入视察任务授权的除外。

点评

"acting on behalf of the TS"是指"以技术秘书处名义行事的"或"代表技术秘书处行事的"，译为"技术秘书处派出的"不准确，"non-scheduled aircraft"是指非定期航班，而不是非定班飞机。事实上，行业中也没有这样的说法，"a scheduled commercial aircraft"是指"定期商业航班"。

批注

① 翻译错误。
② 表述错误。

第 2 段

The time of arrival of the IT at the POE is the time at which the ITL hands the inspection mandate to the ISP representative in accordance with Part Ⅱ, Paragraph 52, of the Protocol.

翻译稿

根据议定书第二部分第 52 款，视察组到达入境点时，视察组组长应立即将视察任务授权递交给被视察缔约国代表。

审校稿

视察组到达入境点的时间应为视察组组长根据议定书第二部分第 52 款之规定向被视察缔约国代表传达视察任务授权之时。

批注

③ 逻辑关系错误。
④ 逻辑错误。

1. 从原文来看，本句的主语是"The time of arrival of the IT at the POE"，即"视察组达到入境点的时间"，"at which the ITL hands the inspection mandate to the ISP representative in accordance with Part Ⅱ, Paragraph 52, of the Protocol"是修饰"time"的定语从句，而翻译稿将定语从句中的一部分即"in accordance with Part Ⅱ, Paragraph 52, of the Protocol"拆出来，放在句首，成了修饰整个句子的作用，显然是弄错了英文的逻辑关系。议定书第二部分第 52 款规定的是"视察组组长向被视察缔约国代表传达视察任务授权的时间，而不是视察组达到入境点的时间"。"hand...to"译为"传达"比"递交"好。

2. 另外，要注意，IT、POE、ITL 和 ISP 等缩写在国际民航组织文件中的含义，要查看国际民航组织词库和参考文件。

第 3 段

The IT and the ISP discuss and agree on how to proceed in parallel with the three following groups of issues: IIP, equipment checking and supportive POE activities such as administrative and logistical discussions. Equipment checking is likely to be an intensive task and should be started as early as possible.

视察组和被视察缔约国应讨论并商定如何同时推进如下三类问题：初次视察计划、设备验证①，以及支持性入境点活动，例如行政和后勤问题讨论②。设备验证③可能是一项繁重④的任务，应尽早开始。

批　注

① 用词错误。
② 位置和表述不佳。
③ 用词错误。
④ 不准确。

视察组和被视察缔约国应讨论并商定如何同时推进以下三类问题：初次视察计划、设备检查以及行政和后勤问题讨论等在入境点开展的资助性活动。设备检查可能是一项密集的任务，应尽早开始。

翻译稿将"equipment checking"译为"设备验证"，这种表述让人费解。验证的含义是"检验……是否正确"，而设备只能检查，看看其是否完好，是否齐全，跟验证没有关系，所以用"设备检查"比"设备验证"好。"such as..."在绝大多数情况下译为"……等"为好。译者将"Equipment checking is likely to be an intensive task"译为"设备验证可能是一项繁重的任务"，在这里，"intensive"应该强调的是"密集"的多，而非"繁重"的重。

第 4 段

The ITL and ISP each nominate points of contact as necessary for coordination purposes (see 4.10.2).

批 注

① 不准确。
② 不准确。

视察组组长和被视察缔约国有必要①分别提名联络点②以便开展协调工作（见 4.10.2）。

视察组组长和被视察缔约国应根据需要各自提名联络人负责协调工作（见第 4.10.2 段）。

"as necessary" 不是 "有必要"，而是 "在必要时""在需要时"。"points of contact" 可以译为 "联络人、联络点"，但在这里，前面接的是 "nominate"，是提名的意思，故提名的对象应该是人，而不是机构，所以译为 "联络人" 比 "联络点" 好。

第 5 段

The ITL gives further explanations of the mandate and the IIP and, if requested, provides the ISP with a copy of all information and data and documentation in its possession related to the inspection, subject to the privileges and immunities of the IT.

批 注

③ 表述不清楚，容易引起逻辑关系混淆。
④ 表述错误且后面存在漏译情况。

视察组组长应进一步解释视察任务授权和初步视察计划，如被视察缔约国提出要求，还应向其③提供视察组掌握的、同视察有关的所有信息和资料以及文件副本④。

视察组组长应进一步解释视察任务授权和初步视察计划，如果被视察缔约国提出要求，还应向被视察缔约国提供视察组已掌握的、同视察有关的所有资料和数据以及文献资料，但应以遵守视察组享有的特权和豁免为前提。

"information" 可以译为 "信息"，也可以译为 "资料"，但在前几段中，翻译稿一直将其译为 "资料"，而且后面还跟有 "data"，另外，"documentation" 译为 "文件副本" 显然不妥，应该做 "文献资料"。

第 6 段

This includes the IA file and the triggering event file. Copies of confidentiality undertaking documents will be provided in accordance with Paragraph 10.2.5.

这其中包括视察区域资料档案以及触发事件卷宗。应根据第 10.2.5 段提供保密承诺书副本⑤。

批 注

⑤ 理解和表述和错误。

其中包括视察区域资料档案以及触发事件卷宗。有保密义务的文件应根据第 10.2.5 段规定提供副本。

原文第二句"Copies of confidentiality undertaking documents will be provided in accordance with Paragraph 10.2.5.",翻译稿将其译为"应根据第 10.2.5 段提供保密承诺书副本",如果光看译文,很难理解这句话是什么意思。实际上,原文是说,有保密义务的文件应根据第 10.2.5 段规定提供副本。在这里,将"undertaking"理解为"义务"比"承诺"更好理解。

第 7 段

To facilitate the checking procedures, preparations are made in accordance with Part Ⅱ, Paragraph 38, of the Protocol and Sections 3.3 and 3.12 of this manual. Part Ⅱ, Subparagraphs 27(d) and (g), of the Protocol are also relevant in this regard.

应根据议定书第二部分第 38 款以及本手册第 3.3 节和第 3.12 节的规定进行筹备,以便协助验证程序①。议定书第二部分第 27 款(d)、(g)两项②也涉及这个问题③。

批 注

① 逻辑关系错误。
② 表述方法错误。
③ 不准确。

为便于检查,应根据议定书第二部分第 38 款以及本手册第 3.3 节和第 3.12 节的规定进行准备。议定书第二部分第 27 款(d)和(g)项也与此有关。

在本段中,"To facilitate the checking procedures"是表示目的,是表示"为了便于检查",也是为了便利开展检查程序的意思,而不是"以便协助验证程序","preparation"译为"准备"比"筹备"好,这里是指为接受检查做好准备,用"筹备"显得用词不当。翻译稿中的"第 27 款(d)、(g)两项"的正确表述应为"第 27 款(d)和(g)项"。另外,"…are also relevant in this regard"译为"也与此有关"比"也涉及这个问题"好。

第 8 段

Documentation prepared in accordance with Paragraph 3.12.2 is handed to the ISP. The IT assists the ISP with the review of these documents at the start of equipment checking at the POE, and subsequently following the arrival of any shipment of approved equipment.

视察组将根据第 3.12.2 段准备的认证文件④递交被视察缔约国。在入境点进行的设备验证开始时⑤,以及任何核准设备送达后⑥,视察组协助被视察缔约国

批 注

④ 表达错误。
⑤ 表述不准确。
⑥ 表述不准确。

检查这些文件。

视察组应将根据第 3.12.2 段准备的证明文件交给被视察缔约国。在入境点开始检查设备时,以及在装运的核准设备到达后,视察组应协助被视察缔约国检查这些文件。

"Documentation"是指随设备一起提供的"证明文件、单证"等,"hand"译为"交给"比"递交"好,"at the start of equipment checking at the POE"应指在入境点开始检查设备时,"following the arrival of any shipment of approved equipment"是指"在装运的核准设备到达后"。另外,后一句的时间状语比较长,拆开来译未尝不可,如果不长,应调整一下主语的位置。

第 9 段

Confirm that equipment items, core and auxiliary, required only for the techniques listed in Part Ⅱ, Subparagraphs 69(f)-(g), of the Protocol have been grouped separately and labelled to make clear that they are for use during different inspection periods as indicated by the mandate.

确认仅供议定书第二部分第 69 款（f）至（g）项所列各技术所需[①]的核心和辅助设备已经分别分组和标记,以明确其根据任务授权所述[②],用于不同的视察阶段。

确认仅采用议定书第二部分第 69 款（f）至（g）项所列技术的核心和辅助设备已经单独分组和标记,以明确其可按照任务授权用于不同视察阶段。

本段话不是一个完整的句子,是一个动宾结构,后面部分都是 confirm 的内容。翻译稿基本上表述清楚,但表述欠妥。首先,"equipment items, core and auxiliary, required only for the techniques listed in Part Ⅱ, Subparagraphs 69(f)-(g)"字面意思是"只需要议定书第二部分第 69 款（f）至（g）项所列技术的核心和辅助设备",意指这些设备使用的技术是议定书第二部分第 69 款（f）至（g）项所列的技术,所以译为"仅供议定书第二部分第 69 款（f）至（g）项所列各技术所需"显然是不准确的,属于硬译。其次,"grouped separately"译为"单独分组"比"分别分组"好。另外,"to make clear that they are for use during different inspection periods as indicated by the mandate"是指"以明确其可按照任务规定用于不同视察阶段"。

批 注

① 表达不符合中文习惯。
② 译法生硬,中文无法理解。

第 10 段

The checking process should be duly recorded, if the IT or the ISP so wishes.

根据视察组和被视察缔约国的要求①，应适当记录验证过程。

如果视察组和被视察缔约国希望记录检查程序，则应适当记录。

"if the IT or the ISP so wishes" 意思是"如果视察组和被视察缔约国希望"，言下之意是希望记录检查程序。因此，这句话的正确译法是"如果视察组和被视察缔约国希望记录检查程序，则应适当记录"。翻译稿的译法有误。

批 注

① 与原文意思不符。

第 11 段

In the event that TIDs are damaged and/or show signs of interference following the transport of equipment while in ISP territory, the ISP and the IT may carry out checks to confirm that the equipment has not been damaged or altered and still functions according to specification.

假如设备在被视察缔约国境内经运输后②，防改装置被破坏和（或）显示出受到干扰的迹象，则被视察缔约国和视察组应进行检查，以确认设备未遭破坏或改动，且仍然按照规范运行③。

在被视察缔约国境内运输完成后，如果设备的防改装置被破坏和（或）显示受到干扰，则被视察缔约国和视察组应进行检查，以确认设备未遭到破坏或改动，且运行仍然符合技术规范。

翻译稿的表述基本准确，但在细节的处理上存在不符合中文表达。例如，"In the event that TIDs are damaged and/or show signs of interference following the transport of equipment while in ISP territory"，从字面意思来看，是指"如果在被视察缔约国境内运输后，设备的防改装置被破坏和（或）显示受到干扰"的意思，在这里，可以将"如果"放在"设备"之前，即"在被视察缔约国境内运输后，如果设备的防改装置被破坏和（或）显示受到干扰"，这样并不影响意思的表达，而且更符合中文的表达方式。从字面意思上看，将"still functions according to specification"译为"仍然按照规范运行"，大概意思是对的，但将其改为"运行仍然符合技术规范"可能更好。

批 注

② 译法生硬，不符合中文表达习惯。

③ 表达不符合中文习惯。

补充练习

1. The IT and the ISP should cooperate in making every reasonable effort to accelerate the passport checking, customs procedures and visa issuance, as applicable, and to otherwise expedite the entry process. The issuance of visas to IT members on arrival, if necessary, should not delay the POE activities according to Paragraphs 4.1.15–4.1.17.

视察组和被视察缔约国应合作开展一切合理努力，从速查验护照、办理海关手续和发放签证（以适用者为准），并以其他方式加快入境程序。在视察组成员抵达被视察缔约国时向其发放签证（如必要），不得延误本手册第4.1.15段至第4.1.17段所述入境点活动。

2. Part Ⅱ, Paragraph 51, of the Protocol gives the ISP the right to check inspection equipment at the POE. This notes, inter alia, that the ISP may exclude equipment that is not in conformity with the inspection mandate or that has not been approved and certified in accordance with Part Ⅱ, Paragraph 38, of the Protocol.

根据议定书第二部分第51款，被视察缔约国有权在入境点检查视察设备。这项规定特别指出，被视察缔约国可以拒绝不符合视察任务授权或没有按照议定书第二部分第38款得到核准及认证的设备入境。

3. The ITL and the ISP coordinate to facilitate timely checking of IT equipment by ISP representatives, including to ensure that relevant experts from within the IT, as determined by the ITL, are present for the checking.

视察组组长应同被视察缔约国协调，以便被视察缔约国的代表及时检查视察组设备，包括确保在视察组组长确定的视察组内部有关专家在场的情况下检查设备。

背景介绍

以下三篇材料均选自联合国和平利用外层空间委员会的技术报告。联合国和平利用外层空间委员会系根据1959年联大第1472号决议设立，其宗旨是制定和平利用外空的原则和规章，促进各国在和平利用外空领域的合作，研究与探索和利用外空有关的科技问题和可能产生的法律问题。外空委员会下设科学技术小组委员会和法律小组委员会，前者主要审议和研究与探索及和平利用外空有关的科技问题，促进空间技术的国际合作和应用问题；后者主要审议和研究和平利用外空活动中产生的法律问题，拟订有关的法律文件和公约草案。外空委员会主要审议两个小组委员会的工作报告以及一般性外空问题，就委员会开展的各项工作做出决定，并向联合国大会提出报告和建议。

基于外空委及两个小组委员会的工作范围，外空委相关文件通常会涉及一些技术性专有名词以及技术应用所在国家/区域的地点、机构名称及相关法律法规等；报告内容包括对联合国内部组织的技术活动的总结，如第六篇关于联合国灾害管理和紧急救援天基信息平台框架内技术活动的总结以及第七篇关于联合国空间技术专题研讨会内容的概述。此外，还有委员会就各国提交的工作文件所做的概述，如第八篇俄罗斯联邦提交的工作文件。因此，译者应具备明确的"主体"意识，注意技术活动属性，即辨别是联合国的技术咨询支助活动，还是各国在联合国框架内各自开展的活动，以更好地把握论述重点，酌情补充省略的主语及成分；鉴于外太空领域的技术与人类和平安全密切相关，也应将这一广阔的背景以及与之有关的国际准则，如《联合国宪章》纳入参考范围；此外，因技术工作报告在编写体例上较一般性会议报告更为严谨，除引用所述规章外，还广泛涉及技术专有词汇，译者需灵活使用"长句化短句"以及词性转换等翻译技巧。

第六篇

Building on the outcomes of previous missions to Guatemala conducted by the programme between 2010 and 2017, UN-SPIDER conducted two expert missions in July and November that included exchanges with a wide range of stakeholders as well as joint seminars together with the National Secretariat for Science and Technology of Guatemala .

The missions were used to meet with high-ranking authorities of the National Institute for Seismology, Volcanology, Meteorology and Hydrology, the Executive Secretariat of the National Coordinating Agency for Disaster Reduction and other government agencies. The missions were also used to conduct meetings with members of the technical inter-institutional team on the use of remote sensing and geographic information systems for risk and disaster management.

Additional advisory support was provided to the Executive Secretariat of the National Coordinating Agency for Disaster Reduction to activate the Charter following a large eruption of the Fuego volcano that took place on 3 June 2018. UN-SPIDER facilitated access to satellite imagery donated by DigitalGlobe to support emergency response efforts and damage assessments.

请自行翻译后查看后文的分析点评

分析点评

第1段

Building on the outcomes of previous missions to Guatemala conducted by the programme between 2010 and 2017, UN-SPIDER conducted two expert missions in July and November that included exchanges with a wide range of stakeholders as well as joint seminars together with the National Secretariat for Science and Technology of Guatemala .

在 2010 年至 2017 年期间对危地马拉多次派遣代表团① 所取得的成果的基础上，天基信息平台于 7 月和 11 月向危地马拉派遣了两个专家访问团，其中包括② 与各类利益攸关方进行了交流，以及与危地马拉国家科学和技术秘书处举行了若干联合研讨会。

批 注
① 专有名词，有固定译法。
② 表述有待完善。

2010 年至 2017 年期间，天基信息平台曾对危地马拉数度进行访问并取得了积极成果，在此基础上，于 7 月和 11 月对危地马拉进行了两次专家访问，访问期间，与各类利益攸关方进行了交流，并与危地马拉国家科学和技术秘书处举行了联合研讨会。

1. 未联系语境处理术语。见"missions"及"expert missions"。"mission"有"任务""特派团""特务任务"等意。联系本段中使用动词为"conduct"而非"dispatch/send"，所以处理为"代表团"实属不该。

2. 化长句为短句的技巧。本段由一个长句构成，翻译稿无论在句式结构还是连接词表述上，都采取了直译，"building on"处理为"在……的基础上"，"that included"处理为"其中包括"，基本意思固然明了，但远称不上佳译，不妨拆分为三个短句，适当重复增译，做到时间线清晰，逻辑关系明确。

第 2 段

The missions were used to meet with high-ranking authorities of the National Institute for Seismology, Volcanology, Meteorology and Hydrology, the Executive Secretariat of the National Coordinating Agency for Disaster Reduction and other government agencies. The missions were also used to conduct meetings with members of the technical inter-institutional team on the use of remote sensing and geographic information systems for risk and disaster management.

这些访问团旨在与国家地震学、火山学、气象学和水文学研究所、国家减灾协调局执行秘书处和其他政府机构的高级官员进行碰面。这些访问团还旨在① 与机构间技术小组的成员举行会议，共同讨论如何利用遥感和地理信息系统进行风险和灾害管理。

批 注

① 两个"旨在"句子在结构上可否优化调整？

专家访问有两个目的，一是与国家地震学、火山学、气象学和水文学研究所，国家减灾协调局执行秘书处和其他政府机构的高级官员会面；二是与机构间技术小组的成员举行会议，讨论利用遥感和地理信息系统进行风险和灾害管理事宜。

翻译中，经常会运用化长句为短句的技巧，但有时也需要运用反向技巧，即整合短句为整句：本段难度不大，由"The missions were used to..."和"The missions were also used to..."两个并列关系的句子组成，点明访问的两个目的。翻译稿沿用了原文的结构，处理也算得当，但审校稿适当增加了几个字眼，将两句整合为总分形式的一个长句，即"有两个目的，一是……；二是……"，译文效果随即得到提升。

第 3 段

Additional advisory support was provided to the Executive Secretariat of the National Coordinating Agency for Disaster Reduction to activate the Charter following a large eruption of the Fuego volcano that took place on 3 June 2018. UN-SPIDER facilitated access to satellite imagery donated by DigitalGlobe to support emergency response efforts and damage assessments.

在 2018 年 6 月 3 日富埃戈火山大规模喷发之后，天基信息平台又向国家减灾协调局执行秘书处提供了额外的咨询支持，以激活《宪章》②。天基信息平台还协助获取③ 由数字地球公司捐赠的卫星图像用于资助开展应急工作和损害评估。

批 注

② 欠明晰。
③ 协助谁？可否具体化？

在 2018 年 6 月 3 日富埃戈火山发生大规模喷发之后，天基信息平台又向该国国家减灾协调局执行秘书处提供了额外的咨询支助，以启动《宪章》机制。天基信息平台还协助该执行秘书处获取由数字地球公司捐赠的卫星图像，以支助开展应急工作和损害评估。

1. 背景知识查阅欠缺，见"activate the Charter"。此短语的处理表面是单词问题，其实是背景知识问题。在此，the Charter 全称为"the International Charter on Space and Major Disasters"（《空间与重大灾害国际宪章》），是欧洲航天局和法国国家空间研究中心在 1999 年 7 月发起的减灾合作机制。2000 年 11 月 1 日，该宪章正式付诸实施，其成员包括加拿大、美国、法国、中国和印度等国的航天机构。《空间与重大灾害国际宪章》规定，在遇到重大自然或人为灾害时，所有宪章成员应免费提供本国卫星获取的灾害资料，以帮助减轻灾害造成的生命和财产损失。据悉，2010 年舟曲特大山洪地质灾害和 2013 年四川雅安地震发生后，中国气象局均曾启动空间与重大灾害国际宪章机制。

2. 逻辑客体不明确，见"facilitated access to"。翻译稿处理为"协助获取"，协助客体不明确，差强人意。在翻译时，通常采用两种方式确认逻辑主体和客体：一是根据上下文确定；二是根据背景知识和常识。就此处而言，先看上下文，前句中提到"the Executive Secretariat of the National Coordinating Agency for Disaster Reduction"，再查阅背景知识，宪章机制的 authorized users，综合考虑之下，可以判定客体就是"执行秘书处"。

补充练习

1. UN-SPIDER and World Vision organized a training course and simulation exercise for emergency response in the case of a typhoon, which was held in Phnom Penh from 29 October to 1 November 2018. The objective was to engage with, and build the capacity of, the Emergency Response to National Disaster Management Team, which comprises international non-governmental organizations and governmental departments. Participants simulated the immediate, initial phase of response to a disaster (i.e., the first month), enacting to the extent possible normal operating procedures in a disaster while still carrying out their regular duties. The activity also generated awareness and understanding of satellite imaging and related mechanisms in the process of emergency management.

2018 年 10 月 29 日至 11 月 1 日，天基信息平台与世界宣明会在金边组办了一期台风应急响应培训班暨模拟演习，目的是与国家灾害管理小组——由国际非

政府组织和政府部门组成——进行接触并对其开展能力建设。参与者模拟了灾后即时/初始应急阶段（即第一个月）的情景，即在继续履行其常规职责的同时，尽可能地按照灾害期间正常作业程序行事。该活动还提高了参与者对应急管理过程中卫星成像及相关机制的认识和了解。

2. Communications were made with the National Committee for Disaster Management of Cambodia with respect to a proposal for a UN-SPIDER technical advisory mission to be conducted in 2019 to support the National Committee and other stakeholder organizations as they strengthened their disaster risk management and emergency response by effectively using space-based information.

此外，天基信息平台还与柬埔寨国家灾害管理委员会就以下提议进行了交流：请天基信息平台在2019年对柬埔寨进行一次技术咨询访问，为国家委员会及其他利益攸关方组织提供支助，以期有效利用天基信息加强自身灾害风险管理和应急工作。

Kenya Space Agency argued that CubeSats were a pathway to space for developing countries. This was illustrated by the first Kenya University nanosatellite-precursor flight (1KUNS-PF), to be launched in 2018, which consisted of a 1U CubeSat being developed by students from Kenya and Italy. The CubeSat was part of an international master's degree programme resulting from collaboration between the University of Nairobi and the University of Rome with the support of the Kenya Space Agency and sponsored by the Italian Space Agency. The 1KUNS-PF CubeSat was selected to be the first beneficiary of the KiboCube programme resulting from collaboration between the Office for Outer Space Affairs and the Japan Aerospace Exploration Agency (JAXA).

A representative of Space Advisory Company focused on the contribution of South Africa to the Netherlands-China lunar explorer, which will be the second lunar lander of China and humanity's first spacecraft to land on the far side of the Moon. The goal is to perform astrophysical studies from translunar locations in the unexplored radio spectrum from 80kHz to 80MHz. The Netherlands-China lunar explorer mission is considered a pathfinder for a future low-frequency space-based or Moon-based radio interferometer.

A representative of Japan Aerospace Exploration Agency (JAXA) introduced the two lunar CubeSats developed in his organization. Omotenashi and Equuleus had been selected as secondary payloads to the EM-1 mission of the National Aeronautics and Space Administration (NASA) of the United States. Omotenashi and Equuleus paved the way for future deep-space CubeSats and cargo vehicles to the cislunar region by demonstrating novel trajectory control techniques with limited fuel requirements.

A representative of the University of Cape Town, South Africa, explained the importance of space-borne synthetic aperture radar using small satellites. Synthetic aperture radar was a mature technology with a diverse range of potential applications. It had advantages over the use of other electromagnetic wave spectrum frequencies, one of which was that it gave access to the whole surface of the Earth regardless of cloud cover.

请自行翻译后查看后文的分析点评

分析点评

第1段

Kenya Space Agency argued that CubeSats were a pathway to space for developing countries. This was illustrated by the first Kenya University nanosatellite-precursor flight (1KUNS-PF), to be launched in 2018, which consisted of a 1U CubeSat being developed by students from Kenya and Italy. The CubeSat was part of an international master's degree programme resulting from collaboration between the University of Nairobi and the University of Rome with the support of the Kenya Space Agency and sponsored by the Italian Space Agency. The 1KUNS-PF CubeSat was selected to be the first beneficiary of the KiboCube programme resulting from collaboration between the Office for Outer Space Affairs and the Japan Aerospace Exploration Agency (JAXA).

翻译稿

肯尼亚航天局认为，立方体卫星是发展中国家通往太空之路①。肯尼亚大学第一次超小型卫星前体飞行（1KUNS-PF）将在2018年启动，其中包括由肯尼亚和意大利的学生开发的1U CubeSat，这表明了这一点。②CubeSat是内罗毕大学与罗马大学在肯尼亚航天局的支持和意大利航天局赞助下，合作开设的国际硕士学位课程的一部分。由于外层空间事务厅与日本宇宙航空研究开发机构之间的合作，1KUNS-PF CubeSat 被选为"希望"号立方舱方案的第一受益人③。

批 注

① 注意用词的微妙区别。
② 注意逻辑关系。
③ 注意语境。

肯尼亚航天局认为，立方体卫星是发展中国家进入空间的一条通道。这方面的证明是，肯尼亚大学第一次超小型卫星先驱飞行（1KUNS-PF）将在 2018 年发射，其中包括由肯尼亚和意大利学生开发的立方体卫星 1U CubeSat。立方体卫星（CubeSat）是内罗毕大学与罗马大学在肯尼亚航天局支持下并在意大利航天局赞助下合作开设的国际硕士学位课程的一部分。由于外层空间事务厅与日本宇宙航空研究开发机构开展合作，1KUNS-PF 立方体卫星任务被选为"希望号立方体卫星"方案支持下的第一轮任务。

1. 联合国文件词汇的特殊性。联合国文件与一般类文件在翻译时的一个区别就是，各类文件翻译有其独特的词汇要求，不能天马行空，自行翻译。翻译时尤其要注意到这一点，拿到文件时先判断属于哪类文件，然后查阅此类的相应词汇来翻译，当然前提是必须结合上下文来判定，不能太过拘泥。这里"Kenya Space Agency argued that CubeSats were a pathway to space for developing countries"，其中"space"一词有多重含义"航空、空间、太空"，在这类文件中，通常会翻译成"空间"，因为总体讲的是空间技术的发明和发展，一些专有名词的翻译则可能多种多样，如 National Aeronautics and Space Administration（NASA）（美国国家航空和航天局）中"space"翻译成"航天"，而在"European Space Policy Institute"（欧洲空间政策研究所）中则翻译为"空间"。

除了上面提到的一点，还要根据上下文来判断。在本文中，词句原译"立方体卫星是发展中国家通往太空之路"，在语义上没有太大问题，但如果结合上下文，就会明白翻译成"通往太空之路"显得有些空泛。这里讲的是发展这种卫星能够帮助发展中国家开辟外层空间，为其助力，可更具体地将其处理为"立方体卫星是发展中国家进入空间的一条通道"，使读者清楚明白。

2. 逻辑关系处理。一些英语句子的表达次序与汉语表达习惯不同，甚至完全相反，这时需要从原文后面翻译起，适当逆着原文的顺序翻译。例如，在此段内容中，"This was illustrated by the first Kenya University nanosatellite-precursor flight (1KUNS-PF), to be launched in 2018, which consisted of a 1U CubeSat being developed by students from Kenya and Italy"一句，如果顺着原文的顺序翻译，处理为"肯尼亚大学第一次超小型卫星前体飞行（1KUNS-PF）将在 2018 年启动，其中包括由肯尼亚和意大利的学生开发的 1U CubeSat，这表明了这一点"。在意义的表达上虽然大意明了，但读起来感到差强人意，显然不符合汉语表达习惯，且在逻辑关系表达上，也有不足。在汉语中，如果前面太长，通常会适当调序，将其处理得简单明了，使短句在前，长句在后，分层次表达含义。故而，审校稿处理时改为"这方面的证明是，肯尼亚大学第一次超小型卫星先驱飞行（1KUNS-PF）将在 2018 年发射，其中包括由肯尼亚和意大利学生开发的立方体卫星 1U CubeSat"，只是小小的改动，一下子就点明了逻辑关系，对句子的含义入木三分，把握精准。

3. 此处还有几个小词值得注意。一个是"precursor"一词，在涉及药品等生物学领域时，指的是被加入培养基的化合物，能够直接在生物合成过程中结合到产物分子中去，而自身的结构并未发生太大变化，却能提高产物的产量的一类小分子物质。还有一个含义是"先驱"，原译将"precursor"直接处理成"前体"跟后面的"飞行"显然是不搭的，因而应该处理成"先驱"。另一个"launch"，该词也有多重含义，通常可以翻译为"启动、开启、发起、发射"等，既然是涉及空间发展的文本，首先就要想到应该是"发射"，而不是其他含义，这涉及译者对词汇的灵敏反应，应多加注意。

4. "The 1KUNS-PF CubeSat was selected to be the first beneficiary of the KiboCube programme resulting from collaboration between the Office for Outer Space Affairs and the Japan Aerospace Exploration Agency (JAXA)."一句中，逻辑关系大致为"由于外层空间事务厅与日本宇宙航空研究开发机构的合作……卫星被选为"，难点在于"beneficiary"一词，该词本义为"受益人、受惠者"，翻译稿将其原搬照用，处理成"受益人"，让读者一头雾水，卫星为何就变成了受益人了，这显然是说不通的。这里涉及的一个翻译小技巧依然是增词，从上下文判断，此处应该指的是一次任务或一次行动被选为这一方案下的一次任务或行动，如此方能理顺逻辑关系，准确表达句子含义，故而审校稿将"A beneficiary"引申处理为"任务"，改为"由于……开展合作，1KUNS-PF 立方体卫星任务被选为'希望号立方体卫星'方案支持下的第一轮任务"，由此使读者一目了然。

第 2 段

A representative of the Space Advisory Company focused on the contribution of South Africa to the Netherlands-China lunar explorer, which will be the second lunar lander of China and humanity's first spacecraft to land on the far side of the Moon. The goal is to perform astrophysical studies from translunar locations in the unexplored radio spectrum from 80kHz to 80MHz. The Netherlands-China lunar explorer mission is considered a pathfinder for a future low-frequency space-based or Moon-based radio interferometer.

翻 译 稿

航天咨询公司的一位代表重点介绍了南非对中荷月球探测器的贡献，该探测器将成为中国的第二枚月球着陆器，并将成为人类第一艘登陆月球远端的航天器。目标是从位于未经探索的无线电频谱为 80kHz 至 80MHz 的月球轨道外地点进行天体物理学研究。荷中月球探测器任务被认为是未来低频空基或基于月球的无线电干涉仪的探路者。

审 校 稿

航天咨询公司的一位代表重点介绍了南非对荷中月球探测器所做的贡献，该探测器将是中国的第二个月球着陆器，也将是人类第一个在月球背面着陆的航天器。其目标是在位于未经探索的无线电频谱为 80kHz 至 80MHz 的月球轨道外地点进行天体物理学研究。荷中月球探测器飞行任务被认为是未来低频天基或月基

批 注

① 专业术语。
② 专业术语。

无线电干涉仪的探路者。

1. 科学科技类文件的第一要义就是要运用专业术语精准表达，除查阅相应的数据库、阅读查阅相关文献资料外，还需要平常的日积月累，关注相关新闻报道等，点点滴滴积累各方面的知识。"will be the second lunar lander of China and humanity's first spacecraft to land on the far side of the Moon"一句中字面意思并不难理解，大意是中国的一个航天器登陆月球，但"far side"成为拦路点，"far side"一词义为"另一边、反面、远侧、远端"，原译将这句话处理为"并将成为人类第一艘登陆月球远端的航天器"，不免让读者疑惑，登陆"月球远端"是哪里，有点摸不着头脑。如果平日多关注这方面的报道，就会很敏锐地知道此处对应的中文表达指的是"月球背面"。当然，局限于有限的时间，译者的知识很难面面俱到，这在所难免，那么就涉及查找资料来弥补这一缺陷，可以借助关键词"登陆"+"far side"就可以轻而易举地查到该词的地道汉语表达方法。翻译过程中遇到类似问题均可以如此处理。

2. 在翻译的过程中，经常会发现有一些词常常是合成词，有时候词汇库中可能未提供相关译法，但翻译的过程中可以参考类似词的翻译表达方法，将其准确地翻译出来。此处在"a future low-frequency space-based or Moon-based radio interferometer"中，我们可以在词汇库或相关文件里找到"space-based"的译法"天基"，但却找不到"Moon-based"的译法，考虑到均是此类文件词汇，完全可以借鉴"space-based"的译法，将"Moon-based"处理成"月基"。这样既不会影响读者理解，也显得非常具有专业水准。

第 3 段

A representative of Japan Aerospace Exploration Agency (JAXA) introduced the two lunar CubeSats developed in his organization. Omotenashi and Equuleus had been selected as secondary payloads to the EM-1 mission of the National Aeronautics and Space Administration (NASA) of the United States. Omotenashi and Equuleus paved the way for future deep-space CubeSats and cargo vehicles to the cislunar region by demonstrating novel trajectory control techniques with limited fuel requirements.

日本宇宙航空研究开发机构的一位代表介绍了他所在组织研制的两个月球立方体卫星。Omotenashi 和 Equuleus 被选为美国国家航空和宇宙航行局 EM-1 任务的次要有效载荷①。Omotenashi 和 Equuleus 通过展示具有有限燃料需求的新型轨迹控制技术，为今后深空立方体卫星和货运车辆②运往地月间区域铺平了道路。

批 注

① 适当增词。

② 望文生义。

日本宇宙航空研究开发机构的一位代表介绍了他所在组织开发的两个月球立方体卫星。Omotenashi 和 Equuleus 被选为美国国家航空和宇宙航行局 EM-1 飞行任务的次级有效载荷。Omotenashi 和 Equuleus 通过展示具有有限燃料要求的新型轨迹控制技术，为今后深空立方体卫星和货运飞行器运往地月间区域铺平了道路。

1. 根据上下文意义上的需要，翻译时既可能要将词类加以转换，又可能要在词量上加以增减，增词是按意义上（或修辞上）和句法上的需要增加一些词来更忠实通顺地表达原文的思想内容。这种增加不是无中生有地随意增词，而是增加原文中虽无其词但有其意的一些词。这里"Omotenashi and Equuleus had been selected as secondary payloads to the EM-1 mission of the National Aeronautics and Space Administration (NASA) of the United States"一句中"EM-1 mission"按照原文意思是"EM-1 任务"，但已知这里指的是一种飞行任务，那么在"任务"前加上"飞行"就显得很有必要，这样更加直观、清晰、明了。"payload"有"有效载荷、工资负担、净载重量"等含义，搭配上"secondary"显然指的是"有效载荷"。

2. 切忌望文生义，成为出色的译者，首要的一条就是细心，时刻提高警惕。有时候越是熟悉的词越要万分小心，否则很容易贻笑大方，犯下大错。"Omotenashi and Equuleus paved the way for future deep-space CubeSats and cargo vehicles to the cislunar region by..."一句中"cargo vehicles"如果不参考上下文考量，很容易上来就下笔将其翻译成"货运车辆"，因为这是大家比较常见的含义。"vehicle"有"运载工具、车辆、媒介物"等含义，搭配上这里的"cargo"很容易直接处理为"货运车辆"，然而根据上下文，前面是"deep-space CubeSats"，指的是"深空立方体卫星"，后面突然间出现"货运车辆"，显然离题万里，将"货运车辆"运送到"地月间区域"逻辑上讲不通，让读者感到不知所云，而事实上，结合前面的卫星，就应该想到这里指的是一种飞行器。对于这些，为了避免错误，首先应该去查相应的词汇库，因为极有可能是"老词新意"，其次是根据上下文将其翻译为适合当下语境的词语。

第 4 段

A representative of the University of Cape Town, South Africa, explained the importance of space-borne synthetic aperture radar using small satellites. Synthetic aperture radar was a mature technology with a diverse range of potential applications. It had advantages over the use of other electromagnetic wave spectrum frequencies, one of which was that it gave access to the whole surface of the Earth regardless of cloud cover.

南非开普敦大学的一位代表解释了使用小卫星的空间合成孔径雷达[1]的重要性。合成孔径雷达是一项成熟技术，具有多种潜在应用。比使用其他电磁波谱频率具有多种优势，其中一个优势是无论云层覆盖如何，都可以进入[2]地球的整个表面。

南非开普敦大学的一位代表解释了使用小卫星的空基合成孔径雷达的重要

批 注

[1] 注意词的精准理解。
[2] 词语运用。

性。合成孔径雷达是一项成熟技术，具有多种潜在用途，比使用其他电磁波频谱有更多优势，其中一个优势是无论云层覆盖如何，都可以到达地球的整个表面。

1. 小词往往在翻译中发挥着大作用，对于这些词的把握显得尤为重要。比如"A representative of the University of Cape Town, South Africa, explained the importance of space-borne synthetic aperture radar using small satellites"一句中"space-borne"非常重要，翻译稿将其翻译为"空间"，仅翻译了"space"的含义，实际上缺了后面一部分的含义没有翻译。"-borne"表示"通过……传播的"这种用法在英语中非常常见，比如"air-borne goods"（空运货物）、"blood-borne diseases"（血液传染病）、"rocket-borne weapons"（火箭运载武器）。这里"space-borne"显然需要把后面一部分翻译出来，而根据上下文，则可参考联合国词汇库里的译法将其处理为"空基"，也更符合此句的语义。

2. 词的适当转换。翻译过程中要注意适当变通处理，不能拘泥于词本身，使其与后面的含义相匹配。"one of which was that it gave access to the whole surface of the Earth regardless of cloud cover"一句中原译将"give access to"处理为最常见的译法"进入"，但后面的内容讲的是"地球的整个表面"，既然是指表面，那显然不能是"进入"，只能是"到达"，不然讲不通，这一点尤其要注意。

1. A representative of HEAD Aerospace Group presented the HEAD-1 Satellite, which provided in-orbit operational data for maritime surveillance. She indicated that the company was planning to create a constellation of 30 small satellites equipped with Automatic Identification System receivers and hyperspectral sensors. The applications would include real-time maritime surveillance services.

HEAD 航空航天集团的一位代表介绍了提供海上监视所需的在轨运行数据的 HEAD-1 号卫星。她表示，该公司正计划创建配有自动识别系统接收器和高光谱传感器的 30 颗小卫星构成的系统。各项应用程序将包括实时海上监视服务。

2. A representative of the Space Advisory Company shared details of the satellite tracking ground station for the nSight-1 CubeSat mission. He addressed hardware and software design from the project perspective. Using readily available off-the-shelf components, the mission could benefit other institutions interested in establishing their own satellite-tracking capabilities.

航天咨询公司的一位代表分享了 nSight-1 号立方体卫星飞行任务卫星跟踪地

面站的详细情况。他从项目角度阐述了硬件和软件设计。使用市面上可用的部件，该飞行任务可使有意于建立自身卫星跟踪能力的其他机构受益。

第八篇

原文

Such models and concepts for creating—on the basis of a rather specific understanding of the relationship between the categories of legality and expediency—a new architecture of "constructive interventionism", formally dictated by reasons of safety of space operations, will lead (by way of response) to the development, in the framework of national doctrines of outer space activities, of concepts of extended deterrence, with more active forms of counterforce planning aimed at entailing high risks for unauthorized supra-jurisdiction actions against foreign space objects.

An expanded positioning of coercive measures, which is characteristic of the draft code of conduct (when coercive measures in self-defense and similar measures dictated by considerations of reducing space debris are treated as equivalent to each other in one and the same context), will quite predictably contribute to fostering the tendency to blur the line between the actual case of self-defense and other essentially unrestricted manifestations of approaches based on the use of force.

Considering the aggregate of pertinent issues in the proposed perspective will make it possible to focus primarily on obvious aspects of outer space security which are implied in the discussion of, and would be conclusively necessary to be factored into, the concept of ensuring the long-term sustainability of outer space activities. It may be expected that a rational order will thus be infused into the consideration and ascertainment of a structure, threshold criteria and ways and means of countering risks and threats of contingencies which are not directly or predominantly linked to the problem of man-made space debris and which may be a result of certain intentional actions into outer space.

请自行翻译后查看后文的分析点评

分析点评

第1段

Such models and concepts for creating—on the basis of a rather specific understanding of the relationship between the categories of legality and expediency—

a new architecture of "constructive interventionism", formally dictated by reasons of safety of space operations, will lead (by way of response) to the development, in the framework of national doctrines of outer space activities, of concepts of extended deterrence, with more active forms of counterforce planning aimed at entailing high risks for unauthorized supra-jurisdiction actions against foreign space objects.

这种在较具体地了解合法性与便利性范畴之间关系的基础上，出于空间作业安全原因正式下令建立"建设性干预主义"新架构的模式和概念将在国家外层空间活动政策主张的框架内，（通过响应的方式）①促使制定延伸威慑的概念，同时采取更加积极形式的反制规划②，目的是限制未经授权对外国空间物体采取超越管辖权的行动的高风险。

批 注

① 理解不到位。
② 词义不准确。

在对合法性与权宜性范畴之间关系的某种特定理解的基础上，这种表面上由空间作业安全原因决定的建立"建设性干预主义"新架构的模式和概念将通过所引起的反应，导致在国家外层空间活动政策主张的框架内制定延伸威慑的概念，同时采取形式更加积极的还击军事力量规划，目的是使未经授权对外国空间物体采取超越管辖权的行动承受高风险。

1. 长句拆分，捋顺逻辑关系。翻译的过程中往往会碰到很长的句子，此段内容就是典型的代表。对于新手译者而言，乍一看往往会觉得无从下手，头痛不已。对于此类长句，一个有效的办法就是要拆分，通过对于原句的关键地方一点点切割，然后再捋顺逻辑关系，最后重组成适合汉语习惯、逻辑关系分明的句式结构。就本段内容而言，"models and concepts"为了创造一种"architecture"，而创建的基础是"a rather specific understanding of..."，而建立这种架构的原因是"by reasons of safety of space operations"，这种"概念和模式"将通过某种方式在一个框架内导致某种结果，然后服务于某种目标。厘清这种逻辑关系后就可以逐层翻译了。而翻译稿显然没有厘清逻辑关系，在理解上难免出现了偏差。这里的两个难点是"formally dictated"和"by response of"，"formally"一般是表示"正式地、正规地"，但也有"形式上"的含义，后面讲的是原因，因而原文译为"正式"显然是不妥的，因为不涉及主语。而"by way of response"中对"response"的处理采取同样的方法，翻译稿拘泥于原文，"通过响应的方式"促使制定某种概念，在逻辑上显然也是讲不通的，而实际上指的是"通过所引起的反应"导致制定某种概念，故而对"response"做了转译处理，这样才会条理分明。

2. 翻译的目的是准确明晰传达原文所要表达的含义，所以一定要讲透，讲到位，"counterforce"有"反作用力、打击军事力量、反力量"等，这里根据后文判断，采用"还击军事力量"要更为准确。

第 2 段

An expanded positioning of coercive measures, which is characteristic of the draft code of conduct (when coercive measures in self-defense and similar measures dictated by considerations of reducing space debris are treated as equivalent to each other in one and the same context), will quite predictably contribute to fostering the tendency to blur the line between the actual case of self-defense and other essentially unrestricted manifestations of approaches based on the use of force.

翻译稿

扩大作为行为守则草案典型特征的强制措施的定位（自卫中的强制措施和出于减少空间碎片的考虑采取的类似措施在相同背景下被视为是等同的）预计在很大程度上将推动促成这种倾向，即使实际自卫情况与其他本质上不受限制使用武力的表现方式之间的界限模糊。

审校稿

行为守则草案的典型特征是扩大部署强制措施（自卫中的强制措施和出于减少空间碎片的考虑因素而必须采取的类似措施在相同背景下被视为是等同的）预计在很大程度上将推动促成一种倾向，即模糊实际自卫情况与其他实际上不限制使用武力的表现形式之间的界限。

点评

1. 关键词的翻译可能影响整个句子的翻译。本文中"An expanded positioning"中的"positioning"通常的对应中文含义是"定位、安置"等，翻译稿使用了"定位"这个含义，但前面是"measures"，搭配起来就变成了"措施的定位"，感觉非常摸不着头脑，而根据上下文判断，既然是扩大措施，那么可以将其"安置"引申为"部署"，这样可以使读者一下子明白要表达的含义。

2. 转换词义和适当切分句子是翻译中的一个非常重要的技巧。"…fostering the tendency to blur the line between the actual case of self-defense and other essentially unrestricted manifestations of approaches based on the use of force"一句中，翻译稿虽然进行了切割，但后面处理的不够妥当，"即使……之间的界限模糊"，容易让读者理解为推动的倾向是"使……界限模糊"，但实际上，这里要表达的含义是这种倾向是"模糊……界限"。因此，在处理这句话时，可以将"模糊"放在前面，明确指出这种倾向到底指的是什么。

第 3 段

Considering the aggregate of pertinent issues in the proposed perspective will make it possible to focus primarily on obvious aspects of outer space security which are implied in the discussion of, and would be conclusively necessary to be factored into, the concept of ensuring the long-term sustainability of outer space activities. It

---

批 注

 理解错误。
② 容易产生歧义。
③ 可适当意译。

may be expected that a rational order will thus be infused into the consideration and ascertainment of a structure, threshold criteria and ways and means of countering risks and threats of contingencies which are not directly or predominantly linked to the problem of man-made space debris and which may be a result of certain intentional actions into outer space.

考虑到从所提议的角度将相关问题聚集在一起将使得有可能主要重点关注确保外层空间活动长期可持续性概念相关讨论所暗含的，并且最终需要被考虑到的外层空间安全的明显方面①。可以预计，在考虑和确定结构、界限标准以及抵制并非直接或主要与人为空间碎片问题相联系和可能是向外层空间进行的特定有意行为结果②的紧急事件风险和威胁的方式和途径时，合理的顺序将融入其中。

批　注

① 句子太长。
② 适当拆分。

从所提议的角度考虑所有相关问题将使得有可能主要关注外层空间安全的明显方面，这些方面暗含在关于确保外层空间活动长期可持续这一概念的相关讨论中并且最终有必要成为该概念的组成部分。或许可以预计这将导致按照合理顺序考虑和确定应对突发事件风险和威胁的结构、最低标准以及方式方法，这些风险和威胁与人为空间碎片问题没有直接关联或永久关联，有可能是某些国际外太空行为造成的。

1. 这里再次涉及句子太长的问题，翻译长句时，往往需要按照汉语表达习惯对句子进行拆分。长句的译法主要有顺序法、逆序法、分译法和综合法。有些英文内容是按时间顺序或逻辑关系顺序安排的，这与汉语表达习惯一致，在翻译的时候可以按照顺序译出即可，但主要句子不要太长。而逆序则恰恰相反，翻译的时候需要逆着原文顺序翻译。有时英语长句中主句与从句或主句与修饰语间的关系并不是十分密切，翻译时可按照汉语多用短句的习惯，把长句中的从句或短语化为句子，分开来表述，适当的时候还可以进行增词。综合法则是在英语长句在其他三种方法都不合适的时候，经过仔细推敲，按照时间先后或者逻辑顺序，有主次地对全句进行综合处理。

2. 具体到本文，则涉及分译法。"which are implied in the discussion of, and would be conclusively necessary to be factored into, the concept of ensuring the long-term sustainability of outer space activities" 修饰的是"aspects"，而"which are not directly or predominantly linked to the problem of man-made space debris and which may be a result of certain intentional actions into outer space" 修饰的是"contingencies"，由于句式结构较长，所以可以将这两个定语从句单独拿出来，使逻辑关系条理分明，又不会使句子显得冗长，读起来颇感吃力。因此，审校稿将两个定语从句拆分出来，使其读起来层次分明。

补充练习

1. Although the 1967 Outer Space Treaty provides that activities of non-governmental entities in outer space shall be authorized and continuously supervised by the relevant State Party to that Treaty, it would be appropriate to consider the grounds for rendering qualification to certain types of action that are carried out by such non-governmental entities (in particular with the aid of space objects belonging to them or managed by them) and may require reciprocal actions, including in self-defense.

尽管1967年《外层空间条约》规定，非政府实体在外层空间的活动应当得到该条约相关缔约国的授权和持续监管，但仍适宜考虑，以何种理由对此类非政府实体（特别是在属于它们或由它们管理的空间物体的协助下）开展的、可能需要对其采取相应行动（包括自卫）的特定类型的行动加以限定。

2. With the participation of States Members of the United Nations, intergovernmental bodies and non-governmental organizations, ICG has become an important platform for communication and cooperation in the field of GNSS. The Office for Outer Space Affairs of the Secretariat continues to support progress towards achieving compatibility and interoperability among global and regional space-based navigation systems. As new systems emerge, signal compatibility and interoperability among GNSS systems and transparency in the provision of open civil services will be key factors in ensuring that civil users around the world receive the maximum benefit from GNSS and its applications.

在联合国会员国、政府间机构和非政府组织的参与下，导航卫星委员会已成为全球导航卫星系统领域交流与合作的重要平台。秘书处外层空间事务厅继续支持推动实现全球和区域天基导航系统之间的兼容性和互操作性。随着新系统的出现，全球导航卫星系统之间的信号兼容性和互操作性以及在提供开放式民用服务方面的透明度，将成为确保全世界民用用户从全球导航卫星系统及其应用中获得最大惠益的关键因素。

本章词汇

profiling　简介、分析
forensic profiling　法医特征分析
sensorimotor deficits　感觉运动缺陷
US gallons of concentrate　美制加仑浓缩物
flammable liquid fires　易燃液体火灾
foam agents　泡沫灭火剂
pool fire tests　油池火灾测试
fluorine-free alternatives　无氟替代品
alcohol resistant firefighting foams　耐酒精消防泡沫
lead implementing agency　牵头执行机构
agency support costs　机构资助费用
tranche implementation plan　付款执行计划
licensing and quota system　许可证和配额制度
allowable level of consumption　允许消费量
refrigerants　制冷剂
low-global warming potential　低全球升温潜能值
list of banned substances　禁用物质清单
identifiers　识别器
certification system　资格认定制度
phase out　淘汰
desk study　案头研究
phase-down targets　逐步减少目标
phase-down plans　逐步削减计划
phase-out management plans　淘汰管理计划
work programme　工作方案
draft format　格式草案
scheduled/non-scheduled aircraft　定期/不定期航班
inspection mandate　视察任务授权
POE（point of entry）　入境点、进入点、进入港、报关港
ISP（inspected State Party）　被视察缔约国
ITL（Inspection Team Leader）　视察组组长
points of contact　联络点

privileges and immunities　特权和豁免
triggering event file　触发事件卷宗
core and auxiliary equipment items　核心和辅助设备
specification　技术规范
outcomes　成果
missions　特派团/特派任务
expert missions　专家访问
stakeholders　利益攸关方
remote sensing　遥感
risk and disaster management　风险和灾害管理
advisory support　咨询支助
emergency response　应急工作
normal operating procedures　正常作业程序
CubeSats　立方体卫星
nanosatellite-precursor flight　超小型卫星先驱飞行
lunar explorer　月球探测器
lunar lander　月球着陆器
translunar locations　月球轨道外地点
space-based or Moon-based　天基或月基
secondary payloads　次级有效载荷
deep-space　深空
cargo vehicles　货运飞行器
cislunar region　地月间区域
space-borne synthetic aperture radar　空基合成孔径雷达
in-orbit operational data　在轨运行数据
receivers　接收器
sensors　传感器
real-time　实时
off-the-shelf components　现成组件
supra-jurisdiction actions　超越管辖权的行动
coercive measures　强制措施
threshold criteria　最低标准

欢迎本书读者关注中译公司官方微信公众号"中译翻译",回复文字"翻译学习资料礼包",即可免费获得电子版学习资源大礼包。

读者也可扫描本书封底二维码,获取配套免费课程。